Munich Studies on Innovation and Competition

Volume 17

The Munich Studies on Innovation and Competition present fundamental research on legal systems that have been created with the objective of promoting and safeguarding innovation and competition as the most important factors for economic growth and prosperity. Accordingly, this series will include monographic works in English in the different fields of intellectual property and competition law such as patent, trademark and copyright law, as well as unfair competition and antitrust law. Rather than describing what the law is, the series strives to contribute to the scholarship on how these legal systems should develop so as to promote innovation and competition. Therefore, its outlook is both international, by not focussing on any specific national legal system, and interdisciplinary. In particular, studies are encouraged that also incorporate the methods and findings of other disciplines such as economics, sociology and anthropology.

More information about this series at https://link.springer.com/bookseries/13275

Giulia Schneider

Health Data Pools Under European Data Protection and Competition Law

Health as a Digital Business

Springer

Giulia Schneider
Scienze bancarie, finanziarie e assicurative
Università Cattolica del Sacro Cuore
Milan, Italy

ISSN 2199-7462 ISSN 2199-7470 (electronic)
Munich Studies on Innovation and Competition
ISBN 978-3-030-95426-0 ISBN 978-3-030-95427-7 (eBook)
https://doi.org/10.1007/978-3-030-95427-7

This Springer imprint is published by the registered company Springer Nature Switzerland AG
The registered company address is: Gewerbestrasse 11, 6330 Cham, Switzerland

To Annette and Thomas Storch

Preface

This study explores the emerging economic reality of health data pools from the perspective of European Union policy and law. The contractual sharing of health data for research purposes is giving rise to a "free movement" of research data, which is strongly encouraged at European policy level within the Digital Single Market Strategy and the European Strategy for Data. However, it has also a strong impact on data subjects' fundamental right to data protection and smaller businesses' and research entities' ability to carry out research and compete in innovation markets. Accordingly, the study questions under which conditions health data sharing is lawful under European data protection and competition law.

For these purposes, the analysis addresses the following sub-questions: (i) Which is the emerging innovation paradigm in digital health research? (ii) How are health data pools addressed at European policy level? (iii) Do European data protection law and competition law promote health data-driven innovation objectives, and how? (iv) Which are the limits posed by the two frameworks to the free pooling of health data?

The underlying assumption of the enquiry is that both branches of European Union law are key regulatory tools for the creation of a "common European health data space" as envisaged in the Commission's 2020 European strategy for data. It thus demonstrates that both European data protection law, as defined under the General Data Protection Regulation, and European competition law and policy set research enabling regimes regarding health data, provided specific normative conditions are met. From a further perspective, both regulatory frameworks place external limits to the freedom to share (or not share) research valuable data.

After having defined the features of emerging digital health research courses, the study assesses the relevance of health data pooling practices as a means of concentrating high-technology resources and stirring innovation in the life sciences sector. In these regards, the practice of health data pools is regarded as an evolution of patent pools in the digital economy. From this perspective, the complex values and interests related to health data are identified. The varied phenomenon of health data pools is proved by some case studies. The analysis then contextualizes the practice of health data pools within the EU Digital Single Market Strategy. At European Union level, digital health and the free flow of information are indeed identified as strategic areas in respect to the set goal of maximizing the innovation potential of the digital internal market. Accordingly, the role of European data protection law is questioned in respect to the identified efficiency-oriented policy goal regarding health data sharing.

The regulation of health data treatment under the GDPR enables health data pools under arts. 9(2) lett. j and 89 GDPR, setting a research exemption and establishing a special data protection regime for the processing of health data for research purposes. In this perspective, it is argued that the research exemption is a rule for the data economy, as the right to data portability, stimulating data mobility among platforms and thus directly serving innovation purposes. Similarly to the GDPR, also European competition law entails a research exemption in the form of a block exemption for research and development agreements, pursuing objectives of economic and technical progress resulting from the sharing of research precious information. The analysis shows how both European data protection and competition law establish specific access regimes regarding research valuable health data, thus enabling the contractual trading of such data. Against this backdrop, attention is given to the data protection safeguards and competition remedies, which are relevant respectively for the *ex ante* and *ex post* design of health data pools. Ultimately, the desirability of a "collaborative governance" of health data pools by data protection and competition authorities is stated.

Milan, Italy — Giulia Schneider

Contents

Chapter 1
Introduction: Object, Methodology and Structure of the Research

The increasing employment of artificial intelligence and machine learning in the biomedical sector as well as the growing number of partnerships aimed at pooling together different types of digital health data for research purposes, stress the importance of an effective regulation and governance of data sharing for innovation purposes in the health and life sciences.

This study explores the emerging economic reality of health data pools from the perspective of European Union policy and law. For these purposes, the analysis addresses the following research questions: (i) which is the emerging innovation paradigm in digital health research?; (ii) how are health data pools addressed at European policy level?; (iii) under which conditions are health data pools lawful under European data protection and competition law?; (iv) which are the limits posed by the two frameworks to the free pooling of health data?

For the purposes of addressing these research questions, the study employs a highly interdisciplinary and comparative methodology, particularly focusing on the mutual interactions between European data protection and competition law in the regulation of the particular phenomenon of health data pools.

The underlying assumption of the study is that both branches of European Union law are key regulatory tools for the creation of a "common European health data space" as envisaged in the Commission's 2020 European strategy for data.[1] The analysis thus demonstrates that both European data protection law, as defined under the General Data Protection Regulation, and European competition law and policy set research enabling regimes regarding health data, provided specific normative conditions are met. From a further perspective, both regulatory frameworks place external limits to the freedom to share (or not share) research valuable data, which is highly incentivised at European policy level within the Digital Single Market Strategy.

[1] European Commission (19 February 2020), p. 7.

G. Schneider, *Health Data Pools Under European Data Protection and Competition Law*, Munich Studies on Innovation and Competition 17,
https://doi.org/10.1007/978-3-030-95427-7_1

Against this backdrop, the research is structured as follows.

After having defined the features of emerging digital health research courses, the second chapter assesses the relevance of health data pooling practices as a means of concentrating high-technology resources and stirring innovation in the life sciences sector. In this respect, the practice of health data pools is regarded as an evolution of patent pools in the digital economy. As argued, health data pools are a form of private ordering of digital health innovation, being a direct expression of businesses' and research entities' freedom of contract and of doing business in the datafied and digitised health research environment. The second chapter thus concludes that in the newly developing data-driven health research environment, contractual solutions of data sharing are emerging as a new innovation paradigm, which appears to be better suited for the achievement of data-driven innovation objectives than an intellectual property-based innovation paradigm.

Against this backdrop, the third chapter highlights the complex values and interests related to health data. The varied phenomenon of health data pools is proved by four case-studies, respectively involving health data sharing between the 23andMe genetic testing company and various pharmaceutical companies; between Google and the pharmaceutical company Sanofi; between Google DeepMind and the Royal Free Hospital; and ultimately between IBM and Italy. The analysis illustrates how health data pools give rise to outright innovation networks, where innovation goals meet health and consumer welfare objectives. At the same time, however, these innovation networks entail some substantial risks related to newly emerging digital health biases. The large scale processing of sensitive data, indeed, directly impacts upon data subjects' fundamental right to data protection and to non-discrimination. Moreover, the sharing of health data among economic actors may lead to anticompetitive market outcomes that impair smaller businesses' and research entities' ability to carry out research and to compete in innovation markets.

With health data pooling practices becoming a means of concentrating high-technology resources and stirring innovation in the life sciences sector, companies' reluctance to aggregate their data with the ones of other companies would lead, according to some commentators, to an outright market failure situation.[2] From this perspective, regulatory incentives and a correspondent legislative action are needed in order to advance research and innovation in the field of health through the aggregation of differently owned datasets.[3] Along similar lines, the innovation-

[2]Lindqvist (2018), pp. 147–148. The point is raised also by Colangelo and Borgogno (5 April 2019).

[3]Mattioli (2017), p. 180, who sees information sharing as a precondition for innovation. Rai (2017), pp. 1642 ff.; Eisenberg and Rai (2006), pp. 1196–1199. Against this backdrop, the proposed legal incentives are both of private nature, as the establishment of a right to property over health data and of public nature, as the creation of public funders resource creation exercising informal or formal regulatory power to promote data pooling. See, e.g., Contreras (2017), pp. 19 ff. Rai and Eisenberg (2003), pp. 289 ff.

driving function of data sharing practices has been variously acknowledged at European level, where the sharing of datasets has been recognised as a key factor for a thriving data economy.[4]

The contractual sharing of health data for research purposes is strongly encouraged within the European Digital Single Market Strategy, where the "free movement" of research data has become a central policy concern. The objective of data sharing has been increasingly considered by the European Commission, which has stated that "it can become efficient for companies to share more data they hold with other companies so that the value resulting from the data can be exploited to the maximum".[5]

Hence, as will be demonstrated in the fourth Chapter, health data transfers are a specific fragment of a much broader economic phenomenon regarding data flows that is increasingly being considered at European regulatory level for its innovative and pro-competitive potential.[6]

However, contracts involving the sharing of data imply the processing of sensitive data, thus falling under the General Data Protection Regulation, and can be—under certain circumstances—qualified as research and development agreements which are relevant under art. 101 TFEU.

After having enquired the developing reality of health data sharing contracts and having acknowledged the emerging efficiency-oriented European policy objective regarding the free flow of research valuable digital data, the second part of the study explores the conditions under which the "free" sharing of health data is lawful under European data protection law and European competition law.

The analysis under Chaps. 5 and 6 thus shows how both the General Data Protection Regulation and art. 101 TFEU interestingly establish a special regime for research data transfers respectively under art. 9(2) let. j GDPR and under art. 101(3) TFEU and the related R&D Block Exemption. These provisions appear to establish outright access regimes regarding scientific data, enabling data mobility among platforms and thus directly serving objectives of economic and technical progress resulting from the flow of research precious information. In this perspective, they both appear to promote freedom of business and contract regarding the transfer of sensitive research data. However, both branches of European law also establish specific sets of conditions to which health data transfers must conform.

Against this backdrop, the third part of the study questions the limits to the freedom of business and freedom of contract in the transfer of health data established under European data protection law and European competition law. Accordingly, the seventh Chapter explores data protection safeguards and competition remedies,

[4]In 2014, the European Commission has advocated the adoption of protocols for "gathering and processing data from different sources in a coherent and interoperable manner across sectors and vertical markets". So European Commission (2 July 2014), p. 6.

[5]European Commission (25 April 2018).

[6]See infra Chap. 4 Sect. 4.3.2.

which are respectively relevant for the *ex ante* and *ex post* design of health data pools.

Data protection safeguards as derived from the General Data Protection's principles and rules assure that sensitive data transfers are compliant to data subjects' rights to data protection as linked to the rights to non-discrimination and non-commodification of health research.

Conversely, competition remedies under both art. 102 TFEU and commitment decisions in merger procedures are relevant for the safeguard of competing research entities' economic freedom. As will be shown, these remedies directly imply the obligation of a dominant market party to share research valuable information to smaller or weaker players. In this perspective, these competition remedies need themselves to comply to the identified data protection safeguards.

At a deeper level, the analysis ultimately reveals the mutual supportiveness of European data protection and competition law in the design of health data pools that serve innovation objectives, for the purposes of diminishing the risks to data subjects' fundamental rights and to distortion of competition within the internal market. As the final part of the study argues, such mutual supportiveness between the two considered regulatory frameworks should be directly substantiated in data protection and competition authorities' collaborative governance of research-based health data pools.

References

Colangelo G, Borgogno O (2019) Data sharing and interoperability: fostering innovation and competition through APIs. Comput Law Secur Rev 35:105314

Contreras JL (2017) Leviathan in the commons: biomedical data and the state. In: Strandburg KJ, Madison MJ, Frischmann BM (eds) Governing medical knowledge commons. Cambridge University Press, Cambridge, pp 19–45

Eisenberg RS, Rai AK (2006) Harnessing and sharing the benefits of state-sponsored research: intellectual property rights and data sharing in California stem's cell initiative. Berkeley Technol Law J 21:1187–1214

European Commission (2 July 2014) Communication from the Commission to the European Parliament, the Council, the European Economic and Social Committee and the Committee of the Regions, 'Towards a thriving data-driven economy', https://ec.europa.eu/digital-single-market/en/news/communication-data-driven-economy

European Commission (25 April 2018) Staff Working Document- Guidance on Sharing Private Sector Data in the European Data Economy, Accompanying the document Communication from the Commission to the European Parliament, the Council, the European economic and social Committee and the Committee of the Regions "towards a common European data space" https://ec.europa.eu/digital-single-market/en/news/staff-working-document-guidance-sharing-private-sector-data-european-data-economy

European Commission (19 February 2020) Communication from the Commission to the European Parliament, the Council, the European Economic and Social Committee and the Committee of the Regions, 'A European Strategy for Data' COM(2020) 66 final. at https://eur-lex.europa.eu/legal-content/EN/TXT/PDF/?uri=CELEX:52020DC0066&from=EN

Lindqvist B (2018) Competition and data pools. J Eur Consum Mark Law 7:146–154
Mattioli M (2017) The Data Pooling Problem. Berkeley Technol. Law J. 32:179–236
Rai AK (2017) Risk regulation and innovation: the case of rights-encumbered biomedical data silos. Notre Dame Law Rev 92:1642–1668
Rai AK, Eisenberg RS (2003) Bayh-Dole reform and the progress of biomedicine. Law Contemp Probl 66:289–314

Chapter 2
Digital Health Research and Health Data Pools

2.1 The Technological and Regulatory Context of Digital Health Research

Over the last decade, with the advent of the digital economy, also the healthcare sector has been increasingly relying on digital technologies.[1]

The phenomenon of the digitization of the healthcare sector has triggered the attention of both European[2] and American[3] legal scholarship, which has been questioning the legal status of electronic health records and the related issues of access,[4] ownership[5] and liability[6] arising from the creation of digital health-datasets.

These concerns were amplified as a consequence of the growing practices of information technology outsourcing by healthcare providers onto third parties providing the needed infrastructure for the management of the large digital health datasets that were coming into existence.[7] Cloud computing services have thus been increasingly relied on by healthcare providers for they enabled to overcome the limitations of hardware and software traditionally used by universities and hospitals.[8]

---

[1] This is why healthcare has been identified by the European Commission as a core business area where digital technologies can play a major role. See European Commission (10 May 2017b), p. 57.

[2] Guarda (26 December 2006); Dumortier and Verhenneman (22 December 2011).

[3] See, among others, Miller and Tucker (2009), pp. 1077 ff. Hoffmann and Podgurski (2008), pp. 2 ff.; Hoffman and Podgurski (2009), pp. 1524 ff.; Terry and Francis (2007), pp. 681 ff.

[4] Hoffmann and Podgurski (2008), pp. 8 ff.

[5] Hall (2010); Zittrain (2000), p. 1201.

[6] Hoffman and Podgurski (2009), pp. 1528 ff.

[7] Gupta et al. (2008).

[8] Pasquale and Ragone (2014), pp. 601 ff.

G. Schneider, *Health Data Pools Under European Data Protection and Competition Law*, Munich Studies on Innovation and Competition 17,
https://doi.org/10.1007/978-3-030-95427-7_2

As foreshadowed by the cited literature, the massive phenomenon of information technology outsourcing was starting to transform the healthcare industry into an intricate net of contractual arrangements regulating health data collection, access and transfer through different sets of platforms, ranging from locked[9] to more collaborative ones.[10] The result of this was soon identified in the creation of a more fluid and less protected health information setting.[11]

Due to massive surveillance technologies and the proliferation of digital monitoring sites pervasively capturing and analysing different data types, biomedical research and healthcare are undergoing deep structural transformations. The availability of a great amount of digital health data and the advancements of the technologies capable of fruitfully harnessing them, such as data mining technologies, is indeed offering new perspectives for the purpose of disease prevention, diagnosis and treatment.[12] Computational capabilities are shaping new opportunities of distance tracking and monitoring that are subverting traditional spatial and temporal restraints of physical trials.

Proof of this is the blossoming of various research projects designed to take advantage of the scientific value of digital data, in the form of individual or quantified self-type self-experiments.[13] Clinical studies are growingly conducted using wearables and enabling new types of population-wide studies and cohorts.[14]

In this context, the dynamics of the algorithmic economy has come to change the sources of health-related information, the means of collection and storage and ultimately the significance of health-related data for health research and policy making: correlations and predictive analytics are expanding the scope of health-inflected data far outside the strictly medical field[15]. Data mining techniques are making it possible to extract sensitive health information from the most disparate and apparently disconnected data points,[16] which directly or indirectly signal actual or future health conditions.[17] Algorithmic computational techniques that are applied to this data are further revolutionising the way in which health data are generated and processed.

---

[9] Hoffmann (2016), p. 1741.

[10] Underlining the growing complexity of health IT infrastructure, Pisto (2013), p. 79.

[11] Pisto (2013), p. 79.

[12] Vayena and Blassime (2018), pp. 119 ff.

[13] This is well described by Lupton (2013), pp. 256 ff.

[14] See the analysis by Izmailova et al. (2018), pp. 42 ff., assessing the future prospects of integration of clinical trials conducted through wearables in traditional clinical trials studies.

[15] Powles and Hodson (2017), pp. 351 ff. Stressing the point also D. Lupton (2017), pp. 562 ff.; Cf. Sharon (2016), p. 6: "in the framework of medical research using digital data (. . .) there is a relatively high risk of context transgression".

[16] Comandè and Malgieri (2017), pp. 229 ff.

[17] Comandè and Schneider (2018), pp. 284 ff.; Sharon (2017), pp. 93 ff.

The algorithmic environment is opening new operational spaces in the healthcare sector for consumer-tech companies that are becoming increasingly active players in the healthcare field.[18] These companies do not solely provide the technological infrastructure needed for the processing of the vast emerging health datasets, but have also acquired the analytical expertise to run experiments on large databases of spam, web documents, internet search queries and consumer purchases.[19] These digital enquiries are ever more becoming essential sources of scientific evidence and are thus architecturally transmuting the processes of health knowledge production.[20]

As a result, the growing employment of algorithmic infrastructures and the advancements in knowledge extraction that are being applied in the healthcare sector, are given rise to a data-intensive health research environment.[21] More precisely, the use of data analytics for the generation of scientifically valuable health knowledge is starting to overturn traditional approaches to health research, with regards to (i) the object of health research; (ii) the epistemiological methodology governing health research courses and (iii) the stakeholders that are involved in health research.

Against this backdrop, the next paragraphs will first enquire how algorithmic methods of collecting, storing and analysing complex and abundant digital health-related data are sensitively altering the traits of traditional biomedical research and thus the resulting markets of health-related products and services. Hence, the detected scientific and economic changes will be enquired from the standpoint of their first reflexes at European regulatory level.

2.1.1 The Object of Health Research: The Evolving Big Health Data Ecosystem

As the World Health Organization has stressed, in the digital environment, patients are encouraged to participate in their own care and become the source of other behavioural information, which comes to integrate strictly medical information.[22] Biomedical big data directly stems from the interaction between users and the technology that support their everyday activities.

This patient-generated information, collected in different domains, forms what the same World Health Organization has described as a "big health data ecosystem". This ecosystem encompasses information not only related to the medical domain, but also information extending wide beyond it.

---

[18] This is what is demonstrated by Mukherjee (20 April 2017a).

[19] Sharon (2016), pp. 3–4.

[20] Krumholz (2014), pp. 1163 ff.

[21] See Christen et al. (2016), pp. 199 ff.

[22] World Health Organization (28 June 2021), p. 21, referring to the Unesco International Bioethics Committee (IBC) (15 September 2017).

With regards to the strictly medical sphere, traditional health-relevant data sources need to be recalled, such as electronic health records and prescription data,[23] diagnostic images and health insurance data. In addition to these, also medical devices, wearable devices, sensors and other digital tools meant to track health and fitness conditions[24] are becoming a very important source of health data. In these regards, nutritional tracking apps, weight management devices, pedometers tracking data subjects' movements, sleep control apps, all contribute to charting users' health conditions and thus to 'quantify' and 'hacking' users' lives.[25]

In addition to health-related services, the WHO identifies as further sources of health data connected to the medical sphere clinical trials records, biobanks, registries and genomic databases[26] as well as.

public health activities, which lead to the creation of health data collections in the form of immunization records, disease surveillance[27] and vital statistics.[28]

Stepping outside the borders of the medical environment, other unconventional sources of health-related data are emerging and becoming growingly important in the new health research eco-system.[29] Indeed, through algorithmic probabilistic inferences also personal data that users decide to share online[30] in exchange of (apparently) free services,[31] are becoming an additional basis of clinical evidence: in an "economics of signalling"[32] the amount of health information spread online through the net in the forms of communities and frequently asked questions has been increasing exponentially.[33] Accordingly, social networks have intensified

---

[23]The shift in format enabled by the creation of comprehensive electronic health records made up by patients' medical data, has opened up the way for previously unthinkable uses of patients' data for both research and clinical-related purposes. In this sense, see Jensen et al. (2012), pp. 395 ff.

[24]Lupton (2017).

[25]Budzinski and Schneider (2017), pp. 89 ff.

[26]The decreasing cost of genomic sequencing has enabled the collection of a vast amount of genomic data over the last years. See Stephens et al. (2015), p. 1002195.

[27]Kandula and Shaman (2 August 2019).

[28]Vayena and Blasimme (2018), p. 119.

[29]Hoffman and Podgurski (2008), p. 86.

[30]For an analysis of the new countenance of contracting techniques in the digital economy, see Grundman and Hacker (2017), pp. 255 ff.

[31]These free services are provided through a complex platform structure that is characterised by a twofold function related on the one side to the provision of free communication services and on the other side to the provision of charged online advertising space. In this way, the losses suffered on the free side are recouped on the paying side. This is the functioning ratio underlying the so-called two-sided markets, which are the distinctive business formula in the digital environment. Hence, on the 'zero-price' side of the platform, digital companies collect multidimensional health data from mobile technologies and through the on- and off-line services they provide. Evans and Schmalensee (2015), pp. 404 ff. Rochet and Tirole (2003), pp. 990 ff.

[32]Pasquale (2014), p. 115.

[33]Solberg (2012), pp. 327 ff. See also Pasquale (2014), p. 103, mentioning the forum PatientsLikeMe, providing a platform in which health issues are specifically addressed.

surveillance specifically over health-inflected data.[34] Facebook, for example, has designed an artificial intelligence application to identify suicidal intent in user-generated content.[35] The algorithm designed by Facebook was intended to scan users' posts, the comments made in response to those posts and also users' private messages in order to identify eventual suicide risk.[36]

Through the employment of associative and probabilistic analytics, also runaway data—apparently not related to physical or mental health conditions, but revealing socioeconomic and lifestyle information about travels or financial transactions, or statistical data referring to crime rates or to house prices in certain areas, have the potential to become silent and unexpected informants of (current and future) health conditions.[37] This data is captured by the technical sensors that constantly keep under surveillance data subjects' sensitive conditions.[38]

Together with socioeconomic and lifestyle data, also environmental data related for example to climate or pollution data as well as wider behavioural or social data, such as GPS information regarding access to an emergency room or apparently neutral actions such as online searches or purchases[39] could signal the occurrence of an illness.[40] In these regards, for example, a credit card website expressly affirmed that credit card purchase information was used as part of a scoring system predicting the probability of consumers getting chronically ill.[41]

If one thinks about the uncountable possible health relations between the most different aspects and expressions of individuals' lives and lifestyles, potentially every type of data spread on the web, could become health inflected,[42] along the

---

[34] On the issue see BBC News (26 August 2016).

[35] Mask (6 November 2018).

[36] Zuckerberg (16 February 2017).

[37] Stressing the point also Comandè and Schneider (2018), pp. 284 ff.

[38] Talking about the need to see clinical care through a massive surveillance lens, Boiten (5 May 2016), where it is stated that "we need all the data on everyone, just in case they require treatment". Sharon (2017), pp. 97–99.

[39] In these regards, famous is the story regarding the American Department Store Target that on the basis of the loyalty card of a teenager were able to predict the pregnant condition of the teenager. Indeed, given her purchase history, Target started to send a series of advertisements coupons targeting needs related to pregnancy, so that the family of the teenager could understand that the girl was pregnant even before that the girl herself new. Duhigg (16 February 2012). The case shows how a shopping list can enable a fairly accurate prediction of a biomedical condition, nearly in the same way as a normal medical test. So Vayena and Gasser (2016), p. 22.

[40] Pasquale (2014), pp. 100–101, giving the example of a woman that had searched online for information regarding multiple sclerosis, subscribing therefore a recommendation service for physicians. That data was collected by the KBM Group, a data analytics and marketing company, that subsequently sent her promotional material for an event for multiple sclerosis sufferers.

[41] Dilworth (14 August 2014).

[42] See Rubinstein (2013), pp. 74 ff. As has been stated, corporations use a huge amount of "'non-traditional' third party data sources, such as consumer buying history, to predict a life insurance applicant's health status with accuracy comparable to a medical exam". So Robinson et al. (September 2014), p. 6, emphasis added.

lines of big data's decontextualization cycles, well described by Helen Nissenbaum.[43]

The above-made examples show that under the current technological developments, health-related big data is an evolving ecosystem,[44] made up of "all health relevant data that can be made interoperable and thus amenable to predictive data mining for health-related purposes".[45] Put altogether this data contains extremely detailed information of users'/citizens'/patients' features at phenotypic, genotypic, behavioural and environmental levels.[46]

This digital data is becoming increasingly relevant for the assessment and enquiry over patients' medical conditions, thus giving rise to what some strand of the literature has been referring to as "digital phenotype".[47] Thanks to the development of data mining and deep-learning techniques, this vast variety of data differently linked to users' health can be valuably exploited in order to infer health-related predictions.[48]

In this strictly interconnected ecosystem, data generated for a wide range of purposes, apparently unrelated to biomedicine, entail an enormous potential for health research.[49]

2.1.2 *New Technological Capabilities and the Emerging Scientific Epistemiological Approach*

The relevance of new types of data for health-related enquiries, is the result of the changed technological landscape, tracing new patterns of health information production.[50] The health-related uses of expanded data sources are indeed stirred by the new analytical capabilities, who are pointing the reflectors of healthcare research outside the walls of clinics, stretching the quantity, the variety and the frequency of health data collection. Hence, together with the tightening of the algorithmic processing infrastructure, health research is increasingly relying on varied and integrated datasets, of which strict biomedical and genomic data are just a minimal

[43] Nissenbaum (2008).

[44] Vayena et al. (2016); Vayena and Blasimme (2018), p. 119; see also Vayena and Blasimme (2017), pp. 501 ff.

[45] Vayena and Blasimme (2017), pp. 502–503.

[46] Vayena and Blasimme (2017), p. 503.

[47] Jain et al. (2015), pp. 462–463.

[48] Krumholz (2014), pp. 1163 ff.

[49] Vayena and Gasser (2016), pp. 17–39. Schneider and Comandè (2018), p. 286; Mendelson and Mendelson (2017), pp. 37 ff.

[50] The National Cancer Institute has expressly declared that the traditional model for analyzing genomic data has become 'unsustainable'. National Cancer Institute (22 October 2021).

portion.[51] Current technological capabilities make it possible to spot correlations and patterns among the collected datasets. As has been observed in the literature, "in data mining, a pattern is a statement that describes relationships in a (sub) set of data such that the statement is simpler than the enumeration of all the facts in the (sub) set of data".[52] Upon the identified patterns, big data analytics construct a model or group profile, through which data are clustered into groups with similar properties.[53] These "pigeonholing" processes are leading to a growing reliance on correlations, which are progressively replacing the more sophisticated and rare causality links.[54] The hidden patterns that are spotted by machine learning processes are in turn the basis for the predictions and inferences about users' health.[55] Accordingly, the algorithmic processing of these variously collected data enables the extraction and the finalisation of the entrenched biomedical value so as to generate new "artificial" scientific knowledge.

The current computational capabilities are thus transmuting the manners in which scientific knowledge is produced, along the lines of a newly emerging epistemological approach:[56] scientific insights are indeed not anymore derived from the combination of theory and physical evidence,[57] but just from data.[58]

It thus seems that the current technological environment is giving rise to a new conception of science, increasingly relying on the advanced capabilities of collecting and mining large datasets, detecting patterns and building predictive models upon these patterns. In this frame, scientific enquiries are growingly turning from factual explanations to data-driven predictions.[59]

The use of automated computational processing methods as a source of scientific evidence appears to be subverting the ordinary patterns of scientific investigations, traditionally determined by the combination of theoretical precepts and physical observations.[60] In the changed technological landscape, these two traditional tools of scientific enquiry- that is theory and practice through physical testing- are increasingly displaced by algorithm-driven models, which provide outputs based on the inputs given by the data that trains the model itself.

The change in the tools used for the production of scientific evidence is linked to a shift in the parameters upon which the scientific evidence is generated: if the

---

[51] Comandè and Schneider (2018), p. 288.

[52] Custers (2013), p. 5, stating further that "a pattern is not likely to be true across all the data. This makes it necessary to express the certainty of the pattern. Certainty may involve several factors, such as the integrity of the data and the size of the sample".

[53] G. Comandè (2017), pp. 169 ff.

[54] In this sense Mayer-Schönberger and Cukier (2013), p. 23.

[55] In this sense Zarsky (2003), p. 1.

[56] Sharon (2016), p. 6, referring to Kitchin (1 April 2014).

[57] Anderson (23 June 2008); Coveney et al. (13 November 2016).

[58] Mayer-Schönberger and Cukier (2013), p. 26.

[59] Skopek (2018), pp. 30 ff.

[60] Comandè (2018), pp. 270 ff.

traditional conception of science was centred upon the paradigm of causality, big data analytics employed for research purposes appear to be governed by the different parameter of correlation.[61] This parameter itself relies on probabilistic and statistical inferences and thus raises some doubts regarding its trustworthiness.[62] Indeed, the correlations that orient predictions and thus the resulting decision-making are hypotheses automatically generated by algorithms that process the premises resulting from a certain set of data.[63] These hypothesis can derive from direct matches when data are close to their original significance as well as from probabilistic links or predictive guesses,[64] which are characterised by a gradually weaker link between the observed or provided data and the inferred ones.[65]

Against this backdrop, this new scientific epistemology has been associated by some authors to the "end of theory"[66] and the rise of a scientific "data fundamentalism",[67] which creates new types of biases, in terms of both *data quality* and *data representativeness.*[68]

2.1.3 Stakeholders Involved in Digital Health

The new technological processing capabilities are not only changing the object of health research and the tools through which the same research is conducted, but appear to be transmuting the courses of health research conduction from a subjective standpoint. Indeed, the growing importance of algorithmic processing methods for both the collection and the processing of health-inflected data is opening up new operational spaces in the field of health research for high tech companies. These companies do not solely provide the technological infrastructure needed for the processing of the vast emerging health datasets, but have also acquired an analytical expertise that has been developed to run investigations on large databases made up by various internet search queries and consumer purchases.

These technological capacities are increasingly needed for the purposes of scientific enquiries. This is progressively attracting digital companies to so called body-based markets.[69] This is a particularly interesting phenomenon given that consumer tech companies did not have an interest in health and medicine in the past.[70]

---

[61] Zarsky (2018), pp. 42 ff.

[62] Stressing the point of the lack of trustworthiness in the current scientific environment and the need to rebuild it, Vayena et al. (2017), pp. 704 ff.

[63] This is well described by Hildebrandt (2008), pp. 17 ff.

[64] Moerel and Prins (25 May 2016).

[65] Reconstruction of OECD (2019), p. 66.

[66] Anderson (23 June 2008).

[67] Stressing the point, Krawford (2013).

[68] See infra Chap. 3, Sect. 3.3.4.

[69] Powles and Hodson (2017), p. 354.

[70] Powles and Hodson (2017), p. 354.

A few examples will suffice to demonstrate the growing attention given to the healthcare sector by high-tech giants. Apple, for instance, launched in September 2014 a so-called 'HealthKit', a software platform that collects users' health, fitness and medical data, bringing these together into one place for users to view. The innovative feature of the platform lied in the fact that it enabled the sharing of the collected data with healthcare professionals. The 'Healthkit' was further developed, resulting in the so-called 'ResearchKit',[71] an open source framework enabling researchers to conduct medical research on iPhones. It is aimed at collecting data of research subjects, handling them back to researchers. Leading medical institutes in universities worldwide have started to use Apple's 'ResearchKit' for the conduction of several studies regarding some important illnesses such as asthma, diabetes, and Parkinson's.[72] More recently, Apple has declared its intention to develop an app enabling the download of electronic medical records collected from participating hospitals and clinics, as well as from Apple devices, directly onto users' smartphones.[73]

Similarly, also Facebook has developed a 'Genes for Good' app aimed at generating and analysing an enormous database of health and genetic information.[74] Facebook's involvement in health research has awaken great discussions in the literature[75] particularly in respect to its 2014 "emotional contagion" study resulting from the testing of the emotional value of nearly 700.000 users.[76]

Ultimately- and maybe most significantly- also Google's investment in the healthcare sector has been radically expanding over the last years, as reflected by projects as Google Flu[77] and Google Health API,[78] or by the foundation of new Google's spin-offs as Google Genomics,[79] Google DeepMind or Verily,[80] Calico[81]

---

[71] The ResearchKit is a software platform that collects a vast range of health, fitness and medical data about a user and brings these together into one place for the user to view. See Apple https://www.apple.com/researchkit/.

[72] Stampa (10 March 2015).

[73] The Economist (1 February 2018).

[74] For a description of the app See Genes for Good, https://genesforgood.sph.umich.edu/.

[75] Auerbach (2015); Crawford (2014); Grimmelmann (2015), pp. 219 ff.; Meyer and Chabris (19 June 2015); Waldman (2014).

[76] Kramer et al. (2014).

[77] Google Flu was a web-service operated by Google, which provided estimates of influenza activities for over 25 countries. Reflecting on the experiences of Google Flu and Ebola tracking, Ginsberg et al. (2009), pp. 1012–1014; Hall (2014), pp. 27 ff.

[78] Google API is a cloud computing infrastructure providing a robust infrastructure to manage some health data types. See Google Cloud (5 March 2018).

[79] MIT Technology (6 November 2014).

[80] "Verily is focused on using technology to better understand health, as well as prevent, detect, and manage disease". So Verily Life Sciences, online available at https://verily.com/.

[81] Calico, for example, targets the spectrum of aging related diseases. See Mukherjee (24 March 2017b).

and City-Block Health[82] and Google Brain.[83] Google Brain's task has been that of analyzing thousands of electronic health records through artificial intelligence tools in order to predict clinical outcomes related to in-hospital mortality and diagnoses at the time of discharge. In a study published in 2018, Google scientists concluded that these models where more accurate than traditional clinical predictive models.[84]

Google has also engaged in other ambitious projects such as the Baseline project[85] and 23&me.[86] Google's action in the healthcare sector has lately become so intense that some scholars have appointed the phenomenon as the "Googlization of health research".[87]

Similar activities have been carried out by other high tech companies, such as IBM and Amazon. The former, for example, has established the business unit Watson Health, delivering cloud-based access to its Watson computer in order to analyse healthcare data. Through the cloud service, researchers and physicians are able to share and analyse health data in order to detect trends and correlations through artificial intelligence tools. The platform thus makes it possible to aggregate health data stemming from the most disparate sources, as clinical claims, accounting, billing, devices and online community.[88]

Likewise, also Amazon has recently come to market a software named "Amazon Comprehend Medical", that uses artificial intelligence in order to identify and analyse text based medical information, extracting health information, as diagnoses and medications from text files, and identifying relationships between different data points.[89]

The new forms of technological and computational expertise that these companies offer is significantly changing the health research environment and has the

[82]City-block Health is building a personalized health system that serves qualifying Medicaid or Medicare in areas that traditionally do not have a good health service. City Block, online available at https://www.cityblock.com/.

[83]Google Brain is a machine intelligence team focused on deep learning, which has the aim to map the human brain. See The Google Brain Team (11 January 2018).

[84]Rajkomar et al. (2018), pp. 1 ff.

[85]Google's spin off Verily, formerly known as 'Google Life Sciences', has launched in July 2014, the so called Baseline Study, in collaboration with Stanford and Duke Universities, with the purpose of enrolling 10.000 volunteers and using testing and sensors to track their clinical, molecular, genetic and microbiome data, in some cases combining these with participants' electronic health records. The ultimate aim of the study is to detect early signs of transition to ill health and develop preventive treatments. See Verily (12 December 2017).

[86]In 2007, Google and Facebook grounded the genetic testing company 23andMe, which in 2015 reached one million genotyped customers, making it the largest database in the world of subjects who had handed out their consent and who were recontactable. 23andMe has pursued its research activities in collaboration with industry and academia, using the genetic and online survey data generated by its customers. Sharon (2016), p. 2.

[87]Sharon (2016), pp. 4–5. The expression 'googlization' is drawn from Vaidhyanathan (2011).

[88]Lohr (13 April 2015).

[89]Evans and Stevens (27 November 2018).

disruptive aptitude to determine the upcoming research agenda.[90] Indeed, the technological infrastructures and the data analytics capacities- in terms of artificial intelligence and machine-learning algorithms- these companies provide are way superior to those that are available to traditional healthcare providers such as universities and hospitals.[91] This is creating new forms of dependencies, since it is becoming increasingly necessary for research institutes to partner with companies providing the relevant research set-up. As a result, big data companies are gaining a key role in enabling and defining scientific research patterns.

2.1.4 The Newly Emerging Paradigm of Health Research

The above-traced developments are significantly subverting that what can be identified as a traditional health research paradigm.

This paradigm is indeed characterised by the following basic features: (i) the research is carried out over human subjects; (ii) the essential precondition for any research endeavour is research subjects' informed consent; (iii) accordingly, the purpose and the context of the research is limited to a specific project and secondary use of the gathered information is exceptional; (iv) the research is based on a physical intervention on the life or body of a human being[92]; (v) the research is site-related, that is, territorially-based and thus territorially-limited; (vi) the research is conducted by one or more, but still *ex ante* identifiable, research sponsors; (vii) the responsibility of the research is thus allocated onto specific actors.

It is to be questioned whether this paradigm of health-related research and the corresponding legal framework are still suitable in the algorithm-driven health research. Indeed, in the networked health research environment, where digital companies are becoming increasingly important players, the health research ecosystem is evolving around different traits, and rather opposite in respect to the ones recalled above.

The newly emerging research patterns are indeed (i) carried over digital data that intrinsically or extrinsically- that meaning in combination with other data- entail health information; (ii) in the interconnected research ecosystem, the importance of informed consent as a mean of controlling and tracing disclosed personal information needs to be reconsidered[93]; (iii) the purpose and the context of health data processing is under constant change, this leading to an unceasing re-use of health data on which current digital health research is based; (iv) digitised research is moving along the lines of remote monitoring, which is increasingly replacing

---

[90] Sharon (2016), p. 2.

[91] Sharon (2016), p. 2.

[92] In respect to the notion of intervention, see Metcalf and Crawford (2016), p. 6.

[93] Nehf (2016). Talking about an "outright" failure of informed consent, Monteleone (2015), pp. 69 ff.

physical intervention in favour of automated analysis of constantly updated datasets; (v) territoriality is being replaced by the ubiquity of data analytics; (vi) in the networked, digitised research environment, both the blossoming of outsourcing practices and partnerships, and the generative nature of algorithmic analytics, renders it highly difficult to trace the actual 'trial sponsors'; (vii) this, ultimately blurs the borders of involved actors' research liabilities.

Against this backdrop, the digital algorithmic environment is shaping a new health-related research paradigm, in respect to which specific regulations based on that what some strand of the literature has defined the "clinical trial model"[94] result to be largely inappropriate. A first demonstration of this is given by some recent regulatory developments occurred at European level, which appear to be a direct response to the changes occurring at the previous stage of health research.

2.1.5 Regulatory Developments from the Perspective of the Data: The Case of Pharmaceutical Research

The above highlighted changes are starting to concretely impact on pharmaceutical research and development.

As the Council of the European Union has highlighted, the "availability of high quality health data for research and innovation enables the creation of new knowledge to prevent diseases, to achieve earlier and more accurate diagnosis and to improve treatment, in particular supporting personalised medicine (...)". Along these lines, the combination of "data sets from different data sources and across borders is especially important in the field of rare and low-prevalence complex diseases". Similarly, the work undertaken by the European Reference Networks is worth taking into consideration, since it has been constituted to establish a dedicated IT platform for pooling expertise, information expertise, information exchange and mutual learning, acknowledging the potential of these networks for enhanced data sharing that would benefit research and innovation, particularly in the area of rare and low prevalence complex diseases.

Outside the institutional context, an increasingly important tool for pharmaceutical research is given by online social networks, where communities of individuals have been formed for the establishment and the pursuing of health research projects. The type of research conducted by these communities is characterised by self-experimentation, self-surveillance, analysis of genomic data, and genome-wide association studies.[95] Moreover, the already recalled mobile technologies are opening new trial endpoints, which also contribute to render the current pharmaceutical research environment more varied.[96]

[94] Laurie (2013), p. 191.

[95] Bhowmick and Hribar (26 August 2016).

[96] Clinical Trials Transformation Initiative (16 December 2019).

This is why some strand of the literature[97] is questioning the future evolution of the notion of clinical trials- and the data deriving from it- in light of the newly emerging needs of novel adaptive trial designs, platform trials, and other novel forms of trials design.[98]

From a further perspective, digital health data are becoming extremely important in those research areas where there is an increased risk of exposure to unknown substances and side effects; where it would be extremely costly to start research or where there are not enough patients to test the substances.[99]

The increasing importance of data analytics in the current research environment is leading to a progressive reconsideration of traditional models of pharmaceutical research. The more sophisticated analytical capabilities are paving the way for new molecular-based testing techniques, relying on the combination of automated processes and the improved understanding of human genetic variation.[100] Additionally, predictions rendered by the available computational means are being employed for the forecast of disease risk among healthy subjects and of the therapeutic response among patients. These predictions are becoming a useful resource for drug development and drug discovery[101] and for tailoring the design of medicinal products and of treatments to specific patient types, especially with regards to smaller subgroups of treatment-eligible patients. Ultimately, projects based on big data are used for comparing the safety and efficacy of drugs in real world settings.[102]

The growing importance of digital health data in the assessment of medicines safety and efficacy is starting to trigger some important developments at regulatory level[103] in terms of faster regulatory approval processes and shorter R&D timelines to market entry.

The European Medicines Agency is taking into consideration adaptive pathways schemes that allow for early and progressive access to medicines to a limited group of patients through conditional approval, with staged approvals and enhanced access prospects based on the emergent evidence on the benefit-risk balance of a product, as

[97] Eichler and Sweeney (16 February 2018).

[98] On the issue, see also, Berry (2015), pp. 951 ff.

[99] Seitz (2017), pp. 301–302, who stresses that health data analytics could be particularly important with regards to rare diseases where it is often difficult to find enough subjects to test active substances. Hence, the use of data could not only reduce the costs for orphan drugs, but could lead to the appraisal of information regarding the effects of new substances and could be key for the parallel sequencing of patients with rare diseases.

[100] These two factors lie at the basis also of the rise of precision medicine based on the idea to deliver a more effective, tailored and targeted treatment "for the right person, at the right time". For an analysis over the legal issues related to precision medicine, see Rai (2017a), pp. 357 ff. European Parliament (2015).

[101] Seitz (2017), p. 296.

[102] Horgan and Kent (2017), p. 198.

[103] Marjanovic et al. (2017), p. 9.

given by a combined evaluation of clinical trials and other 'real-world' data.[104] This means that the assessment of safety and efficacy of pharmaceuticals will likely occur on the basis not only of physical clinical trials data, but also of various "real-world data".[105] As has been clarified, the term "real-world data" is used to describe healthcare-related data that is collected outside of randomized clinical trials. This type of data is more precisely gathered from registries, electronic health records (EHRs), and insurance data either in specific observational studies or through continued monitoring of use, benefits and risks.[106]

The importance of real-world data has been acknowledged by the European Medicines Agency at the joint meeting together with the Human Scientific Committees' Working Parties with Patients' and Consumers' Organisations (PCWP) and Healthcare Professionals' Organisations (HCPWP) on the 17th and 18th April 2018, where the Agency specifically highlighted the importance of real world data for the regulation of pharmaceuticals, especially for the purposes of monitoring unexpected and long-term risk.[107] More specifically, the Agency discussed case studies regarding the enhancement of drug development through the employment of real-world data, and the emergence of contrasting findings between real-world evidence and those from traditional randomized trials.[108] Ultimately, it stressed the importance of real-world evidence for the understanding of therapeutics' complexity.

The key relevance of "real world data" as a support for evaluation and supervision of the safety and efficacy of pharmaceutical products licensed in the EU has been stressed by a Summary Report of the Heads of Medicines Agency (HMA) and EMA Joint Big Data Task Force released on the 13th February 2019.[109] In the report the agencies recognize the importance of a great variety of data in the lifecycle of drug development, which go beyond traditional sources of evidence to support decision making, which is much broader than the traditional clinical

[104] More specifically, the European Medicines Agency has cherished two expedited pathways for the development and thus to the access of medicines that have the potential to offer major therapeutic advantages over current treatment options for serious conditions that match to unmet medical needs. These expedited pathways respectively regard the so-called Promising Innovative Medicine (PIM) and Priority Medicines (PRIME). As the Agency has clarified, "adaptive pathways is a concept of medicines development intended for medicines that address patients' unmet medical needs. It seeks to maximize the positive effect of new medicines by balancing timely access for patients likely to benefit most from a new medicine with the need for adequate, evolving information on their benefits and risks". European Medicines (28 July 2016), p. 13.

[105] On the issue see European Medicines Agency (2017), p. 16.

[106] Heads of Medicines Agencies and European Medicines Agency (13th February 2019), p. 16.

[107] European Medicines Agency (24 April 2018).

[108] European Medicines Agency (24 April 2018), p. 4.

[109] Heads of Medicines Agencies and European Medicines Agency (13 February 2019).

trials data,.[110] More precisely, the report identifies six categories of data which are relevant for pharmaceutical R&D.[111] The report refers to a variety of data, including, amongst others, "observational data", "social media data" and "mobile health data".[112]

The opportunity to integrate the scientific evidence derived from these data into regulatory decision making across the pharmaceutical products' lifecycle are groundbreaking: as the report highlights, the chances given by these data for the research and development of new drugs are related to the improvement of efficiency and cost-effectiveness of the processes of drug discovery and development, through quicker identification of drugs' responsiveness and adverse reactions.[113] Moreover, the consideration of a variety of patients' real world data, signaling also lifestyle factors, can help incorporating a holistic picture of the patient in drugs' design, with that posing the grounds for the advancement of personalized medicines.[114]

As the agencies recognize, these chances need to be maximized through an adequate regulatory recognition assuring that the regulatory system has the capability and the capacity to guide, analyze and interpret these data. In these regards, the agencies stress the importance of defining technological standards for digital data used for regulatory purposes. The definition of these standards is deemed as a fundamental safeguard to overcome problems of uncertainties regarding the quality of the data and the trustworthiness of the generated evidence.[115] Real world data used for the purposes of scientific evidence is indeed of unstructured, heterogeneous and unvalidated nature and it is difficult to determine the exact source of it.

From a strictly legal perspective, the agencies interestingly point out that the ownership of "real world data", otherwise called "observational data", resides onto multiple stakeholders, with many of them having no specific obligations with regards to regulatory agencies. This renders it extremely difficult to level out such data with regards to the quality and accurateness.

In these regards, the agencies stress the need to condition the use of these "real world data" to the respect of quality standards with regards to the source of the data, its transformation and aggregation.[116] Since the obligation to observe these standards cannot be posed onto the stakeholders who generate and own the relevant data but who are not directly involved in the regulatory process, it could be desirable to

---

[110] Heads of Medicines Agencies and European Medicines Agency (13 February 2019), p. 16.

[111] The six identified categories are genomics; bioanalytical omics, clinical trials, observational data (real world data), spontaneous ADR data and social media and m-health data. Heads of Medicines Agencies and European Medicines Agency (13th February 2019), p. 3.

[112] Heads of Medicines Agencies and European Medicines Agency (13 February 2019).

[113] Heads of Medicines Agencies and European Medicines Agency (13 February 2019), p. 1.

[114] The issue of personalised medicines has been addressed by the European Council (7 December 2015).

[115] Heads of Medicines Agencies and European Medicines Agency (13 February 2019), pp. 11–13.

[116] Heads of Medicines Agencies and European Medicines Agency (13 February 2019), pp. 13–15.

set the duty to conform to such standards onto the companies who directly make use of such data for their marketing requests.

According to the agencies, the enactment of quality control measures and findings should be subject to adequate transparency measures which inform the whole regulatory landscape regarding pharmaceuticals.[117] In line with the recent transparency initiatives that have been enacted at regulatory level in the field of both pharmaceuticals and medical devices regulation[118] with the creation of databases regarding regulatory-relevant information, a relevant option could be the establishment of a standardized database managed by the European Medicines Agency regarding non-clinical trials data used for the purposes of the evaluation of medicinals' safety and efficacy.

Although containing very early thoughts on the possible regulatory and policy responses to the datification of health research and market, the report issued by the two regulatory agencies is to be welcomed as a starting point in the reflections regarding the need to adapt the regulatory framework to the occurring shift from a closed- to an open-ended research environment.[119]

The opportunity to modernize regulatory approaches to the developing setting of the pharmaceutical research and development environment is being taking into account also in the United States. Here, the FDA has declared its intention to find new strategies in order to "modernize clinical trials to advance precision medicine, patient protections and more efficient product development".[120] The inclusion of other data different from the ones derived from traditional clinical trials investigations, is recognized as the agency's priority. In this regard, the agency has launched a "clinical trials transformation initiative",[121] evaluating "the role of decentralized

[117]Heads of Medicines Agencies and European Medicines Agency (13 February 2019), pp. 14–16.

[118]The transparency concerns in the field of pharmaceutical regulation have been addressed in the Clinical Trials Regulation EU 536/2014 that has set specific reporting duties onto pharmaceutical companies that have to publish the results of their investigations into the publicly accessible clinical trials database established under art. 81(4). See Regulation EU 536/2014 of the European Parliament and of the Council of 16 April 2014 on clinical trials on medicinal products for human use, repealing Directive 2001/20/EC (27 May 2014) OJ L 158/1. https://ec.europa.eu/health/sites/health/files/files/eudralex/vol-1/reg_2014_536/reg_2014_536_en.pdf. Similarly, also the recently enacted Medical Device Regulation EU 745/2017 has established a database (Eudamed) on medical devices collecting information regarding, amongst others, devices on the market, relevant economic operators, market surveillance issues under art. 33(1). See Regulation EU 2017/745 of the European Parliament and of the Council of 5 April 2017 on medical devices, amending Directive 2001/83/EC, Regulation (EC) No 178/2002 and Regulation (EC) No 1223/2009 and repealing Council Directives 90/385/EEC and 93/42/EEC (5 May 2017) OJ L117/1. https://eur-lex.europa.eu/legal-content/EN/TXT/PDF/?uri=CELEX:32017R0745&from=EN (Medical Device Regulation).

[119]Heads of Medicines Agencies and European Medicines Agency (13 February 2019), p. 14. Reflecting over regulatory hurdles, Colonna (2019), pp. 61–63.

[120]Food and Drug Administration (14 March 2019).

[121]See https://www.ctti-clinicaltrials.org/. As stated, the initiative has "the mission to develop and drive adoption of practices that will increase the quality and efficiency of clinical trials".

clinical trials and mobile technologies".[122] As the European Medicines Agency, also the American drugs' regulatory agency is thus looking at new research paradigms capable of turning down the barriers between digital data and clinical research. The new research frontiers are meant to generate a new type of scientific evidence, ready to be shared among the stakeholders of what is forecasted as a "learning health care system", in which pre-marketing research continues to learn from what occurs after the marketing stage. With regards to the subsequent phase of the marketing of pharmaceutical products, indeed, big health datasets can be used to assess post-marketing adverse events and thus the safety of pharmaceutical products.[123]

2.1.6 Regulatory Developments from the Perspective of the Technology: The Case of Medical Devices

In addition to the transformation of the regulatory pharmaceutical landscape, the rising employment of data analytics in the health sector is also changing the features of medical devices.

Already in 2014 the European Commission was acknowledging the existence of more than 100.000 apps related to mobile health,[124] highlighting that the landscape of mobile health is extremely varied, encompassing "mobile phones, patient monitoring devices, personal digital assistants, and other wireless devices' and 'applications such as lifestyle and wellbeing apps as well as personal guidance systems, health information and medication reminders provided by sms and telemedicine provided wirelessly".

These mobile devices increasingly carry out tasks that are traditionally performed by medical devices, such as the monitoring of symptoms, the diagnosis of disease and the administration of medicines.

From a legal standpoint, e-mobile health technologies and the phenomenon of "appification" is challenging the borders of the legal notion of medical device. In this perspective, it must be noticed that until recently, there has been great regulatory uncertainty with regards to what extent a health app amounts to a medical device and thus falls under the respective regulation. The issue is of utmost importance given that the qualification as a medical device means a greater regulatory burden for manufacturing companies, in terms of enhanced control over the safety and efficacy features of devices that interact with the human body and that thus have an ultimate influence over users' health.

[122] Food and Drug Administration (14 March 2019).

[123] Heads of Medicines Agencies and European Medicines Agency (13 February 2019), p. 29.

[124] European Commission (10 April 2014).

Indeed, the European "medical device framework", which has been amended by the Medical Device Regulation,[125] sets up precise safety requirements as well as a number of documentary and investigative procedures that must be followed in order to provide evidence of compliance. In case the products meets regulatory requirements, the EU certification is issued, which enables the same product to circulate across the European marketplace.[126]

The medical device framework applies also to standalone softwares.[127] In these regards, the same European Court of Justice has stated that art.1(1) and art. 1(2)a of the Council Directive 93/42/EEC of 14 June 1993 concerning medical devices, as amended by Directive 2007/47/EC of the European Parliament and of the Council of 5 September 2007, is to be interpreted as to include also software, "of which at least one of the functions makes it possible to use patient-specific data for the purposes, inter alia, f detecting contraindications, drug interactions and excessive doses, is, in respect of that function, a medical device within the meaning of those provisions, even if that software does not act directly in or on the human body".[128]

Upon these premises, the European medical device framework restricts the scope of medical devices upon the criterion of "intended purpose" of use, this meaning that the manufacturer must have intended the device to serve a medical purpose.[129] Interestingly, the Court of Justice of the European Union has clarified that the criterion of the 'intended purpose' is to be applied also to softwares employed in the medical field.[130]

[125]The Medical Device Framework has been amended by the Medical Device Regulation- Regulation EU 2017/745 of the European Parliament and of the Council of 5 April 2017, on medical devices amending Directive 2001/83/EC, Regulation EC n. 178/2002 and Regulation EC n. 1223/2009 and repealing Council Directives 90/385/EEC and 93/42/EEC.

[126]It must be highlighted that the safety requirements are the more strict the more a device is considered risky. Hence, devices that are considered to be as low risk need to comply to self-compliance and self-notification processes; whereas devices that are considered highly risky more active investigative steps are required under the involvement also of national regulatory bodies.

[127]See art. 1(2) lett.a) of the Council Directive 93/42/EEC of 14 June 1993 concerning medical devices (12 July 1993) OJ L 169/1. https://eur-lex.europa.eu/LexUriServ/LexUriServ.do?uri=CONSLEG:1993L0042:20071011:en:PDF.

[128]European Court of Justice, Snitem and Philips France vs. Premier ministre and Ministre des Affaires sociales et de la Santé, C-329/16 (7 December 2017).

[129]The medical purposes are listed in art. 2 of the new Medical Device Regulation and comprise the "diagnosis, prevention, monitoring, prediction, prognosis, treatment or alleviation of disease; diagnosis, monitoring, treatment, alleviation of, or compensation for, an injury or disability; investigation, replacement or modification of the anatomy or of a physiological or pathological process or state, — providing information by means of in vitro examination of specimens derived from the human body, including organ, blood and tissue donations (. . .)".

[130]European Court of Justice, Brain Products Gmbh vs. Bio Semi VOF, Case C-129/11 (22 November 2012), para 17,stating 'As regards software, the legislature thus made unequivocally clear that in order for it to fall within the scope of Directive 93/42 it is not sufficient that it be used in a medical context, but that it is also necessary that the intended purpose, defined by the manufacturer, is specifically medical'.

As some strand of the literature has acknowledged,[131] the "intended purpose" criterion is double-edged. On the one hand it is meant to free from the rigors of the medical device framework- and with that promote the innovation and spread of-softwares that do not fulfill a medical purpose but that carry out neighboring functions such as well-being apps or similar devices. On the other hand, however, this subjective criterion appears to exempt from compliance to the set safety requirements those self-tracking devices and the wide range of apps that, for example, encourage a healthy living, with that indirectly preventing diseases, or that measure physiological parameters without being specifically destined to 'medical purposes'. This raises some significant concerns if one thinks that these devices actually interact and thus have an impact on users' health.

Facing this problem, the European Commission had issued some guidelines regarding the qualification and classification of standalone software as a medical device.[132] These guidelines appear to be extremely interesting since they identify as a relevant criterion the fact that the software is intended to interpret-or to facilitate the interpretation of- data by modifying or representing health related individual information. Hence, according to these guidelines, an app is to be qualified as a medical device only in case the app transforms and interprets the collected data in order to render and construct a specific image of users' health.[133] Conversely, if the app merely collects, stores and transfers data, then it does not have to comply with the medical device framework.[134] Again, the rationale of this distinction is that only those devices which impact on- and thus pose a risk to users' health- need to comply with the safety requirements established by the medical device framework.

The issue of the qualification as a medical device of health apps has been taken into consideration also by the Court of Justice of the European Union in its decision on the case C-329/16 *Snitem and Philips France*. On this occasion, the Court has argued that a standalone software is to be qualified as a medical device within the meaning of art. 1(2) of the Medical Device Directive disregards the fact that it interacts on or with the human body, in case the app serves a medical purpose, this meaning that it "assists" the "prevention, monitoring, treatment or alleviation of disease".

Both the Guidelines issued by the European Commission and the case brought in front of the Court of Justice of the European Union reveal that the spread of digital tools interacting with users' health are challenging the legal notion of medical device, with that raising a new set of new and rather unexplored safety concerns,

---

[131] Quinn (2017), pp. 361 ff.

[132] European Commission (July 2016).

[133] In this perspective, it must be qualified as medical device an app that provides immediate decision-triggering information, or alters the representation of data in a way that contributes to the interpretative or perceptual tasks performed by medical professionals; and also an app that provides information that contributes to users'/patients' diagnosis or treatments. European Commission (July 2016), pp. 8–9.

[134] Equally falling outside the scope of the Medical Device Framework are the tools that combine medical knowledge with users' physiological parameters. European Commission (July 2016), p. 16.

which would need to be properly addressed by regulators in light of the ductile nature of these apps and the diverse risk to users' health that they pose.

According to a strand of the literature, the issue should be re-considered favoring a risk-based scaled approach, also taking into account the deeper fact that the proliferation of these digital tools is blurring the lines between acts of medicine and activities associated with well-being.[135] Indeed, the increased attention to the prevention of diseases is leading to a heightened use of monitoring devices, which collect physiological and lifestyle data that are often further aggregated into medical data. These combined datasets are then used for the purposes of treatment or other broader medical decisions. In this perspective, it is evident that a wide range of well-being devices are currently carrying out an ancillary function in respect to traditional medical devices. This means that although not "officially" used in the treatment process of a patient, the data rendered by well-being devices are nonetheless important informants used by the patient to orient its treatment and thus- although indirectly- to orient decisions over his/her health conditions. The acknowledgment of this should also lead to the consideration of the risks for users' health stemming from the employment of apps that, although not legally qualified as medical devices, serve an analogous function.[136]

While in the European Union the enactment of a stronger regulation regarding medical devices, establishing higher safety requirements, is opening up a big regulatory gap between the devices falling under the Regulation and those who are not qualified as a medical device, the United States are adopting a more flexible approach.

The FDA has indeed issued a Digital Health Innovation Action Plan, assuring "timely access to high quality, safe and effective digital health products.[137] Amongst other initiatives, the Plan comprises the "digital health software precertification pilot program", which replaces the need for a premarket submission for certain digital health products and provides for faster review of the marketing submission for other similar products. The program proposes a new approach to the regulation of digital health software products, based on the features of the producer rather than of the product. Under this firm-based approach, the FDA evaluates, on the basis of objective criteria, the satisfaction of health software developers' organizational features regarding the software design, validation and testing procedures. The companies that result compliant get a pre-market certification allowing them to market their low-risk digital health devices without additional review of the FDA

[135] Quinn (2017), pp. 368–369. For an analysis of the risk-based US model, see Cortez et al. (2014), pp. 372–379.

[136] Lorchan Lewis and Wyatt (2014), pp. 210 ff.

[137] For an overview of the Action Plan see Food and Drug Administration (7 December 2017c).

or through a more streamlined premarket review, including reduction of submission content or faster review of content.[138]

The firm-based approach proposed by the FDA seems to well suit the digital health environment where the notion of medical devices is stretched not only to include softwares with medical implementation, but is additionally challenged in respect to the digitization of pharmaceutical development. Some of the latest FDA clearances regarding mobile medical applications clearly show the increasing overlap between the medical devices' and the pharmaceutical products' regulatory spheres,[139] for which a same software could qualify as a medical device or as a support for treatment through integration with a medicinal product. In this light, the shift from a product- to a company-based approach could provide the necessary adaptiveness for regulating the fast-evolving health technology market.

In the digital health sector, as a consequence of the convergence between medical devices and pharmaceuticals, the area of 'borderline" digital products is sensitively growing.[140] The emergence of multi-faceted treatment systems, combining software and pharmaceutical products has been taken into consideration by the Medical Device Regulation, which demands stronger collaboration with the European Medicines Agency in the deliberation process regarding the regulatory status of products in borderline cases[141] and requires an appropriate interaction "in terms of consultations during pre-market assessments and of exchange of information in the context of vigilance activities between competent bodies under the same Medical Device Regulation and the Directive 2001/83/EC of the European Parliament and of the Council on the Community code relating to medicinal products for human use.[142]

2.2 The Organizational Patterns of Digital Health Research: The Rising Phenomenon of Health Data Pools

As the above paragraphs have shown, the health-related markets of both medicinal products and medical devices are undergoing a radical transformation due to digitalisation processes. The transformations can be summed up as follows. First, the medical device landscape has become increasingly "appified", triggering the

[138]The FDA observes that the pre-certification status could entitle health software developing firms to collect real world data post-market to affirm the regulatory status of the product or to support new and evolving product functions. See Food and Drug Administration (2017b).

[139]On 10 December 2018 the FDA has announced the clearance of a mobile medical application to treat substance abuse. It is the first time that a mobile app grants marketing license as a prescriptive treatment. Martens (19 December 2018). Nearly a year earlier, the FDA had authorised marketization of a pill combined with a sensor that tracks patients' response to the medication. See Food and Drug Administration (13 November 2017a).

[140]On the issue of so called 'borderline products' see Tseliou (28 March 2015).

[141]Recital 8 of the Medical Device Regulation.

[142]Recital 10 of the Medical Device Regulation.

need to extend the legal notion of medical devices, comprising also stand-alone softwares, as the European Court of Justice has acknowledged. In order to be trained and tested, these softwares need a vast amount of patients' health data.

Likewise, also pharmaceutical research and development processes are relying on a great variety of data that are taken from far outside the restricted scope of clinical trials and comprise also non directly health-related "real world data". The advantages in terms of efficiency and results that the inclusion of this non-strictly clinical data provide, are currently being considered by the European Medicine Agency in the context of regulatory procedures.

Third, the digitisation processes are extending the area of so-called borderline or combined health products, this also leading to the need to reconsider the competence sphere of regulatory authorities or the relationships between them, such as the European Commission and the European Medicines Agency.

As a result of the traced lines of development, innovation in health-related markets, such as the ones of medical devices and pharmaceuticals, is growingly occurring through the door of digitisation and datification patterns.[143] This means that in order to achieve innovation in health-related markets highly complex datasets as well as highly sophisticated analytical techniques.[144]

The importance of technological assets in terms of data and the related processing infrastructure for the advancement of the scientific and technological progress are having direct a direct impact on the organisational patterns that are coming to govern the production of health-related products and services.[145]

In particular, traditional actors in the healthcare setting, such as pharmaceutical companies or public healthcare providers, lack the information and technological expertise needed to exploit the newly available investigation tools and are thus increasingly looking for the support of big data companies owning mass amounts of users' data and controlling the standard technical infrastructure to run more sophisticated experiments and to provide prompter clinical responses. On the other hand, big data companies entering health markets need the more sophisticated health-related data and the expertise traditional stakeholders in the healthcare sector have.

As a result of the matching between these different economic interests, the conduction of healthcare research is starting to evolve around a complex architecture, where courses of biomedical innovation are driven by new forms of

---

[143]This is well expressed by Nicholson Price II (2015), p. 422, affirming that "black-box medicine relies principally on pure information goods: collected data, patterns discovered within that data, and validation of those patterns".

[144]The fact that the processing and exploitation of complex datasets is key for the success and commercial value of companies acting in digital markets is stressed by Fezer (2017), pp. 356–357, stating that "in the reality of the market, behaviour-generated informational data represents a tradable commodity and crucial asset in a booming industry in the digitized world".

[145]Rai (2001b), p. 174, talking about a new era of pharmaceutical innovation as a consequence of information technology advancements, where "biological research will be driven by data".

collaborative networks[146] between high-tech companies and traditional stakeholders in the health sector, such as pharmaceutical companies and public health providers.[147]

In this regard, some strand of the literature has referred to "health data ecosystems" in order to describe the "technical and social arrangements underpinning the environments in which health data is generated, analysed, shared and used".[148]

As will be better shown below, the main features of such networked architecture appear to be the strict interconnection and interoperability[149] between the stakeholders involved in the conduction of health research.

The interconnection that is characterising the current developing health research environment appears to allocate the production of biomedical knowledge onto a "distributed heterarchical network"[150] in which the relationships are subject to continuous change and develop upon the basis of evolving communication processes that ultimately build an eco-system of relationships.

This new social constellation reflects itself into a "network of contracts" governing the composite interests involved in the treatment of digital health-inflected data.[151] In such eco-system every player involved has different tasks and capabilities and brings into the consortium different types of assets and technical background.[152]

Overall, the sharing of the different types of health data among the involved actors is increasingly becoming a means to improve and fasten the design of digital

---

[146]The expression is taken from Camarinha-Matho and Afsarmanesh (2006), pp. 26–40.

[147]From a more general perspective, not strictly related to the medical sector, the emergence of new collaboration scenarios characterising high technology markets, is well highlighted by Colangelo (2008).

[148]Marjanovic et al. (27 April 2017), p. ii. Emphasis added. Similarly, also Vayena and Blasimme (2017), p. 503, where the Authors highlight "the interdependence of the actors and processes that rely on the production and circulation of data as a key resource for their respective activities". See also Purtova (2017), p. 192, stating that the notion of "data ecosystem" "expands on the idea of data as a system resource, first, in that it emphasizes the interconnectedness of, the cause and effect relationship between the elements of the system resource, and, second, in that the notion of ecosystem allows for simultaneous existence and interaction of multiple ecosystems of various sizes and levels, that do or do not overlap, consume smaller ecosystems and are consumed by larger ecosystems".

[149]The notion of 'interoperability' is drawn from the work of Gasser and Palfrey (November 2007), p. 4, where the Authors define 'interoperability' as the "ability to transfer and render useful data and other information across systems, applications, or components".

[150]Ladeur (2016), p. 6.

[151]The concept of network of contracts is drawn from Teubner (2011), where the Author talks about the creation of a hybrid 'network interest' between exchange and collective interests.

[152]See highlighting the complementary nature of the assets in a (patent) pool Mattioli (2018), pp. 225 ff. See also Merges and Mattioli (2017), pp. 281 ff. On the relevance of contract networks in the context of businesses' activities, see Cerrato (2016), Spolidoro (2014) and Musso (2010).

health products, in terms of optimisation and personalisation of the manufacturing processes and with related gains in terms of quality of the resulting products.[153]

As the case studies analysed in the next chapter will better show,[154] the sharing of technological information among involved parties can occur under different legal schemes depending on the object of the transfer- *i.e.* whether solely data or also technology being transferred; the objectives of the partnering actors; and the public or private nature of these same actors. Due to their formal variety, health data sharing practices taking place among old and new actors in digital healthcare markets can be described through the term "data pools".

The phenomenon of data pooling is being increasingly referred to by a strand of the literature with regards to the agreements made by firms for the sharing of "their digitalised information regarding a given market, in reference to a given service or generally in an industry, or within an e-ecosystem".[155]

Pooling practices as a means of concentrating high-technology resources and stirring innovation in health-related markets is a traditionally well-known phenomenon. Patent pooling schemes have indeed been largely used in the pharmaceutical sector,[156] with the purpose of the licensing of complementary patents by means of a single agreement and at a standard royalty fee, with resulting benefits in terms of cost cuts.[157]

At their very essence, patent pools are a form of technological cooperation between different rights owners willing to speed up the process of cumulative innovation.[158] The assembling together of technological assets enables companies to put themselves together to remain at the forefront of information technology developments,[159] through incentivising coordination mechanisms among participants and the prevention of opportunistic free-riding conducts.[160]

Especially in the pharmaceutical sector, the pooling together of patents has been looked at as a remedy for the growing problem of "patent thickets",[161] consisting in a bundle of different and intersecting property rights over technology assets and freezing down-stream innovation.[162] As has been observed, indeed, "numerous issues as intellectual property (IP) protections and funding can be cumbersome or

[153] Lindqvist (2018), pp. 147–148.

[154] See infra Chap. 3 Sect. 3.1.

[155] Lindqvist (2018), p. 146.

[156] For an overall assessment see Owervalle (2009). See also Merges (2001), pp. 123 ff.

[157] For an empirical demonstration of the reduction of transaction costs given by a patent pool, Merges and Mattioli (2017), pp. 281 ff.

[158] Colangelo (16 settembre 2008).

[159] Colangelo (16 settembre 2008), p. 1.

[160] Rai (2001a), pp. 813 ff.

[161] For a general assessment of the issue, Shapiro (2001), pp. 119–150. See also Barnett (2014), pp. 55 ff. arguing that patent pools and other cross-licensing structures overcome problems of patent thickets and related inefficiencies.

[162] Heller and Eisenberg (1998), p. 698; Rai (2001a), p. 813. Talking about "blocking patents" also Merges (1994), pp. 81–82. See also Rai (1992), pp. 77 ff.

completely inhibitory to establishing collaborative ventures and must be overcome to facilitate this process and realize the potentially immense benefits".[163] A way to overcome these hurdles for the stimulation of fruitful research endeavours has been identified in the creation of "IP-free zones" that "would open new areas of R&D to precompetitive collaboration".[164]

As a result of the above-described transformations related to the datification and digitisation of health research, innovation in digital health appears to face an additional barrier in respect to patent thickets, directly related to the emerging phenomenon of "data silos".[165] Data silos are the correspondent of patent thickets in the information-based research environment[166] and directly originate from the enactment of intellectual property protection tools onto valuable informational research assets.[167]

2.2.1 *From Patent Thickets to Research Data Silos in Health-Related Markets*

Already in the context of traditional health research, clinical trials data have been object of strong intellectual property protection under the data exclusivity regime and trade secret law. As several commentators have underlined, these types of protection have come to backup patent protection, extending its market exclusivity effects also long after the expiry of the patent term.[168] The concealment of such strategic data, restricting competitors' access to competitively valuable information has been criticized in the literature for its detrimental effects on competition patterns and long-term innovation outcomes.[169] Along the same lines, also a growingly rich case law of the European Union has come to highlight the public interest underlying the accessibility of scientific testing data in respect to competitors and the broader research community, stressing the essential value of such scientific data for the purposes of both public health and innovation processes.[170]

[163] Olson and Berger (2011), p. 2. More generally about the relationship between IP rights and the transfer of goods, Sarti (1996).

[164] Olson and Berger (2011), p. 49.

[165] Describing this phenomenon, Rai (2001b), p. 177.

[166] Rai (2017a), pp. 92 ff.

[167] Braun and Pugatch (2005), pp. 599–623. This point is also stressed by M. Mattioli (2017).

[168] Nicholson Price II (2017), pp. 1612–1613, talking about so-called "post-expiration monopolies". With specific regards to the pharmaceutical industry, see Feldman and Frondorf (2016), pp. 499 ff.

[169] Rai (2017b), pp. 101 ff.

[170] See European Court of Justice, European Medicines Agency vs. Intermune, Order of the Vice-President C-390/13 (28th November 2013). European Court of Justice, European Medicines Agency vs. AbbVie, Order of the Vice-President, C-389/13 (28th November 2013) not published; European Court of Justice, Opinion od Advocate General Hogan, Therapeutics International vs European Medicines Agency, Case T-175/18 (11 September 2019).

The policy debate over clinical trials data's transparency or disclosure options[171] reflects how scientific data protection schemes, in the form of regulatory protection or factual secrecy, not only raise significant public interest concerns but also lead to substantive market externalities, directly related to the compression of the "information commons" and the obscuring of industry's state of the art.[172] These externalities are certainly destined to be amplified as a result of the digitisation of the health industry and the growing reliance on digital health data for the purposes of manufacturing processes.[173]

The increasing commercial and thus competitive value of information in the dynamics of research and innovation in the health sector[174] has been documented by the US Supreme Court in the well-known *Myriad* case,[175] where the Court has acknowledged how patients' genetic data collected over time by the company owning the patent of the genetic tests had provided to the company a significant competitive advantage over competitors well beyond the date of the patent expiry.[176] Even after the patent's expiry, indeed, competitors would have faced substantial time and cost obstacles for replicating such a database.[177] Likewise, also the European Commission has recently highlighted the particularly important competitive value of "patent databases" and "patent data" in the *Dow-Dupont* merger.[178]

In this respect, some strand of the literature has correctly observed that data generated by a patent could be employed to broaden claim scope or add claims in already existent patent applications.[179]

Moreover, through collected datasets a company could, for example, train an algorithm, which in turn could lead to other patentable data-intensive inventions, this further consolidating the market position of the data-generating patent holder.[180]

From a European perspective, where the patentability of technical processing methods is still debated but excluded according to the more loyal interpretation of

[171] Schneider (2018), pp. 3 ff.

[172] This was already observed by Heller (1998), pp. 621 ff. and similarly by Heller and Eisenberg (1998), pp. 698 ff.

[173] Reichman et al. (2015), pp. 319 ff.

[174] Stressing the point also Rai (2017a), pp. 357–358, where the author notices that the prevalence of trade secrecy in the context of pharmaceutical research is likely to become even more prominent.

[175] US Supreme Court, Myriad Genetics, 133 at 2111–14. For a comment see Evans (2014), pp. 51 ff.

[176] Burk (2015) pp. 253–254; see also Simon and Sichelman (2017), pp. 377 ff.

[177] Oliver (2015) pp. 551–552, stating that "if researchers could create a comparable database through such efforts, it would strip Myriad of trade secret protection for its database".

[178] European Commission (27 March 2017) Dow/DuPont, Case M. 7932, para 102.

[179] Gervais (2019), para 12.

[180] Mattioli (2017), p. 187.

the European patent convention,[181] patent protection appears to be losing its previous central role in the whirls of the digital environment.[182]

This trend is to be particularly perceived in the health sector, where the difficulty of meeting the patentability requirements with regards to new pharmaceutical products has sensitively decreased the number of successful patent applications over the last years.[183] This has in turn triggered the growingly felt need to protect information-based assets, as the ones related to information generated after the filing of the patent, concerning economic complements of a patented invention, generated by patent-protected technology, or other type of information deemed essential for market success.[184]

Thus, the scope of the application of information-based protection tools employed by originators involved in health research endeavours has expanded and is supposedly going to be further expanding as a result of the growing value of health data for the design and testing of health products and services.

2.2.2 *The Intellectual Property Tools over Digital Research Data Silos*

Algorithms processing health information, and more specifically, the software to which algorithms are applied to can find protection, first of all, under copyright rules. Indeed, although there have been long discussions regarding the patentability of "computer implemented inventions",[185] the option of patenting softwares has soon been put aside, due to the legal and practical difficulties related to such an

---

[181] European Patent Convention, Guidelines for Examination- 3.3.1 Artificial Intelligence and Machine Learning, recalling the principles related to mathematical methods.

[182] Goy and Wang (2016), pp. 64 ff.

[183] Stressing this point, see Roin (2009), pp. 503 ff.

[184] See also Nicholson Price II (2017), p. 1613.

[185] Cf. European Commission (20th February 2002). As it has been underlined, mere algorithms cannot be protected by means of patents, given the fact that algorithms are the underlying tasks of a computer program that are not patentable for their being non-technical in nature: a program's functionality cannot indeed be patentable because patent protection cannot cover general ideas and business models, that according to the "fundamental conception of intellectual property rights should remain free". See Drexl et al. (9 September 2016), pp. 5–6, stressing that patent "protection (of algorithms) would pose a risk of two negative effects: first, protection of abstract subject-matter would cause needless—and, in the case of algorithms, unreasonable—restraints on competition that, according to current knowledge, would not be economically justified. In particular, the resulting monopolisation of ideas would hinder technical progress and industrial development. See judgement of European Court of Justice, SAS Institute Inc. vs World Programming Ltd., C-406/10 (2 May 2012), para 40. Second, it is barely foreseeable what markets and sectors would be affected. This makes finding suitable approaches to a regulation seem unrealistic". The debate regarding software's patentability is to be traced back to the Eighties, see Ghidini (1984), pp. 270 ff.

extension.[186] The exclusion of the eligibility of the patent as a tool for the protection of algorithms has caused the shift of focus onto other tools of protection, such as copyright and trade secrets.

With regards to copyright, the 1991 Software Directive,[187] which has been later replaced by the 2009 Directive on the legal protection of computers,[188] has first harmonised European software copyright law, establishing the scope of copyright protection of computer programs.[189] The subject matter of copyright protection has been clarified by the decision of the European Court of Justice *Sas Institute Inc. c. World Programming Ltd.*,[190] where the Court has specified that the protection under copyright law of computer programs extends only to "the forms of expression of a computer program and the preparatory design work capable of leading, respectively, to the reproduction or the subsequent creation of such a program[191]", but does not include the functionalities, the programming language of the program, and the format of data files used in a computer of it.[192] Hence, in the cited case, the European Court of Justice has reaffirmed the basic copyright law principle according to which copyright protects only the original expression of an idea.[193] Against the backdrop of these premises, it is highly debated whether the code source[194] of an algorithm can be protected under copyright.[195] Indeed, code source is on the one hand highly creative, but on the other hand it has an undeniable functional feature.[196] In this

[186]The Supreme Court of the United States, Alice Corp. v. CLS Bank International, 134 S. Ct. 234, 2358 (2014), clarified that abstract inventions, such as algorithms, do not become patentable merely because they are implemented on a computer. For a comment see Nicholson Price II (2017), p. 1425. Hence, softwares can only be patented if they satisfy the requirement of novelty, inventive step and technical effectiveness. These requirements are very difficult to be met. Cf. Lemley (2013), p. 928.

[187]See European Council, Council Directive of 14 May 1991 on the legal protection of computer programs, 91/250/EEC, OJ 17–5-91, N.L. 122/42.

[188]Directive 2009/24/EC of the European Parliament and of the Council of 23 April 2009 on the legal protection of computer programs, OJ L. 111, 5-5-2009.

[189]For the literature see Arezzo (2012).

[190]European Court of Justice, Sas Institute Inc. c. World Programming Ltd., C-406/10 (2 May 2012).

[191]European Court of Justice, Sas Institute Inc. c. World Programming Ltd., C-406/10 (2 May 2012), para 37.

[192]European Court of Justice, Sas Institute Inc. c. World Programming Ltd., C-406/10 (2 May 2012), para 39. For a comment, see Samuelson et al. (2012), p. 158. For an analysis under Us law, see Samuelson (2007), pp. 1921 ff.

[193]See Litman and Samuelson (2010), pp. 1190–1191.

[194]Code source can be defined as "any collection of statements or declarations written in some human readable computer programming language". So Mohan (1 November 2009), p. 2.

[195]It must be however noticed that the issue regarding the copyright protection of the code source has more of theoretical than practical interest. Indeed, there have been a few litigations regarding computer programs involving the copyright protection of code sources. See Horne (1992), pp. 497 ff.

[196]Naughton (2011), pp. 3 ff., where the Author discusses the alleged Google's infringement of the Linux kernel header files.

regard, it must be recalled that in the same *SAS* decision, the Court of Justice of the European Union stated that the programming language in which the source code is expressed, "might be protected, as works, under copyright under Directive 2001/29 if they are the author's own creation".[197]

Along these lines, the Court of Justice of the European Union has stated that where the expression of the components of a computer program, such as a source code, "is dictated by their technical function, the criterion of originality is not met, since the different methods of implementing an idea are so limited that the idea and the expression become indissociable".[198] The court thus appears to suggest that where functionality-related elements are predominant, the residual expressive elements are not protectable due to the lack of originality requirement.[199] Given the impossibility to infer general criteria, the determination of the copyrightability of the source code of an algorithm is to be made on a case by case basis.[200]

Through licensing terms, copyright protection can be used in order to restrict the ability of a third party to use the protected parts of the computer program. Indeed, in case the licenses are established through valid contracts, uses that do not respect the license terms may constitute breach of contract.[201] Hence, copyright protection of algorithms has an important restrictive function regarding the use of the protected technology.[202]

Shifting from the processing infrastructure to the object of the processing, copyright can be employed for the protection of aggregated health data processed by algorithms[203] in case the selection and arrangement of it meets the originality threshold.[204] In this respect, the data undergoing processing operations are mostly of structured nature, for example through an index, and this structure can amount to a selection and arrangement protectable under copyright. However, especially in respect to the arrangement of digital datasets, it is difficult to envisage an expression of originality, as the European Court of Justice has suggested also in the *Football*

---

[197] European Court of Justice, Sas Institute Inc. c. World Programming Ltd., C-406/10 (2 May 2012), para 45.

[198] European Court of Justice, Bezpečnostní softwarová asociace– Svaz softwarové ochrany v. Ministry of Culture of the Czech Republic, C-393/09 (22 December 2010), para 39.

[199] For a comment, see Shemtov (2017), p. 122.

[200] Naughton (2011), p. 5.

[201] Shemtov (2017), p. 136.

[202] Shemtov (2017), p. 151, highlighting the function of copyright as a means to restrictively regulate the use of the protected object.

[203] For a reflection upon the copyrightability of so-called computer-generated works, see Abbott (2020), pp. 322 ff.

[204] It should be however recalled that it is very difficult for a database to accomplish the originality threshold required under European copyright law. On the issue see Gervais (2002), p. 935. For a broader reflection on the originality standard, Margoni (2016), pp. 85 ff.

Dataco case.[205] This holds true especially for the data which are automatically generated by the software.[206] With regards to research valuable and scientific datasets, however, the originality requirement is more likely to be met, in case the processed data and the generated metadata are further arranged into visualizations, figures, charts and graphs, which contribute to the evaluation of the automatically rendered scientific results.[207]

Irrespectively of any inventiveness, digital health datasets can find protection under the 1996 Directive on legal protection of databases,[208] establishing an exclusive *sui generis* rights over databases resulting from a "substantial investment".[209] The right protects against the extraction and reutilization of substantial parts of a protected database.

However, in view of a strict interpretation of such requirement by the European Court of Justice,[210] doubts have been raised in the literature regarding the existence of such a "substantial investment" in the case of automatically processed data.[211] These doubts are further suggested by the statements of the European Commission, which has declared that "the Database Directive did not meant to create a new right in the data".[212]

Despite these acknowledgeable concerns, the possibility that a digital dataset falls under database protection cannot be fully and aprioristically be excluded.[213] This possibility is higher in case of research databases, where there substantial investment could be further given by the analysis and interpretation of data by experts.[214]

[205] European Court of Justice, Football Dataco vs Yahoo! UK Ltd., C-604/10 (1 March 2012), para 42, observing that "significant labour and skill of its author (. . .) cannot as such justify the protection of it by copyright under Directive 96/9, if that labour and skill do not express any originality in the selection and arrangement of that data".

[206] Gervais (2019), paras 26–27.

[207] This is observed by Carrol (2015), p. 5. Stressing the importance of copyright protection in the scientific research environment, Reichman and Okediji (2012), p. 1362 ff., in particular at 1441 ff.

[208] Directive 96/9/EC of the European Parliament and of the Council of 11 March 1996 on the legal Protection of Databases. http://eur-lex.europa.eu/LexUriServ/LexUriServ.do?uri=CELEX:31996L0009:EN:HTML.

[209] Cf. art 7, 4 par. Database Directive. Recently, see Gupta (2017), pp. 11 ff.

[210] European Court of Justice, Fixtures Marketing Ltd. v Oy Veikkaus Ab, C-46/02 (9 November 2004), para 49, where the Court has defined "investment" in obtaining datasets as "resources used to seek out existing materials and collect them in the database" with the exclusion of "the resources used for the creation of materials which make up the contents of the databases".

[211] Gervais (2019), paras 33–34.

[212] European Commission (10 January 2017a), p. 13.

[213] Leistner (2017), pp. 27 ff.

[214] Carrol (2015), p. 6, observing however that the database directive sets an explicit exemption to the protection in case of non-commercial research datasets. See art. 6(2) lett. b of the Database Directive.

Most importantly, however, collected and processed health-related data flowing into the sides of digital platforms are mostly protected through trade secrets.[215] In this regard, it must be recalled that the European Trade Secret Directive[216] provides very broad conditions for protection, encompassing nearly every business confidential information.[217] Despite formal declarations,[218] the Directive provides a proprietary-styled protection over information,[219] which thus offers strong grounds for big data companies to obscure both the processed health data and the procedural information regarding algorithm-driven processing activities. This procedural information encompasses information regarding how algorithms are developed, how they are validated and the data on which they are trained.[220] Hence, the newly designed trade secret protection increases the obscurity of the algorithm-driven health research setting, already given by the intrinsic technical non-interpretability of algorithms.[221]

---

[215] Some recent empirical studies have shown that European businesses are increasingly preferring trade secrets over patent protection. Goy and Wang (2016), pp. 64 ff. European Commission (April 2013). Finally, EUIPO (July 2017), p. 3: "the use of trade secrets for protecting innovations is higher than the use of patents by most types of companies, in most economic sectors and in all Member States".

[216] Directive EU 2016/943 of the European Parliament and of the Council of 8 June 2016 on the protection of undisclosed know-how and business information (trade secrets) against their unlawful acquisition, use and disclosure. http://eur-lex.europa.eu/legal-content/EN/TXT/?uri=CELEX%3A32016L0943.

[217] See art. 2 of the Directive where trade secrets are defined as any information that i) is not generally known among or readily accessible to persons within the circles that normally deal with the kind of information in question; ii) has commercial value because it is secret; and iii) has been subject to reasonable steps to keep it secret. See Sousa-Silva (2014), p. 15.

[218] Recital 10 of the same proposed Directive affirming that its "provisions (...) should not create any exclusive right on the know-how or information protected as trade secrets".

[219] Trade secret protection and enforcement is confined to cases of conducts of "acquisition, use and disclosure" that are to be considered "unlawful". The notion of unlawfulness is very broad and comprehends also any "unauthorised access to, appropriation of, or copy of any documents, objects, materials, substances or electronic files (...) containing the trade secret (...)" carried out "without the consent of the trade secret holder". See artt. 4 n. 56 and 6 of the EU Trade Secret Directive. The specificities of trade secret protection in the context of intellectual property regulations has been widely commented in literature, and still the statements contained in the Trade Secret Directive do not offer decisive grounds for a solution to the problem of whether trade secrets should be considered or not a form of companies' proprietary rights stricto sensu and the debate is still on-going. EU Directorate General for Internal Policies (2014), p. 4, recalling the European Court of Justice ruling in Microsoft Corp. Vs. Commission, T-167-08 (27 June 2012) where the Court mentioned trade secret as a different category from intellectual property rights. The referral of trade secret protection to the sector of intellectual property law has been put into question with the alternative of referring it to the area of unfair competition law. Dias Nunes (25 July 2015). Aplin (2015), p. 426. See also Vanzetti (2011).

[220] All this information regarding algorithms constitute the so-called 'e-trade secrets'. Niebel et al. (2018), p. 3.

[221] Both the technical and the legal means of protection give rise to the phenomenon that the literature has defined as 'black-box medicine', W.N. Price Nicholson II, Regulating Black Box Medicine (2015), pp. 472–473.

In this regard, it must be recalled that the procedural information regarding the development of drugs or medical devices is disclosed to the regulatory authority in the course of the regulatory process and is object of specific disclosure requirements.[222] To the contrary, in absence of specific regulatory provisions regarding health data processing algorithms, the procedural information regarding how digital technologies are trained remains captured under the umbrella of trade secret protection. Trade secret protection is thus used by companies for those market exclusivity purposes that are achieved by the more specific data exclusivity measures regarding traditional pharmaceutical test data, that is clinical trials data.[223]

Against the backdrop of the traced analysis, it appears that the intellectual property framework provides strong grounds for the secretization of companies' digitised research enquiries,[224] thus rendering data collection and processing activities opaque and exclusive.[225] This results, in turn, in likewise opaque and exclusive quantification and categorization practices relying on individuals' health conditions.[226]

In addition to legal measures, also factual and technical measure can further enclose companies' research data silos.[227]

The importance of technical protection measures is to be rooted on the one hand in the legal uncertainty regarding the extent to which intellectual property tools as copyright and the *sui generis* database right can effectively protect digital data, and on the other hand in the unclear allocation of claimed rights in the data market.[228]

In view of the difficulties to make the collaborative and fast-changing digital environment properly adhere to intellectual property rights, control over research-valuable resources is defined on the basis of the practical and technical ability to exclude other market players from the resources at stake, and especially from access to data.[229]

Technical measures of protection have both the effect of factually stretching the limitations regarding the scope of the exclusivities set by the law[230] and, even more interestingly, of factually controlling resources that would not be eligible of protection from both the perspective of objective requirements- as the copyright' originality requirement or database right's substantial investment requirement-, and subjective requirement, because the subjects who enact these measures are not the originators of the resource. This means that a specific resource can be appropriated

[222]On the issue see G. Schneider (2018), pp. 3 ff.

[223]Price Nicholson II (2015), pp. 472–473; Gervais (2019), paras 77–78.

[224]Pasquale (2015), pp. 3–11.

[225]Citron and Pasquale (2014), pp. 102–104. See also Ubertazzi (1997).

[226]Citron and Pasquale (2014), pp. 89 ff.

[227]Hilty (2018), pp. 898 ff.

[228]Drexl (27 April 2018), p. 133.

[229]Purtova (2015), pp. 83 ff.

[230]Hilty (2018), p. 891.

by a player through technical protection measures even if the resource has been originally generated by another company.

In this last respect, a commentator has rightly demonstrated that, in the data marketplace, data-intensive actors are giving rise to an outright battle for the exclusive exploitation of the personal data available in the "free" market zones.[231] Also in respect to resources that are theoretically non-exclusive and non-rivalrous, as personal data, the more powerful market player can obtain a *de facto* control over personal data[232] and thus raise competitors' costs of accessing the collected datasets.[233]

2.2.3 Research Data Silos Contextualized within the Intellectual Property System

The above-illustrated information-based protection tools over digital health data all share the underlying function of protecting digital businesses' competitive advantage deriving from their investments in the collection and production of information.[234]

Indeed, through their direct or indirect secrecy outcomes, companies' valuable R&D information is gradually shielded from the free-riding threats of the public domain.[235] Relying on these tools, digital companies can control and limit access over health information- as it happens with the database right and the copyright- or secretize this same information- as it is the case of trade secrets and of technical protection measures. These different forms of protection over scientific digitised data frequently overlap and create a layered regime of protection over the results of research endeavours, variedly securing scientifically precious information.[236]

As some commentators have correctly stressed,[237] the combination of different protection tools over scientific information gives rise to "hybrid IP regimes" filling "other perceived gaps in the system", with the effect that there are "virtually no products sold on the general products market that do not come freighted up with a bewildering and overlapping array of exclusive property rights that discourage follow-on applications of routine technical know-how".[238] In this perspective, both overlapping and adjacent rights over biomedical data triggers practices

---

[231] Purtova (2015), p. 87.

[232] Purtova (2017), p. 194. On the rise of factual protection schemes, replacing formally legal protection means, see Ricolfi (2019).

[233] Hoffmann and Johannsen (31 May 2019), p. 19, recalling the observations by Rubinfeld and Gal (2017), p. 375.

[234] Romano (2010).

[235] Boyle (2003), pp. 33 ff., and more generally see Stiglitz (2003), pp. 75 ff.

[236] Rai (2017b), pp. 106–112.

[237] Cf. Ullrich (2004), pp. 412 ff.

[238] Maskus and Reichman (2004), p. 297.

of over-appropriation of upstream technology, *i.e.* scientific data and the technical processing infrastructure, by the initial rights' holders. [239]

These "overprotectionist" tendencies[240] regarding research valuable data are at the roots of a data "thicket" problem that exacerbates market accessibility concerns and thus stifles innovation courses.[241]

As opposed to patent thickets, companies' data "silos" have been strongly criticised in the literature for freezing competitors' capacities to compete at a phase that goes well before the marketization of the final product and relates to the previous stage of research over the product itself.[242] As some scholars have observed, indeed, the excessive control over scientific information gives rise to a situation of "innovation bundling" for which "neither the invention nor the complements can be reasonably developed" without access to the protected information.[243] The fragmentation of differently owned datasets covered by a layered regime of rights over pure scientific information assets has been identified as a significant obstacle to the advancements of cumulative innovation.[244]

Traditional justification theories of the industrial intellectual property system and in particular of the patent system[245] rely on the assumption that the more protection is given, the greater are the incentives for producing and thus the greater the innovation pace is.[246] These justification theories are however deeply rooted in two general features of the patent system considered as the main industrial intellectual property right, that is its temporarily limited nature and its transparency function.

Exactly these features of the patent system appear to be challenged in the digital research environment as a consequence of the proliferation of information-based protection tools, with significant reflexes on the alleged causal link between intellectual property protection and innovation.[247]

Indeed, businesses' increasing attention to the safeguard of information assets and the strategic combination of product- and information-centred protection tools, have

---

239 Rai (2017b), p. 102.

240 Ghidini (2006), p. 11.

241 Rai (2001b), p. 813.

242 Nicholson Price II (2017), p. 1613.

243 Nicholson Price II (2017), p. 1613.

244 Reichman and Uhlir (2003), pp. 402–408. See also Nicholson Price II (2015), pp. 447–448, underlining how "keeping data secret" in the area of health research "may significantly hamper the development of black-box medicine. Secrecy slows cumulative innovation and promotes duplicative investment".

245 Nicholson Price II (2017), p. 1612. For an economic analysis see the statements already made by Kitch (1977), pp. 265 ff.

246 See on the issue, Lemley (1997), pp. 1050–1051. Lemley (2004), pp. 129 ff.

247 Heller (2008). Heller (1998), p. 621. More recently, this point has been stressed by Gervais (2019), para 15.

the effect of strengthening and stretching the monopoly conferred by a patent,[248] thus undermining the temporarily limited nature of it[249] and with that distorting that what is commonly referred to as the "patent bargain".[250] This has the effect of retarding the triggering of competition mechanisms that can only blossom after the patent expiry.[251] Moreover, as has been observed, the control in particular of patent-related big data could enable the originator to "predict the next incremental steps in a given field of activity by analysing innovation trajectories".[252] This means that the control of the lines of development in a specific research field, as the one regarding a specific treatment, can enable a company to predict what comes next in terms of innovation.[253]

Second, the trend of secretizing or otherwise restricting access to research valuable data through an array of overlapping rights regarding commercially valuable information,[254] appears to run contrary to patent protection's transparency function given by the disclosure requirement,[255] which is exactly meant to enrich the public domain and thus stir the progress of technology.[256] As has been underlined in the literature, the transparency requirement of the patent system is intimately connected with long-term innovation goals promoted by the public availability of new knowledge.[257]

In view of these developments, the distorting effect of broad information exclusivities appears however to undermine the consequential chain between intellectual property protection and innovation: the innovation driving function of intellectual property rights is indeed destined to decline when the rights over scientifically valuable resources begin to compress the operational space of other players in the same research field, not necessarily competitors.

---

248 For a comment see Simon and Sichelman (2017), pp. 377 ff.

249 Stressing this point Nicholson Price II (2016), pp. 1775–1776.

250 Ghosh (2004), p. 1316, describing the bargaining metaphor underlying the patent system, which grants to the inventor a limited monopoly period in return to the transfer of the invention to society.

251 As soon as the limited exclusivity period expires, broader competition, with the related public benefits, is possible. So Nicholson Price II (2017), p. 1612.

252 Gervais (2019), para 12.

253 Gervais (2019), para 12. Similarly, stressing this point, Burk (2015), pp. 233 ff.

254 Kesselheim and Mello (2007), p. 483. Stressing the point also McGarity and Shapiro (1980), p. 838.

255 As has been stated, "the essence of the patent system is transparency and disclosure". WIPO (2004) 4. However, it must be stated that another strand of the literature stresses the fact that patent disclosure is weak and it focuses on technical information that is only a part of the market-relevant information. For an overview see Müller (1998), p. 615. See also Luzzato (1988). For an assessment on the relationship between patents, disclosure and secrets, see Guglielmetti (2003).

256 This point is well stressed by Nicholson Price II (2017), p. 1612.

257 Correa (2007), p. 94. This is reflected also by latest discussions carried out at both practical and theoretical level, where the disclosure requirement has been put at the centre of reform proposals aimed at tightening patents' sharing benefits. Especially with regard to the disclosure of traditional knowledge, See Gibson (2005), pp. 23–26. WIPO (6 June 2007), p. 4.

The compartmentalisation of scientific knowledge and the resulting erosion of publicly available research resources, thus risks to transform the relationship between intellectual property protection and innovation from a "direct" to an "inverse" proportionality relationship.[258]

The main outcome of this changed scenario is the emerging need of firms to mediate between the possibility to successfully claim exclusivity rights over technological information and the preservation of innovation courses' fruitfulness.[259]

2.2.4 *From the Privatization to the Trading of Research Data Silos: The Features of Health Data Pools*

Concrete organisational responses to the rights' and resources' dispersion affecting the datafied and digitised health research environment are found in collaboration schemes[260] based on data sharing between different actors in the field of medical research. Information alliances achieved through the pooling of intellectual property rights and the establishment of coordination architectures over research resources are capable- if well designed- to overcome the hurdles scientific information silos and thus advance innovation in digital health markets.[261]

The phenomenon of the aggregation of health datasets is certainly not new in the field of biomedical research. Indeed, well before the advent of the digitalisation of the health sector and the expansion of scientifically valuable data sources, companies variously involved in the life science sector had started to establish research collaborations aimed at enriching the variety of scientific data pools.[262] For these purposes, in particular, pharmaceutical companies have sought the support of biotechnology companies in control of genetic or proteomic information, which has become indispensable for the advancement of pharmaceutical research.[263]

---

[258]This is confirmed by some economics studies, which have framed the relationship between intellectual property law and innovation as an "inverted-U relationship". So Furukawa (2010), pp. 99–101. Reflecting about different "intellectual property models", Ottolia (2010).

[259]Colangelo (2009).

[260]Falce (2010).

[261]Ray (2 May 2016). Rai (2001b), p. 845. As will be better assessed later on, the pro-competitiveness of pooling agreements mainly resides on the openness of the pools to other competitors that cannot effectively compete in the relevant R&D market without access to the pool. This is why the pro-competitiveness of the pool ultimately resides on its design features in respect to the adherence of new participants. Rai (2001b), p. 848. See infra Chap. 7 Sect. 7.3.

[262]For an empirical analysis see Lerner and Merges (1998), pp. 125 ff., noting a substantial increase of the collaborations between biotechnology and pharmaceutical companies starting from the Eighties. See also Rai et al. (2008), pp. 1 ff., discussing need to pool small molecule libraries for upstream basic research by university scientists using high-throughput screening technology.

[263]Rai (2001b), p. 816.

As with patent pools, the pooling together of different types of data reduces transaction costs related to data collection and processing operations and enables to aggregate a large quantity of data, which are thus meant to result in more precise and accurate correlations and predictions.[264]

In this perspective, health data sharing agreements are a form of contractual and technology-based private ordering tool of data-driven innovation,[265] intervening there where the intellectual property system alone retards or blocks the generation of fruitful research interactions.[266]

In light of the above traced framework, it appears that health data pools relate to the establishment of technology aggregation practices in an information-based research environment, sharing similar innovation-driving functions of patent pools, but raising completely new challenges.[267]

Similarly to patent pools, data pooling arrangements imply the licensing of different datasets to a central administrator, who provides also the data analytics technologies needed to exploit the full potential of the aggregated data.[268] This is why data pooling agreements are generally integrated with collateral agreements on the processing technology needed for the pooling of the transferred data.[269] The processing infrastructure can be either delivered directly by one of the involved parties or outsourced by a third party.[270]

With regards to the object of the transfer, the distinctive feature of data pooling practices is the difficulty to determine which data is exactly shared, this meaning the difficulty to determine whether only primary users' data are being transferred or also the secondary data that are analytically drawn by the machine learning processes of the involved parties.[271] In these regards some strand of the literature[272] has interestingly observed that contracts regarding high technology projects "have become more and more fluid, because the projects are so complex that it is difficult to figure beforehand what is at stake".[273]

The difficulty of determining the *ex ante* the object and the purpose of the information sharing agreement is the main difference between data and technology

---

[264] Rai (2001b), p. 816.

[265] For an analysis over the contractual dimension of data pools see Ottolia (2017), pp. 273–285. See also Granieri (2013).

[266] For a general assessment over the relationship between intellectual property and private ordering tools, of factual, technical and contractual nature, see Hilty (2018), pp. 898 ff.

[267] Mattioli (2017), p. 187.

[268] Colangelo and Borgogno (2019), p. 12.

[269] Colangelo and Borgogno (2019), p. 12.

[270] Colangelo and Borgogno (2019), p. 12.

[271] Lindqvist (2018), p. 149.

[272] Ladeur (2016), p. 9.

[273] Ladeur (2016), p. 9.

pools, in respect to which the technology object of the transfer is mostly defined in standard-setting agreements.[274] A corollary of this is also that in data pools, more than in technology pools, it is difficult to trace stable rules of data ownership and liability.[275]

In addition to the problem of allocation of rights over the data entering the pool, a newly emerging concern relates to the readability of the pooled data by all the involved players. The aggregation of different types of data triggers indeed the need of the sharing entities to establish specific formats, structures or other technical measures that ensure a high level of readability of the data shared by means of the pool.[276]

The networked countenance of health data pools gives rise to a collaborative research paradigm, which is set in between an individual research paradigm and an open access one:[277] far from the idea of free sharing platforms of scientific information, these collaboration alliances are designed for the purpose of combining technological assets among very few partners. Pooling practices indeed primarily rely on the aggregation and the access to datasets by the involved partners, along the lines of what can be defined as a "restricted" disclosure approach. This means, in other terms, that health data pools are giving rise to an outright big health data shared "anticommons" governing biomedical research.[278]

From this standpoint, some structural traits of data pools can be drawn from the scholarship on the commons, which has gone beyond the traditional private/public dichotomy[279] and has developed a more sophisticated classification of goods in which also more hybrid and complex resource systems, such as common pool resources, have been taken into consideration.[280]

According to the classification of this literature, "common pool resources" are defined as "a resource shared by a group of people that is subject to social dilemmas",[281] with the essential feature of being "system resources", meaning that

[274]Colangelo and Borgogno (2019), p. 3.

[275]Colangelo and Borgogno (2019), p. 6. This is very much observed by Vayena and Blasimme (2018), p. 119.

[276]Colangelo and Borgogno (2019), p. 3 ff.

[277]Unesco International Bioethics Committee (IBC) (15 September 2017), p. 14.

[278]The idea of such "data anticommons" appears to go against some basic assumptions of the dominant view of information economics, according to which any information, just as personal data, is not rival and will not become less available for other actors in the information industry after having been collected once. In this sense Varian (16 October 1998) describing information as a public good; Stiglitz (2000), p. 1448. However the case of research valuable health data is different, since it is highly technical information that can be protected under intellectual property law and through technical measures as illustrated above in Sect. 2.2.2 of this chapter.

[279]Ostrom (2010), pp. 642 ff., where the private/public goods distinction is put in connection with the distinction market/state regulation.

[280]Ostrom (2010), p. 645.

[281]Hess and Ostrom (2007), pp. 3 ff.

they comprise entire "resource ecosystems", which are a "combination of interrelated and interdependent elements that together form a common pool resource".[282]

Also in view of this structural peculiarity, common pool resources are placed in between private and public goods: as private goods, indeed, they are subtractable in use, and as public goods- due to the inter-related nature of the elements that form the pool- they are difficult to exclude from.[283]

The so-described paradigm of common pool resources is an interesting benchmark upon which assessing the considered phenomenon of health data pools. Trough reference to this paradigm, indeed, some additional important features of health data pools can be derived, both analogically and heteronomously.

However, due to the specificities of health data, the paradigm of the common pool resources can only partially be applied to health data pools.

Health data pools, indeed, well fit into the notion of "resource ecosystem", with the peculiarity that the central resource around which the ecosystem evolves is given by sensitive health data.

The health data pooled together is not an isolated economic asset,[284] for its very nature it implies a system of other different resources, which are to be first identified in the physical subjects providing the data and from which the data flows originate and in the processing infrastructure that exploits data's informational value.[285] The consideration of these different components of the data ecosystem highlights the complexity of it, as well as the multiplicity and interdependency of its components.

However, digital data is not subtractable just as a physical good: to the very contrary, the processing and thus exploitation of digital data, leads to a multiplication of (secondary-generated, meta) data, this leading in turn to a greater availability of the resource for the members of the pool. The constant alimentation of the pool with new information enables members of the pool to capture always new resources, with each one of the members having different entitlements and incentives to appropriate the newly generated components.[286]

This generative-rather than subtractable- nature of the pooled resource is strictly related to other two features of health data pools, which can be to the contrary analogically drawn from the common pool resource paradigm. The processing infrastructure under which health data are treated assures the transformation of the

[282]Purtova (2017), p. 194.

[283]Ostrom (2010), pp. 642 ff., where the Author makes the example of fisheries, which are over-exploited this leading to a progressively minor availability of fishes and are very difficult to enclose for the exclusion of others.

[284]Purtova (2015), pp. 83 ff. Personal data as an isolated commodity appears to be, to the contrary, the assumption of the economics of personal data scholarship. See, for example, Acquisti (1 December 2010). The idea of granting data subjects property rights, advanced by some intellectual property scholars, equally underlies the idea of personal data as an isolated and thus fully appropriable. See in this regard, Schwartz (2004), pp. 2056 ff.

[285]Purtova (2017), p. 181.

[286]Purtova (2017), p. 181.

analysed data into always new information that flows from the users' private spheres into the pool.[287]

In this respect, it needs to be observed that health data sharing agreements not only imply the pooling together of research entities' separately held data silos, but—well before—the privatization and propertization of data subjects' sensitive personal information. In this way, information that was in the users' "common" privacy information space entirely governed by data subjects[288] is gradually transferred into a "shared" private space, governed not any more by data subjects but by few data holders.[289] This process of the transfer of resources from a common space to a "common-pool resource", requires the members of the pool to manage, monitor and protect the resource in order to ensure "sustainability and preservation".[290]

Against this backdrop, the generative and interconnected nature of the resources of the system determines a third structural feature of data pools, that is their enclosed nature.

Indeed, in order to shield the resources captured in the pool from external exploitation, its members need to employ costly technical and legal measures to "enclose" the commonly collected and generated data.

In this respect, the interesting feature of health data pools is that they are a means of maximising the research value embedded in different data silos, but replicate the same proprietary schemes characterising the above-illustrated research data silos. In this perspective, they are nothing else than a form of "collaborative" research data silos, which come to exclude the players who are not part to the collaboration from precious research assets.[291]

This means, thus, that also the "social dilemma" related to the "tragedy" of the research-valuable health data anticommons presents itself at a twofold level, the first related to the existence of single companies' and research entities' data silos, the second one related to the emergence of shared, but nonetheless closed, research data silos. In these regards, it has been correctly observed that the technological means improving access to research information, equally can be employed for inhibiting access "in ways that were never before practical",[292] this in turn leading to new sources of innovation courses' distortions.

[287] Purtova (2017), p. 181, underlining how "some resources only become available as resources for appropriation once a certain enabling technology is developed".

[288] In this perspective some authors have advanced the idea of privacy as a common good, in which the choice of some subjects to disclose personal data and opt for a lower level of privacy, risks to decrease the level of privacy enjoyed by other subjects. Reagan (2002), pp. 382 ff. See also, Schwartz (2004), p. 2085, observing that those who disclose their personal data, still try to benefit from the common privacy information space.

[289] This process of appropriation is highlighted by Acquisti (1 December 2010), p. 10.

[290] Hess and Ostrom (2007), p. 10.

[291] See Bertani (2006).

[292] David (2000), p. 10.

"Appropriation" problems[293] can however occur also within an established research data pool.

Indeed, the fact that, as has been already acknowledged, the flexible collaboration agreements based on the sharing of research data often lack a clear definition of entitlements in the pooled resources,[294] can pave the way to darwinian appropriation conducts by the more powerful player in the pool.[295]

The technological superiority of a company in respect to other "resource appropriators" is thus very likely to determine its successful claim over the resource, *i.e.* the data, that was initially equally available to all members of the pool.[296] This is mostly the case of the big tech company who has partnered with traditional actors in the healthcare field and who is in the stronger position of employing the available technological and legal means for protecting data and the connected analytical technology forming the pool.

The above-traced analysis thus shows how digital health research courses are driven by collaborative stances of data sharing, which are meant to overcome established research data silos, but which themselves re-create new forms of enclosed research pools.[297] Here, new risks of takeovers of research valuable assets by the more influent member of an established research consortium arise. The dynamic of digital health research patterns in which digital companies increasingly provide the technological infrastructure needed to run scientific experiments, set the premises for the enactment of appropriation strategies by these same companies, which appear to have the technical and legal superiority to appropriate research valuable data after having pooled them together from different stakeholders. In this perspective, the collaborative alliances aiming at opening up the fragmented research data silos controlled by different research actors, risk to ultimately result into big health data silos controlled just by few digital or high tech companies, which have the market power of excluding smaller companies or weaker public research institutions.

Hence, as a result of the described transformations of the health research setting, health research itself is becoming a data-driven platform market characterised by strong network and lock-in effects where access to research valuable resources might be restricted by the few data gathering entities, in a technological context "that might be otherwise ripe for competitive innovation".[298]

These assertions will be better enquired in the analysis that follows in the next chapters.

[293] Gardner et al. (1990), pp. 335 ff.; Hess and Ostrom (2007), p. 13, observing how "the narrative of enclosure is one of privatization, the haves versus the haves-not, the elite versus the masses".

[294] See para above para 4.1.1 at note 223.

[295] Ricolfi (2002) and Maugeri (2009).

[296] See Ostrom et al. (1994), p. 12 on technological externalities.

[297] Granieri et al. (2009).

[298] Bamberger and Lobel (2017), p. 1089.

2.3 Conclusions: Health Data Pools as Private Ordering Tools of Digital Health Research

The above-traced analysis has shown how the “information revolution” is causing some structural mutations of the health research environment, in terms of object, technological means and stakeholders involved in scientific discoveries.

These changes are in turn determining new organisational arrangements of health research conduction based on the pooling together of complementary technological and informational research resources, among traditional stakeholders in the health research setting, as pharmaceutical companies and public research institutions, and big digital or high-tech companies, acting as new players in the field.

The so emerging health data pools can be considered as the development of patent and technology pooling practices in the emerging digital and data-driven health economy, where innovation increasingly depends on easy access and use of different types of data resources.[299]

As has been demonstrated, the increasing research value of these various types of health data is at the same time grounding their blooming competitive value.

This justifies the growing trend of privatizing scientifically valuable digital data through the enactment of both legal and technical measures of protection capturing both the research valuable datasets and the technological processing infrastructure that serve to their analysis. The consolidation of fragmented research data silos not only reduce the scope of research and development information in the public domain but also risks to impair digital health innovation patterns as alimented by the variety of research assets and the accessibility of always new data.

As other sectors of the digital economy, also digitised health research appears to be affected by the two opposed market tensions respectively related to the secretization of informational resources in respect to other market players, and the search of new and complementary research resources through the establishment of collaborations with other stakeholders.

These research collaborations are exactly based on the trading and sharing of digital health data and the related processing technologies, for the competitive advancement of innovation in digital health products and services. The so emerging health data pools are thus a form of “contractually reconstructed research common”,[300] which open up formed research data silos for the progression of scientific and technological progress.[301]

This has been directly acknowledged also by the World Health Organization, observing that “the isolation that often characterised traditional health actors has become impossible to sustain” and that, as a result, “it is increasingly common” for

[299] Stressing, on a more general level, the impact of technological change on legal schemes, Di Cataldo (2009). On the relevance of licenses in the information society, see Abriani (2002).

[300] This expression is derived from Reichman and Uhlir (2003), pp. 416 ff.

[301] Mattioli (2017), p. 187.

those actors to engage in contractual arrangements with which they "accept mutually binding commitments".[302]

In the digital environment, the contractually-based aggregation of large health datasets owned by different research actors appear to serve innovation goals similar to the one promoted by the patent system in a product-based economy.[303] More precisely, the contractual sharing of research valuable information is emerging as an increasingly important private ordering tool for the achievement of collaborative digital health innovation, in respect to which the intellectual property system alone appears to have too little incentivising function.[304] In this light, it is to be considered as a direct expression of businesses' and research entities' freedom of contract and of business in the datafied and digitised health research environment.

Against this backdrop, the next Chapter will give account of the emerging reality of the network of contracts governing digital health research, highlighting the variety of interests related to health data transfers in the digital economy. Contracts regarding the sharing of health data imply the transfer of very sensitive data, impacting on the diverging interests of data subjects, competing parties and the public at large.

References

Abbott R (2020) Artificial intelligence, big data and intellectual property: protecting computer-generated works in the United Kingdom. In: Aplin T (ed) Research handbook on intellectual property and digital technologies. Edward Elgar, Cheltenham, pp 322–337

Abriani N (2002) Le utilizzazioni libere nella società dell'informazione: considerazioni generali. AIDA:98–124

Acquisti A (1 December 2010) The Economics of Personal Data and the Economics of Privacy, Joint WPISP-WPIE Roundtable The Economics of Personal Data and Privacy: 30 Years after the OECD Privacy Guidelines, Background Paper 3. OECD. https://www.oecd.org/sti/ieconomy/46968784.pdf

Anderson C (23 June 2008) The End of Theory: the Data Deluge Makes the Scientific Method Obsolete. Wired. www.wired.com/2008/06/pb-theory/

Aplin T (2015) Right to property and trade secrets. In: Geiger C (ed) Research handbook on human rights and intellectual property. Edward Elgar, Cheltenham, pp 421–437

Apple ResearchKit and CareKit. https://www.apple.com/researchkit/

Arezzo E (2012) Tutela brevettuale e autoriale dei programmi per elaboratore: profili e critica di una dicotomia normativa. Giuffrè, Milan

Auerbach D (2015) The silicon tower. Slate. https://slate.com/technology/2015/05/facebook-study-why-silicon-valleys-incursion-into-academic-research-is-a-big-big-problem.html

Bamberger KA, Lobel O (2017) Platform market power. Berkeley Technol Law J 32:1051–1092

Barnett J (2014) From patent thickets to patent networks: the legal infrastructure of the digital economy. Jurimetrics 55:1–55

BBC News (26 August 2016) Whatsapp and Facebook Data Sharing Plan Being Investigated. BBC. http://www.bbc.com/news/technology-37198445

[302] World Health Organization https://www.who.int/contracting/arrangements/en/.

[303] World Health Organization https://www.who.int/contracting/arrangements/en/.

[304] Hilty (2018), pp. 898 ff.

Berry DA (2015) The brave New World of clinical cancer research: adaptive biomarker-driven trials integrating clinical practice with clinical research. Mol Oncol 9:951–959

Bertani M (2006) Banche dati ed appropriazione delle informazioni. Europa e diritto privato 319–332

Bhowmick A, Hribar C (26 August 2016) Online health communities: a new frontier of health research. Medium. https://medium.com/@abhowmick1/online-health-communities-a-new-frontier-in-health-research-71fb73edbea2

Boiten E (5 May 2016) Google is now involved with healthcare data – is that a good thing?. The Conversation. https://theconversation.com/google-is-now-involved-withhealthcare-data-is-that-a-good-thing-58901

Boyle J (2003) The second enclosure movement and the construction of the public domain. Law Contemp Probl 66:33–74

Braun J, Pugatch MP (2005) The changing face of the pharmaceutical industry and intellectual property rights. J World Intellect Prop 8:599–623

Budzinski O, Schneider S (2017) Ökonomische Effekte einer Digitalisierung der Selbstvermessung. List Forum für Wirtschafts und Finanzpolitik 2:89–124

Burk DL (2015) Patents as data aggregators in personalized medicine. Bost Univ J Sci Technol Law 21:233–255

Camarinha-Matho LM, Afsarmanesh H (2006) Collaborative networks-value creation in a knowledge society. In: Wang K, Kovacs G, Wozny M, Fang M (eds) Knowledge Enterprise: intelligent strategies in product design, manufacturing, and management. Springer, New York, pp 26–40

Carrol MW (2015) Sharing research data and intellectual property law: a primer. PLoS Biol 13. https://doi.org/10.1371/journal.pbio.1002235

Cerrato SA (2016) Appunti sul contratto di rete: un modello "à la carte" dal contratto all'istituzione… e ritorno. Riv dir imp 3:491–531

Christen M, Domingo-Ferrer J, Draganski B, Spranger T, Walter H (2016) On the compatibility of big data driven research and informed consent: the example of the human brain project. In: Mittelstadt BD, Floridi L (eds) The ethics of biomedical big data. Springer, New York, pp 199–221

Citron DK, Pasquale F (2014) The scored society: due process for automated predictions. Washington Law Rev 89:1–33

Clinical Trials Transformation Initiative (16 December 2019) Developing Novel Endpoints Generated by Mobile Technology for Use in Clinical Trials. http://www.ctti-clinicaltrials.org/projects/novel-endpoints

Colangelo G (2008) Mercato e cooperazione tecnologica. I contratti di patent pooling. Giuffrè-Quaderni di Aida, Milan

Colangelo G (2009) Gli accordi di patent pooling: un'analisi comparata della regolamentazione. Il diritto industriale 17:51–66

Colangelo G, Borgogno O (5 April 2019) Data sharing and interoperability: fostering innovation and competition through APIs. Comput Law Secur Rev 35:105314

Colonna L (2019) Legal and regulatory challenges to utilizing life logging Technologies for the Frail and the sick. Int J Law Inf Technol 27:50–74

Comandè G (2017) Regulating algorithms' regulation? First Ethico-legal principles, problems and opportunities of algorithms. In: Cerquitelli T, Quercia D, Pasquale F (eds) Transparent data Mining for Small and big Data. Springer, New York, pp 169–206

Comandè G (2018) Rotting meat errors from Galileo to Aristotele in data mining? EDPLR 4:270–277

Comandè G, Malgieri G (2017) Sensitive by distance: quasi-health data in the algorithmic era, in inf. Comm Technol Law 26:229–249

Comandè G, Schneider G (2018) Regulatory challenges of data mining practices: the case of the never-ending lifecycles of health data. Eur J Health Law 25:284–307

Correa C (2007) Trade related aspects of intellectual property rights: a commentary on the TRIPS agreement. Oxford University Press, Oxford

Cortez N, Cohen I, Kesselhiem A (2014) FDA regulation of Mobile health technologies. NEJM 371:372–379

Coveney P, Dougherty E, Highfield RR (2016) Big data has not revolutionized medicine – we need big theory alongside it. Philos Trans R Soc A. https://doi.org/10.1098/rsta.2016.0153

Crawford K (2014) The Test We Can—and Should—Run on Facebook. The Atlantic. http://www.theatlantic.com/technology/archive/2014/07/the-test-we-canand-shouldrun-onfacebook/373819/

Custers B (2013) Data dilemmas in the information society: introduction and overview. In: Custers B, Calders T, Schermer B, Zarsky T (eds) Discrimination and privacy in the information society: data mining and profiling in large databases. Springer, New York, pp 3–26

David PA (2000) The Digital Technology Boomerang: New Intellectual Property Rights Threaten Global Open Science. Stanford Department of Economics Working Paper N. 00-006. https://ideas.repec.org/p/wpa/wuwpdc/0502012.html

Di Cataldo V (2009) Nuove tecnologie e nuove regole. Chi inventa le nuove regole e come? In: Rossi S, Storti C (eds) Le matrici del diritto commerciale tra storia e tendenze evolutive. Insubria University Press, Varese, pp 135–152

Dias Nunes P (25 July 2015) The European Trade Secrets Directive (ETSD): Nothing new under the Sun? Lex Research Topics in Innovation 2015-1. http://papers.ssrn.com/sol3/papers.cfm?abstract_id=2635897

Dilworth K (14 August 2014) Health Care Companies Turn to 'Big Data'. https://www.creditcards.com/credit-card-news/health-care-companies-turn-to-big-data-1282.php

Drexl J (27 April 2018) Data Access and Data Control in the Era of Connected Devices. Study on Behalf of the European Consumer Organisation BEUC. https://www.beuc.eu/publications/beuc-x-2018-121_data_access_and_control_in_the_area_of_connected_devices.pdf

Drexl J, Hilty RM et al (9 September 2016) Data ownership and access to data, Position statement of the Max Planck Institute for Innovation and Competition of the 16th August 2016 on the Current European Debate, Max Planck Institute for Innovation and Competition Research Paper No. 16-10. SSRN. https://papers.ssrn.com/sol3/papers.cfm?abstract_id=2833165

Dumortier J, Verhenneman G (22 December 2011) Legal Regulations on Electronic Health Records: a Prerequisite or an Unavoidable By-product?. ICRI Research Paper No. 5. https://papers.ssrn.com/sol3/papers.cfm?abstract_id=1975758

Eichler HG, Sweeney F (2018) The evolution of clinical trials: can we address the challenge of the future?. Sage Journals. https://doi.org/10.1177/1740774518755058

EU Directorate General for Internal Policies (2014) Trade Secrets. http://www.europarl.europa.eu/RegData/etudes/note/join/2014/493055/IPOL-JURI_NT(2014)493055_EN.pdf

EUIPO (July 2017) Protecting innovation through trade secrets and patents: Determinants for European Union Firms. https://euipo.europa.eu/tunnel-web/secure/webdav/guest/document_library/observatory/documents/reports/Trade%20Secrets%20Report_en.pdf

European Commission (20 February 2002) Proposal of a directive related to the patentability of computer implemented inventions. http://eur-lex.europa.eu/legal-content/EN/TXT/?uri=CELEX%3A52002PC0092

European Commission (April 2013) Study on Trade Secrets and Confidential Business Information in the Internal Market. http://ec.europa.eu/internal_market/iprenforcement/docs/trade-secrets/130711_final-study_en.pdf

European Commission (10 April 2014) Green Paper on Mobile Health ('M-health'). https://ec.europa.eu/digitalagenda/en/news/green-papermobile-health-mhealth

European Commission (July 2016) Guidelines on the Qualification and Classification of Standalone Software Used in Healthcare Within the Regulatory Framework of Medical Device. https://ec.europa.eu/docsroom/documents/17921/attachments/1/translations

European Commission (10 January 2017a) Commission Staff Working Document on the Free Flow of Data and Emerging Issues of the European Data Economy. Accompanying the

Communication Building a European Data Economy. https://eur-lex.europa.eu/legal-content/EN/TXT/?uri=CELEX:52017SC0002
European Commission (10 May 2017b) Commission Staff Working Document- Accompanying the Document, Communication from the Commission to the European Parliament, the Council, the European Economic and Social Committee and the Committee of Regions on the Mid-Term Review on the Implementation of the Digital Single Market Strategy, A Connected Digital Single Market For All. https://eur-lex.europa.eu/resource.html?uri=cellar:a4215207-362b-11e7-a08e-01aa75ed71a1.0001.02/DOC_1&format=PDF
European Council (7 December 2015) Council's Conclusions on Personalised Medicine for Patients. https://eur-lex.europa.eu/legal-content/EN/TXT/PDF/?uri=OJ:C:2015:421:FULL&from=EN
European Court of Justice (22 November 2012) Brain Products Gmbh vs. Bio Semi VOF. Case C-129/11
European Court of Justice (7 December 2017) Snitem and Philips France vs. Premier ministre and Ministre des Affaires sociales et de la Santé. C-329/16. https://eur-lex.europa.eu/legal-content/EN/TXT/?uri=CELEX%3A62016CJ0329
European Medicines Agency (28 July 2016) Final Report on the Adaptive Pathways Pilot. http://www.ema.europa.eu/docs/en_GB/document_library/Report/2016/08/WC500211526.pdf
European Medicines Agency (2017) Annual Report 2016 http://www.ema.europa.eu/docs/en_GB/document_library/Annual_report/2017/05/WC500227334.pdf
European Medicines Agency (24 April 2018) Meeting summary Working Parties with Patients' and Consumers' Organisations (PCWP) and Healthcare Professionals' Organisations (HCPWP) joint meeting 17–18 April 2018. https://www.ema.europa.eu/en/documents/minutes/meeting-summary-european-medicines-agency-ema-human-scientific-committees-working-parties-patients_en.pdf
European Parliament (2015) Personalized Treatment: Towards the Right Treatment for the Right Person at the Right Time, Briefing. http://www.europarl.europa.eu/RegData/etudes/BRIE/2015/569009/EPRS_BRI(2015)569009_EN.pdf
Evans BJ (2014) Economic regulation of next-generation sequencing. JLME 42. https://doi.org/10.1111/jlme.12162
Evans DS, Schmalensee R (2015) The antitrust analysis of multi-sided platform businesses. In: Blair R, Sokol D (ed) Oxford handbook on international antitrust economics, 1, Oxford University Press, Oxford pp –447
Evans M, Stevens L (27 November 2018) Big tech expands footprint in health. Wall Street J. https://www.wsj.com/articles/amazon-starts-selling-software-to-mine-patient-health-records-1543352136
Falce V (2010) La sfida del diritto dell'innovazione nei nuovi settori della tecnica. Cenni sui modelli cooperativi. In: Giudici S (ed) Studi in memoria di Paola Frassi. Giuffrè, Milan, pp 293–324
Feldman R, Frondorf E (2016) Drug wars: a new generation of generic pharmaceutical delay. Harv J Legislat 53:499–561
Fezer K (2017) Data ownership of the people-an intrinsic intellectual property law sui generis regarding People's behavior-generated informational data. Zeitschrift für Geistiges Eigentum 9: 356–370
Food and Drug Administration (13 November 2017a) FDA Approves Pill with Sensor that Digitally Tracks if Patients Have Ingested their Medication. https://www.fda.gov/NewsEvents/Newsroom/PressAnnouncements/ucm584933.htm
Food and Drug Administration (2017b) Digital Health Innovation Plan https://www.fda.gov/downloads/MedicalDevices/DigitalHealth/UCM568735.pdf
Food and Drug Administration (7 December 2017c) Statement from FDA Commissioner Scott Gottlieb, M.D., on Advancing New Digital Health Policies to Encourage Innovation, Bring Efficiency and Modernization to Regulation. https://www.prnewswire.com/news-releases/statement-from-fda-commissioner-scott-gottlieb-md-on-advancing-new-digital-health-policies-to-encourage-innovation-bring-efficiency-and modernization-to-regulation-300568421.html

Food and Drug Administration (14 March 2019) Statement by FDA Commissioner Scott Gottlieb, M.D., on new strategies to modernize clinical trials to advance precision medicine, patient protections and more efficient product development. https://www.fda.gov/NewsEvents/Newsroom/PressAnnouncements/ucm633500.htm

Furukawa Y (2010) Intellectual property protection and innovation: an inverted-U relationship. Econ Lett 109:99–101

Gardner R, Ostrom E, Walker JM (1990) The nature of common-Pool resource problems. Ration Soc 2:335–358

Gasser U, Palfrey J (November 2007) Breaking down ICT barriers-when and how ICT interoperability drives innovation. Berkman Publication Series. https://cyber.harvard.edu/interop/pdfs/interop-breaking-barriers.pdf

Genes for Good., https://genesforgood.sph.umich.edu/

Gervais D (2019) Exploring the interfaces between big data and intellectual property law. JIPITEC 10:1–19

Gervais DJ (2002) The internationalisation of intellectual property: new challenges from the very old and the very new. Fordham Intell Prop Law J 12:929–990

Ghidini G (1984) I programmi per Computers tra Brevetto e Diritto d'Autore. Giur Comm 2:251–278

Ghidini G (2006) Intellectual property and competition law: the innovation nexus. Edward Elgar, Cheltenham

Ghosh S (2004) Patents and the regulatory state: rethinking the patent bargain metaphor after elder. Berkeley Technol Law J 19:1315–1388

Gibson J (2005) Intellectual property, international trade and protection of traditional knowledge. Earthscan, London, 2005

Ginsberg J et al (2009) Detecting influenza epidemics using search engine query data. Nature 457:1012–1014

Google Cloud (5 March 2018) Google Cloud for Healthcare: New APIs, Customers, Partners and Security Updates. https://www.blog.google/topics/google-cloud/google-cloud-healthcare-new-apis-customers-partners-and-security-updates/

Goy F, Wang C (2016) Does knowledge tradability make secrecy more attractive than patents? An analysis of IPR strategies and licensing. Oxf Econ Pap 68:64–88

Granieri M (2013) Contratto di rete, programma comune e gestione della proprietà intellettuale nella collaborazione tra imprese. In: Genovese A (ed) Riflessioni sul contratto di rete. Profili privatistici e fiscali, Cacucci, Bari, pp 65–88

Granieri M, Colangelo G, De Michelis F (2009) Introduzione ai contratti per il trasferimento di tecnologia. Cacucci, Bari

Grimmelmann J (2015) The law and ethics of experiments on social media users. Colorado Technol Law J 13:219–271

Grundman S, Hacker P (2017) Digital technology as a challenge to European contract law- from the existing to the future architecture. Eur Rev Contract Law 13:255–293

Guarda P (26 December 2006) Electronic Health Records: Privacy and Security Issues in a Comparative Perspective. Working Paper Series. https://papers.ssrn.com/sol3/papers.cfm?abstract_id=1528461

Guglielmetti G (2003) Brevettazione e segreto. In: VV AA (ed) Le nuove frontiere del diritto dei brevetti. Giappichelli pp 109–225

Gupta A, Goyal RK, Joiner KA, Saini S (2008) Outsourcing in the healthcare industry: information technology, intellectual property, and allied aspects. Inf Resour Manage J 21:1–26

Gupta I (2017) Footprint of feist in European database directive: a legal analysis of IP making in Europe. Springer, Berlin

Hall MA (2010) Property, privacy and the pursuit of integrated electronic medical records. Iowa Law Rev 95:631–663

Hall TS (2014) The quantified self movement: legal challenges and benefits of personal biometric data tracking. Akron Intell Prop J 7:27–37

Heads of Medicines Agencies-European Medicines Agency (13th February 2019) Joint Big Data Task Force-Summary Report. https://www.ema.europa.eu/en/documents/minutes/hma/ema-joint-task-force-big-data-summary-report_en.pdf
Heller MA (1998) The tragedy of the Anticommons: property in the transition from Marx to markets. Harv Law Rev 111:621–688
Heller MA (2008) The Gridlock economy: how too much Ownershi Wrecks markets, stops innovation and costs lives. Basic Books, New York
Heller MA, Eisenberg R (1998) Can patents deter innovation? The anticommons in biomedical research. Science 280:698–701
Hess C, Ostrom E (2007) Introduction: an overview of the knowledge commons. In: Hess C, Ostrom E (eds) Understanding knowledge as commons. MIT Press, Cambridge, pp 3–26
Hildebrandt M (2008) Defining profiling: a new type of knowledge? In: Hildebrandt M, Gutwirth S (eds) Profiling the European citizen- cross-disciplinary perspectives. Springer, New York, pp 17–30
Hilty RM (2018) Intellectual property and private ordering. In: Dreyfuss R, Pila J (eds) The Oxford handbook of intellectual property law. Oxford University Press, Oxford, pp 898–930
Hoffmann J, Johannsen G (31 May 2019) EU-Merger Control in Big Data-Related Merger. Max Planck Institute for Innovation and Competition Research Paper N. 19-05. https://papers.ssrn.com/sol3/papers.cfm?abstract_id=3364792
Hoffmann S (2016) Citizen science: the law and ethics of public access to medical big data. Berkeley Technol Law J 30:1741–1805
Hoffmann S, Podgurski A (2008) Finding a cure: the case for regulation and oversight of electronic health records system. Harv J Law Technol 22:2–64
Hoffmann S, Podgurski A (2009) E-health hazards: provider liability and electronic health records systems. Berkeley Technol Law J 24:1524–1582
Horgan D, Kent A (2017) EU health policy, coherence, stakeholder diversity and their impact on the EMA. BiomedHub 2:481301
Horne AJ (1992) Shared rights to source code: the copyright dilemma. Santa Clara Law Rev 32: 497–538
Izmailova ES, Wagner JA, Perakslis ED (2018) Wearable devices in clinical studies: hypes and hypothesis. Clin Pharmacol Ther 104:42–52
Jain SH, Powers BW, Hawkins JB, Brownstein JS (2015) The digital phenotype. Nat Biotechnol 33:462–463
Jensen PB, Jensen LJ, Brunak S (2012) Mining electronic health records: towards better research applications and clinical care. Nat Rev Genetic 13:395–405
Kandula S, Shaman J (2 August 2019) Reappraising the utility of Google flu trends. PLoS Comput Biol. https://doi.org/10.1371/journal.pcbi.1007258
Kesselheim AS, Mello MM (2007) Confidentiality laws and secrecy in medical research: improving public access to data on drug safety. Health Aff 26:483–491
Kitch E (1977) Nature and function of the patent system. J Law Econ 20:265–290
Kitchin R (1 April 2014) Big data, new epistemologies and paradigm shifts. Big Data Soc. https://doi.org/10.1177/2053951714528481
Kramer ADI, Guillory JE, Hancock JT (2014) Experimental evidence of massive-scale emotional contagion through social networks. Proceedings of the National Academy of Sciences. https://www.pnas.org/content/111/24/8788
Krawford C (2013) The Hidden Biases in Big Data. HBR. https://hbr.org/2013/04/the-hidden-biases-in-big-data
Krumholz HM (2014) Big data and new knowledge in medicine: the thinking, training and tools needed for a learning health system. Health Aff 33:1163–1170
La Stampa (10 March 2015) Researchkit, così l'i-phone aiuterà la ricerca http://www.lastampa.it/2015/03/10/tecnologia/research-kit-cos-liphone-aiuter-la ricercat6kFiTPRpnCtFNE0DiHbRO/pagina.html

Ladeur KH (2016) The Future of Law: Serial Law. EUI Research Papers, Law 2016/19. http://cadmus.eui.eu/bitstream/handle/1814/43345/LAW_2016_19.pdf?sequence=1

Laurie G (2013) Governing the spaces in-between: law and legitimacy in new health technologies. In: Farrell AM, Flear ML, Hervey TK, Murphy T (eds) European law and new health technologies. Oxford University Press, Oxford, pp 191–195

Leistner M (2017) Big data and the EU database Directive 96/9/EC: current law and potential for reform. In: Lohsse S, Schulze R, Staudenmayer D (eds) Trading data in the digital economy: legal concepts and tools-Münster colloquia on EU law and the digital economy III. Nomos, Baden-Baden, pp 27–58

Lemley M (1997) The economics of improvement in intellectual property law. Texas Law Rev 75: 989–1083

Lemley M (2004) Ex ante versus ex post justifications for intellectual property. Univ Chicago Law Rev 71:129–149

Lemley MA (2013) Software patents and the return of functional claiming. Wiscon Law Rev:905–964

Lerner J, Merges RP (1998) The control of strategic alliances: an empirical analysis of biotechnology collaborations. J Ind Econ 46(2):125–156

Lindqvist B (2018) Competition and data pools. EuCML 7:146–154

Litman J, Samuelson P (2010) The copyright principles project: directions for reform. Berkeley Technol Law J 25:1175–1245

Lohr S (13 April 2015) IBM Creates Watson Health to Analyze Medical Data. The New York Times. https://bits.blogs.nytimes.com/2015/04/13/ibm-creates-watson-health-to-analyze-medical-data/

Lorchan Lewis T, Wyatt J (2014) mHealth and Mobile medical apps: a framework to assess risk and promote safer use. J Med Internet Res 16. https://doi.org/10.2196/jmir.3133

Lupton D (2013) The digitally engaged patient: self-monitoring and self-Care in the Digital Health era. Soc Theory Health 11:256–270

Lupton D (2017) Lively data, social fitness and biovalue: the intersections of health self-tracking and social media. In: Bruggess J, Marwick A, Poell T (eds) The sage handbook on social media. Sage, London, pp 562–578

Luzzatto E (1988) I brevetti chimico farmaceutici e il requisito della loro descrizione I: 463–477

Margoni T (2016) The harmonization of Eu copyright law: the originality standard. In: Perry M (ed) Global governance of intellectual property in the 21st century. Springer International Publishing, Switzerland, pp 85–105

Marjanovic S, Ghiga I, Yang M, Knack A (27 April 2017) Understanding value in health data ecosystems- a review of current evidence and ways forward. Rand Corporation https://www.rand.org/pubs/research_reports/RR1972.html

Martens K (19 December 2018) FDA Clears Mobile Medical Application for Patients with Opioid Use Dirsorder. Lexology. https://www.lexology.com/library/detail.aspx?g=21c8632e-22d4-48f5-b66e-78a915bbef34

Mask M (6 November 2018) Artificial Intelligence For Suicide Prediction. Petrie Flom Blog. http://blog.petrieflom.law.harvard.edu/2018/11/06/artificial-intelligence-for-suicide-prediction/

Maskus KE, Reichman J (2004) The globalization of private knowledge goods and the privatization of global public goods. J Int Econ Law 7:279–320

Mattioli M (2017) The data pooling problem. Berkeley Technol Law J 32:179–236

Mattioli M (2018) Patent Pools Outsiders. Berkeley Technol Law J 33:225–286

Maugeri RM (2009) Reti di imprese, contratto di rete e reti contrattuali- Non minor virtus est tueri et perficere rem inventam. . . quam reperire. Obbligazioni e contratti:951–962

Mayer-Schönberger V, Cukier K (2013) Big data: a revolution that will transform how we live, work, and think. John Murray Publishers, London

McGarity TO, Shapiro SA (1980) The trade secret status over health and safety testing information: reforming agency disclosure policies. Harv Law Rev 93:837–888

Mendelson D, Mendelson D (2017) Legal protections for personal health information in the age of big data. Ethics Med Public Health 3:37–55
Merges R (1994) Intellectual property rights and bargaining breakdown: the case of blocking patents. Tenn Law Rev 62:75–106
Merges R, Mattioli M (2017) Measuring the costs and benefits of patent pools. Ohio State Law J 77: 281–347
Merges RP (2001) Institutions for intellectual property transactions: the case of patent pools. In: Dreyfuss RC, Zimmermann DL, First H (eds) Expanding the boundaries of intellectual property: innovation policy for the knowledge society. Oxford University Press, Oxford, pp 123–166
Metcalf J, Crawford K (2016) Where are human subjects in big data research? The emerging ethics divide. Big Data Soc 3. https://doi.org/10.1177/2053951716650211
Meyer MN, Chabris CF (19 June 2015) Please, Corporations, Experiment on Us. The New York Times http://www.nytimes.com/2015/06/21/opinion/sunday/pleasecorporations-experiment-on-us.html
Miller AR, Tucker C (2009) Privacy protection and technology diffusion: the case of electronic medical records. Manag Sci 55:1077–1093
MIT Technology (6 November 2014) Google wants to store your Genome. MIT Technology Review, https://www.technologyreview.com/s/532266/google-wants-to-store-your-genome/
Moerel L, Prins C (25 May 2016) Privacy for the Homo Digitalis: Proposal for a New Regulatory Framework for Data Protection in the Light of Big Data and the Internet of Things. SSRN https://papers.ssrn.com/sol3/papers.cfm?abstract_id=2784123
Mohan A (1 November 2009) Copyright Issues related to Customized Software. SSRN. http://papers.ssrn.com/sol3/papers.cfm?abstract_id=1497363
Monteleone S (2015) Addressing the failure of informed consent in online data protection: learning the lesson from behaviour-aware regulation. Syracuse J Int Law Commer 43:69–119
Mukherjee S (20 April 2017a) Prepare for the Digital Health Revolution. https://fortune.com/2017/04/20/digital-health-revolution/
Mukherjee SY (24 March 2017b) Secretive Google-Backed Startup Calico Just Struck a New Biotech Partnership. Fortune. http://fortune.com/2017/03/24/google-calico-c4-therapeutics/
Müller JM (1998) The evolving application of the written description requirement to biotechnological inventions. Berkeley Technol Law J 13:615–652
Musso A (2010) Reti contrattuali tra imprese e trasferimento della conoscenza innovativa. In: Iamiceli P (ed) Le reti di imprese e i contratti di rete. Gappichelli, Turin, pp 177–224
National Cancer Institute (22 October 2021) NCI Cancer Genomics Cloud pilots. https://cbiit.nci.nih.gov/ncip
Naughton EJ (2011) The bionic library: did Google work around the GPL? Intell Prop Technol Law J 23:3–8
Nehf JP (2016) Protecting privacy with 'heightened' notice and choice. In: Rothchild JA (ed) Research handbook on electronic commerce law. Edward Elgar, Cheltenham, pp 475–492
Nicholson Price W II (2015) Black box medicine. Harv J Law Technol 2:420–467
Nicholson Price W II (2016) Regulating secrecy. Wash Law Rev 91:1769–1812
Nicholson Price W II (2017) Expired patents, trade secrets and stymied competition. Notre Dame Law Rev 92:1611–1640
Niebel R, De Martinis L, Clark B (2018) The Eu trade secrets directive: all change for trade secret protection in Europe?. JIPLP 13:445–457
Nissenbaum H (2008) Privacy in context: technology, policy and the integrity of social life. Stanford University Press, Stanford
OECD (2019) An Introduction to Online Platforms and Their Role in the Digital Transformation. https://read.oecd-ilibrary.org/science-and-technology/an-introduction-to-online-platforms-and-their-role-in-the-digital-transformation_53e5f593-en#page1
Oliver M (2015) Personalized medicine in the information age: Myriad's De facto monopoly on breast cancer research. SMU Law Rev 68:537–566

Olson S, Berger AC (2011) Establishing precompetitive collaborations to stimulate genomic-driven product development: workshop summary-roundtable on translating genomic-based research for health-board on health sciences policy-Institute of Medicine of the National Academies. National Academy Press, Washington

Ostrom E (2010) Beyond markets and states: polycentric governance of complex economic systems. Am Econ Rev 100:641–672

Ostrom E, Garder R, Walker J (1994) Rules, games, and common-Pool resources. The University of Michigan Press, Ann Arbour

Ottolia A (2010) The public interest and intellectual property models. Giappichelli, Turin

Ottolia A (2017) Big data e innovazione computazionale. Giappichelli, Turin

Owervalle GV (2009) Gene patents and collaborative licensing models: patent pools, clearing-houses, open source models and liability regimes. Cambridge University Press, Cambridge

Pasquale F (2014) Redescribing health privacy: the importance of information policy. Hous J Health Law Policy 14:95–128

Pasquale F (2015) The black box society: the secret algorithms that control money and information. Harvard University Press, Cambridge

Pasquale F, Ragone TA (2014) Protecting health privacy in an era of big data processing and Cloud computing. Stanf Technol Law Rev 17:595–654

Pisto LA (2013) The need for privacy-centric role-based access controls to electronic health records. J Health Life Sci Law 7:79–112

Powles J, Hodson H (2017) Google DeepMind and healthcare in an age of algorithms. Heal Technol 7:351–367

Purtova N (2015) The illusion of personal data as no One's property. Law Innov Technol 7:83–111

Purtova N (2017) Health data for common good: defining the boundaries and social dilemmas of data commons. In: Leenes R, Purtova N, Adams S (eds) Under observation: the interplay between e-health and surveillance. Springer, Berlin, pp 177–210

Quinn P (2017) The European Commission's risky choice for a non-risk based strategy on assessment of medical devices. Comput Law Secur Rev 33:361–370

Rai AK (1992) Regulating scientific research: intellectual property rights and the norms of science. Northwest Univ Law Rev 94:77–152

Rai AK (2001a) Fostering cumulative innovation in the biopharmaceutical industry: the role of patents and antitrust. Berkeley Technol Law J 16:813–853

Rai AK (2001b) The information revolution reaches pharmaceuticals: balancing innovation incentives, cost, and access in the post-genomic era. Univ Ill Law Rev 1:173–210

Rai AK (2017a) Legal issues in genomic and precision medicine: intellectual property and beyond. In: Ginsburg G, Willard H (eds) Genomic and personalized medicine: translation and implementation. Elsevier Press, Amsterdam, pp 357–366

Rai AK (2017b) Risk regulation and innovation: the case of rights-encumbered biomedical data silos. Notre Dame Law Rev 92:1642–1668

Rai AK, Reichman JH, Uhlir PF, Crosswell C (2008) Pathways across the valley of death: novel intellectual property strategies for accelerated drug discovery. Yale J Health Policy Law Ethics 8:3–36

Rajkomar A et al (2018) Scalable and accurate deep learning with electronic health records. NPJ Digital Med 18:1–10

Ray T (2 May 2016) Genomic Data Sharing Variant Gains Support. Collaboration Seen as a Key to Interpretation Challenge. Genome Web. https://www.genomeweb.com/informatics/genomic-variant-data-sharing-gains-support-collaboration-seen-keyinterpretation#.XMrTU5MzYb0

Reagan PM (2002) Privacy as a common good. Inf Commun Soc 5:382–405

Reichman J, Okediji RL (2012) When copyright law and science collide: empowering digitally integrated research methods on a global scale. Minn Law Rev 96:1362–1480

Reichman JH, Uhlir PF (2003) A contractually reconstructed research commons for scientific data in a highly protectionist intellectual property environment. Law Contemp Probl 66:315–462

Reichman JH, Uhlir P, Dedeurwaerdere T (2015) Legal and institutional obstacles impeding access and use of scientific literature and data. In: Reichman JH, Uhlir P, Dedeurwaerdere T (eds) Governing digitally integrated genetic resources, data and literature-global intellectual property strategies for a redesigned microbial research commons. Cambridge University Press, Cambridge, pp 319–372

Ricolfi M (2002) La tutela della proprietà intellettuale fra incentivo all'innovazione e scambio ineguale. Riv dir ind I:511–525

Ricolfi M (2019) Il futuro della proprietà intellettuale nella società algoritmica. Giur It 10-36

Robinson D, Yu H, Rieke A (September 2014) Civil rights, big data, and our algorithmic. Future. http://centerformediajustice.org/wp-content/uploads/2014/10/Civil-Rights_Big-Data_Our-Future.pdf

Rochet J, Tirole J (2003) Platform competition in two-sided markets. J Eur Econ 1:990–1029

Roin BN (2009) Unpatentable drugs and the standards of patentability. Texas Law Rev 87:503–570

Romano R (2010) L'innovazione tecnica tra diritti titolati e diritti non titolati (dalla creazione alla segretazione?). In: Giudici S (ed) Studi in memoria di Paola AE Frassi. Giuffrè, Milan, pp 599–619

Rubinfeld D, Gal M (2017) Access barriers to big data. Ariz Law Rev 59:339–381

Rubinstein R (2013) Big data: the end of privacy or a new beginning. Int Data Priv Law 3:74–87

Samuelson P (2007) Why copyright law excludes systems and processes from the scope of its protection. Texas Law Rev 85:1921–1977

Samuelson P, Vinje T, Cornish W (2012) Does copyright protection under the EU software directive extend to computer program behaviour, languages and interfaces? EIPR 34:158–166

Sarti D (1996) Diritti esclusivi e circolazione Dei Beni. Giuffrè, Milan

Schneider G (2018) A European transparency challenge: can commercial confidentiality over clinical trials data be overcome? EPLR 2:3–18

Schwartz PM (2004) Property, privacy and personal data. Harv Law Rev 117:2056–2128

Seitz C (2017) Big data in the pharmaceutical sector. In: Vermeulen G, Lievens E (eds) Data protection and privacy under pressure: transatlantic tensions, EU surveillance and big data. Maklu Verlag, Antwerpen/Apeldoorn/Portland, pp 293–309

Shapiro C (2001) Navigating the patent thicket: cross-licences, patent pools and standard setting. In: Lerner J, Stern S (eds) Innovation policy and the economy. MIT Press, vol. 1, Boston, pp 119–150

Sharon T (2016) The googlization of health research: from disruptive innovation to disruptive ethics. Pers Med 13:563–574

Sharon T (2017) Self-tracking for health and the quantified health: re-articulating autonomy, solidarity, and authenticity in an age of personalized healthcare. Philosophy Technol 30:93–121

Shemtov N (2017) Beyond the code: protection of non-textual features of softwares. Oxford University Press, Oxford

Simon BM, Sichelman T (2017) Data-generating patents. Northwest Univ Law Rev 111:377–437

Skopek JM (2018) Big Data's epistemology and its implications for precision medicine and privacy. In: Glenn Cohen I, Lynch HF, Vayena E, Gasser U (eds) Big data, health law and Biotehics. Harvard University, Cambridge, pp 30–41

Solberg LS (2012) Regulating human subjects research in the information age: data mining on social networking sites. Northern Kentucky Law Rev 39:327–358

Sousa-Silva D (2014) What exactly is a trade secret under the proposed directive? JIPLP 9:923–932

Spolidoro MS (2014) Reti di imprese e diritti di proprietà industriale. Riv di rind 4–5:245–265

Stephens ZD et al (2015) Big Data: Astronomical or Genomical? PLoS Biol 13:1002195

Stiglitz J (2003) Knowledge as a public good. In: Kaul I, Grunberg I, Stern M (eds) Global public goods: international cooperation in the 21st century. Oxford Scholarship Online, Oxford, pp 308–325

Stiglitz JE (2000) The contributions of the economics of information to twentieth century economics. Q J Econ 115:1441–1478

Terry N, Francis LP (2007) Ensuring the privacy and confidentiality of electronic health records. Univ Ill Law Rev 2:681–736
Teubner G (2011) Networks as connected contracts. Hart Publishing, Oxford
The Economist (1 February 2018) A Revolution in Healthcare is Coming- Welcome to Doctor You. https://www.economist.com/leaders/2018/02/01/a-revolution-in-health-care-is-coming
The Google Brain Team (11 January 2018) Looking Back on 2017. https://research.googleblog.com/2018/01/the-google-brain-team-looking-back-on.html
Tseliou T (28 March 2015) Balancing Protection of Public Health and Safety With the Free Movement of Goods in the EU Medical Device Sector: the Case of 'Borderline Products' Classification. TILEC Discussion Paper 2015-008. https://papers.ssrn.com/sol3/papers.cfm?abstract_id=2585539
Ubertazzi LC (1997) Riservatezza informatica e industria culturale. AIDA:529–539
Ullrich H (2004) Expansionist intellectual property protection and reductionist competition rules: a TRIPS perspective. J Int Econ Law 7:401–430
Unesco International Bioethics Committee (IBC) (15 September 2017) Report of the IBC on Big Data and Health. https://unesdoc.unesco.org/ark:/48223/pf0000248724
Vaidhyanathan S (2011) The googlization of everything (and why we should worry). University of California Press, Berkeley
Vanzetti A (2011) La tutela "corretta" delle informazioni segrete. Riv dir ind 60:95–105
Varian H (16 October 1998) Markets for Information Goods. http://people.ischool.berkeley.edu/~hal/Papers/japan/
Vayena E, Blasimme A (2017) Biomedical big data: new models of control over access, use and governance. J Bioeth Inq 14:501–513
Vayena E, Blasimme A (2018) Health research with big data: time for systemic oversight. J Law Med Ethics 46:119–129
Vayena E, Gasser U (2016) Strictly biomedical? Sketching the ethics of the big data ecosystem in biomedicine. In: Mittelstadt BD, Floridi L (eds) The ethics of biomedical big data. Springer, Switzerland, pp 17–38
Vayena E, Dzenowagis J, Langfeld M (2016) Evolving health data ecosystem. WHO https://www.who.int/ehealth/resources/ecosystem.pdf?ua=1
Vayena E, Ienca M, Adjekum A (2017) What is trust? Ethics and risk governance in precision medicine and predictive analytics. OMICS J Integr Biol 21:704–710
Verily (12 December 2017) Establishing a new Baseline of Health and Research Participation for Diverse Populations. https://blog.verily.com/2017/12/establishing-new-baseline-of-health-and.html
Waldman K (2014) Facebook's unethical experiment. Slate. http://www.slate.com/articles/health_and_science/science/2014/06/facebook_unethical_experiment_it_made_news_feeds_happier_or_sadder_to_manipulate.html
WIPO (2004) WIPO technical study on patent disclosure requirements related to genetic resources and traditional knowledge. Study No 3-2004. www.wipo.int/export/sites/www/freepublications/en/tk/786/wipo_pub_786.pdf
WIPO (6 June 2007) Declaration of the Source of Genetic Resources and Traditional Knowledge in Patent Applications: Proposals by Switzerland - Document submitted by Switzerland https://www.wipo.int/meetings/en/doc_details.jsp?doc_id=79175
World Health Organization (28 June 2021) Ethics and Governance of Artificial Intelligence for Health. https://www.who.int/publications/i/item/9789240029200

World Health Organization Contractual Arrangements in Health Systems. https://www.who.int/contracting/arrangements/en/

Zarsky TZ (2003) "Mine your own business!": making the case for the implications of the data mining of personal information in the forum of public opinion. Yale J Law Technol 5:1–56

Zarsky TZ (2018) Correlation versus causation in health-related big data analysis. In: Glenn Cohen I, Lynch HF, Vayena E, Gasser U (eds) Big data, health law and biotehics. Harvard University Press, Cambridge pp, pp 42–55

Zittrain J (2000) What the Publisher can teach the patient: intellectual property and privacy in an era of trusted privication. Stanf Law Rev 52:1201–1250

Chapter 3
Health Data Pools: Case-Studies and Involved Interests

3.1 Health Data Pools: Some Case-Studies

Research collaborations between industries in the life science field have substantially increased over the last decades[1] and have taken up a variety of forms, ranging from complete vertical integration;[2] strategic alliances establishing a tight link between collaborating companies at very early stages of the research processes and involving sharing of R&D costs and final profits; and ultimately joint ventures as well as horizontal or vertical mergers.[3]

As already mentioned in the previous chapter, in recent years, big data companies have been increasingly active in health-related investigations. The agreements and partnerships that big data companies are negotiating enable them to engage in a massive collection of health data, which come to feed their computational capabilities. The channels through which high-tech companies come to collect digital health data can be categorized as follows: (a) the collection of data from other private parties, such as pharmaceutical companies carrying out clinical research; (b) the collection of data from public institutions. The next paragraphs will thus give proof of the complexities of the networks governing algorithm-driven health research.

---

[1]Generally assessing the phenomenon of the emerging collaborative economy in the digital environment, Hatzopoulos (2018), pp. 4–8.

[2]For examples see Rai (2001a), p. 817.

[3]This had been already observed by Balto and Mongoven (1999), p. 255.

G. Schneider, *Health Data Pools Under European Data Protection and Competition Law*, Munich Studies on Innovation and Competition 17,
https://doi.org/10.1007/978-3-030-95427-7_3

3.1.1 Health Data Pools Between Pharmaceutical Companies and Big Data Companies

Pharmaceutical companies have traditionally been at the forefront in the generation and the possession of scientific health data. This data mainly resulted from the health research and the clinical trials carried out in the context of regulatory requirements and of post-marketing pharmacovigilance obligations.[4] Clinical trials data has indeed long been the most valuable research informant, being the result of originators' long, uncertain and costly investments, and thus worthy of peculiar legal protection against the free-riding of competitors.[5] As has been observed,[6] pharmaceutical R&D activities have always been secretive in the sense that they were mostly conducted without external collaboration.[7] This means that the production of pharmaceutical products' safety and efficacy information has long been of exclusive competence of the pharmaceutical sector.

However, as a result of the phenomenon of the digitization of health information, clinical trials data has become only a very small fragment of research valuable health data. Clinical trials data entails a restricted informational significance for it is the result of investigations that are limited in breadth and duration.[8] In other terms, clinical trials data lacks the wealth of longitudinal data about study participants that large tech companies have now access to.[9] Moreover, pharmaceutical companies do not have the analytical capacities to turn data into predictions, which could amount to useful knowledge for drug development and discovery.[10]

The increasing importance of data analytics in the current research environment is leading to a progressive reconsideration of traditional models and traditional value chains in the pharmaceutical industry.[11]

It is on these grounds that new collaborative scenarios between high-tech companies and pharmaceutical companies are taking shape with the ultimate purpose of developing new drugs.[12] In these regards, it is interesting to notice that the

---

[4] Seitz (2017), p. 295.

[5] Both the European and the American legal systems have introduced a special form of protection for clinical trials data, named data exclusivity. For the literature see Fackelmann (2013), pp. 147 ff.; Pugatch (12–16 October 2004).

[6] Cattell et al. (April 2013).

[7] Schuhmacher et al. (2016), p. 105.

[8] Rothwell (1995), p. 1616.

[9] Sharon (2017), pp. 95–96.

[10] Seitz (2017), p. 296.

[11] This evolution is also criticized by some scholars that fear that digitization of pharmaceutical research is likely to increase legal, reputational and financial risks. See Emam et al. (2014).

[12] Google, for example, has increased its partnerships with traditional pharmaceutical companies such as Biogen Idec, Novartis and AbbVie. Through its spin-off Verily, Google has created also a Joint Venture with the drug firm Johnson & Johnson for the development of new kinds of surgical robots. IBM Watson Health partnered with Teva Pharmaceutical Industries. Yildirim et al. (2016), pp. 461 ff. See also Financial Times (15 July 2014); The Economist (3 February 2018) where a

Innovation Partnership on Active and Healthy Ageing[13] has encouraged the promotion of partnerships and bottom-up initiatives, aiming at engaging different stakeholders to work together and supporting the transfer of best practices. The processing infrastructure provided by high tech corporations enables to aggregate and analyze more proficiently electronic databases of chemical substances, disease genes and protein targets.[14]

The agreements between pharmaceutical companies and big data companies are aimed at increasing the speed and efficiency of pharmaceutical testing procedures.[15] As a result, the emerging drug development patterns rely on the human and automated analysis of electronic databases of chemical substances, disease genes and protein targets.[16]

In this regard, predictions enabled by the computational means offered by big data companies are also enabling pharmaceutical companies to predict the disease risk among healthy individuals in the population, and the therapeutic response among patients. The availability and use of digital health data in the context of pharmaceutical research is starting to replace ordinary clinical trials where there is a too high risk of exposure to unknown substances and side effects, and where it would be extremely costly to start research or where there are not enough patients to test the substances.[17] Moreover, for pharmaceutical companies, increased access to health data facilitates the assessment of tested drugs' safety and efficacy.

From an opposite perspective, the digitization of pharmaceutical biometric and genetic data represents a highly attractive opportunity for high-tech companies, who have strong interests in promoting large-scale health screening to identify individuals and users at risk of contracting a diseases. Hence, for big data companies, partnerships with research-based pharmaceutical companies are becoming the source of highly technical and sophisticated health data. More specifically, through these partnerships precious safety and efficacy information regarding pharmaceutical products, post-marketing data, genetic data, and predictive data regarding diseases flows into and, at the same time, is processed by corporations' algorithms. As has

---

collaboration allowing Pfizer to research lupus using 23andMe's "largest dataset of its kind," including over 800,000 individuals' genotyped samples was announced.

[13] European Commission (29 February 2012).

[14] Kim et al. (2016), p. 245.

[15] Sehlstedt et al. (2016), p. 146. Genetic screening has become, for example, a new experimental tool to identify and select a phenotype of a patient on the basis of which the likelihood of contracting a specific disease can be derived. This technology can also be employed for the treatment of certain diseases. See Seitz (2017), p. 300. It must be however recalled that the genetic screening technique has been much debated in the legal literature, see, amongst others Annas and Sherman (1992), p. 291.

[16] Kim et al. (2016), p. 245.

[17] Seitz (2017), pp. 301–302, who stresses that health data analytics could be particularly important with regards to rare diseases where it is often difficult to find enough subjects to test active substances. Hence, the use of data could not only reduce the costs for orphan drugs, but could lead to the appraisal of information regarding the effects of new substances and could be key for the parallel sequencing of patients with rare diseases.

been underlined,[18] the availability of all these data is creating new sources of market power for digital companies, thus giving rise to new competitive scenarios in the pharmaceutical sector where high-tech companies are not only partners but outright competitors of traditional research-based pharmaceutical companies.[19]

Under these premises, a vast range of cooperation activities between high-tech companies and pharmaceutical companies are coming into existence, under various legal forms, from contract to the creation of joint ventures.

3.1.1.1 The Case of Genomics Data: 23andMe's Partnerships with Pharmaceutical Companies

The potential of the employment of digital technologies for the purposes of health research is clearly perceived in respect to genome data.[20] The science of genomics applies information technology to the vast amount of data currently being generated and is deemed to be at the very heart of digitised health-related innovation. New molecular-based testing techniques have been developed, combining automated processes and the improved understanding of human genetic variation.[21] With regards to the technological advancements in the field of genomics, particular attention needs to be given to Genome-Wide Association Studies, which search genetic makers involving rapidly scanning SNPs across the complete set of human genomes in order to find genetic variations associated with a particular disease.[22]

At the preclinical research stage, the employment of genomics data has the capability of diminishing the time necessary to identify the relevant molecular "target" for a specific disease.[23] In addition to this, large-scale processing of genomics data is useful also at the clinical testing stage for the *ex ante* identification of those categories of patients who have genetic variations that render them genetically incompatible with the tested product. In this way, necessarily unsuccessful testing attempts can be avoided.[24]

---

[18] Powles and Hodson (2017), p. 357.

[19] FierceBiotech (October 2015).

[20] Cohen (1997), p. 768; Lockhart and Winzeler (2000), p. 827. The Authors estimate that the amount of biomedical data available increases tenfold every year and that scientists had already at the beginning of 2000 one thousand times as much data as they did in 1985.

[21] These two factors lie at the basis also of the rise of precision medicine based on the idea to deliver a more effective, tailored and targeted treatment "for the right person, at the right time". For an analysis over the legal issues related to precision medicine, see Rai (2017), pp. 357 ff. See in these regards, European Parliament (October 2015).

[22] Ho (2017), p. 90.

[23] More precisely, the technological exploitation of such genomics information can identify the gene sequence that is overexpressed in the cells of people with the studied disease. See Rai (2001b), p. 189.

[24] Rai (2001b), p. 191.

In view of its great scientific and economic value, genetic data has been the object of numerous data sharing agreements between high tech and pharmaceutical companies.[25] A relevant example of this is given by the partnerships between the consumer genomics company 23andMe and various pharmaceutical companies, such as Pfizer,[26] Genetech[27] and lately also Glaxosmithkline.[28] As is well reflected by these partnerships, pharmaceutical companies seek access to whole-genome sequencing data in order to run queries over a vast array of diseases and conditions and identify new associations between genetic markers.[29] For their part, through these partnerships, tech companies who have collected and have the matching infrastructure for processing these data, commercially exploit these valuable assets, enabling third party companies to acquire insights on the most sensitive genetic conditions of millions of consumers, such as cancer risk.[30] In these regards it must be highlighted that in most cases the testing procedures offered by these high tech companies, require the disclosure not only of the strictly genetic data but also of a wide range of other sensitive data, such as family medical history, ethnicity, physical traits, forming the so-called "self-reported information".[31] All this sensitive data is also accessed by partnering pharmaceutical companies.

It is largely unclear whether third party-transfers of genetic data are lawful under the privacy policies governing genetic testing services.[32] Indeed, the collection and processing of this genetic data should be strictly anchored to consumers' determinations expressed through consent. However, there are significant doubts with regards to the actual informed nature of the consent given by consumers for online genetic testing services.[33] Moreover, as some empirical findings illustrate, the consent given is mostly implicit and deemed to be given just through the use of the services' website.[34] Ultimately, genetic testing companies appear to make a wide use of "variation clauses" allowing them to change their terms as needed.[35] Most of

[25] Reflecting on the relevance of genetic data for innovation purposes, Ottolia (2014).

[26] 23andMe (12 January 2015), where a collaboration allowing Pfizer to research lupus using 23andMe's "largest dataset of its kind," including over 800,000 individuals' genotyped samples was announced.

[27] Sullivan (14 January 2015). Lagorio-Chafkin (7 January 2015).

[28] GlaxoSmithKline (25 July 2018); Geggel (26 July 2018).

[29] Sullivan (14 January 2015).

[30] Regalado (11 February 2019).

[31] See 23andMe (30 October 2020), defining "self-reported" information as "information you provide directly to us, including your disease conditions, other health-related information, personal traits, ethnicity, family history, and other information that you enter into surveys, forms, or features while signed in to your 23andMe account".

[32] Phillips (2017), pp. 273 ff.

[33] Hazel and Slobogin (19 April 2018). See also Rimmer (2012), pp. 132 ff.

[34] Phillips (2017), pp. 284–285.

[35] Phillips (2017), pp. 283–284.

the times the changes in policy terms are signalled on the general websites, without directly notifying consumers.[36]

The effects of variation clauses in genetic testing services' privacy policies became apparent when a genetic testing company disavowed the declared condition that it would not have granted access to genetic databases to the police and subsequently gave such access to the FBI.[37] In another case, thanks to the sensitive genetic information acquired, California police was able to identify a rapist and murderer who had been escaping for years.[38] However, blind reliance on evidence given by DNA profiles for law enforcement purposes has soon shown to entail also significant perils, directly related to the risk of charging persons that are wrongly genetically profiled.[39]

With the advancements in DNA sequencing and profiling technologies, the ability of both a vast range of corporations and governments to track and categorise individuals grows. This raises the risk of commodification practices over consumers' sensitive health identities, amplifying corporations' and governments' intrusion in their private spheres.[40] Since these sophisticated processing technologies are controlled by just a few big players, such as 23andMe, it is exactly these companies that decide who can access their genetic data and thus when these intrusions can occur.

From a market perspective, this scenario threatens also free competition in the market of genetic testing services. As the US Supreme Court has highlighted with regards to the genetic testing company Myriad,[41] the collection of patients' genetic data by the company owning the patent of the genetic tests is likely to push the patent owner at the forefront of the competitive edge also after the patent's expiry:[42] the replication of comparable genetic databases by competitors would indeed require extraordinary efforts in terms of time and costs.[43]

3.1.1.2 The Joint Venture Between Google and Sanofi

Cases of joint ventures between pharmaceutical companies and high tech companies are becoming increasingly frequent: in these regards, for example, the Germany pharmaceutical company Merck and the American data analysis and software company Palantir have established a joint venture with the aim of applying digital

[36] Hazel and Slobogin (2018), p. 49.

[37] Haag (4 February 2019).

[38] Smith and Stanton (10 April 2019).

[39] Medvin (20 September 2018).

[40] Pray (2008), p. 75.

[41] US Supreme Court *Association for Molecular Pathology v. Myriad Genetics*, Inc. (13 June 2013) para 2111–2114. For a comment see Evans (2014), pp. 51 ff.

[42] Burk (2015), pp. 253–254.

[43] Oliver (2015), pp. 551–552.

technology in order to accelerate cancer drug research[44]; likewise, also Google and the pharmaceutical company Sanofi have created a joint venture in the field of digital health. This last joint venture has been scrutinized by the European Commission under the Regulation EC 139/2004 Merger Procedure.[45] The Commission's decision raises some interesting issues/points regarding the features of emerging digital health markets and is thus worth discussing in greater detail.

On 19 January 2016 the parties notified to the Commission the proposal of a concentration pursuant to Article 4 of Council Regulation EC N. 139/2004 by which Sanofi S.A., through its subsidiary Aventis Inc., and Google Inc. through its subsidiary Verily Life Science LC acquire control—within the meaning of Art. 3.1.b of the Merger Regulation—of a newly created company constituting a joint venture, by way of purchase of shares.[46]

The joint venture creates an "integrated digital e-medicine platform for the management and treatment of diabetes", with that going beyond the activities of both the parent companies.[47] According to the collaboration agreement, the platform is developed by Google and provides for data collection; data display; data storage; data analysis and data transmission. Through the evidence given by these data, the joint venture is aimed at offering services for the management and treatment of diabetes, including data collection and processing and data analysis. In addition to these research-oriented services, the joint venture intends to market medical devices designed to monitor and treat diabetes, as well as insulin-based medicinal products.[48] These products will be marketed alongside the services. As the Parties underline, the joint venture provides direct responses to the growing demand for integrated solutions of health products and markets.

The integrated nature of the services and products is a direct consequence of digitalization: products and services are indeed trained and thus developed on the basis of the same given datasets and need the evidence reciprocally generated in order to carry out their strictly complementary functions.

Under these premises, the services and product marketed by the joint venture can be divided into three main categories, that are (i) the insulin medicinal products; (ii) the medical devices with monitoring functions; (iii) data analytics services. Accordingly, the Commission has identified five relevant markets,[49] which the Commission has considered separately. As well reflected in the decision, neither

[44] German Federal Ministry For Economic Affairs and Energy (31 January 2019).

[45] European Commission, Sanofi/Google/DMI JV, Case M. 7813 (23 February 2016a).

[46] The Joint Venture was created through a "Collaboration Agreement" signed by the two parties, Google and Sanofi, on the 13 August 2015. European Commission, Sanofi/Google/DMI JV, Case M. 7813 (2016a), p. 2.

[47] European Commission, Sanofi/Google/DMI JV, Case M. 7813 (2016a), p. 3.

[48] European Commission, Sanofi/Google/DMI JV, Case M. 7813 (2016a), p. 2.

[49] The relevant markets assessed by the Commission are related to (i) insulins; (ii) insulin delivery systems; (iii) glucose monitoring systems; (iv) services for the management and treatment of diabetes using an integrated digital e-medicine platform; (v) data analytics services. European Commission, Sanofi/Google/DMI JV, Case M. 7813 (2016a), p. 2.

parties were previously active in the markets of monitoring medical devices relying on an integrated digital e-medicine platform and on data analytics services. The same parties have highlighted that for the development of these products and services a strong technological infrastructure is needed. As the parties claim, this sophisticated infrastructure is usually the result of the collaboration agreements between different companies willing to develop innovative and useful solutions.[50]

Exactly with regards to the technological infrastructure needed to deliver the monitoring services and the data analytics services, the Commission took into consideration two aspects that are worth recalling.

The first one concerns the risk, raised by a competitor, that the employment of the data analysis infrastructure developed by Google would have made patients more dependent on the insulin-based pharmaceutical products that Sanofi was marketing also before the creation of the joint venture.[51]

From the opposite perspective, the use of the insulin-based medicinal product in conjunction with the monitoring service, would have created the risk of a patients' lock-in to the same monitoring services, with the effect of limiting or preventing the portability of their data towards alternative platforms.[52]

In these regards, the Commission has assessed conglomerate effects, resulting from bundling strategies concerning the devices and the services marketed by the joint venture, ultimately denying the risk of foreclosing rivals. Such conclusion was reached on the basis of the possibility for patients to combine the products and services marketed by the joint venture with alternative devices, and of the use made by the same joint venture of open standards, assuring a high level of interoperability.[53]

As the Commission confirmed, users would still have been able to use third-party services and products thanks to the possibility to transfer their data onto other providers' platforms,[54] which has become an outright right pursuant to art. 20 of the General Data Protection Regulation. Portability issues were however not addressed by the Commission that has considered it a matter of data protection law and not of competition law.

In line with previous declarations made in other decisions involving mergers among digital data companies,[55] the Commission stated that "any privacy-related concerns flowing from the use of data within the control of the Parties do not fall within the scope of the EU competition law rules but within the scope of the EU data

[50] European Commission, Sanofi/Google/DMI JV, Case M. 7813 (2016a), p. 10.

[51] European Commission, Sanofi/Google/DMI JV, Case M. 7813 (23 February 2016a), p. 11.

[52] European Commission, Sanofi/Google/DMI JV, Case M. 7813 (23 February 2016a), p. 11.

[53] European Commission, Sanofi/Google/DMI JV, Case M. 7813 (23 February 2016a), p. 13.

[54] European Commission, Sanofi/Google/DMI JV, Case M. 7813 (23 February 2016a), p. 11.

[55] See for example European Commission, Google Double Click, Case N. Comp./M. 4731 (11 March 2008); European Commission, Facebook/Whatsapp, Case N. Comp./M. 7217 (3 October 2014b).

protection rules".[56] The refusal by the Commission to take into consideration data protection concerns in its competition assessment goes against some of the more recent developments occurred at European level, and especially in Germany, where the competition law authority has linked Facebook's abuse of dominant position to the violation of data protection law occurred through the setting of unfair terms.[57]

Secondly, the Commission considered the risk, raised by a competitor, that after the creation of the joint venture Google would refuse to offer its data analytics tools and services used to analyze healthcare data to other third parties owning healthcare datasets.[58] The Commission, however, placed more emphasis to the fact that there are a number of providers offering data analytics services and digital tools for the monitoring of diabetes and did not therefore expect a negative impact of the merger on price and availability of data analytics tools and services used to analyse healthcare data. As was observed, the "advanced analytics of healthcare data is one of the fastest growing segments of both the healthcare IT technology space and data analytics technology overall", this implying the likelihood that "numerous firms will enter the market in some form or fashion in the next five years".[59] In addition to this, the Commission also observed that some competitors had already developed a data analytics tool *in-house*, without the need to rely on third-party services,[60] thus reaching the conclusion that it is possible to independently develop such tools.

In light of these considerations, the Commission concluded that the merger did not have anticompetitive effects in the internal market. This conclusion was reached separately with regards to each of the identified markets.

By ruling so, the Commission appeared however to miss two important points, respectively related (i) to the interdependency between the technological infrastructure and the data processed by it, and (ii) to the possible market power stemming from the collection of vast amount of health datasets.

With regards to the first point, indeed, the Commission appears to have failed to consider the fact that the processing infrastructure needs data alimenting it in order to qualify as a competitive asset. Differently said, the Commission has missed to acknowledge the strategic role played by personal data in the competition equilibria.[61] As other data-driven markets, the market of healthcare analytics is indeed characterized by economies of scale, which is enhanced by the automatic nature, the self-learning and self-generating processing capabilities of algorithmic processing tools: the massive collection and processing of data triggers economies of scale related to the fact that once a sufficient amount of patients' personal data has been collected, the production of new knowledge referring to the same users becomes

[56] European Commission, Sanofi/Google/DMI JV, Case M. 7813 (23 February 2016a), p. 11.

[57] Bundeskartellamt (7 February 2019b).

[58] European Commission, Sanofi/Google/DMI JV, Case M. 7813 (23 February 2016a), p. 11.

[59] European Commission, Sanofi/Google/DMI JV, Case M. 7813 (23 February 2016a), p. 11.

[60] European Commission, Sanofi/Google/DMI JV, Case M. 7813 (23 February 2016a), p. 13.

[61] See infra Chap. 7, Sect. 7.3.1.

quite easy in light of the subsequent and generative nature of algorithmic processing, extracting always new readily usable data from existing databases.[62]

This renders it very difficult for new competitors to have access to a sufficient set of personal data needed as an input for the processing infrastructure. Newcomers face indeed not only the economic trouble of establishing a same technological structure enabling the enactment of this self-reinforcing data generation process,[63] but also the practical difficulty of having a starting pool of data, which is sufficiently updated and sufficiently historically-rich to reproduce at least as precise health profiles as the competitors' ones.

In these regards it must be also observed that health datasets, due to their highly sensitive and scientific value, can hardly be considered of non-rival and ubiquitous nature.[64]

This consideration suggests the existence of a second barrier to entry competitors face in respect to access to personal data considered as a competitive asset. Indeed, not only technological restraints but also legal restraints appear to hamper new-comers entry in the digital market. As illustrated in the previous chapter, personal data collected and subsequently generated through algorithmic processing is often shielded by legal tools of protection, such as trade secrets, the *sui generis* database right and copyright, which obstruct access to third parties.[65]

These considerations lead to the second point regarding the role of data as a source of market power. In denying the risk of patients' technological lock-in to the products and services offered by the joint venture, the Commission did not consider the existence of network effects stemming from algorithmic data processing infra-structures.[66] More precisely, in analyzing the markets separately, the Commission appears to have failed to properly address the interconnected nature of the identified markets. The fact that each of the considered markets rely on the same set of health data which is processed and analysed through the powerful technical infrastructure

[62] Graef (2015), p. 504.

[63] Comandè (2017), pp. 169 ff.

[64] These features are particularly stressed by the literature who does not recognize the competitive nature of data Grunes and Stucke (2015), pp. 1 ff. On the issue also Tucker and Wellford (2014), pp. 1 ff.; Bork and Sidak (2013). The "widespread' collection of consumer data is particularly stressed by Lerner (26 August 2014), pp. 6 ff., who does not acknowledge any link between data and the "entrenchment of dominant online platforms". Also in Facebook/Whatsapp the Commission has affirmed that also in the case the two merging parties datasets would have been combined there would have "continued to be a large amount of internet user data that are valuable for advertising purposes and that are not within Facebook's exclusive control". European Commission, Facebook/Whatsapp, Case M. 7217 (3 October 2014b), para. 184.

[65] For a general assessment of this broader issue see Drexl et al. (9 September 2016). For an assessment over the link between these forms of exclusivities and the constitution of barriers to entry for competitors Newman (2014), pp. 401 ff.

[66] Network effects were taken into consideration in other previous decisions involving digital companies' merger as in the Facebook/Whatsapp merger. Here, however, network effects were not considered as possible source of an anticompetitive behaviour. See European Commission, Facebook/Whatsapp, Case M. 7217 (3 October 2014b), p. 256.

developed by Google, triggers direct network effects resulting from the fact that the more personal data are available, the more precise and thus attractive for patients the monitoring services and data analytics services become.[67]

Direct network effects end up tying a user to a certain service despite his preferences for other services.[68] This means that although a user may prefer to use a different service, he or she remains bound to a same service, because the people he or she is connected to all use this service. The direct network effect increases with the amount of data available to the platform since the more data it has the more precisely the provider can tailor its services and products to users' needs. Direct network effects are thus responsible for higher switching costs and as a result of patients' lock in.[69]

The integrated nature of data-driven markets causes also indirect networks given by the benefits that the other markets of the joint venture experience from the collection of patients' health data occurred on one market side. For example, data collected through the monitoring system or generated through the data analytics service could enable the production of more sophisticated and personalized medicinal products' design on the market of insulin-based pharmaceuticals.

The consideration of these networks effects stemming from the massive collection and generation of patients' health data would have maybe led the Commission to critically assess the joint venture's market position, in light of the existence of data-driven barriers to entry affecting each of the identified market of diabetes-related digital health products and services. The market power acquired through the collection of health datasets could indeed lead to exclusive conducts regarding both the processing infrastructure and the data,[70] but also to other exploitative abuses, in terms of higher prices as well as harmful privacy policies of the marketed health-related digital products and services.[71]

3.1.2 *Health Data Pools Between Public Institutions and Big Data Companies*

Two recent cases respectively involving Google and IBM prove the growing attention of big data companies for health data owned by public institutions. Both these big data companies are at present particularly active in health research. The partnerships that will be described below provide interesting insights into how public institutions and the public at large are being impacted by the emergence of

[67] Katz and Shapiro (1985), pp. 427 ff.

[68] Farrell and Klemperer (2007), p. 2018: "direct network effects increase the opportunity cost that consumers face when considering to switch to another provider".

[69] Farrell and Klemperer (2007), p. 2018.

[70] Graef (2015), pp. 502–504.

[71] These will be dealt with infra in Chap. 7.

data-driven tools and big data in peculiar in highly sensitive sectors such as the healthcare one.

3.1.2.1 The Sharing Agreement Between Google DeepMind and Royal Free Hospital

Google DeepMind is an artificial intelligence company owned by Google, which, until recently, had no previous expertise in the field of healthcare service delivery. Over the past few years, however, Google DeepMind has entered into agreements with various public healthcare institutions within the Royal Free London NHS Foundation Trust, and has recently declared that it intends to reach an agreement with the entire National Health System.[72] Among these agreements, the most interesting- and the most debated- has been the one involving the Royal Free Hospital. This agreement was reached in July 2015 and initially consisted in a five-year partnership, binding the National Health System to provide Google DeepMind with sensitive identifiable medical data.[73] This data was stored on third-party servers that Google had contracted with on behalf of Google DeepMind.[74] The ultimate purpose of the agreement was the development of an app designed for the monitoring of kidney injuries. More specifically, the app was meant to assemble and integrate collected data for the generation of alerts based on these data. These alerts were then to be further transmitted to the clinicians' mobile devices, together with historical data on the patient, thus enabling clinicians to analyze trends.[75]

With regards to the functioning of the app, Google declared that it was not going to rely on machine learning techniques because the app was only supposed to have the function of a data-integrating user interface, thus merely collecting the patient data controlled by Royal Free.[76] However, these public statements did not appear fully consistent with the Information Sharing Agreement that was signed on 29 September 2015.[77] In fact, the Agreement specified that the collected data would primarily serve to deliver a service termed "Patient Rescue" destined to NHS Hospital Trusts.[78] Moreover, the Agreement also mentioned that the same data would have been employed for building "real time clinical analytics, detection,

[72]For an overview see Powles and Hodson (2017), pp. 361–362, documenting the agreement between Google DeepMind and Moorsfield Eye Hospital, and between Google DeepMind and UCL Hospitals NHS Foundation Trust.

[73]DeepMind (2016a). The exact number of transferred data is unknown, but be it sufficient to consider that Royal Free admits an average 1.6 million patients per year: NHS (2016).

[74]Powles and Hodson (2017), p. 353.

[75]Powles and Hodson (2017), p. 353.

[76]Boseley and Lewis (24 February 2016).

[77]Royal Free London-NHS Foundation Trust (29 September 2015).

[78]Royal Free London-NHS Foundation Trust (29 September 2015).

diagnosis and decision to support treatment and avert clinical deterioration across a range of diagnoses and organ systems".[79]

The Information Sharing Agreement did not refer to the processing practices that the data stored by Google would have carried out, also with regards to the combination/matching of other identifiable data owned by Google on other sides of its platform.[80]

Another fundamental concern raised by the agreement is that the transfer of data from Royal Free to Google DeepMind has occurred without the explicit consent of Royal Free's patients. Under UK law, the existence of a direct care relationship between the patient and a third-party is a legitimate basis for processing health data, working as an exception to the consent rule.[81]

Hence, the sharing agreement between Google DeepMind and Royal Free raised some questions concerning the lawfulness of the occurred transfer of health data, given that not only the data of the patients with kidney diseases- whose monitoring was explicitly required by the agreement- was shared: the dataset negotiated with the Information Sharing Agreement was much broader and included the results of every blood test done at Royal Free in the 5 years prior to the transfer, demographic details and patients' electronic records of admissions as well as discharges from clinical care and from accident and emergency.[82] The collected data thus concerned diagnoses for conditions and procedures that were related to kidney injuries, but also diagnoses that were not related to them. This means that the processing of all the data concerning the patients who were not included in the direct care relationship for kidney injury and who did not give a specific and informed consent to the processing of their data, was falling outside the direct care exemption and was thus actually lacking a legal basis for the processing.

While acknowledging the benefits stemming from the "creative use of data" with respect to "patient care and clinical improvement', the English Information

[79] Royal Free London-NHS Foundation Trust (29 September 2015).

[80] These points are raised by Powles and Hodson (2017), p. 352, observing that the sharing agreement did not make any mention regarding the public assurances made by Google DeepMind that Royal Free data would "have never be linked or associated with Google accounts, products or services". This is documented by Boseley and Lewis (24 February 2016).

[81] See UK Data Protection Act 1998 (UK), Schedule 3, par 8. On the issue see Caldicott (2013). The 1998 Data Protection Act has been replaced by the 2018 Data Protection Act setting out a new English data protection framework, which tailors the General Data Protection Regulation EU 679/2016 to the UK. The new framework is to be read alongside the General Data Protection Regulation, which directly applies until Brexit. For a general introduction to the 2018 Data Protection Act see Information Commissioner Office (2018b). Within the new data protection framework the direct care relationship as a ground for processing still remains, under art. 6.1 lett. e) GDPR requiring that the processing of is "necessary" in the "exercise of official authority vested in the controller" and art. 9.2 lett. h), requiring that the processing of health data is necessary for medical diagnosis, the provision of health or social care or treatment (...)". When these two conditions are met no explicit consent for sharing health data is needed. See discussion infra Chap. 5, Sect. 5.3.2.

[82] Powles and Hodson (2017), p. 353.

Commissioner Officer has declared that the "price of innovation does not need to be an erosion of fundamental privacy rights".[83]

The Privacy Impact Assessment that was carried out in accordance with the Information Commissioner Officer's recommendations[84] did not discuss the privacy impact on data subjects that were not affected by kidney injuries and did thus not address fundamental data protection principles such as that of data minimization.[85]

Since the highly sensitive data of Royal Free's patients was collected for the declared purpose of developing a clinical app, the processing of this data by Google DeepMind could have been reasonably qualified as a research activity. However, outside the area of consent and of the direct care relationship, English law requires processing activities on personal data for research purposes to be approved by the Health Research Authority, with the additional approval by the Confidentiality Advisory Group in case the processing activities involve identifiable personal data.[86] Moreover, in case the processing, as it was in this instance, is carried out through a device that serves medical purposes, that device requires regulatory approval under the medical device framework[87] and, as far as England is concerned, specific approval by the Medicines and Healthcare Products Regulatory Agency.[88]

Confirming these infringements, the investigation by the Information Commissioner found that the agreement between Google DeepMind and the Royal Free Hospital failed to comply with the applicable data protection framework.[89] In this perspective, the investigation has highlighted two principal, strictly intertwined, shortcomings of the Agreement, respectively related to the absence of patients' reasonable expectation that their data would have been shared with third parties and the lack of the enactment of adequate transparency measures.[90] As a consequence of these findings, the Parties were asked to commit to changes defined in an undertaking signed between the Information Commissioner Office and the Parties.[91] The remedies required involved (i) the definition of a proper legal basis for the massive treatment of health data employed for the trials' purposes[92]; (ii) the proof of compliance with the duty of confidentiality to be provided to patients in any future trial[93]; (iii) the performance of a privacy impact assessment together with the

[83] Information Commissioner Office (3 July 2017a).

[84] See Information Commissioner Office (2014).

[85] See DeepMind (2016c). 'Waking' was an early product name for the app Streams.

[86] See NHS Health Research Authority (12 October 2018).

[87] See supra Chap. 2, Sect. 2.1.6.

[88] See Medicines and Healthcare Products Regulatory Agency, https://www.gov.uk/topic/medicines-medical-devices-blood/marketing-authorisations-variations-licensing.

[89] Information Commissioner Office (3 July 2017a).

[90] See Information Commissioner Office (3 July 2017b).

[91] Information Commissioner Office (3 July 2017c).

[92] Information Commissioner Office (3 July 2017c), para 14.

[93] Information Commissioner Office (3 July 2017c), para 15.

enactment of transparency measures[94]; (iv) the performance of an audit of the clinical use of the app, the results of which should have been shared with the Information Commissioner Officer.[95]

Consistently with these commitments, the Royal Free Hospital published on the 12th June 2018 the audit carried out by a third party, which found that the employment of the mobile device by the Hospital was lawful and compliant with data protection law.[96] In particular, the audit assured that the Royal Free Hospital's patient data was used by DeepMind only for the purposes of providing the app and its service.[97] The audit however highlighted space for improvement with regard to the protection of patients' rights, relative especially to the scope of the information given to the patients concerning how their personal data was used by Royal Free Hospital.[98] However, no clarification was offered either in the audit or in a separate document with regards to the legal basis of the health data processing.[99]

The correspondence between the Royal Free Hospital and the English Information Commissioner reflects the regulatory uncertainties stemming from the penetration of big data giants, such as Google, into healthcare affairs.

The commitment to process the collected data only for specific clinical research purposes, certified as reliable also by the published audit, has been put under pressure by Google's decision to merge with its subsidiary DeepMind Health Division.[100] This definitely exacerbates the concern that the tech giant will be able to *structurally* access and own a vast array of patients' sensitive and identifiable data without the supervision of an independent board, which has been abolished exactly for the occasion.[101] The merger suggests that health data sharing of the types described above trigger considerations that are even deeper than the data protection infringements lying at the surface, and involve the concentration of the market for health analytics in the hands of one big private corporation. This would threaten not only competing private undertakings in the sector, but also the self-sufficiency of public health services. As Cambridge Professor Ross Anderson has put it, "if Google gets a monopoly on providing some kind of service to the NHS, it will burn the NHS".[102]

Similar legal concerns are destined to grow together with the proliferation of agreements resembling the one between Google DeepMind and Royal Free Hospital: Google DeepMind itself has announced its intention to develop new systems for

---

[94] Information Commissioner Office (3 July 2017c), para 17.

[95] Information Commissioner Office (3 July 2017c), art. 5.

[96] Royal Free London (2018). See Information Commissioner Office (12 June 2018a).

[97] Linklaters (17 May 2018), p. i.

[98] Linklaters (17 May 2018), p. i.

[99] This is well stressed by Lomas (December 2018).

[100] Jee (14 November 2018). See also True Publica (15 November 2018).

[101] Orlowski (14 November 2018).

[102] Newscientist (29 April 2016).

Royal Free as part of a "broad ranging, mutually beneficial partnership to work on genuinely innovative and transformational projects".[103] Accordingly, the company has engaged in similar negotiations with other NHS Trusts, such as the Imperial College NHS Trust and Taunton & Somerset.[104]

Completing the bigger picture is the fact that Google DeepMind is not the only company owned by Google that is engaging in these kind of partnerships: Verily, for example, has also entered into data processing negotiations with the NHS Heywood, Middleton and Rochdale Clinical Commissioning Group, with the aim of looking for patterns that suggest the emergence of long-term diseases such as diabetes, and thus alerting doctors when they are found.[105]

In the USA, the agreements regarding patient data sharing established between Google and the University of Chicago has been object of a lawsuit.[106] The plaintiff is a patient of the University of Chicago Medical Center, accusing the University to have shared with Google large patient datasets. The aggregation of the acquired patient data with Google's other users' personal data is alleged to enable the company to re-identify the patients, in this way violating the Health Insurance Portability and Accountability Act.[107] The complaint stresses that the shared datasets "were not sufficiently anonymized and put the patients' privacy at grave risk",[108] given the threat of the commercial exploitation of the datasets and the patients who are associated to them.[109] This all occurring without the patients' consent.[110]

---

[103] DeepMind (2016b) The document was signed on 28 January 2016 but was uncovered by a freedom of information request only in June 2016. This is recalled by Powles and Hodson (2017), p. 354.

[104] Lomas (14 November 2018).

[105] The Economist (3rd February 2018), recalling also the established partnership between Apple and Standford University to develop algorithms to spot irregular patterns in heartbeat data generated by the AppleWatch.

[106] Illinois Northern District Court Dinerstein v. Google, LLC, 1:19-cv-04 (26 June 2019).

[107] The Health Insurance, Portability and Accountability Act (HIPAA) is the law regulating flows of health information. It is interesting to notice that it applies only to so-called "covered entities" that are defined in the HIPAA rules as (i) health plans; (ii) health care clearinghouses; (iii) health care providers who electronically transmit any health information in connection with transactions for which the US Health and Human Services Department has adopted standards. The fact that the applicability of the HIPAA is restricted to those entities causes a substantial regulatory loophole regarding the processing of health information by non-covered entities, such as big tech corporations. HHS.gov (26 July 2013). This vacuum of protection is well highlighted also in the lawsuit. See Illinois Northern District Court Dinerstein v. Google, LLC, 1:19-cv-04 (26 June 2019), para 32–33. For the literature see Terry (2018), pp. 56 ff.

[108] Illinois Northern District Court Dinerstein v. Google, LLC, 1:19-cv-04 (26 June 2019), para 74.

[109] Illinois Northern District Court Dinerstein v. Google, LLC, 1:19-cv-04 (26 June 2019), para 4; 43; 96–97.

[110] Illinois Northern District Court Dinerstein v. Google, LLC, 1:19-cv-04 (26 June 2019), para 43.

3.1.2.2 The Sharing Agreement Between IBM and Lombardia Region

The IBM Watson Health Centre is specifically aimed at providing scientific evidence in the field of healthcare through the large-scale employment of data analytics on health datasets.[111] In order to provide data to this center, IBM has negotiated with the Italian government the acquisition of Italian citizens' protected health information. A memorandum of understanding was signed on 31 March 2016 and entailed a clause binding the Italian government to subsequently transfer the personal health data of Italian citizens to IBM.[112] The announced acquisition of health data for the training of artificial intelligence health-related tools has been positively welcomed by part of the Italian press[113] as well as by the Italian Data Protection Authority[114] as an important step forward with regards to the strengthening of technology-driven health research.

If it would have been implemented, the transfer would have allow IBM to acquire millions of health-related data, encompassing pharmacologic data, oncologic data, genetic data, treatment data, diagnostic data and reimbursement data.[115] As in the above-analyzed Google DeepMind case, the transfer of this data would occur without data subjects' consent. The confidential document containing the agreement allegedly entitled IBM to process the acquired health datasets for the purposes of the IBM Watson Health project and for other- not much better defined- secondary purposes,[116] thus evidently bypassing the fundamental data protection principles of purpose limitation, necessity and proportionality.

Accordingly, the Italian Data Protection Authority highlighted that the execution of such an agreement would have impacted on the rights of a vast strand of the Italian population, whose sensitive information regarding health conditions were to be sold and processed through new technologies.[117] Thus, it invited the Italian government and the Lombardia Region to involve the same Authority in the implementation of the signed agreement in order to assure compliance with data protection law.[118] However, the legal uncertainties surrounding the legitimacy of the agreement have, to date, blocked the transfer.[119]

Against this backdrop, nearly a year after the signing of the agreement, the Italian Parliament introduced a new provision regarding the treatment of personal data for

---

[111] See IBM https://www.ibm.com/watson/health/.

[112] IBM (31 March 2016a) and IBM (31 March 2016b). For a comment see Barbacetto (21 March 2017b).

[113] Sideri (16 February 2017).

[114] Italian Data Protection Authority (10 May 2017).

[115] Leshem (18 January 2018).

[116] Barbacetto (17 February 2017a).

[117] Italian Data Protection Authority (10 July 2018), para 5.2, 64.

[118] Italian Data Protection Authority (10 July 2018), para 5.2, 64. See also Longo (6 December 2017).

[119] Bernardi (3 April 2018).

scientific research purposes in the form of a new art. 110 *bis* of the Italian Personal Data Protection Code.[120] The first paragraph of the provision enables "the reutilization of personal data, also of a sensitive nature, excluding genetic data, for scientific and statistical purposes, with the previous authorization by the Data Protection Authority, and provided specific safeguards are implemented for the minimization of the processing and for the anonymization of the data for the ultimate protection of data subjects' rights". The provision perfectly echoes art. 89(1) of the General Data Protection Regulation, which entails a specific exemption from the application of the rules laid down in the Regulation, with regards to the "processing for archiving purposes in the public interest, scientific or historical research purposes or statistical purposes". Both the European and the Italian provisions constitute a radical deviation from the golden rule of requiring specific and informed consent as an essential condition for data processing. As has been observed,[121] the absence of any subjective requirement for the application of the lighter regulatory regime of data processing for scientific interest purposes, suggests that also data processing activities carried out by commercial entities for scientific purposes could fall into the exemption. The above-cited norms could thus eventually applied to the transfer of Italian citizens' personal health data to IBM, which has not been finalized to date.

As with regards to the Google DeepMind case, the legal issues arising from the Watson Health Centre case are extremely thought-provoking.

First of all, it should be noted that when the scientific (data-intensive) research activities are carried out by companies such as IBM, the actual link of these data processing activities to public interest-related purposes, should be accurately considered. Indeed, in cases where the processing appears to be carried out not for research but for commercial purposes, as it is very likely for digital companies, the ordinary and full data protection regime should apply. The practical feasibility of the application of general data protection principles and rules, such as the rule of consent and the related purpose and proportionality principles, is however to be reasonably doubted with respect to secondary massive and automated data processing, once these rules and principles have not been respected with regards to the first processing on the basis of the above-recalled research exemption.

Moreover, the accomplishment of the anonymization requirement, expressly taken into consideration by art. 110 *bis* of the Italian Personal Data Protection Code, would anyway exempt processing activities from compliance with the rules laid down by the Data Protection Regulation, even if carried out for commercial purposes. The Regulation indeed applies only to processing activities regarding "identified or identifiable" personal data.[122] However, if, as is widely acknowledged

[120] See art. 110 bis d.lgs. 196/2003, introduced by the law 27 November 2017 n. 277.

[121] Manis (13 December 2017).

[122] See Recital 26 GDPR, further stating that "the principles of data protection should therefore not apply to anonymous information, namely information which does not relate to an identified or identifiable natural person or to personal data rendered anonymous in such a manner that the data subject is not or no longer identifiable".

in the literature,[123] aggregating algorithmic capabilities make anonymization efforts temporary, further secondary processing regarding re-identified personal data would need to comply again with general data protection rules.

Strictly connected to purely data protection-related issues, the IBM case uncovers also the highly controversial issue of the ownership of these datasets,[124] once the transfer has occurred and once the data have been automatically processed by these companies. Both initial and secondary-generated data produced by companies' algorithms that harness publicly-generated datasets are likely to feed digital companies' trade secrets and databases regarding sensitive health information.[125] These protection tools ultimately end up restricting access to highly socially valuable information as health data.

In addition to manifest data protection and (over)propertisation threats, the European Commission has warned against the possible anticompetitive effects of the intended transfer between IBM and the Lombardia Region. These have been signaled by the DG Competition in a letter directed to the Permanent Representation of Italy to the EU, requiring information regarding (i) the selection process of IBM as Italy's partner for the development of the health analytics project; (ii) the specific services and products which the partnership will place on the market; (iii) the allocation of the related intellectual property rights; (iv) the precise nature and amount of health data accessed; (v) the conditions governing the access; (vi) the price of the access; (vii) whether also third competing parties could gain access to IBM's acquired data.[126] The critical points highlighted by the European Commission reflect the core regulatory issues raised by health data sharing practices.

3.2 Health Data Pools as Innovation Networks

The above-analyzed cases provide a very thought-provoking overview of both the structural features of digital health markets and the challenges raised by these.

With regards to the structural features, the analysis shows how the phenomenon of health data pooling is triggered by innovation objectives in the markets of digital health products and services and is giving rise to a collaborative research environment where big high tech companies are taking up an increasingly important role.

More precisely, the case-studies perfectly reflect the essential value of digital health data and of the corresponding technological processing infrastructure for the

[123] Ohm (2010), pp. 1703 ff.

[124] The lack of clear European rules regarding data ownership has been outlined by the European Commission on several occasions. See European Commission (2 July 2014a), where the Commission has stressed the need for guidance on "ownership and liability of data provision". See also European Commission (2017a), pp. 12–15. For the literature see Evans (2011), pp. 70 ff.

[125] Nicholson Price (2015), pp. 446 ff.

[126] European Commission (31 October 2017c).

development of health research projects. In these regards, data pooling agreements represent a means of concentrating around a single research project various types of technological assets and expertise. As each of the illustrated cases suggests, traditional stakeholders in the field of health research, as the pharmaceutical company Sanofi or the Royal Free Hospital, have control of highly specialized and sophisticated health datasets, which represent the very core asset of scientific enquiries. Conversely, big tech companies, as Google in both of the considered cases, appear to offer the algorithmic infrastructure needed for the treatment of these sophisticated datasets, as well as for the collection and the generation of new digital information and the enactment of profiling, statistical analyses and predictions.

The complementary nature of such differently owned assets triggers pooling arrangements, gathering together specialized clinical data and other "real world" digital data under a common processing technology. As a competitor has interestingly observed in the Google-Sanofi merger, "the complexity and regulatory nature of the healthcare analytics industry creates significant *complexity on the data itself, as well as in the structural separation and partitioning*" of the exploited health information, variously related to individuals' health status, access to care, treatment and outcome.[127] This well reflects how digital health markets structurally rely on the intertwining of different types of health datasets, originally owned by mostly non-competing businesses, as has occurred for example in the Google-Sanofi case.

In these regards, the analyzed case-studies confirm the statements made some scholars, stressing how the diversity of (scientific) "knowledge requirements and the more complex technology frontiers imply a need for networks",[128] mainly driven by the desire to achieve efficiency and innovation.[129] This holds true especially for the pharmaceutical sector, where innovation is synonymous of competitiveness.[130]

The aggregation of different kind of datasets enables the development of new digital products and services, as the kidney injury app in the Royal Hospital case or the sophisticated diabetes analysis services and corresponding devices, developed by the joint venture between Google and Sanofi.

As has been interestingly observed, the incentives for innovation in digital markets appear to be stirred by the competitive pressure existing in these same

[127]European Commission, Sanofi/Google/DMI JV, Case M. 7813 (23 February 2016a), p. 8. Emphasis added.

[128]Glader (2001), pp. 513 ff., citing OECD (2000), p. 37. The Author states also that "not surprisingly, the number of networks and strategic alliances between firms is growing rapidly especially in information technology, biotechnology and advanced material industries". Emphasis added. This was also stressed by OECD (1999), p.13.

[129]With regards to the specific issue of pharmaceutical mergers, this is highlighted by Kathuria (2016), pp. 451 ff.

[130]Kettler (1998), p. 9.

markets,[131] rather than by the law, such as intellectual property law.[132] This competitive pressure pushes companies that are active in different markets to aggregate their distinctive resources in order to advance their respective market positions.[133]

Against this backdrop, precious insights in respect to the functioning dynamics of data-driven innovation are provided by studies related to "network theories".[134] These theories assume that in those fields characterized by a rapidly changing knowledge or by complex interdependencies between component technologies, a "network" or "collaborative"[135] governance of the available informational and technological assets is regarded as an efficient means for the delivery of innovative markets outcomes.[136]

As this literature observes, the resulting networks structurally rely on the processing of different types of information.[137] This is deemed especially true with regards to those knowledge-intensive industries that experience rapid and unexpected shifts in competences and in market conditions, just as it is the case of the biotechnology industry.[138] Especially in these markets, where knowledge changes rapidly and there are complex interdependencies between component technologies, companies are induced to modify their organizational structures for the purposes of more promptly responding to the rapid changes in technology and the intensification of global competition[139]. These prompt changes ultimately enable interested businesses to capture the returns in innovative market segments.[140]

The resulting "innovation networks" appear to be characterized by two main features, mainly residing in (i) the uncertainty of the established (contractual) relationships and (ii) the high dynamism and heterogeneity of the involved stakeholders.[141]

---

[131] This is suggested by Marcos (2018), p. 35, stressing that how innovation is the main driver of business performance especially in high-technology sectors as the one of pharmaceuticals and biotechnology and affirming that "firms operating in those industries must innovate to survive and to succeed".

[132] Questioning the role of the law in supporting collaborative exchanges, Jennejohn (2016), p. 294, specifically considering intellectual property and contract law, and their respective interactions.

[133] Drexl (December 2018), p. 7.

[134] Jennejohn (February 2016).

[135] Stressing the importance of collaborative alliances for scientific innovation, David (2000a). See also David (2000b), p. 5, where it is claimed that "technological innovation emerges within the context of a large and complex system, and the character of its effects upon economic development and growth also are shaped by systemic interdependences of equal complexity".

[136] Schrank and Whitford (2011), pp. 151 ff., see in particular the literature review at p. 155–157. See similarly, also Jennejohn (February 2016), p. 297, observing that these alliances have a creative element "at their core" for "their central purpose is to structure a joint discovery process by which new technology is created".

[137] This was already being acknowledged by Stinchcombe (1990).

[138] Schrank and Whitford (September 2011), p. 156.

[139] Svetiev (2007), p. 621.

[140] Schrank and Whitford (September 2011), p. 167.

[141] This is highlighted by Svetiev (2007).

These sociological findings are further supported by the economic analyses, which increasingly acknowledge collaborative arrangements of innovation as a primary pattern of modern economic organization.[142] Here, current innovation processes (especially) in technology-driven markets are observed to cross firm boundaries,[143] along cumulative and complex lines of technical development.[144]

The collaborative nature of innovation courses enables companies to access technology and know-how that would otherwise be difficult to replicate by an individual actor.[145] As prominent intellectual property law scholars have acknowledged, the current complexity of production processes is determining the end of the "myth" of the sole inventor,[146] as replaced by multipart strategic alliances.[147]

From a more strictly legal perspective, the examined cases perfectly reflect how these collaborative networks established for the purposes of health data exchanges mainly fall, as some strand of the literature has effectively pointed out, "in the large grey area between traditional contractual arrangements and corporate acquisitions".[148] The above analysis, indeed, appears to confirm how digital health research partnerships can be performed under a variety of legal forms, ranging from (i) single contractual agreements for the transfer of a single, well-defined dataset, as the example of the data transfers from the company 23andMe and pharmaceutical companies suggest; to (ii) more articulated collaborative alliances, as the one between Google DeepMind and Royal Free Hospital and between IBM and the Italian Lombardia Region, in which the scope of the shared assets and the actual research as well as market objectives of the alliance itself are not *ex ante* defined; to (iii) more structured corporate transactions, as in the case of the joint venture between Google and the pharmaceutical company Sanofi.

Along this spectrum of collaboration arrangements for research purposes, the most interesting is given by the collaborative alliances that lie in between single contractual arrangements and company mergers: these types of alliances are indeed more stable and future-oriented than what occurs under a single contractual agreement, connecting research and development capabilities, without entering into a complete corporate acquisition, as it occurs through a merger.[149]

---

[142] See Evans (2008), pp. 285 ff., stressing how the introduction of new technologies has introduced new business methods for manufacturing in more efficient ways, including contractual innovations that are easing businesses' relationships, and thus changing the way in which businesses' compete.

[143] This is the assumption of the study by Jennejohn (February 2016), pp. 281 ff.

[144] See Arora et al. (2001), pp. 87–89, observing that the complexity of the current technology requires specialization, this leading in turn to "the division of labour" and "expertise fragments", which ultimately render innovation a "group endeavour".

[145] Jennejohn (February 2016), p. 298.

[146] Lemley (2012), pp. 709 ff.

[147] Reflecting over the specificities of "cumulative innovation", Burk and Lemley (2003), pp. 1607–1610.

[148] Villeneuve and Gunderson (2015), pp. 1–2, cited by Jennejohn (February 2016), p. 297.

[149] Jennejohn (February 2016), pp. 284–285, specifically referring to collaborations between big high technology companies such as Google, IBM and Apple and pharmaceutical companies. See

The difficulty of properly qualifying the legal nature of these hybrid collaborations is additionally exacerbated by the fact that the substance of these alliance agreements "typically remains to be completed, and often defined, over time".[150] Indeed, as the Google DeepMind agreement clearly reflects through the reference to the eventual future employment of collected health data for the purposes of the development of other new health devices, the substance of these agreements needs to be structurally open in order to assure the necessary adaptiveness in respect to future (often unexpected) developments of the research consortium,[151] in terms of both the object of the established alliances (i.e. what types of data), the goals of them (i.e. the planned market output) and ultimately the members involved. The flexibility also in terms of the legal tools upon which businesses' inter-relationships rely serve that what some strand of the literature has defined as "continuous innovation", in which firms adjust their decisions and are capable of reacting to unpredictable changes to the market.[152]

Overall, collaborative inter-firm innovation based on data sharing is a multifaceted and complex phenomenon in which innovation outcomes need to be carefully assessed in light of the other interests involved in this collaborative process, mainly related to data subjects' privacy and to the soundness of competitive equilibria.

As the analysed cases show, indeed, health data pools are likely to impact both on data subjects' right to data protection, since they involve the treatment of very sensitive data, and on competitive processes, for they aggregate resources in the hands of few market players, thus potentially triggering foreclosing network effects and setting the conditions for possible exploitative conducts.

From a regulatory standpoint, the case studies have in turn equally reflected that innovation through data exchanges is only partly governed by the private autonomy of the contracting parties, and need to pass the scrutiny of data protection law, as the Google DeepMind and IBM cases reflect, and of competition law, as the Commission's enquiry into the Google-Sanofi merger has shown.

Under these premises the next paragraphs will give account of the variety of stakeholders' interests underlying health data pools. As will be illustrated, these interests are differently related to collaborative data-driven innovation, partly being aligned to it and partly running contrary to it.

---

also Svetiev (2007), p. 620, observing the emergence of a new business organization relying on collaboration rather than integration, and on a "networked" structure, in which "information flows not only from the top down, but also upwards and sideways".

150 Villeneuve and Gunderson (2015), pp. 1–2.

151 Jennejohn (February 2016), p. 297, observing how "these alliance agreements tend to be highly complex and customized to their respective circumstances".

152 Svetiev (2007), p. 621.

3.3 Mapping the Interests in Health Data Pools

Digital health innovation through health data pools touches upon a varied range of interests that are worth to be carefully considered. Indeed, the parties that are somehow involved in and affected by the economic practice of health data pooling appear to have different interests, which can be illustrated along the lines of the following spectrum: (i) health data pools and innovation; (ii) health data pools and consumer welfare; (iii) health data pools and (the right to) digital health; (iv) health data pools and health biases; (v) health data pools and data subjects' interests; (vi) health data pools and commercial interests; (vii) health data pools and competition. Against this backdrop the following paragraphs will give account of the complexity of the interests and risks stemming from health data pooling practices.

3.3.1 *Health Data and Innovation*

As has been illustrated in the previous paragraphs, health data pools serve the marketization of new health-related technologies. In this perspective, they are key for the production and assessment of new scientific evidence resulting from aggregated and analysed health information. The interoperability of the pooled data and technologies is thus likely to trigger the research and development for other devices, which can be related or not to the already designed technology. This has been well expressed by Google that has announced that Royal Free Hospital's data would have been employed also for the testing of other health-related products or services.

New scientific evidence in turn advances medical knowledge[153] and health research[154] for the benefit of the public and of society as a whole. In this context, data is at the same time the output of the scientific process, and these outputs, as aggregated, become themselves input for further scientific enquiries fuelling the pace of innovation.[155]

Under these premises, the free flow of health information among businesses, and among businesses and other public institutions, needs to be assessed from the perspective of the public interest in scientific health advancements.

The social productiveness of the aggregation of scientific information has been expressly considered by a strand of the intellectual property scholarship, which has argued the importance of information interactions among actors in the health research field for the fruitful expansion of the scientific public domain.[156] In this

---

[153] Nicholson Price (2019), p. 66.

[154] Pentland et al. (2013).

[155] Reichman and Uhlir (2003), p. 332. Stressing this point from the economic perspective see Arrow (1962), p. 618.

[156] Maskus and Reichman (2004), pp. 279 ff. See, more generally, Boyle and Jenkins (2003), pp. 10 ff.; Boyle (2003), p. 33.

perspective, the importance of the free flow of scientific information has been grounded in the notion of public science, based on the traditional cooperative and sharing ethos.[157]

Along these lines, strong critiques have been raised in respect to the progressive appropriation[158] of research valuable data by those actors who successfully manage to claim variously-styled proprietary rights over the collected research-valuable information.[159] In the views of these commentators, these claims are supported by an over-protectionist intellectual property framework regarding scientific valuable data, which encourages the capture of this data under commercialization and commodification courses.[160]

In the data-driven research environment, the presence of a solid framework of intellectual property rights over information goods is meant to stimulate the private investments in the production of existing scientific and engineering knowledge.[161] However, the resulting monopolies over scientific knowledge structurally rely on the secretization and imposition of high access charges over information assets.[162] As the literature reflecting on the "tragedy of the anticommons" in biomedical research has argued in this respect,[163] the excessive concentration of property rights in scientific data determines opportunistic behaviours such as hold-outs and excessive pricing,[164] which end up raising the negotiation costs of scientific projects and in this way discourage the conduction of socially valuable scientific enquiries.[165]

In this light, the expansion of property rights in research and the resulting privatization of research endeavours, is ultimately deemed to distort the incentives to conduct research and sensitively influences the type of research conducted by those who have successfully obtained entitlements over the research valuable assets.[166] This hyper-appropriation trend of scientific research prerogatives is in

157 David (2000a, b). For a theoretical assessment of the paradigm of open science, see Polanyi (1962), pp. 59 ff.

158 For a description of the appropriation process of health data both outside and inside health data pools, see supra Chap. 2, Sect. 2.2.4.

159 David (2005), pp. 79 ff.

160 Reichman (2000), pp. 1743 ff.; Rai (1999), pp. 77 ff.

161 David (2000b), p. 7.

162 David (2003), p. 21.

163 Heller and Eisenberg (1998), pp. 698 ff.

164 With regards to these opportunistic conducts, see the discussion below regarding competition effects of health data pools.

165 Heller and Eisenberg (1998). See also David (2003), p. 30, observing that the restriction to access scientific research "raises the cost not simply of research directed toward producing a specific new product (e.g. new diagnostic test kits for a particular class of genetically-transmitted conditions), but also of exploratory research that may enable the future creation of many applications, including those that are undreamed of".

166 Suggesting this, Rai (1999), pp. 116–120. See also Boyle (2003), p. 41, arguing that "the concerns in the informational commons have to do with a different kind of collective action problem: the problem of incentives to create the resource in the first place".

turn considered to generate scientific results that are less socially valuable in the long term,[167] in respect to those who would have been generated by collaborative exchange and cumulative development of scientific knowledge.[168]

It also leads to imbalances within the overall innovation system, in that it interrupts the cycle of information transfers, thus ultimately constraining the production and-maybe even more importantly- the distribution of new knowledge.[169] From a systemic perspective, thus, an over-protectionist intellectual property framework risks to run contrary to its own fundamental goals of stimulating the generation and consumption of new knowledge.[170]

This recognition has triggered deeper reflections on the need to stem monopolistic tendencies over scientific information through a more careful evaluation of the public interest in the common "fair" sharing and use of scientific enabling information as a means of mitigating the securing effect of an over-protectionist- and thus obstructionist- intellectual property framework over digital research data.[171] Accordingly, shared access to reliable and up-to-date information and data has been regarded as key to economic-welfare enhancing innovation, as dependent on the exploitation of the available data by means of new digital technologies.[172]

In this regards the paradigms of open science and of the commons of scientific knowledge have been relied upon as a theoretical basis for counterbalancing the enclosing trend over digital research data[173] and thus for promoting a faster growth of the stock of available scientific knowledge.[174]

In this perspective, it has been observed that scientific health information is a public good because each individual citizen benefits from such information without reducing its value to others.[175] Economic theory regarding public goods has shown that privately supplied public goods will be typically underprovided, this supporting the economic and thus regulatory need to create data interactions and collaboration spaces assuring the provision of socially efficient quantities of these same goods.[176]

It is stressed that the undersupply of health research has concrete impacts on the market side, where a drug's adverse reactions are reflected or where the losses

---

[167]This is the claim made by Eisenberg (1996), pp. 1663 ff.

[168]David (2000b).

[169]David (2000a), p. 6.

[170]This is the assumption by Rai (1999).

[171]Rai (1999), pp. 79–80.

[172]Reichman and Uhlir (2003), p. 356, where it is stated, with reference to digital processing technologies, that "the successful implementation of these data integration functions depends to a large extent on the availability, access to, and unrestricted use of affordable data resources in the public domain".

[173]Reichman (2009), pp. 2 ff.

[174]David (2003), p. 23. See also Darlymple (2003), pp. 35 ff.

[175]Reinhardt (2004), p. 109, highlighting the non-excludable and non-rivalrous nature of the information that "facilitates the proper functioning of a healthcare market, such as that for drugs". See also Taubman (2008), pp. 591 ff.

[176]Reinhardt (2004), p. 109.

resulting from the impossibility to extend a pharmaceutical product to a rear disease are felt.[177]

The resulting gridlock on the side of health research sensitively touches on the market side, showing the ultimate unsustainability of an "individual" health research paradigm not based on information sharing interactions.[178] This is what other scholars have been referring as the "provision problem" affecting excessively privatized health information datasets, and precisely related to the lack of incentives of creating, maintaining and improving the aggregated scientific resources.[179]

In these regards, private exploitation of technological superiority and of obscuring intellectual property tools over scientific information by controllers of formed health datasets is identified as a cause of distraction of upstream information from both the basic and applied science commons, undermining in this way the ability of both private undertakings- *i.e.* other, maybe competing, private companies- and public institutions to harness cumulative data streams for the production of innovative products and services.[180]

Unsustainability and under-provision of scientific health information in turn impacts on the supply of other connected public goods, such as scientific research and health,[181] which are strictly dependent on data availability and on the transferability of technology.[182]

The above debate highlights the theoretical importance of the paradigms of the public domain and of the scientific commons as a benchmark upon which assessing the downsides of an excessively privatizing property regime over scientific information.

Although based on the public/private dichotomy, the debate appears to be of specific relevance in respect to the case of health data pools. As the previous paragraphs have shown, indeed, the phenomenon of health data pools is to be placed in between the spheres of private and public goods and resemble more what the literature on the commons refer to as common pool resources, exactly based on the sharing and the interconnectedness of different resources among different subjects.[183] In light of this structural premise, the just recalled debate over the economic and regulatory complexities of research commons highlights at least two important dynamic features of health data pools.

First of all, the above discussions warn about the risk that the achievement of these long terms efficiency gains is impaired by economic reluctancies to share the data, enabled by an information-based intellectual property system, which appears to

[177] These examples are drawn from Reichman (2009), p. 52.

[178] Reichman (2009), p. 52.

[179] Purtova (2017b), p. 183. See also Gardner et al. (1990), p. 340.

[180] Reichman and Uhlir (2003), p. 367.

[181] For an overview of the debate related to the relevance of health as a public good, see Dees (2018), pp. 20–26. See also the analysis by Moon et al. (2017), pp. 195 ff.

[182] For an analysis in a global perspective, see Maskus and Reichman (2004).

[183] See above Chap. 2, Sect. 2.2.4.

incentivise the "private" accumulation of data and the related short-term economic gains.[184] This risk exists also within the same health data pools, in which the information first aggregated by the pool members for innovation purposes could undergo a progressive process of appropriation under the control of the more powerful and technologically advanced pool partner.[185]

At a deeper level, however, the mentioned scholarly debate well stresses the economic and societal value of information exchanges in data-driven health research activities and thus the importance of the establishment of (quasi-public) areas of collaborative interactions among economic actors.[186] In these regards, some of the economic efficiencies that the cited literature refers to the public domain can be well transposed to the case of health data pools. Indeed, common sharing of scientific information enables different parties to exploit economies of scale and scope in the training and testing of new health-related products and services, minimizing superfluous redundancies and allowing the members of the pool to compare different testing results.[187] As has been observed, greater accessibility of research-valuable information through data pools could also be functional to collaboratively find remedies to investigational obstacles stifling the development of needed treatments.[188]

In addition to this, the accessibility of health information, as also the case of clinical trials disclosure demonstrates,[189] accelerates the manufacturing processes, by reducing research and development costs thanks to triggered network effects[190] and the greater scientific evidence regarding the effectiveness of the products to be marketed.[191]

The reduction of costs on the side of the supply of research material and of the testing risks is in turn very likely to reflect itself on lower prices of the end-marketed products/services.[192] Low product/service prices evidently benefit consumers, with greater access to medicines to low income or more disadvantage patients.[193]

Overall, thus, it appears that information sharing among businesses and among businesses and public institutions serves both short term private gains stemming

[184]See Chap. 2, Sects. 2.2.1 and 2.2.2.

[185]This scenario will be better enquired infra in Chap. 7.

[186]Similarly Reichman and Uhlir (2003), pp. 419 ff.

[187]These are the considerations made by Reichman (2009), p. 51. This is what the literature refers to as the "wasteful duplication" or "rationalization" argument. See Ben-Asher (2000), pp. 271 ff.

[188]Ben-Asher (2000), pp. 271 ff., stressing that collaboration based on information sharing would enable a company whose drug application has been denied to seek remedies to the deficiencies that have affected the application, in order to qualify for a new application.

[189]On the issue, amongst others, Eisenberg (2007), pp. 345 ff.

[190]Hoffmann and Johannsen (2019), p. 22.

[191]Rai et al. (2008), pp. 1 ff.

[192]Reichman and Uhlir (2003), p. 53.

[193]Reichman and Uhlir (2003), p. 54. See, more generally, Lybecker (2011), p. 28.

from a faster marketization of new products[194] and long term efficiencies related to a greater variety of treatments on the market and lower drug prices.[195]

Accessibility of health data is moreover deemed to increase the quality of marketed health products,[196] in terms of greater safety and effectiveness.[197]

Moreover, evidence drawn from health data pools informs diagnostic, therapeutic and prognostic strategies specifically designed to the individual. Accordingly, the new digital health technologies promise to render treatments more effective, on these basis of the consideration of patients' specificities.[198]

The so-identified innovation gains brought about by health data pools can be further qualified, from the particular perspective of the subjects who come benefit from the innovative market outputs, in terms of (i) the enhancement of consumer welfare and (ii) of the standard of health overall enjoyed. The analysis that follows will delve into the assessment of these two points.

3.3.2 Health Data Pools and Consumer Welfare

As argued in the previous paragraph, health data pools, and more precisely data sharing, are supposed to (i) speed up manufacturing processes and thus to increase the quantity of marketed digital health products; (ii) lower the manufacturing processes' costs and thus the ultimate products' costs; (iii) heighten the quality of new health products and services through enhanced personalization and effectiveness. Accordingly, health data pools as a means of conducting health research appear to influence the correspondent health markets in respect to products'/services' quantity, prices and quality. Framed in these terms, health data pools advance consumer welfare in digital health markets.[199] The idea that information concentration among different digital platforms leads to market efficiencies and gains in consumer welfare is emerging in the competition law literature regarding data-driven markets.[200]

In these regards, however, it needs to be observed that neither efficiency nor consumer welfare are clearly defined notions in the competition law reasoning.[201]

---

194 This is observed by Grabowski (2005), pp. 457 ff.

195 Lewis et al. (2007), pp. 1–4.

196 Margolis et al. (2014), pp. 957–958.

197 Stressing this in the context of the debate regarding clinical trials, Reichman (2006), pp. 135 ff.

198 Malanga et al. (2018), p. 105.

199 On the link between access to information, innovation and consumer welfare, see Ghidini (2015).

200 Stressing the efficiency outcomes of "consolidation of data across business platforms", Ohlhausen and Okuliar (2015), p. 151 and more generally in respect to big data Sokol and Comerford (2016), p. 1131, stating that big data creates efficiencies.

201 Brodley (1987), pp. 1020 ff. Stressing the ambiguities of the notion of efficiency, Geradin (12–13 November 2006), pp. 4–5.

Despite having always been a "leading benchmark" in the context of competition law analysis, the notion of consumer welfare- as has been observed- has never "embodied universally agreed properties".[202] The flexibility of the notion is thus currently being reassessed and readapted in respect to the specificities of digital markets. These are triggering a reconsideration of the determinants of consumer welfare, at both a practical and a theoretical level.[203]

Consumer welfare has been traditionally identified in "lower prices, better quality and a wider choice of new or improved goods and services".[204] Among these components, the price parameter has undoubtedly experienced greater success.[205]

However, increasing attention is being given to the non-price related parameters of "quality" or "choice", as complementary parameters of price.[206] According to a re-emerging theory, indeed, consumer welfare is determined by prices and quantities in the short run but it is structurally related also to variety, quality and innovation in the medium and long run.[207]

As the above made analysis suggests, health data pools and the connected data-driven research enquiries are likely to impact on each of these components of consumer welfare in the resulting digital health markets. Each of these consumer welfare parameters have been given new attention by both the scholarship and the case law in the context of digital market analysis.

With regards to the component of product variety, the European Commission has lately come to highlight the importance of "genuine choice and innovation" as essential determinants of the so-called "competition on the merits".[208]The variety

[202]So Ezrachi (2017), p. 61. See also Werden (2011), p. 11, observing that "every favoured policy is said to promote "consumer welfare". But the superficial consensus on this point masks a deep disagreement about what "consumer welfare" means and especially about what policies best to promote it".

[203]On the issue see Orbach (2011), pp. 133 ff. and Cseres (2007), pp. 121 ff.

[204]European Commission, Guidance on the Commission's Enforcement Priorities in Applying art. 82 of the EC Treaty to Abusive Exclusionary Conduct by Dominant Undertakings (2009), p. 10. In the Guidance, the concept of consumer harm is related to all practices restricting competition in the form of high prices, lower innovation or smaller consumer choice. The Commission's approach remains vague: sometimes the guidance refers to "consumer harm" or "detriment to consumers", other times to "consumer welfare" and no clearer definition is actually provided.

[205]This has been due to the phenomenon of the so-called mathematization of competition law. For the literature, see Etro (2009), pp. 327 ff. The attention given by the competition law discourse to price is strictly connected to the efficiency interpretation of competition law as influenced by the orientation of the Chicago School. For a deeper assessment see Averitt et al. (2011), p. 1. See also and Denozza (1988).

[206]This theory is emerging in the context of the debate regarding competition law's goals, Ezrachi and Stucke (2015), p. 1. Tracing the fall of the efficiency-based conception of competition law, Denozza (2010).

[207]Cseres (2007), pp. 121–173. Referring to this conception also Colangelo and Maggiolino (2017), p. 107.

[208]European Commission's investigation on Google Search concluded on the 27th June 2017. See European Commission (27 June 2017b). For the literature assessing the issue of the quality decrease in this specific case, Stucke and Ezrachi (2016), pp. 70 ff.

and thus the quantity of the products available on the market, enable a greater room for consumers' choices, and thus determine consumers' ability to "define his or her own wants and the ability to satisfy these wants at competitive prices".[209]

Likewise, also the relevance of quality as a competitive parameter has been considered in the context of several decisions by the European Commission[210] and has been supported by a strand of the literature, which has juxtaposed the quality criterion to the price parameter.[211]

The newly resulting products are expected to provide more utilities, more safety and more convenience to consumers.[212]

As the previously analysed case law shows,[213] moreover, innovation brought about by data sharing practices and the transfer of the connected processing technology, is to be felt also at the previous stage of the manufacturing process.[214] In this perspective, it appears that data pooling leads to significant benefits in terms of process innovation,[215] resulting in organizational improvements of the manufacturing procedures in the framework of so-called "smart manufacturing" techniques encouraged by digital tools and artificial intelligence.[216]

The scholarly debate regarding the countenance of the quality parameter in digital markets has well highlighted the difficulties in carrying out a quality comparison between competing products.[217] This is also given by the difficulties in clearly defining the determinants of a digital product's or service's quality. In this regard, the acknowledgment of the specificities of data-driven products and services, which are typically based on the access and processing of personal data, has suggested the opportunity of considering as a determinant of quality also the level of data protection assured by the same products or services.

Accordingly, the improvements in the level of data protection of digital products and services have been referred to by some authors as "data protection innovation".[218] Also the European Data Protection Supervisor has observed that in markets where access to services is gained through the disclosure of personal data "privacy

---

[209]In this perspective, the parameter of consumers' choice appears to be still anchored to the quantitative-price parameter. See Lande (2011), pp. 503 ff.

[210]The most relevant is European Court of Justice, France Télécom v. Commission, C-202/07 (2 April 2009), para 112.

[211]Costa-Cabral and Lynskey (2017), p. 30.

[212]Drexl (December 2018), p. 7.

[213]See supra Chap. 3, Sect. 3.1.

[214]So European Commission (1 April 2016b), pp. 3–4.

[215]European Commission (1 April 2016b), pp. 3–4.

[216]European Commission (25 April 2018), p. 9, highlighting how the employment of digital tools fuels optimisation and automatization of production processes.

[217]"From a technical standpoint, quality-driven assessments are difficult to elaborate". So Colangelo and Maggiolino (2017b), pp. 363 ff. Along these lines it needs to be recalled that questions still persist regarding what is the optimal level of quality. This point is stressed also by Ezrachi and Stucke (2015), p. 227.

[218]Zingales (2018), p. 80.

could become a competitive advantage" in the sense that consumers may be oriented to choose one service or another on the basis of the undertaking's data use policy.[219]

In this regard, it can be observed that data protection could work as a structural element for the products' or services' quality especially in respect to data-driven health technologies, which are structurally designed around the collection and processing of very sensitive data- as it is the case of the integrated platform for the management and cure of diabetes delivered by Google and Sanofi- and in respect to which users may evaluate "safe" privacy policies as a determinant component of the safety and thus of the quality of the health-related product/service.[220]

Following this line of reasoning, conversely, merges -such as the Google/Sanofi merger- and other data sharing activities- such as the one between Google DeepMind and Royal Free Hospital-, which come to lower the level of data protection, would impair the resulting services' quality, harm consumer welfare, and thus be deemed anticompetitive.[221]

However, in this respect it needs to be remembered that the relevance of the "quality" of privacy policies as a competitive parameter has been object of the critiques by some commentators who have rightly observed that users have limited choice in selecting the digital services with the better privacy policies because most providers of these services apply the same data-processing conditions.[222]

Moreover, the benefits brought about by digital health technologies' properties of personalization and effectiveness—given, for example, by the real-time features of

---

[219]European Data Protection Supervisor (March 2014), p. 32. In this perspective, the quality of the data use policy emerges as a competitive parameter orienting consumers' choices and thus acting as a parameter of competition between digital platforms. See also European Commission, Facebook/ Whatsapp Case N. Comp./M. 7217 (3 October 2014b), para 81, where the Commission observed for the first time that consumers may see privacy as a significant factor affecting the quality of the goods available on the Internet; European Commission, Microsoft/Linkedin, Case COMP/M.8124 (6 December 2016c), para 330.

[220]The difference indeed between a digital service or product and a specific health-related digital service or product is that the former collect and process every type of information, and by doing so also sensitive health information, whereas the latter are specifically trained and tested upon sensitive health data and are themselves specifically conceived for the analysis of this sensitive data. Reluctancies in using these new technologies and sharing sensitive information with the respective providers, could thus justify consumers' choices in favour of more privacy-friendly health devices and services. This has been empirically demonstrated by a recent British survey, reporting that 63% of the adult population is uncomfortable with allowing personal data to be used to improve healthcare. See Fenech et al. (6 April 2018).

[221]Sharing this perspective, Stucke and Ezrachi (2016), pp. 70 ff.; Grunes and Stucke (2015), p. 7; Grunes (2013), p. 1107; Swire (19 October 2007).

[222]Koops (2014), p. 250, where the Author observes how "often, there is little to choose: if you want to use a service, you have to comply with the conditions—if you do not tick the consent box, access will be denied. And there are no good alternatives: most other providers of the service you want apply the same practice and similar data-processing conditions, and with the most-used major services, such as Facebook, Google, or Twitter, there is no realistic alternative for most people. Underlying this is the fact that there are practically no alternative business models that generate revenue from other sources than user-data-based profiling and advertising".

diagnosis and monitoring functions—could be evaluated as more important by consumers than potential data protection risks. In other terms, health protection and advancements enabled by these digital health products and services could be preferred to data protection.[223] This also because more privacy-friendly digital health devices are very likely to be less innovative.[224] Accordingly, the risk of an outright "privacy paradox"[225] (especially) in digital health markets, suggests that also digital health products and services with low privacy thresholds could still be considered as qualitatively satisfying, or more generally, innovative and thus consumer welfare enhancing.[226]

Innovation is the third component of consumer welfare, which has been recently attracted new attention within the dynamics of digital markets. In the context of competition law analysis, the borders of the notion of innovation remain unsettled.[227] However, in its very essence, innovation relates to the commercialisation of newly invented or upgraded products (product innovation) or production and distribution processes (process innovation).[228] As has been observed, the introduction of new products and services on the market is "the main form of firm rivalry that dissipates supra-economic profits and improves consumer welfare".[229] Innovation is thus related to consumer welfare depending largely on quality advancements, although not always on price decreases.[230]

[223]This is especially the case of health social networks, where an enormous amount of health data is disclosed by users in order to have opinion, recommendations, health forecasts by the corresponding online community. See Li (2013), pp. 704–707.

[224]This has been observed, at a general level, by Chirita (2018).

[225]The so-called "privacy paradox" relates to the fact that also very privacy-sensitive consumers would still be willing to use privacy-invading services despite the accompanying threats for the protection of their personal data. The paradox has been widely acknowledged by both the institutions and the literature. It is what is expressed by the European Data Protection Supervisor (26 March 2014), pp. 23–24; Norberg et al. (2007), p. 100. Kokolakis (2017), pp. 122 ff.; and Tsai et al. (2011), pp. 254 ff.

[226]In these regards, it has been argued that even when privacy is a relevant factor for quality's products and services, it is not a self-standing parameter and should be necessarily assessed together with other more concrete parameters such as price or innovation. So Colangelo and Maggiolino (2017b), pp. 363 ff.

[227]Van Cleynenbreugel (2018), pp. 3–4.

[228]Van Cleynenbreugel (2018), p. 3.

[229]Svetiev (2007), p. 622.

[230]See already Schumpeter (1950), p. 84, stating that "in capitalist reality as distinguished from its textbook picture, it is not [price competition] which counts but the competition from the new commodity. The new technology, the new source of supply, the new type of organization... competition which commands a decisive cost or quality advantages and which strikes not at the margins of the profits and the outputs of the existing firms but at their foundations and their very lives".

3.3.3 Health Data Pools and (the Right to) Digital Health

The paragraphs above have investigated the claim that health data pools, as a means to aggregate different informational resources among different economic stakeholders, enhance consumer welfare in digital health markets by increasing digital health products' variety and quantity, decreasing their costs and advancing their quality.

At a deeper reflection, these alleged economic effects of health data sharing on digital health markets are supposed to also positively favour broader social and fundamental rights-related interests of consumers'/patients' safety and health.

In these regards, it needs to be recalled that just as the notion of efficiency and consumer welfare, also the notion of health is a debated concept in the scholarly literature,[231] who has underlined how the right to health encompasses "a variety of human rights as tools to deal with public health issues",[232] and has an inclusive nature, "incorporating a myriad of freedoms and entitlements".[233]

The right to health is established in various sources of both European and international law.

At European level, the Charter of Fundamental Rights of the European Union interestingly establishes a "right of access to preventive healthcare and the right to benefit from medical treatment under the conditions established by national laws and practices".[234] The international framework regarding the right to health further defines health as "the enjoyment of the highest attainable standard of physical and mental health", which is one of the fundamental rights of every human being without distinction of race, religion, political belief, economic or social condition".[235] The UN Committee on Economic, Social and Cultural Rights has specified that the right to health implies the right *to enjoyment of a variety* of *facilities, goods, services and conditions that are necessary for the realization of the highest attainable standard of health"*.[236] In these respect, the same Committee has stated that the right to health is

---

[231] For a theoretical reconstruction of the right to health, see Ruger (2006), pp. 273 ff.; see also Kinney (2001), pp. 1457 ff.

[232] Lemmens (2013), pp. 163 ff.

[233] Lemmens and Telfer (2012), p. 101, citing U.N. Special Rapporteur on the Right to Health Paul Hunt. See United Nations, Economic and Social Council (1 March 2004).

[234] So art. 35 Charter of the Fundamental Rights of the European Union. At European level, the protection of health has been acknowledged as a concern of European dimension only with the Treaty of Lisbon that came into effect in 2009. In the Lisbon Treaty, it is prescribed that a "high level of human health protection shall be ensured in the definition and implementation of all Community policies and activities". So art. 168, 1 para TFEU. For a broader discussion on the relevance of health protection as a European concern. See Chap. 4, Sect. 4.2.

[235] Art. 12 of the International Covenant on Economic, Social and Cultural Rights. In this perspective, the right to health is intimately connected to the other fundamental right to non-discrimination. United Nations, Economic and Social Council (1 March 2004), para 22.

[236] UN Committee on Social Economic and Cultural Rights, General Comment N. 14: The Right to the Highest Attainable Standard of Health (Art. 12), Adopted at the Twenty-second Session of the Committee on Economic, Social and Cultural Rights (11 August 2000), para 9.

determined first of all by the essential components of availability and accessibility of such facilities, goods and services.[237]

Availability means that these facilities, goods and services have to be available in sufficient quantity, whereas, accessibility means that health facilities, goods and services have to be accessible to everyone without discrimination within a State party.[238]

In addition to the features of availability and accessibility, related to external quantitative aspects of health-related markets, the Committee further identifies as internal qualitative components the ones of acceptability and quality, respectively related to health products' adequacy in respect to minorities', vulnerable people's and communities' specificities and capability of addressing health concerns of the population as a whole.[239]

Against the backdrop of this framework, health data pools and resulting digital health technologies potentially have a sensitive impact on each of the above-identified components of health.

Easy access to health data enables users first of all to become active managers of their health conditions throughout their whole life cycle.[240] The algorithm-based functioning of processes allows for vast quantities of data to be gathered and reported in real-time. The real-time quantification of users' health conditions leads to a prompt identification and evaluation of them.[241] The new devices, such as health

---

[237] UN Committee on Social Economic and Cultural Rights, General Comment N. 14: The Right to the Highest Attainable Standard of Health (Art. 12) (11 August 2000), para 12.

[238] UN Committee on Social Economic and Cultural Rights, General Comment N. 14: The Right to the Highest Attainable Standard of Health (Art. 12) (11 August 2000).

[239] With regards to 'acceptability' issues, the Committee has stressed that health facilities, goods and services need to be culturally appropriate, in the sense that they must respect the culture of individuals, minorities, people and communities, as well as designed to improve the health conditions of these individuals. UN Committee on Social Economic and Cultural Rights, General Comment N. 14: The Right to the Highest Attainable Standard of Health (Art. 12) (11 August 2000).

[240] See Britnell et al. (2016), pp. 14–16.

[241] Lupton (2016) and Lupton (2013b), pp. 25 ff., highlighting how "the data themselves and the algorithms that interpret them and make predictions based on them are social actants" with a "profound impact on how individuals view themselves and the world". As sociological studies are observing, the digitization of the healthcare sector and, more specifically, the digitization of the two above-identified digital health markets is changing attitudes and expectations of people towards health and body. Indeed, health tracking devices enable people individually and socially to understand and care for their bodies, and to identify problems requiring cure or improvement. Algorithms installed in health-tracking devices act to translate physiological signals recorded from the body into data, presented as numbers and visualizations. These enable the bodily self-governing to take place. Algorithms have become powerful classificatory mechanisms for influencing how users' learn about their bodies and health. Such algorithm-driven classificatory system is thus ultimately generating a new conception of health, which is defined through the classificatory scheme written into their algorithms. More specifically, it appears that users' health identity is increasingly shaped by what is reflected by the technical sensors capturing individuals' data signals and rendered back to these same individuals. In this way, users' body are quantified by data and the numbers they return. This is particularly relevant if one thinks that information derived from

apps, and the new digital sites where health data can be shared, are empowering users/patients in the sense that they are becoming active agents of their own health conditions as technologically monitored and displayed. Such monitoring systems thus facilitate the prevention and early cure of diseases, promptly suggesting the needed interventions.

In this perspective, digital health tracking devices permit on the one hand the capturing of updated e-health data and on the other hand the processing of these data for the release of advice, incentives and motivations to improve users' health status.[242] These advancements in health information technology services are thus extending the possibilities of remote consultation, diagnosis, and treatment, with promising effects of inclusion also of the strands of the populations that have greater economic and physical difficulties of accessing health services and products.[243]

With regards to quality and safety aspects, the digital quantification of users' health conditions enables to identify and evaluate them with greater precision: the prevention and early cure of diseases can make healthcare interventions more effective with that reducing healthcare spending.[244] More precisely, the collection and the processing of updated health data makes it possible to deliver patient-tailored health services and health products. Big data analytics are thus paving the way to the rise and development of so-called "precision medicine", based on a patient-centric approach for the delivery of accurate cures based on the available data about a user/ patient.[245] Moreover, with regards to the post-marketing phase of pharmaceutical products, big health datasets can be used to assess post-marketing adverse events and thus the safety of pharmaceutical products.[246]

---

monitoring functions are then mostly transformed into predictions of users' future bodily health. According to both monitoring and predictive data, users take the steps that they deem necessary for the enhancement of their health conditions. In this light, it is interesting to observe that users interact with algorithms as active participants that immediately respond to what the algorithms suggest. As has been observed, digital health tools activate an outright 'dialogue that moves between data as an externalization of self and internal, subjective, qualitative understanding of what the data means'. This constant interaction between users and digital health devices is the result of what sociologists define as a contemporary obsession with 'tuning' and 'perfecting' the body with the 'right' algorithms. Hence, in the present environment, users' body is recorded and reprogrammed, manipulated and improved according to what the norms embedded in algorithmic systems suggest. So Nafus and Sherman (2014), pp. 1784 ff. The above-made considerations suggest how health identities in the digital-algorithmic age are increasingly shaped by the technological devices that have health-related functions and by the "evidence" rendered by algorithmically processed health data.

[242] Lupton (2013a), pp. 256 ff.

[243] World Health Organization (2010), p. 11.

[244] Britnell et al. (2016).

[245] For the literature on the issue, Liddicoat et al. (December 2017). From an American perspective, Rothstein (2017), pp. 274 ff.

[246] See Parasidis (March 2018), pp. 73 ff. See also Heads of Medicines Agencies-European Medicines Agency (13th February 2019), p. 4, stating that "the most natural application of social media data is for pharmacovigilance and signal detection". See also page 36–37; 43 of the report.

On the different side of health products' and services' acceptability, it needs to be observed how the availability of large digital datasets enables to capture demographic and social information that can be useful to address clinical needs in a more uniform way.

For example, selected health indicators can be utilized in order to assess whether minorities and other disadvantaged groups receive the same quality of care as other populations. In these regards, big data analytics are being employed in order to link community-level data with healthcare system data.[247] The rendered results can thus indicate which populations are at greater risk of health disparities.[248]

In this perspective, big data can be used for the identification of patients with serious medical conditions living in social disadvantage, so that the services can be tailored to these subjects with the available resources.[249]

Likewise, data analytics are creating new mechanisms for a faster approval of pharmaceutical products which are specifically designed for the satisfaction of unmet needs and thus for the enhancement of the specific health conditions of certain subgroups of the population.[250]

The improvements in terms of enhanced accessibility, availability, acceptability and quality of health-related products enabled by new health technologies based on the massive processing of health data, need however to be better assessed in the view of some distinctive features of these same health technologies. Indeed, in the evolving digital health markets, health outcomes risk to be impaired by some newly emerging barriers to accessibility and availability of digital health products, as well as by newly emerging sources of quality and thus safety defects rooted in the functioning mechanisms of algorithmic-based processing technologies.

3.3.4 Health Data Pools and the Risks for Digital Health

Traditionally, the scholarly literature has identified among the main barriers obstructing access to health services and products, not only economic factors, *i.e.*

---

[247] Angier et al. (2018), pp. 1 ff.

[248] Place-based health disparities is emerging as an important area of enquiry. In this regard see Zhang et al. (2017), pp. 95 ff. This opportunity is being currently investigated by Google's project, Google City Block, aiming at reaching neighborhoods that face "high poverty rates and accompanying social challenges". See City Block https://www.cityblock.com/about.

[249] In these regards, it is claimed that the distance-tracking and monitoring digital health products and services increase access to healthcare especially for rural populations that lack access to physicians' services, by decreasing travel distance, travel time, and some appointment delay to care. In this way, these services enable access to health services irrespective of where the patient live. So Bashshur (2002), pp. 7 ff.

[250] See supra Chap. 2, Sects. 2.1.5 and 2.1.6 regarding regulatory effects of health digitization.

financial disparities,[251] but also socio-cultural elements.[252] In this respect, language, information availability, working conditions, and ultimately strictly cultural elements, *i.e.* cultural practices and customs, have been considered as obstacles to an equal consumption of health services and products.[253] These obstacles all have been regarded as different causes for the diversification of health products' and services' accessibility among different social groups, with strong exclusionary, and thus discriminatory, outcomes.[254]

In the digital environment, these factors risk to further exacerbate health disparities.[255] The digitization of health products and services indeed requires patients to use technologies that they are not familiar with.[256] Those patients who do not belong to technology-savy group of consumers,[257] such as elderly, disabled or those with low digital literacy could thus face difficulties or even be deterred from using these new technologies.[258] This has been expressly confirmed by a study of the George Washington University Health Workforce Institute, finding that the use of digital health technologies "is most dominant among working age and higher income respondents and those who may have more difficulty leaving the home because of physical and mental limitations".[259]

Among the sources of exclusions in the digital environment, the literature has highlighted the speed of change of technologies; the costs involved in accessing and upgrading the devices; the lack of user-friendliness and the understanding of the meaningfulness of information.[260] All these elements are to be ascribed to the phenomenon of the "digital divide"[261]: with digital technologies becoming increasingly important in the field of healthcare, the gap among those who experience difficulties in accessing and correctly exploiting digital technologies, and those who

[251] For an economic analysis on the issue, see Etienne et al. (2011), pp. 57 ff. See also the less recent analysis by Deaton (May 1999).

[252] Socio-cultural elements are considered to play an increasing important role in the definition of individuals' health status. See generally, World Health Organization, https://www.who.int/teams/social-determinants-of-health.

[253] Gnadinger (22 August 2014), referring to "genetics, behaviour, social circumstances, environmental and physical influences"; similarly, see Bobinski (2003), pp. 363 ff., which stresses education as one of the main drivers of health disparities. Commenting on the notion of health disparities, see Jost (2006), pp. 537 ff.

[254] European Union Agency For Fundamental Rights (2013), especially at pp. 47 ff.

[255] Crawford (1 April 2013).

[256] Uscher-Pines et al. (2016), p. 282.

[257] Generally regarding disparities in the access to Internet, see File and Ryan (November 2014). See also Amante et al. (2015), pp. 106 ff., reporting that Whites were more likely to use the Internet to search for health information compared with other races/ethnicities and the percentage of adults who search for health information increased with education level.

[258] See Stavroulaki (2019a), pp. 171 ff., referring to the observations by Miller (2003), pp. 2 ff.

[259] George Washington University Health Workforce Research Center (3 December 2018).

[260] McAuley (2014), pp. 1118 ff.

[261] Burri (2011), pp. 217 ff.

can easily afford them reflects itself into an increasing gap between those who can access and those who cannot access healthcare services.[262] In other terms, those who have difficulties to use Information and Communication Technologies and those who do not have sufficient information and fewer quality services at their disposal will be precluded from accessing health services rendered through digital channels.[263] This is thought-provoking given that many of the people who are unable to integrate into the "big data trail" are also the very people most in need for health research, intervention and care.

In the digital-algorithmic healthcare environment, access to digital medical devices is of relevance not only for the immediate fruition of these digital services and the above-outlined benefits they provide, but has broader systemic implications. As already mentioned, digital health tracking tools, together with other web-based health services, such as frequently asked questions websites or online disease patient communities, are one of the principal sources of health data.[264] The produced digital health data come to feed in turn the health datasets that are employed for the training of digital medical devices and that are starting to be used by pharmaceutical companies and by regulatory agencies for the testing of the safety and efficacy of pharmaceutical products.

In this light, the exclusion from the health services by some groups, causes the unavailability of health information regarding these groups, this having direct consequences of the other two components of health products' acceptability and quality.

Indeed, incompleteness of the datasets affects the design of digital medical devices that are trained upon these datasets, and the safety and the efficacy features of pharmaceutical products, which are tested upon these same datasets.

In this way, digital health services and products risk to be culturally "exclusive", and thus not fully capable of addressing specific health needs of minority groups.

The impairment of these two elements ultimately affects again accessibility concerns: the less disadvantaged groups are indeed taken into consideration in the design and the structure of products and services, the less they will be able to access them, not only from a financial standpoint, but mostly from a physical and linguistic standpoint. This last consideration shows that there is a circular relationship between the three components of accessibility, acceptability and quality of health services and products: narrow accessibility of final services and products undermines indeed acceptability and quality in the design of these same products; a design that does not take into consideration the needs of minorities newly exacerbates accessibility concerns of marketed services and products.[265]

262 Burri (2011), pp. 217 ff.

263 Stressing this point, Villazor (2004), pp. 35 ff.

264 See supra Chap. 2, Sect. 2.1.1.

265 Council of the European Union (28 November 2017), para 23, where it is observed that differences in digital and health literacy need to be adequately taken into consideration in the implementation and the design of digital medical tools.

Framed in these terms, the issue of the newly emerging health inequalities in the digital-algorithmic environment appears to be strictly intertwined with the different issue of the completeness and quality of the datasets that feed the algorithms structuring digital health products. Attention needs thus to be given to the type of biases that are likely to undermine the completeness and quality of digital health datasets used for the design of digital health products. This will be done in the next section.

3.3.5 Health Data Pools and Health Biases

As illustrated, health data pools aggregate different types of health-related information, ranging from more sophisticated clinical trials-styled information to health-inflected runaway data. In this perspective, health data pools work as large depositories of information regarding citizens' sensitive health conditions. This information is essential for the training and testing of digital health devices and products. It is thus key for the ultimate design of digital health products, in turn reflecting itself upon the overall quality and the accessibility of these same products, once these are marketed.

Ultimately, this means that the nature and the features of the datasets employed by the research actors, as well as the manners in which the data are processed by these entities determine the degree of advancements in the standard of health overall enjoyed by the users of such new technologies. Hence, the way in which the employed health datasets structure the resulting digital health products and services, in turn affects the way in which these same products and services advance the protection of the right to health.

It has been above highlighted that digital health products and services can sensitively advance citizens' health, through faster, more effective, and potentially also cheaper devices and treatments.

However, it cannot be neglected that in the digital dimension, health protection can be impaired by new sources of harm specifically deriving from the digital and thus datafied nature of the new health related products and services. These harms are directly related to the biases potentially affecting the health data pools upon which new digital health technologies are designed and tested.

In these regards, it has been rightly pointed out, that very little is known about the selection, values and assumptions of the 'training data' that machine learning algorithms act upon. Such data may be incomplete, partial, or even incompatible with the data that the algorithm will operate "in the wild".[266]

[266] Gillespie (25 June 2014). With specific regards to the health sector see also Williamson (2015), pp. 133 ff.

Automatically aggregated data or poorly constructed analytic frames may be susceptible to biases and weaknesses.[267]

These biases can result both from ii) the initial stage of collection of the same data, thus referring to the moment of the creation of health data pools and ii) the subsequent phases involving the processing of the collected datasets for the inference of predictive correlations, which are technically drawn from the initial health data pools through the employment of proxies, *i.e.* criteria according to which the initial health data pools are reorganized and sub-grouped.[268]

In this perspective, thus traditional concerns related to the accurateness and quality of research data[269] appear to take a new shape in the digital environment,[270] raising a new set of challenges that are identified below.

First of all, the biases potentially affecting health data pools need to be better contextualized within the broader topic of algorithmic biases. In these regards, the literature distinguishes two major types of algorithmic biases, that is (i) biased training data and (ii) unequal ground truth.[271]

(i) Training data is extremely relevant since on the basis of this data machine learning algorithms optimize a statistical model that links input to output data. The training data is thus the benchmark that assures that the predictions and correlations made on the basis of a certain input are right. Errors in collected data may make patterns harder to identify or lead to false pattern recognition.

One common source of biased training data is given by sampling bias. This bias is obtained when some strands of the population are misrepresented, because there is not a sufficient representation of the features of these strands of the population in the used datasets. In alternative, it can occur that in the datasets there is some data referring to these groups, but this data is less valid and prone to error.[272] Both types of sampling bias lead to misrepresentation distorting the evidence drawn from the same training data. The incorrect handling of training data, indeed, results in an incorrect labelling of the employed data, which means that inputs are associated with

---

[267] For an analysis regarding the analytical errors that inflected Google Flu trends, see Lazer et al. (2014), pp. 1203–1205.

[268] Barocas and Selbst (2016), pp. 671 ff., especially pp. 681–694.

[269] The concerns regarding the accurateness and quality of clinical trials data have been documented by cases regarding access to clinical trials data, as the one involving the European Medicines Agency and the Danish research group Cochrane Collaboration. See Gøtzsche and Jorgensen (2011), p. 342. Dhir (2011), p. 349, underlining the "fact that corporations fail to disclose the totality of studies conducted with respect to particular drugs- and the resulting risk implications, before a drug goes to market". See also, Lemmens and Telfer (2012), pp. 63 ff.

[270] Vayena and Blasimme (March 2018), p. 120; Hiller (2016), p. 59.

[271] Hacker (2018), pp. 1143 ff.

[272] Hacker (2018), pp. 1143 ff.

wrong outputs,[273] such as disease risk.[274] In this way, thus, the bias is incorporated into the statistical model that is drawn from the training data and thus propagates into the output, misleading the rendered results.[275]

Another bias potentially affecting training data is related to that what data scientists call "historical bias", resulting from sociological and/or historical misconceptions that are reflected into the health datasets, likewise skewing their representativeness.[276] As with the first type of bias, also these human-like biases enter into the model and perpetuate themselves through self-learning algorithms. The historical bias can be incorporated in the algorithmic process both unintentionally-as simple mistakes or results of subconscious human bias-, or intentionally.[277] In this last case, for example, the designer of the algorithmic processing technologies could intentionally incorporate these socio-historical biases within the processing infrastructure, associating discriminatory traits with scores in apparently neutral categories, such as educational levels or geographical location.[278] From these considerations, it can be derived that biases in training data can both relate to the substantial nature of the initially collected and employed datasets, as well as to the initial coding of the processing infrastructure employed for the analysis of the given data.

(ii) Biases in training data are also likely to generate biases in the subsequent moment of the analytical processing of collected data. Algorithms construct from input data a score (target variable, such as a risk score), which is the output. However, this output, and thus the scores of the target variable, may excessively correlate with membership in a protected group. In this case, membership with a protected group is automatically associated with the analyzed trait, that is—for example—the studied disease. In an unbiased dataset, data express reality through the best available output-approximation (so-called "equal ground truth"). Conversely, if the algorithmically calculated capacities or risks are distributed in an untruthful way among protected groups, then the employed dataset is affected by a

[273] This occurs in case of what computer scientists call "feature selection", that is given by the construction of the analytical model according to discriminatory criteria. Feature selection derives, for example, from the consideration of an insufficient criteria to infer membership to a certain group; the use of membership to a certain group as a direct input; the reliance on proxies for membership. Kroll et al. (2017), p. 681.

[274] Hiller (2016), p. 28.

[275] Kroll et al. (2017), p. 680.

[276] This can occur for example as a consequence of what the literature refers to as "implicit bias", that are "discriminatory biases based on implicit attitudes or implicit stereotypes". See Greenwald and Krieger (2006), p. 951. In these regards, some socio-linguistic studies have shown that natural language is characterized by discriminatory semantics. Data scientists appoint these "intrinsic" biases, or "human-like biases". See Caliskan et al. (2017), pp. 183–186. From a legal perspective see Croosley (2003), pp. 211–223. For a recent reassessment of the perpetuation in the digital-algorithmic environment of socio-historical biases, as the one related to gender discrimination, see Lambrecht and Tucker (2019), pp. 2947 ff.

[277] Kroll et al. (2017), p. 682.

[278] Hacker (2018).

bias appointed "unequal ground truth". Such bias causes a "proxy discrimination", that is a statistical discrimination,[279] given by "untrue" statistical associations and subsequent scientific inferences.

The consideration of the above-outlined algorithmic biases is extremely relevant in respect to the sensitive context of health data-driven research.

With regards to the initial training data, it has been so far illustrated how the composition of health data pools is varied, combining more sophisticated scientific health data, as clinical trials with other more general health data drawn from various sources such as health tracking devices or online sites, as frequently asked questions sites or social networks.[280] This means that much of the data flowing into health data pools employed for health research purposes are self-reported or distance-tracked.[281]

This type of health data is thus very likely to entail distortive information regarding the identity and the effective health conditions of the data subject.[282] Widely documented problems of false or incorrect reporting appear thus to be amplified in large digital health repositories.[283]

In this perspective, the above-described biases affecting the training data are likely to sensitively impact upon the quality and safety of the to-be-marketed digital products and services.[284] Moreover, the same biased set of training data could be employed for the training and testing of other medical technologies, thus perpetuating the initial errors.[285]

In addition to this, health data pools risk to be biased due to their under-representativeness[286]: indeed, the health data collected from tracking devices or

[279] Kroll et al. (2017), pp. 680–681.

[280] See supra Chap. 2, Sect. 2.1.1. See also Lupton (2014), pp. 856 ff.

[281] Lupton (2017), pp. 562–578.

[282] Lazer et al. (14 March 2014), p. 1203.

[283] See in these regards the observations Hoffmann and Podgurski (2012), pp. 87 ff. See also Mathes et al. (2019), p. 38.

[284] Problems of false reporting of pharmaceuticals' product features have led to the withdrawal of many products that had been granted market authorisations in the EU. For an overview, see McNaughton et al. (2014). In the USA, similarly, the company GlaxoSmithKline was found guilty of selective reporting of positive trial data and hiding of negative data at a premarket stage. See United States District Court Eastern District of New York, New York v. GlaxoSmithKline (16 October 2013). Due to false reporting regarding the safety features of the antidepressant Vioxx, the FDA withdrew the pharmaceutical from the market. FDA (30 September 2004), announcing the "withdrawal of Vioxx from the US market due to safety concerns". For the literature reflecting on the issue of accurateness of the marketed products' safety information, see Faeh (2014), pp. 176–195.

[285] Nicholson Price (2019), p. 90, observing that "it can be difficult to ensure that algorithms trained on data from one electronic health record system can accurately analyze data within the context of another electronic health record system".

[286] Kim (3 November 2018). A concrete example of minorities' under-representation is given by a genetic test that was employed in the US for the identification of a specific heart disease (hypertrophyc cardiomyopathy). Due to under-representation of black Americans in the initial data, these people were diagnosed a high disease risk based on a gene mutation that does not in fact predict a greater disease risk for them. A similar case involved the pharmaceutical Plavix for the

online-based services are very likely to reflect the health conditions of the users who can afford these devices or services.[287] It could thus happen that the data used to conduct the research are not representative of the diseases object of the research or, more generally, do not accurately reflect the health conditions of a sufficient sample of the population.[288]

Problems of under-representativeness affect not only digital health records but also genetic data: participants in genome-wide association studies are indeed mostly of European descent.[289]

As a result, collected health-datasets and the statistical and probabilistic models based on these data could be biased, referring, for example, only to the white, more educated and influent strands of the population.[290] If analytic frames are not sufficiently calibrated to account for society's minorities, big data employed for the design of digital medical devices and digitally tested pharmaceutical products may miss subtle trends related, for example, to ethnic-specific diseases or rare diseases.[291] This could render these digital health products and services not suitable for the monitoring and curing of conditions related to subgroups of the population. This is already being documented, for example, with regards to a dermatological artificial intelligence system, designed to recognize melanoma, which has turned out to be largely ineffective in respect to patients with darker skin.[292]

In light of the illustrated scenario, thus, the existence of the above-outlined biases, as biased training data and unequal ground truth, is likely to undermine the "acceptability" of digital health products.[293] This appears in turn to weaken the quality of these products, as framed above.

The structural features of digital health products and services, as resulting from the health data pools employed for their design, ultimately risk to restrict the accessibility of these new products and services by those groups whose data are not sufficiently or effectively included in the research datasets. These groups could indeed face barriers to access to digital devices, not (only) related to prices but (also)

prevention of heart attacks marketed by Sanofi-Aventis. The manufacturers were sued by the State of Hawaii for false and deceptive marketing deriving from the fact that the producers did not disclose that the treatment had different responses among different strands of the population. In particular, the participants in the clinical studies were all of European descent, this neglecting treatment responses among Pacific Islander or East Asian. See Nicholson Price (2019), pp. 92–93.

287 See, for example, NPD Group (6 January 2015); Sanghavi Goel et al. (3 May 2011), pp. 112 ff.

288 Bol et al. (2018), pp. 183 ff.

289 Nicholson Price (2019), p. 94.

290 The risk of under-representativeness of the employed health datasets is enquired by Malanga et al. (March 2018), pp. 98 ff.

291 Malanga et al. (March 2018), pp. 106–108.

292 Adamson and Smith (2018), pp. 1247–48.

293 From a general perspective, see Lerman (2003), pp. 60–61, arguing for the institution of a principle of "data antisubordination". This principle is drawn from Balkin and Siegel (2003), pp. 9 ff.

to quality concerns,[294] directly stemming from the fact that the marketed devices do not properly read and capture the specificities of their health conditions.

In this perspective, ultimately, the biases related to the under-representativeness of the training data are likely to reflect themselves on an unequal access to digital healthcare products, negatively affecting the standard of health overall enjoyed. In these regards, the need has been acknowledged to develop appropriate political—well before regulatory—responses, assuring "those who live outside or on the margins of data flows some guarantee that their status as persons with light data footprints will not subject them to unequal treatment by the state in the allocation of public goods and services".[295]

A last consideration needs to be made in respect to socio-historical biases. This type of bias is indeed likely to impact, at a more general level, on broader features of digital health research, generating new forms of health-based discrimination.

One of the greatest scientific advancements brought about by digital health research is related to personalization of health treatments.

However, personalization patterns that are positively welcomed as more effective ways to monitor and cure patients' conditions risk to generate new trends of what is referred to in the literature as "group stigmatization".[296] This type of stigmatization occurs when analytical correlation signal that individuals with certain ancestries or genes are more likely than others to contract certain diseases, or have better outcomes with treatments that are different from standard therapy.[297]

In these regards, socio-historical biases affecting the training data or the way in which the initial datasets are analyzed, could cause disease patterns built on the collected phenotypic, biological and behavioral data, to be wrongfully associated with specific groups of the population.[298]

As has been interestingly observed by some authors, specific groups such as low-income, unwell and elderly, are more vulnerable to health information collection endeavors in respect to the wealthier strands of the population who are more educated and have greater financial means to protect their health privacy.[299] As a result of the over-representation of certain groups in the analyzed datasets,[300] these groups risk to find themselves trapped into incorrectly built predictive clusters

---

[294] In these regards, the literature has stressed that accessibility to pharmaceutical products and the related advancements in the standard of health overall enjoyed, are given not only by quantity but also by quality concerns. On the issue see Timmermans (2006), pp. 41 ff. Stressing the importance of quality concerns in antitrust analysis of digital health markets also Stavroulaki (2019b).

[295] Lerman (2003), p. 61.

[296] Hoffmann and Podgurski (2012), pp. 107–108.

[297] Hoffmann and Podgurski (2012), p. 107.

[298] Stressing the discriminatory potential of so-called "implicit biases", Greenwald and Krieger (2006), pp. 961–962.

[299] Konnoth (2017), pp. 1323–1333, describing the phenomenon of inequity of health information collection.

[300] Kroll et al. (2017), p. 681, stressing in respect to the association of high crime rates to black minorities, how "the overrepresentation of black and Hispanic people in this sample may lead an

referring to cultural, ethnic and racial parameters. The health technologies built upon these clusters would be thus unsuitable for other groups of patients who were not adequately reflected in the training datasets.[301]

Moreover, the resulting ethnic-based health profiles are destined not only to affect the production of health-related products and services, but also-as will be better assessed below- to feed more general online discriminatory practices.

The practice of racial profiling in medicine precedes the datification and digitization of the health research setting,[302] and was boosted by the growing importance of genomics for health research.[303] Pharmaceutical companies have started to show increasing economic interest in so-called "race-based" medicine.[304] As a result, in 2005, the FDA approved a drug only for African-Americans[305] for which, very interestingly, the United States Patent and Trademark Office granted a "race-based" patent.[306]

In the USA, the encouragement of racial-based research has been expressly promoted by the National Institute of Health that has issued guidelines stressing the importance of collecting data regarding the different responses to treatments among minority groups.[307] More specifically, the guidelines require researchers to report "racial" and ethnic treatment responses, eventually responding to these differences by developing "racially-developed" therapies.[308] The guidelines' underlying assumption is that the "scientific" consideration of the specificities of ethnic groups could lead to better treatment outcomes for diseases that are more common in those groups than in others.

The personalized character of algorithm-driven health enquiries enables to speed up and advance such objectives, positively meant to decrease health inequalities.

However, from an opposite perspective, the correlation between a certain ethnicity and a disease could potentially lead to under-diagnosis of the same disease among

algorithm to associate typically black or Hispanic traits with stops that lead to crime prevention, simply because those characteristics are overrepresented in the population that was stopped".

[301] Nicholson Price (2019), p. 91: "if the patients in the training data (. . .) differ systematically from the patients in low-resource settings where the algorithm is deployed, the algorithm won't do a good job dealing with those patients".

[302] Hoffmann (2005), pp. 406–410. See also Sullivan (2002), pp. 249 ff.

[303] See supra para. Hoffmann (2005), p. 423, recalling how through genetic testing it was found out that Jews were more likely to have genetic variations associated with a higher risk of breast and ovarian cancer.

[304] See Editorial (19 June 2005).

[305] Hoffmann (2005), pp. 396–397. The FDA's decision has been subject to many critiques, see amongst others the assessment by Kahn (2004), p. 23, reporting that such racially-tailored research had been financially and politically supported. See also Id. (2005), pp. 105 ff.

[306] Kahn (2004), p. 32.

[307] National Institute of Health, Policy and Guidelines on the Inclusion of Women and Minorities as Subjects in Clinical Research (6 December 2017).

[308] National Institute of Health, Policy and Guidelines on the Inclusion of Women and Minorities as Subjects in Clinical Research (6 December 2017).

other groups. Due to scoring charts, these groups could be, for example, less likely than other groups to access the needed testing services.[309] Conversely, the ethnic or societal group that is probabilistically associated with a certain disease or condition could be stigmatized,[310] suffering discriminations which propagate from the health sector to the online commercial environment as well as to the employment sector and the insurance rates.[311]

From this perspective, thus, in the light of both under-representativeness and socio-historical biases, digital health entails the risk of increasing (digital) health divides, with resulting problems of health inequalities. Under these premises, it becomes apparent how, in the digital-algorithmic environment, the identification of the types of biases that are embedded into big health datasets becomes essential in order to properly address health inequalities deriving from both new barriers to access to digital health products and other discriminatory patterns opened up by data-driven health research.[312]

3.3.6 Health Data Pools and Data Subjects

As the analysed case studies have suggested, the innovation goals of health data sharing practices have to be carefully balanced against the threats to users' data protection resulting from the processing of a vast amount of patients' sensitive personal data. The processing of this personal data through machine learning techniques can indeed enable the extraction, through correlations and probabilistic inferences of additional secondary personal data, further feeding controlled health data pools. In a nutshell, health data pools *maximise* health data processing.

At a very general level, health data pools and the "fluid" contractual infrastructure governing them appear to blur the distinction (i) between the private and the public spheres[313] and ultimately (ii) between the dimensions of health research and the broader digital markets.[314]

The blurring between the private and the public spheres ought to be analysed from a double standpoint: on the one hand, the generative potential of business algorithmic processing techniques, together with the speed of data transfers onto third parties, makes it arduous to draw the line between what health information

---

[309]Hoffmann (2005), p. 419.

[310]For an overview, Bobinski (2003), pp. 363 ff.

[311]Kahn (2004), p. 41; Hiller (2016), p. 282. See Pasquale (2014), p. 98.

[312]Khullar (31 January 2019).

[313]In this sense, Teubner (2011), p. 710. Stressing the weakening of the "factual, social and legal conditions of the differentiation of the relationship between the private and the public spheres" in the digital space, Ladeur and Gostomzyk (2011), p. 710.

[314]Powles and Hodson (2017), p. 354; Sharon (2016), p. 7. Similarly, also Marjanovic et al. (2017), p. 4, stressing that "health R&D and the delivery of healthcare are increasingly cross-sectoral activities".

remains in the data subjects' private sphere and the health knowledge that businesses extract and "publicly" employ[315]; on the other hand, with the growing importance of big data companies as facilitators of health research and the resulting expansion of the partnerships between these companies and public research institutes, also the distinction between public and privately conducted health research ends up being distorted.[316]

As a result of the above-highlighted complex and multisided architecture of the digital environment, health-related markets as digitalised appear to be increasingly intertwined with the broader dynamics of digital markets.

This scenario amplifies the concerns already raised back in the 1970s by Richard Titmuss, related to the risk that patients/subjects would be harmed "physically and psychologically, by giving themselves, willingly or unwillingly, knowingly or unknowingly, as teaching material"[317] to scientific research. Indeed, the possible harms faced by data subjects as new research subjects in the digital economy[318] are not only of sector-specific nature, *i.e.* restricted to the health sector as the ones highlighted above, but appear to be of broader and general scope, encompassing prejudices that are common to all digitally-delivered services.

Against this backdrop, the broader data protection harms that data subjects are likely to suffer as a consequence of health data sharing practices can be sub-grouped in the three categories of (i) group profiling and group stigmatization; (ii) online nudging and manipulation upon data subjects' sensitive conditions; (iii) automated-decision making based on data subjects' sensitive conditions.

One of the greatest advancements of algorithmic processing techniques is given by the capability to extract associations and classification patterns from aggregated datasets.[319] The so-identified patterns lie at the very heart of so-called group profiling[320] or clustering techniques,[321] through which data processors construct profiles "pigeonholing" individuals on the basis of similar behavioural features.[322] These collective profiling practices have the specificity of classifying data subjects on the basis not only of the data points directly generated by them but also of the

[315] As some strand of the literature has been observing, in the digital dimension, "electronic communications about "private" issues take place in what is in any case a potentially public manner, so that the participants in the communication no longer address one another privately and individually, but frequently also quite unintentionally can reach a large number of people (. . .)". Ladeur (2016), p. 5.

[316] Sharon (2017), pp. 99–100, talking about a "disintegration of State and collective responsibility for health".

[317] Titmuss (1970), p. 233.

[318] Metcalf and Crawford (2016), pp. 1 ff., providing sensitive information flowing into health research data pools.

[319] Zarsky (2003), pp. 2 ff.

[320] Spina (2014), pp. 249 ff. Moerel and Prins (2016), pp. 20 ff.

[321] Specifically regarding scientific data, see Custers (2003), pp. 291 ff. More generally see Van der Sloot (2017), pp. 197 ff.

[322] For a broader assessment on the issue see Comandè (2017), pp. 169 ff.

ones generated by other, similarly rated, individuals.[323] This means that a certain data subject could be classified on the basis of calculated affinities with other subjects[324] and thus judged by group features he/she does not possess as single individuals.[325] In these regards, it has been interestingly observed in the literature that the boundaries of the so-formed groups are dynamic and thus particularly difficult to identify. Indeed, the groups are developed by constantly updated datasets, which in turn affect the formed models, by modifying and specifying them.[326] The correct association of an individual to a certain group both depends on the group profile itself and on the use that is made of the same profile.[327]

In this perspective, the reliability of the group profile itself can be affected by the previously described biases, and in particular by the wrong selection of target variables- *i.e.* the criteria that the analytics search for- and of the corresponding class labels- *i.e.* the categories formed on the basis of the selected criteria, as well as by biases in training data and in the correlations found among the same training data.[328]

Conversely, the reliability of the group profile's use can be impaired by the interpretation of the group profile and by the decisions that are taken upon the same group profile.[329] In this case, for example, an organisation could intentionally use correlations to discriminate on the basis of users' health conditions, by skewing the training data or selecting criteria of classification with the exact intent of generating discriminatory results.[330]

The group implications of health data pools are particularly evident in the case of genetic data, which as well known contains very sensitive information not only related to the originating data subject, but also to the members of his/her blood group, encompassing both past and future generations.[331]

The practical use of analytically-constructed group profiles provides the grounds for stigmatization courses, directly based on data subjects' collected sensitive information.[332] These stigmatization courses can widely transcend the strictly medical field. Negative health prospects or inferences can indeed activate a chain of

[323] See Cohen (2012), pp. 34 ff. See also Van der Sloot (2016), p. 177.

[324] On the issue, see Wachter (2020).

[325] Custers (2003).

[326] Data subjects are in this way constantly re-grouped into different clusters, without them knowing. Taylor et al. (2017), pp. 225 ff.

[327] Custers (2003), p. 293.

[328] See Council of Europe (2018), pp. 10 ff.

[329] Custers (2003), p. 296.

[330] Council of Europe (2018), pp. 13–14. See also Kroll et al. (2017), p. 682.

[331] Purtova (2017b), p. 192, and accompanying literature. See also Hallinan and De Hert (2017), pp. 175–196.

[332] See Roberts and Weeks Leonard (2017), pp. 484 ff.

"adverse" selection regarding job awards, insurance prices and targeted online advertising practices.[333]

This means that the group profiles formed on the basis of health data inform various businesses' (automated) decision making, giving rise to a profile-based "behavioural discrimination", limiting the autonomy of consumers in choosing products and services on the free market.[334] Such behavioural discrimination does not only imply price discrimination, but also more subtle forms of digital market manipulation,[335] inadvertently impacting on users' autonomy by "nudging" their opinions, interests and ultimately their (commercial) activities.[336]

This means, in other terms, that patients' and users' sensitive health information initially accessed for the conduction of health research, as grouped together along classifying profiles, risk to substantiate also new economic vulnerabilities based on sensitive health conditions[337] as well as new personal harms, deriving for example from the anxiety of having their sensitive conditions exposed to external surveillance and of being harmed because of such exposure.[338]

In the very end, thus, health group profiling and the manipulative implications it entails, ultimately enables the information "bioindustry" to influence patients' and users' knowledge and desires, impairing as a reflex also their ability to challenge and change the surrounding social environment.[339] As has been observed, the actions taken upon citizens' sensitive information, can fundamentally alter the nature of society, classifying and nudging everyone into predictable existences that end up being deprived of the freedom to choose and to self-determination.[340]

All this occurs without data subjects' awareness and control regarding group-based data processing, discriminatory decision-making and nudging. The need to address these concerns has triggered some reflections by the literature, regarding the

[333]Describing the process of de-contextualisation of the employment of health data, Orentlicher (2010), pp. 74 ff.

[334]See generally, Ezrachi and Stucke (2016), pp. 485 ff.

[335]The phenomenon of market manipulation in digital markets has been object of enquiry especially by the law and economics literature, see in particular Calo (2014), pp. 995 ff. See also Susser et al. (8 January 2019); Zarsky (2019), pp. 157 ff.

[336]Well describing the "hidden" nature of these new forms of online manipulation, Susser et al. (8 January 2019), p. 2, stating that "we argue that at its core, manipulation is hidden influence-the covert subversion of another person's decision-making power". This form of manipulation is also known as "nudging", see in this regard, Yeung (2017), pp. 118 ff.

[337]Evans (2009), p. 23, observing that "by trying to maximize profits using patients in any way possible, the unbalanced power of medical stakeholders over patients is perpetuated. Prioritising profits makes patients vulnerable to over-powering providers and undermines the health care system's effectiveness". Emphasis added. See also Comandè (2017), pp. 192–193, citing Moses (2 October 2013).

[338]The literature has lately come to assess the personal harm consisting in the anxiety of having sensitive personal data exposed to "external" collection and surveillance and of being concretely harmed (risk and anxiety as harms). See Solove and Citron (2018), pp. 737 ff.

[339]Purtova (2017b), p. 197.

[340]Radin (1996), pp. 513 ff.

need of a group privacy regulation in the form a collective management of personal data[341] as well as of the application of discriminatory law principles to the digital (health) environment.[342]

The need to find regulatory safeguards to the behavioural discrimination of the less "healthy rated" groups of users, is even more urgent, if one thinks about the possible repercussions of these practices on the same health sector. Indeed, although occurring, as has been shown, largely outside the medical field- and more precisely in the commercial online environment, employment sector and insurance field-, the described discriminatory practices can lead to an outright devaluation and to the lowering of the social status of the targeted groups (for example, smoking people or overweight people),[343] which in turn reduces their health conditions.[344] In these regards, it has been interestingly observed that people living in a stigmatized condition may try to conceal it, with resulting psychological distress and the suffering of additional harms.[345]

3.3.7 Health Data Pools and Commercial Interests

Health research collaborations among different economic parties accelerate production processes with a more sophisticated technologically market outcome.[346] In this perspective, the collection and access to research valuable health data enables the stakeholders involved in data pools initiatives to enjoy significant monetary rewards.[347] Hence, the driving interest underlying companies engaging in data pools is of economic nature, that is profit maximisation.

In the case of public health institutions, as the Royal Free Hospital, the disposal of more effective monitoring and treating technologies enhances the quality of the delivered services, with that eventually also enhancing the institutions' revenues. Conversely, the IBM-Italy case shows an outright attempt carried out by a public administration to monetise health data as such, irrespective of the subsequent market outcomes. Along these lines, also pharmaceutical companies commercially benefit from the exploitation of varied datasets for the digitalisation of their products, with

[341] See Montelero (2016), pp. 238 ff.

[342] See Wachter (2020), pp. 369 ff. and Hacker (2018).

[343] De Hert and Quinn (2014), pp. 19 ff.

[344] This claim is also made by Roberts and Weeks Leonard (2017), in particular at pp. 488–489.

[345] Schabert et al. (2013), pp. 1 ff., making the example of a person trying to conceal her diabetes and making therefore unhealthy eating choices in the effort to hide his/her condition.

[346] Drexl (2018), p. 10.

[347] See Hoffmann and Podgurski (2012), pp. 108–109.

that gaining commercial advantage over their competitors, thanks to the access to cutting edge technologies.

In this context, it needs to be observed that the commercial interests relating to health data pools of big data companies are of broader scope than the ones of the above-mentioned stakeholders. Indeed, pharmaceutical companies and other public institutions involved in health care markets mostly make of the delivery of healthcare products and services their sole commercial activity.[348] This is not the case of big data companies, which are active on multiple market sides.[349]

From a structural standpoint, big data companies are platform-based businesses,[350] working as integrated systems, which "offer a variety of information services under one brand"[351] and in which there are continuous interactions between seemingly separate markets. These interactions generate so-called indirect network effects, leading to the exchange of data between different sides and increasing each side's efficiency. The interoperability between the distinct markets thus enables big data companies to appropriate data originating from one side for the purposes of another side.[352]

In case of data-driven health enquiries, thus, the entrance of big data companies in the field of digital health structurally connects some economic sides with others along the lines of constant information flows.[353] This is because the platform itself relies on a technological processing infrastructure that facilitates interactions between separate market sides.[354] This means that health data are constantly "re-coded" on the various sides of the platforms, enabling big data companies to extract the commercial value embedded in the continuously auto-generating health datasets for the purposes of services and products that are not related to health, but that are relevant for other markets.[355] It thus appears that the commercial interests of big data companies widely transcend the healthcare field and encompass the variety of markets in which their platforms are articulated.

In this perspective, thus, health-inflected data accessed by big data companies shape the scientific evidence needed for the marketing not only of new digital health devices and services, but also of broader-encompassing digital services. This ultimately appears to aggravate the overlap between the spheres of health research and digital markets, that is, between public interest-animated and commercially-oriented activities.

[348] Sharon (2016), p. 6.

[349] The multisided nature of digital platforms, is well described by Cohen (2017), pp. 133 ff.

[350] The literature assessing the so-called new platform economy is extensive, see, amongst others, Bush et al. (2016), pp. 3 ff.; Evans (22 December 2015), pp. 1–48.

[351] Cohen (2016), p. 377.

[352] Ladeur (2016), p. 9.

[353] Cohen (2017), pp. 143–145. Highlighting the flow of personal data into larger networks and economies without users being aware of this, Boyd and Crawford (2012), pp. 662–679.

[354] Cohen (2017), p. 144.

[355] Powles and Hodson (2017), p. 356.

The existence of strong commercial interests is certainly not new to the health research setting, which has been traditionally characterised by conflict of interests between private interests and the public dimension of health research.[356] However, in the digital environment, the attraction of health research activities carried out upon health data pools into the sphere of big corporations' commercial interests results to be more interesting than ever in light of the variety of commercial activities these companies perform. Health data derived from the pool can thus be treated for the tailoring of other non-health related digital activities carried out by these big data companies, as profiling in turn serving the purposes of targeted advertisement practices,[357] personalised pricing strategies[358] and other discriminatory online conducts.[359]

In this perspective, for example, the acquisition of Google DeepMind by Google right after that the subsidiary had accessed Royal Free Hospital's patient data, reflects the risk that, once accessed and collected, health data are employed by big data companies for purposes that are not directly related to health research, but, that are specifically aimed at maximising big data companies' profits.

This exacerbates the overlap between the spheres of health research and health market, that is, between public interest-animated and commercially-oriented activities.

Direct access to health data pools by big data companies that are member of the pool needs to be further distinguished from the indirect access to these same health data pools by a vast range of other corporations that are outside the initial pool but that nonetheless further mine these data pools for their own commercial purposes.[360]

Through health data mining endeavours, mostly mediated and facilitated by data brokering companies, health data are aggregated from different sources and made available for purchase.[361] subsequently employed for other commercial purposes

---

356 See, amongst others, the interesting empirical analysis of Goldner (2009), p. 1211.

357 Enquiring the employment of sensitive data for the purposes of targeted advertisements, Marks (2020).

358 For a description of the phenomenon of personalised pricing and assessment of it from a competition law perspective, see Graef (2018), pp. 541 ff.; Maggiolino and Muraca (2019), pp. 483 ff.

359 For an overview, see Council of Europe (2018), pp. 14 ff., recalling, for example, systems to search for images, or facial recognition systems with difficulties in recognising non-white men. For an overview of the ways platforms' design choices shape and perpetuate discrimination in the contemporary economy, see Levy and Barocas (2018), pp. 1183 ff. Specifically referring to discrimination based on health data within and outside the health sector, see Hiller (2016), pp. 251 ff.; Hoffmann (2018), pp. 85 ff.

360 See Marks (11 October 2017).

361 Pettypiece and Robertson (11 September 2014), documenting the case of the sale of information regarding elderly people health conditions; Hicken (19 December 2013), assessing the case of the sale by consumer data companies to marketers of lists of rape victims and of people who suffered from HIV and AIDS.

such as the calculation of employees' disease risks[362] or of insurance rates,[363] and in these regards, especially of sensitive insurance sectors such as those related to life, health and accident insurances.[364]

Once health data flow outside the strictly medical field, thus, public and commercial interests involved in data-driven health innovation appear not to be aligned anymore, with health data ultimately feeding the commercial interests of the economic players who come to handle health data. Thus, he widespread employment of health data far outside the health research field leads to the commercial (mis-) appropriation of health research results.

This ultimately exacerbates the already well-known problem of the lack of economic returns to research subjects.[365] Indeed, in the case of health data-driven research, the vast range of data subjects, which provide their health data for research purposes, are not only cut-off from the commercial gains deriving from the marketed digital health devices and services tested and designed upon their data, but also, and more interestingly, from all the "underground" profits that are made from the processing of health data for non-health related digital services. The variety of commercial interests involved in the processing of health data ultimately ends up privatizing the "common" value entrenched in health data pools.[366] The considerations made so far entail a further consequence, to be perceived at a regulatory level. Indeed, the private and commercial governance of health data pools by big private corporations, such as high tech corporations, appears to partly supplant- inadvertedly- States' "public" regulation of health research.[367] In respect to the practice of health data pooling carried out by an array of different public and private entities, indeed, traditional health research regulations appear progressively to be eroded by new forms of private governance of research carried out through digital data pools. In this perspective, traditional regulations regarding health

[362] De Armond (2012), pp. 1136–1137. See, more generally also Barocas and Selbst (2016), widely considering the threats of data-driven discrimination in the employment sector, from the moment of collection to the subsequent phase of predictive correlations.

[363] See Chirita (2018), p. 154.

[364] Evans (2009), pp. 37 ff. Brothers and Rothstein (2014), pp. 43–51.

[365] The problem of the over-appropriation of research profits by R&D corporations, who don't share their profits with research subjects has been widely assessed in the literature, see Kahn (2014), especially at pp. 843–849 and 878, where the A. highlights the phenomenon of the turning over of public participation in clinical research to private interests. This is well reflected by the story of Henrietta Lacks, who was the source of the immortal cell line. The story of Henrietta Lacks has been documented by Skloot (2011).

[366] See Kahn (2014), pp. 843–849. See also Purtova (2017b), pp. 177 ff. This is what some other strand of the literature has referred to as the phenomenon of "commodification of data in public science". See Reichman and Uhlir (2003), p. 367.

[367] From a more general perspective and with regards to "online speech platforms", Balkin (2018), pp. 1194 ff., affirming that "platform operators become special-purpose sovereigns who govern populations of end-users".

research reveal their unsuitability in respect to the new digital dimension, raising the need of a new "systemic oversight" of data-driven research.[368]

3.3.8 *Health Data Pools and Competition*

Antitrust scholars have traditionally highlighted the risks entailed in information sharing practices between competitors or potential competitors.[369] Information sharing creates indeed a sort of coordination between some firms—competitors or not—on the market, potentially harming the public interest and with that other market participants and/or consumers.[370]

Under these premises, in the specific case of health data pools, it appears that anticompetitive conducts can occur either outside or inside a same health data pool: anticompetitive conducts can be generated either (i) by the members of the pool considered as a unique economic entity- this is the case for example of a joint venture or (ii) by the stronger member of the health data pool.

In the first case, the massive aggregation of different health datasets could determine exclusionary conducts on health-related markets, such as the refusal to deal/license health data to operators acting outside of the pool. As has been rightly observed, companies controlling the aggregated health datasets could ground such refusal in data protection law's provisions restricting personal data processing by prohibiting secondary transfers of personal data.[371] A refusal to transfer collected health data to actually or potentially competing businesses would mean denying a key research input to both private and public stakeholders involved in health research. These conducts could thus ultimately raise barriers to entry for newcomers intending to develop competitive treatments, diagnoses and services.[372]

In addition to this, the collection of big health datasets by high tech companies is likely to have repercussions also onto non-health related markets, *i.e.* on broader digital markets: health data collected on body-based markets could subsequently be aggregated with other digital datasets collected on the other sides of big data's multisided platforms. This could in turn foster network effects strengthening the market power of already dominant companies and leading to abuses of dominant positions under art. 102 TFEU. These abuses could take the form of traditional exploitative conducts,[373] as the setting of unfair prices, *i.e.* discriminatory or

---

[368] Vayena and Blasimme (2018); Fish (29 October 2018).

[369] See amongst others, Ghezzi and Maggiolino (24 April 2015).

[370] Svetiev (2007), p. 647.

[371] Determann (2020). For a deeper analysis on the data protection regime regarding sensitive personal data, as health data, see infra Chap. 5, Sect. 5.3.

[372] Bundeskartellamt (October 2017). For the literature see Rubinfeld and Gal (2017), p. 375.

[373] See generally Botta and Wiedemann (5 June 2018).

excessive prices, both on the user side and on other sides such as the advertisement side.[374]

Recent case law and scholarship are investigating also less common exploitative conducts deriving from abuses of dominant positions, such as the setting of unfair terms and conditions for digital services[375] as well as the heightening of consumer switching, generating a situation of consumer lock-in.[376]

Ultimately, in case health data pools are connected to pricing algorithms, price collusion practices could likewise occur.[377]

Different considerations need to be conversely made with regards to the anticompetitive threats possibly emerging *within* the same data pool, this meaning among the members of the formed health data pool "agreement".

From this perspective, it has been observed that by establishing collaborative research alliances, the partners of such alliances establish a "pre-competitive space",[378] to be defined as "the time during research and development where there is collaboration but no competition".[379] In these regards, the case studies have shown how such precompetitive space permits partners to access external information and technologies in control of other market participants for the engagement in joint ongoing innovation and the development of new market solutions.[380]

However, as has already been suggested in the first chapter,[381] it could well happen that in the formed collaborative pre-competitive space, power imbalances start to emerge, finally resulting in opportunistic behaviours by the strongest party of the collaboration, which threaten the established collaboration.

The sharing of commercially valuable information structuring a given research collaboration could indeed trigger the attempt by one of the partners to appropriate the information resources pooled together through the collaboration, with that excluding the other collaborators from the innovation process, which had been started together.[382] In other terms, the disclosure of datasets to collaborators could render the disclosing company vulnerable to takeover strategies enacted by the

[374]See Maggiolino (13 June 2017).

[375]The German Antitrust Authority has recently taken clear decisive actions against exploitative digital abuses. See Bundeskartellamt (15 February 2019a). The decision has opened a wide debate in the scholarship regarding the opportunity to extend traditional antitrust tools to new harmful conducts in digital markets, see amongst others, Colangelo and Maggiolino (2019); Schneider (2018).

[376]Sluijs et al. (2012), p. 12.

[377]The issue of algorithmic collusion is currently object of a growing debate among both regulators and the scholarship. See Ezrachi and Stucke (31 May 2017). See also Calvano et al. (27 June 2018) and Picht and Freund (15 May 2018); Beneke and Mackenrodt (2019), pp. 109 ff.

[378]Kahn (2014), pp. 873–874.

[379]Bubela et al. (2012), p. 3, arguing also that "the line between precompetitive and competitive research is in constant flux".

[380]Svetiev (2007), pp. 632–633.

[381]See in particular supra Chap. 2, Sect. 2.2.4.

[382]Svetiev (2007), pp. 632 ff.

same collaborators once the collaboration itself has become stable and has produced its first outputs. More concretely, one party could deny to the other parties of the pool access to the information collected and generated by the pool itself.

Such information takeovers would deprive the weaker collaborators not only from the technological assets they were exclusively controlling before the collaboration, but also from their ability to innovate- ability that was exactly grounded in the resources that are taken over by the more influent party to the collaboration.

Far from being merely abstract hypotheses, such collaboration collapses have passed under the scrutiny of competition authorities both in the United States and in Europe.[383]

In conclusion, it can be overall observed that the anticompetitive conducts occurring both outside and inside the pool are likely to create significant market imbalances in the accessibility and processing of health data for health research and innovation purposes.

Indeed, by taking advantage of the informational assets pooled together through the collaboration, big corporations could increasingly accumulate market power to the detriment of small and medium enterprises, such as innovative start-ups or smaller research institutes, which progressively lose access to important types of data needed to research on innovative treatments and diagnoses.[384]

3.4 Findings: Connecting the Dots in Health Data Pools

Health data pools as the new means in which data-driven health research is carried out touch upon a variety of interests of a range of different stakeholders.

First of all, by satisfying companies' commercial interests in profit maximisation, not only, as has been show, in digital health related markets, but also in other-apparently unrelated- digital markets, information interactions and information availability result to be a precondition for a fruitful exercise of the freedom to conduct business in digital markets.[385]

As has been illustrated, collaboration alliances though health data sharing allow big high tech corporations to exploit to the maximum their sophisticated technological assets for the purposes of scientific research, thus consolidating their presence and role in health-related markets.[386]

Conversely, collaborative health research projects with high tech companies, enable traditional health research actors as public healthcare providers and pharmaceutical companies to keep up with the fast-evolving technological progress and thus

[383] See infra Chap. 7.

[384] Stressing this point, Determann (2020).

[385] Art. 16 CFREU: "The freedom to conduct a business in accordance with Union law and national laws and practices is recognised".

[386] So Sharon (2016).

to competitively re-structure their production and service delivery processes, in line with the developments occurring also in other markets.

Under these premises, innovation outputs resulting from the information synergies in health research appear to have both positive and negative effects, all strictly connected to the specificities of the digital health sector.

As far as the positive effects are concerned, health data pools serve public interests in scientific knowledge and research advancements, benefiting society and the public at large. On the more specific market side, scientific progress stirred by the sharing of information among different economic stakeholders is supposed to lead to faster and more cost-saving research and development processes, enabling a faster design and marketization of new health-related products. The resulting price and quality features are supposed to enhance consumer welfare in the markets of the new digital health products and services. As has been observed, higher consumer welfare in these markets can positively reflect itself on a higher level of health enjoyed by patients.

From a legal perspective, this suggests that health data pools practices promote a variety of rights that are codified at European Union level, as the right to science enshrined in art. 13 ECHR,[387] the right to consumer protection and patients' safety as affirmed at art. 38 ECHR[388] and patients' right to health under art. 35 ECHR,[389] at the same time fostering also their right to access services of general economic interests under art. 36 ECHR.[390]

However, a more careful consideration of these same rights in the context of digital health markets soon reveals the risks possibly originating from health data pooling practices and the resulting scientific evidence. These risks primarily relate to the rise of new socio-economic barriers to the accessibility of digital health products and services, the social inclusiveness of the lines of research explored by collaborating actors, and ultimately the quality of the employed scientific datasets and of the ensuing products. These concerns pose a significant challenge to a full satisfaction of and compliance with the above-considered rights to science, to health and to safe health products and services. Indeed, these rights could be impaired by the newly emerging health disparities and the new discriminatory patterns these disparities give

---

[387] Art. 13 CFREU: "The arts and scientific research shall be free of constraint. Academic freedom shall be respected". For an assessment of the right to science from an international law perspective, see Knoppers and Thorogood (2017), pp. 54–55.

[388] Art. 38 CFREU: "Union policies shall ensure a high level of consumer protection".

[389] Art. 35 CFREU: "Everyone has the right of access to preventive health care and the right to benefit from medical treatment under the conditions established by national laws and practices. A high level of human health protection shall be ensured in the definition and implementation of all the Union's policies and activities".

[390] Art. 36 CFREU: "The Union recognises and respects access to services of general economic interest as provided for in national laws and practices, in accordance with the Treaties, in order to promote the social and territorial cohesion of the Union".

rise to.[391] Moreover, consumers and patients who are supposed to benefit from health data pooling practices and their market outputs risk to suffer different kinds of harms originating in the wider sphere of digital markets and distorting the above-identified benefits.

More precisely, with regards to the data subjects who provide the upstream information for health data pools, massive health information aggregation endeavours pose significant threats to the data protection of the subjects whose identifiable information flows into the always newly alimenting health data pools.

As the case studies have well highlighted, these risks concern the uncontrolled transfer of health data in the data "pockets" of different entities, and the processing of such data for purposes that go widely beyond health-related research projects.[392] Health data can indeed be further employed for the classification of individuals on the basis of their actual or future health conditions, this serving the allocation of the most different (digital) services and, ultimately, the determination of patterns of inclusion and exclusion from society.[393]

The illustrated scenarios thus reflect the dangers to users' fundamental right to data protection[394] as concretised in the General Data Protection Regulation. In these regards, the same Regulation implicitly warns that the compression of data protection law principles and rules in the digital environment can undermine other "rights and freedoms of natural persons", first of all, the right to non-discrimination.[395]

From a different market perspective, the massive processing of health data and connected data misuses, can fuel anticompetitive conducts, which ultimately freeze the innovation in digital health markets. As has been highlighted, indeed, the anticompetitive practices carried out by collaboration groups considered as a unique economic entity could serve the strengthening of the market dominance of the same research consortium, concentrating the health information in the consortium research infrastructure and with that reducing the same consortium's *ex post* incentives to innovate. Different considerations need to be conversely made with regards to the threats of collapses of established data pools as a consequence of data takeovers by the dominant member of the pool. These threats could weaken companies' *ex ante* incentives to collaborate for market innovation purposes. The freezing of incentives to innovate resulting from these anticompetitive behaviours would in turn negatively impact on scientific and health advancements to which innovation in the digital health sector is linked.

---

[391] See art 20 ECHR, stating the everyone's equality before the law and art. 21(1) ECHR, according to which "any discrimination based on any ground such as sex, race, colour, ethnic or social origin, genetic features, language, religion or belief, political or any other opinion, membership of a national minority, property, birth, disability, age or sexual orientation shall be prohibited". Emphasis added.

[392] Purtova (2017a), pp. 64 ff.

[393] Comandè and Schneider (2018), pp. 284 ff.

[394] See art. 8(1) ECHR: "everyone has the right to the protection of personal data concerning him or her".

[395] See recital 75 General Data Protection Regulation.

From a regulatory standpoint, this spectrum of interests involved in health data pooling practices triggers the need to carefully weigh—at regulatory level—the promotion of the free-flow of health information and the related freedom to conduct business in digital health markets, against the risks of emerging data—related harms and anticompetitive behaviors. More precisely, innovation and broader health gains, respectively linked to businesses' fundamental rights to conduct business and to patients' fundamental right to health, need to be carefully outweighed against data protection and anti-discrimination concerns, equally protected as fundamental rights within the European Union.

References

23andMe (12 January 2015) 23andMe announces collaboration with Pfizer Inc. to conduct genetic research through 23andMe's research platform. https://www.prnewswire.com/news-releases/23andme-announces-collaboration-with-pfizer-inc-to-conduct-genetic-research-through-23andmes-research-platform-300018683.html

23andMe Privacy Highlights. https://www.23andme.com/about/privacy/

Adamson AS, Smith A (2018) Machine learning and health care disparities in dermatology. JAMA Dermatol 154:1247–1248

Amante DJ, Hogan TP, Pagoto SL, English TM, Lapane KL (2015) Access to care and use of the internet to search for health information: results from the US National Health Interview Survey. J Med Internet Res 17(e106):1–10

Angier H et al (2018) Progress towards using community context with clinical data in primary care. Family Med Com Health 7:1–5

Annas J, Sherman E (1992) Gene mapping: using law and ethics as guides. Oxford University Press, Oxford

Arora A, Fosfuri A, Gambardella A (2001) Markets for Technology: the economics of innovation and corporate strategy. MIT Press Books, Cambridge

Arrow K (1962) Economic welfare and the allocation of resources for invention. National Bureau of economic research, the rate and directive of inventive activity: economic and social factors. Princeton University Press, Princeton

Averitt W, Lande H, Nihoul P (2011) "Consumer choice" is where we are all going- So Let's go together. Concurrences-Revue Des Droits De La Concurrence 2:1–3

Balkin JM (2018) Free speech in the algorithmic society: big data, private governance, and new school speech regulation. UC Davis Law Rev 51:1149–1210

Balkin JM, Siegel RB (2003) The American civil rights tradition: Anticlassification or Antisubordination? Univ Miami Law Rev 58:9–34

Balto DA, Mongoven JF (1999) Antitrust enforcement in pharmaceutical industry mergers. Food Drug Law J 54:255–278

Barbacetto G (17 February 2017a) A IBM tutti i nostri dati sanitari. In cambio della nuova sede sull'aera Expo. Gianni Barbacetto Blog. http://www.giannibarbacetto.it/2017/02/15/a-ibm-tutti-i-nostri-dati-sanitari-in-cambio-della-nuova-sede-sullarea-expo/

Barbacetto G (21 March 2017b) I nostri dati sanitari all'IBM: il Garante apre un'inchiesta. Il Fatto Quotidiano. https://www.ilfattoquotidiano.it/premium/articoli/i-nostri-dati-sanitari-allibm-il-garante-apre-uninchiesta/

Barocas S, Selbst AD (2016) Big data's disparate impact. Cal Law Rev 104:671–732

Bashshur RL (2002) Telemedicine and health care. Telemed e-health 8:5–12

Ben-Asher D (2000) In need of treatment? Merger control, pharmaceutical innovation and consumer welfare. J Legal Med 21:271–349

Beneke F, Mackenrodt MO (2019) Artificial intelligence and collusion. IIC 50:109–134

Bernardi L (3 April 2018) Ibm, Watson e dati sanitari, cosa sta succedendo davvero in Italia. Start Magazine. https://www.startmag.it/innovazione/watson-ibm-dati-sanitari/

Bobinski MA (2003) Health disparities and the law: wrongs in search for a right. Am J Law Med 29: 363–380

Bol N, Helberger N, Weert JCM (2018) Differences in Mobile health app use: a source of new digital inequalities? Inf Soc 34:183–193

Bork RH, Sidak JG (2013) The misuse of profit margins to infer market power. J Compet Law Econ 9:511–530

Boseley S, Lewis P (24 February 2016) Smart Care: How Google DeepMind is Working with NHS Hospitals. The Guardian. https://www.theguardian.com/technology/2016/feb/24/smartphone-apps-google-deepmind-nhs-hospitals

Botta M, Wiedemann K (5 June 2018) Eu Competition Law Enforcement Vis-À-Vis Exploitative Conducts in the Data Economy-Exploring the Terra Incognita. Max Planck Institute for Innovation and Competition Research Paper N. 18-08. https://papers.ssrn.com/sol3/papers.cfm?abstract_id=3184119

Boyd D, Crawford K (2012) Critical questions for big data: provocations for a cultural, technological, and scholarly phenomenon. Inf Commun Soc 15:662–679

Boyle J (2003) The second enclosure movement and the construction of the public domain. Law Contemp Probl 66:33–74

Boyle J, Jenkins J (2003) The genius of intellectual property and the need of the public domain. In: Esanu JM, Uhlir PF (eds) The role of scientific and technical data and information in the public domain: proceedings of a symposium, National Research Council, steering committee on the role of scientific and technical data and information in the public domain, Office of International Scientific and Technical Information Programs. The National Academies Press, Washington, pp 10–15

Britnell M, Bakalar R, Shehata A (2016) Digital Health: Heaven or Hell?-How Technology Can Drive or Derail the Quest for Efficient, High Quality Health Care. KPMG International https://assets.kpmg/content/dam/kpmg/pdf/2016/03/digital-health-heaven-hell.pdf

Brodley JF (1987) The economic goals of antitrust: efficiency, consumer welfare and technological Progress. New York Univ Law Rev 62:1020–1053

Brothers KB, Rothstein MA (2014) Ethical, legal and social implications of incorporating personalized medicine into healthcare. Future Med 15:43–51

Bubela T, Fitzgerald GA, Gold R (2012) Recalibrating intellectual property rights to enhance translational research collaborations. Sci Transl Med 4:122cm3

Bundeskartellamt (Oktober 2017) Big Data und Wettbewerb Schriftenreihe-Wettbewerb und Verbraucheschutz in der Digitalen Wirtschaft. https://www.bundeskartellamt.de/SharedDocs/Publikation/DE/Schriftenreihe_Digitales/Schriftenreihe_Digitales_1.pdf?__blob=publicationFile&v=3

Bundeskartellamt (15 February 2019a) Facebook, Exploitative Business Terms Pursuant to Section 19(1) GWB For Inadequate Data Processing. https://www.bundeskartellamt.de/SharedDocs/Entscheidung/EN/Fallberichte/Missbrauchsaufsicht/2019/B6-22-16.pdf?__blob=publicationFile&v=3

Bundeskartellamt (7 February 2019b) Bundeskartellamt Prohibits Facebook From Combining User Data From Different Sources. https://www.bundeskartellamt.de/SharedDocs/Meldung/EN/Pressemitteilungen/2019/07_02_2019_Facebook.html

Burk DL (2015) Patents as data aggregators in personalized medicine. Boston Univ J Sci Technol Law 21:233–255

Burk DL, Lemley MA (2003) Policy levers in patent law. Va Law Rev 89:1575–1696

Burri M (2011) Re-conceptualising the global digital divide. J Intell Prop Inf Technol E-Commer Law 3:217–225

Bush C, Sculte-Nölte H, Wiewióroska-Domagalska A, Zoll F (2016) The rise of the platform economy: a new challenge for EU consumer law? Eur J Consum Mark Law 5:3–10

Caldicott F (2013) Information: to Share or not to Share? The Information Governance Review. https://www.gov.uk/government/uploads/system/uploads/attachment_data/file/192572/2900774_InfoGovernance_accv2.pdf
Caliskan A, Bryson JJ, Narayanan A (2017) Semantics derived automatically from language corpora contain human-like biases. Science 356:183–186
Calo R (2014) Digital market manipulation. Geo Wash Law Rev 82:995–1051
Calvano E, Calzolari G, Denicolò V, Pastorello S (27 June 2018) Algorithmic Pricing: What Implications For Antitrust Policy?. SSRN https://papers.ssrn.com/sol3/papers.cfm?abstract_id=3209781
Cattell J, Chilukuri S, Levy M (April 2013) How big data can revolutionize pharmaceutical R&D. Mckinsey. https://www.mckinsey.com/industries/pharmaceuticals-and-medical-products/our-insights/how-big-data-can-revolutionize-pharmaceutical-r-and-d
Chirita AD (2018) The rise of big data and the loss of privacy. In: Bakhoum M, Conde-Gallego B, Mackenrodt MO, Surblytė-Namavičienė G (eds) Personal data in competition, consumer protection and intellectual property law-towards a holistic approach? MPI studies on intellectual property and competition law. Springer, Berlin, pp 153–189
City Block online available at. https://www.cityblock.com/about
Cohen J (1997) The genomics gamble. Science 275:767–772
Cohen J (2012) Configuring the networked self: law, code and the play of everyday practice. Yale University Press, New Haven
Cohen J (2016) The regulatory state in the information age. Theor Enq Law 17:369–414
Cohen JE (2017) The law for the platform economy. Univ Cal Law Rev 51:133–204
Colangelo G, Maggiolino M (2017a) Big data, data protection and antitrust in the wake of the Bundeskartellamt case against Facebook. Ital Antit Rev 1:104–112
Colangelo G, Maggiolino M (2017b) Data protection in attention markets: protecting privacy through competition? JECLAP 8:363–369
Colangelo G, Maggiolino M (2019) Antitrust Über Alles-whither competition law after Facebook? World Compet Law Econ Rev 42:355–376
Comandè G (2017) Regulating algorithms' regulation? First Ethico-legal principles, problems and opportunities of algorithms. In: Cerquitelli T, Quercia D, Pasquale F (eds) Transparent data mining for small and big data. Springer, New York, pp 169–206
Comandè G, Schneider G (2018) Regulatory challenges of data mining practices: the case of the never-ending lifecycles of health data. Eur J Health Law 25:284–307
Costa-Cabral F, Lynskey O (2017) Family ties: the intersection between data protection and competition EU law. Consum Mark Law Rev 54:11–50
Council of Europe (2018) Discrimination, Artificial Intelligence, and Algorithmic Decision-making- Study By Prof. Frederik Zuiderveen Borgesius. https://rm.coe.int/discrimination-artificial-intelligence-and-algorithmic-decision-making/1680925d73
Council of the European Union (28 November 2017) Health in the Digital Society - Making Progress in Data-driven Innovation in the Field of Health. http://data.consilium.europa.eu/doc/document/ST-14078-2017-INIT/en/pdf
Crawford K (1 April 2013) The hidden biases in big data. HBR. https://hbr.org/2013/04/the-hidden-biases-in-big-data
Croosley M (2003) Infected judgment: legal responses to physician's bias. Villanova Law Rev 48: 195–303
Cseres K (2007) The controversies of the consumer welfare standard. Compet Law Rev 3:121–173
Custers B (2003) Effects of unreliable group profiling by means of data mining. In: Grieser G, Tanaka Y, Yamamoto A (eds) Discovery science-6th international conference, DS 2003, Sapporo, Japan, 17–19 October 2003 proceedings. Springer, Berlin, pp 291–296
Darlymple D (2003) Scientific knowledge as a global public good: contribution to innovation and economics. In: Esanu JM, Uhlir PF (eds) The role of scientific and technical data and information in the public domain: proceedings of a symposium, National Research Council, steering committee on the role of scientific and technical data and information in the public domain,

Office of International Scientific and Technical Information Programs. The National Academies Press, Washington, pp pp 35–52
David PA (2000a) Digital Technologies, Research Collaborations and the Extension of Intellectual Property in Science: Will Building "Good Fences" Really Make "Good Neighbours"?. Stanford Institute for Economic Policy Research, Discussion Paper N. 00-33, 2000. https://www.researchgate.net/publication/4787669
David PA (2000b) The Digital Technology Boomerang: New Intellectual Property Rights Threaten Global Open Science. Stanford Department of Economics Working Paper N. 00-006. https://ideas.repec.org/p/wpa/wuwpdc/0502012.html
David PA (2003) The economic logic of 'open science' and the balance between private property rights and the public domain in scientific data and information: A Primer. In: Esanu JM, Uhlir PF (eds) The role of scientific and technical data and information in the public domain: Proceedings of a Symposium, National Research Council, Steering Committee on the Role of Scientific and Technical Data and Information in the Public Domain, Office of International Scientific and Technical Information Programs. The National Academies Press, pp 19–35
David PA (2005) Koyaanisqatsi in cyberspace-the economics of an "out-of-balance" regime of private property rights in digital data and information. In: Maskus KE, Reichman JH (eds) International public goods and transfer of technology under a globalized intellectual property regime. Cambridge University Press, Cambridge, pp 79–120
De Armond ED (2012) To cloak the within: protecting employees from personality testing. DePaul Law Rev 61:1129–1184
De Hert P, Quinn P (2014) Self-respect- "a Rawlsian primary good" unprotected by the European convention on human rights and its lack of a coherent approach to stigmatization. Int J Discrim Law 14:19–53
Deaton A (May 1999) Inequalities in Income and Inequalities in Health. NBER Working Paper 7141. https://www.nber.org/papers/w7141.pdf
DeepMind (2016a) Acute Kidney Injury, Streams. https://deepmind.com/applied/deepmind-health/streams/
DeepMind (2016b) Memorandum of Understanding. Online available at https://storagegoogleapis.com/deepminddata/assets/health/Memorandum%20of%20understanding%20REDACTED%20FINAL.pdf
DeepMind (2016c) Waking Project Privacy Impact Assessment. https://storage.googleapis.com/deepminddata/assets/health/Privacy%20Impact%20Assessment%20for%20Waking%20Project%2027%20Jan%202016%20V0%201%20redacted.pdf
Dees RH (2018) Public health and normative public goods. Public Health Ethics 11:20–26
Denozza F (1988) Chicago, l'efficienza e il diritto antitrust. Giur Comm I:5–34
Denozza F (2010) Il Progetto teorico dell'analisi economica del diritto antitrust e il suo fallimento. In: Rabitti Bedogni C, Barucci P (eds) 20 anni di antitrust, L'evoluzione dell'Autorità Garante della Concorrenza e del Mercato. Giappichelli, Turin, pp 137–153
Determann L (2020) Healthy data protection. Mich Technol Law Rev 26:229–278
Dhir AA (2011) Corporate selective reporting of clinical drug trial results as a violation of the right to health. In: Rioux MH, Basser LA, Jones M (eds) Critical perspectives on human rights and disability law. Martinus Nijhoff Publishers, Leiden, pp 341–366
Drexl J (27 April 2018) Data Access and Data Control in the Era of Connected Devices. Study on Behalf of the European Consumer Organisation BEUC. https://www.beuc.eu/publications/beuc-x-2018-121_data_access_and_control_in_the_area_of_connected_devices.pdf
Drexl J, Hilty RM et al. (9 September 2016) Data ownership and access to data, Position statement of the Max Planck Institute for Innovation and Competition of the 16th August 2016 on the Current European Debate, Max Planck Institute for Innovation and Competition Research Paper No. 16-10. SSRN. https://papers.ssrn.com/sol3/papers.cfm?abstract_id=2833165
Editorial (19 June 2005) The First Race-Based Medicine. https://www.nytimes.com/2005/06/19/opinion/the-first-racebased-medicine.html
Eisenberg R (2007) The role of the FDA in innovation policy. Mich Technol Law Rev 13:345–388

Eisenberg RS (1996) Public research and private development: patents and technology transfer in government-sponsored research. Va Law Rev 82:1663–1727

Emam K, Waldo A, Wright C (2014) Webinar: Fear and Loathing of Data Monetization. Privacy Analytics. https://privacy-analytics.com/de-id-university/webinars/webinar-fear-and-loathing-in-data-monetization/

Etienne JM, Skalli A, Theodossiou I (2011) Do economic inequality harm health? Evidence from Europe. J Income Distrib 20:57–74

Etro F (2009) Antitrust issues in dynamic markets. In: Kokkori I, Lianos I (eds) The reform of EC competition law: new challenges. Kluwer Law International, Houston pp 327–343

European Commission (11 March 2008) Google/DoubleClick, Case N. Comp./M. 4731. http://ec.europa.eu/competition/mergers/cases/decisions/m4731_20080311_20682_en.pdf

European Commission (2009) Guidance on the Commission's enforcement priorities in applying art. 82 of the EC Treaty to abusive exclusionary conduct by dominant undertakings OJ C, 45, 7

European Commission (29 February 2012) Communication from the Commission to the European Parliament and the Council on Taking forward the Strategic Implementation Plan of the European Innovation Partnership on Active and Healthy Ageing. https://eur-lex.europa.eu/legal-content/EN/TXT/PDF/?uri=CELEX:52012DC0083&from=EN

European Commission (2 July 2014a) Communication from the Commission to the European Parliament, the Council, the European Economic and Social Committee and the Committee of the Regions, 'Towards a thriving data-driven economy'. https://ec.europa.eu/digital-single-market/en/news/communication-data-driven-economy

European Commission (3 October 2014b) Facebook/Whatsapp, Case N. Comp./M. 7217. http://ec.europa.eu/competition/mergers/cases/decisions/m7217_20141003_20310_3962132_EN.pdf

European Commission (23 February 2016a) Sanofi/Google/DMI JV, Case M. 7813. http://ec.europa.eu/competition/mergers/cases/decisions/m7813_479_2.pdf

European Commission (1 April 2016b) Competition Policy Brief-EU Merger Control and Innovation. http://ec.europa.eu/competition/publications/cpb/2016/2016_001_en.pdf

European Commission (6 December 2016c) Microsoft/Linkedin, Case COMP/M.8124 http://ec.europa.eu/competition/mergers/cases/decisions/m8124_1349_5.pdf

European Commission (2017a) The Economics of Ownership, Access and Trade in Digital Data. JRC Digital Economy Working Paper. https://ec.europa.eu/jrc/sites/jrcsh/files/jrc104756.pdf,12-15

European Commission (27 June 2017b) Commission Fines Google Eu. 2.42 Billions for Abusing its Dominance as Search Engine by Giving Illegal Advantage to Own Comparison Shopping Service. http://europa.eu/rapid/press-release_MEMO-17-1785_en.htm

European Commission (31 October 2017c) Letter from Director Mørch to the Permanent Representation of Italy to the EU Regarding the Access of Patients' Data to IBM http://www.giannibarbacetto.it/wp-content/uploads/2017/12/ueibm.pdf

European Commission (25 April 2018) Communication from the Commission to the European Parliament, the Council, the European Economic and Social Committee and the Committee of the Regions, Artificial Intelligence for Europe. https://ec.europa.eu/digital-single-market/en/news/communication-artificial-intelligence-europe

European Court of Justice (2 April 2009) France Télécom v. Commission, C-202/07. http://curia.europa.eu/juris/liste.jsf?language=en&num=C-202/07

European Data Protection Supervisor (March 2014) Preliminary Opinion, Privacy and Competitiveness in the Age of Big Data: The Interplay between Data Protection, Competition Law and Consumer Protection in the Age of Big Data. https://edps.europa.eu/sites/edp/files/publication/14-03-26_competitition_law_big_data_en.pdf

European Parliament (October 2015) Personalized Treatment: Towards the Right Treatment For the Right Person at the Right Time, Briefing. http://www.europarl.europa.eu/RegData/etudes/BRIE/2015/569009/EPRS_BRI(2015)569009_EN.pdf

European Union Agency For Fundamental Rights (2013) Inequalities and Multiple Discrimination in Access to and Quality of Healthcare. https://fra.europa.eu/sites/default/files/inequalities-discrimination-healthcare_en.pdf

Evans B (2009) The online advertising industry: economics, evolution, and privacy. J Econ Perspect 23:37–60

Evans BJ (2011) Much ado about data ownership. Harv J Law Technol 25:70–130

Evans BJ (2014) Economic regulation of next-generation sequencing. JLME 42. https://doi.org/10.1111/jlme.12162

Evans DS (2008) Antitrust issues raised by the emerging global internet economy. Northwest Univ Law Rev 102:285–306

Evans DS (2015) Platform economics: essays on multisided businesses. Compet Policy Int 22:1–48

Ezrachi A (2017) Sponge. J Antitrust Enforc 5:49–75

Ezrachi A, Stucke M (2015) The curious case of competition and quality. J Antitrust Enforc 0:1–31

Ezrachi A, Stucke ME (2016) The rise of behavioural discrimination. Eur Compet Law Rev 37: 485–492

Ezrachi A, Stucke ME (31 May 2017) Algorithmic Collusion: Problems and Counter-Measures-OECD Directorate for Financial and Enterprise Affairs Competition Committee. OECD. https://www.oecd.org/officialdocuments/publicdisplaydocumentpdf/?cote=DAF/COMP/WD%282017%2925&docLanguage=En

Fackelmann CR (2013) Clinical data, data exclusivity and private investment protection in Europe. In: Drexl J, Lee N (eds) Pharmaceutical innovation, competition and patent law- a trilateral perspective. Edward Elgar, Cheltenham, pp 141–183

Faeh A (2014) Giving information on medicinal products to the general public-in search of a definition to safeguard the patient. Eur J Health Law 21:176–195

Farrell J, Klemperer P (2007) Coordination and lock-in: competition with switching costs and network effects. In: Armstrong M, Porter R (eds) Handbook of industrial organization. Elsevier, Amsterdam, pp 1967–2072

FDA (30th September 2004) Public Health advisory: Safety of Viox http://www.fda.gov/Drugs/DrugSafety/PostmarketDrugSafetyInformationforPatientsandProviders/ucm106274.htm

Fenech M, Strukelj N, Buston O (6 April 2018) Ethical, Social and Political Challenges of Artificial Intelligence in Health. Future Advocacy. https://wellcome.ac.uk/sites/default/files/ai-in-health-ethical-social-political-challenges.pdf

FierceBiotech (9 October 2015) Is Google a Competitor o Partner to Big Pharma? Roche's CEO doesn't know, yet. https://www.fiercebiotech.com/it/google-a-competitor-or-partner-to-big-pharma-roche-s-ceo-doesn-t-know-yet

File T, Ryan C (November 2014) Computer and Internet Use in the United States: 2013-American Community Survey. https://www2.census.gov/library/publications/2014/acs/acs-28.pdf

Financial Times (15 July 2014) Google and Novartis to Develop 'Smart' Contact Lens For diabetics. https://www.ft.com/content/a4dd1838-0be1-11e4-a096-00144feabdc0

Fish EM (29 October 2018) Key Questions for Regulators Rise With the Dawn of AI-Driven Healthcare. Symposium- The Law and Policy of AI, Robotics, and Telemedicine in Healthcare. Balkin Blog. https://balkin.blogspot.com/2018/10/key-questions-for-regulators-rise-with.html

Gardner R, Ostrom E, Walker JM (1990) The nature of common-pool resource problems. Ration Soc 2:335–358

Geggel L (26 July 2018) 23andMe is sharing its 5 million clients' genetic data with drug Giant GlaxoSmithKline. Livescience https://www.livescience.com/63173-23andme-partnership-glaxosmithkline.html

George Washington University Health Workforce Research Center (3 December 2018) Underserved Populations Least Likely to Use Telehealth Options. GW Today. https://gwtoday.gwu.edu/underserved-populations-least-likely-use-telehealth-options

Geradin D (2006) Efficiency claims in EC competition law and sector-specific regulation. In: Ullrich H (ed) The evolution of European competition law. Edward Elgar, Cheltenham, pp 313–356

German Federal Ministry For Economic Affairs and Energy (31 January 2019) Germany and US launch Joint Venture in Digital Pharmaceutical Research. https://www.exportinitiative-gesundheitswirtschaft.de/EIG/Redaktion/EN/Kurzmeldungen/News/2019/2019-01-31-germany-and-us-launch-joint-venture-in-digital-pharmaceutical-research.html

Ghezzi F, Maggiolino M (24 April 2015) Know Your Enemy: The Dark Side of Information Flows. SSRN. https://papers.ssrn.com/sol3/papers.cfm?abstract_id=2597687

Ghidini G (2015) Profili evolutivi del diritto industrial: innovazione, concorrenza, benessere dei consumatori, accesso alle informazioni. Giuffrè, Milan

Gillespie T (25 June 2014) Algorithm. Culture Digitally. http://culturedigitally.org/2014/06/algorithm-draft-digitalkeyword/

Glader M (2001) Innovation economics and the antitrust guidelines on horizontal co-operation. World Compet 24:513–541

GlaxoSmithKline (25 July 2018) GSK and 23andMe Sign Agreement to Leverage Genetic Insights for the Development of Novel Medicines. https://www.gsk.com/en-gb/media/press-releases/gsk-and-23andme-sign-agreement-to-leverage-genetic-insights-for-the-development-of-novel-medicines/

Gnadinger T (22 August 2014) Health Policy Brief: The Relative Contribution of Multiple Determinants to Health Outcomes. Health Affairs. https://www.healthaffairs.org/do/10.1377/hblog20140822.040952/full/

Goldner J (2009) Regulating conflicts of interests in research: the paper Tiger needs real teeth. St Louis Univ Law J 53:1211–1252

Gøtzsche PC, Jorgensen A (2011) Opening Up Data at the European Medicines Agency. BMJ 342

Grabowski H (2005) Increasing R&D incentives for neglected diseases: lessons from the orphan drug. In: Maskus KE, Reichman JH (eds) International public goods and transfer of technology under a globalized intellectual property regime. Cambridge University Press, Cambridge, pp 457–480

Graef I (2015) Market definition and market power in data: the case of online platforms. World Compet 38:473–506

Graef I (2018) Algorithms and fairness: what role for competition law in targeting Price discrimination towards end consumers? Colum J Eur Law 24:541–559

Greenwald AG, Krieger LH (2006) Implicit bias: scientific foundations. Cal Law Rev 94:945–967

Grunes AP (2013) Another look at privacy. Geo Mason Law Rev 20:1107–1127

Grunes AP, Stucke ME (2015) No mistake about it: the important role of antitrust in the era of big data. Antitrust Source 14:1–14

Haag M (2019) FamilyTreeDNA Admits to Sharing Genetic Data with F.B.I. The New York Times, 4 February 2019, online available at https://www.nytimes.com/2019/02/04/business/family-tree-dna-fbi.html

Hacker P (2018) Teaching fairness to artificial intelligence: existing and novel strategies against algorithmic discrimination under EU law. Common Mark Law Rev 55:1143–1185

Hallinan D, De Hert P (2017) Genetic classes and genetic categories: protecting genetic groups through data protection law. In: Taylor L, Floridi L, Van Der Sloot B (eds) Group privacy-new challenges of data technologies. Springer, Berlin, pp 175–196

Hatzopoulos V (2018) The collaborative economy and EU law. Hart, Oxford

Hazel J, Slobogin C (19 April 2018 last revised 18 October 2018) Who Knows What, and When?: A Survey of the Privacy Policies Proffered by U.S. Direct-to-Consumer Genetic Testing Companies. Cornell Journal of Law and Public Policy and Vanderbilt Law Research Paper No 18–18. https://ssrn.com/abstract=3165765

Heads of Medicines Agencies-European Medicines Agency (13th February 2019) Joint Big Data Task Force- Summary Report. https://www.ema.europa.eu/en/documents/minutes/hma/ema-joint-task-force-big-data-summary-report_en.pdf

Heller MA, Eisenberg R (1998) Can patents deter innovation? The anticommons in biomedical research. Science 280:698–701

HHS.gov Summary of the HIPAA Security Rule. https://www.hhs.gov/hipaa/for-professionals/security/laws-regulations/index.html

Hicken M (19 December 2013) Data Brokers Selling Lists of Rape Victims, AIDS Patients. CNN Money. https://money.cnn.com/2013/12/18/pf/data-broker-lists/

Hiller JS (2016) Healthy predictions? Questions for data analytics in health care. Am Bus Law J 53: 251–314

Ho C (2017) Challenges of the EU general data protection regulation for biobanking and scientific research. J Law Inf Sci 25:84–103

Hoffmann J, Johannsen G (31 May 2019) EU-Merger Control in Big Data-Related Merger. Max Planck Institute for Innovation and Competition Research Paper N. 19-05. https://papers.ssrn.com/sol3/papers.cfm?abstract_id=3364792

Hoffmann S (2005) "Racially-tailored" medicine unravelled. Am Univ Law Rev 55:396–452

Hoffmann S (2018) Big data's new discrimination threats. In: Glenn Cohen I, Lynch HF, Vayena E, Gasser U (eds) Big data, health, law and biotehics. Harvard University, Cambridge, pp 85–98

Hoffmann S, Podgurski A (2012) Balancing privacy, autonomy and scientific needs in electronic health records research. SMU Law Rev 65:85–144

IBM (31 March 2016a) IBM Plans First Watson Health European Center of Excellence in Italy. https://www-03.ibm.com/press/us/en/pressrelease/49436.wss?mhq=watson%20health%20italy&mhsrc=ibmsearch_a

IBM (31 March 2016b) IBM Signs Agreement with Italian Government on First-of-its-Kind Watson Health Center of Excellence in Italy. https://www-03.ibm.com/press/us/en/photo/49450.wss

IBM, Watson Health, online available at. https://www.ibm.com/watson/health/

Illinois Northern District Court (26 June 2019) Dinerstein v. Google, LLC, 1:19-cv-04. https://www.classaction.org/media/dinerstein-v-google-llc-et-al.pdf

Information Commissioner Office (2014) Conducting Privacy Impact Assessments- Code of Practice. https://ico.org.uk/media/about-the-ico/consultations/2052/draft-conducting-privacy-impact-assessments-code-of-practice.pdf

Information Commissioner Office (3 July 2017a) Royal Free-Google DeepMind failed to Comply with Data Protection Law. https://ico.org.uk/about-the-ico/news-and-events/news-and-blogs/2017/07/royal-free-google-deepmind-trial-failed-to-comply-with-data-protection-law/

Information Commissioner Office (3 July 2017b) Letter to Sir David Sloman, Chief Executive Royal Free NHS Foundation Trust. https://ico.org.uk/media/action-weve-taken/undertakings/2014353/undertaking-cover-letter-revised-04072017-to-first-person.pdf

Information Commissioner Office (3 July 2017c) Data Protection Act 1998 Undertaking. https://ico.org.uk/media/action-weve-taken/undertakings/2014352/royal-free-undertaking-03072017.pdf

Information Commissioner Office (12 June 2018a) Statement in Response to Publication of the Royal Free Audit Report. https://ico.org.uk/about-the-ico/news-and-events/news-and-blogs/2018/06/statement-in-response-to-publication-of-the-royal-free-audit-report/

Information Commissioner Office (2018b) About the DPA. https://ico.org.uk/for-organisations/guide-to-data-protection/introduction-to-data-protection/about-the-dpa-2018/

Italian Data Protection Authority (10 May 2017) Letter to the Presidency of the Italian Government. http://www.giannibarbacetto.it/wp-content/uploads/2017/12/garantePrivacyWatson.pdf

Italian Data Protection Authority (10 July 2018). Relazione 2017. https://www.garanteprivacy.it/web/guest/home/docweb/-/docweb-display/docweb/9007915

Jee C (14 November 2018) Google's decision to absorb DeepMind's health division has sparked privacy fears. MIT Technol Rev. https://www.technologyreview.com/f/612418/googles-decision-to-absorb-deepminds-health-division-has-sparked-privacy-fears/

Jennejohn M (2016) The private order of innovation networks. Stan Law Rev 68:281–366

Jost TS (2006) Our broken health care system and how to fix it: an essay on health law and policy. Wake Forest Law Rev 41:537–618

Kahn J (2004) How a drug becomes “ethnic”: law, commerce, and the production of racial categories in medicine. Yale. J Health Policy Law Ethics 4:1–46
Kahn J (2005) From disparity to difference: how race-specific medicines may undermine policies to address inequalities in health care. South Calif Interdiscip Law J 15:105–130
Kahn J (2014) Privatizing biomedical citizenship: risk, duty, and potential in the circle of pharmaceutical life. Minn J Law Sci Technol 15:791–896
Kathuria V (2016) Pharmaceutical mergers and their effect on access and efficiency: a case of emerging markets. World Compet 39:451–478
Katz ML, Shapiro C (1985) Network externalities, competition, and compatibility. Am Econ Rev 75:424–440
Kettler HE (1998) Competition through innovation, innovation through competition. Office of Health Economics, London
Khullar D (31 January 2019) A.I. Could Worsen Health Disparities. New York Times. https://www.nytimes.com/2019/01/31/opinion/ai-bias-healthcare.html
Kim OJ (3 November 2018) The Devil is in the Data, Symposium- The Law and Policy of AI, Robotics, and Telemedicine in Healthcare. Balking Blog https://balkin.blogspot.com/search?q=symposium+healthcare#4117838328430259792
Kim RS, Goossens N, Hoshida Y (2016) Use of big data in drug development for precision medicine. Exp Rev Precision Med Drug Dev 1:245–253
Kinney ED (2001) The international human right to health: what does this mean for our nation and world? Indiana Law Rev 34:1457–1475
Knoppers BM, Thorogood AM (2017) Ethics and big data in health. Curr Opin Syst Biolog 4:53–57
Kokolakis S (2017) Privacy attitudes and privacy behavior: a review of current research on the privacy paradox phenomenon. J Comput Secur 64:122–134
Konnoth C (2017) Governing health information. Univ Pa Law Rev 165:1317–1376
Koops BJ (2014) The trouble with European data protection law. IPDL 4:250–261
Kroll JA, Huey J, Barocas S, Felten EW, Reidenberg JR, Robinson DG, Yu H (2017) Accountable algorithms. Univ Pal Law Rev 165:633–705
Ladeur KH (2016) The Future of Law: Serial Law. EUI Research Papers, Law 2016/19. http://cadmus.eui.eu/bitstream/handle/1814/43345/LAW_2016_19.pdf?sequence=1
Ladeur KH, Gostomzyk T (2011) Der Schutz von Persönlichkeitsrechtsverletzungen gegen Meinungsäußerungen in Blogs. NJW 61:710–715
Lagorio-Chafkin C (7 January 2015) 23andMeExec: You Ain’t Seen Nothing Yet. https://www.inc.com/christine-lagorio/23andme-new-partnerships.html
Lambrecht A, Tucker C (2019) Algorithmic bias? An empirical study of apparent gender-based discrimination in the display of STEM career ads. Manag Sci 65:2947–3448
Lande RH (2011) Consumer choice as the ultimate goal of antitrust. Univ Pitt Law Rev 62:503–525
Lazer D, Kennedy R, King G, Vespignani A (2014) The Parable in Google Flu: traps in big data analysis. Science 343:1203–1205
Lemley MA (2012) The myth of the sole inventor. Mich Law Rev 110:709–760
Lemmens T (2013) Pharmaceutical knowledge governance: a human rights perspective. JLME 41(1):163–184
Lemmens T, Telfer C (2012) Access to information and the right to health: the human rights case for clinical trials transparency. Am J Lifestyle Med 38:63–112
Lerman J (2003) Big data and its exclusions. Stan Law Rev 66:55–63
Lerner AV (26 August 2014) The Role of Big Data in Online Platform Competition. SSRN. https://papers.ssrn.com/sol3/papers.cfm?abstract_id=2482780
Leshem E (18 January 2018) IBM Watson Health AI Gets Access to Full Health Data of 61m Italians. Medium Corporation. https://medium.com/@qData/ibm-watson-health-ai-gets-access-to-full-health-data-of-61m-italians-73f85d90f9c0
Levy K, Barocas S (2018) Designing against discrimination in online markets. Berkeley Technol Law J 32:1183–1238

Lewis TR, Reichman JH, So AD (2007) The case for public funding and public oversight of clinical trials. Economists' Voice 4:1–4

Li J (2013) Privacy policies for health social networking sites. J Am Med Inform Assoc 20:704–707

Liddicoat J, Skopek JM, Liddel K (December 2017) Precision Medicine: Legal and Ethical Challenges. University of Cambridge Legal Studies Research Paper Series, Paper n. 64/2017. https://papers.ssrn.com/sol3/papers.cfm?abstract_id=3070388&download=yes

Linklaters (17 May 2018) Audit of the Acute Kidney Injury Detection System Known as Streams The Royal Free London NHS Foundation Trust. http://s3-eu-west-1.amazonaws.com/files.royalfree.nhs.uk/Reporting/Streams_Report.pdf

Lockhart DJ, Winzeler EA (2000) Genomics, gene expression and DNA arrays. Nature 405:827–836

Lomas N (December 2018) UK watchdog has eyes on Google-DeepMind's health app hand-off'. Tech Crunch. https://techcrunch.com/2018/11/14/uk-watchdog-has-eyes-on-google-deepminds-health-app-hand-off/

Longo A (6 December 2017) Dati degli italiani alle multinazionali, Il Garante Soro "Ecco come tuteleremo la privacy"- intervista ad Antonello Soro presidente del garante per la protezione dei dati personali. La Repubblica. https://www.garanteprivacy.it/web/guest/home/docweb/-/docweb-display/docweb/7274304

Lupton D (2013a) The digitally engaged patient: self-monitoring and self-care in the digital health era. Soc Theory Health 11:256–270

Lupton D (2013b) Understanding the human machine. IEEE Technol Soc Mag 2013:25–30

Lupton D (2014) The commodification of patient opinion: the digital patient experience economy in the age of big data. Sociol Health Ill 36:856–869

Lupton D (2016) The quantified self: a sociology of self-tracking. Polity, Cambridge

Lupton D (2017) Lively data, social fitness and biovalue: the intersections of health self-tracking and social media. In: Bruggess J, Marwick A, Poell T (eds) The sage handbook on social media. Sage, London, pp 562–578

Lybecker KM (2011) The economics of access to medicines: meeting the challenges of pharmaceutical patents, innovation, and access for global health. Harv Int Law J 53:25–43

Maggiolino M (13 June 2017) Personalised prices in European competition law. SSRN: https://papers.ssrn.com/sol3/papers.cfm?abstract_id=2984840

Maggiolino M, Muraca C (2019) Personalized prices under EU antitrust law. Eur Compet Law Rev 10:483–489

Malanga SE, Loe JD, Robertson CT, Ramos KS (2018) Who's left out of big data?. In: Glenn Cohen I, Lynch HF, Vayena E, Gasser U (eds) Big data, health law and biotehics. Harvard University, Cambridge, pp 98–111

Manis ML (13 December 2017) Il caso IBM Watson Health Center pone in luce la mancanza di regole sulla proprietà dei big data. Il Sole 24ore. http://marialuisamanis.nova100.ilsole24ore.com/2017/12/13/il-caso-ibm-watson-health-center-pone-in-luce-la-mancanza-di-regole-sulla-proprieta-dei-big-data/

Marcos F (2018) Innovation by dominant firms in the market: damned if you Don't. . .but damned if you do? In: Nihoul P, Van Cleynenbreugel P (eds) The roles of innovation in competition law analysis. Edward Elgar, Cheltenham, pp 33–50

Margolis R, Derr L, Dunn MC, Huerta M (2014) The National Institutes of Health's big data to knowledge (BD2K) initiative: capitalizing on biomedical big data. J Am Med Inform Assoc 21:957–958

Marjanovic S, Ghiga I, Yang M, Knack A (27 April 2017) Understanding Value in Health Data Ecosystems- A Review of Current Evidence and Ways Forward. Rand Corporation. https://www.rand.org/pubs/research_reports/RR1972.html

Marks M (11 October 2017) Emergent Medical Data. Harvard Law School Bill of Health. http://blog.petrieflom.law.harvard.edu/2017/10/11/emergent-medical-data/

Marks M (2020) Algorithmic disability discrimination. In: Glenn Cohen I, Shachar C, Silvers A, Ashley Stein M (eds) Disability, health law and bioethics. Cambridge University Press, Cambridge, pp 242–255

Maskus KE, Reichman J (2004) The globalization of private knowledge goods and the provatization of global public goods. J Int Econ Law 7:279–320

Mathes SC, McShea MJ, Hanley CL, Ravitz A, Labrique AB, Cohen AB (2019) Digital health: a path to validation. Digital Med 38

McAuley A (2014) Digital health interventions: widening access or widening inequalities? Public Health 128:1118–1120

McNaughton R, Huet G, Shakir S (2014) An investigation into drugs products withdrawn from the EU market between 2001 and 2011 for safety reasons and the evidence used to support the decision making. BMJ Open 4:1–6

Medicines and Healthcare Products Regulatory Agency, Marketing Authorisations, Variations and Licensing Guidance. https://www.gov.uk/topic/medicines-medical-devices-blood/marketing-authorisations-variations-licensing

Medvin M (20 September 2018) Framed by your own cells: how DNA evidence imprisons the innocent. Forbes. https://www.forbes.com/sites/marinamedvin/2018/09/20/framed-by-your-own-cells-how-dna-evidence-imprisons-the-innocent/#50edf464b86b

Metcalf J, Crawford K (2016) Where are human subjects in big data research? The emerging ethics divide. Big Data Soc 3. https://doi.org/10.1177/2053951716650211

Miller EA (2003) The technical and interpersonal aspects of telemedicine: effects on doctor-patient communication. J Telemed Telecare 9:1–7

Moerel L, Prins C (25 May 2016) Privacy for the Homo Digitalis: Proposal for a New Regulatory Framework for Data Protection in the Light of Big Data and the Internet of Things. SSRN https://papers.ssrn.com/sol3/papers.cfm?abstract_id=2784123

Montelero A (2016) Personal data for decisional purposes in the age of analytics: from an individual to a collective dimension of data protection. Compu Law Secur Rev 32:238–255

Moon S, Røttingen JA, Frenk J (2017) Global public goods for health: weaknesses and opportunities in the Global Health System. Health Econ Policy Law 12:195–205

Moses L (2 October 2013) Marketers Should Take Note of When Women Feel Least Attractive. https://www.adweek.com/brand-marketing/marketers-should-take-note-when-women-feel-least-attractive-152753/

Nafus D, Sherman J (2014) This one does not go up to eleven: the quantified self-movement as an alternative big data practice. Int J Commun 8:1784–1794

National Institute of Health (6 December 2017) Policy and Guidelines on the Inclusion of Women and Minorities as Subjects in Clinical Research. https://grants.nih.gov/policy/inclusion/women-and-minorities/guidelines.htm

Newman N (2014) Search, antitrust and the economics of the control of user data. JREG 30(3): 401–454

Newscientist (29 April 2016) Revealed: Google Has Access to Huge Haul of NHS Patient Data. https://www.newscientist.com/article/2086454-revealed-google-ai-has-access-to-huge-haul-of-nhs-patient-data/

NHS (2016) Overview In: Royal Free London NHS Hospital Trust. http://www.nhs.uk/Services/Trusts/Overview/DefaultView.aspx?id=815

NHS Health Research Authority (12 October 2018) HRA Approval. https://www.hra.nhs.uk/approvals-amendments/what-approvals-do-i-need/hra-approval/

Nicholson Price W II (2015) Black box medicine. Harv J Law Technol 2:420–467

Nicholson Price W II (2019) Medical AI and contextual bias. Harv J Law Technol 33:66–116

Norberg PA, Horne DR, Horne DA (2007) The privacy paradox: personal information disclosure intentions versus behaviors. J Consum Aff 41:100–126

NPD Group (6 January 2015) The Demographic Divide: Fitness Trackers and Smartwatches Attracting Very Different Segments of the Market. https://www.npd.com/wps/portal/npd/us/

news/press-releases/2015/the-demographic-divide-fitness-trackers-and-smartwatches-attracting-very-different-segments-of-the market-according-to-the-npd-group/
OECD (1999) Globalisation of Industrial R&D: policy issues. OECD, Paris
OECD (2000) A new economy?: the changing role of innovation and information in growth. OECD, Paris
Ohlhausen M, Okuliar A (2015) Competition, consumer protection and the right (approach) to privacy. Antitrust Law J 80:121–156
Ohm P (2010) Broken promises of privacy: responding to the surprising failure of privacy. UCLA Law Rev 57:1703–1777
Oliver M (2015) Personalized medicine in the information age: Myriad's De facto monopoly on breast cancer research. SMU Law Rev 68:537–566
Orbach B (2011) The antitrust consumer welfare paradox. J Compet Law Econ 7:133–164
Orentlicher D (2010) Prescription data mining and the protection of patients' interests. J Law Med Ethics 38:74–84
Orlowski A (14 November 2018) Google Swallows Up DeepMind Health and Abolishes Independent Board. The Register. https://www.theregister.co.uk/2018/11/14/google_swallows_up_deepmind_health_and_abolishes_independent_board/
Ottolia A (2014) Dati genetici (ed altre materie prime) nella innovazione bioinformatica. In: Olivieri G, Falce V, Arezzo E (eds) Confini e fronti dell'innovazione biotecnologica per la proprietà intellettuale. Giuffrè, Milan, pp 203–224
Parasidis E (2018) The future of pharmacovigilance. In: Glenn Cohen I, Lynch HF, Vayena E, Gasser U (eds) Big data, health law and biotehics. Harvard University Press, Cambridge, pp 73–85
Pasquale F (2014) Redescribing health privacy: the importance of information policy. Hous J Health Law Policy 14:95–128
Pentland A, Reid TG, Heibeck T (2013) Big data and health: revolutionising medicine and public health. WISH Big Data and Health Report. http://kit.mit.edu/sites/default/files/documents/WISH_BigData_Report.pdf
Pettypiece S, Robertson J (11 September 2014) Sick Elderly for Sale by Data Miners for 15 Cents a Name. https://www.bloomberg.com/news/articles/2014-09-11/how-big-data-peers-inside-your-medicine-chest
Phillips AM (2017) Reading the fine print when buying your genetic self online: direct-to-consumer genetic testing terms and conditions. New Genet Soc 36:273–295
Picht PG, Freund B (15 May 2018) Competition (Law) in the Era of Algorithms. Max Planck Institute for Innovation & Competition Research Paper N. 18–10. https://papers.ssrn.com/sol3/papers.cfm?abstract_id=3180550
Polanyi M (1962) The republic of science: its political and economic theory. Minerva 1:54–73
Powles J, Hodson H (2017) Google DeepMind and healthcare in an age of algorithms. Health Technol 7:351–367
Pray LA (2008) Legislative Landmarks of Forensics: California v. Greenwood and Shed DNA. Nat Educ 1:75
Pugatch MP (12–16 October 2004) Intellectual Property, Data exclusivity, Innovation and Market Access. ICTSD-UNCTAD Dialogue on Ensuring Policy Options for affordable Access to Essential Medicines Bellagio. http://www.iprsonline.org/unctadictsd/bellagio/docs/Pugatch_Bellagio3.pdf
Purtova N (2017a) Do property rights in personal data make sense after the big data turn? J Law Econ Regul 10:64–78
Purtova N (2017b) Health data for common good: defining the boundaries and social dilemmas of data commons. In: Leenes R, Purtova N, Adams S (eds) Under observation: the interplay between e-health and surveillance. Springer, Berlin, pp 177–210
Radin MJ (1996) Property evolving in cyberspace. J Law Comput 15:509–526
Rai AK (1999) Regulating scientific research: intellectual property rights and the norms of science. Northwest Univ Law Rev 94:77–152

Rai AK (2001a) Fostering cumulative innovation in the biopharmaceutical industry: the role of patents and antitrust. Berkeley Technol Law J 16:813–853
Rai AK (2001b) The information revolution reaches pharmaceuticals: balancing innovation incentives, cost, and access in the post-genomic era. Univ Ill Law Rev 1:173–210
Rai AK (2017) Legal issues in genomic and precision medicine: intellectual property and beyond. In: Ginsburg G, Willard H (eds) Genomic and personalized medicine: translation and implementation. Elsevier Press, Amsterdam, pp 357–366
Rai AK, Reichman JH, Uhlir PF, Crosswell C (2008) Pathways across the valley of death: novel intellectual property strategies for accelerated drug discovery. Yale J Health Policy Law Ethics 8:3–36
Regalado A (11 February 2019) More than 26 Million People Have Taken an At-home Ancestry Test. MIT Technology Review. https://www.technologyreview.com/s/612880/more-than-26-million-people-have-taken-an-at homeancestry-test/
Reichman JH (2000) Of green tulips and legal kudzu: repackaging rights in subpatentable innovation. Vanderbilt Law Rev 53:1743–1798
Reichman JH (2006) The international legal status of undisclosed clinical trial data: from private to public good. In: Roffe P, Tansey G, Vivas Eugui D (eds) Negotiating health- intellectual property and access to medicines. Earthscan, London, pp 133–150
Reichman JH (2009) Rethinking the role of clinical trial data in international intellectual property law: the case for a public goods approach. Marquette Intell Prop Law Rev 13:3–68
Reichman JH, Uhlir PF (2003) A contractually reconstructed research commons for scientific data in a highly protectionist intellectual property environment. Law Contemp Probl 66:315–462
Reinhardt UE (2004) An information infrastructure for the pharmaceutical market. Health Aff 23: 107–112
Rimmer M (2012) 23andMe Inc.: patent law and lifestyle genetics. J Law Inf Sci 22:132–164
Roberts JL, Weeks Leonard E (2017) Stigmatizing the unhealthy. J Law Med Ethics 45:484–491
Rothstein MA (2017) Structural challenges of precision medicine. J Law Med Ethics 45:274–279
Rothwell PM (1995) Can overall results of clinical trials be applied to all patients? Lancet 345: 1616–1619
Royal Free London-NHS Foundation Trust (12 June 2018) Royal Free London Publishes Audit into Streams App. https://www.royalfree.nhs.uk/news-media/news/royal-free-london-publishes-audit-into-streams-app/
Royal Free London-NHS Foundation Trust (29 September 2015) Information Sharing Agreement. https://drive.google.com/file/d/0BwQ4esYYFC04NFVTRW12TTFFRFE/view
Rubinfeld D, Gal M (2017) Access barriers to big data. Ariz Law Rev 59:339–381
Ruger JP (2006) Toward a theory of a right to health: capability and incompletely theorized agreements. Yale J Law Human 18:273–326
Sanghavi Goel M et al (3 May 2011) Disparities in enrollment and use of an electronic patient portal. J Gen Intern Med 16: 1112–1116
Schabert J et al (2013) Social stigma in diabetes: a framework to understand a growing problem for an increasing epidemic. Patient 6:1–10
Schneider G (2018) Testing art. 102 TFEU in the digital marketplace: insights from the Bundeskartellamt's investigation against Facebook. JECLAP 9:213–225
Schrank A, Whitford J (2011) The anatomy of network failure. Sociol Theory 29:151–177
Schuhmacher A, Gassmann O, Hinder M (2016) Changing R&D models in research-based pharmaceutical companies. J Transnatl Med 14:105
Schumpeter JA (1950) Capitalism, socialism and democracy. Harper Perennial, New York
Sehlstedt U, Bohlin N, de Maré F, Beetz R (2016) Embracing digital health in the pharmaceutical industry. Int J Healthcare Manage 9:145–148
Seitz C (2017) Big data in the pharmaceutical sector. In: Vermeulen G, Lievens E (eds) Data protection and privacy under pressure: transatlantic tensions, EU surveillance and big data. Maklu Verlag, Antwerpen/Apeldoorn/Portland, pp 293–309

Sharon T (2016) The googlization of health research: from disruptive innovation to disruptive ethics. Pers Med 13:563–574

Sharon T (2017) Self-tracking for health and the quantified health: re-articulating autonomy, solidarity, and authenticity in an age of personalized healthcare. Philosophy Technol 30:93–121

Sideri M (16 February 2017) L'intelligenza artificiale del polo IBM a Monaco che ci curerà nel futuro. Il Corriere della Sera. https://www.corriere.it/economia/17_febbraio_17/intelligenza-artificiale-polo-ibm-monaco-che-ci-curera-futuro-77e1069c-f486-11e6-9cca-0c3deaabbf55.shtml

Skloot R (2011) The immortal story of Henrietta lacks. Pen, London

Sluijs JP, Larouche P, Sauter W (2012) Cloud computing in the EU policy sphere. Interoperability, vertical integration and the internal market. JIPITEC 1:12–32

Smith D, Stanton S (10 April 2019) Prosecutors to Seek Death Penalty in Golden State Killer Case. The Mercury News https://www.mercurynews.com/2019/04/10/prosecutors-to-seek-death-penalty-in-golden-state-killer-case/

Sokol D, Comerford R (2016) Antitrust and regulating big data. Geo Mason Law Rev 23:1129–1161

Solove DJ, Citron DK (2018) Risk and anxiety: a theory of data breach harms. Tex Law Rev 96: 737–786

Spina A (2014) Risk regulation of big data: has the time arrived for a paradigm shift in Eu data protection law?, case notes to case C-293/12 and C-594/12 digital rights Ireland and Seitlinger and others. Eur J Risk Regul 5(2):248–252

Stavroulaki T (2019a) Connecting the dots: quality, antitrust and medicine. Loyola Consum Law Rev 31:175–220

Stavroulaki T (2019b) Mind the gap: antitrust, health disparities and telemedicine. Am J Law Med 45:171–187

Stinchcombe A (1990) Information and organizations. University of California Press, Berkeley

Stucke M, Ezrachi A (2016) When competition fails to optimise quality: a look at search engines. Yale J Law Technol 18:70–110

Sullivan C (2002) Racial distinctions in medicine. DePaul J Health Care Law 5:249–256

Sullivan M (14 January 2015) 23andMe Has Signed 12 Other Genetic Data Partnerships Beyond Pfizer and Genentech. VentureBeat https://venturebeat.com/2015/01/14/23andme-hassigned-12-other-genetic-data-partnerships-beyond-pfizer-and-genentech/

Susser D, Roessler B, Nissenbaum H (8 January 2019) Online Manipulation: Hidden Influences in a Digital World. SSRN. https://papers.ssrn.com/sol3/papers.cfm?abstract_id=3306006

Svetiev Y (2007) Antitrust governance: the new wave of antitrust. Loyola Univ Chicago 38:593–694

Swire P (19th October 2007) Protecting Consumers: Privacy Matters in Antitrust Analysis. Center for American Progress. https://www.americanprogress.org/issues/economy/news/2007/10/19/3564/protecting-consumers-privacy-matters-in-antitrust-analysis/

Taubman A (2008) Unfair competition and the financing of public knowledge goods: the problem of test data protection. JIPLP 3:591–606

Taylor L, Floridi L, Van der Sloot B (2017) Conclusion: what do we know about group privacy? In: Taylor L, Floridi L, Van Der Sloot B (eds) Group privacy-new challenges of data technologies. Springer, Berlin, pp 225–237

Terry NP (2018) Big data and regulatory arbitrage in healthcare. In: Glenn Cohen I, Lynch HF, Vayena E, Gasser U (eds) Big data, health law and biotehics. Harvard University, Cambridge, pp 56–68

Teubner G (2011) Networks as connected contracts. Hart Publishing, Oxford

The Economist (3 February 2018) Surgical Intervention- Apple and Amazon's Moves in Health Signal a Coming Transformation. https://www.economist.com/business/2018/02/03/apple-and-amazons-moves-in-health-signal-a-coming-transformation

Timmermans K (2006) Ensuring access to medicine in 2005 and beyond. In: Roffe P, Tansey G, Vivas Eugui D (eds) Negotiating health- intellectual property and access to medicines. Earthscan, London, pp 41–55

Titmuss RM (1970) The gift relationship: from human blood to social policy. Allen and Unwin, London

True Publica (15 November 2018) Google Absorbs Subsidiary with Access to NHS Patient Data. https://truepublica.org.uk/united-kingdom/google-absorbs-subsidiary-with-access-to-nhs-patient-data/

Tsai JY, Egelman S, Cranor L, Acquisti A (2011) The effect of online privacy information on purchasing behavior: an experimental study. Inf Sys Res 22:213–417

Tucker DS, Wellford HB (December 2014) Big mistakes regarding big data Antitrust Source 1–12

UN Committee on Social Economic and Cultural Rights (11 August 2000) General Comment N. 14: The Right to the Highest Attainable Standard of Health (Art. 12), Adopted at the Twenty-second Session of the Committee on Economic, Social and Cultural Rights, on (Contained in Document E/C.12/2000/4). https://www.refworld.org/pdfid/4538838d0.pdf

United Nations, Economic and Social Council, Economic, Social and Cultural Rights (1 March 2004) The Right of Everyone to the Enjoyment of the Highest Attainable Standard of Physical and Mental Health Report of the Special Rapporteur Paul Hunt, Addendun, Mission to the World Trade Organization. https://digitallibrary.un.org/record/517605#record-files-collapse-header

United States District Court Eastern District of New York (16 October 2013) New York v. GlaxoSmithKline

US Supreme Court (13 June 2013) Association for Molecular Pathology v. Myriad Genetics, Inc.

Uscher-Pines L et al (2016) Access and quality of care in direct-to-consumer telemedicine. Telemed E-Health 22:282–287

Van Cleynenbreugel P (2018) Innovation in competition law analysis: making sense of on-going academic and policy debates. In: Nihoul P, Van Cleynenbreugel P (eds) The roles of innovation in competition law analysis. Edward Elgar, Cheltenham, pp 2–13

Van der Sloot B (2016) The individual in the big data era: moving towards an agent-based privacy paradigm. In: Van der Sloot B, Broeders D, Schrijvers E (eds) Exploring the boundaries of big data, exploring the boundaries of big data. Amsterdam University Press, Amsterdam, pp 177–205

Van der Sloot B (2017) Do groups have a right to protect their group interest in privacy and should they? Peeling the onion of rights and interests protected under article 8 ECHR. In: Taylor L, Floridi L, Van Der Sloot B (eds) Group privacy-new challenges of data technologies. Springer, Berlin, pp 197–224

Vayena E, Blasimme A (2018) Health Research with big data: time for systemic oversight. J Law Med Ethics 46:119–129

Villazor RC (2004) Community lawyering: an approach to addressing inequalities in access to healthcare for poor, of color and immigrant communities. N Y Univ J Legis 8:35–62

Villeneuve TF, Gunderson RV (2015) Corporate partnering: Structuring & Negotiating Domestic & international strategic alliances. Wolters Kluwer Legal & Regulatory U.S, New York

Wachter S (2020) Affinity profiling and discrimination by association in online behavioral advertising. Berkeley Technol Law J 35:369–430

Werden GJ (2011) Consumer welfare and competition policy. In: Drexl J, Kerber W, Podszum R (eds) Competition policy and the economic approach: foundations and limitations. Edward Elgar, Cheltenham, pp 11–45

Williamson B (2015) Algorithmic skin: health-tracking technologies, personal analytics and the biopedagogies of digitized health and physical education. Sport Educ Soc 20:133–151

World Health Organization (2010) Telemedicine: Opportunities and Developments in Member States-Second Global Survey in EHealth. https://www.who.int/goe/publications/goe_telemedicine_2010.pdf

World Health Organization, Health Impact Assessment (HIA)-The Determinants of Health. https://www.who.int/hia/evidence/doh/en/
Yeung K (2017) Hypernduge: big data as a mode of regulation by design. iCS 20: 118–136
Yildirim O, Gottwald M, Schûler P, Michel MC (2016) Opportunities and challenges for drug development: public-private partnerships, adaptive designs and big data. Front Pharmacol 7:461
Zarsky T (2019) Privacy and manipulation in the digital age. Theor Enq Law 20:157–188
Zarsky TZ (2003) "Mine your own business!": making the case for the implications of the data mining of personal information in the forum of public opinion. Yale J Law Technol 5:1–56
Zhang X et al (2017) Big data science: opportunities and challenges to address minority health and health disparities in the 21st century. Ethn Dis 27:95–106
Zingales N (2018) Data protection considerations in EU competition law: funnel or straightjacket for innovation? In: Nihoul P, Van Cleynenbreugel P (eds) The roles of innovation in competition law analysis. Edward Elgar, Cheltenham, pp 79–130

Chapter 4
Health Data Pools Under the Digital Single Market Strategy

4.1 Health Data Pools Contextualized in European Policy

As the analysis so far has demonstrated, innovation in health-data driven markets appears to be primarily driven by contractual collaborative schemes among different players, and more precisely, among traditional stakeholders engaged in the healthcare sector, as pharmaceutical companies and public health providers as hospitals, and new players in the field, that are big data companies. As has been illustrated, these last players are getting increasingly important in the field of biomedical research both for their data analytics capabilities and the possession of vast amounts of real world datasets, exploited as a source of scientific evidence. From the other perspective, the pharmaceutical companies and other traditional health providers remain the guardians of the more sophisticated and specialised scientific knowledge and practice needed for keeping up the pace of technological development and thus of biomedical competition.

The resulting networks governing data-driven health research are thus characterised by different types of expertise and assets that the involved stakeholders pool together for designing scientific projects relying on data analytics, such as the delivery of integrated health data analytics platforms or the testing of a new health app. More precisely, as the analysed cases have shown, collaborations in the field of data-driven health rely on the development- usually by high-tech companies- of a needed processing infrastructure and the sharing of both highly technical data-as data resulting from clinical trials or data collected by hospitals, and broader digital health-inflected datasets.

As far as the output of these collaborations is concerned, the examined cases show also that data-driven research ultimately results in new medicinal products and digital services, which are increasingly personalised and interconnected to each other. In this perspective, digital health markets are an example of what antitrust and intellectual property scholars have defined as "innovation markets", defined as

G. Schneider, *Health Data Pools Under European Data Protection and Competition Law*, Munich Studies on Innovation and Competition 17,
https://doi.org/10.1007/978-3-030-95427-7_4

markets in which new products are developed and which are matched to a new demand.[1] Against the backdrop of these findings, this chapter will contextualise health data pools within European policy and law.

From a policy perspective, indeed, the European Union has interestingly identified digital health and free flow of information as two key areas within the Digital Single Market Strategy in respect to the set goal of maximising the innovation potential of the digital internal market.

Both of such key areas result of great interest in respect to the above-described data-driven health research environment.

The European Institutions' interest in the field of digital health has been increasing over the last years, resulting in the issuing by the Commission of several documents stressing the need of advancing innovation in digital health markets for the sake of the achievement of economic efficiencies in the internal market and of the resulting social benefits in a sensitive sector such as that of health services.[2] This has been directly resulting in a growing intervention at a European Union level in the regulation of health markets, concretising in the enactment of specific regulations and directives in the field as well as in the direct enforcement of European competition law in the pharmaceutical sector.[3] As will be shown below, such intervention has been boosted under the General Data Protection Regulation, which entails specific provisions regarding health data and data-driven research activities/practices. It thus seems that although health policy considerations fall outside the scope of European Union's competences, they appear nonetheless to fall back into that realm, triggered by internal market regulatory endeavours.

From a different perspective, health data pools fall under another emerging and increasingly important policy field within the Digital Single Market Strategy, which is related to the sharing of information among businesses (B-to-B) and among businesses and public organisations (B-to-G).

Also in respect to this policy field, initiatives are flourishing, highlighting the economic benefits deriving from the sharing of information among different actors in the internal market. More precisely, the sharing of information is seen as a primary driver for innovation and growth in the digital single market.

Against this backdrop, it appears that the described practice of health data pools is encouraged under the two policy objectives regarding the promotion of digital health markets and the free-flow of information, and thus finds adequate support in the Digital Single Market Strategy.

---

[1] This basic definition of innovation is drawn from Zarsky (2015), p. 126, affirming that innovation is intuitively to be referred to "new or improved processes or services", promoting progress and thus welfare. For a more detailed notion of innovation, see generally OECD (2018), pp. 45 ff.

[2] See infra Sect. 4.3.1.

[3] European Commission (28 January 2019c), p. 3, highlighting the increased antitrust enforcement at both national and also European level in the pharmaceutical sector, and claiming that "the pharmaceutical sector requires close competition law scrutiny" and that "the reported antitrust and merger cases provide a range of examples of how enforcing competition law specifically helps to safeguard EU patients access to affordable and innovative medicines".

4.2 (Digital) Health in the European Union

The ongoing technological changes regarding the conduction of health research have been taken into consideration by European institutions that have given a considerable attention to the phenomenon of e-health within the promotion of the digital single market.[4]

As a general premise, it needs to be outlined that the treaties that constitute the European Union only give very limited policy power over health affairs to the EU: under art. 168, 7 TFEU health and thus healthcare systems are principally the responsibility of Member States.[5] Hence, it is national governments' task to regulate the healthcare sector. [6]

However, these normative statements need to be outweighed against the increasing important role played by internal market principles and provisions that impact on the health sector.[7]

As far as the legal bases are concerned, art. 168, 1 TFEU requires a high level of health protection in the definition and implementation of all European Union's policies and activities. This article is however to be considered only the secondary basis of European Union's intervention in the field of healthcare, since it requires consideration of health protection only within the realm of the defined European Union's policies and activities.[8] To the contrary, art. 114 TFEU enables the stretch of European Union's competences with regards to the protection of health when internal market objectives are to be reached. As it has been stated, the competence of the European Union under art. 114 TFEU is of functional nature, this meaning that the subject matter of a certain established measure is not relevant if the same measure is functional to facilitate trade.[9]

Against this backdrop, market justifications are the drivers for European Union's intervention for standardisation in the field of health and thus for the transfer of Member States' competences at European Union level under art. 4 para. 2 TFEU.[10]

---

[4]In this light, it is worth to mention that Directive 2011/24/EU has set up a e Health Network and there has been a EU Joint Action to support the eHealth Network, which has coordinated Member States' efforts in eHealth, facilitating the cross-border exchange of health data within the EU.

[5]This is expressed under art. 168.7 TFEU, stating that 'the Union shall respect the responsibilities of the Member States for the definition of their health policy and for the organisation and delivery of health services and medical care. The responsibilities of the Member States shall include the management of health services and medical care and the allocation of resources assigned to them'.

[6]Commenting this point, Seitz (2018), p. 132.

[7]Seitz (2018), p. 135.

[8]Art. 168. 5 TFEU provides that the legislature may "adopt incentive measures" designed to, inter alia, "protect and improve human health and in particular to combat the major cross-border health scourges" but this specifically excludes "any harmonisation of the laws and regulations of the Member States". See Flear (2017), p. 76.

[9]See Advocate General Geelhoed (14 December 2004), para 40. Such functionalist approach has been firmly opposed by a strand of early literature, as Crosby (1991).

[10]For similar considerations see. Alemanno and Garde (2013), pp. 1745 ff.

Accordingly, in a series of judgments from 1998 on, the European Court of Justice has established that the principles of the internal market also apply to healthcare policy.[11] Here, the Court of Justice affirmed that healthcare is a service within the meaning of the Treaty[12] and that any barrier to the circulation of such service needed to be removed.[13] As the Court specified, the principle of free movement of services needs to be applied in particular to non-hospital services.[14] The same court subsequently stated that, regardless of individual features, all medical services are "services" within the meaning of the Treaties.[15]

The cited rulings by the European Court of Justice demonstrate that although national healthcare systems fall outside the direct influence of European Union law, significant elements relating to their delivery fall under European principles and rules and have thus to be defined at European Union level.[16] As some strand of the literature has been observing, this has determined a gradual alteration[17] of what has long been a policy sector originally jealously guarded by Member States.[18]

In the last years, however, also several European legislative initiatives in the field of health care-related products, such as the Clinical Trials Regulation and the Medical Device Regulation, have been grounded exactly in art. 114 TFEU.[19]

---

[11] Martinsen (2005), pp. 1035 ff.

[12] So European Court of Justice, Decker v. Caisse de Maladie des Employés Privé, C-120/95 (28 April 1998a) and European Court of Justice, Kohll v. Union de Caisse de Maladie, C-158/96 (28 April 1998b).

[13] European Court of Justice, Geraets-Smits v. Stichting Ziekenfonds, C-157/99 (12 July 2001a), where the Court considered prior authorisation as barrier to the free movement of services, that can be however justified in specific cases identified by the Court, as the existence of 'international medical science' standards orienting the decision on whether or not to grant treatment abroad; and the availability of an equivalent treatment that can be provided in the competent member state "without undue delay".

[14] European Court of Justice, Müller-Fauré and Van Riet Onderlinge Waarborgmaatschappij OZ Zorgverzekeringen UA and E.E.M. van Riet v Onderlinge Waarborgmaatschappij ZAO Zorgverzekeringen, C-385/99 (13 May 2003).

[15] European Court of Justice, Yvonne Watts v Bedford Primary Care Trust and Secretary of State for Health, C-372/04 (16 May 2006), para. 86.

[16] Mossialos et al. (2010), pp. 4–5, stressing the contradictory nature of the regulation of health at European level.

[17] Stressing this point, Neergard (2011), pp. 19 ff. More generally, commenting the move of competences from national to the European level as a consequence of globalisation and the emergence of a multi-level governance system, Altenstetter (2011), pp. 227 ff.

[18] Greer (2006), pp. 134 ff.

[19] Bache et al. (2013), p. 21. This is well expressed by recital 4 of the Directive 2001/83/EC on the Community Code relating to medicinal products for human use, where it is stated that "trade in medicinal products within the EU is hindered by disparities between certain national provisions, in particular between provisions relating to medicinal products (. . .), and such disparities directly affect the functioning of the internal market". See also Recitals 3 and 4 of the Regulation 141/2000 on orphan drugs, affirming that action to stimulate the development of orphan medicinal products "is best taken at EU level, in order to take advantage of the widest possible market and to avoid the dispersion of limited resources".

Under the objective of the internal market, hence, the European Parliament and the Council have been implementing a strong harmonization in the field of health-related products and services through the use of regulations,[20] e.g. in the fields of clinical trials and medical devices, and directives, e.g. in the sector of research and development[21] and pharmacovigilance,[22] signaling the European legislator's intention to intervene more decisively in the integration process of health-care related markets.

In some cases, the promotion of the market rationale is mediated by safety concerns: as the community code for medicinal products and the medical device framework suggest, a key precondition for the free movements of products within the internal market is the harmonisation of the same products' safety levels.[23]

As a result of the above-traced scenario, a substantial part of the products and services that form Member States healthcare systems' structure have ended up being regulated by European internal market- oriented provisions.[24] Market justifications thus appear to have stimulated "exceptional" and highly sectorial European Union interventions in the field of health. This has ultimately determined many national health activities to be captured and thus regulated by European Union lawin its ultimate objective to establish and promote the internal market.[25]

The process of the "Europeanization" of health is being further advanced by the technological progress made in the healthcare sector, and more precisely by two newly emerging features respectively related to the digitalisation and datification of health services and products, which are growingly designed and tested upon digital health data. The importance of health data for market purposes has also determined the increase of health-related cross-border activities, involving health data transfers between Member States for treatment and other purposes.[26]

The digitalisation and datification of healthcare services and products[27] are sensitively transforming health systems with the consequent need of establishing a correspondent legal framework.[28] Technology advancements and the delivery of

---

[20] In this respect, the case of the framework regarding medical devices is particularly interesting since it has been initiated with directives and recently reformed with the adoption of a regulation, thus determining a shift to stronger regulation. See also the Clinical Trials Regulation.

[21] Directive 2001/20/EC of the European Parliament and of the Council of 4 April 2001 on the approximation of the laws, regulations and administrative provisions of the Member States relating to the implementation of good clinical practice in the conduct of clinical trials on medicinal products for human use, 2001, OJL 121.

[22] Directive 2001/83/EC of the European Parliament and of the Council of 6 November 2001 on the Community Code relating to medicinal products for human use (2001) OJL 262.

[23] Bache et al. (2013), p. 23.

[24] Seitz (2018), pp. 132 ff.

[25] On the issue, more broadly, see McKeee et al. (2002).

[26] Callens (2010), pp. 561–562.

[27] Mossialos et al. (2004), pp. 498 ff.

[28] S. Callens (2010), p. 562.

new digital health-related services and products are urgently requiring new regulatory responses.[29]

Since this transformation of the healthcare sector is primarily driven by technology advancements and the marketization of new health-related services and products, such the relevant framework is to be primarily found at European level.

The European Union has indeed become the first-stance regulator of technological developments[30] and correspondently the promoter of the Digital Single Market Strategy.[31] As a consequence of the technological transformations occurred in several markets,[32] European internal market law has become a primary source of regulation of technological risks,[33] designed in order to promote innovative technology not only for the efficiency of the internal market but also for the preservation of European businesses' competitive advantage in the global market.[34] The innovation rationale is thus at the very heart of the need for harmonisation in technology-driven health markets.[35]

An example of this is given by the European Union Directive 98/44/EC on the legal protection of biotechnological inventions, which was a direct response to the need to overcome differences in legal protection for biotechnological inventions among different Member States. These differences were deemed to create barriers to trade in the international market,[36] and were causing damages to the unity of the internal market, as also the European Court of Justice has come to acknowledge.[37]

---

[29] See Horgan and Kent (2017), pp. 191 ff., in particular pp. 193–194, stressing the still existing "limitation's to EU health agenda".

[30] See lately, European Commission (7 December 2018k) stressing the need to establish a solid European framework with regards to artificial intelligence.

[31] European Commission https://ec.europa.eu/digital-single-market/en/policies/shaping-digital-single-market.

[32] In this regard, the digital transformation occurred in the financial markets is of particular interest. See European Commission (8 March 2018a). For the literature on the issue see, for example, Zetsche et al. (2017–2018), pp. 393 ff.

[33] Flear (2017), p. 76.

[34] Bache et al. (2013), p. 21.

[35] This was already very well expressed in recital 2 of the Council Directive 87/22/EEC of 22 December 1986 on the approximation of national measures relating to the placing on the market of high-technology medicinal products, particularly those derived from biotechnology, OJ L15/38, where it is stated that "high-technology medicinal products requiring lengthy periods of costly research will continue to be developed in Europe only if they benefit from a favourable regulatory environment, particularly identical conditions governing their placing on the market throughout the EU".

[36] See Recital 5-6-7 of the Parliament and Council Directive 98/44/EC of 6 July 1998 on the legal protection of biotechnological inventions, 1998, OJ L213/13. In particular, recital 7 stresses that "uncoordinated development of national laws on the legal protection of biotechnological inventions in the EU could lead to further disincentives to trade, to the detriment of the industrial development of such inventions and of the smooth operation of the internal market".

[37] European Court of Justice, Netherlands vs. Parliament and Council (Biotechnology), C-377/98 (9 October 2001b).

Against this backdrop, through the door of regulated technology, the European Union is acquiring an additional important role in the regulation of the health sector as increasingly relying on new technologies. Proof of this is given by the emphasis specifically placed on digital health within the Digital Single Market Strategy[38] as well as the specific provisions regarding health data treatment within the General Data Protection Regulation.

As will be better shown in the next paragraphs, under the pace of digital transformation, thus, healthcare services and products, and what stands behind them, that is health data sharing practices, appear to be increasingly placed within the broader dynamics of European digital markets. This means that the regulation of digital technologies at European Union level is causing an interesting spill-over regulatory effect in the more specific field of healthcare. This spillover effect is to be perceived from a double standpoint: one the one hand the regulation of digital technologies at European Union level attracts within this specific regulatory sphere health matters, as growingly digitised; [39] on the other hand the inclusion of specific provisions regarding health in general policy and legislative endeavours as the Digital Single Market Strategy and the General Data Protection Regulation, suggests that health is being increasingly treated as just one part of the broader, multi-sided (digital) internal market.

4.3 Health Data Pools within the Digital Single Market Strategy

Health data pools as described in the first chapter involve (i) massive processing of health data for the purposes of the delivery of digital health products and services and (ii) the aggregation of different types of data among different stakeholders.

The first identified feature relates to the application of new processing infrastructures, such as algorithms and machine learning, for the treatment of health data, serving the development of new tools and services based on information communication technologies (ICT).

In this perspective, health data pools are to be inscribed in the broader economic phenomenon of digital health. In the words of the European Commission, "digital health and care refers to tools and services that use information and communication technologies (ICTs) to improve prevention, diagnosis, treatment, monitoring and management of health and lifestyle. Digital health and care has the potential to

[38] European Commission (10 May 2017d), p. 8. European Commission (25 April 2018b), pp. 3–4.

[39] In these regards, it is interesting to highlight that in respect to artificial intelligence and the related regulatory issues, the European Commission is stressing health as one of the key sector for the deployment of these new technologies. European Commission (25 April 2018c), pp. 2; 4; 5; 7; 8; 9; 11, where reference to the health sector is made.

innovate and improve access to care, quality of care, and to increase the overall efficiency of the health sector".[40]

From a further and different perspective, it has been showed that health data pools imply the sharing of scientifically valuable information originating from different sources. In these regards, health data pools are to be placed in the other broader economic practice regarding information exchanges among different stakeholders.

Information exchanges have been recently under increasing consideration by the European Commission, which has been stressing the importance of data sharing practices for the efficient development of the digital internal market. In this context, the Commission has been employing the term "data sharing" in order to refer to "all possible forms and models" implying "data access or transfer" among different players, of both private and public nature.[41] As the Commission further acknowledges, data sharing can be carried out through different technical mechanisms and under a variety of legal forms.[42] The definition given by the Commission is thus extremely broad and likely to encompass a variety of means of data exchange and the different range of potentially involved actors.[43]

The Data Governance Act has ultimately provided a normative definition of the notion of data sharing, meaning "the provision of data by a data subject or a data holder to a data user for the purpose of joint or individual use of such data, based on voluntary agreements or Union or national law, directly or through an intermediary, for example under open or commercial licenses, for free or against remuneration".[44] Data access is conversely defined as "data use, in accordance with specific technical, legal, or organisational requirements, without necessarily implying the transmission or downloading of such data".[45] Under these premises, the practice of health data pools is to be contextualised in the two European policies regarding digital health and the free-flow of data. Far from being separate, these policies are both a fragment of the much wider European Digital Single Market Strategy.

More precisely, digital health and the free flow of information are identified as strategic areas in respect to the set goal of maximising the innovation potential of the digital internal market.

The European Commission has indeed given wide attention to both these fields as strategic economic sectors, in need to be promoted for the advancements of the whole internal market as well as for the enhancement of the level of health enjoyed by European society. In parallel to this, several recent initiatives signal the growing recognition of the importance of data sharing practices for the development of new digital products and services, and thus, ultimately for the fuelling of the digital single market in which digitised health markets are to be inscribed.

40 So European Commission https://ec.europa.eu/health/ehealth/overview_en.

41 So European Commission (25 April 2018e), p. 5.

42 European Commission (25 April 2018e), p. 12.

43 Richter and Slowinski (2019), pp. 8–9.

44 Council of the European Union (10 December 2021), Art. 2(7) DGA.

45 Council of the European Union (10 December 2021), Art. 2(8) DGA.

Against this backdrop, the next paragraphs will give account of the growing focus given at European level to these two identified policy areas, highlighting the emergence of an outright regulatory paradigm regarding the free flow of commercially valuable information in the digital single market. In view of the great emphasis placed on digital health, this regulatory paradigm should especially apply to health data pools, and thus to digital health markets considered as a segment of the broader European digital single market.

Once having defined the coordinates of this efficiency-oriented regulatory paradigm over data sharing, the European legal framework applicable to health data pools will be tested against it. The analysis in the following chapters will enquire whether under European data protection and competition law there are some provisions that upheld the outlined regulatory paradigm, liberalising the digital flows—and thus the digital markets—of such sensitive data; or whether there are some conditions and breaking points that the stakeholders involved in digital health markets must respect.

4.3.1 Digital Health Within the Digital Single Market Strategy

The European Union's attention to the phenomenon of digital health dates back to the early 2000 where the Commission launched the so-called e-Europe initiative (e-Europe- an information society for all).[46] It is in this context that the European Union recognised the strategic relevance of the exploitation of technologies in healthcare.[47] The opportunities offered by digital health have been soon identified in the empowerment of patients, becoming active agents in the course of their health treatment[48] through more involving and participatory approaches[49] and recipients of personalized treatments.[50] In these regards, the European Commission has stressed the importance of digital health tools in order to strengthen health education and awareness, thanks to the continuous monitoring of patients' health status and the

[46] European Commission (19 April 2001). See also Commission of the European Communities (28 May 2002). For the literature see Mărcut (2017), pp. 24 ff., retracing the shift from the Information Society to the Digital Market.

[47] For a historical reconstruction, Beurden (2003), pp. 106–108.

[48] In these regards, in an recent interview with EURACTIV, the European Commissioner for Health and Food Safety Vytenis Andriukaitis has stressed the potential of eHealth to make European health systems more accessible and sustainable and to empower patients to manage their own health. See European Commission (25 January 2019b).

[49] European Commission (10 April 2014a), p. 2. This is also stressed by the Council of the European Union (8 December 2017), p. 5.

[50] Council of the European Union (8 December 2017), p. 5.

faster identification of the needed treatments.[51] The gains in terms of safety enhancement have been likewise highlighted.[52]

As the European Data Protection Supervisor has summarized in respect to mobile health applications, healthcare technology developments enable to lower the costs of healthcare and enhance patients' control over their health conditions. This occurs thanks to a constant flow of information from the patients to the providers' datacenters that form and shape patients' digital image.[53]

The benefits of precision-medicine primarily reside in the capability of identifying the actions that are likely to improve health outcomes. In these regards, digital health tools have been evaluated for their significant economic impact, given by the fact that they make it possible to make savings from unnecessary and ineffective medical treatment and improve health providers' planning.[54]

The heightened efficiency of digitised healthcare systems is regarded by the Commission as the precondition to unlock innovation in health and well-being markets.[55]

With regards to digital health, the efficiency rationale appears to be very much intertwined with equality concerns.[56] Indeed, savings from unnecessary and ineffective medical treatment can be used to expand services to those previously without access to the healthcare system.[57] In this perspective, it is argued that the new analytical tools will decrease health inequalities among populations. This has been stated by the European Commission in its e-Health Action Plan 2012–2020, where it is affirmed that eHealth is destined to play a central part in facilitating "socio-economic inclusion and equality, quality of life and patient empowerment through

---

[51] European Commission (10 April 2014a), p. 5. Council of the European Union (8 December 2017), p. 2.

[52] Attention to safety concerns has been given by the European Parliament in a resolution on safer healthcare, stressing the importance of e-health in improving patients' safety, in particular in light of the opportunities given by mobile health tools. See European Parliament (19 May 2015).

[53] European Data Protection Supervisor (21 May 2015), p. 3.

[54] European Commission (10 April 2014a), p. 5.

[55] European Commission (7 December 2012b), pp. 10–12.

[56] In these regards, in its e-health Action Plan 2012–2020, the European Commission explicitly mentions that, "e-health – when applied effectively— delivers more personalized "citizen-centric" healthcare, which is more targeted, effective and efficient and helps reduce errors, as well as the length of hospitalization. It facilitates socio-economic inclusion and equality, quality of life and patient empowerment through greater transparency, access to services and information and the use of social media for health." European Commission (7 December 2012b), p. 4. See also European Parliament (14 January 2014).

[57] Highlighting equality concerns also the "Digital Health Society Declaration" has also listed among the benefits arising from the employment of digital tools in health, "inclusiveness and equality" through "better communication and access to healthcare services and professionals". The Digital Health Society Declaration has been adopted at the high-level "Health in Digital Society. Digital Society for Health" conference, which took place on 16–18 October 2017 in Tallin, launching multi-stakeholder task forces to work on actions addressing the main challenges of large-scale deployment of digital innovation in the field of health. European Commission (14 July 2017e).

greater transparency, access to services and information and the use of social media for health".[58]

In view of these statements, however, the European Data Protection Supervisor has issued a call for caution, stressing the need to align the promised gains for consumers in terms of market efficiency and for patients in terms of social equality to the protection of data subjects' fundamental rights to data protection, dignity and self-determination.[59] As the Supervisor has observed, indeed, these rights are highly impacted in the context of personalized digital health technologies, mostly implying the creation of profiles of patients on the basis of data differently collected from various sources.[60] These health profiles could be further used not only for treatment and research purposes but also for other commercial purposes, such as the determination of insurance rates.[61]

The concerns highlighted by the European Data Protection Supervisor, however, do not appear to have been properly addressed in the further developed policy debate regarding digital health. To the very contrary, it seems that digital health and the connected treatment of health information have been increasingly considered at policy level by the European Commission for their innovation potential in the context of the digital internal market, rather than for their sensitive impact on patients' health conditions and related rights.[62]

This has ultimately led the Commission to comprehensively include digital health within the Digital Single Market Strategy for Europe.[63] Hence, the digital

---

[58] European Parliament (14 January 2014). Emphasis added.

[59] European Data Protection Supervisor (27 March 2013), pp. 3–6.

[60] European Data Protection Supervisor (27 March 2013), p. 6.

[61] European Data Protection Supervisor (27 March 2013), p. 6.

[62] Data-driven (or data-based) health tools are having a significant impact on users' and thus patients' health conditions. More precisely, users' health conditions are determined by the design and the processing criteria on the basis of which these same devices and products function. As far as medical devices are concerned, their design is given by the collected and alimenting data and by who can and who cannot access these devices or apps. Differently, as far as algorithm-tested pharmaceutical products are concerned, the definition of which pharmaceutical product will be allowed to the market, will be determined on the basis of the dataset alimenting the automated testing procedures, and more specifically of whose data- i.e. which groups of the population- form these datasets. These last acknowledgments become particularly interesting if one thinks that algorithmic processes are not neutral, objective, sources of knowledge. Indeed, digital health databases alimenting artificial machine learning processes do not undergo the same development and validation of clinical databases. Little is thus known about the selection, values and assumptions of the 'training data' that machine learning algorithms act upon. As a strand of the literature has stressed such data may well be incomplete or partial. So Ajunwa et al. (2016), pp. 474 ff. For a more general assessment over algorithmic bias see Richardson et al. (2019). Given that users' healthiness is- or may be- increasingly determined by automated procedures and the value systems embedded in algorithms' codes, the issue of the partiality and approximation of algorithmically processed data becomes even more relevant and raises newly emerging legal concerns in the markets of digitized health-related products. For a broader discussion on this issue see supra Chap. 3, Sect. 3.3.4.

[63] See lately, European Commission (10 May 2017d).

transformation of European health and care has determined health services and products to be considered in the general perspective of European digital markets.

Interestingly, the 2015 Digital Single Market Strategy for Europe[64] did not focus specifically on health and care, but already made some references to e-health. References to e-health were made as an example of another sector, amongst the others mentioned,[65] where digital services would bring benefits to both users/consumers and businesses, particularly in terms of standardization and interoperability.[66]

In May 2017, in the Communication on the Mid-Term Review on the implementation of the Digital Single Market Strategy, the European Commission came to strengthen the focus on digital health, particularly stressing the two policy objectives (i) of providing citizens' secure access to electronic health records and (ii) of supporting data infrastructure to advance research, disease prevention and personalized health.[67]

Ultimately, in its Communication on "enabling the digital transformation of health and care in the Digital Single Market: empowering citizens and building a healthier society",[68] the Commission has stressed the importance of the development of the European digital market for the achievement of "equal access to high quality care through the meaningful use of digital innovations".[69] Here, the Commission affirms the role of the European Union in the promotion of the digital health industry through a wider deployment of digital products and services in health and care.

Interestingly, it is stressed that through the convergence between information communication technologies and healthcare devices, new businesses are emerging.

From a broader perspective, as the Commission points out, European health systems would benefit of digitization processes, in terms of resilience and sustainability.[70] Digital health tools are indeed deemed to improve patients' safety, reduce the number of avoidable mistakes, and improve the coordination and continuity of care and better adherence to treatment.[71]

---

[64] European Commission (6 May 2015).

[65] E-Health has indeed been considered by the Commission together with other digital services in the context of e-government, e-energy-e-transport. European Commission (6 May 2015), p. 15.

[66] European Commission (25 April 2018b), pp. 3–4.

[67] European Commission (10 May 2017d), p. 19.

[68] European Commission (25 April 2018i).

[69] European Commission (25 April 2018b), p. 5.

[70] European Commission (25 April 2018b), p. 3. Stressing the same also Council of the European Union, Council Conclusions on Health in the Digital Society- Making Progress in Data-driven Innovation in the Field of Health, cit., 5. The market efficiency gains of digitisation of healthcare has been stressed by the Council of Europe on several occasions. See Council of the European Union (10 December 2013), p. 3; Council of the European Union (20 June 2014); Council of the European Union (7 December 2015).

[71] Council of the European Union (8 December 2017), p. 5.

The European Commission thus clearly links technological developments in health to the central goal of economic optimization and innovation.[72] More precisely, according to the Commission, the wider deployment of digital products and services in healthcare would stimulate growth and promote the European industry in this specific domain, with that overall maximizing the potential of the digital internal market.[73] The resulting efficiency gains in data-driven markets are in turn deemed to increase the standard of health personally enjoyed by European citizens with subsequent broader public health achievements such as early detection of infectious outbreaks.[74] It thus seems that the European Commission is considering the promotion of economic innovation through digitization in the specific field of health also for its connected social advancements.

Accordingly, it is claimed that the European Union is developing "strong approaches in high performance computing, data analytics and artificial intelligence, which can help design and test new healthcare products, provide faster diagnosis and better treatments".[75] Against the backdrop of the technological transformations relevant for the healthcare sector, the European Commission highlights the need for health and care authorities to face the emerging common challenges jointly. These challenges primarily concern the development of EU-wide standards for data quality, reliability and cybersecurity and the EU-wide standardization of electronic health records and a better interoperability through open exchange formats.[76]

Under these premises, the European Commission calls for further action at EU level to accelerate the meaningful use of digital solutions in healthcare in Europe.[77]

In these regards, the same Commission lists the relevant legislative initiatives that have been enacted in order to provide first European regulatory responses in respect to the phenomenon of e-health and advance progress in the field of data-driven health. In these regards, mention is made to the Directive on patients' rights in cross-border healthcare,[78] establishing an e-health network to advance the interoperability of e-health solutions for the promotion of health data exchanges among Member States.[79]

In addition to specific interventions, the Commission refers also to laws that are of general relevance for the digital single market and that turn out to be key regulatory tools for data-driven health markets. This more general framework is made up by a

---

[72] Flear (2017), p. 76.

[73] European Commission (25 April 2018b), p. 5.

[74] European Commission (25 April 2018b), p. 9.

[75] European Commission (25 April 2018b), p. 3.

[76] European Commission (25 April 2018b), p. 5.

[77] European Commission (25 April 2018b), p. 3.

[78] Directive 2011/24/EU of the European Parliament and of the Council of 9 March 2011, on the application of patients' rights in cross-border healthcare (2 April 2011) OJL 88/45.

[79] Art. 13 Directive 2011/24/EU. Stressing the relevance of this e-health network for the purposes of overcoming legal, organisational, technical and semantic interoperability challenges in the context of the cross-border exchange of personal health data, European Commission (21 September 2018j), p. 13.

diverse range of bodies of law,[80] amongst which particular attention is to be given to data protection and competition law. As will be shown below, indeed, the specificities of health-related markets, increasingly networked and information-intensive, trigger the application of specific provisions of the two frameworks.

4.3.2 *The Free Flow of Information within the Digital Single Market Strategy*

Moving from a substantial to a procedural perspective, health data pools are data sharing practices enabling the free-flow of scientifically and thus commercially valuable information between different stakeholders, both of public and private nature, acting within the borders of the European internal market. From this perspective, health data pools are to be contextualised also in the other branch of European policy concerning the free-flow of information, lately concretised in the more specific policy promoting the accessibility and re-use of data.

Together with the rise of the digital economy, driven by "digital data, computation and automation",[81] the Commission soon identified "the insufficient access to

[80]The European Commission mentions the e-commerce directive, which may be applied to online medicines purchases, to health services based on the transmission of information via a communication network or providing access to a communication network, to services that transfer medical information among physicians. The Directive obliges e-health companies providing an information society service to communicate to the recipients of the service and competent authorities, easily, directly and permanently accessible information on the service providers. Under the Directive, e-health actors must also indicate any relevant codes of conduct to which they subscribe with the relevant information on how the code can be consulted electronically. Ultimately, it is worth recalling that art. 4 para 1 of the Directive requires Member States to ensure that the pursuit of the activity of an information society service provider including an e-health actor, may not be made subject to a prior authorization or any other requirement having equivalent effect. This important rule promoting the free movement of information society services, is a challenge for e-health networks or telemedicine projects for which the competent national public authorities intend to provide reimbursements under certain conditions. European Parliament and Council Directive 2000/31/EC on certain legal aspects of information society services, in particular electronic commerce in the internal market, OJ 2000 N. L178/1. For a comment see Callens (2002), pp. 93 ff. In the Communication, the Commission stresses the relevance for digital health markets purposes also of the Directive on Electronic Signatures. Regulation UE 910/2014 of the European Parliament and of the Council of 23 July 2014, on electronic identification and trust services for electronic transactions in the internal market and repealing Directive 1999/93/EC, OJ L 257. Finally, also the Regulation regarding the security of network and information systems is mentioned. Regulation UE 910/2014 of the European Parliament and of the Council of 23 July 2014, on electronic identification and trust services for electronic transactions in the internal market and repealing Directive 1999/93/EC, OJ L 257.

[81]European Commission (2 July 2014b), p. 2.

large datasets and the enabling infrastructure" as obstacles to market entry and to innovation.[82]

This is why the Digital Single Market Strategy acknowledged information exchanges as a precondition for "maximising the growth potential of the digital economy" and assuring an efficient use of data across the EU.[83] The efficiencies related to data sharing among different stakeholders have been confirmed by some economic studies.[84]

Accordingly, the free-flow of information initiative[85] has become a key action within the project of building a Digital Single Market Strategy.[86] In this context, the Commission set as a major goal the one of establishing a policy and legal framework regarding the issue of data ownership and data access.[87]

This objective was further assessed in the Commission's Communication "Building a European Data Economy", setting a list of general principles meant to help shaping an EU framework for the free-flow of data and the improved sharing of commercial and machine-generated data.[88] In these regards, the Commission has distinguished between a non-legislative and a legislative approach to the free-flow of data, the first resulting in mere guidance documents and the second objectifying in outright legislative proposals and reforms.[89]

Against this backdrop, among the areas deemed to be critical for the fostering of the free-flow of data, the Commission has addressed amongst others, the issue of data ownership[90] to be concretised in the introduction at European Union level of a data producer's right over data,[91] supposed to enact a full legal recognition of the

---

[82] European Commission (2 July 2014b), pp. 2–3. These concerns had already been addressed with regards to cloud computing systems. European Commission (17 September 2012a).

[83] European Commission (6 May 2015), pp. 14–15.

[84] Amongst others, with specific regards to the efficiencies related to the development of artificial intelligence tools see Cockburn et al. (2019), pp. 115–146, stressing the essential nature of data and thus of data sharing among businesses for the development of technological innovation.

[85] The free flow of information initiative was first announced in the "Mid-Term Review on the implementation of the Digital Single Market Strategy". European Commission (10 May 2017d), p. 11, where it was announced that the Commission would have prepared "a legislative proposal on the EU free flow of data cooperation framework which takes into account the principle of free flow of data within the EU, the principle of porting non-personal data, including when switching business services like cloud services as well as the principle of availability of certain data for regulatory control purposes also when that data is stored in another Member State".

[86] European Commission (6 May 2015), pp. 14–15. Drexl (27 April 2018), pp. 22–23.

[87] European Commission (6 May 2015), p. 15. For a critical appraisal of the policy initiative, see Kim (2017), p. 699.

[88] European Commission (10 January 2017a).

[89] European Commission (10 January 2017a), pp. 30-31. See Duch-Brown et al. (2017).

[90] See also European Commission (10 January 2017a), pp. 11–15; 33–36.

[91] This is highlighted by Zech (2017), pp. 51 ff. The introduction of a specific ownership right over digital data has been commented by many authors. For a critical assessment see Drexl et al. (16 August 2016), p. 12 and also Kerber (2016), pp. 989 ff.

economic value of data in the internal market. This proposed right has however not been supported in any subsequent legislative intervention.[92]

In view of the Commission, access to machine-processed and machine-generated data is to be further addressed through (i) the employment of technical solutions for the reliable identification and exchange of data, such as application programming interfaces; (ii) the establishment of default contractual rules for contracts relating to data; (iii) the renewed consideration of scientific purposes as a ground for data access; and, ultimately, (iv) the encouragement of access to data against remuneration.[93] All these four identified tools are meant to differently foster data access and transfer within the internal market.[94]

As the latest documents by the Commission suggest, the objective of data sharing has become of central relevance within the policy for the free-flow of data, which has been consolidating around this major concern.

Consistently with other declarations released at both international and national,[95] the Commission has highlighted that the acquisition of data and their processing through data analytics is source to firms' competitive advantage in the digital market.[96] In the view of the Commission, barriers preventing businesses and especially SMEs and start-ups from innovating on data resources need to be eliminated[97] so that the value resulting from the shared data is exploited to the maximum.[98]

For the purposes of strengthening the relevant regulatory framework, the Commission has recently announced a new package of measures, meant to create a European common data space, in which new products and services are developed upon the shared data.[99]

Within this reform package, the proposed measures differently consider data sharing from a subjective perspective, that is from the perspective of the *subjects* who have control of the data to be shared, and from an objective perspective, that is from the perspective of the *type of data* to be shared.

From a subjective standpoint, the recipients of the proposed measures are private and public stakeholders, both considered as promising sources for data sharing endeavours.

---

[92] For a comment, Drexl (2019), pp. 19 ff.

[93] European Commission (10 January 2017a), pp. 12–13 and European Commission (10 January 2017b), pp. 30–36.

[94] European Commission (10 January 2017a), pp. 8 ff.

[95] At international level, the competitive value of data has been acknowledged by OECD (6 October 2015), pp. 42–43. For a national expression of this view, see in particular Autorité de la Concurrence and Bundeskartellamt (10 May 2016).

[96] European Commission (10 January 2017a), p. 3.

[97] European Commission (4 April 2019d).

[98] Stressing this point also, Martens (December 2018), p. 19.

[99] European Commission (25 April 2018d), p. 1.

In this respect, the Commission has come to stress the relevance of privately held data for the purposes of business to business (B2B) sharing agreements.[100] It is highlighted that access and use of a same set of shared data can be employed by businesses for the development and the testing of products meant to be delivered in different markets.[101] The issue of B2B relations had been already examined by the Commission with respect to the fairness of the online platform to business relations.[102] One of the main concerns that resulted from the analysis was exactly platforms' refusal to provide access to essential business data,[103] this leading to an inefficient underuse of data in the market, which harms businesses' activities and inhibit the development of new data-related innovations.[104]

In addition to this, also data transfers occurring within public-private partnerships have been considered by the Commission for their economic potential.[105] The sharing of private and public data is encouraged at a bi-directional level, both with regards to the public employment of privately generated data[106] and with regards to the private access to government data.[107] The aggregation of data resulting from industry, research institutions and other public institutions has been identified as key for the improvement of data-related research and innovation.[108] In this perspective, it is interesting to highlight that the reform of the Public Sector Information Directive places a particular emphasis on research data, to be included within the scope of the new Directive.[109] In this respect, the new Open Data Directive[110] expressly

[100] European Commission (25 April 2018d), pp. 8–11; European Commission (2020c).

[101] European Commission (25 April 2018d), p. 2.

[102] European Commission (25 May 2016b).

[103] European Commission (25 May 2016b), p. 12.

[104] Commenting this, Graef et al. (September 2018), p. 11.

[105] European Commission (24 January 2017c).

[106] European Commission (25 April 2018d), pp. 12–14. The issue of the growing use by public sector bodies of corporations' collected data (business-to-government sharing) for the delivery of public services, has been enquired with regards to the reflexes on public accountability and democracy. See in these regards, Schneider (2019), pp. 134 ff. See also Brauneis and Goodman (2018), pp. 111 ff. and Edwards (2016), pp. 28 ff.

[107] The issue re-use of public information has been recently given renewed attention together with the recent adoption of a new Open Data and Public Sector Information Directive, reforming the previous Public Sector Information Directive. Directive 2003/98/EC of the European Parliament and of the Council of 17 November 2003 on the re-use of public sector information on the re-use of public sector information. See European Commission (24 January 2019a). The new Open Data and Public Sector Information Directive encourages Member States to facilitate the re-use and thus the sharing of public sector data. For the purpose encouraging the sharing of information in the public sector, the Commission has also proposed the establishment of a Support Centre for Data Sharing under the Connecting Europe Facility Programme. European Commission (25 April 2018d), p. 6.

[108] See Big Data Value Association (October 2017), pp. 71–72, specifically highlighting the importance of health data sharing among public and private actors.

[109] European Commission, (25 April 2018d), pp. 6–7.

[110] Directive EU 2019/1024 of the European Parliament and of the Council of 20 June 2019 on open data and the re-use of public sector information (26 June 2019) OJ L 172/56.

considers research data under art. 10 stating that "member states shall support the availability of research data (...)" on the basis of "open access policies". In this direction, the Data Governance Act has come to complement the Open Data Directive, establishing a data sharing mechanism for public interest purposes, evolving around the new notion of "data altruism", related to the sharing of data "without seeking a reward, for purposes of general interest, such as scientific research purposes or improving public services"[111]. Research interests have been ultimately taken into consideration also under the proposed Digital Service Act, which sets an obligation onto "very large online platforms" to provide access to data to researchers "for the sole purpose of conducting research that contributes to the identification and understanding of systemic risks"[112].

Access to and reuse of publicly funded research data is additionally encouraged by the renewed Recommendation on access to and preservation of scientific information.[113]

The advancement of the availability of scientific information is to be placed at the crossroads of the policy regarding the free-flow of information of the Digital Single Market Strategy and the different European Open Science Agenda,[114] calling for research processes conducted by any type of researcher- of public, private and independent nature[115]- to be transparent so as to facilitate follow on research.[116]

Accordingly, the Recommendation on access to and preservation of scientific information adapts these goals to the new datification patterns and the enhanced data analytics capabilities.[117] Big data are indeed deemed to change the way research is performed and knowledge is shared,[118] along the lines of a paradigm shift towards more collaborative methods of carrying out scientific research.[119] This is in turn leading to a more open and transparent research approach, which in the view of

[111]Council of the European Union (10 December 2021), Art. 2(10) DGA.

[112]European Commission (15 December 2020), Art. 31 DSA.

[113]European Commission (25 April 2018f). The 2018 Recommendation revises the previous 2012 Recommendation. See European Commission (17 July 2012). See also European Commission (25 April 2018g).

[114]European Commission (2020b). European Open Science Cloud (2021).

[115]Among the independent actors in the research field, also mere citizens are included. See European Commission (4 March 2016a), where the involvement of citizens in scientific research projects is deemed functional to the achievement of the broader objectives of the democratisation of science and greater public participation.

[116]European Commission (25 April 2018d), p. 7. This was additionally highlighted by Council of the European Union (27 May 2016).

[117]See in particular recital 12 of the Recommendation on access to and preservation of scientific information, European Commission (25 April 2018f) and European Commission (2020c).

[118]Recital 2 of the Recommendation, European Commission (25 April 2018f).

[119]Recital 9 of the Recommendation, European Commission (25 April 2018f), stressing that "technological progress has over time caused a major shift in the world of science towards increasingly collaborative methods, and has steadily contributed to an increasing volume of scientific material".

the Commission needs to be further encouraged and incentivised.[120] In this frame, the Recommendation considers the new text and data mining technologies[121] and the technical standards for data[122] as important catalysts for the access and reuse of extracted scientific information generated by public stakeholders.

With regards to the object of the data transfers among the mentioned stakeholders, it needs to be acknowledged that at its origins, the free-flow of information initiatives appeared to specifically refer to non-personal data.[123] The 2017 Mid-Term Review of the Digital Market Strategy indeed recognizes the objective of creating an "effective and trustworthy cross-border free-flow of non-personal data", which builds upon the "principle of free movement of data within the EU".[124] As the Commission further specifies, non-personal data can either be per se of non-personal nature or derive from anonymization processes of originally personal data.[125] In this last case, the Commission requires "full anonymisation", rendering any additional re-anonymisation on the basis of further information impossible.[126]

Personal data are said to fall outside the scope of the free-flow of data initiative since this data is already regulated in the different regulatory sector covered by the General Data Protection Regulation and the e-Privacy Directive, specifically setting the framework with respect to processing of personal data.[127] Hence, it seems that the Commission sees the regulatory framework regarding personal data and the free-flow of non-personal data as complementary.[128]

A first legislative step towards the strengthening of the policy in question is to be found in the recently enacted regulation regarding the free-flow of non-personal data.[129] This regulation is meant to complete the framework established by the

---

[120] Recital 10 and para 9 of the Recommendation "Incentives and Rewards". European Commission (25 April 2018f).

[121] See para. 3 of the Recommendation "Management of Research Data, including Open Access". European Commission (25 April 2018f).

[122] See para 6 and 7 of the Recommendation "Infrastructures for Open Data". European Commission (25 April 2018f).

[123] European Commission (25 April 2018d).

[124] European Commission (10 May 2017d), p. 10.

[125] European Commission (10 May 2017d), p. 4, stressing that the EU framework for the free-flow of data and improved sharing of commercial data and in particular machine-generated data, shall regard "data which are either non-personal in nature or personal data that have been anonymised". See also European Commission (10 January 2017a), pp. 5–6.

[126] European Commission (10 January 2017a), p. 9. This point is acknowledged by Drexl (2019). See also European Data Protection Supervisor (8 June 2018), p. 2.

[127] European Commission (10 January 2017b), p. 2.

[128] This point is stressed by Graef et al. (September 2018), pp. 2 ff.

[129] European Parliament and Council of the European Union, 'Regulation (EU) 2018/1807 of the European Parliament and of the Council of 14 November 2018 on a framework for the free flow of non-personal data in the European Union' 28 November 2018, OJ L 303/59. It is still largely unclear how this Regulation will practically interact with the General Data Protection Regulation. In these regards, the European Data Protection Supervisor has observed that "the Proposal carries significant risks of overlap or conflict with the GDPR, thus undermining legal certainty and causing difficulties of practical application". See European Data Protection Supervisor (8 June 2018), p. 3.

General Data Protection Regulation with regards to the free flow of data across the internal market, emerging as the fifth freedom, in addition to the four traditional ones.[130] Interestingly, recital 10 states that the regulation regarding the free-flow of non-personal data establishes the same "principle of free movement" of non-personal data, which the General data protection regulation lays down in respect to the flow of personal data, which "Member States may neither restrict nor prohibit (...) for reasons connected to the protection of natural persons". This means, in other terms, that data protection law as newly framed under the General Data Protection Regulation has to be interpreted in a way that poses restrictions to the free movement of personal data only on grounds of data protection reasons. Accordingly, a European support centre for data sharing has been recently announced under the Connecting Europe Facility Programme in April 2018 and was established on the 15th July 2019.[131] The centre has the main objective of assisting companies in developing model contracts and providing to them technical and legal advice with regards to data sharing initiatives for efficiency purposes.[132]

4.3.2.1 The Free Flow of Information Initiative and Personal Data

The reference to non-personal data appears to be appropriate in respect to datafied sectors, where there is little or no involvement of physical subjects and the generated data are thus necessarily of non-personal nature. This is the case, for example, of agricultural data[133] or geo-spatial or satellite data to which the free-flow of information policy makes explicit reference, also within the European Strategy for Data.[134]

To the very contrary, in most sectors of the digital market, the circulating data are of highly personally-inflected nature. More precisely, as largely recognised by the literature, algorithmic processing of data and the constant data de-contextualisation

[130] Colangelo and Borgogno (5 April 2019). See art. 4 of the mentioned Regulation.

[131] European Commission (8 September 2021). Colangelo and Borgogno (5 April 2019), p. 7.

[132] Colangelo and Borgogno (5 April 2019), p. 7.

[133] With regards to agricultural data, a number of stakeholders in the agricultural sector has issued a code of conduct regarding the sharing of agricultural data. See EU Code of conduct on agricultural data sharing by contractual agreement (2020).

[134] The sharing of geo-spatial and satellite data is taken into consideration respectively by two Commission initiatives, the INSPIRE and the COPERNICUS programmes. The INSPIRE Directive facilitates access to geo-spatial information. See Directive 2007/2/EC establishing an Infrastructure for Spatial Information in the European Community. Similarly, through the COPERNICU programme the Commission collects earth observation data making it available to public bodies, researchers, business and citizens through a free and open data policy. See Regulation (EU) No 377/2014 of 3 April 2014 establishing the Copernicus Programme and repealing Regulation (EU) No 911/2010. See European Commission (10 January 2017a), pp. 11–12.

processes occurring in the network of hyper-connected devices, render it extremely difficult to draw an absolute line between personal and non-personal data.[135]

Moreover, as the case of health data described in the previous chapter perfectly shows, the Commission's focus on solely non-personal data appears to clearly underestimate the innovation potential of personal data.[136] As it occurs with health data, in many cases, it is exactly the personal nature of the data that renders it precious for research and thus for market innovation purposes.

Hence, this approach taken by the European Commission with respect to the free-flow of data policy has been strongly criticised by the literature, calling for a more comprehensive policy and regulatory approach.[137]

In these regards, it needs to be observed that personal data have been somehow taken into consideration by the Commission, acknowledging that actors in the data economy "deal both with personal and non-personal data and that data flows and datasets will regularly contain both types".[138] It is also further affirmed that "any policy measure must take account of this economic reality and of the legal framework on the protection of personal data, while respecting the fundamental rights of individuals".[139] These words by the Commission reflect that the object of the policy regarding the free-flow of information remains relatively unclear.[140]

There are however some evident stances in favour of the inclusion of personal data within the policy promoting data access and reuse.

The Open Data Directive as well as the Data Governance Act, for example, expressly mention the need for compliance with the General Data Protection Regulation[141] and with that seem to suggest the inclusion of personal data within their scope.

In addition to this, the frequent reference in the mentioned policy documents to the health sector signal the manifest inclusion within the data accessibility policies also of sectors where there is a high gradient of personal information. This is further proved by the explicit consideration of health data sharing as a key concern with regards to the objective of boosting the data availability within the digital single market.[142]

---

[135] Stressing the re-identifiability of data in view of the current technological capabilities, Purtova (2018), pp. 40 ff. and Koops (2014), pp. 250 ff. There have been also many cases of re-identification in data-sets that were deemed to be anonymised. See Blackman and Forge (November 2017). For a deeper assessment on the issue see infra para.

[136] Highlighting the same point on a more general level, Graef et al. (September 2018), p. 3.

[137] With specific regard to the free-flow of information initiative, Graef et al. (September 2018), p. 5; Drexl (2019), pp. 19 ff.

[138] European Commission (10 January 2017a), p. 9.

[139] European Commission (10 January 2017a), p. 9.

[140] Noticing a certain ambivalence by the Commission with regards the relationship between the free-flow of data policy and data protection law, Graef et al. (September 2018), p. 2.

[141] European Commission (4 April 2019d); Council of the European Union (10 December 2021), art. 1(2a) DGA.

[142] European Commission (25 April 2018h).

The great emphasis over non-personal data could suggest that the European Commission refers to non-personal health data, that is anonymised data. However, as already suggested above, it needs to be noticed that anonymization processes, especially with regards to health data, would risk to undermine exactly the innovation capabilities that data sharing policies wish to promote. Hence, the importance given to health data and the health industry by free-flow of data policy documents, together with the above mentioned explicit references by the Commission to personal data and the General Data Protection Regulation, could be regarded as further grounds to include also personal data within the object of the policy regarding the liberalisation of data flows among various stakeholders acting within the digital internal market.

A clearer definition of the object of the considered policy of data sharing and the understanding of whether also personal data are considered within it or not, are of great relevance at a legal, and thus in turn at a practical, level.

The option of the inclusion of personal data within the policy objective of the free-flow of information, does not challenge the effectiveness of the data protection regime established under the General Data Protection Regulation and the e-Privacy Directive. To the very contrary, as acknowledged by the Commission itself, the data protection framework is the first and essential regulatory basis for the transfer and thus the processing of personal data. As will be further illustrated, the treatment of sensitive personal data is object of an even higher regulatory threshold. Data protection law under the reformed framework has exacerbated controllers' obligations and data subjects' rights in respect to the treatment of personal data. This evidently renders personal data sharing subject to more burdensome procedural and substantial requirements, which evidently have the effect of curbing and restricting personal data transfers among different parties. Data subjects' fundamental rights in respect to the trading of their personal data are in this way meant to be safeguarded.

Under these premises, the consideration and inclusion of personal data within the free-flow of information policy does not interfere with the material application of the data protection regime *as such* (that is, it does not impact on the '*an*' of application of data protection law), but can be relevant at a secondary interpretative level, for the purposes of the definition of how data protection rules must be interpreted and thus applied in respect to the same data protection law's regulatory objectives. In these regards, as will be better shown in the next chapters, the *social* objective of protecting data subjects' fundamental rights need to be carefully weighed against the other data protection law's *economic* objective of advancing market integration through the promotion of the free flow of personal data.[143] In respect to this last objective, data protection law under the General Data Protection Law is to be considered not only a fundamental rights-based law but also a form of market regulation,[144] as suggested in particular by some specific provisions.[145]

[143] Identifying this dual objective of Lynskey (2015), pp. 76–80.

[144] Lynskey (2015), pp. 86–87.

[145] See analysis infra Chap. 5, Sects. 5.3.2.3 and 5.4.

In this perspective, the emerging policy objective regarding (personal) data sharing and re-use within the digital market, strictly connected to broader data-related innovation goals, shall function as an interpretative benchmark guiding the application of European Union's market regulation framework.[146]

This means, ultimately, that the growingly pressing policy objectives of data accessibility and digital efficiency shall be taken into account for the analysis of the legal framework relevant for the health data sharing, starting from data protection law- regulating the market relationship between private and public entities and individual data subjects-, and competition law- regulating the market relationship between undertakings.

4.4 The Free Movement of Research Data as an Emerging European Principle

Overall, the analysis shows the emergence of a policy objective regarding (personal) data sharing and re-use within the digital market, strictly connected to broader data-related innovation goals. If considered together with the EU Commission's documents regarding digital health and the importance of health data sharing, a specific efficiency-oriented policy goal regarding health data sharing can be distinguished at the forefront of the European Union's policy agenda.

The importance of access to health data for these purposes has been lately highlighted by the European Commission in the recently enacted "European strategy for data".[147] Here, the creation of a "Common European health data space" has been considered among the nine European data spaces the European Commission intends to encourage. The common European health data space is consistent with the principle of the free movement of research data that is emerging in some of the latest above-recalled regulatory interventions, as the Regulation on the free flow of non-personal data, the Open Data Directive as well as the Data Governance Act. It is further supported by the more general innovation principle, which, as the Commission underlines, ensures that "legislation is designed in a way that creates the best possible conditions for innovation to flourish".[148]

As has been highlighted in the previous chapters, health data pooling practices is a varied phenomenon encompassing mergers or partnerships established through contractual agreements specifically designed for the transfer of digital health data. Although extremely varied, health data pooling practices appear to share two essential features, for they basically involve (i) health data processing activities and (ii) an agreement over the sharing of scientifically valuable health data. In this

[146] Stressing the emergence of an outright regulatory paradigm of the free-flow of data, Richter and Slowinski (2019), pp. 4 ff.

[147] European Commission (19 February 2020a), p. 7.

[148] European Commission (25 November 2019e).

perspective, health data pooling practices are relevant under both data protection and competition law. Hence, the analysis that follows will question under which conditions health data pools are lawful under European data protection and competition law. In other terms, it will enquire under which conditions European data protection and competition law promote innovation objectives achieved through the sharing of health data.

Such innovation objectives underlying contractual arrangements of health data and supported by European Union's policy in the digital single market need thus to be weighed against the regulatory objectives—respectively underlying European data protection and competition law—respectively related to the protection of data subjects' fundamental right to data protection and the protection of free competition. Under these premises, the following chapters will test health data pools and their related efficiency-objectives against the backdrop of the provisions of both European data protection and competition law.

It is indeed questioned whether EU data protection and competition law promote such innovation-oriented goals, or rather curb them for the purposes of the protection of other interests.

While European competition law has always played a role in regulating innovation resulting from research and development endeavours, the General Data Protection Regulation has lately come to provide additional regulatory responses to data-driven innovation. The specificities of health-related markets, which are highly technology-inflected and with a highly scientific content, trigger the relevance of specific provisions of the two frameworks.

As far as data protection law is concerned, the General Data Protection Regulation entails some specific provisions regarding the treatment of health data under art. 9 GDPR, which prohibits the treatment of health data unless specific exceptional conditions are met, related, amongst others, also to the processing of heath data for scientific and statistical purposes.

Shifting from a vertical business-to-consumer perspective to a horizontal business-to-business perspective, also the European competition law framework similarly appears to lay down a prohibition regarding health data sharing agreements, potentially relevant as horizontal agreements under art. 101, 1 TFEU. However, also this prohibition is exempted under the so-called block exemptions regarding research and development agreements and technology transfer agreements. As far as competition law is concerned, also the recent merger case law in the pharmaceutical sector shows a renewed attention by the Commission for innovation achievements in such a sensitive sector, also despite resulting market concentrations.

References

Advocate General Geelhoed (14 December 2004) Opinion in case of the European Court of Justice Arnold André GmbH & Co. KG v Landrat des Kreises Herford, C-434/02. http://curia.europa.eu/juris/showPdf.jsf?text=&docid=49762&pageIndex=0&doclang=en&mode=lst&dir=&occ=first&part=1&cid=4981214

Ajunwa I, Crawford K, Schulz J (2016) Health and big data: an ethical framework for health information collection by corporate wellness programs. J Law Med Ethics 44:474–480

Alemanno A, Garde A (2013) The emergence of an EU lifestyle policy-the case of alcohol, tobacco and unhealthy diets. Common Mark Law Rev 50:1745–1786

Altenstetter C (2011) Medical device regulation and nanotechnologies: determining the role of safety concerns in policymaking. Law Policy 33:227–255

Autorité de la Concurrence-Bundeskartellamt (10 May 2016) Competition Law and Data. https://www.bundeskartellamt.de/SharedDocs/Publikation/DE/Berichte/Big%20Data%20Papier.pdf?__blob=publicationFile&v=2

Bache G, Flear ML, Hervey TK (2013) The defining features of the European Union's approach to regulating new health technologies. In: Farrell AM, Flear ML, Hervey TK, Murphy T (eds) European law and new health technologies. Oxford University Press, Oxford, pp 7–45

Beurden A (2003) The European perspective on E-health. In: Callens S (ed) E-health and the law. Kluwer, Den Haag, pp 106–108

Big Data Value Association (October 2017) European Big Data Value-Strategic Research and Innovation Agenda, online available at http://www.bdva.eu/sites/default/files/BDVA_SRIA_v4_Ed1.1.pdf

Blackman C, Forge S (November 2017) Data Flows-Future Scenarios: In-Depth Analysis for the ITRE Committee, European Parliament, Directorate-General for Internal Policies- Policy Department Economic and Scientific Policy http://www.europarl.europa.eu/RegData/etudes/IDAN/2017/607362/IPOL_IDA(2017)607362_EN.pdf

Brauneis R, Goodman EP (2018) Algorithmic transparency for the Smart City. Yearb J Law Technol 103:111–176

Callens S (2002) Tele-medicine and the E-commerce directive. Eur J Health Law 9:93–109

Callens S (2010) The EU legal framework on E-health. In: Mossialos E, Permanand G, Baeten R, Hervey T (eds) Health systems governance in Europe: the role of European Union law and policy. Cambridge University Press, Cambridge, pp 561–588

Cockburn IM, Henderson R, Stern S (2019) The impact of artificial intelligence on innovation: an exploratory analysis. In: Grawal AK, Gans J, Goldfarb A (eds) The economics of artificial intelligence. University of Chicago Press, Chicago, pp 115–146

Colangelo G, Borgogno O (5 April 2019) Data sharing and interoperability: fostering innovation and competition through APIs. Comput Law Secur Rev 35: 105314

Commission of the European Communities (28 May 2002) Communication from the Commission to the Council, the European Parliament, the Economic and Social Committee and the Committee of the Regions-eEurope 2005, An Information Society for All. https://eur-lex.europa.eu/LexUriServ/LexUriServ.do?uri=COM:2002:0263:FIN:EN:PDF

Council of the European Union (10 December 2013) Council conclusions on the "Reflection process on modern, responsive and sustainable health systems". https://www.consilium.europa.eu/uedocs/cms_data/docs/pressdata/en/lsa/140004.pdf

Council of the European Union (20 June 2014) Council Conclusions on the Economic Crisis and Healthcare. https://www.consilium.europa.eu/media/28051/143283.pdf

Council of the European Union (7 December 2015) Council Conclusions on Personalised Medicine for Patients. http://data.consilium.europa.eu/doc/document/ST-15054-2015-INIT/en/pdf

Council of the European Union (27 May 2016) The Transition Towards an Open Science System-Council Conclusions. http://data.consilium.europa.eu/doc/document/ST-9526-2016-INIT/en/pdf

Council of the European Union (8 December 2017) Council Conclusions on Health in the Digital Society- Making Progress in Data-driven Innovation in the Field of Health. http://data.consilium.europa.eu/doc/document/ST-14079-2017-INIT/en/pdf

Council of the European Union (10 December 2021) "Proposal for a Regulation of the European Parliament and of the Council on European data governance (Data Governance Act) - Analysis of the final compromise text in view to agreement and Council of the European Union" 2020/0340(COD) https://www.consilium.europa.eu/en/press/press-releases/2021/11/30/promoting-data-sharing-presidency-reaches-deal-with-parliament-on-data-governance-act/

Crosby S (1991) The single market and the rule of law. Eur Law Rev 16:451–465

Drexl J (27 April 2018) Data Access and Data Control in the Era of Connected Devices. Study on Behalf of the European Consumer Organisation BEUC https://www.beuc.eu/publications/beuc-x-2018-121_data_access_and_control_in_the_area_of_connected_devices.pdf

Drexl J (2019) Legal challenges of the changing role of personal and non-personal data in the data economy. In: De Franceschi A, Schulze R (eds) Digital revolution: data protection, smart products, blockchain technology and bitcoins challenges for law in practice. Beck, München, pp 19–41

Drexl J, Hilty R et al (16 August 2016) On the Current Debate on Exclusive Rights and Access Rights to Data at the European Level- Max Planck for Innovation and Competition Position Statement. https://pure.mpg.de/rest/items/item_2339820_16/component/file_2339821/content

Duch-Brown N, Martens B, Müller-Langer F (2017) The Economics of Ownership, Access and Trade in Digital Data- European Commission Joint Research Centre Digital Economy Working Paper 2017-01. https://ec.europa.eu/jrc/sites/jrcsh/files/jrc104756.pdf

Edwards L (2016) Privacy, security and data protection in smart cities: a critical EU law perspective. EDPL 2:28–58

European Commission (19 April 2001) E-Europe- an Information Society for All. https://ec.europa.eu/digital-single-market/en/news/eeurope-information-society-all

European Commission (17 September 2012a) Communication from the Commission to the European Parliament, the Council, the European Economic and Social Committee and the Committee of the Regions- Unleashing the Potential of Cloud Computing in Europe. https://www.pdpjournals.com/docs/88053.pdf

European Commission (7 December 2012b) eHealth Action Plan 2012-2020: Innovative Healthcare for the 21st Century. https://ec.europa.eu/digital-single-market/en/news/ehealth-action-plan-2012-2020-innovative-healthcare-21st-century

European Commission (10 April 2014a) Green Paper on Mobile Health. https://ec.europa.eu/digital-single-market/en/news/green-paper-mobile-health-mhealth

European Commission (2 July 2014b) Communication from the Commission to the European Parliament, the Council, the European Economic and Social Committee and the Committee of the Regions- Towards a Thriving Data Economy. https://eur-lex.europa.eu/legal-content/EN/TXT/PDF/?uri=CELEX:52014DC0442&from=EN

European Commission (6 May 2015) Communication from the Commission to the European Parliament, the Council, the European Economic and Social Committee and the Committee of the Regions- A Digital Single Strategy for Europe, 2015 Digital Single Market Strategy for Europe. https://eur-lex.europa.eu/legal-content/EN/TXT/?uri=COM%3A2015%3A192%3AFIN

European Commission (4 March 2016a) Citizens Science. https://ec.europa.eu/digital-single-market/en/citizen-science

European Commission (25 May 2016b) Communication from the Commission to the European Parliament, the Council, the European Economic and Social Committee and the Committee of the Regions, Online Platforms and the Digital Single Market – Opportunities and Challenges for Europe. https://eur-lex.europa.eu/legal-content/EN/TXT/PDF/?uri=CELEX:52016DC0288&from=EN

European Commission (10 January 2017a) Communication from the Commission to the European Parliament, the Council, the European Economic and Social Committee and the Committee of the Regions-Building a European Data Economy. https://eur-lex.europa.eu/legal-content/EN/TXT/?uri=COM:2017:9:FIN

European Commission (10 January 2017b) Commission Staff Working Document on the Free Flow of Data and Emerging Issues of the European Data Economy. Accompanying the Communication Building a European Data Economy. https://eur-lex.europa.eu/legal-content/EN/TXT/?uri=CELEX:52017SC0002

European Commission (24 January 2017c) Big Data Value Private-Public Partnership. https://ec.europa.eu/digital-single-market/en/big-data-value-public-private-partnership

European Commission (10 May 2017d) Commission Communication on the Mid-Term Review on the implementation of the Digital Single Market Strategy. A Connected Digital Single Market for All. https://eur-lex.europa.eu/legal-content/EN/TXT/?qid=1496330315823&uri=CELEX:52017DC0228

European Commission (14 July 2017e) The Digital Health Society Declaration. https://digital-strategy.ec.europa.eu/en/news/digital-health-society-declaration

European Commission (8 March 2018a) Communication from the Commission to the European Parliament, the European Council, the Council, the European Economic and Social Committee and the Committee of the Regions- Fin Tech Action Plan: For a More Competitive and Innovative European Financial Sector. https://eur-lex.europa.eu/resource.html?uri=cellar:6793c578-22e6-11e8-ac73-01aa75ed71a1.0001.02/DOC_1&format=PDF

European Commission (25 April 2018b) Communication from the Commission to the European Parliament, the Council, the European Economic and Social Committee and the Committee of the Regions Enabling the Digital Transformation of Health and Care in the Digital Single Market; Empowering Citizens and Building a Healthier Society. https://ec.europa.eu/digital-single-market/en/news/communicationenabling-digital-transformation-health-and-care-digital-single-market-empowering

European Commission (25 April 2018c) Staff Working Document, Accompanying the Document-Communication from the Commission to the European Parliament, the Council, the European Economic and Social Committee and the Committee of the Regions on Enabling the Digital Transformation of Health and Care in the Digital Single Market; Empowering Citizens and Building a Healthier Society. https://ec.europa.eu/digital-single-market/en/news/staff-working-document-enabling-digital-transformation-health-and-care-digital-single-market

European Commission (25 April 2018d) Communication from the Commission to the European Parliament, the European Council, the Council, the European Economic and Social Committee and the Committee of the Regions- Artificial Intelligence for Europe. https://eur-lex.europa.eu/legal-content/EN/TXT/PDF/?uri=CELEX:52018DC0237&from=EN

European Commission (25 April 2018e) Communication from the Commission to the European Parliament, the Council, the European Economic and Social Committee and the Committee of the Regions, "Towards a European Common Data Space". https://eur-lex.europa.eu/legal-content/EN/TXT/PDF/?uri=CELEX:52018DC0232&from=EN

European Commission (25 April 2018f) Commission Staff Working Document, Guidance on Sharing Private Sector Data in the European Data Economy, Accompanying the Document Communication from the Commission to the European Parliament, the Council, the European economic and social Committee and the Committee of the Regions "Towards a common European data space". https://eur-lex.europa.eu/legal-content/EN/TXT/PDF/?uri=CELEX:52018SC0125&from=EN

European Commission (25April 2018g) Commission Recommendation EU 2018/790 of 25 April 2018 on access to and preservation of scientific information. https://www.eoscportal.eu/sites/default/files/CELEX_32018H0790_EN_TXT.pdf

European Commission (25 April 2018h) Commission Staff Working Document Accompanying the Document Commission Recommendation on access to and preservation of scientific information. http://edz.bib.uni-mannheim.de/edz/pdf/swd/2018/swd-2018-0123-en.pdf

European Commission (25 April 2018i) Data in the EU: Commission Steps Up Efforts to Increase Availability and Boost Healthcare Data Sharing. http://europa.eu/rapid/press-release_IP-18-3364_en.htm

European Commission (21 September 2018j) Report from the Commission to the European Parliament and the Council on the Operation of Directive 2011/24/EU on the Application of Patients' Rights in Cross-border Healthcare. https://eur-lex.europa.eu/resource.html?uri=cellar:bc5ac6d2-bd7c-11e8-99ee-01aa75ed71a1.0019.02/DOC_1&format=PDF

European Commission (7 December 2018k) Communication from the Commission to the European Parliament, the European Council, the Council, the European Economic and Social Committee and the Committee of the Regions- Coordinated Plan on Artificial Intelligence. https://eur-lex.europa.eu/legal-content/EN/TXT/PDF/?uri=CELEX:52018DC0237&from=EN

European Commission (24 January 2019a) Proposal for a Revision of the Public Sector Information (PSI) Directive https://ec.europa.eu/digital-single-market/en/proposal-revision-public-sector-information-psi-directive

European Commission (25 January 2019b) Speech by Commissioner For Health and Food Safety Vytenis Andriukaitis at the Event: "EU's Role in Promoting Health of Europeans Beyond East & West". https://ec.europa.eu/commission/commissioners/2014-2019/andriukaitis/announcements/speech-commissioner-health-and-food-safety-vytenis-andriukaitis-event-eus-role-promoting-health_en

European Commission (28 January 2019c) Report from the Commission to the Council and the European Parliament- Competition Enforcement in the Pharmaceutical Sector- European Competition Authorities Working Together for Affordable and Innovative Medicines. http://ec.europa.eu/competition/publications/reports/kd0718081enn.pdf

European Commission (4 April 2019d) Digital Single Market: Commission Welcomes European Parliament's Vote on New Rules for Sharing Public Sector Data. http://europa.eu/rapid/press-release_STATEMENT-19-1935_en.htm

European Commission (25 November 2019e) Ensuring EU Legislation Supports Innovation. https://ec.europa.eu/info/research-and-innovation/law-and-regulations/innovation-friendly-legislation_en

European Commission (19 February 2020a) Communication from the Commission to the European Parliament, the Council, the European Economic and Social Committee and the Committee of the Regions, 'A European Strategy for Data', , COM(2020) 66 final. https://eur-lex.europa.eu/legal-content/EN/TXT/PDF/?uri=CELEX:52020DC0066&from=EN

European Commission (15 December 2020) Proposal for a Regulation of the European Parliament and of the Council on a Single Market For Digital Services (Digital Services Act) and amending Directive 2000/31/EC COM(2020) 825 final https://eur-lex.europa.eu/legal-content/EN/TXT/PDF/?uri=CELEX:52020PC0825&from=IT

European Commission (2020b) Guidance on Private Sector Data Sharing. https://ec.europa.eu/digital-single-market/en/guidance-private-sector-data-sharing

European Commission (2020c) Open Science. https://ec.europa.eu/info/research-and-innovation/strategy/strategy-2020-2024/our-digital-future/open-science_en

European Commission, Digital Single Market-Shaping the Digital Single Market https://ec.europa.eu/digital-single-market/en/policies/shaping-digital-single-market

European Commission, eHealth: Digital Health and Care. https://ec.europa.eu/health/ehealth/overview_en

European Commission, Big Data (8 September 2021) online available at https://ec.europa.eu/digital-single-market/en/big-data

European Court of Justice (28 April 1998a) Decker v. Caisse de Maladie des Employés Privé, C-120/95. http://curia.europa.eu/juris/showPdf.jsf;jsessionid=5137B71DB7448092D44F4547FB48BFF9?text=&docid=43791&pageIndex=0&doclang=EN&mode=lst&dir=&occ=first&part=1&cid=4959036

European Court of Justice (28 April 1998b) Kohll v. Union de Caisse de Maladie, C-158/96. https://eur-lex.europa.eu/legal-content/EN/TXT/PDF/?uri=CELEX:61996CJ0158&from=EN

European Court of Justice (12 July 2001a) Geraets-Smits v. Stichting Ziekenfonds, C-157/99. http://curia.europa.eu/juris/showPdf.jsf?text=&docid=46529&pageIndex=0&doclang=EN&mode=lst&dir=&occ=first&part=1&cid=4961917

European Court of Justice (9 October 2001b) Netherlands vs. Parliament and Council (Biotechnology), C-377/98. http://curia.europa.eu/juris/showPdf.jsf?text=&docid=46255&pageIndex=0&doclang=EN&mode=lst&dir=&occ=first&part=1&cid=1770869

European Court of Justice (13 May 2003) Müller-Fauré and Van Riet Onderlinge Waarborgmaatschappij OZ Zorgverzekeringen UA and E.E.M. van Riet v Onderlinge Waarborgmaatschappij ZAO Zorgverzekeringen, C-385/99. http://curia.europa.eu/juris/showPdf.jsf?text=&docid=48278&pageIndex=0&doclang=EN&mode=lst&dir=&occ=first&part=1&cid=4966274

European Court of Justice (16 May 2006) Yvonne Watts v Bedford Primary Care Trust and Secretary of State for Health, C-372/04. http://curia.europa.eu/juris/showPdf.jsf?text=&docid=56965&pageIndex=0&doclang=EN&mode=lst&dir=&occ=first&part=1&cid=4973720

European Data Protection Supervisor (27 March 2013) Opinion on the Communication from the Commission on 'eHealth Action Plan 2012-2020- Innovative Healthcare for the 21st Century'. https://edps.europa.eu/sites/edp/files/publication/13-03-27_ehealth_action_en.pdf

European Data Protection Supervisor (21 May 2015) Opinion 1/2015- Mobile Health-Reconciling Technological Innovation with Data Protection. https://edps.europa.eu/sites/edp/files/publication/15-05-21_mhealth_en_0.pdf

European Data Protection Supervisor (8 June 2018) Comments of the EDPS on a Proposal for a Regulation of the European Parliament and of the Council on a Framework for the Free-Flow of Non-Personal Data in the European Union. https://edps.europa.eu/sites/edp/files/publication/18-06-08edps_formal_comments_freeflow_non_personal_data_en.pdf

European Open Science Cloud (2021) EOSC- A Gateway to information and resources in EOSC. https://eosc-portal.eu/about/eosc

European Parliament (14 January 2014) Resolution of 14 January 2014 on the eHealth Action Plan 2012-2020- Innovative healthcare for the 21st century. http://www.europarl.europa.eu/sides/getDoc.do?pubRef=-//EP//TEXT+TA+P7-TA-20140010+0+DOC+XML+V0//EN

European Parliament (19 May 2015) Report on Safer Healthcare in Europe: Improving Patient Safety and Improving Antimicrobial Resistance http://www.europarl.europa.eu/sides/getDoc.do?pubRef=-//EP//TEXT+TA+P8-TA-20150197+0+DOC+XML+V0//EN

European Parliament and Council of the European Union (28 November 2018) 'Regulation (EU) 2018/1807 of the European Parliament and of the Council of 14 November 2018 on a framework for the free flow of non-personal data in the European Union', OJ L 303/59. https://eurlex.europa.eu/legalcontent/EN/TXT/PDF/?uri=CELEX:32018R1807&from=EN

Flear ML (2017) Regulating new technologies: EU internal market law, risk and socio-technical order. In: Cremona M (ed) New technologies and EU law. Oxford University Press, Oxford, pp 74–120

Graef I, Gellert R, Husovec M (September 2018) Towards a Holistic Regulatory Approach for the European Data Economy: Why the Illusive Notion of Non-Personal Data is Counterproductive to Data Innovation. https://papers.ssrn.com/sol3/papers.cfm?abstract_id=3256189

Greer SL (2006) Uninvited Europeanization: neo-functionalism and the EU in health policy. J Eur Public Policy 13:134–152

Horgan D, Kent A (2017) EU health policy, coherence, stakeholder diversity and their impact on the EMA. BiomedHub 2:191–201

Kerber W (2016) A new (intellectual) property right for non-personal data? An economic analysis. GRUR Int:989–999

Kim D (2017) No One's ownership as the status quo and a possible way forward: a note on the public consultation on building a European data economy. J Intell Prop Law Pract 13:154–165

Koops BJ (2014) The trouble with European data protection law. IDPL 4:250–261

Lynskey O (2015) The foundations of EU data protection law. Oxford University Press, Oxford

Mārcut (2017) Crystalising the EU digital policy- an exploration of the EU digital single market. Springer, Basel

Martens B (December 2018) The Importance of Data Access Regimes for Artificial Intelligence and Machine Learning, European Commission- JRC Digital Economy Working Papers 2018-09. https://papers.ssrn.com/sol3/papers.cfm?abstract_id=3357652

Martinsen DS (2005) Towards an internal health market with the European court. West Eur Polit 28(5):1035–1056

McKeee M, Mossialos E, Baeten R (2002) The impact of EU law on health care systems. Peter Lang, Brussels

Mossialos E, Thomson S, Linden AT (2004) Information technology law and health Systems in the European Union. Int J Technol Assess Health Care 20:498–508

Mossialos E, Permanand G, Baeten R, Hervey T (2010) Health systems governance in Europe: the role of European Union law and policy. In: Mossialos E, Permanand G, Baeten R, Hervey T (eds) Health systems governance in Europe: the role of European Union law and policy. Cambridge University Press, Cambridge, pp 1–83

Neergard U (2011) EU healthcare law in a constitutional light: distributions of competence, notions of 'solidarity', and 'social Europe'. In: Van De Gronden JW, Szyszczak E, Neergaard U, Krajewski M (eds) Healthcare and EU law, legal issues of services of general interest. TMC Asser Press, The Hague, pp 19–58

OECD (6 October 2015) Data-driven Innovation-Big Data for Growth and Wellbeing. https://www.oecd.org/sti/data-driven-innovation-9789264229358-en.htm

OECD (2018) Oslo Manual 2018- Guidelines for Collecting, Reporting and Using Data Innovation- The Measurment of Scientific, Technological and Innovation Activities. OECD Publishing, Paris/Eurostat, Luxembourg

Purtova N (2018) The law of everything. Broad concept of personal data and future of EU data protection law. Law Innov Technol 10:40–81

Richardson R, Schultz J, Crawford K (2019) Dirty data, bad predictions: how civil rights violations impact police data, predictive policing systems, and justice. New York Univ Law Rev 94:15–55

Richter H, Slowinski PR (2019) The data sharing economy: on the emergence of new intermediaries. IIC 50:4–29

Schneider G (2019) The algorithmic governance of public-decision making: towards an integrated European framework for public accountability, in big data and public law: new challenges beyond data protection. Eurojus Special Issue 4:134–148

Seitz C (2018) Healthcare systems and competition: challenges and boundaries for the application of competition law in highly regulated Markets in the Healthcare Sector in the European Union. In: Nihoul P, Van Cleynenbreugel P (eds) The roles of innovation in competition law analysis. Edward Elgar, Cheltenham, pp 131–161

Zarsky T (2015) The privacy-innovation conundrum. LCLR 19:115–168

Zech H (2017) Data as a tradable commodity. In: De Franceschi A (ed) European contract law and the digital single market- the implications of the digital revolution. Intersentia, Cambridge, pp 51–80

Zetsche DA, Buckley RP, Arner DW, Barberis JN (2017-2018) From fin-tech to tech-fin: the regulatory challenges of data-driven finance. New York Univ J Law Bus 14: 393-446

Chapter 5
Health Data Pools Under European Data Protection Law

5.1 Health Data Pooling as Health Data Treatment Under Data Protection Law

Health data sharing practices imply first of all a treatment of health data, which is regulated under data protection law. In these regards, the General Data Protection provides a very complex regulatory framework specifically regarding health data. Indeed, it provides specific definitions of different types of health data, such as genetic data or biometric data under art. 4, para. 13, 14 and 15 GDPR. In addition, it categorizes health data as a "special category of data" the processing of which is prohibited under art. 9, 1 para GDPR. Ultimately, it sets some broad exemptions to such prohibitions that allow the processing of health data if it is carried out for certain purposes and provided specific conditions are met. By establishing a general prohibition of health data treatment and some grounds of exceptions to that prohibition, the regulatory status of health data treatment appears to be defined by a layered—if not contradictory—regime and triggers some challenging interpretative efforts.

Before digging deeper into the multifaceted data protection law provisions regarding the treatment of health data, some theoretical background considerations are needed. Indeed, the contradictory regime established with regards to health data is the result of a much deeper tension within European data protection law, which the General Data Protection Regulation has inherited from the previous Directive and partly exacerbated. This tension relates to the two seemingly contrasting objectives of data protection law, on the one hand the protection of data subjects' fundamental rights in the digital environment and on the other hand the promotion of lawful data flows fuelling efficiency outcomes within the digital single market.

G. Schneider, *Health Data Pools Under European Data Protection and Competition Law*, Munich Studies on Innovation and Competition 17,
https://doi.org/10.1007/978-3-030-95427-7_5

5.2 European Data Protection Law's Pillars

5.2.1 The Fundamental Rights' Pillar

European Data Protection Law has its roots deeply planted in the fundamental rights' rationale.[1] As widely acknowledged in the scholarly literature, the European conception of privacy is strongly civil rights-oriented, as opposed to the American utilitarian model.[2] Born from the rib of the right to privacy,[3] the right to data protection has been itself elevated to an autonomous fundamental right in the European Charter of Fundamental Rights under art. 8 EU Charter.[4] This is directly reflected in the General Data Protection Regulation, which is legally rooted in art. 16 TFEU and recalls art. 8 EU Charter in recital 1.[5]

The fundamental rights dimension of the right to data protection has however broadened in the digital economy: here, the right to data protection is not only to be regarded as a self-standing fundamental right but rather a foundational precondition for the protection of other data subjects' fundamental rights, as the same recital n. 75 GDPR highlights.[6]

Indeed, in the current technical and economic environment, data has become the key asset for corporations' decision-making along the lines of technically established

[1] For a historical reconstruction, see Van Der Sloot (2017), pp. 3 ff.; Hustinx (2014).

[2] Samuelson (1999), p. 1127.

[3] For a comment on the relationship between privacy and data protection, Gellert and Gutwirth (2013), pp. 522–530. Lynskey (2014), pp. 569 ff.

[4] For a critical assessment of the fundamental rights nature of the right to data protection, see Van Der Sloot (2017).

[5] Lynskey (2014), p. 573.

[6] Recital 75 GDPR: "the risk to the rights and freedoms of natural persons, of varying likelihood and severity, may result from personal data processing which could lead to physical, material or non-material damage, in particular: where the processing may give rise to discrimination, identity theft or fraud, financial loss, damage to the reputation, loss of confidentiality of personal data protected by professional secrecy, unauthorised reversal of pseudonymisation, or any other significant economic or social disadvantage; where data subjects might be deprived of their rights and freedoms or prevented from exercising control over their personal data; where personal data are processed which reveal racial or ethnic origin, political opinions, religion or philosophical beliefs, trade union membership, and the processing of genetic data, data concerning health or data concerning sex life or criminal convictions and offences or related security measures; where personal aspects are evaluated, in particular analysing or predicting aspects concerning performance at work, economic situation, health, personal preferences or interests, reliability or behaviour, location or movements, in order to create or use personal profiles; where personal data of vulnerable natural persons, in particular of children, are processed; or where processing involves a large amount of personal data and affects a large number of data subjects". Emphasis added. See also recital 76 GDPR, stating that "the likelihood and severity of the risk to the rights and freedoms of the data subject should be determined by reference to the nature, scope, context and purposes of the processing. Risk should be evaluated on the basis of an objective assessment, by which it is established whether data processing operations involve a risk or a high risk".

schemes in which individuals are arbitrarily included or excluded,[7] leading to labelling and stigmatization patterbs that end up compromising due processing guarantees[8] and causing that what some scholars have defined as an outright "disruption of human lives".[9] Uncontrolled circulation of a huge quantity of information about individuals and the uncontrolled use that is made of it by businesses produce a range of harms- such as the loss of a job or a higher charge for services-, which is very likely to provoke a chilling effect directly related to a general "sense of insecurity" and to the constant "infringement of freedom of communications as well as that of the right to live in a free society without fear".[10] In this perspective, data processing activities conducted on a massive scale as the current technological capabilities allow,[11] is to be considered as a risky practice,[12] posing substantial threats not only to individuals' rights, first of all to individuals' autonomy,[13] but also to broader collective interests.[14]

Against this backdrop, the right to data protection in the form of the right to a fair, transparent and accountable[15] data collection, processing and practical use in the

[7]The point is again stressed by Gellert (2015), p. 4.

[8]For a deeper assessment on the issue see Crawford and Schultz (2014), pp. 93 ff., stressing the analogies between "real" and "technological" due process.

[9]US Department of Health Education & Welfare (1973), p. 14.

[10]Gellert (2015), p. 5, stating that "the biggest issues stemming from automated data processing systems are not violations of privacy, but rather, social sorting practices, which are discriminating". With these regards, Miller (1971), p. 49, underlining an alienation and de-humanisation process that individuals undergo in the classifying society.

[11]See Recital 6 observing how "rapid technological developments and globalisation have brought new challenges for the protection of personal data. The scale of the collection and sharing of personal data has increased significantly. Technology allows both private companies and public authorities to make use of personal data on an unprecedented scale in order to pursue their activities".

[12]See Recitals 75–76 GDPR. For the literature see Rubinstein (2013), pp. 74 ff., talking about "systemic risks" and. Gellert (2015), pp. 6 ff. For a broader assessment see Mantelero (2018), pp. 289 ff.

[13]Spina (2014), p. 251, commenting on the statements of the European Court of Justice, affirming that the various collected "(..) data, taken as a whole may allow very precise conclusions to be drawn concerning the private lives of the persons whose data has been retained" (par. 27, ECJ Digital Rights Ireland and Seitlinger and others). Moreover, the author underlines that the court appears to adopt a teleological interpretation by highlighting the possible risks of certain processing of personal data. Indeed, the collection of traffic data could have "chilling effects" on individuals' autonomy, especially with regard to freedom of expression (para. 28), the right to self-determination. The case appears to be of particular importance since it stresses the potential risks of a chilling effect caused by unconstrained data processing. With specific regard to the issue of the relationship between automatic data processing and chilling effect see Burri and Schär (2016) and Casarez (2015–2016).

[14]Spina (2014), p. 256, stating how "the market failures associated with forms of Big Data encourage us to look at privacy risks and at privacy as not only an individual right but a collective interest".

[15]See art. 5 GDPR.

context of businesses' decision making[16] becomes a structural and technical precondition to the protection of other fundamental rights, jeopardised by data-driven algorithmic models,[17] first of all the right to self-determination, the right to equality and non-discrimination.[18] This means that in the digital environment, the right to data protection as recently reshaped in the face of current technological developments, is not "an end in itself",[19] but is rather to be considered in a dynamic perspective, capable of highlighting the intrinsic interrelation between the right to data protection and other fundamental rights. Where data protection in the traditional conception of informational control and self-determination is difficult to be accomplished,[20] data protection law itself thus appears to have acquired the new function of a framework[21] for assessing the risks to other fundamental rights caused by massive-scale data processing activities.

The specificities of the economic and technical environment, where few big businesses' come to collect a vast amount of users' data and the information asymmetries between users and undertakings have widened more than ever,[22] have thus justified a turnaround of data protection law's regulatory barycentre, which under the General Data Protection Regulation has largely shifted from data subjects to processing undertakings. This means that the individual-based model, relying on the paradigm of consent and control of personal data[23] has been integrated and strengthened with what some strand of the literature has called an "agent-based"

[16]Nissenbaum (2008), pp. 24 ff., stressing how the fairness of privacy principles directly stems from social norms defining what constitutes an appropriate intrusion. It is important to stress that fair information practices are already applied by some statutes with regard to biobank research. It however needs a very solid structure assuring good governance, thus raising the problem of the efficacy of data protection authorities' intervention. On the issue see also Lemmens and Austin (2009), p. 251.

[17]Bennet (1992); Mayer-Schönberger and Cukier (2013), p. 20, noticing that data protection was generated as a risk regulation, aimed at controlling the different steps of data processing operations, made up by "complex and rich procedures to control and regulate the use of technology"; Burkert (1996), stressing that the function of data protection regulation is the one of reconciling basic values with technological change and development; Bygrave (2001), pp. 17 ff., stating that "data protection is a risk regulation to safeguard constitutional structure of the state against all risks entailed by automatic data processing", and with that recalling a data protection regulation of the German Land of Hesse, where at art. 1.2 the purpose of preventing "harm to any personal interests of the person concerned warrant protection", was pointed out.

[18]Wachter (22 January 2017).

[19]For a distinction between an "empty" right to data protection, and a "full" right to privacy, see Gellert and Gutwirth (2013), pp. 522 ff.

[20]It should be sufficient to think that without the disclosure of personal data, the innumerous services provided on the net would become inaccessible. Data is the actual money.

[21]Comandè (2015), pp. 121 ff.

[22]Cohen (2016), pp. 369 ff.

[23]For an assessment of the privacy as control theory, see Liebenau (2016), pp. 285 ff., especially 288 ff. In the big data environment the paradigm of individual control of personal data has soon come to show its weaknesses. This has been widely commented in the scholarly literature. See amongst others, Thierer (2013), pp. 409 ff.; Cate and Mayer-Schönberger (2013), p. 67.

paradigm,[24] with focus on the subject who actively comes to process the data.[25] In these regards, if the previous data protection framework under the 1995 Directive was focused on the phase of generation of the data and the moment when the use of the data has an impact on single individuals, The General Data Protection Regulation has started to shed regulatory light on the phase in between, where computational analysis aggregates the data on a massive scale and defines the profiles upon which businesses act.[26]

Upon these premises, the General Data Protection Regulation has come to set new safety standards to which data practices must comply to, expressing the need to establish anticipatory—or more technically speaking precautionary[27]—safeguards in respect to harms whose relationship with data processing practices is not any more determined by causality but rather by correlation.[28] Such safety standards have the form of outright obligations for processing businesses,[29] which are required to carry out their activities in a "lawful and fair" manner.[30] Through the tightening of processing companies' obligations, the General Data Protection Regulation has come to "proceduralize" data protection law, by tailoring companies' data processing activities to the protection of data subjects' rights and interests, and not by curtailing or prohibiting them.[31]

[24] Stressing the point Van der Sloot (2016), p. 197. The need of such a shift had been already acknowledged by See Pasquale (2013), pp. 1009 ff.

[25] The need of a coexistence of the consent-based model and a new model based on the direct intervention on businesses' conduct has been highlighted by the literature well before the enactment of the General Data Protection Regulation. See Tene and Polonetsky (2013), p. 245, stressing the need to view the data protection framework as a "set of levers that must be adjusted to adapt to varying business and technological conditions", in which "data minimisation and consent requirements" stand in second line, to leave room for the enactment of transparency, access and accuracy rules.

[26] De Hert and Lammerant (2016), pp. 146 ff.

[27] See with this regard the De Hert and Christianen (April 2013) calls upon the use of the precautionary principle as a useful tool for the risk regulation. For a comment on this see Gellert (2015), p. 7.

[28] Van der Sloot (2016), p. 178. On the issue see also Rubinstein (2013), p. 76, affirming how in the era of big data it is not any more a matter of causality, but rather of correlation. On the issue see supra Chap. 2, Sect. 2.1.2.

[29] In these regards see the provisions under articles 30–36 specifically regulate controllers' and processors' conduct in the form of the obligation to record the processing activities (art. 30); to cooperate with the supervisory authority (art. 31); to implement "appropriate technical and organisational measures to ensure a level of security appropriate to the risk (. . .)" (art. 32); to notify personal data breaches to the supervisory authority (art. 33) and to the data subject (art. 34); to carry out the data impact assessment (art. 35) with prior consultation of the same supervisory authority (art. 36).

[30] See art. 6 GDPR.

[31] Van Der Sloot (2017), p. 23.

This is well reflected in the central role given in the Regulation to the principle of accountability, related to data controllers' and processors' "responsabilisation".[32] This principle establishes a "burden of care" onto processing corporations regarding the compliance to fundamental principles of data protection law, such as the principle of lawfulness, transparency and fairness, and to the rules that substantiate these principles.[33] The accountability principle thus commands the processing entities to structure their business activities so as to render them adherent to the normative data protection requirements, as well as externally verifiable by both data subjects and data protection authorities.[34] Both data subjects and data protection authorities are indeed the recipients of various information duties, respectively under art. 13–15 GDPR and art. 58, 1 para lett. a) GDPR, which enable these in turn to exercise their rights and powers in order to effectively protect data subjects' fundamental right to data protection and the other fundamental rights that are incidentally involved.

Under these premises, the principle of accountability and especially the rules giving data subjects' information rights and the supervisory authorities investigation powers, well reflect how through the recent reform European data protection law has ever more become a primary source of regulation of businesses' conduct and, as a reflex, of data-driven markets.[35]

In this perspective, it appears that the objective of the protection of the fundamental right to data protection is achieved through the regulation of personal data processing activities considered as an "innovative technology".[36]

5.2.2 *The Market-Oriented Pillar*

Right from its very origins, European data protection law under the Directive had the primary objective of facilitating the establishment of the internal market. This economic and market-oriented objective was placed aside the rights-based goal of protecting the data subjects' personal rights when their personal data is processed.[37] The explanatory Memorandum of the Directive stresses that personal data needed to be transferred between Member States by business people acting at transnational level and taking advantage of their Treaty Freedoms, by national authorities cooperating as a direct result of the abolition of the borders within the internal market and, most interestingly, for scientific purposes.[38]

---

[32] The principle of accountability is established at art. 5.2 GDPR, affirming that "the controller shall be responsible for, and be able to demonstrate compliance with paragraph 1 (accountability)".

[33] See art. 5, 1 para.

[34] In these regards see Schneider (2019), p. 327 ff.

[35] F. Pasquale, Privacy, Antitrust and Power (2013), pp. 1009 ff.

[36] Gasser (18 March 2014), p. 2.

[37] Lynskey (2015), pp. 46 ff.

[38] See Commission of the European Communities (13 September 1990), para 7, stating that "a Community approach towards the protection of individuals in relation to the processing of personal

Since the European Union was lacking the competence with regards to the enactment of fundamental rights legislation before the Lisbon Treaty, the market-integration objective has been much emphasized by the European Court of Justice.

The great academic and policy debate- that has accompanied the drafting procedure and has followed the approval of the General Data Protection Regulation-, regarding the effectiveness of the tools provided by the Regulation in respect to the declared objective of protecting European citizens' fundamental rights from the intrusiveness of new data processing technologies,[39] has however perhaps left out of sight the other fundamental pillar on which the General Data Protection Regulation resides, that is the free flow of information as a precondition for the integration and consolidation of the internal market.

This pillar had a primary importance within the Data Protection Directive, whose legal foundations were to be found exactly in the regulation of the internal market under art. 100 of the Treaty establishing the European Community.[40] It has however not lost its hold within the normative system of the General Data Protection Regulation, under which the fundamental rights and the market integration purposes appear to be "on equal footing".[41]

Here, the market-related objective comes right behind the one of data subjects' fundamental rights in the changed technological and economic landscape, and it is expressed in recital 2 GDPR, stating how the Regulation is intended to contribute, amongst others, "to the economic and social progress" and "to the strengthening and the convergence of the economies within the internal market". Accordingly, recital 5 GDPR acknowledges how the flows of personal data have increased as a consequence of the "economic and social integration resulting from the functioning of the internal market" and with that also the "exchange of personal data between public and private actors". These statements reflect the acknowledgment by the European legislator of the economic value of personal data within the whirls of the digital economy. This is confirmed also by recital 13 GDPR, where the free movement of personal data is considered as a requirement for the proper functioning of the internal market.

---

data is also essential to the development of the data processing industry and of value-added data communication services. The speedy introduction of harmonized provisions concerning the protection of data and privacy in the context of digital telecommunications networks is a key element in the completion of the internal market in telecommunications equipment and services". See in these regards also the European Court of Justice, Österreichischer Rundfunk and Others, Joined Cases C-465/00, C-138/01 and C-139/01 (20 May 2003a), para 39, and European Court of Justice, Commission v. Germany, Case C-518/07, Gran Chamber (9 March 2010), para 3.

[39] In these regards it must be said that the academic scholarship is widely divided, and the positions range from more positive views to more critical ones, requiring additional regulatory endeavours to the protection of users' right in the digital-algorithmic dimension. For a critical assessment of the insufficiencies of the protection provided by the GDPR in respect to algorithmic inferences, Wachter and Mittelstadt (2019).

[40] Van Der Sloot (2017), p. 25.

[41] Lynskey (2015), p. 47.

Along these lines, the European Commission has lately come to pair the General Data Protection Regulation with the Regulation on the free flow of non-personal data, considering the two bodies of law as a comprehensive and coherent framework to the free movement of data in the European Union.[42]

From this second regulatory perspective, personal data—and the sharing of it—are not an object of protection but rather an "innovation enabling technology"[43] and with that a fundamental means for the establishment of the Digital Single Market, being the policy cornerstone of the European Commission.[44]

Against the backdrop of the cited recitals, it appears that under the Regulation more than it occurred in the Directive, European data protection law is characterised by an internal tension between two apparently conflicting aims, on the one hand the restriction of personal data processing for the sake of the protection of subjects' rights and on the other hand the maximisation of personal data flows for a development of the internal market, and in particular, of the digital economy that is blossoming in it.[45] This tension is again suggested in recital 123 GDPR, where supervisory authorities are given the task of monitoring and contributing to the application of data protection rules "in order to protect natural persons in relation to the processing of their personal data and to facilitate the free flow of personal data within the internal market".[46]

Under these premises, in addition to the new procedural obligations borne by data controllers[47] and the users' new digital rights[48] established by the General Data Protection, which either prohibit or curtail data processing activities, there is a parallel set of provisions that appears to encourage and facilitate data processing operations.[49] This set of provisions promotes the prospering of a free economic market for personal data, and with that the development of the broader digital economy.[50] As some strand of the literature had been observing already in the wakes of the approval of the new European data protection regime, the General Data Protection Regulation opens up "concrete doors" for personal data analytics to flourish.[51]

This occurs through a special data protection regime, which is variedly characterised by the three basic features of (i) allowing large-scale data processing

[42] European Commission (22 October 2021). See in these regards, Drexl (2019), p. 20, observing that "personal data are no longer only objects of a privacy interest but are increasingly recognised in their role as a valuable asset used by businesses in the digital sector".

[43] This expression is employed by Gasser (18 March 2014), p. 2.

[44] Marelli and Testa (4 May 2018), p. 497–498.

[45] For a reconstruction of the "hybrid nature of EU data protection law", Lynskey (2015), pp. 8–9.

[46] So Recital 123 GDPR.

[47] Maxwell (2015), pp. 205 ff.

[48] Mitrou (2017), pp. 42–48.

[49] This has been also observed by Mayer-Schönberger and Padova (2016), pp. 315 ff.

[50] See discussion supra Chap. 4, Sect. 4.3.2.

[51] Mayer-Schönberger and Padova (2016), pp. 317–318.

upon a legal basis that is different from data subjects' consent; (ii) providing derogations from controllers' obligations and from data subjects' rights; (iii) leaving greater discretion to Member States in the definition of the rules that data processing activities must observe and in particular in the definition of the additional organisational and technical measures assuring the protection of data subjects' fundamental rights.

Hence, not very far from what occurred through the Directive, also the Regulation leaves to Member States great space for shaping the regulatory landscape,[52] this raising the likelihood that some Member States will legislate in a more permissive way to personal data processing and others in a more restrictive way.[53] Moreover, in the absence of implementation by national member states, the definition of the relevant safeguards is additionally left to the discretionary choice of processing entities, this amplifying the room for regulatory divergences.[54]

This makes European Data Protection law overall an extremely nuanced regulatory landscape, in which the different regime layers established by the General Data Protection Regulation are rendered additionally complex by national divergences.[55]

Against this backdrop, an accurate and overall assessment of the General Data Protection Regulation reveals the existence of regulatory loopholes within the (fundamental rights-oriented) architecture of data subjects' protection and reaction tools, not only permitting but also effectively encouraging massive retention and reuse of personal data.

In these regards, the European legislator appears to have upheld some of the arguments put forward by EU policy makers during the GDPR's drafting procedures, stressing the need to foster innovation and enact economic growth through flexible regimes of data access and analysis.[56] This assumption is also shared by a strand of the scholarship acknowledging the gains in efficiency stemming from the "free" analysis of personal data and the consolidation of data across business

[52] Mayer-Schönberger and Padova (2016), p. 325. See recital 10 GDPR,

[53] This partly appears to threat the declared objective of enhancing legal certainty in the field of data protection. See recital 13 GDPR.

[54] Stressing this point, Marelli and Testa (4 May 2018), p. 498. The room for single entities' discretionary choice, although undermining legal certainty, can help them to react to and address more promptly the peculiarities of the environments in which the same processing entities act. See Von Grafenstein (11 March 2019), p. 5.

[55] Highlighting GDPR's regulatory flexibilities, Marelli and Testa (4 May 2018), p. 49, observing how different national data protection regimes are likely to enable and advantage massive data protection activities carried out by established national players employing big data analytics, which are less impacted- in respect to small and medium undertakings- by the costs needed for the adjustments to the different national regimes.

[56] Voss and Padova (25 June 2015).

platforms.[57] In these regards, the law and economics literature has traditionally criticised privacy laws[58] for establishing limits on consumer information flows, hampering businesses' freedom to innovate,[59] posing barriers to market entry and otherwise harming competition.[60]

Along these lines, the tightening of data controllers' obligations enacted by the new European data protection law has been criticised for raising compliance costs borne by companies, in this way (once again) competitively disadvantaging the small and medium enterprises, facing greater difficulties of collecting and processing personal data for the delivery of new digital products and services.[61]

Ultimately, the overall restriction of data processing activities resulting from the stricter data protection rules stemming from the data minimization principle under art. 5, 1 para lett. c) GDPR, has arisen concerns of associations of researchers in the biomedical sector,[62] highlighting the related prejudices to the developments of data-driven research.[63] In these regards, scientific researchers stressed that without the creation of necessary "safe harbours" regarding data processing, the General Data Protection Regulation would have impaired scientific research and the resulting innovation.[64]

Exactly these critiques have been concretised in a subset of provisions within the General Data Protection Regulation, which express a more liberal approach towards data processing activities carried out for purposes of research and development.[65]

These are well expressed in respect to the notion of research under recital 159 GDPR, stating that "(. . .) for the purposes of this Regulation, the processing of personal data for scientific research purposes should be interpreted in a broad

---

57 See in particular, Ohlhausen and Okuliar (2015), p. 151, stating that "consolidation of data across business platforms often creates significant efficiencies and gains in consumer welfare".

58 See generally, Laudon (1996), pp. 92 ff. For an overview and re-consideration of the relationship between privacy law and markets, see Calo (2016), pp. 649 ff.

59 Thierer (2014), p. 468, observing that privacy is on a "collusion course with the general freedom to innovate that has thus far powered the Internet revolution".

60 Grunes (2013), p. 1119.

61 Goodman (2016), p. 6. Highlighting this also Price et al. (1 February 2019), pp. 448–450, observing that new data protection laws "enable competition in big-data research in a way that affirmatively protects individuals' privacy and autonomy, that is progress", but highlighting also the risk that "additional hurdles—such as notifying individuals and gaining affirmative consent for sensitive-data processing—may exacerbate differences in innovative capacity between big players in the health and life sciences (or big-data competitors such as Google and Amazon) and smaller firms that lack resources to ensure compliance. For an economic analysis see Blades and Herrera-Gonzáles (September 2016).

62 For a comment, Ho (2017), pp. 84 ff. See also in respect to the consideration of research interests during the Regulation's drafting procedures, Forgò (2015), pp. 54 ff.

63 Ploem et al. (2013), p. 3534.

64 Stressing this point Forgò (2015), p. 55, observing that in medicine, "data protection risks to be seen as a hindering factor for the development and the exploitation of new knowledge in the patient's best interest".

65 Dove et al. (2016), pp. 1374–1375.

manner including for example technological development and demonstration, fundamental research, applied research and privately funded research. In addition, it should take into account the Union's objective under art. 179 (1) TFEU of achieving a European Research Area. Scientific research purposes should also include studies conducted in the public interest in the area of public health. (...)". Although the recital appears to link data processing carried out for research purposes to broader public interest purposes, as it is expressed with regards to public health studies, the reference to "privately funded research" suggests that within the same notion of research also research performed by private organisations for connected marketing purposes is to be included.[66] It is not by coincidence, that the mentioned recital refers to art. 179 (1) TFEU, which among other things highlights the value of research as a means for EU to become more competitive in the global market.[67]

Under these premises, it seems that the General Data Protection Regulation, by layering the data protection regime-one the one hand through the tightening of data subjects' rights *vis à vis* technological developments, on the other hand through the provision of some relatively free "open harbours" to the processing of personal data-, has controversially leveraged the market constituting effects of data protection law.[68] This will be better shown below with regards to some interpretative uncertainties raised exactly by that what will be referred to as the "market-oriented regime".[69]

The next paragraphs will thus give account of the fact that in the intertwined algorithmic digital health environment described in Chap. 3, the processing regime for research purposes is likely to de-regulate corporations' health data processing activities carried out under the façade of public interest-leaning health research activities. From a policy perspective, hence, it seems that the public interest-related purpose of research ultimately reveals to be strictly interconnected to innovation and thus efficiency purposes in data-driven (health) markets.

Under these premises, it needs to be said right from the beginning that the highlighted data protection law's intimate tension between the two subject- and market- oriented objectives does not seem to be irreconcilable, if one considers that also the goal of protecting users' fundamental rights has the effect of promoting a

---

[66] Stressing this point, Tene and Polonetsky (2016), pp. 458 ff. More recently also, Wachter and Mittelstadt (2019), pp. 495 ff.

[67] Van Veen (2018), p. 75.

[68] Stressing the market-constituting effects of data protection law, Hoffmann and Johanssen (9 April 2019). From a more general perspective, the role of law as a "leveller of innovation" is highlighted by Mayer-Schönberger (2010), p. 157, stressing that "specific privacy laws for health and financial services, for example, may prevent entrepreneurs from reusing and linking personal data for targeted marketing or resale to other corporations, thus reducing the value of data the entrepreneur has collected at significant cost". The controversial relationship between law and innovation is stressed also by Gasser (18 March 2014).

[69] Von Grafenstein (11 March 2019), pp. 5–6, highlighting that the establishment of broad legal principles and of broad legal terms is considered by a strand of the scholarship the most effective regulatory approach with regards to complex, dynamic and innovative environments. In these regards, see Eifert (2012), pp. 1318 ff.

lawful processing and circulation of personal data. In this perspective, the two highlighted opposed objectives appear to find a connection point in respect to two factors, that are respectively related to harmonisation objectives and trust concerns.

With regards to the first element, the enactment of the reformed data protection regime through a Regulation is meant, at least formally, to align national data protection regimes in order to create a level playing field for the processing of personal data, which removes obstacles to the free flow of it through Member States and in this way advances innovation through data processing.[70]

As far as the second element is concerned, recital 7 GDPR highlights that the data protection framework, and compliance to it, has the related spillover effect of building the trust that allows the development of the digital economy across the internal market[71] in that what the Commission itself has defined as a "sustainable" manner.[72] In light of these statements, the fundamental rights protection dimension of European data protection law appears to have an ultimate efficiency "externality" at which the European legislator intends to hint exactly in recital 7 GDPR.[73]

More precisely, the object of protection of data subjects' fundamental rights under art. 8 Charter of Fundamental Rights has as natural side effect that of creating common legal obligations onto data processing entities, which end up being market constituting in a technological economic environment where the flow of personal data is a structural feature of new business models.[74] In the digital environment, hence, adherence to data protection safeguards can become a source of competitive advantage[75] and with that a key means to enhance a data-driven innovation.[76]

[70]Harmonization objectives lied at the very heart of the data protection directive that has been the first step towards a positive integration of data protection regimes, to the benefit of the functioning of the internal market. The Regulation is the direct expression of the need to achieve a greater level of harmonization in the field. European Commission (25 January 2012a). For the literature see Lynskey (2015), pp. 46; 49–50.

[71]So recital 7 GDPR. In these regards see also European Data Protection Supervisor (27 March 2013), p. 3, stating that "effective data protection is vital for building trust in eHealth". It is also a key driver for its successful cross-border deployment, in which harmonisation of rules concerning cross border exchange of health data is essential". Emphasis added. Also the European Commission has observed that the General Data Protection Regulation creates a solid framework for the processing of personal data meant to "create digital trust which is a key precondition for any data sharing". So European Commission (25 April 2018b), p. 1.

[72]European Commission (25 April 2018a), p. 1.

[73]This is argued by Von Grafenstein (11 March 2019).

[74]This is observed by Hoffmann and Johannsen (31 May 2019), note 91 pp. 35–36.

[75]With regards to data protection as a source of competitive advantage, see European Commission (4 July 2013). This point is stressed also by the German scholarly literature, see Rossnagel (2007), p. 195; and also Bäumler (2001), pp. 1–11.

[76]Generally reflecting on the law's role in shaping "responsible innovation", Hoffmann-Riem (1998), pp. 513 ff. Similar conclusions are shared by Graef et al. (September 2018a), pp. 15–16, considering data protection law as an "organising principle for data markets".

As already observed,[77] innovation patterns in the health sector, if well directed, are likely to enhance patients'/consumers' welfare, and with that also to heighten the standard of health enjoyed within the European Union. This is the view taken by the European Commission within the Digital Single Market Strategy.[78] Nonetheless, it should be acknowledged that the degree of advancements achieved with regards to digital markets' efficiency and the protection of health largely depend on the level of data protection safeguards[79] observed during the training and testing procedures of digital health products. The implementation of data protection measures indeed comes to guarantee the quality and safety of the resulting digital health products.[80]

5.3 The Regulation of Health Data Treatment Under the General Data Protection Regulation

The two above-highlighted objectives of European data protection law are well reflected in the regulation of health data established by the General Data Protection Regulation: indeed, the general prohibition of processing special categories of sensitive data constitutes an (over-)regulatory response to the objective of protecting data subjects' fundamental rights against not consented accesses to very intimate subjective spheres such as the one of health;[81] conversely, the exceptions to this prohibition, as shaped in the form that will be illustrated below, attest the acknowledgement of the scientific- and thus, of the innovation-enabling value- of these sensitive data within the European digital market.

As will be shown in the next paragraphs, these exceptions appear to provide some fertile grounds to the flourishing of health data pools aimed at developing and placing new digital health products and services on the market. Hence, the regulation of health data treatments directly internalizes the principle of the free flow of personal data, thus providing strong support to the above-outlined policy goals of stirring digital (health) markets' efficiency through health data sharing practices.

If correctly implemented, these exceptions do not totally back out fundamental rights protection goals. However, they open some loopholes that risk doing so.[82]

---

[77] See supra Chap. 3, Sects. 3.3.1–3.3.3.

[78] See supra Chap. 4, Sect. 4.3.1.

[79] This was already acknowledged by Schwartz (1997), pp. 74–75.

[80] The issue will be discussed infra Chap. 7, Sect. 7.2.

[81] Art. 3 European Charter of Fundamental Rights.

[82] See infra Chap. 7, Sect. 7.2.

5.3.1 *The Object of Protection: The Notion of Health Data*

5.3.1.1 The Notion of Personal Data

The General Data Protection Regulation regulates the processing of personal data.[83] Under art. 4 (a) GDPR personal data is not only "information relating to an identified natural person", but extends also to information that *can* identify a natural person and thus through which a natural person becomes *identifiable*. Recital 26 GDPR specifies that identifiability should be assessed taking account "of all the means reasonably likely to be used, such as singling out, either by the controller or by another person to identify the natural person *directly* or *indirectly*".[84] Hence, identifiability results from the additional information available to the data processor.[85] For the purposes of identifiability, "account should be taken to *all objective factors*, such as the costs of and the amount of time required for identification, taking into consideration *the available technology at the time of the processing and technological developments*".[86] The corollary of this is that "the principles of data protection should therefore not apply to anonymous information, namely information which does not relate to an *identified* or *identifiable* natural person or to personal data rendered anonymous in such a manner that the data subject is not or no longer identifiable".[87]

As a wide strand of the literature has been observing, however, the available technological processing means render anonymity a temporarily restricted status[88] and with that identifiability a natural outcome of machine-learning and algorithmic processing techniques collecting and aggregating different data points,[89] which, combined, will very easily identify a single natural person.[90]

As a result, the borders of the notion of personal data remain object of a heated debate among the scholarly literature,[91] which is divided into the ones who stress the

---

[83] See Art. 20 Data Protection Working Party (20 June 2007).
Art. 6, 1 para lett. e) GDPR.

[84] Recital 26 GDPR. Emphasis added.

[85] Drexl (2019), pp. 19 ff.

[86] Recital 26 GDPR. Emphasis added.

[87] Recital 26 GDPR. Emphasis added.

[88] Ohm (2010), pp. 1703 ff. See also Voss (2014/2015), pp. 253 ff.

[89] Barocas and Nissenbaum (2014), pp. 44 ff. Similarly, Tene and Polonetsky (2013), pp. 241–243. In more distant times, Sweeney (1997), pp. 98 ff.

[90] Ernst (2018), pp. 8–13. See Barth-Jones (July 2012), pp. 8 ff. In these regards also, Art. 29 Data Protection Working Party (10 April 2014b), p. 8. It needs to be however recalled that according to the Court of Justice of the European Union, the likelihood of identifiability does not have to imply "a disproportionate effort in terms of time, cost and man-power, so that the risk of identification appears in reality to be insignificant". So Court of Justice of the European Union, Patrick Breyer v. Bundesrepublik Deutschland, C-582/14 (19 October 2016), para 46.

[91] For an overview of the concept of personal data, see. Korff (20 January 2010), pp. 38–58.

opportunity to overcome the traditional distinction personal data/non personal data[92] and others who share the view that this traditional dichotomy needs to be maintained, but nonetheless reconsidered.[93] In this last regard, it is currently being questioned whether the notion of personal data as defined above shall include also inferences drawn by data analytics:[94] Art. 29 Data Protection Working Party's interpretative guidance seems to provide an affirmative answer to such questions.

In its opinions regarding the General Data Protection Regulation, the Art.29 Data Protection Working Party has made a distinction between provided and observed data, which are to be in turn distinguished from derived and inferred data.[95] Provided data are data that are directly provided by the individuals concerned, whereas observed data are indirectly provided by the individual in the form of so-called runaway data, such as location data or data relating to clicking activities.[96] Conversely, derived and inferred data are generated by the controller through the processing of provided and observed data.[97]

According to the Art. 29 Data Protection Working Party, in order to qualify as personal data, either (i) the content, (ii) the purpose or (iii) the result of the data must relate to an identifiable person either directly or indirectly.[98] The Working Party specifies that the "result" of data relates to the likelihood of "impact on a certain person's rights and interests".[99] Under the interpretation given by the Working Party, thus, not only data that *describe* the data subject (content) or that "evaluate, treat in a certain way or influence the status or behaviour"[100] of the data subject (purpose), but also data that is extracted from other available data and that is likely to impact on the data subject's rights and interests (result) falls within the scope of personal data.[101] In this perspective, inferences that are derived from initial provided

---

[92] Purtova (2018), pp. 40 ff.

[93] Drexl (2019).

[94] Wachter and Mittelstadt (2019), p. 498; Quinn and Quinn (2018).

[95] Art. 29 Data Protection Working Party (3 October 2017b), p. 8, stating that "automated decision making can be based on any type of data: (i) data provided directly by the individuals concerned (such as responses to a questionnaire); (ii) data observed about the individuals (such as location data collected via an application); (iii) derived or inferred data such as a profile of the individual that has already been created (e.g. a credit score)". Emphasis added.

[96] Observed data was mentioned already in a previous opinion by the Working Party. See Art. 29 Data Protection Working Party (20 June 2007b), p. 8.

[97] See also Article 29 Data Protection Working Party (13 December 2016, last revised on 5 April 2017). Art. 29 Data Protection Working Party (3 October 2017b, last revised on 6 February 2018) 9, stating that profiling "works by creating derived or inferred data about individuals- 'new' personal data that has not been provided directly by the data subjects themselves".

[98] Art. 29 Data Protection Working Party (20 June 2007b), pp. 10–11. D. Korff (20 January 2010), pp. 42–43.

[99] Art. 29 Data Protection Working Party (20 June 2007b), p. 11.

[100] Art. 29 Data Protection Working Party (20 June 2007b), p. 10.

[101] The broad scope of personal data is further supported by the reference to "any information" contained in art. 4, 1 para GDPR and already present in the Directive. See Korff (20 January 2010), pp. 39–40.

or observed datasets need to be considered personal data for the purposes of data protection law, with the resulting obligations and rights. As has been observed, however, under the definition given to derived and inferred data, this data can also result from non-personal data, provided it impacts on the data subject's rights and interests.[102] Hence, also non-personal data can be transformed into personal data through linkage to an identified or identifiable individual.[103]

If according to the above-recalled interpretation, inferences drawn from personal or non-personal data are subject to data protection law as it is currently framed by the General Data Protection Regulation, the case-law of the Court of Justice of the European Union has traditionally shaped a narrower notion of personal data.[104] In line with this restrictive approach to the concept of personal data, the Court has circumscribed the relevance of inferences for the purposes of data protection law, excluding the relevance of "assessments" and "non-verifiable data".[105] By ruling so, the Court upheld the view of the Advocate General that "only information relating *to facts* about an individual can be personal data".[106] In the view of the Advocate General a distinction needs to be made between "objective facts" that are verifiable and "subjective analysis" that is not verifiable,[107] being only the formers object of data protection law.[108] Under this interpretation, the personal data status of predictions, statistical and probabilistic analyses such as scoring would be excluded.

To the contrary, the Art. 29 Data Protection Working Party has claimed that inferred and derived data should enjoy the protection of the individual rights

[102] This is suggested by S. Wachter-B. Mittelstadt (2019), pp. 515 ff.

[103] Korff (20 January 2010), p. 41, observing that the transformation of non personal data into personal inferred or derived data, through the matching of other personal data, will be an increasingly common phenomenon in light of the available technological capabilities. As the Author stresses, in the present technological environment, "there will be increasing (indeed, exponentially increasing), amounts of such "closely-but-perhaps-not-fully" person-related data". As an example of this, the case of IP addresses is mentioned. In respect to IP addresses, the same Art. 29 Data Protection Working Party has stated that "unless an Internet Service Provider is in the position to distinguish with absolute certainty that the data correspond to users that cannot be identified, it will have to treat all IP addresses as personal data, to be on the safe side". So Art. 29 Data Protection Working Party (20 June 2007b), p. 17.

[104] For an in-depth overview of the ECJ'ss concept of persona data, see European Court of Justice, Bodil Lindqvist, C-101/01 (6 November 2003b), para 24; European court of Justice, Joined Cases C-465/00, C-138/01 and C-139/01 (20 May 2003a), para 64.

[105] European Court of Justice, YS, M and S v Minister Voor Immigratie, Integratie en Asiel Joined cases C-141/12 and C-372/12 (17 July 2014), para 38–39.

[106] Opinion of the Advocate General Sharpston, YS, M and S v Minister Voor Immigratie, Integratie en Asiel, Joined cases C-141/12 and C-372/12 (12 December 2013), para 56. Emphasis added.

[107] Opinion of the Advocate General Sharpston, YS, M and S v Minister Voor Immigratie, Integratie en Asiel, Joined cases C-141/12 and C-372/12 (12 December 2013), para 57.

[108] Opinion of the Advocate General Sharpston, YS, M and S v Minister Voor Immigratie, Integratie en Asiel, Joined cases C-141/12 and C-372/12 (12 December 2013), para 57. For a comment on the decision see Wachter and Mittelstadt (2019), pp. 521 ff.

provided by the General Data Protection Regulation.[109] By referring to the case of profiling containing the prediction that a patient will suffer from a heart disease,[110] the Working Party expressly appears to include also non-verifiable predictions as the ones resulting from a statistical or probabilistic analysis.

5.3.1.2 The Notion of Sensitive Personal Data

Within the category of personal data, the General Data Protection Regulation includes the subcategory of "special categories of personal data" under art. 9 GDPR, encompassing sensitive personal data that are "by their nature particularly *sensitive in relation to fundamental rights and freedom*" and whose processing "could create significant *risks* to the fundamental rights and freedoms".[111] These special categories of data are defined under art. 9 GDPR[112] and are object of a higher regulatory burden in respect to non-special personal data, encountering an outright prohibition of processing.

Under art. 9 GDPR, these special categories of personal data encompass amongst others, (i) genetic data, (ii) biometric data and, more generally, (iii) "data concerning health".

5.3.1.2.1 "Genetic Data"

Under art. 4, para 13 GDPR Genetic data are defined as "personal data relating to the inherited or acquired genetic characteristics of a natural person which give unique information about the physiology or the health of that natural person and which result, in particular, from an analysis of a biological sample from the natural person in question". Recital 34 GDPR further specifies that the "analysis of biological sample" encompasses, in particular, "chromosomal, deoxyribonucleic acid (DNA), or ribonucleic acid (RNA) analysis", or "the analysis of other elements that enables equivalent information to be obtained". This definition suggests that also genetic information that could be derived from analysis of other materials such as molecular and biological materials is considered genetic data for the purposes of the General Data Protection Regulation. Moreover, the reference to "other elements that enable equivalent information to be obtained" seems to broaden the scope of genetic data

[109] Art. 29 Data Protection Working Party (3 October 2017b, last revised on 6 February 2018), pp. 17–18.

[110] Art. 29 Data Protection Working Party (3 October 2017b, last revised on 6 February 2018).

[111] Recital 51 GDPR. Emphasis added. Stressing the risks stemming from the processing of sensitive data, see Ohm (2015), p. 1125.

[112] Under art. 9, 1 para GDPR special categories of personal data are "personal data revealing racial or ethnic origin, political opinions, religious or philosophical beliefs, or trade union membership, and the processing of genetic data, biometric data for the purpose of uniquely identifying a natural person, data concerning health or data concerning a natural person's sex life or sexual orientation".

also up to include genetic information that is derived from the most disparate sources, such as "genealogical information gathered through various questionnaires".[113]

As has been observed by some strand in the literature,[114] the capability of providing "*unique*" information about the data subject, highlighted by the normative definition of genetic data, is not completely adherent to the real nature of genetic data, which in most of the cases *uniquely* identifies not a single natural person, but rather a genetic family as a group.

The consequence of this is that this narrow definition linking genetic data just to a data subject risks to exclude from the scope of the notion of sensitive data, data that do not uniquely identify a natural person as art. 4, 13 para GDPR require, but just a group.

Through inclusion within the special categories of personal data under art. 9, 1 para GDPR, the Regulation affirms the automatic sensitive nature of genetic data.[115] The qualification of genetic data as sensitive data in the Regulation is the legislative acknowledgement of the increasing relevance of genetic data for health research purposes and thus of the resulting spread of processing activities regarding genetic data. This has in turn required a more direct regulatory intervention,[116] which has come to consider genetic data along with other types of data, as biometric data and data regarding health.[117] This was not the case under the previous Directive, which did not provide a definition of genetic data nor defined its legal status.[118]

The Art. 29 Data Protection Working Party took into specific consideration the case of genetic data under the previous regime, stating that it was to be intended as "health data" under the Directive, and thus subject to stricter regulatory requirements such as the one of explicit consent.[119] In order to qualify as health data, genetic data needed to provide an "indication" as to "the health status of an identifiable

[113]Questioning this statement, Chassang (2017).

[114]Dove (2018a), pp. 163–164.

[115]Quinn and Quinn (2018), pp. 4–5. The specific reference to genetic data within the General Data Protection Regulation has been encouraged by the call for greater privacy in the genetic field contained in the UNESCO International Declaration on Human Genetic Data, issued on the 16 October 2003, as a complement to the Universal Declaration on Human Genome and Human Rights of 11 November 1997. So Shabani and Borry (2018), p. 149. It needs to be remembered that genetic data were already considered as personal data under some Member States law. See Art. 29 Data Protection Working Party (20 April 2011a), p. 7.

[116]Sariyar et al. (2017), p. 498.

[117]By regulating the treatment of genetic data in the same way as other types of health data, such as biometric data, the European legislator appears to have opted against the so-called "genetic exceptionalism", which intends to treat genetic data differently than other health-related data. Sariyar et al. (2017), p. 499.

[118]Quinn and Quinn (2018), p. 5.

[119]Art. 29 Data Protection Working Party (17 March 2004).

individual".[120] A difficult case by case assessment regarding the capability of indicating such health status thus had to be put in place.[121]

Although referring to genetic data in various recitals[122] and although referring to the case of biological samples,[123] the General Data Protection Regulation has failed to provide direct answers to the question regarding whether the use of human tissues has to respect data protection law.[124] The issue was addressed by the European Court of Human Rights in the case *S. and Marper v. United Kingdom,*[125] where it was specified that DNA profiles and cellular samples could be considered as personal data within the UK previous Data Protection Act of 1998, as long as they could be referred to an identifiable individual. The decision thus reflects that biological material is not per se protected under data protection law, but it becomes relevant for purposes of it as soon as it is "datafied", that meaning scanned, analysed, sequenced.[126] Since the use for any purpose of such material, implies the extraction of information from it, this implies that biological material would need to be processed consistent with the General Data Protection Regulation, unless it is so incomplete that it is impossible to refer it to an individual.[127]

In these regards, it has been observed how advancements in the field of computational genetics leave to date quite little room for anonymity of genome sequences. In the past, researchers have tried to argue the anonymity of their genetic datasets in order to avoid compliance to data protection law, on the grounds that the datasets were kept separate from data that could render them identifiable.[128] The anonym status of genetic data is however largely unrealistic due to the great likelihood of linkage to an identifiable individual that the accessibility in the world wide web not only of genetic sequencing but also of complementary information;[129] the growth in computer capabilities; and the development of powerful algorithmic processing

[120] Art. 29 Data Protection Working Party (20 April 2011), p. 10.

[121] Quinn and Quinn (2018), p. 5.

[122] Recital 34; 35; 53; 75 GDPR.

[123] Recital 35 GDPR.

[124] Shabani and Borry (2018), p. 155.

[125] European Court of Human Rights, S. and Marper v. United Kingdom (4 December 2008).

[126] Reflecting on the issue, Hallinan and De Hert (2016), pp. 119 ff.

[127] Dove (2018b), p. 1020.

[128] Roewer (2013), p. 22; and also Gutmann and Wagner (2013), p. 16, stating that "while any whole genome is uniquely identifiable (because DNA is unique to only one person), genomic data stripped of traditional identifiers are not readily identifiable because there is no key matching particular data to a particular person".

[129] Gutmann and Wagner (2013), p. 15, "the more genomic data collected, and the more refined the connections between genetic variations, disease states, and other personal characteristics, the easier it becomes to re-identify an individual and discover".

techniques.[130] These three factors render it thus extremely easy to identify individual through statistical processing of genetic sequences and other available data.[131]

5.3.1.2.2 "Biometric Data"

Art. 4, para 14 GDPR, biometric data are "personal data resulting from specific technical processing relating to the physical, physiological or behavioural characteristics of a natural person, which allow or confirm the unique identification of that natural person, such as facial images or dactyloscopic data".[132] The definition reflects that biometric data are captured by peculiar technologies that scan individuals' features. In these regards, it has been observed that biometric data is not the initial data, but rather the specific technical processing operations applied to this data and the resulting data.[133]

This means that for the purposes of the Regulation, biometric data are the ones resulting from biometrical technical processing operations, which are capable of transforming also ordinary personal data, as photos or videos, into sensitive biometric data. In these regards, Google publicly declared the technological ease of identifying users through the pictures they post online.[134]

Traditionally, biometric technologies were used for special purposes, such as crime investigation.[135] With the spread of Internet of Things technologies, the collection of human characteristics has become embedded in everyday life devices providing personalised services, and registering unique qualities and behaviours of data subjects.[136] In addition to this, more sophisticated sensors recording fingerprints, voices, retina and vein structure, walking gaits[137] are being developed and used for identification and authentication purposes in various specific fields,[138] such as the workplace.[139]

Similarly as it occurs with genetic data, the expanding collection of biometric data aliments databases enabling identification and various forms of profiling based on

---

[130] Quinn and Quinn (2018), p. 2. With regards to the technological advancements in the field of genomics, mention needs to be made to Genome-Wide Association Studies, that search genetic makers involving rapidly scanning SNPs across the complete set of human genomes in order to find genetic variations associated with a particular disease. See Ho (2017), p. 90.

[131] Niemiec and Howard (2016), pp. 23–30.

[132] See Art. 29 Data Protection Working Party (1 August 2003), p. 2.

[133] European Data Protection Board (10 July 2019a), pp. 15–16.

[134] Gannes (7 September 2010).

[135] Kaye (2006), pp. 188 ff.

[136] Kindt (2018), pp. 523 ff.

[137] See Krishan and Mostafavi (2018), pp. 19 ff.

[138] Sprokkereef (2007), pp. 277 ff.

[139] Selinger and Hartzog (17 October 2019).

individuals' physical, physiological and behavioural traits.[140] Based on these sensitive features, inferences can be drawn in the form of predictions and statistical probabilities,[141] opening the floor to various discriminatory practices, in the employment, insurance, as well as advertisement sectors.[142]

On these grounds, the Constitutional Court of France has stated that the keeping of a database with biometric identity information that allows for identification violates the fundamental right to privacy.[143] Biometric data and its uses have gained renewed attention within the French legal system with the issuing of new Guidelines by the French Data Protection Authority (*Commission Nationale de l'Informatiques et des Libertés, CNIL*), distinguishing between biometric data stored on the used devices and biometric data stored on other premises.[144] According to the CNIL, the collection and storage of biometric data is to be considered as an "autonomous" use of biometric data provided certain conditions are met, which involve (i) the decision of the user alone to use biometric authentication,[145] this implying the possibility to choose between biometric authentication and other methods of authentication such as a traditional PIN code; (ii) the storage of the data on the used device, without the possibility of sharing the data with other devices or with other third parties; (iii) the securing of data through encryption technologies; (iv) the use of the processing technology only for private purposes. Under the given interpretation, when these conditions are met, the processing of biometric data falls within the household exception under art. 2, 2 para lett. c) GDPR and, accordingly, is not protected by data protection law.[146] It needs however to be recalled that according to recital 18 GDPR, the Regulation, and thus data protection law provisions, apply "to controllers or processors which provide the means for processing personal data for such personal or household activities". This means that the application of the household exceptions does not totally relief data controllers from data protection obligations regarding the application. In these regards, for example, security obligations regarding the applications are of utmost importance.[147]

Conversely, according to the CNIL's guidelines, when biometric data are stored on remote services and can be accessed by third parties, these same data are not under the control of the data subject itself but of the service provider. In this case, the processing of this data is covered by data protection law and the controller has the

[140] Kindt (2018), pp. 538–539.

[141] Cantore (2011), pp. 84 ff.

[142] For some examples see, Peppet (2014), p. 85.

[143] Constitutional Court of France, n. 2012-652, 22 March 2012, Art. 6 Loi Protection De L'Identité, stating that "la création d'un fichier d'identité biométrique (. . .) dont les caractéristiques rendent possible l'identification d'une personne à partir de ses empreintes digitales porte atteinte inconstitutionnelle au droit au respect de la vie privée"'.

[144] Commission Nationale de l'Informatiques et des Libertés (24 July 2018).

[145] This condition is not met if the biometric authentication is imposed by the employers. Commission Nationale de l'Informatiques et des Libertés (24 July 2018).

[146] Commission Nationale de l'Informatiques et des Libertés (24 July 2018).

[147] See Notermans (8 January 2019).

obligation to make a careful assessment regarding the impact of the processing of such data on individuals' fundamental rights.[148]

More recently, the French Data Protection Authority has taken into consideration the case of biometric data, by issuing a Regulation regarding the processing of biometric data as workplace access control.[149] The Regulation prescribes specific requirements for the processing of biometric data by public or private employers using biometric systems to control access to premises, devices and applications at work. The Regulation distinguishes between biometric authentication techniques based on morphological characteristics, in respect to which the biometric means used must be described and justified; and biometrical authentication based on biological samples, which is to the contrary prohibited.[150] In addition, the CNIL Regulation identifies three categories of biometric templates, being a set of measurements of an individuals' morphological characteristics, on grounds of the level of control data subjects' have over the collected biometric data. Where biometric data are controlled jointly by the employer and the individual or solely by the employer, the use of such templates shall only be used under exceptional and justified circumstances for critical environments, where the exclusive control of the data by the data subject is not possible.[151]

The cited interventions by the French Data Protection Authority reflect the national regulator's attention of regulating processing activities of biometric data also for verification purposes, as is the case of using biometric technologies authentication in the workplace.

In these regards, it needs however to be observed that for the purposes of the General Data Protection Regulation, biometric data are considered a special category of personal data under art. 9, 1 para GDPR "for the purpose of uniquely identifying a natural person".[152] According to some commentators, the explicit reference only to identification purposes made by art. 9, 1 para GDPR, would exclude the application of the special regime of sensitive data in case biometric data are used for purposes that are different than identification, as verification.[153] However, the fact that the

[148] Commission Nationale de l'Informatiques et des Libertés (24 July 2018), referring to the controller's obligation to carry out a Data Protection Impact Assessment under art. 35 GDPR.

[149] Commission Nationale de l'Informatiques et des Libertés (10 January 2019). The Regulation has been issued on grounds of art. 9, 4 para GDPR, according to which "Member States may maintain or introduce further conditions, including limitations, with regard to the processing of genetic data, biometric data or data regarding health". Under the French Data Protection Act, as revised in 2016, has granted the Data Protection Authority the power to issue "standard regulations to ensure the security of personal data processing systems and to regulate the processing of genetic data, biometric and health data. See Leabeau-Marianna and Balducci (11 April 2019).

[150] Commission Nationale de l'Informatiques et des Libertés (10 January 2019), art. 5.

[151] Commission Nationale de l'Informatiques et des Libertés (10 January 2019), art. 6.

[152] So art. 9, 1 para GDPR.

[153] Kindt (2018), pp. 526–527, where the Author distinguishes between "identification", implying a "one-to-many search and comparison and requires in principle a database in which several individuals are listed" and "verification", implying to the contrary "a one-to-one comparison and is used to verify and confirm by biometric comparison whether an individual is the same person as the one

definition under art. 4, 14 para GDPR mentions both the functionalities of identification and verification through the wording "allow *or* confirm identification",[154] suggests the opportunity of a combined reading of articles 4, 14 para GDPR and 9, 1 para GDPR, according to which also biometric data employed for mere verification purposes fall under the stricter regulatory requirements regarding special categories of personal data, in which biometric data are included.[155] Clear support for this interpretation is given by the already recalled ruling by the European Court of Human Rights in *S. and Marper vs. United Kingdom,* where the Court regarded the retention and storage of biometric data as an interference with the fundamental right to privacy, *regardless of any subsequent use.*[156]

In this perspective, it needs to be further mentioned that the risks related to the employment of biometric processing technologies were shown by an increasing number of studies spotting significant discriminatory biases based on gender and race affecting the functioning of such same technologies.[157] The findings of these studies are fuelling discussions about the legitimacy of patents regarding facial recognition technologies employed for massive identification purposes[158] and are triggering big companies themselves to call for additional regulatory action regarding the uses of such technologies.[159] As a latest response to this, the first ban regarding the use of facial recognition softwares by the police and other agencies has been issued.[160]

5.3.1.2.3 "Data Concerning Health"

Ultimately, art. 9, 1 para GDPR includes among the special categories of personal data, "data regarding health". These are very broadly defined under art. 4, para 15 GDPR, as "personal data related to the physical or mental health of a natural person, including the provision of health care services, which reveal information about his or her health status".

from whom the biometric data originates", concluding that "verification is hence inherently another kind of use and purpose than identification".

[154] Emphasis added.

[155] Art. 29 Data Protection Working Party (23 March 2012), p. 10.

[156] European Court of Human Rights, S. and Marper v. United Kingdom (4 December 2008), para. 121. Emphasis added.

[157] Singer (24 January 2019). See Buolamwini and Gebru (2018), pp. 1–15.

[158] An example of this is facial recognition technology, gathering biometric data and identifying through that people considered to be "suspicious". In these regards, a technology and civil liberties attorney at the Civil Liberties Union of Northern California highlighted that the patent application reflects that technology can be used for the creation of a "massive, decentralised surveillance network". See Holley (18 December 2018).

[159] See Singer (13 July 2018). The need for regulatory responses is clearly more felt in the United States where no federal data protection law has been enacted to date.

[160] Conger et al. (14 May 2019).

Recital 35 GDPR specifies that this type of data "should include all data pertaining to the health status of a data subject which reveal information relating to the past, current or future physical or mental health status of the data subject". According to this definition, thus, information regarding health is objectively and chronologically very broadly defined.

From an objective standpoint, as the recital clarifies, this special category of personal data encompasses data regarding health status. Accordingly, the recital lists some possible types of health data as "information about the natural person collected in the course of the registration for, or the provision of, health care services" and "a number, symbol or particular assigned to a natural person to uniquely identify the natural person for health purposes".

Interestingly, the recital also mentions "information derived from the testing or examination of a body part or bodily substance, including from genetic data and biological samples". Through the reference to genetic data, it seems that the legislator has intended to subtly distinguish between genetic data and more general data regarding individuals' health conditions that can be inferred from genetic sequences.[161] It needs however to be observed that it is a merely descriptive distinction since both genetic data and data regarding health are object to the same special regime under art. 9 GDPR.

Ultimately, the recital lists various other types of health data containing information regarding, for example, "a disease, disability, disease risk, medical history, clinical treatment or the physiological or biomedical state of the data subject *independent of its source*".[162] By stating so, the Regulation implicitly acknowledges that health-related information can be derived from various sources, which are very likely to be unrelated to the strict health care context. In this way, thus, it recognises the de-contextualisation process that health data is undergoing in the current technological processing environment,[163] where sensitive health conditions can be extracted from apparently neutral data, in the form, for example, of disease risk prediction the same recital refers to. Practical evidence of this directly found in the above-recalled employment of so-called real world data by the European Medicines Agency for pharmaceutical regulatory purposes.[164]

With regard to disease risk prediction, it is interesting to observe that the recital n. 35 GDPR itself mentions also information relating to the "*future* physical or mental health status of the data subject", thus implicitly including within the notion of health data also health-related inferences and predictions. Since these ones can be drawn also from the aggregation and analysis of non-sensitive personal data,[165] the

[161] Dove (2018b), p. 121.

[162] Emphasis added.

[163] Nissenbaum (2008).

[164] See supra Chap. 2, Sect. 2.1.5.

[165] This is technically confirmed by some studies, such as Romei and Ruggieri (2014), p. 582.

notion of health data itself appears to be pretty much widely-encompassing and comprising also (non-directly sensitive) data from which sensitive information regarding an individual can be derived.[166] As the same Art. 29 Data Protection Working Party had been observing under the previous data protection framework, also data with a different degree of sensitivity appears to fall under this broad notion of health data, ranging from non-sensitive data with sensitive signalling capabilities, to minor sensitive data such as "data regarding a cold", to "stigmatising information about illnesses or disabilities".[167] In this perspective, the sensitive category of data concerning health was already acknowledged as "one of the most complex areas of sensitive data and one where the Member States display a great deal of legal uncertainty".[168]

Against this backdrop, it can be argued that the difficulties of clearly defining the borders of the notion of health data persist under the definition given in the General Data Protection Regulation[169] and are further exacerbated together with the advancement of the current technical processing capabilities,[170] this adding even greater concerns to the definition of the borders between non-personal, personal and personal sensitive data. This creates in turn significant uncertainties with regards to the applicability of the different regulatory regimes that are established in respect to each of these categories.[171]

In view of the difficulty of drawing a clear line between non-sensitive data that are excluded from the special regime regarding sensitive data and non-sensitive data that are conversely attracted within the higher standard of protection due to their sensitive proximities,[172] some strand of the literature is being referring to "shadow health records" comprising these data stemming from various different sources that would not directly qualify as health records but which processed and combined with each

---

[166]This had already been observed by Art. 29 Data Protection Working Party (20 April 2011), pp. 5–6, referring to the notion of sensitive data under art. 8 of the previous Data Protection Directive. The breadth of the category of data concerning health has been recently acknowledged by the Council of Europe in a recent Recommendation regarding health-related data. See Council of Europe (27 March 2019), replacing Recommendation N. R(97) 5 of the Committee of Ministers to Member States on the Protection of Medical Data, and using the more general term "health-related data".

[167]Council of Europe (27 March 2019), p. 8, observing that this diversity leads to some "difficulties in practice, as the individual's consent is required even for unproblematic processing of such data".

[168]Council of Europe (27 March 2019), p. 10.

[169]This was being acknowledged already by European Data Protection Supervisor (21 May 2015), p. 6, stating that the list of examples of health data provided by GDPR's recitals "does not specifically address the question whether and to what extent lifestyle and well-being information comes within the scope of health information".

[170]Stressing this Art. 29 Data Protection Working Party (16 September 2014c), p. 5, where the Working Party underlines that "quantified self" technologies are "challenging with regard to the types of data collected that are health-related". For the literature, Malgieri and Comandè (2017), pp. 229 ff.; Comandè and Schneider (2018), pp. 284 ff.

[171]Quinn and Quinn (2018), p. 5.

[172]For a more precise categorisation see Malgieri and Comandè (2017).

other can provide exactly the same information as "standard health records".[173] As this strand of scholarship observes, these shadow health records, made up by masses of health-related data and linked health inferences, although having a sensitive "capacity", risk to be placed in a less regulated area in respect to standard health records.[174]

This risk has been taken into specific consideration by the Art. 29 Data Protection Working Party, which has come to define the notion of health data in respect to apps and devices,[175] providing some additional indications that can be of useful guidance also under the General Data Protection Regulation.

Personal data originating from apps and devices are expressly mentioned in recital n. 35 GDPR that identifies among the possible sources of health data, together with health professionals and hospitals, also medical devices.[176] Starting exactly from this definition, Art. 29 Data Protection Working Party first makes reference to strict medical data, originating from a health-care context in the course of diagnoses and treatment procedures carried out by providers of health services.[177]

In addition to this strictly medical data, the Art. 29 Data Protection Working Party considers the broader category of health data, encompassing data signalling individuals' health conditions from the most diverse settings such as employment or administrative actions.[178] In this perspective, a second type of health data is found in that what is referred to by the Working Party as "raw sensor data that can be used in itself or in combination with other data to draw a conclusion about the actual health status or health risk of a person".[179]

This second type of health data is further distinguished from another sub-category of health data defined on grounds of its processing purpose. This last sub-category is made up by "any personal data (health data or not)" processed for the purpose of determining the health status of an individual, such as the already mentioned disease risk.[180] As the Working Party interestingly highlights this often occurs in the context of medical research using big data.[181]

---

[173] Price et al. (1 February 2019), p. 450.

[174] Price et al. (1 February 2019).

[175] See Art. 29 Data Protection Working Party (5 February 2015). The Annex was requested by the European Commission within the mHealth initiative. See International Association of Privacy Professionals (10 February 2015).

[176] With regards to the difficulty of distinguishing between medical devices and apps see supra Chap. 2, Sect. 2.1.6.

[177] Art. 29 Data Protection Working Party (5 February 2015), p. 2. Strict medical data have been taken into consideration also by the Council of Europe (13 February 1997).

[178] In these regards, also the European Data Protection Supervisor has acknowledged that personal data relating to the health status of a person encompass also administrative documents such as medical certificates, forms concerning sick leaves or the reimbursement of medical expenses. So European Data Protection Supervisor (September 2009).

[179] European Data Protection Supervisor (September 2009), p. 5.

[180] European Data Protection Supervisor (September 2009), p. 3.

[181] European Data Protection Supervisor (September 2009).

To sum up, the three identifying criteria suggested by the Working Party for the purposes of the definition of the category of health data are to be found in (i) the medical context in which health data is originated; (ii) the capacity of signalling an individual's health status; (iii) the processing purpose of defining an individual's health status.[182]

In light of this categorisation, it appears that the scope of health data largely depends upon the definition of what is an individuals' health status. In these regards, the Working Party only affirms that health status is not only confined to "ill health".[183] A useful definition of health status is given by the World Health Organisation, which refers to a "state of complete physical, mental and social well-being", and not merely as "the absence of disease or infirmity".[184] Such a broad conception of health well reflects the importance of other types of data that are different from strict health records: these data render indeed a more "complete" image of individuals' "physical, mental and social well-being" and thus contribute to more clearly picture their health status. A broad interpretation of health-related data has been endorsed also by the Court of Justice of the European Union, which in the well know *Lindqvist* case has ruled that the term "data concerning health" must be given a "wide interpretation so as to include information concerning all aspects, both physical and mental, of the health of an individual".[185]

In these regards, however, the same Art. 29 Data Protection Working Party has affirmed that data relating to the well-being of individuals does not constitute health data *as such* but it can contribute in defining an individual's health "as the data is registered in time, thus making it possible to derive inferences from its variability over a given period".[186]

Hence, following the above-recalled reconstruction, well-being data are very likely to extract, mostly in combination with other data, disease risk or predictions, and are thus likely to fall under the category of data concerning health under art. 9, 1 para GDPR.

Along the same lines, the European Data Protection Supervisor has acknowledged that the relevance as health data of lifestyle and well-being data originated from devices or apps is to be assessed on a case by case basis, taking into particular account also "the circumstances surrounding the gathering and processing of such information".[187]

The burden in assessing whether personal data, such as lifestyle and well-being data are health-data according to the above-identified criteria is to be ultimately

---

[182] For a critical evaluation of this last criteria see Malgieri and Comandè (2017), pp. 237–238.

[183] Malgieri and Comandè (2017), pp. 237–238.

[184] This is the definition of the Constitution of World Health Organization https://www.who.int/governance/eb/who_constitution_en.pdf.

[185] Court of Justice of the European Union, Bodil Lindqvist, C-101/01 (6 November 2003), para 50.

[186] Art. 29 Data Protection Working Party (16 September 2014c), p. 17.

[187] European Data Protection Supervisor (21 May 2015), p. 5. See also European Data Protection Supervisor (7 December 2012), p. 3, paras 10–11.

placed upon the controllers who come to process the data and who are most of the times in possession of the relevant elements to qualify the processed information as health data.[188]

5.3.2 The Legal Bases for the Treatment of Health Data

The above-defined category of sensitive health data is object of a special regulatory regime.[189] Indeed, in line with the previous Data Protection Directive,[190] also the General Data Protection Regulation conditions the processing of such special category of personal data to stricter data protection rules. In these regards, the Council of Europe has recently welcomed the higher threshold of protection regarding data concerning health, in view of the need to regulate its use so as to "guarantee due regard for the rights and fundamental freedom of every individual, in particular the right to protection of privacy and data protection".[191] Along the same lines, also the European Court of Human Rights has underlined the importance of protecting health data in the context of article 8 of the European Convention on Human Rights, stressing that "the protection of personal data, in particular medical data, is of fundamental importance to a person's enjoyment of his or her right to respect for private and family life as guaranteed by Art. 8 of the Convention".[192]

In this perspective, the prohibition to process special categories of sensitive data under art. 9, 1 para GDPR is one of the most apparent expressions of the fundamental rights orientation of the General Data Protection Regulation.[193]

This prohibition nonetheless has some exceptions allowing the processing of sensitive health data on the basis of different legal grounds listed under art. 9, 2 para GDPR. These different legal bases build up a mosaic of processing possibilities regarding health data, which need to be carefully interpreted in respect to the general prohibition regarding the same processing of special categories of personal data.

Under art. 9,2 para GDPR, the processing exceptions regarding sensitive personal data as health data are of great interest in respect to health data sharing agreements. These agreements, indeed, involve the treatment of health data and thus need to be rooted in a precise legal basis.[194]

---

[188] European Data Protection Supervisor (21 May 2015), p. 7.

[189] For a critical assessment regarding this special regulatory regime see Zarsky (2017), pp. 1012 ff.

[190] See art. 8 Data Protection Directive. Art. 29 Data Protection Working Party (5 February 2015), p. 1; European Data Protection Supervisor (27 March 2013), p. 3; Article 29 Data Protection Working Party (15 February 2007a), p. 8.

[191] Council of Europe (27 March 2019), p. 2.

[192] European Court of Human Rights, I v Finland (appl. No 20511/03) (17 July 2008), para. 38; European Court of Human Rights, Armonienė v Lithuania (appl. No 36919/02) (25 February 2008), para. 40.

[193] Stressing the symbolic value of this provision Zarsky (2017), p. 1014.

[194] Zingales (2018), p. 108, considering data protection law as a "permission based" regime.

These legal grounds can be respectively sub-grouped as follows: (i) data subject's consent under art. 9, 2 para lett. a) GDPR and, strictly related to it, the need to protect a vital interest of the data subject under art. 9, 2 para lett. c) GDPR as well as the manifest publicity of the personal data under art. 9, 2 para lett. e) GDPR; (ii) the processing is necessary for reasons of substantial public interest under art. 9, 2 para lett. g) GDPR, for the purposes of preventive or occupational medicine, medical diagnosis, the provision of health or social care or treatment or the management of health or social care and systems and services under art. 9, 2 para lett. h) and for reasons of public interest in the area of public health under art. 9, 2 para lett. i) GDPR; (iii) the processing is necessary for scientific or historical research purposes or statistical purposes under art. 9, 2 para lett. j) GDPR.

The first category of legal bases for the processing of health data is based on the data subjects' subjective perspective, concretised through his/her determinations in the form of consent or in respect to his/her fundamental interests. Conversely, the other two identified categories take a rather objective perspective and rely on objective features of data controllers' processing activities, related to their public interest or research-oriented nature.[195]

As a general premise it needs to recalled that the mentioned legal bases established under art. 9, 2 para GDPR for the processing of sensitive data need to be linked to the legal grounds generally established under art 6 GDPR setting the conditions for the lawfulness of the processing. In these regards, there are two possible interpretative options.

According to a first position, the legal grounds under art. 9, 2 para GDPR are complementary to the general requirements for a lawful data processing under art. 6 GDPR.[196] This means that the existence of a general lawful basis under art. 6 GDPR is a precondition for the processing of sensitive personal data under the special conditions laid down under art. 9, 2 para GDPR.[197]

Conversely, another solution regards the legal bases for the processing of special categories of data as a *lex specialis* in respect to the *lex generalis* under art. 6 GDPR.[198] This latter solution appears to be more adherent to the special data protection regime provided under some of the legal bases listed by art. 9(2) GDPR. These will be described below.

The choice of which of the listed legal bases is to be applied in specific cases is not only of theoretical but also of great practical relevance: as will be shown below, indeed, it influences the scope of data subjects' applicable rights. A correct interpretation of the scope of these legal bases is thus of crucial importance in order to determine the severity of the data protection regime to be applied, and thus the reaction capabilities of involved data subjects.

---

[195] In this direction see, Marelli and Testa (4 May 2018), p. 496, observing a "shift toward a decentralized, controller-anchored, and accountability-based model".

[196] Van Veen (2018), p. 72.

[197] This is the solution given by Dove (2018b), p. 1024. See also Schulz (2018), p. 365.

[198] Molnár-Gábor (2018), p. 620.

5.3.2.1 Data Subject's Consent and Related Legal Bases for Processing

The first exception to the prohibition regarding the processing of health data processing relates to the data subject's consent under art. 9, 2 para lett. a) GDPR. According to the mentioned provisions, the given consent[199] needs to be explicit and must be given for one or more specified purposes in accordance to the principle of purpose limitation.[200] As newly required by the Regulation, consent must be "freely given" in a contractual relationship where there is no "significant imbalance" between the data subject and the controller[201] and the performance of which is not conditional on the processing of personal data that is not necessary for the performance of a contract.[202]

Through the reference to explicit consent needed for the processing of data concerning health, the Regulation reaffirms the role of data subject's consent as a fundamental condition for the processing of sensitive data, as variously established in international declarations and guidelines regarding medical research.[203] Explicit consent is considered as the default regime for the processing of health data in the

---

[199] Under art. 4, 11 para GDPR, consent is defined as "any freely given, specific, informed and unambiguous indication of the data subject's wishes by which he or she, by a statement or by a clear affirmative action, signifies agreement to the processing of personal data relating to him or her". For an overview of the notion of consent see Art. 29 Data Protection Working Party (13 July 2011b) and Art. 29 Data Protection Working Party (28 November 2017a and last revised and adopted 10 April 2018). Art. 7 GDPR outlines some additional organisational and procedural requirements the data controller shall comply with in respect to the consent. The controller shall request the consent "in a manner which is clearly distinguishable from the other matters, in an intelligible and easily accessible form, using clear and plain language" (art. 7, 2 para GDPR); and thus shall be able, through adequate measures of data governance, "demonstrate that the data subject has consented to processing of his or her personal data" (art. 7, 1 para GDPR). For a comment, see Comandè (2019), pp. 189 ff.

[200] See, similarly art. 6, 1 para lett. a) GDPR.

[201] See Recital 43 GDPR.

[202] So art. 7(4) GDPR.

[203] The World Medical Association's Declaration of Helsinki, calls for "informed consent, preferably in writing" and establishes the right of the data subject "to refuse to participate in the study or to withdraw consent to participate at any time without reprisal". See World Medical Association (27 November 2013), para 25–32. For a critical assessment on the Helsinki Declaration, see Sharon et al. (2 November 2016); similarly see, Convention on Human Rights and Biomedicine under art. 5, stating that art. 5 states that "an intervention in the health field may only be carried out after the person concerned has given free and informed consent to it", provided appropriated information to the purpose and nature of the intervention, consequence and risks, and with the right to freely withdraw consent "at any time". See also artt. 6 to 9 of the Convention; International Ethical Guidelines for Biomedical Research Involving Human Subjects, establishing that for the processing of health data "voluntary informed consent of the prospective subject" must be obtained and that "waiver of informed consent is to be regarded as uncommon and exceptional, and must in all cases be approved by an ethical review committee". For a comment Dove (2018b), pp. 1021–1022.

context of scientific research[204] and is additionally required for the processing of personal data in the context of automated individual decision making, such as profiling.[205]

The Art. 29 Data Protection Working Party has specified that explicit consent must be given through an "express statement", such as a written statement signed by the data subject "in order to remove all possible doubt and potential lack of evidence in the future".[206]

As widely stressed by the literature, in the traditional data protection law architecture, consent is the fundamental means of control over the course of data processing activities[207] and with that a fundamental means of data subject's self-determination and self-empowerment.[208] To these purposes, consent is to be associated to the reaction means newly provided by the General Data Protection strengthening data subjects' control over personal data.[209] Ultimately, the centrality of consent in respect to data protection is strictly related to the individual values of autonomy and dignity,[210] functioning as constituting elements of the individual fundamental right to data protection.

Under these premises, just as the prohibition of processing under art. 9, 1 para GDPR, explicit consent as a legal basis for the processing of sensitive categories of personal data such as health data, is to be directly contextualised in the individual fundamental rights' dimension of the General Data Protection Regulation above-identified as the first pillar of the renewed European data protection law.

In this perspective, the legal basis of the explicit consent is to be aligned to a further legal basis for the processing of sensitive health data expressed under art. 9, 2 para lett. c) and related to the "protection of a vital interest of the data subject". Also in this case, indeed, the processing of sensitive data is residually[211] allowed for the

---

[204] Quinn and Quinn (2018), p. 11; Secretary's Advisory Committee on Human Research Protections (SACHRP) (13 March 2018) where it is stated that "consent is the basis most typically relied upon for processing personal data in research."

[205] Art. 22, 2 para lett. c) GDPR.

[206] See Art. 29 Data Protection Working Party (28 November 2017a and last revised and adopted 10 April 2018), pp. 18–19, adding that "in the digital or online context, a data subject may be able to issue the required statement by filling in an electronic form, by sending an email, by uploading a scanned document carrying the signature of the data subject, or by using an electronic signature".

[207] See Recital 7 GDPR: "natural persons should have control over their personal data". The perspective of consent as a means of control well suits the "will theory" of rights. So McDermott (2017), p. 3, recalling the reconstruction of HLA. Hart (1955), pp. 175 ff.

[208] See in this regard, the famous case Federal German Constitutional Court (Bundesverfassungsgericht) (15 December 1983) where the court developed the concept of "informational self-determination". For the literature see Cheung (2018), pp. 15 ff.

[209] Schneider (2018), pp. 230–231; Lynskey (2014), pp. 569–597.

[210] McDermott (2017), p. 3.

[211] See recital 46 GDPR: "(. . .) Processing of personal data based on the vital interest of another natural person should in principle take place only where the processing cannot be manifestly based on another legal basis. (. . .)". See also Article 29 Data Protection Working Party (15 February 2007a), p. 9.

protection of a vital interest of the data subject, to be intended as an interest that is "essential for someone's life",[212] such as the right to health in the context of medical care, especially in emergency cases.[213]

Both the legal bases regarding consent and the protection of a vital interest of the data subject, thus, relate to the protection of an essential interest of the data subject: in the first case the subject's interest in self-determination and in the second case the subject's vital interest.[214]

Both the legal bases regarding consent and the protection of a vital interest of the data subject appear to restrict processing activities over sensitive personal data. These ones are indeed limited either to the determinations of the data subjects as a result of the exercise of its fundamental right to autonomy and self-determination through consent or to what is strictly necessary to the protection of the above-mentioned "vital interest" of the data subject. Hence, the two analysed legal bases are a direct expression of the principle of data minimisation newly introduced by the General Data Protection Regulation under art. 5, 1 para lett. c) GDPR.[215]

The principle of data minimisation, in particular in respect to consent, is however being currently challenged in the digital environment. Indeed, the effectiveness of consent as a primary means to control data subjects' personal information appears to be threatened by mainly two factors, the first one given by the impossibility to quantify the actual amount of the data being processed on the basis of a single consent given and the second one given by the technological difficulty of detecting data processors and their processing activities.[216] In this context, users' self-determination through consent is sensitively weakened in view of the broad information asymmetries characterising the relationship between big data processors and individual data subjects.[217] As has been largely observed, the control paradigm

[212] Article 29 Data Protection Working Party (15 February 2007a), p. 9: "the processing must relate to essential individual interests of the data subject or of another person and it must – in the medical context – be necessary for a life-saving treatment in a situation where the data subject is not able to express his intentions".

[213] See Information Commissioner's Officer https://ico.org.uk/for-organisations/guide-to-data-protection/guide-to-the-general-data-protection-regulation-gdpr/lawful-basis forprocessing/vital-interests/.

[214] Article 29 Data Protection Working Party (15 February 2007a), p. 10.

[215] Art. 5, 1 para lett. c) GDPR: "personal data shall be adequate, relevant and limited to what is necessary in relation to the purposes for which they are processed ('data minimisation')".

[216] On the issue see European Commission (September 2012c), p. 2: "We believe explicit consent is difficult to implement in practice in a digital environment and may place a significant burden on businesses and a cumbersome online experience for users. We support the principle of twenty-first century consent: one that is consumer-friendly and contextual. The IAB believes that such affirmative action may introduce a 'tick box' consent culture to the internet making it futile for consumers to even participate. An increasing focus on explicit consent could also jeopardise innovation".

[217] Stressing this point Mantelero (2014), pp. 643 ff. With regards to the information asymmetries emerging in the information society, see Balkin (2010), pp. 232–246 and Lynskey (2014), pp. 592–597.

appears to be overturned in favour of data controllers and processors,[218] whose massive processing activities render it difficult for data subjects to discern to whom their consent is actually given to and for what processing activities the consent has been given and at what risks.[219]

Against this backdrop, the suitability of the legal basis of consent has been much debated especially in regards to health research, as increasingly relying on the sharing, aggregation and, in particular, on the repurposing of data processing activities[220] having transformative potential.[221] Data-intensive health research has thus sensitively expanded the borders of research projects, which have become ever more interconnected and open-ended,[222] and thus resulting structurally unsuitable in respect to the consent paradigm, conversely designed for specific and "closed" research projects.[223]

As a result, some strand of the literature has been starting to think of alternative forms of informed consent, considering more open and dynamic forms of consent as more appropriate for the governance of the uncertainty and unpredictability of data-driven health research.[224]

This opportunity has been concretely acknowledged within the General Data Protection Regulation, which under recital 33 GDPR appears to consider the difficulty for data processors of retrieving a specific and explicit consent exactly in the context of scientific research.[225] The recital indeed paves the way to broad forms of consent in those cases where it is not possible to define the specific purposes of the processing for scientific research purposes.[226] In these cases, the recital allows the data subject to give a broad form of consent widely related to certain areas of scientific research, under the only condition that these areas of research respect the "recognised ethical standards for scientific research".[227] According to the literature,

---

[218]This was already acknowledged by Froomkin (2000), p. 1464. See also Lemmens and Austin (2009), pp. 243 ff.

[219]Nehf (2016).

[220]Mittelstadt and Floridi (2016), pp. 303 ff.

[221]Mantelero (2014), p. 643.

[222]See supra Chap. 3, Sect. 3.2.

[223]Metcalf and Crawford (2016).

[224]Cheung (2018), pp. 25 ff.; Hallinan and Friedewald (2015), pp. 1 ff. In the context of bio-banking, forms of broad consent have already become the norm under the so-called FAIR (findable, acceptable, interoperable and reusable) principles, see The Dutch Techcentre for Life Sciences https://www.dtls.nl/fair-data/fair-principles-explained/.

[225]Marelli and Testa (4 May 2018), p. 497.

[226]Ho (2017), pp. 93–94.

[227]Recital 33 GDPR: "It is often not possible to fully identify the purpose of personal data processing for scientific research purposes at the time of data collection. Therefore, data subjects should be allowed to give their consent to certain areas of scientific research when in keeping with recognised ethical standards for scientific research. Data subjects should have the opportunity to give their consent only to certain areas of research or parts of research projects to the extent allowed by the intended purpose". For a comment see Comandè (2019); Quinn and Quinn (2018), p. 11.

the reference to ethical standards imply approval by ethics committees[228] and the determinations set by codes of conduct.[229]

The legitimacy of such broad forms of consent has been confirmed by Art. 29 Data Protection Working Party[230] which has clarified that research purposes need to be "well-described", however admitting the possibility that they are not "fully specified".[231] In the case of a lack of specified purpose, however, the Working Party advises data controllers to implement additional safeguards as the provision of a comprehensive research plan before the commencement of the project, as well as the implementation of adequate transparency measures enabling data subjects also to retrieve consent. Despite the requirement to conform data processing activities to the mentioned safeguards, the interpretation given by the Working Party supports the option of broad consent for research purposes, with the resulting weakening of informational self-determination objectives underlying consent.[232]

In these regards, it needs however to be observed that the option of broad consent is placed within a recital, which has no binding force: the breadth of consent is thus still restrained by the binding requirement of the purpose limitation expressed under art. 9, 2 para lett. a) GDPR.[233] It is thus the purpose limitation requirement that can be stretched, and thus be defined more generally in accordance with the needs of research purposes in accordance to the interpretative guidelines provided by both recital 33 GDPR and the Art. 29 Data Protection Working Party.[234]

The so-defined broad consent thus appears to open some spaces for the maximisation of health data processing activities carried out for research purposes. In the practice, however, this risks to lead to great uncertainties.[235]

In this perspective, this broad version of consent considered legitimate under the mentioned interpretative guidelines, is to be aligned with the legal basis for processing expressed under art. 9, 2 para lett. e) GDPR, regarding the processing of sensitive data that are "manifestly made public by the data subject". This legal basis appears to be particularly problematic, since it could be applied to all the data that are "made public" online, in social networks or in specific online communities, without the need of a consent, be it of specific or of broad nature.

In these regards, it must be also recalled that the consent rule, derogating under art. 9,2 para lett. a) GDPR the prohibition to process health data, is itself derogated

[228] Ho (2017), p. 94.

[229] Marelli and Testa (4 May 2018), p. 498.

[230] Art. 29 Data Protection Working Party (28 November 2017a and last revised and adopted 10 April 2018), pp. 27–30.

[231] Art. 29 Data Protection Working Party (28 November 2017a and last revised and adopted 10 April 2018) p. 28.

[232] Van Veen (2018), p. 76.

[233] Quinn and Quinn (2018), p. 12.

[234] Art. 29 Data Protection Working Party (28 November 2017a and last revised and adopted 10 April 2018), p. 28. For the literature see Shabani and Borry (2018), p. 154; Dove (2018b), p. 1022.

[235] Townend (2018), pp. 657 ff.

by art. 6, 4 para GDPR, which states that processing for a purpose other than that for which the personal data has been collected is lawful when it is compatible with the initial purpose. This provision needs to be in turn linked to art. 5, 1 para lett. b) GDPR ruling that "further processing for archiving purposes in *the public interest, scientific or historical research purposes or statistical purposes* shall, in accordance with Article 89(1), not considered to be incompatible with the initial purposes".[236] The combined reading of art. 6, 4 para and art. 5, 1 para lett. b) GDPR thus suggests that if personal data, also of sensitive nature, are processed for secondary research purposes, the processing is lawful for it is *per se* or *by default* compatible with the initial purpose, even if the processing is not based on the data subject's consent. This default compatibility rule with regards processing activities carried out for research purposes constitutes an important derogation from the principle of purpose limitation.

5.3.2.2 Public Interest-Related Legal Bases for Processing

Shifting from a subjective to an objective and controller-based legal basis for the processing of health data, art. 9, 2 para lett. g.) GDPR allows processing activities regarding sensitive health data when these are necessary "for reasons of substantial public interest",[237] which is additionally concretised by the following provisions under art. 9, 2 para lett. i) GDPR in the context of public health, referring to the purposes of "protecting against serious cross-border threats to health or ensuring high standards of quality and safety of health care and of medicinal products or medical devices", and under art. 9, 1 para lett. h) GDPR, referring to the purposes of "preventive or occupational medicine, for the assessment of the working capacity of the employee, medical diagnosis, the provision of health or social care or treatment or the management of health or social care systems and services". These reasons of public interest legitimately enable controller to override data subjects' individual rights,[238] such as the right to consent.[239] As the Art. 29 Data Protection Working

[236] Emphasis added. The rule is further confirmed also by recital 50 GDPR. Art. 6, 4 para GDPR introduces also criteria for the compatibility test, which the data controller has to carry out on a case-by-case basis, taking into account, amongst other factors, "any link between the purposes for which the personal data have been collected and the purposes of the intended further processing" (Art. 6(4)(a)); "the context in which the personal data have been collected" (Art. 6(4)(b)); "the nature of the personal data, in particular whether special categories of personal data are processed" (Art. 6(4)(c)); and as expressed by recital 50 GDPR also "the reasonable expectations of data subjects on the basis of their relationship with the controller as to their further use". For the literature, Marelli and Testa (4 May 2018), pp. 496–497.

[237] See art. 8, 4 para Directive 95/46/EC. This legal basis specifically regarding sensitive data is to be aligned to the one envisaged under art. 6, 1 para lett. e) GDPR, regarding the processing activities that are "necessary for the performance of a task carried out in the public interest".

[238] European Data Protection Supervisor (7 March 2012), pp. 83–85. For the literature see Townend (2004), pp. 89 ff.

[239] See recital 54 GDPR.

Party had outlined under the Directive, the public interest clause is an expression of the flexibilities within data protection law, enabling to strike the appropriate balance between the protection of data subjects' rights and other collective interests.[240]

It is important to stress that art. 9, 2 para lett. g) GDPR requires the "reasons of substantial public interest" to be grounded in "Union or Member State law".[241] As stressed in the literature, however the public interest clause is employed, at both normative and policy level, in many different ways and is mostly defined on a case-by-case basis.[242] In these regards, it has been observed that the employment of such a general clause as a legal basis for the processing of sensitive personal data will have the effect of leading to greater heterogeneity across the EU despite the choice of a regulation.[243]

In absence of a determination by national legislators, the guidelines of data protection authorities are to be taken into consideration.[244]

As the Directive had already done, also the Regulation provides some examples of public interest under recital 45 GDPR, relating to public health, social protection and the management of health services. With particular regard to the field of health, the Art. 29 Data Protection Working Party has linked the public interest to the protection of the right to health as enshrined in some Member States' constitutions.[245] With regards to the protection of the right to health, individual and collective interests are aligned. This means that the individual and collective dimensions are strictly intertwined.

As the Working Party underlines, the treatment of sensitive health data can be necessary to guarantee adequate medical assistance to patients and thus be functional to the satisfaction of the general interest.[246]

---

[240] Article 29 Data Protection Working Party (15 February 2007a), p. 12. Schulz (2018), p. 374.

[241] See art. 6, 2–3 para GDPR and recital 10 GDPR, stating that "regarding the processing of personal data for compliance with a legal obligation, for the performance of a task carried out in the public interest or in the exercise of official authority vested in the controller, Member States should be allowed to maintain or introduce national provisions to further specify the application of the rules of this Regulation". Emphasis added. See Van Veen (2018), p. 76, stressing that that the decision regarding what constitute a reason of public interest must be defined by a democratically accountable body. Article 29 Data Protection Working Party (15 February 2007a), pp. 12–13, where the Working Party recalls the European Court of Human Rights jurisprudence, defining the features of the law causing the interference with a fundamental right such as the one of to private and family life under art. 8 ECHR, highlighting that the law "must indicate the scope of any such discretion conferred on the competent authorities and the manner of its exercise with sufficient clarity, having regard to the legitimate aim of the measure in question, to give the individual adequate protection against arbitrary interference". This principle is expressed by European Court of Human Rights, Rotaru v. Romania, n. 28341/95 (4 May 2000b), para 55; European Court of Human Rights, Hasan and Chaush v. Bulgaria, n. 30985/96 (26 October 2000a), para 84.

[242] Townend (2004), p. 98.

[243] Quinn and Quinn (2018), p. 13.

[244] Riccio et al. (2018), p. 101.

[245] Article 29 Data Protection Working Party (15 February 2007a), p. 13.

[246] Article 29 Data Protection Working Party (15 February 2007a), p. 13.

Within the system of the General Data Protection Regulation, the legal basis under art. 9, 2 para lett. g) GDPR regarding sensitive data is to be aligned to the one generally envisaged under art. 6, 1 para lett. e) GDPR, regarding processing activities that are "necessary for the performance of a task carried out in the public interest".[247] The parallel with this provision is interesting for interpretative reasons: the definition of the task carried out in the public interest has indeed been enquired by the English Data Protection Authority that has stressed how any organisation either private or public can rely on this basis.[248] In the cited provisions, indeed, the Regulation adopts an objective criterion based on the nature of the purpose of the processing and not on the nature of the controller.[249] In these regards, for example, the European Data Protection Board, has clarified that processing of personal data for the purposes of clinical trials' procedures is to be considered as necessary for the performance of a task carried out in the public interest, when "the conduct of clinical trials directly falls within the mandate, missions and tasks vested in a public or private body by national law".[250]

Under these premises, the ground of processing in the public interest provides greater room for flexibilities than the other ground for processing sensitive data under art. 9(2)(d) GDPR, which allows the processing of sensitive data carried out in the course of a "legitimate interest" by "a foundation, association, or any other not-for-profit bodies (...) and on condition that the processing relates solely to the members or to former members of the body or to persons who have regular contact with it in connection with its purposes and that the personal data are not disclosed outside that body without the consent of the data subjects".[251] Similarly to what occurs under to the legal basis relating to the processing for the public interest, the legal basis regarding the legitimate interest allows controllers to bypass the strict requirements of consent.[252] As the cited provision suggests, however, this ground for processing is limited only to specific controllers carrying out non-commercial activities. Conversely, this limit is not set in respect to the grounds of public interest.

[247] Dove (2018b), p. 1023.

[248] See also recital 45 GDPR. Fir the definition of the public task, see Information Commissioner's Office https://ico.org.uk/for-organisations/guide-to-data-protection/guide-to-the-general-data-protection-regulationgdpr/lawful-basis-for-processing/public-task/. See also Comandè (2019), p. 1012.

[249] Stressing this point, De La Torre (5 February 2019).

[250] European Data Protection Board (23 January 2019b), p. 7.

[251] The provision is to be matched with the general provision under art. 6(1)(f) GDPR, establishing the grounds of legal processing for the purposes of legitimate interests. According to the interpretation given by the Art. 29 Data Protection Working Party, the legitimate interest needs to be real, i.e. non-speculative, sufficiently specific and "accepted by law". Art. 29 Data Protection Working Party (9 April 2014a).

[252] So Zingales (2018), p. 110.

Under the Directive, Art. 29 Data Protection Working Party[253] stressed the need to narrowly interpret the notion of public interest.[254]

This approach appears to have been conversely overturned by the European Data Protection Supervisor, which has underlined that the concept of public interest within the Regulation, due to the lack of further normative clarifications, is to be envisaged broadly, also from an economic perspective, extending also to health and social security.[255] This interpretation is thus particularly interesting for it amplifies the scope of public interest-related data processing activities not only to activities that are directly functional to the protection of fundamental rights such as the right to health, considered in its collective dimension, with regards to the mentioned protection "against serious cross-border threats to health" or the safeguard "of high standards of quality and safety of health care", but also to activities that have the effect of promoting the overall economic public interest, as in the words of the European Commission, the maximisation of European internal market's efficiency, which in turn, indirectly assures a higher standard of protection of health through the achieved innovation. In this perspective, the notion of public interest in the General Data Protection Regulation appears, amongst others, to be strictly connected to the principle of the free flow of information and thus to market functioning objectives, opening up also in this case, as already observed with regards to the basis of broad consent, to data maximisation outcomes.

These outcomes are nonetheless limited by the same art. 9, 2 para lett. g) GDPR, affirming that processing activities carried out in the public interest need to respect "the essence of the right to data protection" and be accompanied by "specific measures to safeguard the fundamental rights and interests of the data subject". These measures will be object of analysis of the next chapter. Be it sufficient for now to say that these measures work as outright conditionalities for the processing of personal data under the public interest, to be, again, defined by the Member State legislation in place in each jurisdiction.

As specified by the Regulation, first safeguards in these regards, can be found in the general principles of proportionality and necessity.[256] The importance of anchoring personal data processing activities carried out for public interest purposes to the parameters of proportionality and necessity has been underlined also by a recent ruling by the European Court of Justice,[257] where it has been affirmed that "the protection of the fundamental right to respect for private life at the European Union

[253] Article 29 Data Protection Working Party (15 February 2007a), pp. 12–13.

[254] See also BBMRI-ERIC- Biobanking and Biomolecular Resources Research Infrastructure (October 2014), pp. 8–9, underlining the risk of a 'politicization' of research under the general clause of the public interest, which in the previous drafts of the Regulation was formulated as 'high public interest'.

[255] European Data Protection Supervisor (7 March 2012), p. 83.

[256] Art. 9, 2 para lett. g) GDPR, "processing is necessary for reasons of substantial public interest, on the basis of Union or Member State law which shall be proportionate to the aim pursued".

[257] European Court of Justice, Puskar v Finance Directorate of the Slovak Republic, Case C-73/16 (27 September 2017), regarding the interpretation of the notion of "task carried out in the public

level requires that derogations from the protection of personal data and its limitations be carried out within the limits of what is strictly necessary".[258] This means that if another legal basis more respectful of the data subjects' rights and interests, such as consent, can be relied upon by the controller for the achievement of the same purpose, then this legal basis must be relied.[259] In any case, the processing of personal data concerning health cannot result in personal data being processed for other purposes by third parties.[260]

In the absence of any further clarification given by the Regulation, the definition of the notion of public interest is additionally left to the interpretation given by Data Protection Authorities and the jurisprudence.[261]

5.3.2.3 Research and Statistical Purposes

Ultimately, the processing of health-related data is allowed under art. 9, 2 para lett. j) GDPR when it is "necessary for reasons of public interest, scientific or historical research purposes or statistical purposes".

The promises of health data processing for scientific research projects is acknowledged under recital 157 GDPR, where it is stated that "by coupling information from registries researchers can obtain new knowledge of great value with regard to widespread medical conditions such as cardiovascular disease, cancer and depression. (...) In order to facilitate scientific research personal data can be processed for scientific research purposes, subject to appropriate conditions and safeguards set out in Union or Member State law".

Processing for research purposes seems indeed to have a privileged position within the General Data Protection Regulation, which provides various definitions of data-driven research. The Recitals do in fact treat different types of research separately, distinguishing between "scientific research", "historical research", "statistical research".

5.3.2.3.1 The Notion of Research

With regards to scientific research, recital 159 GDPR defines it as "the technological development and demonstration, fundamental research, applied research, and

---

interest" as a legitimate basis for processing personal data under art. 7 lett. e) of the previous Data Protection Directive.

[258] European Court of Justice, Puskar v Finance Directorate of the Slovak Republic, Case C-73/16 (27 September 2017), para 112.

[259] In this sense, Quinn and Quinn (2018), p. 1013.

[260] See recital 54 GDPR. Stressing this point Price et al. (1 February 2019), p. 450.

[261] For an assessment of the American case-law regarding public interest-related grounds of health data processing, see Kaplan (2016), pp. 312 ff.

privately funded research",[262] as well as public health research. The recital expressly refers to Article 179(1) of the Treaty on the Functioning of the European Union, which encourages "the objective of strengthening its scientific and technological bases by achieving a European research area in which researchers, scientific knowledge and technology circulate freely".

Interestingly, Recital 54 GDPR defines public health according to Regulation (EC) No. 1338/2008 as "all elements related to health, namely health status, including morbidity and disability, the determinants having an effect on that health status, health care needs, resources allocated to health care, the provision of, and universal access to, health care as well as health care expenditure and financing, and the causes of mortality." Given this broad definition, the activities of social media and other online platforms may well qualify as public health research.

Along these lines, as clarified by recital 160 GDPR, historical research comprises genealogical research. However, recital 160 GDPR expressly excludes from its scope processing activities on deceased persons.

Ultimately, "statistical research" is defined under recital 162 GDPR, as "any operation of collection and the processing of personal data necessary for statistical surveys or for the production of statistical results". As the same recital affirms, statistical research "implies that the result of processing for statistical purposes is not personal data, but aggregate data." While statistical research may be used in support of scientific research, it cannot be "used in support of measures or decisions regarding any particular natural person". The Recital specifies that the EU or the Member States should legislate around the scope of the statistical research exemptions, including defining the appropriate safeguards for assuring "statistical confidentiality". A strand of the literature commenting the research exemption under art. 9, 2 para lett. j) GDPR, has observed that the notion of processing for statistical purposes could encompass also processing activities carried out through big data analytics as they rely exactly on statistical methods.[263]

As can be derived from the mentioned recitals, the General Data Protection Regulation adopts a broad definition of research,[264] likely to encompass the activities of both public and private entities.[265]

These considerations lead to the question of the nature of the link between the legal grounds of processing for research purposes and for public interest. Indeed, although it is true that art. 9(2) lett. j) GDPR refers both to processing activities carried out in the public interest and for research purposes, the public interest and the research purpose ground two different legal bases for processing under of arts. 9(2) lett. i) and j) GDPR.

---

[262] Emphasis added.

[263] Wachter and Mittelstadt (2019), p. 593; similarly, Zarsky (2017), p. 1013.

[264] This is directly affirmed by recital 159 GDPR, which affirms that "for the purposes of this Regulation, the processing of personal data for scientific research purposes should be interpreted in a broad manner".

[265] Similarly, Pormeister (2017), pp. 137 ff.

By considering the research purpose autonomously, thus, the Regulation appears to overcome the approach adopted by the previous Directive, which mentioned the scientific research as an example of "reasons of substantial public interest" under recital 34.[266]

Moreover, the broad interpretation of the notion of "research" required by the same recital 159 GDPR suggests that this ground for processing can encompass processing activities also by private entities that are not public interest-, but, conversely, profit-oriented.[267]

Hence, the definition of scientific research under the General Data Protection Regulation is likely to encompass also commercial and thus market-oriented research.[268] As the German Data Ethics Committee[269] has highlighted in this respect, substantial uncertainties nonetheless persist in respect to whether research includes also product development and enhancement.

It thus seems that, differently from what was the case under the Directive, under the Regulation, scientific research is not a specification of the public interest. This is further confirmed by some of the Regulation's recitals that consider the research purpose not only as an autonomous legal basis for processing but also as a possible example of a controllers' legitimate interest under art. 6, 1 para lett. f) GDPR.[270] This is also the interpretation also given by the Art. 29 Data Protection Working Party, which has included scientific research as a legitimate interest.[271]

In view of the risk of reliance on the legal grounds of scientific research also for commercially-oriented activities, the Biobanking and BioMolecular Resources Research Infrastructure- European Research Infrastructure Consortium (BBMRI-ERIC) has stressed the need to restrict the broad interpretation given to the General Data Protection Regulation of scientific research so as to consider only public interest-oriented research activities.[272]

However, in light of the above-described networked environment, in which private organizations increasingly collaborate with public entities, also this restrictive approach would not provide greater certainties as regards the scope of the research exemption: in the intertwined algorithmic digital health data processing activities, health data could indeed end up being freely processed by large

[266] Shabani and Borry (2018), p. 153. It must be additionally recalled that under the Previous Directive, the legal base of the processing in the public interest, has been used by Member States to permit processing for a range of purposes, as scientific research. This has occurred for example in Germany. See Quinn and Quinn (2018), p. 1013.

[267] Mayer-Schönberger and Padova (2016), p. 326. Similarly, Richter (2016), p. 583.

[268] Ho (2017), pp. 98–99, where the Author cites some empirical studies showing the mistrust of consumers with regards the use of health data by private commercial entities. See Royal Statistical Society (22 July 2014).

[269] Bundesministerium für Justiz und Verbraucherschutz (22 January 2020), p. 125.

[270] See recitals 47 and 113 GDPR. Shabani and Borry (2018), p. 154.

[271] Article 29 Data Protection Working Party (9 April 2014a).

[272] BBMRI-ERIC- Biobanking and Biomolecular Resources Research Infrastructure (October 2014), p. 3. This is the view shared also by another strand of the literature, Raum (2017), pp. 41–42.

commercial corporations under the façade of public interest-leaning health research activities, directly benefiting from a major leeway in favor of data controllers over data subjects.[273]

Against this backdrop, it appears that the General Data Protection Regulation leaves much more room for interpretation regarding the link between the processing for research- be it scientific or statistical- purposes and secondary commercially-oriented purposes. In these regards, more specific and decisive interpretative guidelines from the European Court of Justice or the European Data Protection Board are certainly required and awaited.[274]

For these purposes, a look at the solutions provided by other legal systems can be fruitful. In the USA, for example, where there are notoriously weaker data protection regimes, due to the fragmentation and sectorial nature of data protection laws, such as the Health Insurance Portability and Accountability Act regarding health information,[275] the California Consumer Privacy Act,[276] coming into force in 2020, similarly establishes a research exemption for the processing of personal data,[277] limiting the same research exemption to deidentified information employed for processing activities "that are compatible with the context in which the personal information was collected" with the explicit limit of commercial purposes, broadly defined as "the use of personal information for the business's or a service provider's operational purposes, or other notified purposes"[278] in order "to advance a person's commercial or economic interests, such as by inducing another person to buy, rent, lease, join, subscribe to, provide, or exchange products, goods, property, information, or services, or enabling or effecting, directly or indirectly, a commercial transaction".[279]

Similarly, in the European Union, the 2019 Copyright Directive draws a distinction between not-for profit and public interest-oriented research entities and organisations operating for commercial purposes. Recital 12 of the Copyright Directive indeed excludes from the notion of "research organisations" and thus from the research regime "organisations upon which commercial undertakings have a decisive influence allowing such undertakings to exercise control because of structural situations, such as through their quality of shareholder or member, which could result in preferential access to the results of the research".

[273] Stressing this point, Tene and Polonetsky (2016), pp. 458 ff. More recently also, Wachter and Mittelstadt (2019), pp. 592–599.

[274] The need for a clarification regarding the scope of the GDPR's research exemption is stressed by Nicholson Price et al. (1 February 2019), p. 450.

[275] Nicholson Price (2018), pp. 295 ff.; Terry (2018), pp. 56 ff.

[276] California Consumer Privacy Act (CCPA) (2018). See for the literature, Determann (2018), pp. 1 ff.

[277] Nicholson Price et al. (1 February 2019).

[278] This is the definition of "business purpose" under section 1798. 140 lett.d) CCPA.

[279] So section 1798.140 lett.f) CCPA.

In light of these statements, the California data protection law as well as the European Copyright Directive appear to take a different approach in respect to the General Data Protection Regulation, by expressly defining the commercial purpose and with that more clearly defining *a contrario* the scope of the established research exemptions.

The broad notion of research provided by the GDPR reveals its problematic nature especially in respect to health data transfers occurring among different organizations. This has become apparent in a recent Italian ruling by the Tribunal of Cagliari,[280] which has overturned the decision by the Italian Data Protection Authority regarding the transfer of genetic data from an Italian genomic biobank named Shardna, storing genetic and health data of Sardinian data subject, to the UK-based for-profit corporation Tiziana Life Science plc.[281]

The Italian Data Protection Authority[282] had indeed blocked the transfer with an interim injunction, ordering the company Tiziana to inform the data subjects of the change of data controller and of the new research purposes for which the transferred genetic data would have been processed for. In addition to this, it required the company to recollect consent from all the data subject whose data was transferred.[283]

The Tribunal of Cagliari, conversely, ruled for the lawfulness of the processing of the genetic and health data acquired by the English company in view of the same research processing purpose shared with the genomic biobank.[284] Although both the administrative and the judicial decisions have been given under the Italian data protection law framework preceding the European reform of the General Data Protection Regulation, both of the decisions appear to anticipate some rules that have been further developed by the General Data Protection Regulation, such as the obligation codified under art. 14 GDPR to provide to the data subject information when the data are not directly obtained from the data subject- as occurs in the case of mergers- and the legal basis for processing related to research purposes under art. 9, 2 para lett. j) GDPR.

The mentioned case raises interesting questions regarding whether the processing activities for research purposes carried out by the third party recipient of a certain dataset are to be considered secondary processing activities for which a new specific consent is required. In accordance to the default compatibility rule set out under the above-recalled artt. 6,4 and 5, 1 para lett b) GDPR, if the purposes of the processing are related to research activities the default compatibility should exempt from requiring a new consent. However, also in this case, the solution will largely depend on the definition of the scope of such research purpose: the question relates to whether the mentioned compatibility rule applies also to a different third party organization,

---

[280] Tribunal of Cagliari, Sentenza n. 1569 (6 June 2017).

[281] Commenting the case, see Marelli and Testa (4 May 2018), p. 498.

[282] Italian Data Protection Authority (6 October 2016).

[283] Italian Data Protection Authority (6 October 2016).

[284] Tribunal of Cagliari, Sentenza n. 1569 (6 June 2017).

carrying out private and for-profit oriented research activities-as the one carried out by a company as Tiziana- in the form of different research projects that are not strictly related to the research projects for which the health data were originally collected.[285]

According to the interpretative suggestions under recital 159 GDPR the answer to this question should be positive, this rendering the decision of the Tribunal of Cagliari more adherent to the newly established- controller-friendly- data protection framework.[286]

The further developments of the case involving the Sardinian genetic and health database trigger additional considerations regarding the relationship of the research exemption in respect to other rules of the data protection framework such as the one of consent.

Indeed, with a subsequent decision, the Italian data protection authority has again ordered the English company to block the processing of health data referring to the data subjects that had withdrawn their consent directly as a consequence of the data transfer to the for-profit company.[287]

Under art. 7, 2 para of the General Data Protection Regulation, withdrawal of consent is always possible. However, since the one regarding processing for research purposes is a legal basis alternative to the one of consent under the list provided under art. 9, 2 para GDPR for the processing of special categories of personal data, questions again arise with regards to whether the withdrawal of consent by data subjects renders the research ground ineligible.

Possible solutions in this respect are given by the realignment of research processing activities to public interest-oriented purposes, through a more fundamental-rights compliant interpretation, which respects first of all data subjects' right to self-determination; and by the re-application of the ordinary and "full" data protection law regime, in case sensitive data are used for further commercial purposes, i.e. the "practical" economic employment of the statistical models designed and constructed in the context of research projects.[288]

This interpretation is directly suggested by recital recital 162 GDPR, which prohibits the use of personal data in the context of research activities "in support of measures or decisions regarding any particular natural person".[289]

---

[285] Leaving the interpretative question open, Dove (2018b), p. 1025.

[286] See Grifeo (11 July 2017) and more generally, Bassini (2019), pp. 109 ff.

[287] Italian Data Protection Authority (21 December 2017).

[288] Raum (2017), p. 41. In this regard, a controller would need to have a different legal basis, such as consent or a task in the public interest, in order to employ a statistical model designed under the statistical research exemption. Stressing this point also, Wachter and Mittelstadt (2019), p. 593.

[289] In these regards, some clarifications have been provided by the Art. 29 Data Protection Working Party that has identified some examples in which companies carry out processing activities over personal data, without finalising them to individual decisions regarding natural persons, as in the case a business may wish to "classify its customers according to their age or gender for statistical purposes and to acquire an aggregated overview of its clients without making any predictions or drawing any conclusions about an individual. In this case the purpose is not assessing individual

As the recital suggests, thus, processing of personal data carried out for research purposes cannot result in profiling activities and other decisions regarding single natural persons. This statement is extremely important and poses some interesting normative grounds for interpreting the special data protection regime regarding data-driven research in a way that prevents research processing activities over health data from triggering further, "secondary", commercial actions.

5.3.2.3.2 The Special Data Protection Regime for Research-Oriented Processing Activities

With regards to the legal framework concerning research-oriented processing activities, the broad definition of research given by the mentioned recitals, is nonetheless counterbalanced by the requirement under art. 9, 2 para lett. j) GDPR to base the processing activities on Union or Member State law. It will be thus Union or Member State law's competence to define more clearly which exact activities can fall under the scope of research as a legitimate basis for the processing. With regards to European Union law, an example of such specific regulation is given by the Clinical Trial Regulation,[290] which the European Data Protection Board has lately clarified as a "sectoral law containing specific provisions relevant from a data protection viewpoint but no derogations to the GDPR", thus clarifying that the two frameworks both apply simultaneously.[291]

In addition to this, as in the case of the processing of sensitive data on public interest grounds, the provision under art. 9, 2 para lett. j) GDPR requires the processing activities to be proportionate to the aim pursued consistently with the proportionality and data minimization principles under art. 5, 1 para lett. b) and c) GDPR, to respect the essence of the data protection right and be subject to specific safeguards for the protection of the data subjects' fundamental rights and interests.[292]

These safeguards are ever more important because in case of processing for research purposes important data protection law principles, as the principle of storage limitation under art. 5, 1 lett. e) GDPR and the principle of purpose limitation under the above-recalled default compatibility rule under art. 6, 4 para and art. 5, 1 para lett. b) GDPR, are derogated.

Also data subjects' rights as the right to be forgotten under art. 17, 3 para GDPR can be derogated in case the enactment of the right impairs the achievement of the

characteristics and is therefore not profiling". So Art. 29 Data Protection Working Party (3 October 2017b), p. 7.

[290] Regulation EU n. 536/2014 of the European Parliament and of the Council of 16 April 2014 on clinical trials on medicinal products for human use, and repealing Directive 2001/20/EC, OJ L 158/1 (27 May 2014).

[291] European Data Protection Board (23 January 2019), p. 3.

[292] Comandè (2019), p. 1013.

research objectives; equally, data subjects' right to be informed when the processed data is collected from third party sources and not from the data subjects, can be derogated under art. 14, 5 para lett. b) GDPR in case the "provision of such information proves impossible or would involve a disproportionate effort".[293] This last derogation is quite far-reaching since it is allows controllers processing for research purposes to diminish the information they have to disclose to the data subjects in the so-called privacy notice, which according to art. 14, 1 para GDPR should include information regarding the contact details of the Data Protection Officer, the purposes and the legal basis for processing, and- most interestingly- information about whom the data is shared with.[294] This information should be provided in general organizational documents as well as in project-specific documents or participant information sheets, such as consent forms.[295] Data subjects must receive this information prior to the processing or in reasonable time, depending on the circumstances of the case, when the processed data is acquired from another source, such as from a third-party organization.[296] In case the origin of the processed data is not identifiable since various sources have been used, general information should be provided.[297]

Conversely, when the data processed for research purposes are directly collected from the data subject, the controller's information duties under art. 13 GDPR remain effective, unless, as specified by recital 62 GDPR, also in this case, "the provision of information to the data subject proves to be impossible or would involve a disproportionate effort".

The derogations to such right to information in case of processing for research purposes, well reflects the controller-oriented nature of the considered legal basis for processing, which is to be placed at the exact opposite in respect to the legal basis of the consent and its control and data minimization rationales. Allowing for these derogations, the special regime for research purposes appears to disavow data subjects' control prerogatives over their sensitive data. Under the ordinary data protection regime, these prerogatives are satisfied through the strengthening of the transparency obligations of data controllers enacted by the Regulation. The mention derogations thus allow the data controller to fully take control over the data

[293] As observed by some scholars, compliance with the transparency requirements within long data-driven research projects could be disproportionate and substantially impair the objectives of the processing, especially when there are many data subjects involved and the data has been heavily pseudonymised. So Quinn and Quinn (2018), p. 1014.

[294] Dove (2018b), p. 1024.

[295] Dove (2018b).

[296] So recital 61 GDPR; art. 13–14 GDPR. See also Health Research Authority https://www.hra.nhs.uk/planning-and-improving-research/policies-standards-legislation/data-protection-and-information-governance/gdpr-detailed-guidance/transparency/; and Information Commissioner's Office https://ico.org.uk/for-organisations/guide-to-data-protection/guide-to-the-general-data-protection-regulation-gdpr/individual-rights/right-to-be-informed/.

[297] Recital 61 GDPR.

processed for research purposes, with that entirely transferring the control barycenter onto the processing entities, without the data subjects knowing the features and conditions under which their sensitive personal data are processed.[298] The derogation to the principle of storage limitation- this meaning that health data may be stored for longer periods if necessary for research purposes- additionally allows for an uncontrolled data maximization of the processing of sensitive data for research purposes.[299]

Furthermore, additional derogations from the ordinary data protection regime set out by the Regulation can be further provided by Member State law: art. 89, 2 para GDPR specifically enables Union or Member State law to provide derogations from data subjects' right to access under art. 15 GDPR; right to rectification under art. 16 GDPR; right to restriction of processing under art. 18 GDPR and ultimately the right to object under art. 21 GDPR.[300] These derogations can be provided when the satisfaction of data subjects' rights "are likely to render impossible or seriously impair the achievement" and these derogations are necessary for the fulfilment of the purpose.[301] Also in this case, however, national legislation needs to assure that appropriate conditions and safeguards for the processing are enacted and respected.

Also under the special regime regarding the processing of sensitive data for research purposes, nonetheless, some relevant data subjects' rights remain effective, as users' right to data portability under art. 20 GDPR. This right is extremely important in respect to health data since it enables patients to transfer their data from a platform to another. Moreover, also the right not to be subject to automated decisions under art. 22 GDPR cannot be object of derogations, not even at national level.[302]

As has been observed in the literature, the restraints to processing activities regarding sensitive data will largely depend on how burdensome the conditions

---

[298] Pormeister (2017), p. 139, observing that "the exceptions from the storage and purpose limitations afforded to the research exemption create an outcome in which consent will become more irrelevant over time in correlation with advancements in personal medicine".

[299] Pormeister (2017), p. 138.

[300] It must be observed that the possibility granted to national legislations to derogate from the right to object under art. 21 GDPR expressly recalled by art. 89, 2 para GDPR, is to be reconciled with the provision under the same art. 21, 6 para GDPR, affirming the endurance of the right at stake in case of processing carried out for "scientific or historical research purposes or statistical purposes pursuant to art. 89, 1 GDPR". As can be derived from art. 21, 6 para GDPR, derogation to the data subjects' right to object are admitted when "the processing is necessary for the performance of a task carried out for reasons of public interest". This is thus the rule in absence of any national legislation. Conversely, a national legislation can under art. 89, 2 para GDPR derogate to the rule in case the exercise of the right is likely to render impossible or seriously impair the achievement of the specific (research) purposes and in case the restrictions are necessary to fulfil the purpose. Dove (2018b), p. 1025.

[301] Art. 89,2 para GDPR. With regards to processing for scientific purposes, the English Data Protection Bill approved in 2018, has established derogations with regards to the right to access under art. 15 GDPR; to rectification under art. 16 GDPR; to object under art. 21 GDPR.

[302] See infra Chap. 7, Sect. 7.2.2.

and safeguards defined at national level will be.[303] With specific regards to health-related data, art. 9, 4 para GDPR additionally allows Member States to establish "further conditions, including limitations, with regard to the processing of genetic data, biometric data or data concerning health". Ultimately, thus, the scope of the research exemption under art. 9, 2 para; 5, 1 lett. b and e); 6, 4 para and 89 GDPR will largely depend on these national determinations and thus, ultimately, on Member States' discretion in establishing adequate safeguards.[304]

However, it needs to be observed that in absence of these national determinations the research exemption is directly applicable as defined by the Regulation, with the direct applicability of the derogations to the above-mentioned principles and rights that the Regulation itself provides.[305] As has been observed, this resulting "relaxation of the law" encourages big data controllers to create new statistical models for the massive processing of sensitive data and resulting categorization of data subjects, which have no reaction means over the results of such statistical processing.[306]

Against this backdrop, however, a first limitation to the further processing of health data, and thus to the sharing of health data for research purposes has been recently suggested by the European Data Protection Supervisor in its preliminary Opinion on data protection and scientific research.[307] The Supervisor has indeed observed that the special regime regarding the processing of sensitive data for research purpose cannot disown the "essence of the (fundamental) right to data protection". This means, first of all, that the derogations provided by the special regime cannot be abused by data controllers acting for research purposes. The Supervisor suggests therefore a highly restrictive interpretation of the research exemption.[308]

Following such an interpretative approach, a possible restriction to the creeping application of the above traced special data protection regime also to further processing of health data, can be found in the distinction between public interest and commercial-oriented research. In the previous paragraph it has been indeed shown that the GDPR's notion of research encompasses both public and privately-funded research, differently from other normative definitions of research as the ones enshrined in the California Consumer Protection Act or the Copyright Directive. In these regulations, the distinction between these two types of research triggers the application of the ordinary regulatory regime to commercially-oriented (research) activities, and of the special regulatory regime to public interest-oriented research activities. Conversely, in the General Data Protection Regulation both the commercially and the public interest-oriented activities trigger the application of the special data protection regime.

[303] Quinn (2016), pp. 1 ff.

[304] Pormeister (2017), p. 138.

[305] Pormeister (2017), p. 138.

[306] Wachter and Mittelstadt (2019), p. 593.

[307] European Data Protection Supervisor (6 January 2020).

[308] European Data Protection Supervisor (6 January 2020), pp. 18 and 22.

In this respect, the German Data Ethics Commission has underlined the need to exploit to the maximum the research privileges existing under European data protection law, as well as the need to consider research as a "particularly valuable good" when compared with other competing interests.[309] For these purposes it encourages the adoption of a broad notion of research irrespective of its privately or publicly funded nature.[310]

However, it could be worth reviving such distinction for the purposes of scaling the flexibilities or "privileges"- as the recalled Data Ethics Commission defines them- of the special data protection regime. As has been shown above, these flexibilities are directly given by the national definitions, which are relevant, as well as the modulation of the derogations and the safeguards, which are enacted in respect to each health data-driven research project. Under these premises, a restrictive interpretative approach as the one required by the European Data Protection Supervisor suggests the opportunity to regulate these flexibilities differently in respect to public interest-oriented research and privately-governed one.

Both the derogations and the safeguards required under the exemption should indeed be respectively restricted to the minimum and stretched to the highest when it comes to commercially-oriented research data processing. Conversely, public health-oriented research activities could enjoy a more enabling regulatory regime, designed around deeper derogations, if needed, and less burdensome safeguards. As suggested under the already recalled recital 12 of the Copyright Directive, this public-oriented aim of research activities could be "reflected through public funding or through provisions in national laws or public contracts".

This distinction could however prove to be difficult in respect to private-public partnerships established for grounds of public health protection, as has occurred in the fight against the Coronavirus pandemic. In this respect, the collaboration between private and public actors, as in the "Innovative Medicines Initiative", based on a public-private partnership between the European Commission and the pharmaceutical industry,[311] should trigger the enactment of higher data protection safeguards and lower derogations from the ordinary regime, because of the presence of commercially-oriented stakeholders. Nonetheless, purposes of public health protection, and the need of immediate research actions, could conversely require a relaxation of data protection checkpoints. Against this backdrop, in respect to mixed private-public health datasets employed for research purposes, the special regime should be calibrated based on the influence that commercial undertakings have in the established research partnership or organisation. In case these have a "decisive influence" over the established research partnership or organisation, this meaning that they are able to exercise a dominant control over initiated research patterns because of their direct control over research infrastructures and thus because of a

[309] Bundesministerium für Justiz und Verbraucherschutz (22 January 2020), p. 124.

[310] Bundesministerium für Justiz und Verbraucherschutz (22 January 2020), p. 124.

[311] See IMI-Innovative Medicines Initiative https://www.imi.europa.eu/.

"preferential access to the results of the research",[312] safeguards should be as strict as in the case of a fully privately-conducted research. Conversely, in case the control of the research endeavours over mixed private-public datasets primarily resides onto the public entity, the mentioned data protection flexibilities could be exploited to the maximum.

5.4 The GDPR's Research Exemption as a New Efficiency Defense for Health Data Pools

The above-traced framework leads to deeper considerations regarding the nature of the research exemptions within the system of the General Data Protection Regulation. The detachment from the consent/control rule and the direct or possible (based on national legislation) derogations from some of data protection law's principles as the purpose limitation and the storage limitation principle, as well as from important data subjects' rights suggests that the considered research exemption substantiates a regulatory paradigm that is not directly aligned to the objective of the protection of data subjects' fundamental rights.

With regards to sensitive health data, this objective is clearly satisfied by the prohibition of processing special categories of data under art. 9, 1 para GDPR. As has been illustrated, however, this prohibition results to be largely weakened by the exceptions that overall come to liberalize the processing of sensitive personal data, as health data, on grounds of a (broad) consent, a public interest-oriented purpose or a scientific research purpose. Especially the last two legal grounds for processing sensitive personal data are characterized by a high degree of intrinsic and extrinsic vagueness:[313] the intrinsic vagueness stems from the difficulties of clearly defining the notion of both public interest and scientific and statistical research; conversely, the extrinsic vagueness is given by the Regulation's deferral of these exemptions to Member States' legislation.[314]

In this context, the research exemption appears to ultimately embed a substantially different rationale in respect to the other legal basis for processing. Indeed, the ground for processing related to the explicit consent, although opening up the way for a broad consent in case of research activities, is strictly rooted in data subjects' control and self-determination interests, which are in turn related to the individual fundamental rights of autonomy and dignity. This legal basis thus allows data subjects to autonomously and freely decide over their most sensitive information.

Conversely, under the public interest-related ground of exception, the processing and use of sensitive personal data is allowed for the achievement of higher societal

[312] The wording is taken from recital 12 of the Copyright Directive.

[313] In this regard, Wendehorst (2017), pp. 327 ff.

[314] Stressing this point also Zarsky (2017), p. 1009.

and collective interests, which could, under a more relaxed interpretation suggested by the Art. 29 Data Protection Working Party, comprise also economic interests. The processing of sensitive data is in this case justified by higher interests, transcending individual data subjects' autonomy and self-determination expectations.[315]

With the introduction of a specific scientific and statistical research exemption, the notion of scientific and statistical research appears to have gained an autonomous status in respect to the processing ground related to the public interest.[316]

This is well acknowledged under recital 157 GDPR, which highlights the very functional nature of research, being an essential precondition for the "formulation and implementation of knowledge-based policy, improve the quality of life for a number of people and improve the efficiency of social services".[317] At a deeper understanding, this recital perfectly echoes the statements made by the European Commission with regards to the digital single market strategy.[318] In this perspective, indeed, scientific and statistical research involving the processing of personal data is a key driver for the development and advancement of the digital single market as fueled by the free flow of personal data. This holds especially true in respect to sensitive health data that entail a highly sophisticated scientific value, which in turn renders this same data essential for the design of new products and services in the healthcare sector.

Under these premises, the research exemption under art. 9, 2 para lett. j) GDPR appears to be the direct expression of what has been identified above as the second pillar of the General Data Protection Regulation, namely the objective regarding the free-flow of information and the promotion of digital innovation within the internal market.[319] In this perspective, the research exemption does not align with the fundamental rights nature of data protection law, and reveals itself to be a new safe harbor for the processing of sensitive data that aims to stimulate competition and innovation in data-driven markets such as health data-driven markets.[320]

Hence, the very nature of the analyzed research exemption is not that of a *data protection* rule but rather that of a rule of the data economy, with data protection concerns, expressed in the requirement of the enactment of safeguards for the respect of data subjects' fundamental rights.[321]

---

[315] Stressing the paternalistic nature of the data protection law regime under the General Data Protection Regulation, Hermstrüwer (2016), pp. 359–363.

[316] Quinn and Quinn (2018), p. 1015.

[317] See Purtova (2017), p. 178.

[318] See supra Chap. 4, Sect. 4.3.2.

[319] A similar position is taken by Mayer-Schönberger and Padova (2016), pp. 323 ff.

[320] Stressing a similar point in respect to the nature of the right to data portability, Graef et al. (2018b), pp. 1359 ff. and also Graef et al. (2018a), p. 16, highlighting that "data portability of Art. 20 GDPR is an example of an innovation policy embedded in data protection law". With regards to the research exemption, see Wachter and Mittelstadt (2019), pp. 594–595.

[321] For a distinction between the rules regarding data protection and data economy, see, Wendehorst (2017), p. 332.

In the practice, this means that the research exemption could work as a sort of efficiency defense under data protection law for the transfer and the processing of health data for research purposes, with subsequent market outcomes. Within the regulatory architecture of the General Data Protection Regulation, the research exemption seems to serve the original data protection law's internal market objectives.

From a regulatory standpoint, thus, the General Data Protection Regulation appears to reflect aspects of economic regulation, which ultimately facilitate the creation of a market of personal health data and in this way set the conditions for an efficient functioning of other markets,[322] such as the one for digital medical devices and pharmaceuticals.

In consistency with the European Commission's support for digital health, the General Data Protection Regulation incentivizes data-driven research activities by establishing a special regime regarding processing activities over sensitive health data carried out for research purposes.

The research environment emerging under the pressure of technological change and the growing employment of algorithmic processing techniques in health research, is very complex, characterized by a deep interconnection between traditional research centers and large high tech corporations.

As shown, the networked nature of the current health research environment renders it particularly arduous to draw the line between processing activities carried out for health research purposes and processing activities differently employed for non-health related, commercial purposes. This renders the distinction between the spheres of (health) market and (health) research, on which articles 9(1) and 9(2) GDPR rely, quite obsolete.

The prohibition regarding the treatment of special categories of personal data, such as data regarding health, serves the General Data Protection Regulation's primary goal of protecting data subjects' fundamental rights.[323] However, without a careful interpretative effort for the establishment of appropriate safeguards, this objective risks being undermined by the liberalization of health data processing for health research purposes.

The General Data Protection Regulation's research provisions indeed ultimately appear to serve the different parallel objective of promoting the free flow of personal information as an essential precondition of the efficient development of the internal market.[324]

In this perspective, the analyzed provisions regarding the processing of special categories of data for scientific and statistical research purposes are to be systemically aligned with other provisions that appear to serve similar objectives.

[322] This is highlighted from a general perspective by Lynskey (2015), pp. 76–77.

[323] See recital 1 GDPR.

[324] See recital 2 GDPR.

In these regards, a parallelism emerges between the examined research exemptions and the right to data portability under art. 20 GDPR. This right has been indeed expressly welcomed by the Commission as a new means of promotion of the data economy, providing the data subject with the right to transfer his/her data from a service provider to another.[325] Through this new right, thus, the data subject acquires an enhanced control over the data shared with businesses.[326] Together with control rationales, however, the right to data portability ultimately stimulates data mobility across platforms, through data subjects' impulses.[327] From this perspective, hence, the right to data portability has been recognized by a strand of the literature as a tool for data-innovation and the promotion of the free-flow of personal-information.[328]

Against this backdrop, if data portability enhances and promotes data sharing from consumer to businesses; the research exemption appears to promote health data sharing among businesses or among businesses and other stakeholders, thus enabling the re-use of this information.

However, as has been observed,[329] the right to data portability is still based on data subjects' control over their data in respect to processing platforms, since the flow of data is enacted only upon the data subjects' determinations. To the very contrary, under the research exemption the data subjects appears to be totally excluded from control over their sensitive data. From a broader perspective, moreover, these research exemptions are to be thus paired with the regulation regarding the free-flow of non-personal data,[330] which highlights the importance of access to data for the purposes of the "ability of research and development companies to facilitate collaboration between firms, universities and other research organisations with the aim of driving innovation".[331]

It appears that health data sharing agreements among various private and public actors could find a valid legal basis for the involved treatment of health data exactly within the GDPR's efficiency-tailored research regime.

The need to maintain high standards of protection regarding data subjects' rights especially in a very sensitive environment such as that of health research, has pushed the European Commission to start considering "health data markets" as a special, which is to be placed right beyond the digital market/research dichotomy. In this area, the data protection safeguards listed above constitute just the starting point of a much-needed intervention in the developing networked digital health research field, where ethical and regulatory standards as well as competition analysis must be

[325] European Commission (14 February 2012b), p. 53.

[326] Drexl (27 April 2018), p. 12.

[327] Graef et al. (2018a), p. 3.

[328] Graef et al. (2018b), pp. 1359 ff.

[329] Graef et al. (2018b), pp. 1359 ff.

[330] Regulation (EU) 2018/1807 of the European Parliament and of the Council of 14 November 2018 on a framework for the free flow of non-personal data in the European Union (28 November 2018) OJL 303/59.

[331] See recital n. 6.

solicited in order to "collaboratively" fill the regulatory gaps left open by the market-oriented GDPR's research provisions.

References

Art. 29 Data Protection Working Party (1 August 2003) Working Document on Biometrics. https://ec.europa.eu/justice/article-29/documentation/opinion-recommendation/files/2003/wp80_en.pdf

Art. 29 Data Protection Working Party (17 March 2004) Working Document on Genetic Data. https://iapp.org/media/pdf/knowledge_center/wp91_Genetic-Data_03-2004.pdf

Art. 29 Data Protection Working Party (15 February 2007a) Working Document on the processing of personal data relating to health in electronic health records, .https://www.dataprotection.ro/servlet/ViewDocument?id=228

Art. 29 Data Protection Working Party (20 June 2007b) Opinion 4/2007 on the Concept of Personal Data. https://ec.europa.eu/justice/article-29/documentation/opinion-recommendation/files/2007/wp136_en.pdf

Art. 29 Data Protection Working Party (20 April 2011a) Advice Paper on Special Categories of Data ("Sensitive Data"). https://www.pdpjournals.com/docs/88417.pdf

Art. 29 Data Protection Working Party (13 July 2011b) Opinion 5/2011 on Consent. https://www.pdpjournals.com/docs/88081.pdf

Art. 29 Data Protection Working Party (23 March 2012) Opinion 01/2012 on the Data Protection Reform Proposals. https://ec.europa.eu/justice/article-29/documentation/opinion-recommendation/files/2012/wp191_en.pdf

Art. 29 Data Protection Working Party (9 April 2014a) Opinion 06/14 on the notion of legitimate interests of the data controller under Article 7 of the Directive 95/46/EC. https://www.dataprotection.ro/servlet/ViewDocument?id=1086

Art. 29 Data Protection Working Party (10 April 2014b) Opinion 4/2014 on Surveillance of Electronic Communications for Intelligence and National Security Purposes. http://ec.europa.eu/justice/data-protection/article-29/documentation/opinion-recommendation/files/2014/wp215_en.pdf

Art. 29 Data Protection Working Party (16 September 2014c) Opinion 8/2014 on the Recent Developments on the Internet of Things. https://www.pdpjournals.com/docs/88440.pdf

Art. 29 Data Protection Working Party (5 February 2015) Annex-Health Data in Apps and Devices. https://ec.europa.eu/justice/article-29/documentation/other-document/files/2015/20150205_letter_art29wp_ec_health_data_after_plenary_annex_en.pdf

Art. 29 Data Protection Working Party (28 November 2017a and last revised and adopted 10 April 2018) Guidelines on consent under Regulation 2016/679. https://ec.europa.eu/newsroom/article29/item-detail.cfm?item_id=623051

Art. 29 Data Protection Working Party (3 October 2017b last modified 6 February 2018) Guidelines on Automated Individual Decision-Making and Profiling for the Purposes of Regulation 2016/679. https://ec.europa.eu/newsroom/article29/item-detail.cfm?item_id=612053

Article 29 Data Protection Working Party (13 December 2016, last revised on 5 April 2017) Guidelines on the Right to Data Portability. http://ec.europa.eu/information_society/newsroom/image/document/2016-51/wp242_en_40852.pdf

Association of Privacy Professionals (10 February 2015) Working Party Clarifies Health Data Definition in Apps. https://iapp.org/news/a/working-party-clarifies-health-data-definition-in-apps/

Balkin J (2010) Information power: the information society from an Antihumanist perspective. In: Subramanian R, Katz E (eds) The global flow of information: legal, social and cultural perspective. NYU Press, New York, pp 232–246

Barocas S, Nissenbaum H (2014) Big Data's end run around anonymity and consent. In: Lane J, Stodden V, Benden S, Nissenbaum H (eds) Privacy, big data, and the public good: frameworks for engagement. Cambridge University Press, Cambridge, pp 44–75

Barth-Jones C (2012) The "Re-identification" of Governor William Weld's Medical Information: A Critical Re-examination of Health Data Identification Risks and Privacy Protections, Then and now. SSRN https://papers.ssrn.com/sol3/papers.cfm?abstract_id=2076397

Bassini M (2019) Il nuovo regolamento generale sulla protezione dei dati personali e il settore farmaceutico. In: Ferrari GF (ed) Osservatorio del Farmaco. Egea, Milan, pp 109–145

Bäumler H (2001) Der Konkurrennz einen Schritt Voraus. In: Bäumler H, Von Mutis A (eds) Datenschutz als Wettbewerbsvorteil-Privacy Sells: mit Modernen Datenschutzkomponenten Erfolg beim Kunden. Vieweg und Teubner Verlag, Berlin, pp 1–11

BBMRI-ERIC-Biobanking and Biomolecular Resources Research Infrastructure (October 2014) Position Paper on the General Data Protection Regulation. http://www.bbmri-eric.eu/wp-content/uploads/BBMRI-ERIC-Position-Paper-General-Data-Protection-Regulation-October-2015_rev1_title.pdf

Bennet CJ (1992) Regulating privacy. Cornell University Press, Ithace

Blades Nm Herrera-Gonzáles F (September 2016) An Economic Analysis of Personal Data Protection: Obligations in the European Union, Conference Paper. In: 27th European Regional Conference of the International Telecommunications Society (ITS). Cambridge, United Kingdom, 7th–9th September 2016. https://www.econstor.eu/bitstream/10419/148661/1/Blades-Herrera-Gonzalez.pdf

Bundesministerium für Justiz und Verbraucherschutz (22 January 2020) Opinion of the Data Ethics Commission. https://www.bmjv.de/SharedDocs/Downloads/DE/Themen/Fokusthemen/Gutachten_DEK_EN_lang.html;jsessionid=A6A9519779DDF3581BA26837A1481B6D.1_cid334?nn=11678512

Buolamwini J, Gebru T (2018) Gender shades: intersectional accuracy disparities in commercial gender classification. Proc Machine Learn Res 81:1–15

Burkert H (1996) Data-protection legislation and the modernization of public administration. Int Rev Adm Sci 4:557–567

Burri M, Schär R (2016) The reform of the EU data protection framework: outlining key changes and assessing their fitness for a data driven economy. J Inf Policy 6:479–511

Bygrave LA (2001) Minding the machine: Art. 15 of the EC data protection directive and automated profiling. CLSR 17:17–24

California Consumer Privacy Act (CCPA) (2018). https://leginfo.legislature.ca.gov/faces/billTextClient.xhtml?bill_id=201720180SB1121

Calo R (2016) Privacy and markets: a love story. Notre Dame Law Rev 91:649–690

Cantore D (2011) On biometrics and profiling: a challenge for privacy and democracy? Int J Technoeth 2:84–93

Casarez NB (2015–2016) The synergy of privacy and speech. Univ Pa J Const Law 18:813–894

Cate FH, Mayer-Schönberger V (2013) Notice and consent in a world of big data. IDPL 3:67–73

Chassang G (2017) The impact of the EU general data protection regulation on scientific research. Ecancermedicalscience 11:1–12

Cheung ASY (2018) Moving beyond consent for citizen science in big data health and medical research. Nw J Technol Intell Prop 16:15–40

Cohen J (2016) The regulatory state in the information age. Theoret Enq Law 17:369–414

Comandè G (2015) Tortious privacy 3.0: a quest for research. In: Potgieter J, Knobel J, Jansen RM (eds) Essays in honour of/Huldigingsbundel vir Johann Neethling. Durban, LexisNexis, pp 121–131

Comandè G (2019) Ricerca in sanità e data protection... un puzzle risolvibile. RIML 1:183–203

Comandè G, Schneider G (2018) Regulatory challenges of data mining practices: the case of the never-ending lifecycles of health data. Eur J Health Law 25:284–307

Commission Nationale de l'Informatiques et des Libertés (24 July 2018) Biométrie dans les smartphones des particuliers: application du cadre de protection des données. https://www.

cnil.fr/fr/biometrie-dans-les-smartphones-des-particuliers-application-du-cadre-de-protection-des-donnees

Commission Nationale de l'Informatiques et des Libertés (10 January 2019) Délibération n° 2019-001 du 10 janvier 2019 portant règlement type relatif à la mise en œuvre de dispositifs ayant pour finalité le contrôle d'accès par authentification biométrique aux locaux, aux appareils et aux applications informatiques sur les lieux de travail. https://www.cnil.fr/sites/default/files/atoms/files/deliberation-2019-001-10-01-2019-reglement-type-controle-dacces-biometrique.pdf

Commission of the European Communities (13 September 1990) Communication on the Protection of Individuals in Relation to the Processing of Personal Data in the Community and Information Security. COM(90)314 final- SYN 287 and 288 https://resources.law.cam.ac.uk/cipil/travaux/97-66-EC_TRAVEAU_TELECOMMUNICATIONS.pdf#page=3

Conger K, Fausset R, Kovaleski SF (14 May 2019) San Francisco Bans Facial Recognition Technology. New York Times. https://www.nytimes.com/2019/05/14/us/facial-recognition-ban-san-francisco.html

Council of Europe (13 February 1997) Recommendation N.R (97) 5 of the Committee of Ministers to Member States on the Protection of Medical Data. http://hrlibrary.umn.edu/instree/coerecr97-5.html

Council of Europe (27 March 2019) Recommendation CM/Rec(2019)2 of the Committee of Ministers to Member States on the protection of health-related data. https://www.apda.ad/sites/default/files/2019-03/CM_Rec%282019%292E_EN.pdf

Court of Justice of the European Union (19 October 2016) Patrick Breyer v. Bundesrepublik Deutschland, C-582/14. online available at http://curia.europa.eu/juris/document/document.jsf?docid=184668&doclang=EN

Crawford K, Schultz J (2014) Big data and due process: toward a framework to redress predictive privacy harms. Boston Coll Law Rev 55:93–128

De Hert P, Christianen K (April 2013) Progress Report on the Application of the Principles of Convention 108 to the Collection and Processing of Biometric Data- Commissioned by the Council of Europe. https://rm.coe.int/progress-report-on-the-application-of-the-principles-of-convention-108/1680744d81

De Hert P, Lammerant H (2016) Predictive profiling and its legal limits: effectiveness gone forever? In: Van der Sloot B, Broeders D, Schrijvers E (eds) Exploring the boundaries of big data, exploring the boundaries of big data. Amsterdam University Press, Amsterdam, pp 145–177

De La Torre LF (5 February 2019) What is 'Public Interest' Under EU Data Protection Law?. Medium. https://medium.com/golden-data/what-is-public-interest-under-eu-data-protection-law-a8ef4637724a

Determann L (2018) New California law against data sharing. Comp Internet Lawyer 35:1–10

Dove ES (2018a) Collection and protection of genomic data. In: Gibbon S et al (eds) Routledge handbook of genomics, health and society. Routledge, New York, pp 161–168

Dove ES (2018b) The EU general data protection regulation: implications for international scientific research in the digital era. JLME 46:1013–1030

Dove ES, Thompson B, Knoppers BM (2016) A step forward for data protection and biomedical research. Lancet 387:1374–1375

Drexl J (27 April 2018) Data Access and Data Control in the Era of Connected Devices. Study on Behalf of the European Consumer Organisation BEUC https://www.beuc.eu/publications/beuc-x-2018-121_data_access_and_control_in_the_area_of_connected_devices.pdf

Drexl J (2019) Legal challenges of the changing role of personal and non-personal data in the data economy. In: De Franceschi A, Schulze R (eds) Digital revolution: data protection, smart products, blockchain technology and bitcoins challenges for law in practice. Beck, München, pp 19–41

Eifert M (2012) Regulierungstrategien. In: Hoffmann-Riem W, Schmidt-Aßmann E, Voßkuhle A (eds) Grundlagen des Verwaltungsrechts -Methoden –Maßstäbe-Aufgaben-Organisation, vol. 1. C.H. Beck, Munich pp 1318–1394

Ernst S (2018) DS-GVO Art. 4 Begriffsbestimmungen. In: Paal B, Pauly DA (eds) Datenschutz Grundverordnung. Beck Online pp 8–13

European Commission (25 January 2012a) Communication from the Commission to the European Parliament, the Council, the European Economic and Social Committee, and the Committee of the Regions, 'Safeguarding Privacy in a Connected World: A European Data Protection Framework for the 21st Century'. https://eur-lex.europa.eu/legal-content/EN/TXT/PDF/?uri=CELEX:52012DC0009&from=en

European Commission (14 February 2012b) Commission Staff Working Paper Impact Assessment Accompanying the Document Regulation of the European Parliament and of the Council on the Protection of Individuals with Regard to the Processing of Personal Data and on the Free Movement of such Data (General Data Protection Regulation) and the Directive of the European Parliament and of the Council on the Protection of Individuals with Regard to the Processing of Personal Data by Competent Authorities for the Purposes of Prevention, Investigation, Detection or Prosecution of Criminal Offences or the Execution of Criminal Penalties, and the Free Movement of such Data, SEC (2012) 72/2. https://ec.europa.eu/transparency/regdoc/rep/2/2012/EN/SEC-2012-72-2-EN-MAIN-PART-1.PDF

European Commission (September 2012c) General Data Protection Regulation: IAB UK Response to Ministry of Justice Call for Evidence. https://www.iabuk.net/sites/default/files/EC%20Data%20Protection%20Rules%20%20IAB%20UK%20response%20to%20MoJ%20Call%20for%20Evidence.pdf

European Commission (4 July 2013) Statement by Vice President Neelie Kroes "on the Consequences of Living in an Age of Total Information". http://europa.eu/rapid/press-release_MEMO-13-654_en.htm

European Commission (25 April 2018a) Communication from the Commission to the European Parliament, the Council, the European Economic and Social Committee and the Committee of the Regions- Towards a Common European Data Space. https://eur-lex.europa.eu/legal-content/EN/TXT/PDF/?uri=CELEX:52018DC0232&from=EN

European Commission (25 April 2018b) Commission Staff Working Document, Guidance on Sharing Private Sector Data in the European Data Economy, Accompanying the Document Communication from the Commission to the European Parliament, the Council, the European economic and social Committee and the Committee of the Regions "Towards a Common European Data Space". https://eur-lex.europa.eu/legal-content/EN/TXT/PDF/?uri=CELEX:52018SC0125&from=EN

European Commission (22 October 2021) Free Flow of Non Personal Data. https://ec.europa.eu/digital-single-market/en/free-flow-non-personal-data

European Court of Human Rights (26 October 2000a) Hasan and Chaush v. Bulgaria, n. 30985/96. https://minorityrights.org/wp-content/uploads/old-site-downloads/download-382-Hasan-and-Chaush-v-Bulgaria.pdf

European Court of Human Rights (4 May 2000b) Rotaru v. Romania, n. 28341/95. https://hudoc.echr.coe.int/eng#{%22itemid%22:[%22001-58586%22]}

European Court of Human Rights (4 December 2008) S. and Marper v. United Kingdom. https://rm.coe.int/168067d216

European Court of Human Rights, Armonienė v Lithuania (25 November 2008) appl. No 36919/02. https://hudoc.echr.coe.int/eng#{%22fulltext%22:[%22Armonas%22],%22documentcollectionid2%22:[%22GRANDCHAMBER%22,%22CHAMBER%22],%22itemid%22:[%22001-89823%22]}

European Court of Human Rights I v Finland (17 July 2008). appl. No 20511/03. https://www.5rb.com/wp-content/uploads/2013/10/I-v-Finland-ECHR-17-July-2008.pdf

European Court of Justice (20 May 2003a) Österreichischer Rundfunk and Others, Joined Cases C-465/00, C-138/01 and C-139/01

European court of Justice (6 November 2003b) Bodil Lindqvist, C-101/01. http://curia.europa.eu/juris/document/document.jsf?docid=48382&doclang=en

European Court of Justice (9 March 2010) Commission v. Germany, Case C-518/07, Gran Chamber. http://curia.europa.eu/juris/document/document.jsf?text=&docid=79752&pageIndex=0&doclang=EN&mode=lst&dir=&occ=first&part=1&cid=8240530

European Court of Justice (17 July 2014) YS, M and S v Minister Voor Immigratie, Integratie en Asiel, Judgment of the Court (Third Chamber), Joined cases C-141/12 and C-372/12. http://curia.europa.eu/juris/document/document.jsf?docid=155114&doclang=EN

European Court of Justice (27 September 2017) Puskar v Finance Directorate of the Slovak Republic, Case C-73/16. http://curia.europa.eu/juris/document/document.jsf?text=&docid=195046&doclang=EN

European Data Protection Board (10 July 2019a) Guidelines 3/2019 on Processing of Personal Data Through Video Devices. https://edpb.europa.eu/sites/edpb/files/consultation/edpb_guidelines_201903_videosurveillance.pdf

European Data Protection Board (23 January 2019b) Opinion 3/2019 Concerning the Questions and the Answers on the Interplay Between the Clinical Trials Regulation (CTR) and the General Data Protection Regulation (GDPR) (Art. 70.1.b). https://edpb.europa.eu/our-work-tools/our-documents/avis-art-70/opinion-32019-concerning-questions-and-answers-interplay_es

European Data Protection Supervisor (September 2009) Guidelines regarding the processing of health data in the workplace by community institutions and bodies. https://edps.europa.eu/sites/edp/files/publication/09-09-28_guidelines_healthdata_atwork_en.pdf

European Data Protection Supervisor (7 March 2012) Opinion of the European Data Protection Supervisor on the Data Protection Reform Package. http://www.europarl.europa.eu/document/activities/cont/201205/20120524ATT45776/20120524ATT45776EN.pdf

European Data Protection Supervisor (27 March 2013) Opinion on the Communication from the Commission on 'eHealth Action Plan 2012-2020- Innovative Healthcare for the 21st Century'. https://edps.europa.eu/sites/edp/files/publication/13-03-27_ehealth_action_en.pdf

European Data Protection Supervisor (6 January 2020) A Preliminary Opinion on Data Protection and Scientific Research. https://edps.europa.eu/sites/edp/files/publication/20-01-06_opinion_research_en.pdf

Federal German Constitutional Court (Bundesverfassungsgericht) (15 December 1983) Federal Census Act. https://www.bundesverfassungsgericht.de/SharedDocs/Entscheidungen/EN/1983/12/rs19831215_1bvr020983en.html

Forgò N (2015) My health data-your research: some preliminary thoughts on different values in the general data protection regulation. IDPL 5:54–63

Froomkin MA (2000) The death of privacy? SLR 52(5):1461–1543

Gannes L (7 September 2010) Eric Schmidt: welcome to "age of augmented humanity". Gigaom http://gigaom.com/2010/09/07/eric-schmidt-welcome-to-the-age-of-augmented-humanity/

Gasser U (18 March 2014) Cloud innovation and the law: issues, approaches and interplay. Berkman Center Research Publication

Gellert R (2015) Understanding data protection as risk regulation. J Internet Law:3–15

Gellert R, Gutwirth S (2013) The legal construction of privacy and data protection. CLSR 29:522–530

Goodman B (2016) A step towards accountable algorithms? Algorithmic Discrimination and the European Union. http://www.mlandthelaw.org/papers/goodman1.pdf

Graef I, Gellert R, Husovec M (September 2018a) Towards a Holistic Regulatory Approach for the European Data Economy: Why the Illusive Notion of Non-personal Data is Counterproductive to Data Innovation. TILEC Discussion Paper, DP 2018-028. https://papers.ssrn.com/sol3/papers.cfm?abstract_id=3256189

Graef I, Husovec M, Purtova N (2018b) Data portability and data control: lessons from an emerging concept in EU law, in German Law J, 19: 1359–1398

Grifeo FM (11 July 2017) Banche dati genetiche trasferibili se la finalità scientifica non muta. Il Sole 24 Ore. http://www.diritto24.ilsole24ore.com/art/guidaAlDiritto/dirittoCivile/2017-07-11/banche-dati-genetiche-trasferibili-se-finalita-scientifica-non-muta%2D%2D181318.php?refresh_ce=1

Grunes AP (2013) Another look at privacy. Geo Mason Law Rev 20:1107–1127

Gutmann A, Wagner JW (2013) Found your DNA on the web: reconciling privacy and Progress. Hastings Centre Report 43:15–18

Hallinan D, De Hert P (2016) Many have it wrong-samples do contain personal data: the data protection regulation as a superior framework to protect donor interests in biobanking and genomic research. In: Mittelstadt BD, Floridi L (eds) The ethics of biomedical big data. Springer, Berlin, pp 119–137

Hallinan D, Friedewald M (2015) Open consent, biobanking and data protection law: can open consent be 'informed' under the new general data protection regulation. Life Sci Soc Policy 11: 1–36

Hart HLA (1955) Are there any natural rights? Philosophical Rev 64:175–191

Health Research Authority, GDPR Guidance. https://www.hra.nhs.uk/planning-and-improving-research/policies-standards-legislation/data-protection-and-information-governance/gdpr-detailed-guidance/transparency/

Hermstrüwer Y (2016) Informationelle Selbstgefährdung. Mohr Siebeck, Tübingen

Ho C (2017) Challenges of the EU general data protection regulation for biobanking and scientific research. J Law Inf Sci 25:84–103

Hoffmann J, Johannsen G (31 May 2019) EU-Merger Control in Big Data-Related Merger Max Planck Institute for Innovation and Competition Research Paper N. 19-05. https://papers.ssrn.com/sol3/papers.cfm?abstract_id=3364792

Hoffmann-Riem W (1998) Innovationsoffenheit und Innovationsverantwortung durch Recht-Aufgaben Rechtswissenschaftlicher Innovationsforschung. Archiv des Öffentlichen Rechts 123:513–540

Holley P (18 December 2018) This patent shows Amazon may seek to create 'a database of suspicious persons' using facial recognition technology. Washington Post. https://www.washingtonpost.com/gdprconsent/?destination=%2ftechnology%2f2018%2f12%2f13%2fthis-patentshows-amazon-may-seek-create-database-suspicious-persons-using-facial-recognition technology%2f%3f&utm_term=.30e2c8f734b8

http://curia.europa.eu/juris/showPdf.jsf?text=&docid=48330&pageIndex=0&doclang=EN&mode=lst&dir=&occ=first&part=1&cid=8237402

Hustinx P (2014) EU data protection law: the review of Directive 95/46/EC and the proposed general data protection regulation. European Data Protection Supervisor. https://secure.edps.europa.eu/EDPSWEB/webdav/site/mySite/shared/Documents/EDPS/Publications/Speeches/2014/14-09-15_Article_EUI_EN.pdf

IMI-Innovative Medicines Initiative. https://www.imi.europa.eu/

Information Commissioner's Office, Public Task. https://ico.org.uk/for-organisations/guide-to-data-protection/guide-to-the-general-data-protection-regulationgdpr/lawful-basis-for-processing/public-task/

Information Commissioner's Office, Right to be Informed. https://ico.org.uk/for-organisations/guide-to-data-protection/guide-to-the-general-data-protection-regulation-gdpr/individual-rights/right-to-be-informed/

Information Commissioner's Officer, Vital Interests. https://ico.org.uk/for-organisations/guide-to-data-protection/guide-to-the-general-data-protection-regulation-gdpr/lawful-basisforprocessing/vital-interests/

Italian Data Protection Authority (6 October 2016) Provvedimento di blocco del trattamento dei dati personali contenuti in una biobanca n 389. https://www.garanteprivacy.it/web/guest/home/docweb/-/docweb-display/docweb/5508051

Italian Data Protection Authority (21 December 2017) Provvedimento 21 dicembre 2017 n 561. https://www.garanteprivacy.it/web/guest/home/docweb/-/docweb-display/docweb/7465896

Kaplan B (2016) How should health data be used? Privacy, secondary use & big data sales. Camb Q Health Anal 25:312–329

Kaye DH (2006) Who needs special needs? On the constitutionality of collecting DNA and other biometric data from arrestees. JLME 34:188–198

Kindt EJ (2018) Having yes, using no? About the new legal regime for biometric data. CLSR 34: 523–538

Korff D (20 January 2010) Working Paper n. 2: Data Protection Laws in the EU: The Difficulties in Meeting the Challenges Posed by Global, Social and Technical Developments. European Commission-Directorate-General Justice, Freedom and Security, Comparative Study on Different Approaches to New Privacy Challenges in Particular in the Light of Technological Developments. SSRN https://papers.ssrn.com/sol3/papers.cfm?abstract_id=1638949&download=yes

Krishan R, Mostafavi R (2018) Biometric technology: security and privacy concerns. J Internet Law 22:19–23

Laudon KC (1996) Markets and privacy. Commun ACM 39:92–104

Leabeau-Marianna D, Balducci A (11 April 2019) France: the First CNIL Standard Biometric Regulation for Biometric Systems in the Workplace. DLA Piper Blog. https://blogs.dlapiper.com/privacymatters/france-the-first-cnil-standard-regulation-for-biometric-systems-in-the-workplace/

Lemmens T, Austin L (2009) The end of individual control over health information: promoting fair information practices and the governance of biobank research. In: Kaye J, Stranger M (eds) Principles and practice in biobank governance. Routledge, London, pp 243–266

Liebenau D (2016) What intellectual property can learn from informational privacy and Viceversa. Harv J Law Technol 30:285–307

Lynskey O (2014) Deconstructing data protection: the 'added-value' of a right to data protection in the EU legal order. Int Comp Law Q 63:569–597

Lynskey O (2015) The foundations of EU data protection law. Oxford University Press, Oxford

Malgieri G, Comandè G (2017) Sensitive by distance: quasi-health data in the algorithmic era. Inf Commun Technol Law 26:229–249

Mantelero A (2014) The future of consumer data protection in the EU. Rethinking the 'notice and consent' paradigm in the new era of predictive analytics. CLSR 30:643–660

Mantelero A (2018) La gestione del rischio nel GDPR: limiti e sfide nel contesto dei Big Data e delle applicazioni di Artificial Intelligence. In: Mantelero A, Poletti D (eds) Regolare la tecnologia: il Reg. 2016/679 e la protezione dei dati personali. Un dialogo tra Italia e Spagna. Pisa University Press, pp 289–305

Marelli L, Testa G (4 May 2018) Scrutinizing the EU general data protection regulation- how will new decentralized governance impact research?. Science 360: 496–498

Maxwell WJ (2015) Principle-based regulation of personal data: the case of 'fair processing'. IDPL 5:205–216

Mayer-Schönberger V (2010) The law as stimulus: the role of law in fostering innovative entrepreneurship. I/S: a journal of law and policy for the. Inf Soc 6:153–188

Mayer-Schönberger V, Cukier K (2013) Big data: a revolution that will transform how we live, work, and think. John Murray Publishers, London

Mayer-Schönberger V, Padova Y (2016) Regime change? Enabling big data through Europe's new data protection regulation. Colum Sci Technol Law Rev 17:315–335

Metcalf J, Crawford K (2016) Where are human subjects in big data research? The emerging ethics divide. Big Data Soc 3. https://doi.org/10.1177/2053951716650211

McDermott Y (2017) Conceptualising the right to data protection in an era of big data. Big Data Soc:1–7

Miller AR (1971) The assault on privacy: computers, data banks, and dossiers. The University of Michigan Press, Ann Arbour

Mitrou L (2017) The general data protection regulation: a law for the digital age? In: Synodinou TE, Jougleux P, Markou C, Prastitou T (eds) EU internet law- regulation and enforcement. Springer, Cham, pp 19–57

Mittelstadt BD, Floridi L (2016) The ethics of big data: current and foreseeable issues in biomedical contexts. Sci Eng Ethics 22:303–341

Molnár-Gábor F (2018) Germany: a fair balance between scientific freedom and data subjects' rights? Hum Genet 137:619–626
Nehf JP (2016) Protecting privacy with 'heightened' notice and choice. In: Rothchild JA (ed) Research handbook on electronic commerce law. Edward Elgar, Cheltenham, pp 475–491
Niemiec E, Howard H (2016) Ethical issues in consumer genome sequencing: use of consumers' samples and data. Appl Transl Genet 8:23–30
Nissenbaum H (2008) Privacy in context: technology, policy and the integrity of social life. Stanford University Press, Stanford
Notermans P (8 January 2019) Biometrics & Household Excpetion: A Responsibility Limitation by the French CNIL?, Ku Leuven Citip Blog. https://www.law.kuleuven.be/citip/blog/biometrics-household-exception-a-responsibility-limitation-by-the-french-cnil/
Ohlhausen MK, Okuliar AP (2015) Competition, consumer protection and the (right) approach to privacy. Antitrust Law J 80:121–156
Ohm P (2010) Broken promises of privacy: responding to the surprising failure of privacy. UCLA Law Rev 57:1703–1777
Ohm P (2015) Sensitive Information. South Cal Law Rev 88:1125–1196
Pasquale F (2013) Privacy, antitrust and power. Geo Mason Law Rev 20:1009–1024
Peppet R (2014) Regulating the internet of things: first steps toward managing discrimination, privacy, security and consent. Texas Law Rev 93:85–176
Ploem MC, Essink-Bot ML, Stronks K (2013) Proposed EU data protection regulation is a threat to medical research. BMJ 346:f 3534
Pormeister K (2017) Genetic data and the research exemption: is the GDPR going too far? IDPL 7: 137–146
Price WN II (2018) Medical malpractice and black box medicine. In: Glenn Cohen I, Lynch HF, Vayena E, Gasser U (eds) Big data, health law and Biotehics. Harvard University, Cambridge, pp 295–307
Price WN, Kaminski ME, Minssen T, Spector-Bagdady K (1 February 2019) Shadow health records meet new privacy Laws-how will research respond to a changing regulatory space?. Science 363: 448–450
Purtova N (2017) Health data for common good: defining the boundaries and social dilemmas of data commons. In: Leenes R, Purtova N, Adams S (eds) Under observation: the interplay between e-health and surveillance. Springer, Berlin, pp 177–210
Purtova N (2018) The law of everything. Broad concept of personal data and future of EU data protection law. Law Innov Technol 10:40–81
Quinn P (2016) The anonymisation of research data- a pyric victory for privacy that should not be pushed too hard by the EU data protection framework? Eur J Health Law 24:1–21
Quinn P, Quinn L (2018) Big genetic data and its big data protection challenges. CLSR 0:1–19
Raum B (2017) DS-GVO Art. 89 Verarbeitung zu Archivzwecken, Forschungszwecken. In: Ehmann E, Selmayr M (eds) Datenschutz-Grundverordnung. C.H. Beck, München pp, pp 41–42
Regulation EU n. 536/2014 of the European Parliament and of the Council of 16 April 2014 on clinical trials on medicinal products for human use, and repealing Directive 2001/20/EC, online available at https://ec.europa.eu/health/sites/health/files/files/eudralex/vol-1/reg_2014_536/reg_2014_536_en.pdf
Riccio GM, Scorza G, Belisario E (2018) GDPR e Normativa Privacy-Commentario. Wolters Kluwer, Milan, p 101
Richter P (2016) Big Data, Statistik Und Die Datenschutz-Grundverordnung. Datenschutz und Datensicherheit 40:581–586
Roewer L (2013) DNA fingerprinting in forensics: past, present, future. Investig Genet 4:1–10
Romei A, Ruggieri S (2014) A multidisciplinary survey on discrimination analysis. Knowl Eng Rev 29:582–638
Rossnagel A (2007) Datenschutz in einem Informatisierten Alltag, 2007, Gutachten im Auftrag der Friedrich-Ebert-Stiftung. Stabsabteilung der Friedrich-Ebert-Stiftung, Berlin

Royal Statistical Society (22 July 2014) Royal Statistical Society research on trust in data and attitudes toward data use/data sharing-Briefing Note. http://www.statslife.org.uk/images/pdf/rss-data-trust-data-sharingattitudes-research-note.pdf

Rubinstein R (2013) Big data: the end of privacy or a new beginning. IDPL 3:74–87

Samuelson P (1999) Privacy as intellectual property? SLR 52:1125–1173

Sariyar M, Suhr S, Schlünder I (2017) How sensitive is genetic data? Biopreserv Biobank 15(6): 494–501

Schneider G (2018) European intellectual property and data protection in the digital-algorithmic economy. JIPLP 13:229–237

Schneider G (2019) Algoritmi, "verificabilità" del trattamento automatizzato dei dati personali e tutela del segreto commerciale nel quadro europeo. Concorrenza Mercato e Regole 2:353–382

Schulz S (2018) Art. 9 Verarbeitung besonderer Kategorien personenbezogener Daten. In Gola P (ed) Datenschutz-Grundverordnung VO (EU) 2016/679- Kommentar. C.H. Beck, Munich pp 361–381

Schwartz PM (1997) Privacy and the economics of personal health care information. Texas Law Rev 76:1–75

Secretary's Advisory Committee on Human Research Protections (SACHRP) (13 March 2018) Attachment B-European Union's General Data Protection Regulations. https://www.hhs.gov/ohrp/sachrp-committee/recommendations/attachment-b-implementation-of-the-european-unions-general-data-protection-regulation-and-its-impact-on-human-subjects-research/index.html

Selinger E, Hartzog W (17 October 2019) What Happens if Employers Can Read Your Facial Expression?. New York Times. https://www.nytimes.com/2019/10/17/opinion/facial-recognition-ban.html

Shabani M, Borry P (2018) Rules for processing genetic data for research purposes in view of the new general data protection regulation. Eur J Hum Gen 26:149–156

Sharon T et al (2 November 2016) Shortcomings of the revised 'Helsinki Declaration' on Ethical Use of Databases, in Clinical Trials and Human Subjects Research. The Hastings Center. https://www.thehastingscenter.org/shortcomings-world-medical-associations-revised-declaration-ethical-use-health-databases/

Singer N (13 July 2018) Microsoft Urges Congress to Regulate Use of Facial Recognition. New York Times. https://www.nytimes.com/2018/07/13/technology/microsoft-facial-recognition.html

Singer N (24 January 2019) Amazon is pushing facial technology that a study says could be biased. New York Times. https://www.nytimes.com/2019/01/24/technology/amazon-facial-technology-study.html

Spina A (2014) Risk Regulation of Big Data: Has the time arrived for a Paradigm shift in Eu Data Protection Law?, Case notes to Case C-293/12 and C-594/12 Digital Rights Ireland and Seitlinger and others. Eur J Risk Regul 5:248–252

Sprokkereef A (2007) Data protection and the use of biometric data in the EU. In: Fischer Hübner S, Duquenoy P, Zuccato A, Martucci L (eds) The Future of Identity in the Information Society-Proceedings of the Third IFIP WG 9.2, 9.6/11.6, 11.7/FIDIS International Summer School on The Future of Identity in the Information Society, Karlstad University, Sweden, August 4–10, 2007. Springer, New York, pp 277–284

Sweeney L (1997) Weaving technology and policy together to maintain confidentiality. JLME 25: 98–110

Tene O, Polonetsky J (2013) Big data for all: privacy and user control in the age of analytics. Northwest J Technol Intell Prop 1:2239–2273

Tene O, Polonetsky J (2016) Beyond IRBs: ethical guidelines for data research. Wash Lee Law Rev 72:458–471

Terry NP (2018) Big data and regulatory arbitrage in healthcare. In: Glenn Cohen I, Lynch HF, Vayena E, Gasser U (eds) Big data, health law and Biotehics. Harvard University, Cambridge, pp 56–68

The Dutch Techcentre for Life Sciences, The FAIR Data Principles Explained. https://www.dtls.nl/fair-data/fair-principles-explained/
Thierer A (2014) Privacy Law's precautionary principle problem. Maine Law Rev 66:467–486
Thierer AM (2013) The pursuit of privacy in a world where information control is failing. Harv J Law Public Policy 36:409–455
Townend D (2004) Overriding data subjects' rights in the public interest. In: Townend D, Wright J, Beyleveld D, Rouillè-Mirza S (eds) The data protection directive and medical research across Europe. Routledge, London, pp 89–102
Townend D (2018) Conclusion: harmonization in genomic and health data sharing for research: an impossible dream? Hum Genet 137:657–664
Tribunal of Cagliari, Sentenza n. 1569, 6 June 2017
US Department of Health Education & Welfare (1973) Records, computers, and the rights of citizens. The MIT Press, Cambridge. https://www.justice.gov/opcl/docs/rec-com-rights.pdf
Van der Sloot B (2016) The individual in the big data era: moving towards an agent-based privacy paradigm. In: Van der Sloot B, Broeders D, Schrijvers E (eds) Exploring the boundaries of big data, exploring the boundaries of big data. Amsterdam University Press, Amsterdam, pp 177–205
Van Der Sloot B (2017) Legal fundamentalism: is data protection really a fundamental right? In: Leenes R, Van Brakel R, Gutwirth S, De Hert P (eds) Data protection and privacy: (in)-visibilities and infrastructures. Springer, Switzerland, pp 3–30
Van Veen EB (2018) Observational Health Research in Europe: understanding the general data protection regulation and underlying debate. Eur J Cancer 104:70–80
Von Grafenstein M (11 March 2019) Co-Regulation and the Competitive Advantage in the GDPR: Data protection Certification Mechanisms, Codes of Conduct and the "State of the Art" of Data Protection-by-design. SSRN. https://papers.ssrn.com/sol3/papers.cfm?abstract_id=3336990
Voss A, Padova Y (25 June 2015) We Need to Make Big Data Into an Opportunity for Europe. Euractive. https://www.euractiv.com/section/digital/opinion/we-need-to-make-big-data-into-an-opportunity-for-europe/
Voss WG (2014/2015) European data privacy law developments. Business Lawyer 70:253–260
Wachter S (22 January 2017) Primus inter Pares: Privacy as a Precondition for Self-development, Personal Fulfilment and the Free Enjoyment of Fundamental Rights. SSRN. https://papers.ssrn.com/sol3/papers.cfm?abstract_id=2903514&download=yes
Wachter S, Mittelstadt B (2019) A right to reasonable inferences: re-thinking data protection law in the age of big data and AI. Columbia Bus Law Rev 2:497–620
Wendehorst C (2017) Of elephants in the room and paper tigers: how to reconcile data protection and the data economy. In: Lohsse S, Schulze R, Staudenmayer D (eds) Trading data in the digital economy: legal concepts and tools. Nomos/Hart Publishing, Baden-Baden, pp 327–357
World Health Organization, Constitution of the World Health Organization. https://www.who.int/governance/eb/who_constitution_en.pdf
World Medical Association (2013) Declaration of Helsinki- Ethical principles for Medical Research involving Human beings. http://jama.jamanetwork.com/article.aspx?articleid=1760318
Zarsky T (2017) Incompatible: the GDPR in the age of big data. Seton Hall Law Rev 47:995–1020
Zingales N (2018) Data protection considerations in EU competition law: funnel or straightjacket for innovation? In: Nihoul P, Van Cleynenbreugel P (eds) The roles of innovation in competition law analysis. Edward Elgar, Cheltenham, pp 79–130

Chapter 6
Health Data Pools Under European Competition Law

6.1 Health Data Pools as Competitively Relevant Information Sharing Agreements

It has been illustrated how the phenomenon of data pooling is an extremely widely-encompassing phenomenon that can occur through partnerships established through contractual agreements specifically designed for the transfer of digital health data,[1] or even through mergers.[2]

As the previous chapter has shown, all these various forms of collaborative research alliances structured upon health data pools imply the processing of health data and thus fall under the data protection framework. In this context, the analysis of the legal bases of health data processing under the General Data Protection Regulation has shown how the data protection framework regarding the treatment of special categories of personal data under art. 9 GDPR, primarily based on the protection of individuals' fundamental rights and/or of the public interest, entails also some market-based and innovation-oriented rules, which relax the regulatory regime of health data pools for research purposes.

From a further perspective, health data pools imply the sharing of competitively relevant scientific health data and can thus be considered as a form of aggregation of research-valuable data and technology.

---

[1] This is the case, for example of the agreement between the Royal Free Hospital and Google Deep Mind, or between the Lombaria Region and IBM. See supra Chap. 3, Sect. 3.1.1.1 and 3.1.2.1.

[2] This has been the case of the merger between Google and Sanofi. In these regards it needs to be however recalled that the pharmaceutical sector is traditionally characterised by mergers having the exact aim of strengthening the merging entities' research capacities. This case will be better assessed in Chap. 7, regarding legal remedies to the health data pooling phenomenon.

G. Schneider, *Health Data Pools Under European Data Protection and Competition Law*, Munich Studies on Innovation and Competition 17,
https://doi.org/10.1007/978-3-030-95427-7_6

In this respect, the new theories of data as a key economic asset enabling firms to gain and hold market power within digital markets[3] suggest that the sharing of digital health data for research and innovation purposes and the related cooperation coalitions, could themselves potentially determine a concentrated nature of the digital health markets in which the same data transfers occur, with the related risk of a drift of monopolistic market dominance by the companies involved in the same health data exchanges.

Such market concentrations can either directly or indirectly stem from the aggregation of health data, depending on the particular legal form in which the research collaboration is established: in the case of a merger the market concentration directly derives from the creation of a new entity controlling the aggregated research-valuable datasets, whereas in the case of a contractual transfer between two or more entities, the flow of information, is likely to strengthen the market position of each of the involved research actors, potentially leading to oligopolistic interdependencies, ultimately advantaging the stronger parties to the research consortium.

Exactly because of its structural market reflexes, the phenomenon of health data aggregation needs thus to be enquired through the lenses of European competition law. The question in this respect relates to how competition law treats these research-oriented information sharing agreements, and more precisely whether these agreements are promoted or rather restrained under the same competition framework.

As generally known, indeed European competition law regulates under art. 101(1) TFEU arrangements that have as their object or effect the prevention, restriction or distortion of competition. Merger operations on their side are regulated by a specific merger control procedure.[4]

From this standpoint, the following points need to be enquired, respectively regarding (i) whether health data pools as described in the previous chapters can fall under the notion of agreement and/or concerted practices that art. 101(1) TFEU prohibits; and (ii) whether the exception under art. 101(3) TFEU can be applied to and thus positively favour health information exchanges for their innovation and pro-competitive effects on the market. Furthermore, in case the health data pool occurs through a merger, the question arises whether under merger control procedures the consideration of specific research related efficiencies can ground a more favourable treatment of the merger itself, and whether there are in this context tools

[3] See, ex multis, for similar considerations, see Haucap and Heimeshoff (2014), pp. 49 ff.; Newman (2014), pp. 402 ff. See also Kerber (2016), pp. 856 ff.; Bundeskartellamt (October 2017), pp. 7–8. This view, shared for the purposes of the present analysis, is however opposed by a strand of the literature, arguing that big data does not give rise to barrier to entry, because of the non-exclusive and non-rivalrous nature of digital data. See amongst others Rubinfeld and Gal (2017), pp. 339 ff.; Tucker and Wellford (2014), pp. 1 ff.; Spulber and Yoo (2014), pp. 380 ff.; Ohlhausen and Okuliar (2015), pp. 121 ff. However, it needs to be observed that these studies refer to the general markets of personal data, from which the market of health data, due to its very specificities needs to be distinguished.

[4] Council Regulation EC N. 139/2004 of 20 January 2004 on the control of concentrations between undertakings (the EC Merger Regulation) (29 January 2004) OJ L 24/1.

that competition authorities can enact in order to maximise the efficiencies stemming from a merger.[5]

Under these premises, just as it has been done in the previous data protection law chapter, the analysis that follows will enquire whether also in the European competition law framework—as it occurs with the research exceptions to the general prohibition of health data processing under art. 9(1) GDPR—there are exceptions to the provision under art. 101(1) TFEU or, in case of mergers, a lenient merger policy, which upheld and promote the newly emerging European policy goal related to health data driven innovation.

On the background of these questions, a preliminary concern relates to which exact market the competition law analysis regarding health data pools shall refer to, and whether health data pools can themselves be regarded as autonomous relevant markets in which health data are traded.

For these purposes, the chapter will first do some brief general premises regarding the traditional goals of competition law and the emerging "subversive" role of the innovation parameter in the competition assessment of digital markets; then assess the relevance of health data pools as competitively relevant arrangements; from here enquire when health data pools fall within the scope of art. 101(1) TFEU; and when although potentially infringing the provision, they can be exempted under innovation-based exemptions. Ultimately, the treatment of health data pools in the context of European merger policy will be evaluated.

6.2 European Competition Law's Goals Under Review: Some General Premises

The objectives of competition law have never been enshrined in any document or specific provision.[6] This makes the identification of the European competition law framework's goals not an easy hermeneutical task.[7]

According to the traditional line of reasoning of the Court of Justice of the European Union, the European competition law framework aims to protect "the structure of the market",[8] "competition as an institution"[9] and "competition as

[5]This second part of the question will be better assessed in the following Chapter regarding competition remedies. See infra Chap. 7, Sect. 7.3.4.

[6]An overview has been given by the OECD Global Forum on Competition (29 January 2009).

[7]Ezrachi (2018).

[8]European Court of Justice (13 February 1979) Opinion in Hoffmann La Roche AG v. Commission, C-85/76 para 91.

[9]See Opinion of the Advocate General Kokott (23 February 2003) Opinion in British Airways vs. Commission, C-95/04, para 69.

such".[10] From this perspective, the competition framework protects the existence and the regularity of the competitive process, the safeguard of which is connected to broader goals as the promotion of the competitiveness of the European economy and the spreading of an entrepreneurial culture inspired by the competition on the merit paradigm.[11]

The European Commission, on its side, has conversely placed greater emphasis on the notion of consumer welfare as protected and promoted through an efficient allocation of resources.[12]

From this perspective, the goal of competition law is the protection of the well functioning of the market as measured by consumer surplus. This means that competition enforcement is triggered when a firm's behaviour infringing a competition law prohibition may lead to a worsening of the well functioning of the market as measured by a reduction in consumer surplus.

Consumer welfare has been traditionally positioned at the centre of competition law enforcement as the guiding benchmark upon which assessing insufficiently competitive market structures and anti-competitive business behaviour, with a negative impact on consumers.[13]

As prominent scholarship has observed,[14] the protection of consumer welfare has been traditionally linked to the broader economic goals of competition law, to be respectively found in the protection of economic efficiency, as directly deriving from the protection of economic freedom; the constrain of economic power; and, ultimately, the promotion of economic change, that is innovation.[15] Although quite

---

[10]European Court of Justice, Post Danmark A/S v Konkurrencerådet, C-209/10 (27 March 2012), para 21–24. See also European court of justice, GlaxoSmithKline Services Unlimited v Commission, C-501/06 (6 October 2009b), par. 63 where in respect to art. 101 TFEU the Court has claimed that "Art. 81 EC aims to protect not only the interests of competitors or of consumers, but also the structure of the market and, in so doing, competition as such". Emphasis added. Cf. also European Court of Justice (4 June 2009a), T-Mobile vs. Commission, C-8/08. On the issue see also European Commission (2000), Guidelines on Vertical Restraints, OJ C291/1 para. 7, where the "protection of competition" is identified as the primary goal of competition law.

[11]This is observed by Daskalova (2015), pp. 133 ff.

[12]In these regards, former Commissioner for Competition Policy, Mario Monti, has interestingly summarised, the same European Treaties assign to competition law the fundamental role of "guaranteeing consumer welfare", by "encouraging the optimal allocation of resources", and by "granting to economic agents the appropriate incentives to pursue productive efficiency, quality, and innovation". This is reported by Glader (2001), p. 513 ff. See also Kroes (15 September 2005): "consumer welfare is now well established as the standard the Commission applies when assessing mergers and infringements of the Treaty rules on cartels and monopolies. Our aim is simple: to protect competition as a means of enhancing consumer welfare and ensuring an efficient allocation of resources".

[13]Ezrachi (2018), p. 6.

[14]Gerber (1998).

[15]Fox (2010), pp. 1375 ff.

varied, the mentioned economic factors can be all directly or indirectly linked to the notion of consumer welfare.[16]

This purely economic approach has been traditionally prominent in competition enforcement assessments[17] and over time it has been variously modulated, with different weight respectively given to the mentioned economic elements in accordance to the peculiarities of the specific case.

The technological changes stirring the development of digital markets are progressively displacing the traditional market model,[18] this triggering a reconsideration of established legal and enforcement schemes.[19] One of the main directions of this readjustment efforts is given by the newly attention given to non-price related components of consumer welfare.[20] This is directly resulting from the decrease of importance- if not the outright absence- of price criteria in data-driven markets.[21] Here, indeed, digitally delivered services often cannot be monetized and the marginal costs related to their production are negligible.[22]

The consideration of non-price dimensions of consumer welfare is a direct result of the challenges faced by competition regulators to identify apt tools for the competition assessment in markets where competition is majorly occurring in respect to the type and degree of innovation. In these regards, some strand of the literature has highlighted the shift occurring in modern markets from price competition to innovation concerns.[23]

These structural features have thus induced first antitrust scholars, then enforcers to look at other parameters, different from prices, to be employed as yardsticks for the assessment of anticompetitive practices.[24]

The effort in the adaption of competition law tools to the peculiar reality of the digitalized and online business environment has had both the theoretical effect of triggering deeper reflections regarding the changing goals of competition law in the digital economy and the more practical consequence of triggering tangible turnarounds in competition law enforcement policies.[25]

These turnarounds can be traced back to two major enforcement trajectories, the first one regarding the inclusion within competition assessments of the consideration of non-economic values related to broader public policy objectives to be addressed

[16] See in these regards, Brodley (1987), p. 1020, arguing that innovation efficiency is the most important form of efficiency.

[17] Ahlborn and Padilla (2008), pp. 61–62.

[18] Christensen et al. (2015), pp. 44 ff.; Sokol (2017), pp. 43 ff.; Sokol and Comerford (2016), pp. 1129 ff.

[19] With regards to merger analysis, see Todino et al. (2018), pp. 1 ff.

[20] Kroes (15 September 2005). See also supra Chap. 3, Sect. 3.3.2.

[21] In this sense, see Kokkoris (2020), p. 58.

[22] Kokkoris (2020), p. 58.

[23] Glader (2001), p. 523.

[24] Glader (2001), p. 523.

[25] Ezrachi (2018).

in digital markets, the second one regarding the emerging importance of a non-price related measure of dynamic economic efficiency, namely innovation.

6.2.1 The Protection of Non-Economic Efficiencies

Along the lines of the first identified enforcement trajectory, the new countenance of digital markets has determined a renewed attention given by the European Commission, in the person of Commissioner Vestager, to the relevance of the non-price related dimension of the fairness of competition dynamics.[26] As the Commissioner has come to underline,[27] the fairness parameter pushes antitrust regulators to consider anticompetitive market conducts that deprive consumers with the possibility to arbitrate between different competitive options. This means, in other terms, that a fairness-based analysis should investigate firms' behaviour from the consumers' perspective, with the ultimate goal of preserving consumers' abilities to choose and to self-determination in the evolving "ubiquitous" marketplace.[28]

According to this perspective, thus, attention to the fairness of competition interactions' process at a horizontal level,[29] is likely to reflect itself also onto vertical fairness, that is fairness towards consumers.[30] This instrumental conception of fairness for the purposes of competition law assessments,[31] ultimately suggests that far from being an additional element in respect to the objective of consumer welfare as interpreted in terms of market efficiency, the fairness criterion could indeed be interpreted as a component of the notion of consumer welfare itself.[32]

Under these premises, part of the literature has noted that for the pursuing of consumer welfare protection, the fairness principle safeguards "the protection of economic freedom, the protection of rivalry and the protection of small and medium size firms".[33]

---

[26] See in this regard the editorial by Gerard (2018), pp. 211–212.

[27] Commissioner Vestager (25 January 2018).

[28] Commissioner Vestager (25 January 2018).

[29] Lianos (2013), p. 11.

[30] Motta (2004), p. 24. In the same sense Faull and Nickpay (2014), p. 333, stating that the prohibition of exploitative behavior is primarily aimed at effectively regulating market outcomes. In this sense also Nazzini (2011), p. 279. Gerber (5 March 2002).

[31] For a distinction between the two conceptions of fair processing, i.e. the "autosufficient" and the "instrumental" one, see Faull and Nickpay (2014), pp. 332–333. Cf. also Zimmer (2008), p. 106. Contra Ohlhausen and Okuliar (2015), p. 156, who reject the interpretative option of including non-economic considerations in light of the risk of re-introducing subjective non-competition elements.

[32] Shelanski (2013), pp. 1663 ff.

[33] Fairness objectives have been introduced by ordoliberalism. The control of unilateral conducts has traditionally been governed by the fairness parameter as substantiated in the need of protection of rivalry and economic freedom with specific regards to small and medium enterprises. So Ahlborn

These concerns are increasingly felt in the context of digital markets, where network effects and economies of scale quickly give rise, as will be shown below, to strong market imbalances. As a result, the need of preserving businesses' equal opportunities is felt more than ever and suggests the extension of relevant anticompetitive conducts to those, which undermine the fairness of the competitive process.[34]

Exactly due to its functional link to the detection of market imbalances, the general clause of fairness has been regarded by some authors as a gateway for the inclusion within competition assessments of non economic interests such as data protection and consumer protection interests, as impaired by the market conducts of digital undertakings.[35]

A first concrete expression of such a more comprehensive approach to competition enforcement, has been given in the Bundeskartellamts' decision against Facebook, which has widened the scope of unfair trading terms relevant under art. 102 TFEU, up to include users' data protection concerns.[36]

Interestingly, the decision has rooted the relevance for competition law purposes of data protection concerns in the constitutional foundations of users' data protection interests, and in particular if users' right to self-information, resulting impaired by the digital company's market behaviour.[37]

From this perspective, the discussion regarding the opportunity to include in the competition law assessments of digital markets non-economic interests,[38] is to be inscribed within the broader debate regarding the possibility to incorporate within the notion of consumer welfare wider social interests for which there is no market price in competition law analysis.[39]

Ultimately, hence the consideration of the parameter of fairness triggers the deeper question regarding whether competition authorities should assess market efficiency in a strictly economic sense, or include within such assessment also non-directly economic but public-interest related efficiencies. The question is of great relevance for the analysis of digital health markets, because it queries the possible relevance of health-related efficiencies for the purposes of competition assessments. Interestingly, indeed health-related efficiencies, entail also non-economic values, as the ones related to the quality of digital health products,

and Padilla (2008), p. 73, observing how the reconsideration of the notion of fairness among the objectives of competition law equals to a return to the origins. As some strand of literature has indeed underlined, (US) antitrust policy has shifted from the fairness criteria to the one of consumer welfare in the Seventies.

[34] Reflecting on this Graef et al. (2018), pp. 200 ff.

[35] Graef et al. (2018), pp. 200 ff.

[36] Bundeskartellamt (7 February 2019a).

[37] Bundeskartellamt (7 February 2019b), p. 5.

[38] The decision has triggered various critiques by a strand of the scholarship, opposing the extension of competition analysis to a "special privacy responsibility". See among others Colangelo and Maggiolino (2019), pp. 355 ff.

[39] Townley (2009).

their safety and trust. These criteria are all strictly related to the respect of data protection standards by the health data exchanges and the resulting manufacturing processes. This is why, following the lines of the German antitrust authority, antitrust regulators may take into account also these specific non-economic efficiencies in the analysis of digital health markets.

However, given that the decision by the *Bundeskartellamt* is only a first attempt to broaden the scope of competition enforcement, which occurred at national level and which has been very much debated in the literature, whether similar lines of enforcement will be followed by other authorities and also at European level is still surrounded by great uncertainties.

6.2.2 The Protection of Economic (Dynamic) Efficiencies

The second trajectory differently relates to the growing importance given by the European Commission to the protection and promotion of one particular economic component of consumer welfare related to the protection of competing firms' "innovation paths", by ensuring firms' ability to present new products and services to consumers.[40] These very recent lines of enforcement appear to have ultimately evaluated European competition law's potential as a regulatory tool relevant for the purposes of the more general European innovation policy, and more precisely for the maximisation of dynamic efficiencies in existing and "developing" markets.[41] This will be better enquired in the next paragraph.

6.3 Innovation as a "Subversive" Parameter in the Competition Law Analysis of Digital Markets

6.3.1 Competition and Innovation: The Relevant Market Perspective

The growing importance of innovation considerations within European competition law and policy assessments can be, to a certain extent, rooted in the economic changes brought about by the digital transformation of products and services.[42]

[40] Larouche and Schinckel (2014), pp. 153 ff.

[41] Weber (2015), pp. 239 ff.

[42] So Todino et al. (2018), pp. 1–2, expressly observing how "impressive acceleration of technology, internet and digital economy has put the issue of innovation at the (controversial) centre of the current antitrust debate".

Also within the variety of positions regarding the roles of innovation in competition law analysis,[43] there is a general consensus about the fact that the growing importance of the innovation parameter for competition purposes is a direct result of the specific economic nature of technology-driven markets.[44]

As has been observed, the fast-changing technologies shorten services' and products' lifecycles making continuous innovation an essential component of businesses' success.[45] This has direct effects on digital markets' structure: the competitive pressure to innovate pushes indeed companies to aggregate complementary assets and collaborate on costly research and development lines through the sharing of precious know-how.[46]

The collaborative countenance of technology driven markets is directly reflected in the industrial consolidation trends that are starting to become apparent in these same markets especially in the United States.[47] As empirical studies show, these consolidation trends are the result of the blossoming of arrangements increasing the market power of involved firms.[48] Although less pronounced, also in the European Union similar consolidation trends are starting to take shape.[49] Along these lines, the OECD has acknowledged that the number of networks and strategic alliances between firms is growing rapidly especially in information technology and biotechnology industries.[50]

Interestingly, this line of economic studies shows how these consolidation trends are facilitated, not only by the technological selection process, heightening barriers to market entry[51] but also, on the legal side, by a permissive competition enforcement by antitrust agencies, especially in the context of merger procedures.[52]

In light of the newly reinvigorated need for firms to collaborate and outsource in the digital economy,[53] also the scholarship has acknowledged the difficulty for antitrust law to approach the phenomenon of information based inter-firm collaborations.[54]

At a closer examination, indeed, these collaborative stances are to be considered as a direct by-result of the functioning mechanisms of so-called dynamic markets,

---

[43] See the summary by Van Cleynenbreugel (2018), pp. 2 ff.

[44] Kokkoris (2020), p. 59.

[45] Glader (2001), pp. 513 ff.

[46] This was already observed by Gellhorn and Miller (1997), p. 851.

[47] Reflecting on this point, Todino et al. (2018), p. 3.

[48] see Grullon et al. (2019), pp. 697 ff.

[49] Weche and Wambach (January 2018).

[50] OECD (2017), pp. 134–136 highlighting the new emerging phenomenon of collaboration on innovation.

[51] Andrews et al. (2015).

[52] Motta and Peitz (March 2019). It needs to be underlined that this trend relates not only to digital markets.

[53] See supra Chap. 3, Sect. 3.2.

[54] Shapiro and Varian (1999).

which work very differently from traditional static markets. Indeed, in dynamic markets, as high tech markets, and information technology markets, firms compete so as to create products with the highest quality, with the likelihood that a dominant firm is overthrown by entrants or rivals with better technology, higher quality or a different business model.[55] As has been expressively highlighted, in dynamic markets the competitive process is stirred by the "continuous, self-reinforcing innovation and creativity drive" of incumbents,[56] ultimately leading to the introduction of new products and technologies.[57]

Overall, thus, dynamic markets are characterised by ongoing investments in research and development with the ultimate purpose of enhancing consumer needs regarding improved technology. In these markets, thus, technological progress is the primary driver of innovation.[58]

Accordingly, in technology driven markets the competitive mechanism does not work on the basis of competition *in* the market—as it occurs in traditional static markets—but of competition *for* the market.[59] In these markets, indeed, the competitive pressure does not refer to existing markets—that is to existing products or services-, but rather to markets that are in course of development for they are based on the research and development of new products or new business models.[60]

From an economic perspective, hence, innovation driven markets are said to be characterised by dynamic efficiencies to be opposed to static efficiencies.[61] The parameter of dynamic efficiency has been considered especially by American enforcers as a structural component of consumer welfare.[62]

As firms increasingly compete on research and development of new products and services, also the European Commission has started to regard innovation as a key parameter within competition law assessments, moving it at the top of its enforcement priorities.[63]

However, the parameter of innovation- especially in the digital environment- is extremely complex and antitrust analysis faces a concrete problem of developing an

[55] Todino et al. (2018), p. 3.

[56] Kokkoris (2020), p. 78.

[57] Glader (2001), pp. 513 ff.

[58] Glader (2001), p. 519.

[59] Todino et al. (2018), p. 3.

[60] Todino et al. (2018), p. 2.

[61] See Kokkoris (2020), p. 61.

[62] See speech by G.F. Masoudi- Deputy Assistant Attorney General, DOJ Antitrust Division (18 January 2007), p. 2, where he stated "static efficiency is a powerful force for increasing consumer welfare, but an even greater driver of consumer welfare is dynamic efficiency, which results from entirely new ways of doing business. (...) It follows that policymakers should pay particular attention to the impact of laws and enforcement decisions on dynamic efficiency. Intellectual property laws are aimed directly at encouraging dynamic efficiency".

[63] Todino et al. (2018), pp. 2–4. See in this regard Crèmer et al. (2019).

appropriate- and sufficiently sophisticated- framework to address competition law concerns related to innovation.[64]

The consideration of innovation concerns in digital markets has brought about the demand of defining the relevant markets, the applicable framework and the appropriate lines of enforcement.

The features of dynamic markets have pushed regulators to update the regulatory approach in respect to practices in innovation transactions, in particular with regards to research and development collaborations and mergers.

Well before the prompting of such complex assessment, the need has emerged to reconsider the perimeter of the relevant market in which the anticompetitive assessment is conducted.[65]

From the perspective of the definition of the relevant market, the difficulties of defining a proper relevant market with regards to markets that are in course of development through research and development activities have triggered a reassessment of relevant markets, which share different features in respect to defined static markets. Competition law analysis has referred to these "to-be developed" markets as "innovation markets", where the dynamics of competition exactly relate to innovation.[66]

At a very general level, innovation markets are those markets in which new products are developed, creating a completely new demand.[67]

In these regards, the term "innovation market" has been used by the Federal Trade Commission for describing dynamic industries where "innovation, intellectual property and technological change" are central features.[68] A particular type of innovation market is given by research and development markets, defined by the Federal Trade Commission, as markets consisting "of the assets comprising research and development related to the identification of a commercializable product, or directed to particular new or improved goods or processes, and the close substitutes for that research and development" and linked to "specialised assets or characteristics of specific firms".[69]

The European Commission, on its side, has traditionally employed the notion of innovation market more rarely mainly for analysing competition in R&D for certain

64 Galloway (2011), pp. 73 ff.

65 Kern (2014), pp. 173 ff.

66 See infra Sect. 6.4.

67 Carrier (2009), pp. 303 ff., specifically referring to the pharmaceutical industry.

68 See Shapiro (8 November 2005).

69 U.S. Department of Justice and Federal Trade Commission (12 January 2017), pp. 11–12.

products[70] and mainly with the purpose of defining the markets of future products, that is where no product has been yet introduced.[71]

The European Commission has however acknowledged that "cooperation in research and development and in the exploitation of the results is most likely to promote technical and economic progress if the parties contribute complementary skills, assets or activities to the cooperation".[72] Already in 2004, with the issuing of the Technology Transfer Guidelines, innovation markets were considered as a third type of relevant market, in addition to product and technology markets.[73]

The possibility to consider an innovation market autonomously has been confirmed, although without an explicit reference to the innovation market, in the latest Technology Transfer Guidelines,[74] as well as in the Guidelines on Horizontal Cooperation,[75] both relying on the notion of "competition in innovation". More recently, also European merger policy has given a renewed attention to "future markets".[76]

---

[70]The European Commission has been indeed very sceptical about the use of such notion for the purposes of its assessments, as well reflected in some statements of John Temple Lang, former Director at DG Competition, saying that "(if) there is a 'market for R&D', it is only if companies are selling the service of providing R&D to other companies. That is a present service, and it is not the same as the question of whether R&D activities for the researchers' own use is a good measure of future market power". So Temple Lang (1997), p. 764. The careful approach to so-defined "innovation markets" by the Commission can however be explained in light of the disinterest in innovation markets imposed on competition law by the "block exemptions" regarding both technology transfer and research and development agreements. Here it is indeed stressed that the efficiency enhancing and pro-competitive effects of technology transfers is likely to "outweigh any anticompetitive effects". So European Commission, Regulation EU n. 316/2014, 21 March 2014 on the application of Art. 101.3 of the Treaty on the Functioning of the European Union to Categories of Technology Transfer Agreements, OJ L 93 (28 March 2014b), pp. 17–23, recital 5.

[71]Lindqvist (2015), p. 199, recalling the broad analysis of the innovation market under the EU merger regime and the US Licensing Guidelines. See also OECD (1997), p. 90.

[72]European Commission, Regulation EU n. 1217/2010 of 14 December 2010 on the application of Article 101(3) of the Treaty on the Functioning of the European Union to certain categories of research and development agreements, recital 8.

[73]For a historical reconstruction, see Glader (2006), p. 3.

[74]European Commission, Communication from the Commission, Guidelines on the application of Article 101 of the Treaty on the Functioning of the European Union to technology transfer agreements, 2014/C 89/03, OJ C 89/3 (28 March 2014a), para 26.

[75]European Commission, Communication from the Commission- Guidelines on the Applicability of Art. 101 of the Treaty on the Functioning of the European Union to Horizontal Co-operation Agreements, 2011/C 11/01 (14 January 2011), para 119.

[76]The concept of future market has been for the first time employed by the European Commission, Ciba-Geigy/Sandoz Case No. IV/M.737 OJ L 201/1 (29 July 1997), para. 42 and 44. This notion will be better assessed in respect to health data pools infra Sect. 6.4.1.

6.3.2 Competition and Innovation: The Theoretical Debate

The analysis of innovation markets triggers the need to identify the relevant competition law framework and the competition enforcement policies that are sufficiently adherent to the peculiarities of innovation-based markets. This goes not without substantial difficulties: as some scholars have indeed rightly observed, there are no "overall well-suited generalisations for analysing the competitive impact of various transactional arrangements" occurring in innovation markets, "since these are very closely connected to the underlying needs of the innovation and commercialisation processes".[77]

These difficulties have triggered a theoretical debate regarding the roles of innovation in competition analysis,[78] which is worth to briefly recall.

On a theoretical level, the legal difficulties of competition analysis to respond to the emerging complexity of the new technology-driven research environment, in the effort of both upholding its benefits and detecting it harms, are rooted in the old economic dilemma regarding which market structure fosters innovation.[79] This dilemma is to be traced back to the well-known debate between Schumpeter and Arrow, the first one assuming that big firms with static market power would be more inclined to engage in risky and long research and development initiatives that would generate great societal benefits[80]; the second one highlighting that a dominant firms' incentive to innovate would be narrower than that of a firm acting in conditions of rivalry, which would have a greater incentive to innovate so as to grab market power under competitive pressure.[81]

Both theoretical and empirical economic studies have rendered various, often contrasting, results as to which of the above traced positions is more rooted in economic findings.[82]

The resulting economic debate has triggered the legal discussions regarding the way competition enforcement should be enacted in innovation markets.

In this regard, an emerging strand of the literature following Schumpeter's line of reasoning, regards innovation as a ground for a lenient competition analysis.

In view of the need to promote innovation-fruitful market transactions, some scholars have thus suggested to update the assessment of horizontal arrangements from a standard cartel theory to the inclusion of the assessment regarding the

[77] Glader (2001), p. 522.

[78] Ibanez Colomo (2018), pp. 561 ff.

[79] See the analysis of Kerber (2010), pp. 173 ff.

[80] Schumpeter expressed this theory in the famous work, Schumpeter (1943).

[81] Arrow (1962), pp. 609 ff. The link between competition- in terms of rivalry- and innovation has been traditionally expressly acknowledged in the context of the pharmaceutical market. This is particularly stressed by Carrier (2008), pp. 396 ff.

[82] Kerber (2010), pp. 173 ff., recalling nonetheless studies showing how R&D ventures bring about more innovations than mergers.

beneficial impact of innovation on consumer welfare.[83] Drawing on such considerations, the lines of the debate have been further weaved by Carl Shapiro that has pointed out that collaboration restricting rivalry in research and development could still be treated leniently under a competition law assessment, provided the collaboration creates synergy effects—*i.e.* the parties to the collaboration achieve innovation that they may not achieve independently—and/or increase appropriability—*i.e.* the collaboration creates economies of scale on research and development endeavours.[84]

Arguments have been raised that the positive correlation between innovation and technological markets, would justify outright exceptions in terms of competition enforcement as the market structurally tends to the accumulation of market power in order to generate innovative market outputs.[85] More precisely, it has been claimed that a dominant position provides stronger incentives for breakthrough innovation, since the return for innovation efforts is given exactly by the "appropriability" of the whole new market.[86] In this perspective, a call for caution has been issued regarding the competition law interventions that could potentially curtail innovation in industries that enhance consumer welfare majorly through innovation.[87] Indeed, it is claimed that even if innovation-driven research collaborations can exclude, thus harm competitors, they can still benefit consumers thanks to the innovation they bring about. This is why it is argued that dynamic and rapidly changing industries—where the pace of innovation is high and determining a short life of marketed technologies and products—require a more flexible and holistic competition assessment, taking into account different variables such as R&D investment, the quality and variety of products.[88]

According to this line of reasoning, thus, the outweighing of the benefits on consumers resulting from innovation against the eventual harm to competition, could well ground a non-interventionist competition law enforcement.[89] In view of this possibility, the considered literature suggests the opportunity to approach novel arrangements in innovative markets under a rule of reason capable of promoting a firm's innovation drive for product development and distribution, ensuring at the same time competitors' access to necessary assets.[90] Such rule of reason, primarily structured around the innovation parameter, could help antitrust enforcers to identify

[83] Brodley (1987), p. 1020, arguing that innovation efficiency should be given priority in antitrust policy.

[84] Shapiro (2012), pp. 361 ff.

[85] Stressing this point, Manne and Wright (2010), p. 171.

[86] Larouche (2009), pp. 933 ff.

[87] Kokkoris (2020), p. 78.

[88] Bejcek (2005), p. 821.

[89] Kokkoris (2020), p. 73.

[90] This is the view expressed also by Jorde and Teece (1993), pp. 611 ff.

the social costs resulting from a situation of over-enforcement,[91] thus concluding for the convenience of under-enforcement.[92]

The highlighted approach ultimately suggests that agencies enforcing antitrust should take into account also the innovation drive of research collaborations, thus taking a step back and not intervening in the case of consumer welfare enhancing arrangements.[93]

In this perspective, hence, the innovation parameter appears to have a "subversive" role in competition law assessments, restricting thus the scope of antitrust enforcement intervention in the assessments of conducts in research-based markets, when these generate also efficiency outcomes, thus restricting the sphere of anti-competitive conducts.[94]

The opportunity of a "restrictive" competition enforcement in the view of innovation considerations, is however debunked by another strand of the literature that, even in the acknowledgment that competition tools should remove unnecessary impediments to organisational arrangements promoting innovation, has nonetheless stressed the need for competition law and policy to promote, at its very essence, competitive rivalry.[95] More precisely, attention has started to be given to the need to preserve competition *in* innovation. In these specific regards, it has been further highlighted that, although it is true that collaborative research arrangements can have innovative market outcomes, the market power accumulated by the same research consortium directly leads to a decrease of its incentive to innovate, with the resulting generation of consumer harms.[96]

From this different viewpoint, theoretically to be linked to Arrow's lines of reasoning, the new relevance of the innovation parameter has suggested the expansion of the margin of intervention of competition enforcement in the case a research collaboration deriving from any type of arrangement has the effect of combining the only innovators in the market and thus foreclose potential other innovators to access the relevant markets.[97] According to this perspective, hence, competition policy should include within its objectives the ones of spurring companies' incentives to invest in innovation.[98] In this respect, the innovation parameter has brought about the concern related to the protection of firms' freedom to compete through

[91] See the literature assessing the regarding the limits of antitrust, in particular highlighting the social costs related to over-enforcement, Easterbrook (1984), p. 1; Manne and Wright (2010), p. 171.

[92] It needs to be specified that both over-enforcement and under-enforcement are outright enforcement errors, thus respectively above and below the optimal line of enforcement. However, it is argued that the market should self-correct under-enforcement errors with greater ease than over-enforcement errors. See Galloway (2011), pp. 73 ff.

[93] Rai (2001), pp. 813 ff.

[94] See in this regard, interestingly, Holzweber (2019), pp. 41 ff.

[95] Scherer (1987), p. 1001.

[96] Aghion et al. (2005), pp. 701 ff. See also Carrier (2008), pp. 396 ff., applying the Schumpeter-Arrow debate to the case of pharmaceutical innovation market.

[97] Larouche and Schinckel (2014), pp. 153 ff.

[98] Glader (2001), p. 519.

innovation,[99] suggesting the opportunity of an interventionist competition policy for the detection of new harms to firms' ability to research and to innovate, thus broadening the sphere of anticompetitive conduct.

Under these premises, it needs to be observed that the competitive impact of transactional arrangements occurring in research-based markets cannot be constrained into a one-size-fits it all model.[100]

Especially in digitally driven markets, which are characterised by new market arrangements evolving around data transfers, competition authorities face the problem of discerning whether a dominant company aggregating increasingly more data harmfully forecloses competitors' access in the corresponding data-driven markets, or, disregarding a certain foreclosure effect, advance consumers and their welfare through the innovative products it brings to the market. Hence, the practical challenge arises with regards the need to find the critical point in which "innovation exclusion" resulting from undistorted competition on the merits driven by collaborative research and development turns into harmful market power.[101]

6.3.3 *Competition and Innovation: The Responses by European Law and Policy*

The two strands of the above-highlighted economic and legal debate, one calling for a contraction of competition enforcement in respect to innovation markets, the other one suggesting the need to activate competition law remedies in respect to innovation-related harms, appear to be both "positively" embedded in the European competition framework.

In a first Schumpeterian perspective, indeed, some European competition law provisions support research-based collaborative organizations established on dynamic markets, expressly allowing for certain arrangements and thus for a (temporary) suspension of the competitive process in the view of the resulting innovation achievements and welfare gains. As will be shown below, the European framework, as defined by the Commission's Guidelines regarding horizontal agreements, expands the area of lawful research-based collaborations, which thus structurally fall outside any competition scrutiny. This shows an underlying favour by the same Commission for these kinds of alliances.

Furthermore, also transactions infringing competition law provisions, and especially art. 101(1) TFEU, are granted a favourable treatment either in the form of an outright safe harbour regarding these research-based collaborations, provided normatively set conditions are respected by the same collaborations, or in the form of a broader efficiency-based exemption to be found in art. 101(3) TFEU.

---

[99] Akman (2014), pp. 183 ff.

[100] Kokkoris (2020), p. 78.

[101] Kokkoris (2020), p. 78.

The European competition law framework, as the American one, has expressly recognised the importance of innovation concerns with the implementation and extension of so-called block exemptions. These can be considered as the direct result of the acknowledgment that collaborative innovation is important and that the blocking of such collaborative synergies, in the name of protection of competitive rivalry "as such", could be source of consumer harm and thus generally diminish the creation of wealth.[102] Accordingly, the European Commission, has stated that "consumers can generally be expected to benefit from the increased volume and effectiveness of research and development through the introduction of new or improved products or services, a quicker launch of those products or services, or the reduction of prices brought about by new or improved technologies or processes".[103]

Hence, very similarly to the data protection regime established under the General Data Protection Regulation, also European competition law framework appears to entail an innovation-based set of provisions, potentially promoting research-based health data pooling practices and the resulting market concentrations. This innovation-based framework thus ultimately appears to uphold the Digital Single Market Strategy's health data driven innovation objectives.

From the very opposite perspective, conversely, innovation is considered within the European framework as a parameter of competition intended as rivalry, alongside price and outputs. The Guidelines on the assessment of horizontal mergers[104] indeed consider the decrease of the rate of innovation as one of the possible grounds of competitive harm deriving from "increased market power".[105] Similarly, also the Guidelines on Horizontal Co-operation acknowledge the anticompetitive nature of agreements that negatively impact on innovation, thus giving autonomous recognition to harms to innovation.[106]

In both Guidelines, thus, the Commission appears to suggest that the competitive harm resulting from a reduction of competition should deserve the same attention granted to price increases and reductions of outputs by competition enforcers.[107] By doing so, the Commission appears to consider innovation not only as a key core value requiring protection- even despite contractions of the competitive process-, but

[102] Rai (2001), p. 820.

[103] European Commission, Regulation EU n. 1217/2010 of 14 December 2010 on the application of Article 101(3) of the Treaty on the Functioning of the European Union to certain categories of research and development agreements, recital 10.

[104] European Commission, Guidelines on the Assessment of Horizontal Mergers Under Council Regulation on the Control of Concentrations Between Undertakings (5 February 2004a).

[105] European Commission, Guidelines on the Assessment of Horizontal Mergers Under Council Regulation on the Control of Concentrations Between Undertakings (5 February 2004a), para 8.

[106] European Commission, Communication from the Commission- Guidelines on the Applicability of Art. 101 of the Treaty on the Functioning of the European Union to Horizontal Co-operation Agreements (14 January 2011), para 27.

[107] Todino et al. (2018), p. 5.

rather a policy value that should also guide the assessment and the condemnation of anticompetitive practices.[108]

Along these lines, closer to Arrow's ideas, European merger policy has lately come to regard innovation as a self-standing object of rivalry, with the resulting activation of competition enforcement when market concentrations have been suspected to block the overall competitive pressure over research endeavours on innovation markets.

These concerns have been addressed by some decisions by the European Commission, as the ones related to the *Dow/DuPont* and *Bayer/Monsanto* mergers.[109] Here the European Court of Justice has acknowledged the relevance of innovation as "an input activity for both the upstream technology markets and the downstream [...] markets",[110] which needs to be protected in the assessment of potentially anticompetitive practices. As a result, the Commission has bound competition enforcement to the protection of the ability of competing firms to innovate through the re-establishment of a certain degree of market fragmentation regarding innovation efforts.

In this regard, the European Commission has been said to establish a new theory of competitive harm,[111] occurring when the foreclosure of innovating competitors also reflects itself into harm to consumers directly deriving from the loss of at least equally innovative competitors.[112]

Under these premises, it needs to be acknowledged that both of the highlighted perspectives in which the European competition framework regards innovation ultimately consider innovation as a competitively relevant parameter that the framework itself either promotes, through a set of lenient rules, or protects, through direct competition intervention.

Against the backdrop of the traced innovation-based competition framework, the analysis will explore the regulatory framework applicable to contractual agreements or outright mergers implying the sharing of research valuable information, and thus the creation of research-based health data pools.

With regards to the relevant market, it can be indeed argued that health data pools are outright data-driven innovation markets, in which health data are traded for the purposes of the conduction of research that aims to develop and test new products and services.

In these regards, the more specific question arises whether these contractual agreements or outright mergers implying the sharing of research valuable

[108] Stressing this point, Colomo (2016), pp. 201 ff. and Van Cleynenbreugel (2018), p. 7.

[109] See also case law cited infra Chap. 7, Sect. 7.3.4.

[110] European Commission, Dow/DuPont, Merger Procedure Regulation (EC) 139/2004, Case M. 7932 (27 March 2017).

[111] Werner et al. (2018), pp. 133 ff. and Denicolò and Polo (22 March 2018).

[112] See Kokkoris (2020), pp. 56 ff.

information could be redeemed on the basis of innovation considerations, and thus of efficiency claims, in these health data-driven markets.[113]

For these purposes, it needs to be first assessed whether novel practices related to data-driven research and innovation based on health data pooling can be subsumed in traditional competition law schemes.[114] More precisely, a preliminary enquiry needs to be made with regards to the possible qualification of health data pools as agreements relevant under European competition law.

6.4 Health Data Pools as Research and Development Agreements Under Art. 101 TFEU

The European competition law framework moves from the general normative postulate, enshrined under art. 101(1) TFEU, that all the agreements between undertakings, decisions by associations, or concerted practices that restrict by their object or effect competition are prohibited.[115]

In light of this provision, the first issue to be addressed is whether health data pools can be included within the notion of arrangement and thus be assessed under art. 101(1) TFEU.

From a subjective standpoint, it needs to be acknowledged that also arrangements between private and public institutions fall within the competition law scrutiny under art. 101(1) TFEU. Indeed, the notion of undertaking for the purposes of competition law is anchored to the requirement of the conduction of an economic activity, implying the offering of services and products on a given market,[116] "regardless of the legal status of the entity and the way in which it is financed".[117]

---

[113]The different aspect of the competition enforcement policies relevant in respect to the innovation-related harms possibly emerging in the markets of health data sharing, will be addressed in the next chapter, specifically dedicated to the framework regarding needed regulatory remedies in health data pooling practices. See infra Chap. 7, Sect. 7.3.

[114]Highlighting the need to investigate more deeply the competition concerns arising from data collection, Almunia (26 November 2012).

[115]The restrictions by object are to be found in the so-called black-listed conducts, outlined in the Commission's Guidelines and Notices.

[116]According to the case law, an economic activity consists in offering "services and products on a given market". European Court of Justice, Commission of the European Communities v Italian Republic, C-35/96 (18 June 1998b), para 36.

[117]European Court of Justice, Höfner and Elser v Macrotron GmbH, C-41/90 (23 April 1991), para 21.

Such functional approach to the notion of undertaking can thus encompass both private and public health care providers,[118] as hospitals.[119] In this perspective, health data sharing agreements like the ones established between Google DeepMind and London's Royal Free Hospital and between IBM and the Lombardia Region, could fall under the scrutiny of competition law, given that in the context of health data sharing practices carried out for research purposes, the public institutions offer a product, i.e. the health data, on the (innovation) market involving the defined research activity, and will subsequently offer the service that has been designed and tested upon the data, in the market of the service.

From an objective standpoint, it has been shown how health data pools are factually information exchanges both between private and between private and public entities.

The European Commission has expressly acknowledged the relevance of information exchanges for the purposes of art. 101 TFEU in the 2011 Guidelines on Horizontal Co-operation Agreements.[120] Although the information exchanges to which the Commission refers to are of a different kind in respect to digital data exchanges,[121] some general considerations seem to be applicable also to this latter type of information exchange.

In this respect, for the purposes of art. 101(1) TFEU, the Commission affirms the relevance not only of bilateral information exchanges, but also of unilateral conducts of information disclosure by just one of the involved parties.[122] According to the Commission, indeed, also a unilateral information disclosure from one party to another, can generate the risk of restricting competition.[123]

---

[118]The notion of undertaking however excludes entities exercising public powers. See European Court of Justice, Commission of the European Communities v Italian Republic, C-118/85 (16 June 1987) para 7; European Court of Justice, Jean Reyners v Belgian State, C-2/74 (21 June 1974), paras 664–665, where it is affirmed that "official authority is that which arises from the sovereignty and majesty of the State; for him who exercises it, it implies the power of enjoying the prerogatives outside the general law, privileges of official power and powers of coercion over citizens". Moreover, it needs to be recalled that the European Court of Justice has excluded from the notion of undertaking relevant for competition law purposes, sickness funds and organizations involved in the management of the public social security system, fulfilling a social function based on the principle of solidarity and thus non-profit-making. European Court of Justice, Christian Poucet v Assurances Générales de France and Caisse Mutuelle Régionale du Languedoc-Roussillon, Joined Cases C-159/91 and C-160/91 (17 February 1993), para 18–20.

[119]This positive solution is given by Odudu (2011), pp. 231 ff. Highlighting the difficulties in applying the notion of undertaking to state-owned hospitals, Seitz (2018), pp. 131 ff.

[120]European Commission, Communication from the Commission- Guidelines on the Applicability of Art. 101 of the Treaty on the Functioning of the European Union to Horizontal Co-operation Agreements, 2011/C 11/01 (14 January 2011), paras 55 ff.

[121]This will be better assessed infra para 8.

[122]Ghezzi and Maggiolino (20 June 2015).

[123]European Commission, Communication from the Commission- Guidelines on the Applicability of Art. 101 of the Treaty on the Functioning of the European Union to Horizontal Co-operation Agreements, 2011/C 11/01 (14 January 2011), para 62. See also Advocate General Kokott (19 February 2009) Opinion in T-Mobile Netherlands BV and Others, C-8/08, ECR I-4529, para 54.

What is however more important is that the Commission further distinguishes between information exchanges that are linked to broader arrangements and self-standing information exchanges with the ultimate goal of sharing competitively relevant information pieces.[124] In the first case, indeed, the competition law assessment of information exchanges is absorbed by the competition analysis of the broader economic operation in which the information exchange is inscribed, whereas in the second case the standalone information exchange is made object of an autonomous competition assessment.[125]

As has been pointed out in the previous chapters, health data pools can be part of broader economic operations, such as the creation of a joint venture or a merger, as it has occurred in the Google Sanofi merger case,[126] or exist as standalone agreements, as it was the case of the Google DeepMind-Royal Free Hospital or in the IBM-Italy partnership.[127]

Although not occurring through a merger operation, it can however be that health data pools established for research purposes are placed in the context of a broader agreement regarding a research and development project. In this case, the health data exchange, considered as a new digital form of research and development collaboration, would thus fall under the corresponding legal framework regarding research and development agreements.

These are considered in the Guidelines for Horizontal Cooperation as a peculiar form of information-based alliance and are the object of a special regime under the Research and Development block exemption,[128] which provides a safe harbour under art. 101(3) TFEU of research and development agreements that meet certain normatively set requirements.

For the purposes of this competition law regime, the Commission recognizes the variety of Research and Development agreements, which can range from outsourcing contracts concerning certain R&D activities, the joint improvement of existing technologies, to broader agreements involving the cooperation for the

---

[124]See, in these regards, Ghezzi and Maggiolino (20 June 2015), p. 2.

[125]European Commission, Communication from the Commission- Guidelines on the Applicability of Art. 101 of the Treaty on the Functioning of the European Union to Horizontal Co-operation Agreements, 2011/C 11/01 (14 January 2011), para 62. See also Ghezzi and Maggiolino (20 June 2015), p. 9, where the Authors add another type of information exchange occurring in the view of other future concerted practices. These would need to be treated under a competition law assessment together with the principal concerted practice.

[126]See supra Chap. 3, Sect. 3.1.1.2.

[127]See supra Chap. 3., Sect. 3.1.2.

[128]European Commission, Communication from the Commission- Guidelines on the Applicability of Art. 101 of the Treaty on the Functioning of the European Union to Horizontal Co-operation Agreements, 2011/C 11/01 (14 January 2011), paras 111 ff. European Commission, Commission Regulation EU N. 1217/2010 of 14 December 2010 on the application of Article 101(3) of the Treaty on the Functioning of the European Union to certain categories of research and development agreements (18 December 2010b) (hereafter R&D Block Exemption). For the literature see Seitz (2011), pp. 452 ff.

research, development and marketing of new products or the creation of a joint controlled company.[129]

Under these premises, the next paragraphs will enquire the competition law regime of research and development agreements under art. 101 TFEU. For these purposes, following the Guidelines, the questions needs to be addressed regarding how to determine the relevant market; when research and development agreement are lawful under art. 101(1) TFEU; when they infringe art. 101(1) TFEU and when, although violating the provision at stake, they can be exempted under art. 101(3) TFEU and the related block exemption.

Outside the context of research and development agreements, it will ultimately be assessed whether health data pools as "pure" information exchanges detached from a specific research purpose can be object of an autonomous assessment under art. 101(1) TFEU and 101(3) TFEU.

6.4.1 The Relevant Market: Health Data Pools as Multi-Sided Data-Driven Innovation Markets

In case of research and development agreements, the definition of the relevant market needs to be made with reference to the products, technologies or research and development efforts that will act as a main competitive constraint on the parties.[130]

In case the research and development agreement is means to improve an existing product or technology then the relevant market concerned by the cooperation is to be determined through reference to these products, technologies or their close substitutes.[131]

Conversely, the exact definition of a relevant research market, as detached from a specific product or service, is not an easy task and risks to become a very abstract endeavour. In these regards, the European Commission's Guidelines on Horizontal Co-operation distinguish two types of possible relevant innovation markets.[132]

---

[129] So European Commission, Communication from the Commission- Guidelines on the Applicability of Art. 101 of the Treaty on the Functioning of the European Union to Horizontal Co-operation Agreements, 2011/C 11/01 (14 January 2011), para 111.

[130] European Commission, Communication from the Commission- Guidelines on the Applicability of Art. 101 of the Treaty on the Functioning of the European Union to Horizontal Co-operation Agreements, 2011/C 11/01 (14 January 2011), para 112.

[131] European Commission, Communication from the Commission- Guidelines on the Applicability of Art. 101 of the Treaty on the Functioning of the European Union to Horizontal Co-operation Agreements, 2011/C 11/01 (14 January 2011), para 113; 116.

[132] European Commission, Communication from the Commission- Guidelines on the Applicability of Art. 101 of the Treaty on the Functioning of the European Union to Horizontal Co-operation Agreements, 2011/C 11/01 (14 January 2011), para 119.

The first ones is related to an innovation process that is structured and in respect to which precise research poles can be identified.

In the first case, the Commission suggests to analyse competition between the identified research and development poles, by assessing the closeness of such competition between the parties and the existence of other competing poles.[133] For the purposes of this assessment the Commission highlights the need of an analysis regarding the nature, scope and size of the other identified research and development poles on the market, their access to the needed intellectual property rights and other specialised assets and their capability to exploit possible results. Within this assessment, the identification of competing research and development poles is given by their substitutable nature, that is when the research poles are aimed at developing substitutable products or technologies.[134] As the Commission specifies, research and development poles are considered as competing on the basis of the assessment of specific factors, as, amongst others, their access to know-how and patents or to other specialised assets, their timing and capability to exploit the achieved results.[135] For these purposes, it needs to be observed that specific regulatory requirements to render research information public, as it is the case of clinical trials data,[136] may help identify the research carried out by market players, and thus defining rivals that are targeting a same demand.[137]

To the very contrast, when research & development poles cannot be clearly defined, and the innovation process appears to be unstructured, the definition of a specific relevant market would be too speculative, and the assessment of the relevant market needs thus to be made, if possible, with reference to "existing product and/or technology markets which are related to the R&D co-operation in question".[138]

The distinction made by the Commission between structured and unstructured innovation processes thus suggests that when research poles can be identified, they are treated as object of the so-defined innovation market, just as specific products or technologies are treated as objects of traditional products' or technologies' markets. In this perspective, interestingly, research poles, which are exactly given by research

[133] European Commission, Communication from the Commission- Guidelines on the Applicability of Art. 101 of the Treaty on the Functioning of the European Union to Horizontal Co-operation Agreements, 2011/C 11/01 (14 January 2011), para 120.

[134] European Commission, Communication from the Commission- Guidelines on the Applicability of Art. 101 of the Treaty on the Functioning of the European Union to Horizontal Co-operation Agreements, 2011/C 11/01 (14 January 2011), para 120.

[135] European Commission, Communication from the Commission- Guidelines on the Applicability of Art. 101 of the Treaty on the Functioning of the European Union to Horizontal Co-operation Agreements, 2011/C 11/01 (14 January 2011), para 120.

[136] As under art. 81 Clinical Trials Regulation EC 536/2014.

[137] European Commission, Communication from the Commission- Guidelines on the Applicability of Art. 101 of the Treaty on the Functioning of the European Union to Horizontal Co-operation Agreements, 2011/C 11/01 (14 January 2011), para 120.

[138] European Commission, Communication from the Commission- Guidelines on the Applicability of Art. 101 of the Treaty on the Functioning of the European Union to Horizontal Co-operation Agreements, 2011/C 11/01 (14 January 2011), para 122.

valuable information, are considered the self-standing "products" or "technologies" of innovation markets.

The application of these general statements to health data-driven innovation markets, implies that, in order to be properly defined, these need to be traced around well identified research poles, which are given by the health data aggregated for a precise research purpose, as for example health data regarding a specific disease or disease group, which thus serve the research purpose regarding such specific disease or disease group.

Hence, in case of aggregated health data that are not structured around a specific research pole, and thus have no specific research purpose, no precise innovation market can be identified, this preventing the analysis of this unstructured health data under competition law schemes.

With regards to health-data driven innovation markets, it needs to be further observed that the identification of relevant research poles can be facilitated by the connection, mostly occurring in both digital and high tech markets, of health data-driven research poles to specific digital health products or services. These generate health data flows that in turn come to define the relevant data-driven innovation market. An example of this is given by the kidney app developed by Google DeepMind on the basis of Royal Free Hospital's patient data. In this case, the health data-driven research pole was exactly given by the hospital's patient data regarding kidney injuries. Once the kidney app was developed, the health data generated by the same app would thus aliment the research-relevant health data pool, and with that the "pure" health data-driven innovation market. In this perspective, it can be said that health data pools established for research purposes are often connected to the different markets of already existing digital products or technologies, or will be connected to such newly delivered products or technologies, after the research is carried out. As already suggested elsewhere,[139] in case digital companies are part of the research agreement, it is very likely that the "research market" is attracted into the functioning of digital platforms and thus connected also to other, more general, products and technology markets.

Under these premises, health data-driven research markets are very likely to be part of multi-sided platforms, which process health data for research and other purposes.

This multi-sided structure is very likely to be characterised by economies of scale,[140] direct network effects[141] within and indirect network effects among the

[139] See supra Chap. 3, Sects. 3.3.6 and 3.3.7.

[140] Economies of scale are related to the fact that once a sufficient amount of health data has been collected, the production of new scientifically valuable knowledge becomes easier and less costly as a result of the generative nature of algorithmic processing, extracting always new research significant data from existing databases. This is well highlighted by Mattioli (2017), pp. 179 ff.

[141] Direct network effects are related to the fact that the utility that a user derives from a good depends "on the number of other users who are in the same network as he or she". This means, with specific regards to the health sector, that the bigger the health data pool is, the more efficient the health product or service is, this leading to a greater number of patients/users that are attracted to the

various sides. These externalities in turn determine the consolidation of the market power of undertakings who are active in digital health research and who engage in health data exchanges,[142] along the lines of what some strand of the literature has regarded as a "self-reinforcing data advantage of dominant firms".[143]

6.4.2 (Pro)Competitive Health Data Pools Under Art. 101(1) TFEU

In the Guidelines on Horizontal Cooperation, the Commission moves from the assumption that research-based alliances "generally" do not violate art. 101(1) TFEU.[144]

In particular, the Guidelines state that the exchanges of research-valuable information occurring between non-competing parties do not produce restrictive effects on competition and should thus not be captured under rules on restrictive agreements under art. 101(1) TFEU.[145]

For the purposes of the application of art. 101(1) TFEU to research and development agreements, the notion of non-competing parties is quite broad and encompasses also companies who are active in the same product markets but in different geographic markets, without being potential competitors".[146]

Interestingly, in the context of research agreements, also companies who cannot carry out the research independently[147] and who target a new market, which they

same product or service. The greater amount of health information that is in this way pooled together, determines in turn an increased efficiency of the rendered products or services, which are increasingly patient-tailored. In a nutshell, the more users the digital product or services has, the more data about them it collects. Katz and Shapiro (1985), pp. 427 ff. Direct network effects in turn determine higher switching costs. With regards to switching costs, see Farrell and Klemperer (2007), pp. 1967 ff.

[142] From a general perspective on the issue, see Autoritè de la Concurrence-Bundeskartellamt (10 May 2016), p. 27. Stucke and Grunes (May 2015), p. 6; Harbour and Koslov (2010), p. 794.

[143] So Pasquale (2013), p. 1015.

[144] See Recital 6 R&D Block Exemption.

[145] European Commission, Communication from the Commission- Guidelines on the Applicability of Art. 101 of the Treaty on the Functioning of the European Union to Horizontal Co-operation Agreements, 2011/C 11/01 (14 January 2011), para 130.

[146] European Commission, Communication from the Commission- Guidelines on the Applicability of Art. 101 of the Treaty on the Functioning of the European Union to Horizontal Co-operation Agreements, 2011/C 11/01 (14 January 2011), para 1.

[147] This means that in case a party can initiate the research independently, the agreement is not per se lawful. Interestingly the Guidelines on Horizontal Co-operation define those parties that cannot initiate the research independently as non-competing parties. European Commission, Communication from the Commission- Guidelines on the Applicability of Art. 101 of the Treaty on the Functioning of the European Union to Horizontal Co-operation Agreements, 2011/C 11/01 (14 January 2011), para 130.

could not have reached independently,[148] are considered as non-competing parties, with the resulting research agreement falling outside the scope of art. 101(1) TFEU.[149]

In this respect, for example, the Commission refers to the case of outsourcing of research and development to a specialized company, as research institutes or academic bodies. In this case it is exactly the complementary nature of the parties' research assets that grounds the lawfulness of the research agreement under art. 101(1) TFEU.[150]

Against this backdrop, thus, also parties holding strong market positions would be able to take part to joint R&D agreements with the objective of creating a new technology associated to a new demand, without falling under the scrutiny of art. 101(1) TFEU. The broad notion of non-competing parties provided by the Commission both in the Guidelines on Horizontal Cooperation and in the R&D block exemption could thus incentivise the parties to claim a broad scope of the research in order to be considered non-competing businesses.[151]

Whenever the above-mentioned subjective requirements are met, the research and development agreement is considered per se lawful and thus falling outside the scope of art. 101(1) TFEU.

From a different objective perspective, for the purposes of art. 101(1) TFEU a first assessment shall regard the possible anticompetitive effects of such a conduct and the eventual efficiency outcomes that are related to the same conduct.[152]

Among the primary benefits brought about research-based cooperation, the Commission identifies the reduction of duplication of unnecessary costs, the cross-fertilization of ideas and experience, resulting in a faster development of new products and technologies as well as the means of establishing a consortium of

---

[148] European Commission, Communication from the Commission- Guidelines on the Applicability of Art. 101 of the Treaty on the Functioning of the European Union to Horizontal Co-operation Agreements, 2011/C 11/01 (14 January 2011), para 130.

[149] The Guidelines clarify that the assessment of the non-competing nature of the involved parties need to be carried out on a realistic basis, considering whether the parties independently have the resources to carry out a research project, in terms, for example, of know-how and expertise. European Commission, Communication from the Commission- Guidelines on the Applicability of Art. 101 of the Treaty on the Functioning of the European Union to Horizontal Co-operation Agreements, 2011/C 11/01 (14 January 2011), para 130.

[150] European Commission, Communication from the Commission- Guidelines on the Applicability of Art. 101 of the Treaty on the Functioning of the European Union to Horizontal Co-operation Agreements, 2011/C 11/01 (14 January 2011), para 131.

[151] B. Lindqvist (2015), p. 192.

[152] This is highlighted by the European Commission, Commission Notice: Guidelines on the Application of Article 81(3) of the Treaty, 2004/C 101/08 (27 April 2004b), para 17. For the literature stressing this, see Zingales (2018), pp. 89–91 and case law cited.

small and medium companies able to innovate and thus to compete with bigger market players.[153]

These aspects have been evaluated by Mario Monti who has observed how the "Horizontal guidelines recognise that companies need to respond to increasing competitive pressure and a changing market place driven by globalisation, the speed of technological progress and the generally more dynamic nature of markets. Co-operation can often be a way to share risk, save costs, pool know-how and launch innovation faster".[154]

These efficiencies related to information-based research cooperations are being increasingly highlighted at policy level in the context of data-driven research and innovation.

As Commissioner Vestager has indeed pointed out, combining companies' data might provide insights that could not be otherwise and independently achieved,[155] suggesting that for innovation purposes, the bigger the datasets, and thus the businesses, the better it is for innovation purposes.[156] Also in the Report "Competition Policy for the Digital Era",[157] the European Commission expresses a positive view of collaborative data innovation.

At national level, this view is shared also by the German Competition Authority[158] which has acknowledged that the co-operations between companies in the collection and processing of data can lead to efficiencies and pro-competitive effects, in particular in the context of connected industry applications such as it is in the case of pharmaceuticals combined with medical devices.[159]

Accordingly, the Statement on Competition Law and Data jointly issued by the German and the French Competition Authorities appears to interestingly suggest that research collaborations based on data sharing can enable also smaller entities to enter research-based markets, the penetration of which would require investments these entities could otherwise not afford.[160]

The acknowledgement of efficiency effects of research valuable information exchanges is upheld by the literature especially in respect to the context of innovation and technology markets.[161] In the acknowledgment of the peculiar dynamics of

---

[153] European Commission, Communication from the Commission- Guidelines on the Applicability of Art. 101 of the Treaty on the Functioning of the European Union to Horizontal Co-operation Agreements, 2011/C 11/01 (14 January 2011), para 2. This is stressed by Glader (2001), p. 531.

[154] Monti (20 October 2000).

[155] Commissioner Vestager (29 September 2016).

[156] Carli (2018), pp. 397 ff.

[157] Crèmer et al. (2019), p. 12.

[158] Bundeskartellamt (Oktober 2017), pp. 9 ff.

[159] See supra Chap. 2, Sect. 2.1.5 and 2.1.6.

[160] Autoritè De La Concurrence and Bundeskartellamt (10 May 2016), p. 38.

[161] See Di Porto (2014), pp. 296 ff., stressing that the "pro-competitive virtues of exchanges of information are as relevant as anti-competitive risks in the assessment of any exchange under art. 101(1) TFEU". See also Bennet and Collins (2016), pp. 311 ff., especially at 318–320; stressing the efficiencies of big data and concluding thus for the Sokol and Comerford (2016), pp. 1133 ff.

competition in innovation markets, this literature has underlined that there can be forms of co-operations also between competing undertakings, which enhance the innovation process and the technological development.[162] It is indeed argued that the flow of knowledge among businesses that are active in innovation intensive industries, such as the health industry, can sometimes lead to the reduction of uncertainties related to research and development processes.[163] The reduction of uncertainties, would favour the individual firms' competitiveness, with that stirring the development of the industry sector.[164]

In particular, information sharing can improve allocative efficiency, ensuring that scarce resources are allocated to those who want or need them most.[165] From a further perspective, through the acquisition of new information, firms can better understand market trends and thus more readily match supply with demands, this being extremely important especially in markets undergoing rapid technological change.[166] Ultimately, the availability of information regarding consumer risk—this being also the case of personal health information- can reduce companies' problems of adverse selection, occurring when firms cannot distinguish good consumers from bad consumers.[167]

For the purposes of data-driven health research, the knowledge about the patients who are less at risk of contracting diseases and those who conversely suffer the greater risk, is essential for the enactment of more precise predictions, which in turn reduce problems of adverse selection in health research courses.

The above-outlined efficiencies can ground the lawfulness of the same agreement in respect to art. 101(1) TFEU, in accordance to the so-called "ancillarity test".

According to this test, an arrangement falls out of the scope of art. 101(1) TFEU in case the anticompetitive effects it produces are necessary, thus ancillary, to the production of efficiencies.[168]

The notion of ancillarity relevant for the test has been progressively narrowed by the European Court of Justice that has been increasingly referring to the notion of ancillarity outlined with regards to joint venture operations, for the purposes of the

---

[162] Teece (1994), pp. 465 ff.; Jorde and Teece (1993), pp. 611 ff.; Jorde and Teece (1990), pp. 75 ff.

[163] This is stressed by Capobianco (2004), p. 1274.

[164] Jorde and Teece (1990), p. 79.

[165] Bennet and Collins (2016), p. 318.

[166] Bennet and Collins (2016), p. 318.

[167] Bennet and Collins (2016), p. 319.

[168] See European Court of Justice, Société Technique Minière v Mascinenbau Ulm, C-56/65 (30 June 1966), para 250, where the Court held that an exclusive license to a distributor does not infringe art. 101(1) TFEU, to the extent that is "really necessary for the penetration of a new area by an undertaking". See also European Court of Justice, Nungesser KG and Kurt Eisele vs. Commission of the European Communities, C-258/78 (8 June 1982a) and European Court of Justice, Coditel SA, Compagnie générale pour la diffusion de la télévision, and others v Ciné-Vog Films SA and others, C-262/81 (6 October 1982b), where the Court admitted restrictions commensurate to securing the appropriate incentives for investments, thus incorporating dynamic considerations through the backdoor of article 101(1) TFEU.

ancillarity test under art. 101(1) TFEU.[169] Drawing from the notion of ancillarity in the context of the assessment of joint ventures, the General Court in *Métropole*[170] ruled that "ancillary restraints" are only those who are "objectively necessary" for the performance of the operation under assessment.[171]

This approach was further followed by other decisions of the Court, as *Mastercard v. Commission*,[172] in which it was observed that the mere fact that the operation is *more difficult* to implement without the restriction is not sufficient to meet the "objective necessity" threshold.[173] In light of this interpretation, the ancillarity test under art. 101(1) TFEU requires that in the absence of the restriction to competition, the arrangement would not have been pursued.[174]

Provided this objective necessity threshold is met, the ancillary test is interesting because it admits some restrictions of competition, provided the main arrangement pursues legitimate objectives, such as innovation, and the restrictions are an objectively necessary means to achieve these objectives.

For the purposes of the ancillarity test, the European Court of Justice has stated that competition authorities may under certain circumstances take into account the specificities of the sector interested by the restrictions, also admitting inherent restrictions when objectives in the general interest are at stake.[175]

Under these premises, it is interesting to recall that in the *Meca-Medina* case a regulation regarding anti-doping was accepted, in light of the consideration of the legitimate objectives pursued by it. These were interestingly related to health.[176]

---

[169] European Commission, Commission Notice on Restrictions Directly Related and Necessary to Concentrations, 2005/C 56/24 (5 March 2005a).

[170] European Court of Justice, Métropole Télévision (M6), Suez-Lyonnaise des eaux, France Télécom and Télévision française 1 SA (TF1) v Commission of the European Communities, C-T-112/99 (18 September 2001), para 62.

[171] It has been in these regards highlighted how the notion of "objectively necessary" does not imply the assessment of efficiencies related, for example, to the commercial success of the operation or the establishment on the market on a long-term basis of the undertakings part to the operation. Zingales (2018), p. 92.

[172] European Court of Justice, Mastercard Inc. and Others v. European Commission, C-382/12 (11 September 2014), para 91.

[173] Zingales (2018), p. 93.

[174] This is what is suggested by the European Commission's Guidelines, European Commission, Communication from the Commission- Guidelines on the Applicability of Art. 101 of the Treaty on the Functioning of the European Union to Horizontal Co-operation Agreements, 2011/C 11/01 (14 January 2011), para 74.

[175] European Court of Justice, J.C.J. Wouters and Others v. Algemene Raad van de Nederlandse Orde van Advocaten, C-309/99 (19 February 2002), dealing with a partnerships between lawyers and accountants, which was held as not infringing art. 101(1) TFEU because it was found to be necessary for the proper exercise of the legal profession.

[176] European Court of Justice, David Meca-Medina and Igor Majcen vs. European Commission and Republic of Finland, C-519/04 (18 July 2006a), involving an anti-doping regulation developed by sports organisations, that was deemed as not infringing art. 101(1) TFEU for the legitimate (public) objectives pursued by these same regulations.

From this further perspective, the ancillary test could be of great relevance for the assessment of health data pools, by requiring competition authorities to strike a balance between the aim of preserving undistorted competition and the consideration of health-related innovation objectives. To the contrary, if the ancillarity test is not fulfilled, research and development agreements would fall under the scope of art. 101(1) TFEU.

6.4.3 Anticompetitive Health Data Pools Under Art. 101(1) TFEU

The research and development collaboration between competing[177] or "potentially" competing parties[178] can have, in some circumstances, restrictive effects on competition, thus violating art. 101(1) TFEU.

More precisely, research and development based on data exchanges can negatively influence market structures and decrease consumer welfare, by inducing the market to a situation of oligopoly and adversely impacting on certain competition parameters as market price and output, product quality and variety, innovation.[179] This is both acknowledged by Commissione Vestager, who has stressed the relevance of the Guidelines on Horizontal Cooperation for the detection of anticompetitive outcomes of information sharing agreements[180] and the *Bundeskartellamt* that has warned that data sharing can facilitate collusion, obstruct access to data for third parties and raise entry barriers.[181]

Under these premises, although generally expressing a positive approach to research and development collaboration, the Guidelines on Horizontal Cooperation do not fail to highlight how these can negatively affect competition in various ways.

In this respect, the Commission acknowledges the potential anticompetitive effects of research and development agreements in case the involved parties have

---

[177] For the purposes of the Block Exemption Regulation, parties are competing when they are active on the same product or technology market as a result of the research and development agreement. See art. 1 lett.s) R&D Exemption.

[178] A Potential competitor is defined under the Block Exemption Regulation as an undertaking that, in the absence of the R&D agreement, would, on realistic grounds and not just as a mere theoretical possibility, be likely to undertake, within no more than 3 years, the necessary additional investments or other necessary switching costs to supply a product, technology or process capable of being improved, substituted or replaced by the contract product. Critically on the definition of potential competitor, Lindqvist (2015), p. 187 and similarly Drexl et al. (2010), para. 24, commenting the absence in the same Block Exemption of the innovation market concept.

[179] European Commission, Communication from the Commission- Guidelines on the Applicability of Art. 101 of the Treaty on the Functioning of the European Union to Horizontal Co-operation Agreements, 2011/C 11/01 (14 January 2011), p. 16.

[180] Commissioner Vestager (29 September 2016).

[181] Bundeskartellamt (Oktober 2017), pp. 5–6.

market power on existing product or technology markets.[182] Hence, the market power of the parties can be an indicator of the anticompetitive nature of a research and development agreement.

Moreover it is acknowledged that research cooperations, by decreasing external competitive pressure, can slow down the pace of innovation in the considered sector, this leading to a slower development of new products and services, and also affect competition concerning the final products or services, with resulting price increases.[183]

Especially in case the research and development is directed at a fully new product or service, the anticompetitive effects can regard innovation itself, in terms of reduced quality and variety of possible future products or technologies and, more in general, reduced innovation speed.[184] This occurs in particular when the parties could achieve the research objective fully autonomously, thus also in absence of any collaborating party[185] or when significant competitors on an existing technology market cooperate to develop a new technology that may substitute the old one.[186] In this last case, the cooperation between the two companies may slow down the research process on the new technology, exactly because the parties to the research and development agreement have a strong market position both on the technology and the research market.[187]

Interestingly the Commission also refers to foreclosure effects, arising when the research cooperation involves a player with significant market power, especially in respect to a key technology.[188] This statement is particularly interesting for the case of health data pools that, as illustrated in the analysed case-studies, often involve a digital company, as Google or IBM, with significant market power especially in

[182] European Commission, Communication from the Commission- Guidelines on the Applicability of Art. 101 of the Treaty on the Functioning of the European Union to Horizontal Co-operation Agreements, 2011/C 11/01 (14 January 2011), para 133.

[183] European Commission, Communication from the Commission- Guidelines on the Applicability of Art. 101 of the Treaty on the Functioning of the European Union to Horizontal Co-operation Agreements, 2011/C 11/01 (14 January 2011), para 127.

[184] European Commission, Communication from the Commission- Guidelines on the Applicability of Art. 101 of the Treaty on the Functioning of the European Union to Horizontal Co-operation Agreements, 2011/C 11/01 (14 January 2011), para 138.

[185] European Commission, Communication from the Commission- Guidelines on the Applicability of Art. 101 of the Treaty on the Functioning of the European Union to Horizontal Co-operation Agreements, 2011/C 11/01 (14 January 2011), para 138.

[186] European Commission, Communication from the Commission- Guidelines on the Applicability of Art. 101 of the Treaty on the Functioning of the European Union to Horizontal Co-operation Agreements, 2011/C 11/01 (14 January 2011), para 139.

[187] European Commission, Communication from the Commission- Guidelines on the Applicability of Art. 101 of the Treaty on the Functioning of the European Union to Horizontal Co-operation Agreements, 2011/C 11/01 (14 January 2011), para 139.

[188] European Commission, Communication from the Commission- Guidelines on the Applicability of Art. 101 of the Treaty on the Functioning of the European Union to Horizontal Co-operation Agreements, 2011/C 11/01 (14 January 2011), para 139.

respect to the algorithmic processing infrastructure needed to run the digital research enquiries.[189]

However, the Commission also acknowledges that the foreclosing effects of research and development agreements mostly stem from the related agreements regarding the joint production and marketing of the products or technologies research and development agreements aims at improving or at newly producing, in case these are already sufficiently defined. When this is the case, the foreclosing effects occur mostly in the related products and technology markets.

Moreover, as has been observed in the literature, foreclosure effects particularly often result exactly from public-private partnerships established for the purposes of joint R&D collaborations. Here indeed the agreements usually entail restrictions preventing the public institution to conduct similar competing research after the conclusion of the co-operation.[190] Similarly, smaller firms risks to be foreclosed by larger firms under R&D agreements in the pharmaceutical sector, as a result of agreements with which the larger firm trades its development, testing and distribution skills with the venture or with which the stronger party prohibits the institutions part to the research project to autonomously research and develop the compound or substance object of the agreement.[191]

In respect to restrictions of competition by object, the Commission observes that research and development agreements can serve as a tool to engage in a cartels, this implying the coordination in terms of price fixation, output limitation or market allocation.[192] According to the Commission, the restrictive effects of research and development agreements are likely to occur if the same parties to the agreement entail a strong market position, the entry in the research market is difficult and the innovation rate in respect to the considered research activities is already low.[193]

Similarly, anticompetitive effects can result also from a research agreement between a dominant undertaking and a smaller or even potential competitor who is just about to enter the research market, potentially endangering the incumbent's market power.[194]

---

[189] See supra Chap. 3, Sects. 3.1.1 and 3.1.2.

[190] So Lindqvist (2015), p. 183.

[191] Zain (2006) pp. 350 ff.

[192] European Commission, Communication from the Commission- Guidelines on the Applicability of Art. 101 of the Treaty on the Functioning of the European Union to Horizontal Co-operation Agreements, 2011/C 11/01 (14 January 2011), para 128.

[193] European Commission, Communication from the Commission- Guidelines on the Applicability of Art. 101 of the Treaty on the Functioning of the European Union to Horizontal Co-operation Agreements, 2011/C 11/01 (14 January 2011), para 136.

[194] European Commission, Communication from the Commission- Guidelines on the Applicability of Art. 101 of the Treaty on the Functioning of the European Union to Horizontal Co-operation Agreements, 2011/C 11/01 (14 January 2011), para 136.

6.4.4 Health Data Pools under Art. 101(3) TFEU

Although producing anticompetitive effects, a research and development agreement can be exempted for its efficiency outcomes.

Efficiency considerations are directly incorporated within Article 101(3) TFEU, which allows for exemptions of agreements and practices, which, while having some anticompetitive attributes, have the beneficial effect of contributing to the promotion of technical or economic progress. Hence it is exactly under art. 101(3) TFEU that the innovative potential of a transaction, such as the one involving an information exchange, can be relied on as a defence to a conduct that would be otherwise prohibited.[195]

The conditions under which antitrust enforcers are normatively allowed to positively judge an exchange of information for its efficiency outcomes, even if falling under the prohibition of art. 101(1) TFEU for its anticompetitive effects, are listed under art. 101(3) TFEU and are cumulative.[196] Here it is stated that an agreement can be exempted if it (i) contributes to improving the production or distribution of goods or contribute to promoting technical or economic progress; (ii) allows consumers a fair share of the resulting benefits; (iii) the restrictions it causes are indispensable to the attainment of these objectives; (iv) the agreement must not afford the parties the possibility of climinating competition in respect of a substantial part of the products in question.

Art. 101(3) TFEU is thus the acknowledgment that sometimes an effect-based approach or an "intelligent-design approach", may be exceptionally valuable, provided that a conduct that impairs a proper development of the competitive process still results in some efficiencies and leaves a certain margin for the competitive process to have some margin of development.[197] In this perspective, the exemption to art. 101(1) TFEU reflects a consideration of consumer welfare concerns that goes beyond the safeguard of the mere competition process, in accordance to a more economic approach in the application of competition rules and in the pursuing of the objective of consumer welfare protection.[198]

Following the Commission's Guidelines, once having inferred the anticompetitive effects of information exchanges, these need to be balanced against the countervailing positive, pro-competitive aspects.[199] It could indeed be that the anticompetitive effects are outweighed by the achievement of efficiency-enhancing

[195] Zingales (2018), p. 94.

[196] European Commission, Commission Notice on Restrictions Directly Related and Necessary to Concentrations, 2005/C 56/24 (5 March 2005a), para 38.

[197] Wagner-von Papp (2013), p. 143.

[198] Lindqvist (2015), p. 127.

[199] This is what occurred in the Asnef Equifax case where the European Court of Justice held that although the occurred information exchange could have led to collusive outcomes, the positive outcome stemming from the removal of information asymmetry could outweigh the restrictive effects. See European Court of Justice, Asnef Equifax v. Ausbanc, C-238/05 (23 November 2006).

effects.[200] As the Commission however clarifies, although positively considering efficiencies generated by a transaction, art. 101(3) TFEU relies on the presumption that the elimination of competition generates long term welfare losses that cannot be compensated by short-term efficiencies.[201]

As for the assessment of the anticompetitive effects of the agreements under art. 101(1) TFEU, also the assessment under art. 101(3) TFEU, involving a balancing between the possible anticompetitive effects and the efficiency outcomes, needs to be carried out with regards to the specific market context in which the exchange occurs.[202] In these regards, it has been acknowledged that the main difficulty of the balancing between efficiencies and consumer harm generated by arrangements involving information exchanges is that these can occur in different markets.[203] In this case, a balancing could nonetheless be carried out if the two markets in which the efficiencies and the consumer harm occur are related and both the positive and negative effects occur in respect to the same consumers.[204] The latest interpretation of cross-market efficiencies, however, admits the analysis of efficiencies in a connected market even without consumer commonality, as long as those benefits produce objective advantages for the consumers in the related market.[205]

Overall, the balancing under art. 101(3) TFEU is a multifactor test that expressly takes into account innovation concerns.

The European Commission Guidelines regarding art. 101(3) TFEU provide useful specifications with regards to the exercise required by the provision at stake.[206] First of all the Commission requires a so-called counterfactual comparison between the state of competition in absence of the agreement and the one established as a result of it.[207] For these purposes, the relevant market needs to be defined and regard needs to be taken to the "nature of the products, the market position of the

---

[200] See European Court of Justice, Métropole télévision (M6), Suez-Lyonnaise des eaux, France Télécom and Télévision française 1 SA (TF1) v Commission of the European Communities C-T-112/99 (18 September 2001), para. 74; European Court of Justice, Van den Bergh Foods vs. Commission, C T-65/98 (23 October 2003), para. 107.

[201] European Commission, Commission Notice: Guidelines on the Application of Article 81(3) of the Treaty, 2004/C 101/08 (27 April 2004b), para. 105.

[202] See, with regards to the specific case of price information exchanges, see Stucke (2005), p. 86, stating with regards to the balancing between anticompetitive and pro-competitive effects of information exchanges that "there is no bright-line rule… nor can there be one, given the fact-intensive inquiry and the varying likelihood of pro- and anticompetitive effects".

[203] Kathuria (2016), p. 474.

[204] European Commission, Commission Notice: Guidelines on the Application of Article 81(3) of the Treaty, 2004/C 101/08 (27 April 2004b), para. 43. In addition to this case some strand of the literature has admitted a balancing also in the case of cross-market efficiency, when the market in which the efficiency results is significantly larger than the market in which competition is threatened. Hovenkamp (2011), pp. 556 ff.

[205] Hovenkamp (2011).

[206] European Commission, Commission Notice: Guidelines on the Application of Article 81(3) of the Treaty, 2004/C 101/08 (27 April 2004b), para 74.

[207] Geradin and Girgenson (2013), p. 211.

parties, the market position of competitors, the market position of buyers, the existence of potential competitors and the level of entry barriers".[208]

With regards to the indispensability of the restrictions for the achievements of the legitimate objectives as the improvement of production, the distribution of goods and the promotion of the technical and economic progress, although it apparently resembles the requirement under the ancillarity test, the Commission has provided a more flexible interpretation of the requirement of indispensability under art. 101(3) TFEU, referring it to restrictions that are "reasonably necessary" for the efficiency in question.[209] This means that under art. 101(3) TFEU the assessment concerns whether more efficiencies are produced with the agreement and the related restrictions, than in the absence of such agreement and restrictions.[210]

6.4.4.1 Technological and Economic Progress Under Art. 101(3) TFEU

The efficiencies stemming from potentially anticompetitive agreements relevant under art. 101(3) TFEU are mainly of economic nature.

This is suggested by the Guidelines regarding art. 101(3) TFEU that specify how the consideration of goals set by other Treaty provisions is allowed only to the extent that they cannot be included under the four conditions set under art. 101(3) TFEU.[211] This clarification reflects a strictly economic evaluation of efficiencies under art. 101(3) TFEU, which allows for the consideration of broader welfare benefits, of social nature, only to the extent these are connected to economic efficiencies.[212]

Accordingly, the European Commission has granted the exception under art. 101(3) TFEU to research and development agreements combining research and development departments of competitors or potential competitors, for their contribution to the technical and economic progress and, as a reflex of that, for their promotion of the creation of the internal market.[213]

---

[208] European Commission, Commission Notice: Guidelines on the Application of Article 81(3) of the Treaty, 2004/C 101/08 (27 April 2004b), para 27.

[209] European Commission, Commission Notice: Guidelines on the Application of Article 81(3) of the Treaty, 2004/C 101/08 (27 April 2004b), para. 73. In this perspective, the test under art. 101(3) TFEU allows for greater discretion than what occurs under the ancillarity test under art. 101(1) TFEU. See supra Sect. 6.4.2.

[210] European Commission, Commission Notice: Guidelines on the Application of Article 81(3) of the Treaty, 2004/C 101/08 (27 April 2004b), para 74.

[211] European Commission, Commission Notice: Guidelines on the Application of Article 81(3) of the Treaty, 2004/C 101/08 (27 April 2004b), para. 42.

[212] This is what occurred with regards to the assessment of social concerns, related to environmental protection, considered by the European Commission, Exxon/Shell (18 May 1994b); to sustainable development, as considered in European Commission, CECED (24 January 1999a); European Commission, Ford/Volkswagen, N. IV/33.814 (23 December 1992); European Commission, Stichting Baksteen (29 April 1994a). For the literature see, Rosenboom (December 2013), p. 19.

[213] for a case law on the Commission's decisions regarding anticompetitive but exempted R&D Collaborations, see Lindqvist (2015), pp. 127 ff., highlighting an evolution from a very first phase,

A similar favourable treatment has been given in the case law of the European Commission to collaborations established for industrial restructuring purposes. These have been expressly taken into consideration by the European Commission under art. 101(3) TFEU as means to increase the competitiveness of European businesses.[214]

In the *BPCL/ICI*[215] and *ENI/Montedison* cases,[216] the Commission maintained that the agreements made for the purposes of overcoming industry's structural process problems, would have been more effective than if the undertakings would have faced such issues separately.[217]

Along the same lines, the Commission also granted exemption to an agreement between *Bayer* and *BP Chemicals*, especially highlighting the technological improvements to the industrial organisation of the involved companies, capable of boosting companies' competitiveness.[218]

The advancements in terms of competitiveness brought about by an agreement have been positively evaluated also in the *Optical Fibre* decision, where the creation of a joint venture has been considered by the Commission as a means for technology transfer from the United States to the European Community. This transfer has been deemed "essential to enable the European companies to withstand competition from non-Community producers, especially in the USA and Japan, in an area of fast moving technology".[219]

Lastly, the notion of technological progress under art. 101(3) TFEU has been employed to include also consumer protection concerns.[220] As a result, the *Asahi/*

---

in which the Commission affirmed that arrangements between non-competing parties or arrangements between competitors that neither limit third parties' ability to compete, nor their market position would be deemed per se lawful and thus not falling under the prohibition under art. 101 TFEU; to a second phase, in which this lenient approach was then reconsidered, in respect to research & development agreements performed by large undertakings. See also Ullrich (2003), pp. 191 ff.

[214] See lately, European Commission (19 April 2014c).

[215] European Commission, BPCL/ICI (19 July 1984).

[216] European Commission, ENI/Montedison (4 December 1986b).

[217] European Commission, BPCL/ICI (19 July 1984) para 37; European Commission, ENI/Montedison (4 December 1986b), para 31.

[218] European Commission, Bayer/BP Chemicals (6 June 1994c), para 27.

[219] European Commission, Optical Fibre (14 July 1986a), para 59. See also European Commission, Olivetti/Canon (22 December 1987), para 54.

[220] For a critical assessment of the policy option of including consumer protection concerns within the notion of technological progress under art. 101(3) TFEU, see Monti (2002), p. 1076, where the Author observes how "using the power to exempt as a means of forcing the parties to accept unrelated obligations appears to be a misuse of powers by the Commission", in that "it forces the parties to rewrite their bargain to comply with regulatory norms to protect consumers which were not legislated according to the appropriate procedures established by EC Law, but merely imposed by the Commission".

Saint Gobain agreement was exempted in the view of the enhancement of product safety it was deemed to bring about.[221]

The recalled case law provides an interesting benchmark for the inclusion of health data-driven innovation under the art. 101(3) TFEU exemption, in view of the specific industrial and consumer-related efficiencies- generated by both process and product innovation- health data exchange agreements can lead to.

In respect to the specific case of health data sharing agreements, the question needs to be addressed regarding whether also public health benefits stemming exactly from the pooling of health data could gain relevance under the exemption to art. 101(1) TFEU.

Interestingly, in the *Mètropole* ruling, the European Court of Justice has provided a wide interpretation of art. 101(3) TFEU, stating that "the Commission is entitled to base itself on considerations connected with the pursuit of the public interest in order to grant exemption under art. 81(3)".[222]

Despite the acknowledgment of the possibility of incorporating public interest concerns within the analysis under art. 101 TFEU, health concerns have been rarely considered by the European case law under art. 101(3) TFEU,[223] and mainly in combination to environmental interests.[224]

The failure to properly assess the public interest dimension of agreements in the pharmaceutical sector has been well highlighted by the European Court of Justice, in the *GlaxosmithKline* case,[225] where the Court, upheld the argument made by the Court of First Instance, which had criticised the insufficient the analysis by the Commission of the efficiencies related to the transaction, and had in particular stressed the importance of considering the specific legal and economic context of the pharmaceutical sector for the purposes of the evaluation of efficiencies under art. 101(3) TFEU.[226]

---

[221] European Commission, Asahi/Saint-Gobain (16 December 1994d).

[222] European Court of Justice, Métropole télévision (M6), Suez-Lyonnaise des eaux, France Télécom and Télévision française 1 SA (TF1) v Commission of the European Communities C- T-112/99 (18 September 2001), para 118.

[223] Van de Gronden (2011), p. 275.

[224] In the Exxon/Shell case, for example, the avoidance of health risks related to the environmental advancements deriving from the transactions were considered as a further reason to exempt the transaction under art. 101(3) TFEU. In the specific case, indeed, the reduction in the use of raw materials and the production of plastic waste has been considered by the Commission as "beneficial to many consumers". As a result, the related environmental and health improvements were deemed by the agency as "of increasing public concern". European Commission, Exxon/Shell (18 May 1994b), para 71.

[225] European Court of Justice, GlaxoSmithKline Services Unlimited vs. Commission of the European Communities, Joined Cases C 501/06 P, C-513/06 P, C-515/06 P and C 519/06 P (6 October 2009b), paras 111 ff. The case involved an agreement regarding the restrictions on parallel trade, which the Commission had found to infringe art. 101(1) TFEU.

[226] European Court of Justice, GlaxoSmithKline Services Unlimited vs. Commission of the European Communities, Joined Cases C 501/06 P, C-513/06 P, C-515/06 P and C 519/06 P (6 October 2009b), para 118.

However, it needs to be acknowledged that the failed inclusion of the consideration of health-related efficiencies largely depends on the fact that the health sector is regulated and protected by other branches of European Union law, especially after Lisbon, and mostly by other provisions at national level.

The so far missed inclusion within art. 101(3) TFEU assessments of public interest considerations related to health[227] could be however restored as a consequence of the growing attention given to health-related issues at European level, and in particular in the context of the Digital Single Market Strategy. As has been shown, in particular within the Digital Single Market Strategy, health efficiencies are treated in the context of digital economic efficiencies, if not *as outright* economic efficiencies.[228]

This could maybe ground a greater consideration of health-related efficiencies brought about by the digitalisation of health products—as deriving from arrangements regarding the exchange of health information-, both in terms of health products innovations (*i.e.* personalisation of health products) and health process innovations (*i.e.* faster delivery of health care services through digitalisation).[229]

These efficiencies could be worth of autonomous consideration- and not only for their purely economic relevance- for the purposes of the competition law assessment of health information exchanges under art. 101(3) TFEU.[230]

However, the possible consideration of health data pools under art. 101-(3) requires a hermeneutical operation that takes into account the peculiarities of both data-driven innovation and the health sector: in the digital environment, innovation patterns are strongly affected by uncertainty and unpredictability, both wit regards the subjects taking part to it and the object of research and development. The uncertainty and unpredictability, together with the speed, characterising data-driven innovation are greater than what occurs in respect to non-digital innovation.[231]

At a deeper level, thus, the very features of data-driven innovation trigger a careful assessment of how data-driven innovation can fit into the notion of "technical and economic progress" as expressed under art. 101(3) TFEU.

[227] See also Monti (2002), p. 1090.

[228] See supra Chap. 4, Sect. 4.3.1.

[229] See supra Chap. 3, Sect. 3.3.2.

[230] This is suggested, with regards to more general data-driven efficiencies, by Lindqvist (6 November 2018b), p. 7.

[231] It needs however to be underlined that uncertainty is a structural feature of every type of innovation. See in these regards the observations by Jalonen and Lehtonen (2012), pp. 12 ff. where the Authors highlight eight forms of uncertainty affecting the innovation process: technological uncertainty, market uncertainty, regulatory uncertainty, social and political uncertainty, acceptance and legitimacy uncertainty, managerial uncertainty, timing uncertainty, and consequence uncertainty. Uncertainty of data-driven innovation is in particular stressed by. Zarsky (2015), pp. 115 ff.

For these purposes, there are significant obstacles to the incorporation of data-driven innovation concerns into the considered exemption.[232]

Indeed, for the application of the exemption, the Commission requires a detailed explanation and description regarding “the nature of the efficiencies and how and why they constitute an objective economic benefit”.[233] This means that the parties to the agreement, and more precisely to the information exchange, must give proof of the precise efficiencies that will be generated by the transaction and that will positively impact the market.[234] In these regards, the precise description of the efficiencies stemming from data sharing agreements and the related research activities proves to be problematic first because of the difficulties to figure out beforehand where data-driven innovation efforts will lead to, given the different epistemiological approach that data-driven innovation follows operationally. As has already pointed out,[235] indeed, data-driven research does not follow the traditional hypothesis/testing process but rather subverts this traditional scientific discovery process by delivering hypothesis only after the analytical process has been run. As a result, the idea of predetermining ex ante the outcomes of the innovation process appears to be inadequate in respect to the above-highlighted features of the big data discovery process, if not directly in harsh contrast with it.

A first steps towards a greater consideration of data-driven innovation under art. 101(3) TFEU could be given by the relaxation of the requirements of specificities and quantifiability of the efficiencies by competition law authorities, eventually substituting these parameters to others more adherent to the specificities of the data-driven innovation process.[236]

These other parameters could relate for example to the disclosure of the functioning criteria of the analytical models used to process the pooled information, and the provision of an “impact assessment” of the operation involving health data exchanges. This information could indeed well forecast expected technological efficiencies brought about by an established data pool. This procedural information could be acquired by competition authorities through collaboration with data protection authorities.[237]

[232] Zingales (2018), pp. 94 ff.

[233] European Commission, Commission Notice: Guidelines on the Application of Article 81(3) of the Treaty, 2004/C 101/08 (27 April 2004b), para 57.

[234] European Commission, Commission Notice: Guidelines on the Application of Article 81(3) of the Treaty, 2004/C 101/08 (27 April 2004b), para 58.

[235] See supra Chap. 2, Sect. 2.1.2.

[236] A departure from the specificities and quantifiability parameters in light of the different features of the new economy is suggested by De La Mano (13 February 2009), para. 52.

[237] The issue will be better addressed infra in Chap. 7, regarding remedies to health data pooling practices, under Sects. 7.2.2 and 7.3.6.

6.4.5 Health Data Pools under the Research and Development Block Exemption

The European Commission has specifically considered the peculiarities of innovation markets and the innovation-based transactions occurring in the context of them, by specifying the application of the exemption under art. 101(3) TFEU to so-called research and development collaborations.

Indeed, the consideration of the very features of research and development collaboration for innovation purposes has justified an autonomous consideration of them under the competition framework, in the form of a regulatory approach that generally evaluates them positively, provided certain normatively set conditions are met.

The direct acknowledgment that the combination of complementary skills or assets is source to substantial efficiencies in the field of research and development, has resulted into a block exemption regulation exactly based on art. 101(3) TFEU and specifically regarding research and development agreements.[238]

The Block Exemption needs to be complemented with the statements in the already mentioned Guidelines on Horizontal Co-operation Agreements,[239] that have the exact aim to guide the competition law analysis in the assessment of agreements structuring multi-firm innovation processes.

The R&D Block Exemption is based on the presumption that research and development agreements do not cause restrictive effects on competition[240] and should thus fall outside competition law enforcement's sphere. As the same R&D Block Exemption specifies, indeed, the exemption shall apply only to those agreements that violate art. 101(1) TFEU.[241]

Hence, for the purposes of the Research and Development block exemption, the notion of research and development collaboration encompasses a wide range of agreements that need to be examined in relation to the specific characteristics of the transaction and the underlying market conditions. Indeed, the definition of research and development agreement given by art. 1(a) of the Block Exemption is quite broad, potentially including "joint research and development of contract products or contract technologies" linked to "joint exploitation of the results of the research and development".

Interestingly, the Commission expressly acknowledges that research and development agreements may include the transfer of know-how between competitors.

[238]European Commission, Commission Regulation EU N. 1217/2010 of 14 December 2010 on the application of Article 101(3) of the Treaty on the Functioning of the European Union to certain categories of research and development agreements (18 December 2010b). Block exemption.

[239]European Commission, Communication from the Commission- Guidelines on the Applicability of Art. 101 of the Treaty on the Functioning of the European Union to Horizontal Co-operation Agreements, 2011/C 11/01 (14 January 2011), para 50.

[240]See Recital 4 R&D Block Exemption.

[241]Art. 2(1) R&D Block Exemption.

According to the Commission, know-how includes a "package of non-patented information, resulting from experience and testing, which is *secret*, *substantial* and *identified*".[242] In these specific regard, the same Block Exemption Regulation specifies that "secret" means that the know-how is not generally known or accessible[243]; "substantial" means that the know-how includes information that is "*indispensable* for the manufacture of the contract product or the application of the contract processes"[244]; and "identified" means that the know-how "is described in a sufficiently comprehensive manner so as to make it possible to verify that it fulfils the criteria of secrecy and substantiality".[245]

These statements are particularly interesting for they admit that research and development agreements can involve the transfer of information that is necessary for the conduction of research. This means, more concretely, that provided the information shared among the parties adheres to the features of secretness, substantiality and identification outlined in art. 1 of the block exemption, health data pools established for digital health research purposes could fall under the special regime provided for research and development agreements.

The Research and Development Block Exemption considers research and development agreements as benign research co-operations subject to specific conditions and requirements.

As a general premise, it needs to be recalled that the application of the R&D block exemption is conditioned upon the respect of a market ceiling above which the favourable regime is not applicable anymore[246] and upon the absence of "hard core"[247] or "black-clauses" codified in the Block Exemption.[248]

The Black clauses outlined in the Block Exemption concern the restriction of the freedom of participants to carry out research independently or in cooperation with others in fields disconnected from the relevant field of research or prohibiting the challenging of the validity of intellectual property rights resulting from the research cooperation.

If such clauses are absent, the block exemption works as an outright safe harbour for companies engaging in research and development collaboration.

---

[242] Art. 1(i) R&D Block Exemption. Emphasis added.

[243] Art. 1(j) R&D Block Exemption.

[244] Art. 1(k) R&D Block Exemption.

[245] So art. 2(10) of the R&D Block Exemption.

[246] Art. 4(2) R&D Exemption, under which the application of the exemption is conditioned to the requirement that the involved parties' market share does not exceed 25% on the relevant product and technology.

[247] Hard core clauses traditionally concern price fixing, output restrictions, naked allocation of markets or customers.

[248] Black clauses outlined in the Block Exemption concern the restriction of the freedom of participants to carry out research independently or in cooperation with others in fields disconnected from the relevant field of research or prohibiting the challenging of the validity of intellectual property rights resulting from the research cooperation.

Against the backdrop of these premises, in the case the agreement is thus not per se illegal because of the presence of hard clauses or not per se legal according to the parameters established by the Guidelines on Horizontal Co-operation,[249] but has rather anticompetitive outcomes not outweighed by efficiencies, the safe harbour of the block exemption is still applicable.

The application of the R&D exemption is subject to the conditions highlighted under art. 3 R&D Block Exemption, requiring that the results of the research cooperation are made available to all the involved parties, without exclusions, including "any resulting intellectual property right and know-how, for the purposes of further research and development and exploitation, as soon as they become available"[250]; that all the parties have access to any pre-existing know how to which one or more of the parties to the agreement are entitled and that results to be "indispensable" for the exploitation of the research's results[251]; that any joint exploitation may only pertain to results that are protected through intellectual property rights or know-how, and that are, again, indispensable for the manufacture of the contract products or technologies[252]; and that the parties having the obligation of manufacture contract products or technologies fulfil orders for suppliers of the contract products also from other parties.[253]

Ultimately, the exemption covers collaborative research endeavours only for a timeframe of 7 years.[254]

The analysis of the provisions of the research and development block exemption together with the statements entailed in the Guidelines on Horizontal Co-operation shows that very few research and development agreements actually would trigger a competition law enforcement.[255] Indeed, research and development collaborations either do not infringe art. 101(1) TFEU in accordance with the broad interpretation given to the notion of non-competing parties by the Guidelines on Horizontal Co-operation, or they would violate art. 101(1) TFEU but be exempted under the block exemption, provided the conditions set by the same block exemption are met. As a result, it could be said that the only research and development agreements that happen to infringe art. 101(1) TFEU are those that do not meet the conditions established under art. 3 of the R&D Block Exemption or that exceed the market share thresholds set under the Block Exemption.

Still, in these cases, the Commission highlights that the agreements falling outside the scope of the Block Exemption do not necessarily have anticompetitive

[249] See supra Sect. 6.4.2.
[250] Art. 3(2) R&D Exemption.
[251] Art. 3(3) R&D Exemption.
[252] Art. 3(4) R&D Exemption.
[253] Art. 3(5) R&D Exemption.
[254] Art. 4(1) R&D Exemption.
[255] Lindqvist (2015), p. 195.

effects.[256] However, it is observed that the stronger the market power of the parties is the greater the reduction of competition in innovation is, this making the chances higher that the considered agreement has restrictive effects on competition.

The efficiencies of the research alliances can nonetheless be still evaluated up to be exempted under art. 101(3) TFEU.[257]

Under these premises, the R&D Block Exemption reflects the Commission's intent to regulate the increasing number of research and development-based firms, promoting their existence for the sake of the technological development of the internal market and the European economy more generally.[258]

Against this backdrop, the R&D Block Exemption positively considers competition restrictions when they are generated by an overall welfare enhancing research and development agreement. In this case, indeed, also these apparently anticompetitive restrictions serve the purposes of the agreement and are thus worth of being exempted from the competition enforcement.

In these regards, indeed, it is interesting to observe that the same R&D Block Exemption allows for restrictions to the rights of exploitation of the results of the research and development and to the access of the correspondent results for the purposes of the exploitation of them.[259] In addition to this it admits that research entities which supply research and development as a commercial service without normally exploiting the results of the research itself, can suffer restrictions regarding future research.[260] Finally, it allows also reciprocal compensation among the parties for the access to the results for the purposes of further research or exploitation.[261]

The favourable approach regarding research collaborations is already reflected in some early R&D cases, as *Asahi/StGobain*,[262] *KSB/Goulds/Lowara/ITT*[263] and *Continental/Michelin*,[264] where the Commission allowed for collaboration between undertakings, which held a considerable market power on their respective product

[256] European Commission, Communication from the Commission- Guidelines on the Applicability of Art. 101 of the Treaty on the Functioning of the European Union to Horizontal Co-operation Agreements, 2011/C 11/01 (14 January 2011), para 135.

[257] Lindqvist (2015), pp. 206–207.

[258] Lindqvist (2015), p. 208.

[259] Art.3(2) R&D Exemption.

[260] Art.3(2) R&D Exemption.

[261] Art.3(2) R&D Exemption. The compensation needs however to be reasonably low and thus not be so high as to impede actual access of the results.

[262] European Commission, Asahi/Saint-Gobain (31 December 1994e). In this case the research collaboration has been exempted under art. 101(3) TFEU and not under the Block Exemption. However, since it concerns a research and development collaboration, it seemed appropriate to mention it in this paragraph specifically dedicated to research and development agreements.

[263] European Commission, KSB/Goulds/Lowara/ITT (25 January 1991).

[264] European Commission, Continental/Michelin (10 November 1988).

markets and were the very few research poles in the relevant industries.[265] In all these cases the Commission positively welcomed that such research collaborations were aimed at creating new technology standards, that are new basic technologies for future markets, in which old technologies will be substituted by newly developed technology.

The mentioned cases thus well reflect how research collaborations have been treated leniently and even promoted by the Commission, despite the risk, expressly acknowledged by the Commission,[266] of the creation of monopoly positions on future markets and of the exclusion of minor research institutions from current lines of technological research.

Under these premises, it can be said that in respect to research and development collaborations, the European competition law embraces a Schumpeterian conception of innovation, according to which the analysis' barycentre is not placed on the market structure but rather on the technological progress a same research agreement brings about.[267]

From a first, more practical perspective, the lenient treatment granted to research collaborations can also be rooted in the practical difficulty of figuring out beforehand the anticompetitive outcomes that research and development collaborations will have in new technology markets.[268]

However, it needs to be observed that the rising importance of research collaborations have lately triggered a renewed attention by the Commission regarding the competitive harms exactly deriving from research-based market concentrations. The issue will be assessed in the next chapter concerning the legal remedies needed in the data-driven health research environment.

From a second- more systematic- perspective, by preventing inefficient market segmentation in the field of technological and research cooperation, both the R&D Exemption and art. 101(3) TFEU ultimately appear to serve market integration objectives, as promoted by the "free flow" of research and technological assets among companies.[269] In this light, the exemptions are to be considered as a regulatory subset of the European competition framework, which calibrate the competitive process in a way that is adherent to the attainment of the broader objectives of the European Treaties, "in particular the creation of a single market achieving conditions similar to those of a domestic market".[270]

---

[265] European Commission, Asahi/Saint-Gobain (31 December 1994e), para. 16; European Commission, KSB/Goulds/Lowara/ITT (25 January 1991), para. 24; 34; European Commission, Continental/Michelin (10 November 1988), para. 20; 29.

[266] European Commission, KSB/Goulds/Lowara/ITT (25 January 1991), para 13.

[267] For similar considerations, although in a US perspective, see Carrier (2008), p. 403.

[268] Lindqvist (2015), p. 127.

[269] The link between art. 101 TFEU (formerly art. 81) and market integration objectives had been already stressed by the Commission in the White Paper on Modernization. See European Commission (28 April 1999b) executive summary points 4 and 8.

[270] This is the definition of workable competition by the European Court of Justice, Metro I vs. Commission of the European Communities, C-26/76 (25 October 1977), para 20.

Against this backdrop, the R&D Block Exemption appears to reaffirm the hierarchy of European policy objectives already expressed by the European Commission in its White Paper on Modernization, where free movement principles take priority over competition.[271]

The competition law framework concerning research and development collaboration is very likely to gain new relevance in the context of the digital economy, and especially in the pharmaceutical sector, which, as has been illustrated, is ever more evolving around a collaborative paradigm putting in connection traditional health research stakeholders with technology-based undertakings.[272]

In light of the new digital health research context, the research and development block exemption could well provide a normative ground for the promotion of new research alliances based on health data pools.[273] Indeed, as has been illustrated, the newly emerging digital health collaborations, appear to be conducted among businesses active in different markets, which thus would be considered as non-competing businesses under the above-recalled criteria established by the Guidelines on Horizontal Co-operation.

The fact that these collaborations are established among what under the Commission's interpretation are to be regarded as non-competing businesses would presumably make these same collaborations fall outside the scope of art. 101(1) TFEU. Moreover, even if the parties to such research projects would be considered potential competitors[274] and the resulting agreement would be found violating art. 101(1) TFEU with the need to resort to the R&D block exemption- the wide notion of research and development agreement provided under art. 1 R&D block exemption, expressly encompassing data transfers, appears suited to include also health research data pools.

Hence, the R&D Block Exemption could well favour the free flow of research valuable information in accordance to the market integration objectives related to the digital single market.[275]

As it has been already observed in respect to the General Data Protection Law's research exemption, also under the competition law's block exemption, a positive attention to what is data-driven research, meaning data analytical enquiries effectively promoting technological and thus economic progress, and what are conversely ordinary commercial data-driven activities, would be needed to avoid the risk that sensitive data exchanges between various actors in the digital internal market bypass a proper competition law scrutiny.

Surely, the conditions set out by art. 2 as well as the market share thresholds are first, useful, safeguards for an excessive application of the R&D block exemptions to

[271] European Commission (28 April 1999b), para 6.

[272] See supra Chap. 3, Sects. 3.1 and 3.2.

[273] Similar considerations are made by Richter and Slowinski (2019), pp. 22–23.

[274] See in these regards, the considerations concerning the new competitive courses between traditional pharmaceutical companies and high-tech companies. See supra Chap. 3, Sects. 3.1.2.1.

[275] See supra Chap. 4, Sect. 4.3.2.

data-driven research collaborations. However, a proper reconsideration of the competition law exemption to art. 101(1) TFEU in light of the peculiar features of the digital research would be needed in a near future, given the increase of the importance of pre-market competition in the digital economy,[276] as well as the difficulty to define market shares in digital multi-sided markets.[277]

6.4.6 *Health Data Pools under the Technology Transfer Block Exemption*

In the second chapter it has been observed how (health) data pools involve most of the times not only the sharing a varied type of data, but also the pooling of the processing technology needed to analyse the data and thus to run scientific enquiries over it. With regards to the processing technology, hence, health data pools could find further grounds for exemption under another block exemption, regarding technology transfers.[278]

The Commission establishes a presumption of lawfulness of technology transfers "irrespective of the market position of the parties"[279]: as it is observed, indeed, "most licence agreements do not restrict competition and create procompetitive efficiencies. Indeed, licensing as such is procompetitive as it leads to dissemination of technology and promotes innovation by the licensor and the licensee(s)".[280]

In the Guidelines, the Commission specifies that a technology transfer agreement is to be deemed as pro-competitive especially in case the "(a) participation in the pool creation process is open to all interested technology rights owners; (b) sufficient safeguards are adopted to ensure that only essential technologies (which therefore necessarily are also complements) are pooled; (c) sufficient safeguards are adopted to ensure that exchange of sensitive information (such as pricing and output data) is restricted to what is necessary for the creation and operation of the pool; (d) the pooled technologies are licensed into the pool on a non-exclusive basis; (e) the pooled technologies are licensed out to all potential licensees on FRAND terms; (f) the parties contributing technology to the pool and the licensees are free to

276 Lindqvist (2018b), p. 213.

277 See M. Patterson (2013), pp. 509–513, observing how the possibility to share information also at low cost, require a reassessment of the notion of market power in the digital environment, and, in particular of the concepts underlying the notion of market power. In these regards, for example, the notion of market share would fail to provide a strong basis for the definition of dominance or market power.

278 European Commission, Commission Regulation EU N. 316/2014 of 21 March 2014 on the application of Article 101(3) of the Treaty on the Functioning of the European Union to Categories of Technology Transfer Agreements (28 March 2014a) (hereafter TT block exemption). For the literature see Rab (2014), pp. 436 ff.

279 TT block exemption, para 261.

280 TT block exemption, para 9.

challenge the validity and the essentiality of the pooled technologies, and; (g) the parties contributing technology to the pool and the licensee remain free to develop competing products and technology".[281]

Under these premises, it can nonetheless be that technology transfers have restrictive effects on competition, thus infringing art. 101(1) TFEU. Also in this case, however, these agreements could still be exempted under the Technology Transfer Exemption.

In this respect, the potential relevance of health data pools under the technology transfer block exemption is quite controversial.[282]

The concerns regarding the application of the rules concerning technology transfers to data pools mainly relate to the fact that traditional technology transfers normally include non-competing patents and are devices to collect royalties, in which technologies are defined in the standard setting agreements. Data pools, conversely, are agreements involving exchanges of information that are the testing material and the design material for technologies that cannot be *ex ante* properly defined,[283] also in the view of the generation of always new secondary-generated data as a result of the processing investigations.

Despite these hurdles, the qualification of health data pools as technology transfers is nonetheless suggested by both a normative and a practical perspective.

From the first standpoint, as has been already acknowledged under the R&D block exemption, also the TT block exemption makes reference to data as possible object of a technology transfer agreement, allowing the licensor to transfer know-how, defined as "practical information, resulting from experience and testing".[284] Under the TT block exemption, know-how shares exactly the same above-recalled features of secretness, substantiality and identifiability.[285]

From a practical perspective, it has been acknowledged that the technical infrastructure employed to set up a health data pool is very similar to a patent pool,[286] this triggering the relevance also of the soft regulation entailed in the Technology Transfer Guidelines specifically regarding the establishment of technology pools.[287] As occurs with patent pools, that can involve the licensing of essential[288]

[281] TT block exemption, para 261.

[282] Colangelo and Borgogno (5 April 2019), p. 12.

[283] Colangelo and Borgogno (5 April 2019), p. 13.

[284] Art. 1(i) TT Block Exemption.

[285] Art. 1(i) TT Block Exemption.

[286] Lindqvist (6 November 2018b), p. 17.

[287] TT Block Exemption, para 244 ff., where technology pools are defined as "arrangements whereby two or more parties assemble a package of technology which is licensed not only to contributors to the pool but also to third parties. In terms of their structure technology pools can take the form of simple arrangements between a limited number of parties or of elaborate organisational arrangements whereby the organisation of the licensing of the pooled technologies is entrusted to a separate entity".

[288] TT Block Exemption, para 252 providing the definition of "essential technology".

and non-substitutable[289] patents, also some data pools, as health research data pools can involve the aggregation of data that can be both *essential* for the programmed research and of *non-substitutable* nature, such it is the case of sophisticated clinical trials data owned by pharmaceutical companies and "real world" digital health-related data collected by digital companies.

Moreover, it can be argued that as in traditional technology pools where technology are protected by patent that are licensed within the pools, also in (health) data pools, the data are usually covered by some form of intellectual property rights,[290] mainly trade secrets and database rights that are "licensed" to the pool members.[291]

However, it needs to be remembered, that just as the R&D block exemption, also the TT block exemption is conditioned upon the respect of some requirements.[292] These relate to the absence of any obligation of the licensee to grant an exclusive license,[293] the absence of the prohibition borne by a party to challenge the validity of an intellectual property right[294] and ultimately the absence of a clause limiting the ability of any of the parties to the agreement to carry out research and development and to exploit their own technology rights.[295]

The applicability of the technology transfer block exemption to health data pools is further restrained by a last provision of the same block exemption regulation, stating that in case of applicability of the Research and development block exemption, this last exemption absorbs the technology transfer exemption, which thus becomes not applicable.[296]

Hence, if a health data pool is linked to a research and development agreement relevant for the purposes of the application of the R&D block exemption, the same health data pool will be granted leniency under the R&D block exemption, instead of under the TT block exemption.

6.5 Health Data Pools as Information Exchanges Under Arts. 101(1) and 101(3) TFEU

The analysis above has illustrated the competitive relevance of health data pools as part of research and development agreements. It has shown how both exceptions under art. 101.3 TFEU and under the relevant block exemptions could ground a favourable treatment of health information exchanges that are inscribed in a specific

289 TT Block Exemption, para 254 providing the definition of "substitutable technology".

290 In these regards, see supra Chap. 2, Sect. 2.2.2.

291 Supra Chap. 2, Sect. 2.2.4.

292 Art. 5 TT Block Exemption.

293 Art. 5(1-a) TT Block Exemption.

294 Art. 5(1-b) TT Block Exemption.

295 Art. 5(2) TT Block Exemption.

296 Art. 9 TT Block Exemption.

research project. The link of research alliances conducted through the sharing of data to a promised technical development is positively regarded under European competition law, which therefore tolerates also possible anticompetitive effects, exempting them.

Different considerations are to be conversely made if health data pools, that is health information exchanges are not part of a research and development agreement and are thus self-standing information exchanges.

As research and development agreements, also self-standing information exchanges are expressly taken into consideration in the Commission's Guidelines on Horizontal Cooperation.

As a premise, however, it needs to be said that the Commission's Guidelines appear to refer to information exchanges in non-digital markets, where information exchanges—as the Commission clearly suggests—involve the sharing of information regarding firms' future conduct on the market,[297] such as the firms' respective commercial policies[298] or data concerning future prices or quantities.[299] More precisely, the information exchanges the Guidelines refer to, are the ones that reduce market uncertainties[300] and thus increase the likelihood of anticompetitive outcomes.[301]

Hence, the Guidelines do not appear to be properly tailored to exchanges having the specific object of digital personal data. Nonetheless some interesting suggestions can be drawn in respect to the competitive relevance of sensitive personal data exchanges. Indeed, the same Guidelines include within the list of strategically relevant information also, customer lists, that is information regarding customers,[302] which can well include also personal data.

---

[297] See in this regard, European Commission, Cobelpa/VNP (8 September 1977), para. 29, where the Commission refers the exchange of information concerning prices, discounts, price increases and reductions, rebates and general terms of sale, supply and payment to "the desire to coordinate market strategies and to create conditions of competition deriving from normal market conditions, by replacing the risks of pricing competition by practical cooperation".

[298] European Commission, Communication from the Commission- Guidelines on the Applicability of Art. 101 of the Treaty on the Functioning of the European Union to Horizontal Co-operation Agreements, 2011/C 11/01 (14 January 2011), para 62.

[299] European Commission, Communication from the Commission- Guidelines on the Applicability of Art. 101 of the Treaty on the Functioning of the European Union to Horizontal Co-operation Agreements, 2011/C 11/01 (14 January 2011), para 74.

[300] European Commission, Communication from the Commission- Guidelines on the Applicability of Art. 101 of the Treaty on the Functioning of the European Union to Horizontal Co-operation Agreements, 2011/C 11/01 (14 January 2011), para 78.

[301] See in this regard Advocate General Darmond, Opinion in, Ahlström Osakeyhtiö and Others vs. Commission of the European Communities, C-89/85, 104/85, C-114/85, C-116/85, C-117/85 and C-125/85 to C-129/85 (7 July 1992), para 173, observing that information exchanges between competitors enable the involved firms to get an assurance with regard to "the conduct to be expected of their competitors" so that each of them get to know the future actions of the others.

[302] European Commission, Communication from the Commission- Guidelines on the Applicability of Art. 101 of the Treaty on the Functioning of the European Union to Horizontal Co-operation Agreements, 2011/C 11/01 (14 January 2011), para 86.

From a first perspective, the Guidelines on horizontal co-operation affirm that information exchanges are not related to a presumption of unlawfulness under art. 101(1) TFEU. To the very contrary, information exchanges are positively regarded as "a common feature of many competitive markets and may generate various types of efficiency gains. It may solve problems of information asymmetries, thereby making markets more efficient".[303] Moreover, it is suggested that if the exchanges regard complementary informational assets, they are likely to generate "great economic benefits", as, amongst others, faster innovation rates.[304]

Along these lines, the Commission stresses the efficiency outcomes of information exchanges, acknowledging their structural relevance in many competitive markets. In these regards, information exchanges are considered for their efficiency gains in terms of, *inter alia*, the improvement of "internal efficiency through benchmarking against each other's best practices"; the saving of costs related to the "reduction of inventories"; the "quicker delivery of perishable products to consumers"; and the reduction of consumer search costs and their improvement of choice.[305] In addition to this, the Commission stresses the advantages of information exchanges for the purposes of risk sharing between the firms involved in the exchange, the creation of economies of scale and the related cost savings, the reduction of information asymmetries, the transfer of know-how and ultimately the enhancement of product variety and quality, with the resulting overall fostering of the pace of innovation.[306]

Against this backdrop, the Commission first highlights that information sharing can be a means for firms to coordinate, resulting in restrictive effects of competition as result of the reach of a common understanding on the terms of coordination or of the increase of the internal stability of a collusive outcome on the market.[307]

The collusion effect is the primary antitrust concern associated to information exchanges,[308] providing the firms with complete information and thus helping them to find a particular collusive equilibrium.

---

[303] European Commission, Communication from the Commission- Guidelines on the Applicability of Art. 101 of the Treaty on the Functioning of the European Union to Horizontal Co-operation Agreements, 2011/C 11/01 (14 January 2011), para 56.

[304] European Commission, Communication from the Commission- Guidelines on the Applicability of Art. 101 of the Treaty on the Functioning of the European Union to Horizontal Co-operation Agreements, 2011/C 11/01 (14 January 2011), para 2.

[305] European Commission, Communication from the Commission- Guidelines on the Applicability of Art. 101 of the Treaty on the Functioning of the European Union to Horizontal Co-operation Agreements, 2011/C 11/01 (14 January 2011), para 57.

[306] European Commission, Communication from the Commission- Guidelines on the Applicability of Art. 101 of the Treaty on the Functioning of the European Union to Horizontal Co-operation Agreements, 2011/C 11/01 (14 January 2011), para 59. For the literature see Lindqvist (2018c), p. 152.

[307] European Commission, Communication from the Commission- Guidelines on the Applicability of Art. 101 of the Treaty on the Functioning of the European Union to Horizontal Co-operation Agreements, 2011/C 11/01 (14 January 2011), p. 15.

[308] Wagner-von Papp (2013), pp. 130 ff.

The collusive effect of an information exchange appears however to be a concern especially related to information *regarding* marketed products or services, that is mostly related to firms behaviours, such as information regarding price settings, geographical markets or sales.[309]

Conversely, with regards to information working as a structural component and thus as an input for digital services and products—as it is the case of health data—the risk of collusive practices is narrower, because such information is not really relevant for enacting coordination mechanisms, in the forms, recalled by the Commission, of monitoring deviations by other firms from a collusive or of monitoring market entrance efforts of incumbents.[310] In these regards, health information sharing agreements, given their little collusive value, should mostly fall outside the scope of art. 101(1) TFEU.[311]

However, the European Commission interestingly considers another ground of competitive harm stemming from information exchanges, which is separate from collusion and is related to the different case of anticompetitive foreclosure.

From this different perspective, the Commission acknowledges that information sharing is capable of leading to anti-competitive foreclosure effects on the market where the information exchange has taken place.[312] As the Commission observes this occurs when the exchange of the commercially sensitive information leaves competitors who have been left outside the arrangement with a competitive disadvantage as compared to the companies affiliated within the exchange system.[313]

The information exchange could for example determine the raising of competitors' costs to enter the market in which the information exchange has occurred, as a consequence of the high costs either for replicating the datasets needed to entering the concerned markets or for the acquisition of the same datasets by the parties

---

[309] This point is particularly highlighted by Lindqvist (6 November 2018b), p. 9, stressing that the consideration of this type of information relates to old fashioned cartels and does not fit well with the new competitive relevance of data in the digital economy.

[310] European Commission, Communication from the Commission- Guidelines on the Applicability of Art. 101 of the Treaty on the Functioning of the European Union to Horizontal Co-operation Agreements, 2011/C 11/01 (14 January 2011), p. 15.

[311] See, the already cited statements by European Commission, Communication from the Commission- Guidelines on the Applicability of Art. 101 of the Treaty on the Functioning of the European Union to Horizontal Co-operation Agreements, 2011/C 11/01 (14 January 2011), para 130. European Commission, Guidelines on the Assessment of Horizontal Mergers Under Council Regulation on the Control of Concentrations Between Undertakings, 2004/C 31/03 (5 February 2004a), para 45.

[312] European Commission, Communication from the Commission- Guidelines on the Applicability of Art. 101 of the Treaty on the Functioning of the European Union to Horizontal Co-operation Agreements, 2011/C 11/01 (14 January 2011), p. 15. Commenting the apparently exceptional consideration by the Commission of anticompetitive foreclosure effects within art. 101(1) TFEU, Di Porto (2014), p. 306.

[313] European Commission, Communication from the Commission- Guidelines on the Applicability of Art. 101 of the Treaty on the Functioning of the European Union to Horizontal Co-operation Agreements, 2011/C 11/01 (14 January 2011), p. 15, where the Commission specifies that this type of foreclosure is only possible if the information concerned is very strategic for competition.

involved in the exchange. With regards to this last case, for example, firms involved in the information exchange could indeed raise the price of the same exchanged dataset that a competitor wants to have access to.[314]

In this respect, it is particularly interesting that the Commission expressly acknowledges that information exchanges of competitively valuable information can be source to market power for the firms engaging in the information arrangement, with the connected effect of raising their rivals' costs needed to enter the downstream market.[315]

Hence, the Commission appears to take into consideration the value of data as an input consolidating firms' market position and raising cost barriers for rivals' market entrance. This consideration gains a particular relevance in the context of digital markets and in the even more specific context of health data pools in light of the current view of the value of data as a source of market power in digital environments.[316] Firms exchanging information in digital health innovation markets could thus raise the price of the same shared information or refuse to supply it at all. These conducts could well preclude competitors the access to digital health data, being key component for a market downstream, such as the provision of a digital health service.[317]

The risk of exclusion by raising rivals' costs has been expressly taken into consideration by the European Court of Justice especially in the two cases of *John Deere*[318] and *Asnef Aquifax*.[319] In these cases the Court expressly took into consideration the exclusion of some competitors from strategic collaboration and, more generally, from sharing agreements regarding a precious information facility. Although both of the mentioned cases assess the conducts under art. 101 TFEU, they appear to suggest that information exchanges lead to anticompetitive effects when they are related to a refusal to supply or to a refusal to deal conduct.[320]

This last consideration proves to be particular relevant in respect to conducts related to sharing of information that is an input for the conduction of research and for the development of new products or services, as health data.

---

[314] See Wagner-von Papp (2013), p. 138.

[315] European Commission, Communication from the Commission- Guidelines on the Applicability of Art. 101 of the Treaty on the Functioning of the European Union to Horizontal Co-operation Agreements, 2011/C 11/01 (14 January 2011), p. 15.

[316] See supra Sect. 6.1.

[317] This will be better assessed infra Chap. 7, Sect. 7.3.2.

[318] European Court of Justice, John Deere v. Commission C-7/95 (28 May 1998a), para 52.

[319] European Court of Justice, Asnef Equifax v. Ausbanc, C-238/05 (23 November 2006), para 60.

[320] Criticizing the qualification made by the Court in the two mentioned cases of the anticompetitive conduct under art. 101 TFEU instead of art. 102 TFEU, Wagner-von Papp (2013), p. 142, observing that the anticompetitive conduct is not related to the information exchange itself but to the different conduct of refusal to license/deal.

Indeed, if collusive effects are in this case difficult to identify, the risk of foreclosure effects is surely more grounded in the dynamics of the emerging collaborative research alliances.

However, a careful distinction need to be made between the foreclosure effects that arise as a consequence of a refusal by the formed pools' members to share their aggregated research valuable data with third—eventually competing—parties, and the foreclosure effects that arise as a result of the establishment of the pool itself.

The first type of foreclosure effect can be relevant under art. 102 TFEU when the refusal from which it stems is linked to a dominant position of the members of the research alliance.[321] This foreclosure effect however derives from a conduct carried out by parties of an already established information pool.

Conversely, the analysis under art. 101(1) TFEU captures eventual foreclosure effects that originate from the same conduct of exchanging data, thus of the establishment of an information pool. In respect to the creation of health data pools, the foreclosure effect would stem from the conduct of appropriation of the health information enacted by the members of the pool, implementing stronger intellectual property measures over the collected and secondary-generated health predictions, and in this way foreclosing the access to such research valuable information to other competing entities. For those who remain outside the so-formed health data pool, the complexity and sophisticated nature of health datasets deriving from health data pooling efforts render the same exchanged health data highly difficult for competitors to replicate.[322] Moreover the scientific, and thus market value of these health datasets is strictly intertwined with the technological infrastructure that extract research valuable analytics from the aggregated health data pools.[323] Usually this technological infrastructure is equally not readily available or replicable to every market entrant, but is rather the exclusive property of one of the market players involved in the exchange.

For the purposes of the assessment of the foreclosing effects of information exchanges under art. 101(1) TFEU, the Commissions' Guidelines stress that the analysis of the concrete anticompetitive outcomes of information exchanges under art. 101(1) TFEU is to be made highly dependent on the specific circumstances of the singular case, and more specific on the economic conditions on the relevant markets and the characteristics of the exchanged information.[324]

---

[321] This case will be better assessed infra Chap. 7, Sect. 7.3.1.2.

[322] The issue of the replicability of health datasets will be better addressed infra Chap. 7, Sects. 7.3.3.1.

[323] This is acknowledged, from a general perspective by Graef (2015), pp. 476 ff.; Geradin and Kuschewsky (2013), pp. 2–4.

[324] European Commission, Communication from the Commission- Guidelines on the Applicability of Art. 101 of the Treaty on the Functioning of the European Union to Horizontal Co-operation Agreements, 2011/C 11/01 (14 January 2011), para 76. In these regards, some authors have critically observed that the very context-specific nature of information exchanges renders the guidance of the Guidelines of little value. So Wagner-von Papp (2013), pp. 130 ff. Seitz (2011), pp. 460–462.

The very peculiar nature of exchanges of personal data in digital markets certainly requires a specific consideration of their anticompetitive value.

In these regards, interestingly, the relevance of information exchanges as arrangements under art. 101(1) TFEU has been recently taken in consideration by the European Court of Justice with regards to a computerised information system, working as a technological infrastructure for the exchange of information between the parties.[325] The case constitutes a first acknowledgment of the need to adapt the notion of information-based concerted practices to the reality of digital information flows. The judgment clarifies that participation to a technology platform sharing information among businesses using the platform can give rise to an anticompetitive agreement between the platform administrator and the platform's users, with the technological information-exchange platform working as a facilitator of a collusive conduct.[326]

This first recognition of the peculiar technological ecosystem in which digital data exchanges occur has however not yet followed by a more comprehensive evaluation by the Commission of the potential relevance under art. 101 TFEU of digital information exchanges.

The criteria set by the Guidelines as indicators of the anticompetitive effects of information exchanges do not appear to be suitable to the specificities of digital markets' functioning.

The redaction of Guidelines specifically concerning the assessment cooperation arrangements stemming from digital data exchanges would thus be desirable. Such operation could be done directly moving from some of the criteria considered by the present Guidelines on Horizontal Cooperation, which identify as relevant indicators the structure of the market, considered before and after the performance of the information exchange; the subject matter of the shared information; its degree of aggregation; its novelty; its degree of secretness; the frequency of exchanges; the size and materiality of the market covered. All these criteria would need to be reconsidered in light of the very features of digital data exchanges.

In the absence of a more developed case law and more specific policy guidelines, the assessment under art. 101(1) TFEU of "pure" data exchanges, that is disconnected from a broader research and development agreement, proves to be difficult.

Just as the reflection about the anticompetitive effects of digital data exchanges under art. 101(1) TFEU, also the reflection about the possibility to exempt digital data exchanges under art. 101(3)TFEU is still at an early stage.

In the *John Deere* case, involving the creation of a data pool regarding tractors' sale, the Court denied application of art. 101(3) TFEU, because, interestingly, it held that the data sharing agreements created restrictions of competition that were not

[325] European Court of Justice, Eturas UAB and others v. Lietuvos Respublikos konkurencijos taryba, C-74/14 (21 January 2016).

[326] European Court of Justice, Eturas UAB and others v. Lietuvos Respublikos konkurencijos taryba, C-74/14 (21 January 2016), para 42, stressing the causal link between the element of concertation and the ensuing collusive behaviour on the market.

indispensable for the generation of efficiencies related to the possibility of identifying and comparing sales of individual tractors on the basis of the pooled data.[327] Indeed, the Court observed that businesses could well operate in the agricultural tractor market also relying just on own company data and aggregate industry data that was already available on the market.[328]

This statement is particularly interesting because it implies, *a contrario*, that the restrictions of competition resulting from a data pool can be considered indispensable only if the data that are shared among competitors are indispensable to operate in the considered market, just as it occurs with health data needed for the development of digital health services and products.

A more generous approach under art. 101(3) TFEU with regards to the establishment of data pools has been more recently adopted in the *Asnef Equifax* case.[329]

Here, the European Court of Justice has come to acknowledge efficiency outcomes of information exchanges among firms, involving the creation of a financial data pool. The Court highlighted that the sharing of information regarding the creditworthiness of potential borrowers was related to the purpose of reducing the risk of lending through the reduction of the information asymmetry between credit institutions and borrowers. In this perspective, the information exchange was deemed to reduce the number of borrowers who did not manage to repay the loan, thus enhancing the functioning of the credit supply system as a whole with more efficient market outcomes.[330] Overall, hence, the court identified the benefits of the data pool, stressing however that the assessment of the efficiencies stemming from the creation of data pools needs to be carried out on a case by case analysis.[331]

In this perspective, the peculiar efficiencies highlighted in the *Asnef Equifax* could be somehow applied to the case of health data pools, to the extent that the aggregation of health information reduces the information asymmetry between healthcare providers and patients, thus reducing the numbers of diagnostic or treatment errors with an enhancement of the efficiencies of the specific health care service to which the health data exchange relates.

These are however only first considerations. The assessment of the technological and economic progress related to a data exchange that is not inscribed into a research and development agreement proves to be surely more challenging, and as the European Court of Justice has stressed in the *Asnef Equifax* case, needs to be deeply rooted in the specific circumstances of the single exchanges.

---

[327] European Court of Justice, Eturas UAB and others v. Lietuvos Respublikos konkurencijos taryba, C-74/14 (21 January 2016), para 15.

[328] European Court of Justice, Eturas UAB and others v. Lietuvos Respublikos konkurencijos taryba, C-74/14 (21 January 2016), para 105.

[329] European Court of Justice, Asnef Equifax v. Ausbanc, C-238/05 (23 November 2006b).

[330] European Court of Justice, Asnef Equifax v. Ausbanc, C-238/05 (23 November 2006b), para 47 and 55.

[331] European Court of Justice, Asnef Equifax v. Ausbanc, C-238/05 (23 November 2006b), para 72.

It can however be forecasted, as some strand of the literature has already highlighted, that future case law will give explicit consideration to data-driven efficiency outcomes of self-standing data sharing practices for the purposes of the effect-based analysis under art. 101(3) TFEU.[332]

6.6 Health Data Pools Under European Merger Policy

With regards to information exchanges occurring in the context of a broader arrangement between undertakings, also the "extreme" case of information exchanges occurring in the context of merger operations between undertakings needs to be taken into consideration.

In the case of information exchange analysed in the previous paragraphs, the exchange creates a new data pool to which the involved entities have common access to. In these cases, the parties maintain a separate economic and legal subjectivity.

Things are quite different in the case two entities merge. Through the merger, indeed, a new economic entity is created, in which among other things such as payoffs, also the information assets that were previously under the separate control of each of the merging entities are ultimately pooled together. In this way, together with a unity of interests in payoffs, the merger also creates a unit of interests in information.[333]

In the context of merger analysis, innovation concerns are expressly taken into account under recital 29 of the merger Regulation, which affirms that the assessment of efficiencies constitutes an integral part of the merger analysis, thus implying that mergers can have efficiency outcomes. Accordingly, art. 2 of the Regulation compels the European Commission to take into account "the development of technical and economic progress".[334]

With regards to merger-related efficiencies, the Non-horizontal Merger Guidelines interestingly affirm that non-horizontal mergers are more likely to create pro-competitive efficiencies than horizontal mergers between competitors.[335]

Moreover, expressly taking into consideration innovation concerns, the Horizontal Merger Guidelines specify that in markets where innovation is an important competitive force, a merger may increase firms' ability and incentives to produce innovative market outputs, in turn increasing the competitive pressure on rivals to

---

[332] This view is shared especially by Lindqvist (2018a).

[333] Wagner-von Papp (2013), p. 147.

[334] Article 2 of the Merger Regulation compels the European Commission to take into account "the development of technical and economic progress".

[335] European Commission, Guidelines on the assessment of non-horizontal mergers under the Council Regulation on the control of concentrations between undertakings, 2008/C 265/07 (18 October 2010a), para 13.

innovate in that market.[336] As a result, consumers may benefit from new or improved products resulting from increased research and development.[337] The same Guidelines require however specific proof by the parties of the claimed innovation-related efficiencies. More precisely, the parties to the transaction are required to show that such efficiencies will be passed on to consumers, are verifiable and are merger-specific specific, this meaning that these efficiencies can be achieved only through the merger and not through another, less market invasive transaction, such as a cooperation agreement.[338]

Against this backdrop, a strand of the literature has underlined how, especially in the pharmaceutical sector, mergers have been driven by firms' aspiration to achieve higher efficiency and innovation outcomes.[339]

In recent years, the antitrust literature has placed an increasingly strong attention to innovation concerns within merger analysis.[340]

The impact of corporate mergers on innovation has been the subject of a heated controversy in the field of antitrust scholarship.[341]

Some economic studies find that mergers have a negative externality related to the decrease of firms' incentives to innovate, ultimately harming innovation, both considered in terms of process and product innovation.[342] Thus, a merger- in the absence of innovation-specific efficiencies or research spillover effects- would generally cause harm to consumer welfare, as a consequence not only of the traditionally acknowledged price increases caused by mergers, but also of the diminishment of innovation rates.[343]

Along similar lines, others, focusing on sole product innovation, stress how through mergers firms coordinate their commercialization decisions, so that if one—or even both—of the merged research laboratories innovate, the other free rides on the innovation successes of the other laboratory. This possibility to free ride thus ultimately reduces the merged laboratories' overall research efforts.[344]

---

336 See European Commission, Guidelines on the Assessment of Horizontal Mergers Under Council Regulation on the Control of Concentrations Between Undertakings, 2004/C 31/03 (5 February 2004a), para 82.

337 European Commission, Guidelines on the Assessment of Horizontal Mergers Under Council Regulation on the Control of Concentrations Between Undertakings, 2004/C 31/03 (5 February 2004a), para 81.

338 European Commission, Guidelines on the Assessment of Horizontal Mergers Under Council Regulation on the Control of Concentrations Between Undertakings, 2004/C 31/03 (5 February 2004a), para 81.

339 Kathuria (2016), pp. 451 ff.

340 For an assessment on how innovation is accounted for in mergers in EU see Colomo (2016), pp. 201 ff.

341 For a comprehensive literature review, see Jullien and Lefouili (2018), pp. 364 ff.

342 So Motta and Tarantino (30 August 2017).

343 Motta and Tarantino (30 August 2017).

344 So Federico et al. (2017), pp. 136 ff.; Federico et al. (2018), pp. 1 ff.

From a different perspective, mergers can possibly also have positive externalities, directly related to "knowledge spillover effects" triggered by mergers, through which merging firms internalise positive knowledge externalities, as well as by "margin expansion effects" or, more simply, scale effects, directly related to the fact that the merger reduces the overall cost of a fixed investment like research and development.[345]

Merger-related efficiencies have been ultimately highlighted by another strand of the literature, which has carefully explored the efficiencies on the side of research and development that a merger, combining research and development resources, can bring about.[346] These efficiencies relate to the knowledge diffusion occurring within the merged entity[347]; the technological and research spillovers, leading to the heightening of incentives to innovate[348]; enhancement of technological appropriability[349]; the coordination of research and development investments, leading to significant cost savings related to the avoidance of duplicating efforts, with a positive effect on the expected amount of realized innovation[350]; the stirring of cumulative innovation, especially in case the innovation acquired by a party through the merger could not be licensed or could not be properly exploited by the original right owner[351]; ultimately, the increase of legal certainty, given by the fact that a merger, by forming a new entity out of previous two, reduces legal uncertainties regarding the allocation of intellectual property rights in the market and the risk of legal conflicts.[352]

---

[345]So Jullien and Lefouili (2018), pp. 364 ff. It needs however to be stressed that the mentioned efficiencies have been taken into consideration also by the literature that focuses more on the negative externalities related to mergers. See Motta and Tarantino (30 August 2017) especially at pp. 27 ff., highlighting that mergers can also lead to large efficiency gains or spillovers in research. As the Authors interestingly observe, these are more likely to be generated by agreements that fall short of a full merger, such as a network sharing agreements and research and development joint ventures. Ibid. 32.

[346]Régibeau and Rockett (2019), pp. 38 ff.

[347]Régibeau and Rockett (2019), pp. 38–39.

[348]Régibeau and Rockett (2019), pp. 39–40.

[349]Régibeau and Rockett (2019), p. 40, where it is recalled that appropriability relates to the innovator's ability to capture the benefits from the use of innovation by others.

[350]Régibeau and Rockett (2019), p. 41.

[351]Régibeau and Rockett (2019), pp. 41–43, where the Authors consider also the case in which the merger reduces incentives for follow on innovation.

[352]Régibeau and Rockett (2019), p. 43. Interestingly the Authors observe that problems of legal uncertainties surrounding intellectual property rights allocation is more felt in industries where the intellectual property rights are not easily defined, as in the software industry and in some branches of electronics. According to this reasoning, thus the highlighted efficiencies should be less perceived in industries where there is a clearer allocation of rights, as it is in the pharmaceutical industry, which majorly relies on patents. However, the increasingly value of digital data, for which the related intellectual property rights as trade secrets are not formally allocated, as it occurs with regards to patent protection, could make such source of efficiency more relevant in mergers occurring in the digital health research sector.

In light of the above-traced efficiencies, and in respect to the specific case of the pharmaceutical market, some scholars have underlined how pharmaceutical mergers are a means of aggregating technically and scientifically valuable assets, thus enabling firms to fruitfully combine their research and development skills with sensitive efficiency outcomes in innovation markets.[353] In particular, the combination of research and development assets through a merger is regarded as a means for smaller companies to overcome the high entrance barriers given by high research and development and marketing costs needed to enter pharmaceutical markets.[354]

Against this backdrop, the literature stressing the potential efficiencies related to mergers claim that, exactly in the view of these efficiencies, mergers with a dynamic innovative twist, should be treated more leniently than static transactions.[355]

For the purposes of the incorporation of innovation considerations in the context of merger analysis, proxies have been developed, regarding the number of patents, the number of new products, and R&D spending.[356]

Nonetheless, the above-outlined theoretical developments have not yet been fully internalized in the practical context of merger analysis.

In these regards, the Commission has highlighted the key importance of the existence of a potential third party competitor in the innovation market in which the merger occurs, to the point that the Commission has cleared some mergers in the pharmaceutical market exactly based on the existence of the pressure of potential third party competitors.[357]

This means that traditional market analysis by the European Commission has taken into consideration innovation aspects of mergers, positively evaluating them.[358]

The practical attempt to incorporate innovation consideration into merger analysis has however not gone without significant difficulties given the inconvenience of interpreting and detecting such vague efficiency parameter in light of the heterogeneity of the merger cases.[359]

---

[353] Kathuria (2016), pp. 467–468.

[354] Kathuria (2016), p. 470.

[355] P Régibeau and Rockett (2019), p. 44.

[356] See European Commission, Guidelines on the Assessment of Horizontal Mergers Under Council Regulation on the Control of Concentrations Between Undertakings, 2004/C 31/03 (5 February 2004a), para 45, affirming that in the context of dynamic markets "volatile demand, substantial internal growth by some firms in the market or frequent entry by new firms may indicate that the current situation is not sufficiently stable to make coordination likely. In markets where innovation is important, coordination may be more difficult since innovations, particularly significant ones, may allow one firm to gain a major advantage over its rivals". See more broadly, Kokkoris and Shelanski (2014), pp. 127 ff.

[357] European Commission (25 August 2005b). See also the comment by Bacchiega et al. (2005), pp. 87 ff. For the literature see Kern (2014), pp. 177 ff.

[358] See Todino et al. (2018), p. 5.

[359] The difficulty for antitrust regulators in assessing innovation outcomes of mergers, is well highlighted by Kokkoris and Shelanski (2014), para 12.19.

Similarly to what has occurred in the US,[360] although efficiency considerations have been given attention in some merger decisions, there haven't been so far any mergers that have been approved by the Commission on the basis of "pure" merger-specific efficiencies, outweighing consumer harm.[361]

As a strand of the literature has observed, indeed, the efficiency defence in mergers has been so far of weak impact, because the intervention of European antitrust regulators has been majorly aimed at protecting the market structure and thus at safeguarding an effective competitive process, *without establishing whether the merger operation has actually generated a consumer harm.*[362]

Moreover, the Horizontal Merger Guidelines themselves exclude that a merger leading to a monopoly or to a close degree of market power can be declared legitimate in the internal market, on the grounds that efficiency claims outweigh the potential anticompetitive effects, in the form, ultimately, of consumer harm.[363]

Finally, from a more practical standpoint, merger-related efficiency claims have been cautiously assessed by antitrust agencies, because of the lack of evidence related to the claimed efficiencies.[364] Information regarding the efficiencies produced by a merger is indeed mostly in the sole firms' possession.[365]

Against the backdrop of these premises, it needs to be observed that innovation concerns have been given consideration in the context of the more recent pharmaceutical merger policy especially with regards to the harm to innovation, thus to research, caused by a merger involving research-based companies. Hence, the *harm* to innovation instead of the innovation outcome of a merger has lately come under the focus of European merger policy. This means that in merger policy the innovation parameter has been relied on for the purposes of expanding the scope of

---

[360] In the US, the FTC approved the Novazyme/Genzyme merger—leading to monopoly scenario—for its potentially beneficial effects on innovation. For the literature commenting see Kathuria (2016), p. 465. Assessing the role of innovation in the context of USA merger analysis, Jullien and Lefouili (2018), pp. 364 ff.

[361] In some cases, however, efficiency claims made by merging parties were partially accepted by the Commission and balanced against the competition harm. This occurred in European Commission, UPS/TNT Express, COMP/M.6570 (30 January 2013); European Commission, Ineos/Solvay, COMP/M.6905 (8 May 2014d) https://ec.europa.eu/competition/mergers/cases/decisions/m6905_20140508_20600_3967413_EN.pdf; European Commission, Orange/Jazztel, COMP/M.7421 (19 May 2015).

[362] So Ibanez Colomo (2016), p. 205.

[363] European Commission, Guidelines on the Assessment of Horizontal Mergers Under Council Regulation on the Control of Concentrations Between Undertakings, 2004/C 31/03 (5 February 2004a), para 84.

[364] For a historical assessment of the consideration of efficiencies in EU merger control, see Cardwell (2017), pp. 552–554.

[365] See OECD (2012), p. 29, stressing that "since information about potential efficiency gains in mergers is solely in the merging firms' possession (which puts competition authorities at disadvantage), or sketchy or non-existing at all in some cases, it is not surprising that most agencies adopt a cautious approach when they evaluate efficiency claims".

competition law enforcement, rather than for the purposes of curbing it[366] as it occurs under art. 101(3) TFEU and the related analysed block exemptions.

The interventionist merger policy in pharmaceutical innovation markets has been triggered by the acknowledgment of the threats to research-based innovation given by the consolidation of research information under the control of one or few big research entities. In these regards, it is however interesting to acknowledge that exactly in the context of pharmaceutical merger policy, many mergers have been granted clearance by the Commission, that has conditioned the permission of the operation upon commitments specifically aiming at impeding the freezing of the innovation process, through the "targeted" sharing of research valuable information to other market players.

Since these commitments attain to the realm of competition law enforcement's remedies, these will be more accurately analysed in the context of the next chapter, generally identifying the relevant remedial tools for the risks stemming from health data pools.

As a premise, merger policy in pharmaceutical innovation markets reflects the intent of the European antitrust regulator to tailor the concentration of research pipelines to efficiency goals directly related to the advancement of technical and economic progress these same concentrations can, under specific circumstances, lead to.[367]

In this perspective, this merger policy appears to be somehow aligned to art. 101(3) TFEU and the cited statements of the block exemptions, because both acknowledge, although in different ways, the efficiency outcomes of research-based operations relying on the sharing of scientifically valuable information. Such efficiency outcomes are favorably regarded by European competition regulators upon the respect of specific conditions, which in the case of mergers are established by the European Commission's decision in the form of commitments and in the case of art. 101.3 TFEU and the related block exemptions are legislatively set.

---

[366] See analysis supra under Sect. 6.3.

[367] This is supported also by economic findings, see in this respect Denicolò and Polo (22 March 2018), p. 26, concluding that that there are cases in which two merging firms share the basic innovation, thus increasing "the R&D investment both in the research stage and in the development stage. The investment in the research stage increases as the basic innovation can be applied to the research projects of both divisions of the merged firm and hence is more valuable. The investment in the development stage increases, on average, as it is more likely that R&D expenditure is more productive thanks to the basic innovation". Recognising, up to certain limits, the positive impacts on innovation of collaborations, Aghion et al. (2005), p. 701 ff.

References

Advocate General Darmond (7 July 1992) Opinion in Ahlström Osakeyhtiö and Others vs. Commission of the European Communitie. C-89/85, 104/85, C-114/85, C-116/85, C-117/85 and C-125/85 to C-129/85. https://eur-lex.europa.eu/legalcontent/EN/TXT/PDF/?uri=CELEX:61985CC0089(01)&from=EN

Advocate General Kokott (23 February 2003) Opinion in British Airways vs. Commission C-95/04 https://eur-lex.europa.eu/legal-content/EN/TXT/PDF/?uri=CELEX:62004CC0095&from=EN

Advocate General Kokott (19 February 2009) Opinion in T-Mobile Netherlands BV and Others, C-8/08, ECR I-4529. https://eur-lex.europa.eu/legal-content/EN/TXT/HTML/?uri=CELEX:62008CC0008&from=EN

Aghion P, Bloom N, Blundell R, Griffith R, Howitt P (2005) Competition and innovation: an inverted U relationship. Q J Econ 120:701–728

Ahlborn C, Padilla AJ (2008) From fairness to welfare: implications for the assessment of unilateral conduct under EC competition law. In: Ehlermann CD, Marquis M (eds) European competition law annual 2007: a reformed approach to article 82 EC. Hart Publishing, Oxford, pp 55–102

Akman P (2014) The role of freedom in competition law. Oxf J Leg Stud 34:183–213

Almunia J (26 November 2012) Competition and Personal Data Protection, Speech given at the European Commission event, Privacy Platform Event: Competition and Privacy in Markets of Data. https://europa.eu/rapid/press-release_SPEECH-12-860_en.htm

Andrews D, Criscuolo C, Gal PN (2015) Frontier firms, technology diffusion and public policy: micro-evidence from OECD countries. OECD Background Paper. OECD Publishing, Paris

Arrow K (1962) Economic Welfare and the Allocation of Resources to Invention. In: Universities-National Bureau Committee for Economic Research, Committee on Economic Growth of the Social Science Research Council (ed) The Rate and Direction of Inventive Activity: Economic and Social Factor. Princeton University Press, Princeton, pp 609–626

Autorité de la Concurrence-Bundeskartellamt (10 May 2016) Competition Law and Data. https://www.bundeskartellamt.de/SharedDocs/Publikation/DE/Berichte/Big%20Data%20Papier.pdf?__blob=publicationFile&v=2

Bacchiega A, Todino M, Macewen C (2005) Johnson & Johnson/Guidant: potential competition and unilateral effects in innovative markets. Competition Policy Newsl 3:87–94

Bejcek J (2005) Mergers and new technologies. IIC 36:809–835

Bennet M, Collins P (2016) The law and economics of information sharing: the good, the bad and the ugly. Eur Comp J 6:311–337

Brodley J (1987) The economic goals of antitrust: efficiency, consumer welfare and technological Progress. New York Univ Law Rev 62:1020–1053

Bundeskartellamt (Oktober 2017) Big Data und Wettbewerb Schriftenreihe- Wettbewerb und Verbraucheschutz in der Digitalen Wirtschaft. https://www.bundeskartellamt.de/SharedDocs/Publikation/DE/Schriftenreihe_Digitales/Schriftenreihe_Digitales_1.pdf?__blob=publicationFile&v=3

Bundeskartellamt (7 February 2019a) Bundeskartellamt Prohibits Facebook From Combining User Data From Different Sources, Press Release. https://www.bundeskartellamt.de/SharedDocs/Publikation/EN/Pressemitteilungen/2019/07_02_2019_Facebook.pdf?__blob=publicationFile&v=2

Bundeskartellamt (7 February 2019b) Bundeskartellamt Prohibits Facebook From Combining User Data From Different Sources- Background information on the Bundeskartellamt's Facebook proceeding. https://www.bundeskartellamt.de/SharedDocs/Publikation/EN/Pressemitteilungen/2019/07_02_2019_Facebook_FAQs.pdf?__blob=publicationFile&v=5

Capobianco A (2004) Information exchange under EC competition law. Common Mark Law Rev 41:1247–1276

Cardwell D (2017) The role of the efficiency defence in EU merger control proceedings following UPS/TNT, FedEx/TNT and UPS v Commission. JECLAP 8:551–560

Carli C (2018) Big (digital): is it really bad? Mercato Concorrenza Regole 3:397–418

Carrier MA (2008) Two puzzles resolved: Schumpeter-Arrow stalemate and pharmaceutical innovation markets. Iowa Law Rev 93:396–450
Carrier MA (2009) Innovation for the 21st century: harnessing the power of intellectual property and antitrust law. Oxford Scholarship Online, Oxford
Christensen CM, Raynor ME, McDonald R (2015) Disruptive technologies: catching the wave, what is disruptive innovation? HBLR:44–53
Colangelo G, Borgogno O (5 April 2019) Data sharing and interoperability: fostering innovation and competition through APIs. CLSR 35: 105314
Colangelo G, Maggiolino M (2019) Antitrust Über Alles-whither competition law after Facebook? World Competition Law Econ Rev 42:355–376
Colomo PI (2016) Restrictions on innovation in EU competition law. Eur Law Rev 41:201–219
Commissioner Vestager (29 September 2016) Big Data and Competition. https://ec.europa.eu/commission/commissioners/2014-2019/vestager/announcements/big-data-and-competition_en
Commissioner Vestager (25 January 2018) Fairness and Competition, Speech delivered at the GCLC Annual Conference, Brussels. https://ec.europa.eu/commission/commissioners/2014-2019/vestager/announcements/fairness-and-competition_en
Council Regulation EC N. 139/2004 of 20 January 2004 on the control of concentrations between undertakings (the EC Merger Regulation) (29 January 2004) OJ L 24/1
Crèmer J, De Montjoye Y, Schweitzer H (2019) Competition Policy For the Digital Era- Report for the European Commission. https://ec.europa.eu/competition/publications/reports/kd0419345enn.pdf
Daskalova V (2015) Consumer welfare in EU competition law: what is it (not) about? Compet Law Rev 11:133–162
De La Mano M (13 February 2009) For the Customer's Sake: The Competitive Effects of Efficiencies on the European Merger Control. European Commission's Enterprise Directorate-General Enterprise Papers. https://ec.europa.eu/growth/content/customer%E2%80%99s-sake-competitive-effects-efficiencies-european-merger-control-0_ga
Denicolò V, Polo M (22 March 2018) The Innovation Theory of Harm- an Appraisal. SSRN. https://papers.ssrn.com/sol3/papers.cfm?abstract_id=3146731
Di Porto F (2014) Abuses of information and informational remedies: rethinking exchange of information under competition law? In: Di Porto F, Drexl J (eds) Competition law as regulation. Edward Elgar, Cheltenham, pp 296–340
Drexl J, Frueh A, Mackenrodt MO, Ullrich H, Picht PG, Pulyer B (15 November 2010) Comments of the Max Planck Institute for IP, Competition and Tax Law on the Draft Commission Block Exemption on R&D Agreements and the Draft Guidelines on Horizontal Cooperation Agreements. Max Planck Institute for IP, Competition & Tax Law Research Paper N. 10-12. https://papers.ssrn.com/sol3/papers.cfm?abstract_id=1695421
Easterbrook F (1984) The limits of antitrust. Texas Law Rev 63:1–40
European Commission (8 September 1977) Cobelpa/VNP. 77/592/EEC. https://eur-lex.europa.eu/legal-content/EN/TXT/PDF/?uri=CELEX:31977D0592&from=en
European Commission (19 July 1984) BPCL/ICI, N. IV/30.863, 84 / 387 / EEC. https://eur-lex.europa.eu/legal-content/EN/TXT/PDF/?uri=CELEX:31984D0387&from=EN
European Commission (14 July 1986a) Optical Fibre, IV/30.320, 86/405/EEC. https://eur-lex.europa.eu/legal-content/EN/TXT/PDF/?uri=CELEX:31986D0405&from=en
European Commission (4 December 1986b) ENI/Montedison, N. IV/31.055, 87/3/EEC. https://eur-lex.europa.eu/legal-content/EN/TXT/PDF/?uri=CELEX:31987D0003&from=en
European Commission (22 December 1987) Olivetti/Canon, IV/32306, 88/88/EEC. https://eur-lex.europa.eu/legal-content/EN/TXT/PDF/?uri=CELEX:31988D0088&from=EN
European Commission (10 November 1988) No IV/32.173 - Continental/Michelin. OJ L 305/33. https://eur-lex.europa.eu/legal-content/EN/TXT/PDF/?uri=CELEX:31988D0555&from=EN
European Commission (25 January 1991) No IV/32.363 — KSB/Goulds/Lowara/ITT, 91/38/EEC. OJ L 19/25. https://eur-lex.europa.eu/legal-content/EN/TXT/PDF/?uri=CELEX:31991D0038&from=DE

European Commission (23 December 1992) Ford/Volkswagen, N. IV/33.814. https://eur-lex.europa.eu/legal-content/EN/TXT/PDF/?uri=CELEX:31993D0049&from=en

European Commission (29 April 1994a) Stichting Baksteen, N. IV/34.456. https://eur-lex.europa.eu/legal-content/EN/TXT/PDF/?uri=CELEX:31994D0296&from=EN

European Commission (18 May 1994b) Exxon/Shell, N. IV/33.640. https://eur-lex.europa.eu/legal-content/EN/TXT/PDF/?uri=CELEX:31994D0322&from=EN

European Commission (6 June 1994c) Bayer/BP Chemicals, IV/32.07S, 94/384/EC. https://eur-lex.europa.eu/legal-content/EN/TXT/PDF/?uri=CELEX:31994D0384&from=IT

European Commission (16 December 1994d) Asahi/Saint-Gobain, IV/33.863, 94/896/EC. https://eur-lex.europa.eu/legal-content/EN/TXT/PDF/?uri=CELEX:31994D0896&from=EN

European Commission (31 December 1994e) N. IV/33.863 - Asahi/Saint-Gobain, 94/896/EC. OJ L 354/87. https://eur-lex.europa.eu/legal-content/EN/TXT/PDF/?uri=CELEX:31994D0896&from=DE

European Commission (29 July 1997) Ciba-Geigy/Sandoz, Case No. IV/M.737. OJ L 201/1. https://eur-lex.europa.eu/legal-content/EN/TXT/PDF/?uri=CELEX:31997D0469&from=en

European Commission (24 January 1999a) CECED, N. IV.F.1/36.718. https://eur-lex.europa.eu/legal-content/EN/TXT/PDF/?uri=CELEX:32000D0475&from=EN

European Commission (28 April 1999b) White Paper on Modernisation of the Rules Implementing Articles 85 and 86 of the EC Treaty. https://europa.eu/documents/comm/white_papers/pdf/com99_101_en.pdf

European Commission (2000) Guidelines on Vertical Restraints, OJ C291/1. http://ec.europa.eu/competition/antitrust/legislation/guidelines_vertical_en.pdf

European Commission (5 February 2004a) Guidelines on the Assessment of Horizontal Mergers Under Council Regulation on the Control of Concentrations Between Undertakings, 2004/C 31/03. OJ C 31/5

European Commission (27 April 2004b) Commission Notice: Guidelines on the Application of Article 81(3) of the Treaty, 2004/C 101/08, OJ C101/97. https://eur-lex.europa.eu/legal-content/EN/TXT/PDF/?uri=CELEX:52004XC0427(07)&from=EN

European Commission (5 March 2005a) Commission Notice on Restrictions Directly Related and Necessary to Concentrations, 2005/C 56/24. https://eur-lex.europa.eu/legal-content/EN/TXT/PDF/?uri=CELEX:52005XC0305(02)&from=EN

European Commission (25 August 2005b) Mergers: Commission Approves Takeover of Guidant Corporation by Johnson & Johnson, Subject to Conditions. https://europa.eu/rapid/press-release_IP-05-1065_en.htm

European Commission (18 October 2010a) Guidelines on the Assessment of Non-horizontal Mergers under the Council Regulation on the Control of Concentrations Between Undertakings, 2008/C 265/07, OJ C 265/6. https://eur-lex.europa.eu/legal-content/EN/TXT/PDF/?uri=CELEX:52008XC1018(03)&from=EN

European Commission (18 December 2010b) Regulation EU n. 1217/2010 of 14 December 2010 on the application of Article 101(3) of the Treaty on the Functioning of the European Union to certain categories of research and development agreements, OJ 335/36. https://eur-lex.europa.eu/LexUriServ/LexUriServ.do?uri=OJ:L:2010:335:0036:0042:EN:PDF

European Commission (14 January 2011) Communication from the Commission- Guidelines on the Applicability of Art. 101 of the Treaty on the Functioning of the European Union to Horizontal Co-operation Agreements. 2011/C 11/01. https://eur-lex.europa.eu/legal-content/EN/TXT/PDF/?uri=CELEX:52011XC0114(04)&from=EN

European Commission (30 January 2013) UPS/TNT Express, COMP/M.6570. https://ec.europa.eu/competition/mergers/cases/decisions/m6570_20130130_20610_4241141_EN.pdf

European Commission (28 March 2014a) Communication from the Commission, Guidelines on the application of Article 101 of the Treaty on the Functioning of the European Union to technology transfer agreements, 2014/C 89/03. OJ C 89/3, https://eur-lex.europa.eu/legal content/EN/TXT/PDF/?uri=CELEX:52014XC0328(01)&from=EN

European Commission (28 March 2014b) Commission Regulation EU N. 316/2014 of 21 March 2014 on the application of Article 101(3) of the Treaty on the Functioning of the European Union to Categories of Technology Transfer Agreements. OJ L 93/17. https://eur-lex.europa.eu/legal-content/EN/TXT/PDF/?uri=CELEX:32014R0316&from=EN

European Commission (19 April 2014c) Communication: Digitising European Industry, Reaping the Full Benefits of a Digital Single Market. https://eur-lex.europa.eu/legal-content/EN/TXT/PDF/?uri=CELEX:52016DC0180&from=EN

European Commission (8 May 2014d) Ineos/Solvay, COMP/M.6905. https://ec.europa.eu/competition/mergers/cases/decisions/m6905_20140508_20600_3967413_EN.pdf

European Commission (19 May 2015) Orange/Jazztel, COMP/M.7421. https://ec.europa.eu/competition/mergers/cases/decisions/m7421_3169_4.pdf

European Commission (27 March 2017) Dow/DuPont, Merger Procedure Regulation (EC) 139/2004, Case M. 7932. http://ec.europa.eu/competition/mergers/cases/decisions/m7932_13668_3.pdf

European Commission, Regulation EU n. 316/2014 of 21 March 2014 on the application of Art. 101.3 of the Treaty on the Functioning of the European Union to Categories of Technology Transfer Agreements (28 March 2014) OJ L 93

European Court of Justice (30 June 1966) Société Technique Minière v Mascinenbau Ulm, C-56/65. https://eur-lex.europa.eu/legal-content/EN/TXT/PDF/?uri=CELEX:61965CJ0056&from=EN

European Court of Justice (21 June 1974) Jean Reyners v Belgian State, C-2/74. https://eur-lex.europa.eu/legal-content/EN/TXT/PDF/?uri=CELEX:61974CJ0002&from=EN

European Court of Justice (25 October 1977) Metro I vs. Commission of the European Communities, C-26/76. http://curia.europa.eu/juris/documents.jsf?num=C-26/76

European Court of Justice (13 February 1979) Hoffmann La Roche AG v. Commission, C-85/76. https://eur-lex.europa.eu/legal-content/EN/TXT/?uri=CELEX%3A61976CJ0085

European Court of Justice (8 June 1982a) Nungesser KG and Kurt Eisele vs. Commission of the European Communities, C-258/78. https://eur-lex.europa.eu/legal-content/EN/TXT/PDF/?uri=CELEX:61978CJ0258&from=EN

European Court of Justice (6 October 1982b) Coditel SA, Compagnie générale pour la diffusion de la télévision, and others v Ciné-Vog Films SA and others, C-262/81. https://eur-lex.europa.eu/legal-content/EN/TXT/?uri=CELEX%3A61981CJ0262

European Court of Justice (16 June 1987) Commission of the European Communities v Italian Republic, C-118/85. https://eur-lex.europa.eu/resource.html?uri=cellar:6d636a50-0f4d-49d0-8500-36085568f785.0002.03/DOC_2&format=PDF

European Court of Justice (23 April 1991) Höfner and Elser v Macrotron GmbH, C-41/90. https://eurlex.europa.eu/resource.html?uri=cellar:1689d9868f434ecca389bb324927dfc5.0002.06/DOC_1&format=PDF

European Court of Justice (17 February 1993) Christian Poucet v Assurances Générales de France and Caisse Mutuelle Régionale du Languedoc-Roussillon, Joined Cases C-159/91 and C-160/91. https://eur-lex.europa.eu/resource.html?uri=cellar:db3e29e0-8215-4085-a7f1-170f5d0d7e0c.0002.06/DOC_2&format=PDF

European Court of Justice (28 May 1998a) John Deere v. Commission, John Deere Ltd vs. Commission of the European Communities, C-7/95, 28 May 1998. http://curia.europa.eu/juris/liste.jsf?language=en&num=C-7/95

European Court of Justice (18 June 1998b) Commission of the European Communities v Italian Republic, C-35/96. http://curia.europa.eu/juris/showPdf.jsf?text=&docid=43942&pageIndex=0&doclang=EN&mode=lst&dir=&occ=first&part=1&cid=595842

European Court of Justice (18 September 2001) Métropole Télévision (M6), Suez-Lyonnaise des eaux, France Télécom and Télévision française 1 SA (TF1) v Commission of the European Communities, C- T-112/99. http://curia.europa.eu/juris/liste.jsf?language=en&num=T-112/99

European Court of Justice (19 February 2002) J.C.J. Wouters and Others v. Algemene Raad van de Nederlandse Orde van Advocaten, C-309/99. http://curia.europa.eu/juris/showPdf.jsf?text=&

docid=46722&pageIndex=0&doclang=EN&mode=lst&dir=&occ=first&part=1&cid=1885470
European Court of Justice (23 October 2003) Van den Bergh Foods vs. Commission, C T-65/98. http://curia.europa.eu/juris/liste.jsf?language=en&num=T-65/98
European Court of Justice (18 July 2006a) David Meca-Medina and Igor Majcen vs. European Commission and Republic of Finland, C- 519/04. https://eur-lex.europa.eu/legal-content/EN/TXT/PDF/?uri=CELEX:62004CJ0519&from=EN
European Court of Justice (23 November 2006b) Asnef Equifax v. Ausbanc, C-238/05. https://eur-lex.europa.eu/legal-content/EN/TXT/PDF/?uri=CELEX:62005CJ0238&from=EN
European Court of Justice (4 June 2009a) T-Mobile vs. Commission, C-8/08. http://curia.europa.eu/juris/liste.jsf?language=en&num=C-8/08
European Court of Justice (6 October 2009b) GlaxoSmithKline Services Unlimited vs. Commission of the European Communities, Joined Cases C 501/06 P, C-513/06 P, C-515/06 P and C 519/06 P. http://curia.europa.eu/juris/document/document_print.jsf?docid=77866&text=&dir=&doclang=EN&part=1&occ=first&mode=lst&pageIndex=0&cid=1907452
European Court of Justice (27 March 2012) Post Danmark A/S v Konkurrencerådet, C-209/10. http://curia.europa.eu/juris/document/document.jsf;jsessionid=1D4EC982DE8D5866F2E69D075D321FCD?text=&docid=121061&pageIndex=0&doclang=EN&mode=lst&dir=&occ=first&part=1&cid=1987032
European Court of Justice (11 September 2014) Mastercard Inc. and Others v. European Commission, C-382/12. http://curia.europa.eu/juris/liste.jsf?num=C-382/12&language=en
European Court of Justice (21 January 2016) Eturas UAB and others v. Lietuvos Respublikos konkurencijos taryba, C-74/14. http://curia.europa.eu/juris/document/document.jsf?text=&docid=173680&pageIndex=0&doclang=EN&mode=lst&dir=&occ=first&part=1&cid=563912
Ezrachi A (2018) The Goals of Competition Law and the Digital Economy-Discussion Paper. BEUC Study. https://www.beuc.eu/publications/beuc-x-2018-071_goals_of_eu_competition_law_and_digital_economy.pdf
Farrell J, Klemperer P (2007) Coordination and lock-in: competition with switching costs and network effects. In: Armstrong M, Porter R (eds) Handbook of industrial organization. Elsevier, Amsterdam, pp 1967–2072
Faull J, Nickpay A (2014) The EU law of competition. Oxford University Press, Oxford
Federico G, Langus G, Valletti T (2017) A simple model of mergers and innovation. Econ Lett 157: 136–140
Federico G, Langus G, Valletti T (2018) Horizontal mergers and product innovation. Int J Ind Organ 59:1–23
Fox E (2010) "Antitrust welfare"- the Broadley synthesis. Boston Univ Law Rev 90:1375–1383
Galloway J (2011) Driving innovation: a case for targeted competition policy in dynamic markets. World Competition 34:73–96
Gellhorn E, Miller WT (1997) Competitor collaboration guidelines- a recommendation. Antitrust Bull 42:851–870
Geradin D, Girgenson I (2013) The counterfactual method in EU competition law: the cornerstone of the effects-based approach. In: Bourgeois J, Waelbroeck D (eds) Ten years of effects-based approach in EU competition law. Bruylant, Bruxelles, pp 211–241
Geradin D, Kuschewsky M (13 February 2013) Competition Law and Personal Data: Preliminary Thoughts on a Complex Issue. Concurrences. SSRN. https://papers.ssrn.com/sol3/papers.cfm?abstract_id=2216088
Gerard D (2018) Fairness in EU competition policy: significance and implications. JECLAP 9:211–212
Gerber D (1998) Law and competition in twentieth century Europe: protecting Prometheus. Oxford University Press, Oxford

Gerber DJ (5 March 2002) Fairness in competition law: European and US Experience, paper presented at the Conference on Fairness and Asian Competition Laws. http://archive.kyotogakuen.ac.jp/o_ied/information/fairness_in_competition_law.pdf

Ghezzi F, Maggiolino M (24 April 2015) Know Your Enemy: The Dark Side Of Information Flows. SSRN. https://papers.ssrn.com/sol3/papers.cfm?abstract_id=2597687

Glader M (2001) Innovation economics and the antitrust guidelines on horizontal co-operation. World Competition 24:513–541

Glader M (2006) Innovation markets and competition analysis- EU competition law and US antitrust law. Edward Elgar, Cheltenham

Graef I (2015) Market definition and market power in data: the case of online platforms. World Competition 38:473–506

Graef I, Clifford D, Valcke P (2018) Fairness and enforcement: bridging competition, data protection and consumer law. IDPL 8:200–223

Grullon G, Larkin Y, Michaely R (2019) Are US industries becoming more concentrated? Rev Finance 23:697–743

Harbour PJ, Koslov TI (2010) Section 2 in a web 2.0 world: an expanded vision of relevant product markets. Antitrust Law J 76:769–794

Haucap J, Heimeshoff U (2014) Google, Facebook, Amazon eBay: is the internet driving competition or market monopolization? Int Econ Econ Policy 11:49–61

Holzweber S (2019) Innovation-Defence? Innovation als Einschränkender Parameter in der Marktmachtmissbrauchkontrolle. In: Maute L, Mackenrodt MO (eds) Recht als Infrastruktur für Innovation. Nomos Verlag- GRUR Junge Wissenschaft, Baden Baden, pp 41–60

Hovenkamp H (2011) Federal antitrust policy, the law of competition and its practice. Thomson Reuters, Toronto

Ibanez Colomo I (2018) Competition law and innovation: where do we stand? JECLAP 9:561–562

Jalonen H, Lehtonen A (2012) Uncertainty in the innovation process. J Manag Res 4:1–47

Jorde TM, Teece DJ (1990) Innovation and cooperation: implication for competition and antitrust. J Eon Perspect 4:75–96

Jorde TM, Teece DJ (1993) Rule of reason analysis of horizontal arrangements: agreements designed to advance innovation and commercialize technology. Antitrust Law J 61:579–619

Jullien B, Lefouili Y (2018) Horizontal mergers and innovation. J Compet Law Econ 14:364–392

Kathuria V (2016) Pharmaceutical mergers and their effect on access and efficiency: a case of emerging markets. World Compet 39:451–478

Katz ML, Shapiro C (1985) Network externalities, competition, and compatibility. Am Econ Rev 75:424–440

Kerber W (2010) Competition, innovation and maintaining diversity through competition law. In: Drexel J, Kerber W, Podszun R (eds) Economic approaches to competition law: foundations and limitations. Edward Elgar, Cheltenham, pp 173–202

Kerber W (2016) Digital markets, data, and privacy: competition law, consumer law, and data protection. JIPLP 11:856–866

Kern BJ (2014) Innovation markets, future markets or potential competition: how should competition authorities account for innovation competition in merger reviews? World Compet 37:173–206

Kokkoris I (2020) Innovation considerations in merger control and unilateral conduct enforcement. J Antitrust Enforc 8:56–85

Kokkoris I, Shelanski H (2014) EU merger control: a legal and economic analysis. Oxford University Press, Oxford

Kroes N (15 September 2005) European Competition Policy – Delivering Better Markets and Better Choices. Sppech 05/512, London. http://europa.eu/rapid/press-release_SPEECH-05-512_en.htm

Larouche P (2009) The European Microsoft case at the crossroads of competition policy and innovation. Antitrust Law J 75:933–963

Larouche P, Schinckel MP (2014) Continental drift in the treatment of dominant firms: article 102 TFUE in contrast to section 2 Sherman act. In: Sokol D (ed) Oxford handbook of international antitrust economics, vol 2. Oxford University Press, Oxford, pp 153–187
Lianos I (2013) Some Reflections on the Question of the Goals of EU Competition Law. CLES Working Paper Series 3/2013. https://papers.ssrn.com/sol3/papers.cfm?abstract_id=2235875
Lindqvist B (2015) Joint research and development under US antitrust and EU competition law. Edward Elgar, Cheltenham
Lindqvist B (2018a) Competition and data pools. Eur Consum Mark Law 7:146–154
Lindqvist B (6 November 2018b) Data Collaboration, Pooling and Hoarding Under Competition Law Stockholm Faculty of Law Research Paper Series 61 https://papers.ssrn.com/sol3/papers.cfm?abstract_id=3278578
Lindqvist B (2018c) Joint Research and Development collaborations under competition law. In: Nihoul P, Van Cleynenbreugel P (eds) The roles of innovation in competition law analysis. Edward Elgar, Cheltenham, pp 179–214
Manne G, Wright J (2010) Innovation and the limits of antitrust. J Compet Law Econ 6:153–202
Masoudi GF -Deputy Assistant Attorney General, DOJ Antitrust Division (18 January 2007) Efficiency in Analysis of Antitrust, Standard Setting, and Intellectual Property. Brussels. https://www.justice.gov/atr/file/519331/download
Mattioli M (2017) The data pooling problem. Berkeley Technol Law J 32:179–236
Monti G (2002) Art. 81 EC and public policy. Common Mark Law Rev 39:1057–1099
Monti M (20 October 2000) European Competition Policy for the 21st Century. Speech at The Fordham Corporate Law Institute, 28 Annual Conference on International Antitrust Law and Policy. https://ec.europa.eu/commission/presscorner/api/integration/rapid2/start/cgi/guesten.ksh?p_action.gettxt=gt&doc=SPEECH/00/389|0|RAPID&lg=EN
Motta M (2004) Competition policy: theory and practice. Cambridge University Press, Cambridge
Motta M, Peitz M (March 2019) Challenges for EU Merger Control, Discussion Paper Series-CRC TR 224, Discussion Paper No. 077 Project B 05. https://www.crctr224.de/en/research-output/discussion-papers/discussion-paper-archive/2019/challenges-for-eu-merger-control-massimo-motta-martin-peitz-1/view
Motta M, Tarantino E (30 August 2017) The Effect of Horizontal Mergers-When Firms Compete in Prices and Investments. https://pdfs.semanticscholar.org/2709/12148ff62a37fc2d572a8edf74b155299a96.pdf
Nazzini R (2011) The foundations of European Union competition law. Oxford University Press, Oxford
Newman N (2014) Search, antitrust and the economics of the control of user data. Yale J Reg 31: 402–454
Odudu O (2011) Are state-owned health-care providers undertakings subject to competition law? Eur Comp Law Rev 32:231–241
OECD (1997) Application of Competition policy to High Tech Markets. OECD Working Papers, Series Roundtables on Competition Policy n.9. Paris
OECD (2012) The Role of Efficiency Claims in Antitrust Proceedings. http://www.oecd.org/competition/EfficiencyClaims2012.pdf
OECD (2017) OECD science, technology and industry scoreboard 2017- the digital transformation. OECD Publishing, Paris
OECD Global Forum on Competition (29 January 2009) The objectives of Competition Law and Policy- Note by the Secretariat. http://www.oecd.org/daf/competition/2486329.pdf
Ohlhausen MK, Okuliar AP (2015) Competition, consumer protection, and the right [approach] to privacy. Antitrust Law J 80:121–156
Pasquale F (2013) Privacy, antitrust and power. Geo Mason Law Rev 20:1009–1024
Patterson M (2013) Antitrust and informational restraints. In: Hawk B (ed) International antitrust law & policy: Fordham Competition Law 2012, pp 493–537
Rab S (2014) New EU technology transfer block exemption: a note for caution. J Eur Compet Law Pract 5:436–450

Rai AK (2001) Fostering cumulative innovation in the biopharmaceutical industry: the role of patents and antitrust. Berkeley Technol Law J 16:813–853

Régibeau P, Rockett KE (2019) Mergers and innovation. The. Antitrust Bull 64:31–53

Richter H, Slowinski PR (2019) The data sharing economy: on the emergence of new intermediaries. IIC 50:4–29

Rosenboom NSR (December 2013) How Does Article 101(3) TFUE Case Law Relate to EC Guidelines and the Welfare Perspective?. Seo Economic Research, Amsterdam. https://pdfs.semanticscholar.org/d6ff/567e0fdd600a1143e8ef2b406fce00d84bdd.pdf

Rubinfeld D, Gal M (2017) Access barriers to big data. Ariz Law Rev 59:339–381

Scherer FM (1987) Antitrust, efficiency, and Progress. New York Univ Law Rev 62:998–1020

Schumpeter J (1943) Capitalism, socialism and democracy. George Allen & Unwin, Crows Nest

Seitz C (2011) One step in the right direction- the new horizontal guidelines and the restated block exemption regulations. J Eur Compet Law Pract 2:452–462

Seitz C (2018) Healthcare systems and competition: challenges and boundaries for the application of competition law in highly regulated markets in the healthcare sector in the European Union. In: Nihoul P, Van Cleynenbreugel P (eds) The roles of innovation in competition law analysis. Edward Elgar, Cheltenham, pp 131–161

Shapiro C (8 November 2005) Antitrust, Innovation and Intellectual Property- Testimony Before the Antitrust Modernization Commission. https://faculty.haas.berkeley.edu/shapiro/amcinnovation.pdf

Shapiro C (2012) Competition and innovation: did Arrow hit the Bull's eye? In: Lerner J, Stern S (eds) The rate & direction of economic activity revisited. University of Chicago Press, Chicago, pp 361–404

Shapiro C, Varian HR (1999) Information rules: a strategic guide to the network economy. Harvard Business School Press, Boston

Shelanski HA (2013) Information, innovation and competition policy for the internet. Univ Pa Law Rev 161:1663–1705

Sokol D (2017) Understanding online markets and antitrust analysis. Northwest J Technol Intell Prop 15:43–52

Sokol D, Comerford R (2016) Antitrust and regulating big data. Geo Mason Law Rev 23:1129–1161

Spulber DF, Yoo CS (2014) Antitrust, the internet and the economics of networks. In: Blair RD, Sokol D (eds) Oxford handbook of international antitrust economics. Oxford University Press, Oxford, pp 380–403

Stucke M (2005) Evaluating the risks of increased price transparency. Antitrust 19:81–88

Stucke ME, Grunes A (May 2015) Debunking the myths over Big Data and Antitrust. CPI Antitrust Chronicle. https://papers.ssrn.com/sol3/papers.cfm?abstract_id=2612562

Teece DJ (1994) Information sharing, innovation and antitrust. Antitrust Law J 62:465–481

Temple Lang J (1997) European Communities antitrust law: innovation markets and high technology industries. Fordham Int Law J 20:717–818

Todino M, Van De Walle G, Stoican L (2018) Eu merger control and harm to innovation- a long walk to freedom (from the chains of causation). Antitrust Bull XX:1–20

Townley C (2009) Article 81 EC and public policy. Hart Publishing, Oxford

Tucker DS, Wellford HB (2014) Big mistakes regarding big data. Antitrust Source:1–12

U.S. Department of Justice and Federal Trade Commission (12 January 2017) Antitrust Guidelines for the Licensing of Intellectual Property ("IP Guidelines") https://www.justice.gov/atr/IPguidelines/download

Ullrich H (2003) Competitor cooperation and the evolution of competition law: issues for research in a perspective of globalisation. In: Drexl J (ed) The future of transnational antitrust from comparative to common competition law. Kluwer Law International, Alphen aan den Rijn, pp 159–223

Van Cleynenbreugel P (2018) Innovation in competition law analysis: making sense of on-going academic and policy debates. In: Nihoul P, Van Cleynenbreugel P (eds) The roles of innovation in competition law analysis. Edward Elgar, Cheltenham, pp 2–13
Van de Gronden JW (2011) The treaty provisions on competition and health care. In: Van de Gronden JW, Szyszczak E, Neergaard U, Krajewski M (eds) Health care and EU law. TMC Asser Press, The Hague, pp 265–294
Wagner-von Papp F (2013) Information exchange agreements. In: Lianos I, Geradin D (eds) Handbook on European competition law. Edward Elgar, Cheltenham, pp 130–173
Weber RH (2015) From competition law to sector-specific regulation in internet markets? A critical assessment of a possible structural change. In: Drexel J, Di Porto F (eds) Competition law as regulation. Edward Elgar, Cheltenham, pp 239–267
Weche JP, Wambach A (January 2018) The Fall and Rise of Market Power in Europe. Discussion Paper N. 18-003, Zentrum Für Europäische Wirtschaftsforschung. http://ftp.zew.de/pub/zew-docs/dp/dp18003.pdf
Werner P, Clerckx S, De La Barre H (2018) Commission expansionism in EU merger control: fact and fiction. J Eur Compet Law Pract 9:133–145
Zain S (2006) Suppression of innovation or collaborative efficiencies? An antitrust analysis of a research and development collaboration that led to the shelving of a promising drug. J Marshall Rev Intell Prop 5:347–381
Zarsky T (2015) The privacy-innovation conundrum. LCLR 19:115–168
Zimmer D (2008) On fairness and welfare: the objectives of competition policy. In: Ehlerman CD, Marquis M (eds) European competition law annual. Hart Publishing, Oxford, pp 103–107
Zingales N (2018b) Data protection considerations in EU competition law: funnel or straightjacket for innovation? In: Nihoul P, Van Cleynenbreugel P (eds) The roles of innovation in competition law analysis. Edward Elgar, Cheltenham, pp 79–130

Chapter 7
Designing Health Data Pools: Data Protection Safeguards and Competition Remedies

7.1 The Regulatory Design of Health Data Pools Under European Data Protection and Competition Law

The analysis made in the previous chapters has illustrated how health data represent a highly scientifically valuable asset, the accessibility and the treatment of which is ever more becoming essential for research and market innovation purposes in the field of digital health. As the analysed cases have shown, the interactions between various market players specifically designed for the pooling together of different types of research valuable health data, appear to have increased, creating a networked digital health innovation environment.

In line with these developments, the consideration of the two emerging policy objectives at European level respectively regarding the advancement of the European digital health sector and the promotion of the free flow of information within the digital single market, suggests the emergence at European level of the policy objective regarding the free flow of research valuable (health) data.

Against the backdrop of this identified policy objective, it has been demonstrated how the General Data Protection Regulation under the research exemption *ex* art. 9(2) lett. j) GDPR establishes a special access regime specifically regarding sensitive personal data- as health data- for research purposes. Similarly also under European competition law, research alliances based on the sharing of health data could, under specific circumstances, find a favourable treatment under art. 101.3 TFEU and the related Block Exemption regarding research and development agreements.

Framed in these terms, the analysed provisions both under European data protection and competition law appear to provide normative grounds for the promotion of the sharing of health data for research purposes in consistency with the objectives of the free flow of information, of technical progress and ultimately of the consolidation of the internal market in the digital health sector.

G. Schneider, *Health Data Pools Under European Data Protection and Competition Law*, Munich Studies on Innovation and Competition 17,
https://doi.org/10.1007/978-3-030-95427-7_7

In this perspective, the considered provisions and the corresponding policy objectives directly satisfy economic fundamental rights, related to the freedom of business and the right to scientific progress. As a result of the health advancements stemming from analytical research enquiries over health data, the personal fundamental right to health is ultimately promoted.

However, the free flow of health data both among private businesses and among private businesses and public institutions, as enabled under the considered data protection and competition law access regimes and promoted by European policy initiatives within the Digital Single Market Strategy, cannot be left to the free digital market play. As has been acknowledged, the unrestricted flow of information could create legal uncertainty negatively affecting not only the data subjects who are the originators of these data, as well as the consumers'/patients' who ultimately come to use the resulting digital products and services, but also the same "merchants" of these sensitive data.[1]

These concerns have been upheld by Commissioner Vestager, stressing how the European Commission welcomes the pooling of data "as long as companies do it in a way that protects people's privacy and doesn't hurt competition".[2]

In this perspective, the acknowledgment of the market-oriented provisions enabling the sharing of health data for research purposes among market players, is the starting point for a deeper reflection the regulatory tools, which need to be enacted for the creation of a digital health research environment that is compliant to data subjects'/patients' fundamental rights to data protection, to non-commodification of research valuable health data as well as to research entities' economic freedom and right to non-discrimination.

For these purposes, the following chapter will identify the *ex ante* data protection safeguards that have to structure the creation of research-based health data pools, as well as the *ex post* competition remedies that correct anticompetitive aggregations of research valuable data.

As will be shown, data protection safeguards and competition remedies have very different tasks.

The formers are indeed related to the proceduralization of businesses' research activities through the imposition of specific obligations to which the sharing, aggregation and processing of health data for research purposes need to conform under the General Data Protection Regulation. These obligations majorly assure that the transfer and use of health data for research purposes are strictly anchored to the production of adequate information regarding the features of such processing activities and, in particular, to the identification of possible discriminatory outcomes of data-driven research patterns. In other terms, the data protection safeguards that will be assessed below are mainly functional to the generation of information regarding how health data pools are structured and the impact of the processing activities that occur therein on data subjects and on the consumers of the research results. Such

[1] So Graef et al. (2018b), p. 1359.

[2] Commissioner Vestager (29 September 2016).

procedural information regarding the processing of research information is addressed mainly at data subjects and, most relevantly, at data protection authorities.

From a very different perspective, the recent enforcement policies enacted by the European Commission in high technology innovation markets- both in the field of market abuses under art. 102 TFEU and in the context of merger procedures-, shows the emergence of competition remedies aimed at opening up established research pools in order to disclose research valuable informational assets to weaker competing parties. If applied to the case of health data pools, these competition remedies could be employed by competition authorities for the imposition of the creation of new health data pools among market players, as research entities, which would otherwise be foreclosed. In these regards, the setting of a disclosure obligation onto a dominant or merged entity of closely pooled health data could be functional to aliment competition in data-driven health research and with that the otherwise compromised well-functioning of digital health innovation markets.

Against this backdrop, the following analysis demonstrates how both data protection law and competition law have a significant role in shaping the design of research valuable data flows, although with different tasks.

Data protection law indeed sets some precise obligations that need to be followed by research stakeholders handling sensitive personal data before and during the transfer and processing of health data. In this perspective, it thus sets a general normative architecture for data driven research to which every player in the market of health research is subject. In this respect, it is argued that data protection law under the General Data Protection Regulation sets the *ex ante* safeguards for the establishment of research-based health data pools, rendering health data aggregation practices and the resulting data-driven research patterns, respectful of data subjects' right to data protection and to non-discrimination.

Differently, the competition remedies developed under the latest interpretations of the essential facilities doctrine and under commitment decisions in the pharmaceutical markets, set case-specific obligations exceptionally designed by competition authorities targeting either dominant or merged research entities, respectively as a result or in forecast of an identified antitrust harm. In this respect, it is deemed that competition law can intervene setting *ex post* remedies into formed health data pools, rendering the competition process evolving around the formed research poles *fairer* and more respectful of competing parties' freedom to conduct research.

Notwithstanding these structural differences, some interesting commonalities can be found, at a more general level, between the *ex ante* data protection safeguards and the *ex post* competition remedies. Indeed, both provide tools for the design of data-driven health innovation, in a way that curbs the risks to both data subjects' and minor businesses' rights stemming from the free flows of research information that both branches primarily encourage under their access regimes. For these purposes, it is interesting to observe that both regimes react with transparency measures either regarding how the pooled health data is processed and employed- as it occurs with the data protection safeguards-, or concerning the research data itself- as it occurs under competition remedies.

In these regards, both data protection authorities and competition authorities have a very important role, the former having large investigating powers regarding the structuring of collaborative data-driven research endeavours, the latter being themselves encumbered of the power of deciding when and how to activate pro-competitive sharing remedies.

In this respect, it will be shown how the data protection rules and principles work as a structural basis for the design of competition remedies regarding the sharing of personal research data by competition authorities. Moreover, the information that data protection authorities are entitled to access can be extremely relevant for competition authorities in order to better define the terms of the sharing remedy, *i. e.* the information that needs to be made object of the remedy and the timeframe that the sharing remedy has to cover. This suggests the opportunity of a close collaboration between the two authorities for a joint governance of shared research data.

Furthermore, as will be demonstrated below, both data protection safeguards and competition remedies, and the connected authorities' powers, sensitively interfere with the intellectual property protections enacted by pools' members onto research data and related processing infrastructures, thus running against the obscuring trends of centralized research propertization patterns.[3]

From a theoretical standpoint, exactly in the view of the impact of data protection safeguards and competition remedies on the design of research data sharing alliances, data protection law and competition law appear to have gained, respectively with the enactment of the General Data Protection Regulation and the European Court of Justice's and European Commission's policies in the field of competition in innovation, a newly emerging regulatory function in respect to data-driven innovation.

In respect to data-driven innovation, both data protection and competition law have complementary regulatory tasks, the first one setting the basic rules of the research play, the second determining how many players can enter the research field considered as a self-standing market. In this perspective, thus they shape and model data-driven innovation patterns around collaborative paradigms, established by data protection law between research entities and the data subjects whose data are being employed, and established by competition law between research entities and other competing parties. Although from these different perspectives, both laws ultimately appear to promote technical progress stemming from the flows of research valuable data.

By doing this, both laws appear to attract within their spheres, the task of both regulating and incentivising innovation, which traditionally resided in the domain of intellectual property law.

As has already been suggested in previous parts of the present study and by a strand of intellectual property scholars, the obscuring and over-propertizing intellectual property protections regarding research assets, and mostly informational

---

[3] See Von Braun and Pugatch (2005), pp. 599 ff. See also supra Chap. 2, Sects. 2.2.1 and 2.2.2.

assets, risk to run against the original innovation stirring function of the intellectual property system.[4]

In this respect, it has already illustrated how the phenomenon of pools of research valuable resources has been partly regarded as a contractually reaction against the proliferation of propertized data silos.

Under these premises, the peculiarities of data-driven innovation and the collaborative interactions characterising its flows appear to be better captured by both data protection and competition law, which respectively have provided provisions and developed policies on the one hand encouraging research fruitful data aggregations and on the other hand invasively directing their form. In other terms, the comprehensive regulatory framework set by both data protection and competition law for health data pools, comprises both carrots for their flourishing and sticks for their design.

Against this backdrop, the following analysis will enquire the data protection safeguards and the competition remedies that have been developed at both normative and policy level in respect to research data pools.

7.2 The *Ex Ante* Design of Health Data Pools: Data Protection Safeguards

In acknowledging research as an autonomous legal basis for the processing of sensitive data under art. 9(2) lett. j GDPR, the same General Data Protection Regulation conditions the processing of sensitive data to the enactment of "suitable and specific measures to safeguard the fundamental rights and the interests of the data subject". Likewise, art. 89(1) GDPR, which art. 9(2) lett. j GDPR expressly recalls, affirms that controllers must put in place "technical and organizational measures" to ensure that they process only the personal data that are necessary for the research purposes.

These technical and organizational measures need to be first of all rooted in the fundamental data protection law principles. Against the backdrop of these principles, relevant measures for the safeguard of the fundamental rights and the interests of the data subjects can be systematically drawn from the General Data Protection Regulation's texture.

[4] See supra Chap. 2, Sect. 2.2.2.

7.2.1 *The GDPR's Data Protection Principles for Health Research*

Art. 89 (1) GDPR clarifies that the processing of personal data for research purposes needs to respect, first of all, the principle of data minimization. This principle has been introduced under the General Data Protection Regulation as a direct response to the massive data processing activities over personal data enabled by new technologies. Art. 5(1) lett. c GDPR requires processing activities to be "adequate, relevant and limited to what is necessary in relation to the purposes for which they are processed". The importance of such principle in the context of scientific research is expressly acknowledged under recital 156 GDPR that demands that research entities calibrate the amount of data processed in order to avoid unnecessary analysis of personal data, and thus reduce the risks of harms to data subjects.[5]

The principle of data minimization is strictly related to other general data protection principles, as the principle of purpose limitation and storage limitation, which are likewise bound to restricting the scope and duration of processing activities. However as has already been illustrated, art. 5(1) lett. b) and art. 5(1) lett. e) GDPR respectively allow exceptions to the principles of purpose limitations and storage limitation in case of data processing for research purposes.[6]

The exceptions to these principles renders the reference to the principle of data minimization even more important, for it needs to permeate research processing activities notwithstanding the exceptions to the two above recalled principles.

However, it has been interestingly observed that a proper compliance to the principle of data minimisation could risk to run contrary to the very purposes of data-driven research, which renders the more accurate and valuable results the bigger and the more heterogenoues the analyzed datasets are.[7] This triggers the need for research entities to design their data-driven enquiries in a way that mediates between the adequate implementation of the said principle and the achievement of the purposes for which the data have been pooled together and processed.

In order to adequately comply with the principle of data minimization, members of established health data pools need thus to *demonstrate* that the processing activities that they are conducting are strictly necessary and proportionate to the set research goals. A direct application of the principle of data minimization would require data controllers, for example, to consider whether the research objectives can be achieved also with anonymized data.[8]

Exactly the difficulty of properly implementing the data minimization principle in the research context determines the crucial relevance of other two general data protection law principles, namely the principles of transparency and accountability,

---

[5]These have been mapped supra Chap. 3, Sect. 3.3.

[6]This had been already discussed supra Chap. 5, Sect. 5.3.2.3.2.

[7]In this perspective Quinn and Quinn (2018), p. 1006.

[8]European Parliament (July 2019), pp. 26–27.

respectively enshrined in art. 5(1) lett. a and 5(2) GDPR. These principles are complementary to the principle of data minimization: they indeed require that, if data processing activities cannot be avoided, at least they have to be conducted in a transparent way, with data processing entities taking full responsibility of the enquiries they carry out under the principles of accountability.

Also as far as the principle of transparency is concerned, data processing activities carried out for research purposes can undergo significant exceptions regarding the information that data controllers have to release to data subjects under art. 14(5) lett. b).[9] The provision refers to the duties of data controllers to provide specific information to data subjects over ongoing processing activities when the processed data are not directly retrieved from data subjects but from third party sources. Since this is the case of most of the data pooled together from different sources in order to conduct research enquiries, the exception to this transparency-based rule is quite far reaching.

The derogation to such transparency rule enhances the relevance of the principle of accountability in the context of data-driven research. Accountability is related to data controllers and processors 'responsabilization'. It is established at art. 5.2 GDPR, affirming that 'the controller shall be responsible for, and be able to demonstrate compliance with paragraph 1 (accountability)'. By stating so, art. 5.2 GDPR declares the autonomy of the principle of accountability in the data protection law ecosystem, and at the same time the strict operational connection to other principles relating to the processing of personal data—such as the principle of lawfulness, of fairness and of transparency—and to the rules that substantiate these principles.

Defined in these terms, the principle of accountability has a twofold dimension, an internal one, related to the 'burden of care' borne by processing corporations, and an external one, related to the capability of the same processing corporations to demonstrate that such "burden of care" has been correctly performed.

Operationally, accountability means compliance with other data protection principles, as the principle of accuracy[10] and with data controllers' and processors' procedural obligations set by the General Data Protection Regulation with regards to processing activities, such as the data protection by design and by default rule under art. 25 GDPR; the data protection impact assessment and prior consultation under art. 35 and 36 GDPR; the reporting duties as the breach notification obligation under art. 33 GDPR. In this perspective, the accountability principle as expressed in corporations' procedural obligations entails the essential function of the *ex ante*

[9]See supra Chap. 5, Sect. 5.3.2.3.2.

[10]In respect to the accuracy principle it needs to be recalled that the principle is deemed to apply only to collected data and not to the inferences drawn from the data. This is the interpretation given by the European Parliament following the European Court of Justice judgment in YS v Minister voor Immigratie, Integratie en Asiel. This interpretation would sensitively limit the accuracy obligations of research entities in respect to the scientific results drawn from personal data. See European Parliament (July 2019) 31 and European Court of Justice, YS v Minister voor Immigratie, Integratie en Asiel, in Joined Cases C-141/12 and C-372/12 (17 July 2014).

prevention and management of the risks stemming from massive machine-driven processing operations.

As the same wording of art. 5(1) GDPR clarifies, the accountability parameter demands that compliance to normative requirements is externally verifiable, thus traceable. In these regards, if the transparency obligations in respect to data subjects are sensitively weakened in the context of data processing activities carried out for research purposes, the same principle of accountability requires that such activities are externally verifiable by data protection authorities in the exercise of their investigative powers under art. 58(1) lett. b) GDPR.[11]

Ultimately, the special regime established for data processing activities carried out for research purposes should ground the relevance in the context of data-driven research projects of another data protection principle, which is strictly related to the principle of accountability.

Enshrined in art. 5(1) lett. a) GDPR, the principle of fairness has been appointed by the European Data Protection Supervisor as "a core principle of data protection law".[12] The principle of fairness builds on the principle of lawfulness but requires an evaluation of a specific processing conduct that goes beyond the mere lawfulness. Indeed, a specific processing operation may be, on the basis of an *ex ante* assessment, lawful for it fully satisfies mandatory legal requirements (such as the informed consent rule) but may result, from an *ex post* perspective, unfair.

Although there is no definition as such of the principle of fairness in positive European data protection law, fairness of the processing is related to the balancing of competing interests and more precisely of fundamental rights and freedoms of the subjects involved, that is, on the one side the data subject and on the other side the data controllers and processors. More precisely, fairness requires that in pursuing their data-processing objectives, data controllers and processors take into consideration the interests and the reasonable expectations of data subjects. For a "fair" protection of these interests, corporations may need to go beyond the minimum legal requirements.[13]

Fair balancing is of theoretical nature and its application relies on the particular context in which it is applied. From an operational perspective, fair balancing incorporates the principles of proportionality and necessity, which are explicitly recognised in the GDPR and more precisely in art. 6(1) GDPR: the necessity and proportionality criteria substantiate the fair balancing test and enable the assessment of the appropriateness of controllers'/processors' actions, through the evaluation of the peculiar circumstances, *i.e.* the research context, in which the processing operation has occurred.

Against this backdrop, the principle of fairness carries out an overarching function of re-balancing of the data-subject/controller relationship in case the collection and processing of personal data undermines data subjects' interests. In this

[11] See European Data Protection Supervisor (February 2018).

[12] European Data Protection Supervisor (23 September 2016).

[13] Clifford and Ausloos (7 August 2017).

perspective, the fairness criterion assures the protection of data subjects from controllers'/processors' abuse, by preventing disproportionate harms stemming from the power asymmetries characterising the data-driven research environment.[14]

Since, as has been illustrated,[15] the special data protection regime regarding processing activities for research purposes, admits exceptions to data subjects' rights such as the right of erasure under art. 17 GDPR and the right to object under art. 21 GDPR, data subjects' reaction means to counteract the power asymmetries arising in data-driven research enquiries can result sensitively weakened. Through these derogations, data subjects are deprived from the possibility of having a proactive role in protecting their legal position *vis à vis* data controllers/processors and in neutralizing existing imbalances.

In this context, thus, the principle of fairness shifts the perspective onto the controllers'/processors' perspective, demanding that processing operations do not infringe data subject' fundamental rights and freedoms, in particular the fundamental right to freedom from unfair discrimination. In these regards, recital 71 GDPR, requires the controller to "implement technical and organisational measures appropriate to ensure, in particular, that (. . .) the risk of errors is minimised" and to "secure personal data in a manner that takes account of the potential risks involved for the interests and rights of the data and that prevents, inter alia, discriminatory effects on natural persons on the basis of racial or ethnic origin, political opinion, religion or beliefs, trade union membership, genetic or health status or sexual orientation, or that result in measures having such an effect".

The mentioned recital establishes a deep connection between the principle of fairness and of non-discrimination. In this perspective, it suggests that large scale processing operations conducted over sensitive health data should respect both "individual fairness" and "group fairness". The former is safeguarded when similar individuals are treated by the processing system alike and is thus violated when two individuals sharing similar features, except for a certain (discriminatory) criterion, are treated differently. Conversely, "group fairness" is safeguarded through statistical parity, which occurs when each group determined by the model bears similar outcome distributions.[16]

Under these premises, it can be concluded that the principles of transparency, accountability, fairness and non-discrimination, provide a basic data protection framework, upon which the specific data protection safeguards for research activities have to be rooted and measured.

In this perspective, these principles have the fundamental function of structuring health data-driven research enquiries and the resulting digital health innovation patterns in a way that enhances the digital trust in the final digital health products and services. The creation of trust has been acknowledged by the European Commission as an "essential precondition for the sustainable development of the data

[14] Maxwell (2015), pp. 205 ff.

[15] Chapter 5, Sect. 5.3.2.3.2.

[16] This is assessed by Hacker (2018).

economy", and, as far as the digital health sector is concerned, of the innovation market related to health research.[17]

7.2.2 The GDPR's Data Protection Obligations for Health Research: An Overview

By setting the requirement of the implementation of adequate "technical and organizational measures" in the context of processing activities carried out for research purposes, art.89 GDPR expressly refers to pseudonymization techniques, stating that the employment of such technique is encouraged "as long as (the research purposes) can be fulfilled in this manner". Under art. 4(3) lett. b GDPR, pseudonymization is "the processing of personal data in such a way that the data can no longer be attributed to a specific data subject without the use of additional information, as long as such additional information is kept separately and subject to technical and organizational measures to ensure non-attribution to an identified or identifiable individual".

Unlike anonymous data, the processing of pseudonymous data falls within the scope of the Regulation. It must however be observed that the distinction between anonymous and pseudonymous data is not always easy and requires a fact-specific inquiry.[18] Under Recital 26, data is to be considered anonymous only if it cannot be identified by any means "reasonably likely to be used... either by the controller or by another person". This means that although a researcher no longer has the ability to re-identify the dataset, the processing activities regarding these data may still be regulated by the Regulation, in case the datasets can be re-identified with reasonable effort.[19]

In addition to this, it needs to be recalled that the possibility to re-identify the analyzed data is most of the times an essential component of the research enquiry, this rendering the option of pseudonymisation most of the times more useful, from a research perspective, than anonymization.[20]

This distinction between anonymous and pseudonymous data goes not without significant regulatory consequences. Indeed, in case pseudonymous health data is processed for research purposes through automated processing techniques, as profiling, the General Data Protection Regulation establishes an important restriction under art. 22 GDPR, which prohibits such processing if not occurring pursuant to a contract or to the data subject's consent. This provision is fully applicable to automated processing for research purposes.[21]

[17] European Commission (25 April 2018c), p. 1.

[18] Maldoff (12 February 2016).

[19] Maldoff (12 February 2016).

[20] This is highlighted by Quinn (2016), pp. 2–3. Comandè (2019), p. 198.

[21] European Parliament (July 2019), p. 33.

The right not to be subject to automated processing appears to be specifically taken into consideration in respect to the processing of personal data for research purposes under the already mentioned recital 162 GDPR, which in respect to statistical research endeavours prohibits the use of personal data "in support of measures or decisions regarding any particular natural person".[22] As the recital suggests, thus, processing of personal data carried out for research purposes cannot result in profiling activities and other decisions regarding single natural persons.[23] This statement, although only contained in a recital, is extremely important and poses some interesting interpretative grounds for the prevention of research processing activities resulting into further, "secondary", commercial actions.

However, art. 22(2) GDPR clarifies that the data subjects' right to object to the automated processing is limited to the cases in which, amongst others, the decision is based *solely* on automated processing.[24] This means that if the decision, as the evaluation of rendered scientific results drawn from data analytics, is made with the *aid of* automated decision making techniques, then the prohibition under art. 22 GDPR could be circumvented.[25] Hence, in order to determine whether the provision under art. 22 GDPR applies or not to a specific research project, research entities using automated processing techniques should define beforehand how decisions are taken within the project.[26]

Since art. 89 (1) GDPR generally refers to "technical and organizational measures" without specifying them properly, these have to be systematically derived from the general provisions of the General Data Protection Regulation.

As a general premise it needs to be recalled that especially in the context of data sharing for research purposes among multiple research entities these may fall under the joint controllership rule ex art. 26 GDPR. This means that all the research entities members to the pool who jointly determine the purposes and the means of the processing, shall be considered joint controllers under art. 26 GDPR and thus be jointly liable in respect to the obligations under data protection law, as the enactment of the technical and organizational measures in the context of data-driven research

---

[22] In these regards, some clarifications have been provided by the Art. 29 Data Protection Working Party that has identified some examples in which companies carry out processing activities over personal data, without finalising them to individual decisions regarding natural persons, as in the case a business may wish to "classify its customers according to their age or gender for statistical purposes and to acquire an aggregated overview of its clients without making any predictions or drawing any conclusions about an individual. In this case the purpose is not assessing individual characteristics and is therefore not profiling". So Art. 29 Data Protection Working Party (3 October 2017, last revised on 6 February 2018), p. 7.

[23] Zarsky (2017), p. 1008. It must however be said that in the context of big data analytics it is extremely difficult to identify secondary uses. So, Richter (2016), p. 585, highlighting the difficulties of detecting in which way the statistical models are employed, i.e. for which purposes and by which controllers.

[24] Mendoza and Bygrave (2017), pp. 77 ff.

[25] So Wachter (2018), pp. 266 ff.

[26] This is suggested by European Parliament (July 2019), p. 34, stressing the importance for these purposes of the involvement of research ethics committees.

projects. According to recital 76 GDPR this joint liability rule regards also the processing entities who run data processing operations on behalf of the controllers, as cloud processors or scientific computer centers.[27]

Against this backdrop, in order to reverse the normatively set presumption of joint liability in the context of research collaborations, the European Parliament has recommended the establishment of a joint contractual agreement between the involved research parties. The contract should identify the specific obligations of each of the involved parties exactly with regards to the enactment of the technical and organizational measures needed to render the data-driven research project respectful of data subjects' rights and freedoms.[28]

The identification of these specific measures in the context of health data sharing-based collaborations is still surrounded by great uncertainties. Some of the general obligations set by the General Data Protection Regulation could be of great interest for these purposes. Their specific implementation in the health data research context should be however better specified by both guidelines specifically referring to this peculiar context and by the evolving practice.

Under these premises, an interesting tool for a more precise definition of such technical and organizational measures in the field of digital health innovation is to be found in the redaction of codes of conduct encouraged under art. 40 GDPR. The provision recommends designated bodies to "prepare codes of conduct (...) for the purpose of specifying the application of this Regulation, such as with regard to: (a) *fair and transparent processing* (...)".[29] Relying on art. 40 GDPR, the Biobanking and Biomolecular resources Research Infrastructure-European Research Infrastructure Consortium (BBMRI-ERIC) is currently developing a GDPR Code of Conduct for Health Research as a means to comply with and to contribute to a proper implementation of the GDPR in the field of health research.[30]

In the wakes of the redaction of this code of conduct, some suggestions regarding which could be the relevant data protection safeguards for data-driven research projects can still be drawn from the General Data Protection's provisions.

Particularly important are the provisions under articles 24 and 25 GDPR, respectively requiring controllers to enact data protection measures by design and default, which would structurally internalize and assure compliance to data protection principles.[31] For the purposes of data protection by design and by default, art. 42 GDPR authorizes "the establishment of data protection certification mechanisms and data protection seals and marks" that shall "be available *via a process that is*

---

[27] So Dove (2018), p. 1015.

[28] European Parliament (July 2019), pp. 34–35 expressly citing the case of the Google DeepMind-Royal Free Hospital partnership as an example of lack of a clear allocation of liabilities among involved research entities.

[29] Emphasis added.

[30] BBMRI-ERIC http://www.bbmri-eric.eu/news-events/code-of-conduct-for-health-research/.

[31] This is stressed by European Parliament (July 2019), p. 34.

transparent".[32] Certification measures of data-driven research activities could be a relevant safeguard for preventing processing practices of sensitive health data for research purposes from resulting in commercially-employed categorizations of data subjects' health conditions.

Among other safeguards established by the Regulation that can be useful in order to prevent the employment of sensitive research data for purposes that are different from research purposes, the transparency requirements set out by the same Regulation are worth of deeper assessment.

Art. 13 GDPR requires controllers to provide data subjects with information regarding the features of the ongoing processing when the personal data are collected from the data subject. In particular, they oblige controllers to provide "meaningful information" regarding the "existence of automated decision-making, including profiling, referred to in artt. 22(1) and 22(4), and at least in those cases, *meaningful information* about the logic involved, as well as the *significance* and the *envisaged consequences* of such processing for the data subject".[33] Likewise, the above-recalled art. 22 GDPR requires the data controller to "implement suitable measures to safeguard the data subject's rights and freedoms and legitimate interests, at least *the right to obtain human intervention on the part of the controller, to express his or her point of view and to contest the decision*".[34]

It should be however noticed that these transparency requirements directed to data subjects are difficult to implement in the context of big data research projects, first of all because it is difficult identify who the data subjects are in a research context mainly centred on a group perspective rather than on an individual perspective.[35] In second stance, even if the data subjects that are the recipients of the information by the data controllers would be identified, it is very probably that the effective fulfilment of the transparency requirements would be impaired by the intellectual property, and in particular trade secrets, exceptions that the same General Data Protection Regulation takes into account under recital 63 GDPR.[36] Especially in the context of health research, where there are strong intellectual property safeguards,[37] the impact of related exceptions onto controllers transparency obligations could be significant.

Moreover, the data employed for research purposes are most of the times collected not directly from the data subject but from third parties: in this case the data controllers in the context of a research project are exempted from complying to art. 14 GDPR, setting the transparency obligations related to data that are not directly collected from data subjects.[38]

---

[32] Emphasis added.

[33] Art. 13, 2 lett. f) of the General Data Protection Regulation. Emphasis added.

[34] Emphasis added.

[35] This has been assessed supra Chap. 5, Sect. 5.3.1.1.

[36] For a deeper analysis on the issue, see Schneider (2019), pp. 327 ff.

[37] See supra Chap. 2, Sect. 2.2.1.

[38] This exception has been already assessed supra Chap. 5, Sect. 5.3.2.

Both the legal exceptions to the transparency requirements under art. 14 GDPR and the practical difficulty of implementing the transparency requirement under art. 13 GDPR, renders the transparency obligations in respect to the data subjects quite weak.

This acknowledgment should thus ground a stronger transparency burden placed onto research entities in respect to supervisory authorities through the "data protection impact assessment", required under art. 35 GDPR, in case the processing operations are likely to result in "a high risk to the rights and freedoms of natural persons".[39]

As the provision clarifies, such risk is to be found in case the processing activities involve a "systematic and extensive evaluation *of personal aspects* relating to natural persons which is based on automated processing"[40] and, in case they involve the "processing on a large scale of special categories of data referred to in article 9(1) GDPR (. . .)".[41] Since health data pools involve exactly the massive processing of sensitive data for research purposes that are related to the evaluation of health conditions, that are personal aspects of data subjects, it is clear that the requirement of a data protection impact assessment becomes a key obligation in the context of data-driven research enquiries. However, also in the absence of the processing "on a large scale" of sensitive data, the Working Party 29 has recommended the conduction of a data impact assessment also in case the processing involves a significant "volume of data" or, a "range of different data items", as it distinctively occurs with health data pools.[42] In this respect, the Working Party has highlighted the need of a data protection impact assessment exactly where sensitive data are aggregated with other non-sensitive data and thus where "innovative uses" of sensitive data are made.[43] The processing of sensitive data through new technologies for research purposes can be considered as an "innovative use", also because the personal and social consequences of such processing in the frame of data-driven research enquiries may be unknown.[44]

As far as the content is concerned, the data protection impact assessment is a document with which controllers map the various interests involved and the rights impacted in a data-driven research project conducted through the "use of new technologies". The document has to entail "a systematic description of the envisaged processing operations and the purposes of the processing";[45] "an assessment of the necessity and proportionality of the processing operations in relation to the purposes"[46] of the research as well as of "the risks to the rights and freedoms of the data

[39] Art. 35(1) GDPR.

[40] Art. 35(3) lett. a) GDPR. Emphasis added.

[41] Art. 35(3) lett. b) GDPR.

[42] Article 29 Working Party (4 April 2017), p. 9.

[43] Article 29 Working Party (4 April 2017), p. 9.

[44] Article 29 Working Party (4 April 2017), p. 9.

[45] Art. 35(7) lett. a) GDPR.

[46] Art. 35(7) lett. b) GDPR.

subjects".[47] Moreover, interestingly, the data protection impact assessment has to contain a description of "the measures envisaged to address the risks, including safeguards, security measures and mechanisms to ensure the protection of personal data and to *demonstrate compliance* with this Regulation taking into account the rights and legitimate interests of data subjects and other persons concerned".[48]

Under these premises, thus, the function of the Data Protection Impact Assessment is exactly that of being an *ex ante* tool of appraisal of the possible threats to the data subjects' rights through a systematic evaluation of the processing activities performed under the responsibility of the controller, with the release of specific information regarding the structural features of the technologies employed for the processing.[49]

As the Article 29 Working Party has underlined, the description of the architectural features of the processing needs to be preceded by the enactment of measures that are functional to the prevention of errors, inaccuracies and discriminatory factors.[50] These safeguards have to be enacted not only in the initial moment of the design of the technological processing infrastructure, but need to accompany the whole processing operation, whenever it concretely impacts on a data subject.[51] This means, in other terms, that the auditing procedures need to follow and monitor the auto-generative and auto-alimenting cycles of automated processing operations.

However, it has been underlined how there is still a great uncertainty as to what should be the risks to the rights and freedoms of data subjects and the measures that controllers should enact for the purposes of the limitation of such risks.[52] An even greater uncertainty resides in the definition of the relevant risks and corresponding preventive measures in the context of data-driven research enquiries.[53] Indeed the rights and freedoms that could be impacted by such research enquiries are potentially unlimited, ranging from harms related to access to healthcare, to social and group harms and more broader, non health-related harms.[54]

The consideration of all such harms and the measures needed to address these would thus imply a disproportionate effort on the controllers' side, which could only be demanded to well established corporations, such as big digital companies, who can have the resources to outsource the conduction of such impact assessments to external expertise, such as consultancies or external advisors who are specializing in impact assessments.

---

[47] Art. 35(7) lett. c) GDPR.

[48] Art. 35(7) lett. d) GDPR.

[49] Article 29 Data Protection Working Party (4 April 2017), pp. 17–18.

[50] Article 29 Data Protection Working Party (3 October 2017, last revised on 6 February 2018), p. 28.

[51] Article 29 Data Protection Working Party (3 October 2017, last revised on 6 February 2018), p. 28.

[52] For a proposal see. Mantelero (2018), pp. 754 ff.

[53] Quinn and Quinn (2018), p. 1008.

[54] See mapping of interests conducted supra Chap. 3, Sect. 3.3.

With specific regards to data-driven research projects that involve only small research entities, some strand of the literature has suggested the sharing of resources needed for the conduction of impact assessments.[55] This could occur through the circulation of data protection impact assessment models for smaller research projects, or the creation of specific units within research institutions, releasing advice to research groups as to when and how a data protection impact assessment would be needed.

As art. 36(1) GDPR demands, the controller has the obligation to consult the supervisory authority prior to the processing when the data protection impact assessment shows that the processing would result in a high risk in the absence of measures taken by the controller to mitigate the risk. For the purposes of this prior consultation, the controller shall provide the supervisory authority with the data protection impact assessment performed under art. 35 GDPR,[56] together with any other information requested by the same supervisory authority.[57]

In this light, it appears that art. 36 GDPR establishes onto processing research entities an outright duty to collaborate with the data protection authority, which is entitled to access very sensitive information regarding the structuring of data-driven research projects, the information that is processed and the risks for the data subjects it entails.

Supervisory authorities, on their side, also have the power to carry out "investigations in the form of data protection audits". These audits are functional to the monitoring of the processing activities by data protection authorities so as to identify eventual biases affecting the research enquiries.[58] They thus involve outright investigations of the functioning of the technologies employed for the purposes of the processing[59] and they enable the same data protection authorities to access "all personal data" and "all information necessary for the performance of its tasks".[60] This means that through their investigative powers, data protection authorities can enquire which data are object of the research enquiries and how exactly they are technically processed.

Similarly, also art. 30 GDPR imposes onto controllers the obligation to redact an "internal record of processing" that must "be made available to the supervisory authority on request".

Overall, thus, the combined reading of artt. 30; 35; 36(1) and 58(1) lett. b) GDPR grounds the duty of controllers, and thus of research entities, to structure their health

---

[55] Quinn and Quinn (2018), p. 1009.

[56] Art. 36(3) lett. e) GDPR.

[57] Art. 36(3) lett. f) GDPR.

[58] See Casey et al. (2019), pp. 143 ff.

[59] Article 29 Working Party (3 October 2017, last revised on 6 February 2018), p. 32, where it is underlined that algorithmic audits are a means of "testing the algorithms used and developed by machine learning systems to prove that they are actually performing as intended and not producing discriminatory, erroneous or unjustified results". For the literature see Hacker (2018), pp. 1170–1173.

[60] So art. 58(1) lett. e) GDPR.

data pools and the related processing operations carried out in the context of a research task, in a manner that is externally verifiable by the supervisory authorities. These thus gain a central role in the enquiry and thus monitoring of research projects based on the sharing and analysis of sensitive information.

From a further perspective, it needs to be observed that the auditing powers of supervisory authorities are also capable of investigating both substantial and procedural information that is very likely covered by intellectual property protections. As has been illustrated above, indeed, supervisory authorities' auditing powers exactly concern the structural features of the technological processing infrastructures that mostly constitute the core know-how of research entities.

However, if the intellectual property exceptions can have a wide reach when it comes to disclosure of protected information onto data subjects or competing research entities, these undergo substantial limitations in case the recipient of the disclosure is a public authority. This principle is made explicit in the Trade Secret Directive, that affirms in recital 11, that the same directive "should not affect the application of Union or national rules that require the disclosure of information, including trade secrets, to the public or to public authorities", and should thus not impair "the application of rules that allow public authorities to collect information for the performance of their duties". Moreover, recital 18 of the same Directive further specifies that the disclosure of trade secrets should be considered lawful under the Directive, amongst others, "in the context of statutory audits performed in accordance with Union or national law". The ability of supervisory authorities to access trade secret protected information is itself safeguarded by the confidentiality obligations borne by the same supervisory authorities.[61]

Against the backdrop of this general overview of the potential relevant safeguards, which the General Data Protection Regulation either requires—as it occurs with the data protection impact assessments under art. 35 GDPR—or recommends—as it occurs with the recalled data protection certification mechanisms under art 42 GDPR—it needs to be ultimately signalled that other safeguards that are relevant for the purposes of data-driven research are found not at normative level but in the other neighbouring field of ethics.

This is what is expressly recognized by recital 33 GDPR, stating that controllers should act "in keeping with recognized ethical standards for scientific research".[62] These ethical guidelines are to be found at national level. In Italy, for example, the Italian Data Protection Authority has issued the "regole deontologiche per trattamenti a fini statistici o di ricerca scientifica".[63] These ethical rules establish

[61] See Recital 18 Trade Secret Directive, stating that the same Directive "should not release public authorities from the confidentiality obligations to which they are subject in respect of information passed on by trade secret holders, irrespective of whether those obligations are laid down in Union or national law".

[62] For an assessment over the ethical standards applicable to data-driven research see Vayena and Blasimme (2017), pp. 501 ff.

[63] Garante per l protezione dei dati personali, Regole deontologiche per trattamenti a fini statistici o di ricerca scientifica, pubblicate ai sensi dell'art. 20, comma 4, del d.lgs. 10 agosto 2018, n. 101 (19 December 2018).

additional burdens of care onto data controllers in the context of data-driven research. According to these rules, for example, controllers need to further distinguish between data processing activities carried out for research purposes and for more specific health treatment purposes.[64]

Exactly in respect to ethical safeguards, the Data Ethics Committee[65] has underlined the importance in the context of data-driven research projects of the employment of privacy management tools (PMT) and personal information management systems (PIMS). These tools are to be contextualized in the broader category of "data trust schemes". For the purposes of a uniform enactment of these software tools and applications, however, the same Data Ethics Committee stresses the need of the creation of adequate standards in relation to software tools and services of this kind.

As the Ethics Guidelines for a Trustworthy AI drafted by the High-level Expert Group on AI have clarified, the enactment of standards function as outright quality management systems, especially in the context of data-driven research.

7.2.3 Data Protection Safeguards and the "Scaled" Special Data Protection Regime for Research

In accordance to the scaled special data protection regime approach previously suggested,[66] the invasiveness of the above-recalled normative and technical safeguards would need to be modulated in consistency with the private or public-oriented nature of the enacted research activities. This means that in case the research is conducted by public interest-oriented entities, as universities or hospitals, the safeguards could be restrained to the minimum of normative requirements, in a proportionate balance between the reasons of protection of data subjects' fundamental rights and other fundamental rights, such as the right to health, promoted by research over health datasets.

Conversely, research endeavours by private entities, or anyway involving private entities along the lines of private-public partnerships' schemes, should be subject to a stricter safeguard regime, suggested by the same risk-based approach expressed in the General Data Protection Regulation, requiring higher technical and organizational measures- also in respect to basic normative requirements—whenever the risks to data subjects' rights and freedoms are evaluated as higher in accordance to an *ex ante* precautionary assessment.

[64] Garante per l protezione dei dati personali, Regole deontologiche per trattamenti a fini statistici o di ricerca scientifica, pubblicate ai sensi dell'art. 20, comma 4, del d.lgs. 10 agosto 2018, n. 101, art. 8(3).

[65] Bundesministerium für Justiz und Verbraucherschutz (22 January 2020).

[66] See supra Chap. 5, Sect. 5.3.2.3.2.

Exactly in the case of privately-conducted research the risks to data subjects' rights and freedoms are higher, because there is a higher risk that sensitive personal data is employed outside of the scope of strict research and innovation purposes, and is conversely used for commercial purposes. The Regulation's risk-based approach suggests the enactment of higher context-sensitive safeguards for the prevention of this scenario: as has been illustrated elsewhere,[67] the treatment of health data for commercial purposes is basically prohibited under art. 9(1) GDPR, unless the data subject provides explicit consent in this respect as required under art. 9(2) lett. a) GDPR.

Moreover, the higher protection safeguards required to private entities would be consistent with the above-recalled principle of fairness, which assures the protection of data subjects from controllers'/processors' abuse, by preventing disproportionate harms stemming from the power asymmetries that characterise the technology-driven processing environment, and in particular the research processing environment. In this respect, however, a careful consideration of the principle of fairness in the context of health data pools' design suggests further considerations.

As the outlined safeguards assure that the processing of health data for research purposes is not (ab)used for other different purposes potentially harming data subjects' rights and freedoms, also an opposite scenario needs to be considered, regarding the exploitation of these same data protection safeguards by the data controller for the refusal or limitation of third-party access to collected research data. In this second scenario, thus data protection safeguards could be relied on by commercially-oriented stakeholders for the concealment of privately-collected or generated research data, with a resulting monopolization of the research opportunities entrenched in existing health datasets.

From a first ethical perspective, this would shield privately-conducted data-driven research activities from the enquiry of independent or public research entities, which would in this way be prevented from evaluating these research patterns.[68] However, such abuse by private entities of the data protection safeguards required under art. 89 GDPR could amount to an outright abuse relevant under competition law as an abuse of dominant position directly resulting from the refusal, justified in data protection law, to give access to collected datasets to third-party research entities.

In recent years, the relationship between data protection law and competition law has been assessed at theoretical level by the scholarship and at practical level by national competition authorities. As especially the German Facebook case reflects, the main enquiries in this sense have tried to put competition law violations in direct relation with violations of data protection law. As here suggested, conversely, it could well be the case that over-reliance on data protection law requirements entrenching the market dominance of a company directly deriving from collected research datasets could be relevant under competition law. In other terms, it could be that the lack of exploitation of data protection law's flexibilities regarding research

[67] supra Chap. 5, Sect. 5.3.2.

[68] This is underlined by the European Data Protection Supervisor (6 January 2020), p. 26.

resulting in the refusal to share research valuable data as health data could have anticompetitive effects and thus be sanctionable under competition law.

In this regard, competition law remedies could thus be a tool for re-designing health data pools, which strict data protection safeguards risk to enclose, hindering a pro-competitive and thus pro-innovative circulation of research data. The feasibility of a competition law-based sharing remedy will be enquired in the paragraphs that follow.

It is however interesting to observe right from the beginning that in the considered scenario, a competition law remedy is not a means to *enforce* data protection law, but becomes rather a means *to take advantage of* and *govern* data protection law's flexibilities regarding research for direct innovation purposes. As the analysis below will illustrate, competition interventions have recently become increasingly sensitive in respect to innovation goals in the enforcement of anticompetitive conducts as abuses of dominant position as well as in the context of merger procedures.

7.3 The Ex Post Design of Health Data Pools: Competition Remedies

7.3.1 The Emerging Reality of Informational Abuses

Information aggregation can facilitate abusive conducts directly stemming from the informational advantage acquired through massive data collection.[69] The competitive advantage stemming from the collection of digital information is indeed very likely to result in an informational "super-dominance" or quasi-monopoly.[70]

The phenomenon of this informational "super-dominance" has started to become mostly visible in information-based industries, such as network, media, software and IT industries.[71]

The growing relevance of both information and software technologies in these industries has determined the expansion of such informational dominances also in other economic sectors,[72] this widening the risks of related market distortions.

The European Commission has started to acknowledge the need to investigate the competition concerns arising from data collection in the *Google/DoubleClick* merger,[73] highlighting that the accumulation of data could have distorting market effects, leading to anticompetitive outcomes.[74]

---

[69] Graef (2016).

[70] Szyszczak (2011), p. 1756.

[71] Waller (2012), p. 575.

[72] Waller (2012), p. 575.

[73] European Commission, Google/DoubleClick Case N. Comp./M. 4731 (11 March 2008), para. 6.

[74] Almunia (26 November 2012).

In the *Magill* case, the Court of Justice of the European Union recognised that the involved undertakings, in species three broadcasters, had a de facto monopoly over the provision of the relevant information.[75] Similar acknowledgments were made in the Microsoft decision.[76]

With regards to information generating market power, the literature has observed that "the line between the sensible use and the abuse of this kind of information is very thin".[77]

On the enforcement side, thus, the new complexities of information-based markets have suggested a shift of the enforcement focus from collusive conducts under art. 101 TFEU to abusive conducts under art. 102 TFEU.

As the analysis above has indeed shown, bilateral as well unilateral information disclosures mostly do not infringe art. 101 TFEU, and in case they produce an anticompetitive effect, these are possibly treated leniently and even encouraged under art. 101(3) TFEU.[78] However, these information flows that the same art. 101(1) TFEU and art. 101(3) TFEU promote for the purposes of the advancement of technological progress and research and development, could be distorted and thus misused by the stakeholder or stakeholders who have accumulated research valuable information exactly thanks to art. 101 TFEU's leniency. More precisely, the parties having access to the formed health data pool could employ their asymmetric information—and thus research—advantage to abuse the market power they have conquered exactly through the access to the data flown in the pool.[79]

This new connection between data aggregation and abusive conducts, is deemed to trigger new problems, which will, according to some of the scholarship's forecasts "become systemic".[80] As has been observed in this respect, these major problems firstly relate to the lack of legal certainty brought about by the effect-based approach to art. 102 TFEU[81] triggered by the changed digital economic environment, in which

[75] European Court of Justice, Radio Telefis Eireann (RTE) and Independent Television Publications Ltd. (ITP) supported by Intellectual Property Owners Inc. (IPO) vs. Commission of the European Communities supported by Magill TV Guide Ltd., Joined Cases C-241/91 P and C-242/91 P (6 April 1995), para 47.

[76] European Court of Justice- Court of First Instance, Microsoft Corp. vs. Commission of the European Communities, Case T-201/04 (17 September 2007), para 319–320.

[77] Almunia (26 November 2012).

[78] See supra Chap. 6, Sect. 6.4.

[79] These considerations are shared by Lindqvist (6 November 2018), p. 12.

[80] B. Lindqvist (6 November 2018), p. 12.

[81] See European Commission, Guidance on Enforcement Priorities in Applying Article 82 of the EC Treaty to Abusive Exclusionary Conduct by Dominant Undertakings, C 45/02 (24 February 2009). For a scholarly assessment of the effect-based approach to art. 102 TFEU, see Ghidini and Arezzo (2010), pp. 115 ff.

"atypical" conducts—that are not included in the list of possible abuses in Article 102[82]—have become increasingly relevant.[83]

Following the traditional classifications under art. 102 TFEU, aggregation of data shall be prohibited under competition law when it gives rise to exploitative or exclusionary behaviours, ultimately hindering the rise of new innovative technologies.[84]

Hence, in respect to the conducts through which a research actor or a research consortium abuses the market power acquired in research markets as a consequence of the aggregation of valuable health research data, can be of exploitative or exclusionary nature.

With specific regards to abuses carried out over health innovation valuable data, the scope of relevant health-information abuses can be defined—and properly circumscribed—through the consideration of the same research and development objectives that ground the favourable treatment of research information exchanges (or unilateral disclosure) under art. 101 TFEU.

7.3.1.1 Exploitative Health Information-Related Abuses

With regards to exploitative health information-related abuses, abuses can stem from unfair trading terms for digital services, which the dominant undertaking can impose because of its acquired market power.[85] In this perspective, the infringement of art. 102 TFEU would thus be triggered by the infringement of data protection rules, and more precisely of the mandatory data protection safeguards mentioned above.[86] Along these lines, health information abuses could thus result from the harm suffered by users/patients as a result of the imposition of unfair trading conditions regarding the collection and use of the health data acquired through digital health products or services. In this case, it needs however to be observed that the abuse occurs not in the data-driven research market but rather in the market of the new digital health product or service to which the data-driven innovation market is connected.[87]

---

[82] These are listed in the European Commission's Guidance on Enforcement, see European Commission, European Commission, Guidance on Enforcement Priorities in Applying Article 82 of the EC Treaty to Abusive Exclusionary Conduct by Dominant Undertakings, C 45/02 (24 February 2009), para IV.

[83] See Di Porto (2014), p. 312.

[84] See Colangelo and Borgogno (5 April 2019), p. 13. More generally on the abuse of dominant position, Osti (2011) and Meli (2003).

[85] This has been part of the reasoning of the Bundeskartellamt's decision in the Facebook case, Bundeskartellamt (7 February 2019). However, it needs to be recalled that in this specific case, the Bundeskartellamt ultimately based its decision on a theory of harm based on the exclusionary effects of Facebook's actions. See Kathuria (2019), p. 100.

[86] See supra Sects. 7.2.1 and 7.2.2.

[87] For this distinction see supra Chap. 6, Sect. 6.4.1.

Nonetheless, such an abuse can reflect itself also in the outright data-driven research market, in case the further processing of health data acquired through these digital health products and services do not respect the research relevant data protection rules as set out in the General Data Protection Regulation, especially under art. 9(2) and 89 GDPR. The processing of health data for research purposes should indeed be considered as abusive from a competition law perspective, in case it does not respect the above traced rules provided by the data protection framework regarding *fair* and *sustainable* health data-driven research.

In this regard, the remedy to be imposed by competition authorities should concern the imposition of fair and transparent conditions of collecting and processing health information.[88] This would imply, more precisely, the respect of the health research relevant data protection rules, which assure the availability to both data subjects and, more importantly, data protection authorities of substantial and procedural information regarding the processing of sensitive data for research purposes. Since the respect of data protection rules is an exclusive competence of data protection authorities, the imposition of the remedy should be conducted by competition authorities in strict collaboration with data protection authorities.[89] Such scenario of collaboration of antitrust and data protection authorities, and indirectly, to ethics committees, for the prevention of abuses in data-driven research markets would be particular desirable.

7.3.1.2 Exclusionary Health Information-Related Abuses

With regards to exclusionary health information-related abuses, the conduct of a refuse to access efficient health data flows needed for conducting research, could be deemed abusive, and thus anticompetitive, under art. 102 TFEU.

Differently than the above forecasted exploitative health information-related abuses, these exclusionary health information-related abuses entirely occur within the health data-driven innovation market.

In these regards, two abusive scenarios appear to be possible. The first relates to the abuse possibly reflecting itself outside the health data pool as a result of the refusal by the members of the health data pool considered as a unique research consortium to further exchange data with other market players willing to engage in research activities. The second conversely relates to the abuse possibly occurring within the health data pool as a result of the refuse by the more powerful member of the data pool to continue to provide health information to the other members of the pool, thus blocking ongoing and future research developments. In this second scenario, the abuse is conducted within—and in respect to—the health data pool

[88] This is suggested, from a general perspective, by Di Porto (2014), p. 316.

[89] See paper Graef et al. (2018), pp. 200 ff.

by the party who has acquired its market dominance exactly through access to the health data pool.[90]

As generally known, the European Commission has deemed as anticompetitive under art. 102 TFEU the conduct of refusal to supply, as possibly occurring in the form of a refusal to supply a product to existing or new customers; a refusal to license intellectual property rights[91] or a refusal to grant access to an essential facility or a network.[92]

Against the backdrop of this classification, a refusal to disclose health data, pooled together by a research consortium, can be potentially qualified under each of the identified conducts of refusal to supply. Health information can indeed be regarded as a product of the research activities of the stakeholders that have first processed health datasets; as an intellectual property right itself, in particular trade secrets and database rights that mostly protect the health information pooled together;[93] or as an essential facility in respect to health research purposes.

Specifically regarding the refusal to disclose research valuable health information, it is worth to recall that the Italian antitrust authority has found the pharmaceutical company Bayer liable for abusing its dominant position as a result of the refusal to provide the results of the toxicological studies it had conducted to its competing generics producers.[94]

---

[90] In this regard an interesting parallel with this second scenario is to be found in the Huawei decision by the European Court of Justice. In this case, thus, the Court stipulated that a firm that has agreed to a standard-setting agreement and its correspondent policy, establishing when and how to enforce intellectual property rights from the standard, can resort to an injunction against an infringer. This however did not preclude that the injunction that was legitimate under the standard-setting agreement, amounted to a an abuse of dominant position under art. 102 TFEU, and where the dominant position was exactly derived from the success resulting from the conclusion of a standard-setting agreement. See European Court of Justice, Huawei Technologies Co. Ltd. vs. ZTE Corp. and ZTE Deutschland GmbH, C-170/13 (16 July 2015), paras 45–47. Under these premises, a strand of the literature has observed that the Huawei case could be applied in analogy to data pools, arguing that a similar mechanism of reaction of members to an agreement against abuses occurred within a collaborative alliance by a party to the same alliance, could be applied under art. 102 TFEU also to data pools. This could occur, for example, in case the dominant member of the data pool intends to (legitimately) apply trade secret rules against another data pool member. See Lindqvist (6 November 2018), p. 25.

[91] For the literature on the refusal to license intellectual property rights, see the general reflections by Denozza (2010).

[92] European Commission, Guidance on Enforcement Priorities in Applying Article 82 of the EC Treaty to Abusive Exclusionary Conduct by Dominant Undertakings, C 45/02 (24 February 2009), para 78.

[93] See analysis supra Chap. 2, Sect. 2.2.1.

[94] Autorità Garante della Concorrenza e del Mercato, Sapec Agro/Bayer-Helm, Case A415, Decision n. 22558 (18 February 2010). The case is particularly interesting because Bayer's conduct was found to be abusive because the information contained in Bayer's toxicological studies was necessary for generic competitors not only for the conduction of their own research studies, but also, and in particular, for the granting of marketing authorisation. In this perspective, thus, Bayer's refusal to disclose its research information had the effect of distorting regulatory procedures, and in particular of violating the obligation posed at European level onto originators to either find an

In the United States, for example, Intel, a company with a dominant position in the market of microprocessors, broke a collaborative relationship with other three companies producing micro-processor related technology, by blocking the supply of collected technical information to its collaborators.[95]

At European level, the conduct of refusing to share information with competitors has been mainly analysed by the case law under the essential facilities doctrine.

In the Magill decision, the abuse was found to be stemming from the refuse of the broadcasters to supply information "duly in advance" so that the delay in the disclosure impeded the competing undertaking Magill to develop its own product.[96]

Similarly, in the Microsoft decision, the Commission first and then the Court of Justice of the European Union,[97] found the company abusing its dominant position by failing to provide its downstream competitors with information that was necessary for its downstream competitors to allow interoperability and to develop and distribute competing products. Interestingly, the work group servers who were denied the information, had previously gained access to it exactly in virtue of the collaboration with Microsoft.[98] Because of Microsoft's refusal to share key technical information, competitors were impaired to "viably compete in the work group server operating system market".[99] The Commission ultimately ordered Microsoft to

agreement concerning the results of studies on vertebrates or, in absence of such agreement, to share these same results with generic producers requesting an authorisation. The refusal to share these scientific results was deemed by the Italian antitrust authority to have exclusionary effects ultimately harming consumers. See Council Directive 91/414/EEC of 15 July 1991 concerning the placing of plant protection products on the market, 19 August 1991, OJ L 230/1, subsequently repealed by Regulation (EC) No 1107/2009 of the European Parliament and of the Council of 21 October 2009 concerning the placing of plant protection products on the market, 24 November 2011, OJ L 309/1.

[95] Intel's conduct was a self-help measure against the collaborators' litigation regarding Intel's alleged infringement of their patents. Free trade Commission, Complaint in the matter of Intel Corporation, N. 9288 (8 June 1998). Intel ultimately received an order by the Free Trade Commission to "cease and desist" from "impeding, altering, suspending, withdrawing, withholding or refusing to provide access by any microprocessor customer to AT Information for reasons related to an Intellectual Property Dispute (. . .); basing any supply decisions for general purpose microprocessors upon the existence of an IP Dispute". So Free trade Commission, Docket n. 9288-Decision and Order (3 August 1999a).

[96] European Court of Justice, European Court of Justice, Radio Telefis Eireann (RTE) and Independent Television Publications Ltd. (ITP) supported by Intellectual Property Owners Inc. (IPO) vs. Commission of the European Communities supported by Magill TV Guide Ltd., Joined Cases C-241/91 P and C-242/91 P (6 April 1995), para 52.

[97] European Court of Justice- Court of First Instance, Microsoft Corp. vs. Commission of the European Communities, Case T-201/04 (17 September 2007).

[98] European Commission, Microsoft vs. Commission, Case C-3/37.792 (24 March 2004), para 578 ff., stating that "Microsoft's conduct involves a disruption of previous levels of supply".

[99] European Commission, Microsoft vs. Commission, Case C-3/37.792 (24 March 2004), para 1064.

disclose the information needed by competitors to remain on the market and more precisely to develop and distribute work group server operating system products.[100]

The rationale of the Commission's order to disclose the information is thus more precisely related to the preservation of follow-on innovation based on the same information.[101] Along these lines, some authors have observed that the order to disclose interoperability information serves more profound purposes of protecting "the incentives and modalities for collaboration necessary to acquire knowledge that spurs innovation"[102] and the introduction of new products and services.[103]

The importance of information disclosure for collaborative cumulative innovation purposes has been stressed also by the European Court of Justice in the case *IMS Health vs. NDC Health*.[104] As in the above-described cases, also this one concerned the refusal by a healthcare technology company to grant the previous partner access to a technological "structure" that was used for the presentation of regional sales data in the pharmaceutical industry. The structure was protected by IMS Health copyright,[105] although the participation of pharmaceutical laboratories collaborating with the copyright holder had been determinant in the development of the structure itself.[106] In assessing the anticompetitiveness of such refusal to licence the use of the brick structure, the Court ultimately relied upon the fact that the structure had become the industry standard upon which the collaborators could have developed new and improved products serving consumers' needs.[107] The takeover by one member of the collaboration was thus found to block collaborative research in the sector, and thus the market's ability to develop.

The described cases all show that anticompetitive threats could emerge also within collaboration pools, becoming source of stronger market power and of subsequent abuses by one of the collaborators.

In these regards, the mentioned cases reflect how usually the party that is more influent in the collaboration is the one who controls the technological infrastructure in which the information aggregated through the collaboration is stored, processed and rendered available to the parties of the research pool. The control of the technological platform confers the company the privileged position of gatekeeper

[100] European Commission, Microsoft vs. Commission, Case C-3/37.792 (24 March 2004), art. 5 of the Commission's decision.

[101] European Commission, Microsoft vs. Commission, Case C-3/37.792 (24 March 2004), para 696.

[102] Svetiev (2007), p. 639.

[103] See, European Commission, Microsoft vs. Commission, Case C-3/37.792 (24 March 2004), amongst others, para 694.

[104] European Court of Justice, IMS Health GmbH & Co. OHG vs. NDC Health GmbH & Co. KG, C-418/01 (29 April 2004).

[105] European Court of Justice, IMS Health GmbH & Co. OHG vs. NDC Health GmbH & Co. KG, C-418/01 (29 April 2004), para 26.

[106] European Court of Justice, IMS Health GmbH & Co. OHG vs. NDC Health GmbH & Co. KG, C-418/01 (29 April 2004), paras 5; 27; 29.

[107] European Court of Justice, IMS Health GmbH & Co. OHG vs. NDC Health GmbH & Co. KG, C-418/01 (29 April 2004), para 49.

of the aggregated information, and thus the (market) power to withdraw it from the collaborators' availability. The resulting abuses are thus rooted exactly in the ownership of intellectual property rights over the technological infrastructure around which the collaboration develops (in the Microsoft case Microsoft's ownership of intellectual property rights in the operating system and in the IMS Health case IMS Health's copyright over the "brick structure").

The cases well suggest the risk of the attempt by the company "dominating" the collaboration to extend their exclusive control also onto the information product resulting from the joint collaboration process and to block upstream information fluxes. This erosion of the collaboration freezes the capabilities and thus the incentives of other companies—regardless of whether they compete om the same markets—to engage in innovation-fruitful investigations.

Interestingly, this sort of conducts has been declared as anticompetitive under European competition law in the Microsoft and IMS Health cases under art. 102 TFEU.

Conversely, the American approach in the Intel case has been more careful, since no evidence of the harm to competition was found by Intel's refusal to give access to its data. However, although anticompetitive effects deriving from the collaboration collapse were not positively affirmed by the Free Trade Commission, the fact that the commissioners' majority gave relevance to the re-establishment of the same collaboration, already signals—*a contrario*—the acknowledgment of the pro-competitiveness of joint follow-on enquiries.[108]

Interestingly, the expansive interpretation given by the European case law of the essential facilities doctrine exactly in the context of high tech markets has resulted into an expansive interpretation of the scope of abuses consisting in refusal to disclose information. The conduct of refusal to disclose information has indeed been deemed abusive in case it has the effect of impeding the collaborative development of technological progress through the concentration of research efforts under the control of few research market players. This interpretation has in turn determined the expansion of remedies imposing exchanges of information or duties to disclose information deemed essential to competitors for the conduction of research and development.

Against this backdrop, the analysis of the essential facilities doctrine under art. 102 TFEU, and in particular the related remedial obligation to share research valuable resources, is extremely interesting for the case of health data-related exclusionary abuses and is thus worth of a deeper assessment.

[108] This was the view of the majority of commissioners in the Intel case. See Free Trade Commission (6 August 1999b).

7.3.2 *Information Sharing Remedies Under Art. 102 TFEU*

The leniency under both the data protection research exemption under art. 9(2) lett. j and art. 89 GDPR and the block exemptions under art. 101(3) TFEU, allowing information exchanges for the establishment of research collaborations and the development of new products and services, should trigger a more sophisticated analysis—and stronger enforcement intervention—with regards to the abuses possibly stemming from massive health data aggregation, under art. 102 TFEU.[109]

With specific regards to exclusionary abuses stemming from the refusal to disclose research valuable informational assets, an analysis of the essential facilities case law under art. 102 TFEU suggests the legitimacy, as well as the opportunity of the adoption of behavioural remedies, mandating access to or disclosure of research information. Such remedies would indeed be adherent to the complexity of the collaborative networked digital health environment.

In this respect, the particular suitability of information sharing remedies for the purposes of advancing research in high tech markets has led to a revival of the essential facilities doctrine.[110]

Under these premises, this section will first illustrate the evolution of the European case law regarding the interpretation of the notion of essential facilities in respect to research and technological progress objectives; then it contextualises the analysed case law in the debate regarding the applicability of the essential facilities doctrine to digital personal data (in general); ultimately it concludes in favour of the applicability of sharing remedies in case of exclusionary abuses specifically regarding the refuse to share research valuable health information.

7.3.2.1 The Evolution of the European Case Law

Traditionally, the essential facilities doctrine and the related sharing remedies have been regarded as applicable to exclusionary abuses under art. 102 TFEU only in "exceptional circumstances".[111] This means that the essential facilities doctrine framework was traditionally anchored to strict conditions defined by the relevant case law, which sensitively restricted the scope of exclusionary conducts relevant under art. 102 TFEU.

---

[109]This is suggested also by Lindqvist (6 November 2018), p. 27.

[110]Waller (2012), p. 593; Newman (2014), pp. 15–16, stressing the competitive relevance of data portability.

[111]In the Magill exceptional circumstances were listed, European Court of Justice, European Court of Justice, Radio Telefis Eireann (RTE) and Independent Television Publications Ltd. (ITP) supported by Intellectual Property Owners Inc. (IPO) vs. Commission of the European Communities supported by Magill TV Guide Ltd., Joined Cases C-241/91 P and C-242/91 P (6 April 1995), paras 52–53.

Under these premises, the two cases of *Magill* and *IMS Health* first defined the test for the assessment of whether a refusal to license an intellectual property right should be considered abusive under art. 102 TFEU.

The "exceptional circumstances" for the application of the essential facilities doctrine were related to (i) the indispensable nature of the refused product or service for the exercise of a particular business in a downstream market; (ii) the exclusion of effective competition in the considered market as a result of the refuse; (iii) the prevention of the development of a new product for which there is consumer demand; and ultimately (iv) the unjustified nature of the refusal.[112]

In this test, the principal condition, from which also the other ones depend, is the one related to the essential nature of the requested facility. In this respect, the Magill decision has specified that the refusal to give access to a facility amounts to an abuse when the facility is an "indispensable raw material" for the provision of a derivative service or product.[113] The requirement of indispensability of the requested facility has been further developed by the case law. In particular, in the Bronner case, it was stressed how the requirement of indispensability attains to the fact that it is not economically viable for the competitor to autonomously reproduce a facility that is comparable in scope to the one held by the dominant company.[114] More precisely, the Bronner decision, affirms that access to an input is not indispensable in case there are no "technical, legal, or even economic obstacles capable of making it impossible, or even unreasonably difficult" to replicate.[115] According to the *Bronner* decision, thus, access to the facility is not indispensable if alternatives are available, even though less valuable.

This restrictive approach was then broadened by the General Court in the Microsoft case, where the indispensability requirement was linked to the fact that thanks to the access to the essential facility, the requesting undertaking would have

[112]European Court of Justice, European Court of Justice, Radio Telefis Eireann (RTE) and Independent Television Publications Ltd. (ITP) supported by Intellectual Property Owners Inc. (IPO) vs. Commission of the European Communities supported by Magill TV Guide Ltd., Joined Cases C-241/91 P and C-242/91 P (6 April 1995), para 52–56. For a comment see Drexl (2017), pp. 282 ff.

[113]European Court of Justice, European Court of Justice, Radio Telefis Eireann (RTE) and Independent Television Publications Ltd. (ITP) supported by Intellectual Property Owners Inc. (IPO) vs. Commission of the European Communities supported by Magill TV Guide Ltd., Joined Cases C-241/91 P and C-242/91 P (6 April 1995), para 52.

[114]European Court of Justice, Oscar Bronner GmbH & Co. KG vs. Mediaprint Zeitungs, C-7/97 (26 November 1998), para 43–46. The indispensability requirement has been further specified in the IMS Health case, see European Court of Justice, IMS Health GmbH & Co. OHG vs. Commission of the European Communities, C-418/01 (29 April 2004), para 38.

[115]European Court of Justice, Oscar Bronner GmbH & Co. KG vs. Mediaprint Zeitungs, C-7/97 (26 November 1998), para 44.

been able to compete with the incumbent "on an equal footing"[116] for the development a new product.[117]

Against this backdrop, the consideration of the specificities of high-technology markets and the peculiar effects generated by refusals to disclose research valuable information on innovation has led to a progressive reconsideration of the essential facilities doctrine's requirements in the context of innovation markets. This interpretative evolution has thus come to re-define the "exceptional" conditions upon which the imposition on a dominant undertaking of a positive duty to disclose can work as a remedy to re-balance an occurred informational abuse occurred in a high technology research market.

Such interpretative evolution has regarded in particular the two conditions of (i) the exclusion of effective competition on the considered market and, strictly related to the former, (ii) the prevention of the emergence of a new downstream product.

More precisely, the initial focus of the exclusion of competition has been progressively expanded around the requirement of a restriction of future competition in innovation markets: the focus of the analysis for the purposes of an infringement of art. 102 TFEU appears to have thus shifted from the consideration of the occurred exclusion or restriction of effective competition, to the consideration of a potential restriction on future innovation. As a result, also the new product requirement, has been expansively interpreted and referred to the research process as such: the requirement of the prevention of the development of new products or services has been expanded up to considering also more general impairments of research and innovation processes, irrespective of the identification of a new product or service to which such research and innovation processes are targeted.

This interpretative evolution of the test for the essential facilities doctrine has progressively untightened the pillars of the European essential facilities doctrine framework.

According to a previous approach, the requirement of exclusion of the requirement of effective competition has been identified in the fact that the facility holder would reserve the downstream market to itself, excluding the competitors who were denied access to the facility.

This approach was first affirmed in the *Commercial Solvents* case, where the Court argued that a dominant supplier abuses its dominant position when it refuses to provide a facility to a customer, which is at the same time a competitor in the downstream market "with the object of reserving such raw material for

---

[116] European Court of Justice-Court of First Instance, Microsoft Corp. vs. Commission of the European Communities, Case T-201/04 (17 September 2007), para 421.

[117] European Court of Justice-Court of First Instance, Microsoft Corp. vs. Commission of the European Communities, Case T-201/04 (17 September 2007), para 334.

manufacturing its own derivatives" and "therefore risks *eliminating* competition on the part of this customer".[118]

A similar line of reasoning was further followed in the Magill case, where the Court of Justice observed that the Irish broadcasting stations had "reserved to themselves the secondary market of weekly television guides by *excluding all* competitors on that market".[119] The Court thus found that the refusal was infringing art. 102 TFEU because it impeded the entrance on the market of an equally efficient- i.e. equally likely to innovate- competitor in the market. In the *Magill* decision, the Court further specified that for the sharing remedy to be triggered, the impairment of competitors' research and development processes determined by the unavailability of the "essential" resource, must result into a harm to consumer welfare directly related to the loss of the benefit that consumers would have experienced with the marketization of a new product.[120]

Likewise, also in the *IMS Health* ruling the Court highlighted that the refusal had the effect of reserving for the dominant company "the market for the supply of data on sales of pharmaceutical products in the Member States concerned by eliminating all competition on that market".[121] In this case, the holder of the essential facility was itself active in the downstream market and had tried to entrench its dominant position through the refuse to license its intellectual property rights.[122] On that occasion, the Court particularly highlighted the existence of a vertical relationship between two or more markets and the fact that the refusal of granting access to an upstream right blocks the development of a new downstream product for which there is a potential consumer demand and which can be delivered only through access to the upstream right.[123] As the Court has observed in the same decision, the upstream right—whose access is refused—was operating as a connecting link between the two markets, in the sense that the right is essential for the development of the new products, and not only beneficial or important for its design.[124] As the Court however recognized in

---

[118]European Court of Justice, Istituto Chemioterapeutico Italiano and Commercial Solvents vs. Commission, Joined Cases C-6 and 7/73 (6 March 1974), para 25. Emphasis added.

[119]European Court of Justice, European Court of Justice, Radio Telefis Eireann (RTE) and Independent Television Publications Ltd. (ITP) supported by Intellectual Property Owners Inc. (IPO) vs. Commission of the European Communities supported by Magill TV Guide Ltd., Joined Cases C-241/91 P and C-242/91 P (6 April 1995), para 56. Emphasis added.

[120]European Court of Justice, European Court of Justice, Radio Telefis Eireann (RTE) and Independent Television Publications Ltd. (ITP) supported by Intellectual Property Owners Inc. (IPO) vs. Commission of the European Communities supported by Magill TV Guide Ltd., Joined Cases C-241/91 P and C-242/91 P (6 April 1995), para 54.

[121]European Court of Justice, IMS Health GmbH & Co. OHG vs. Commission of the European Communities, C-418/01 (29 April 2004), para 52.

[122]Graef (13 May 2019), p. 20.

[123]European Court of Justice, IMS Health GmbH & Co. OHG vs. Commission of the European Communities, C-418/01 (29 April 2004), para 48–49. For the literature commenting the IMS Health Case, see Houdijk (2005), pp. 467 ff.

[124]European Court of Justice, IMS Health GmbH & Co. OHG vs. Commission of the European Communities, C-418/01 (29 April 2004), para 48–49.

this same case, these new products or services need to be sufficiently identified so as to identify a "potential consumer demand".[125] In this same perspective, however, the Court already appeared to consider the possibility that the essential facility doctrine could be applied also with reference to a "potential or even hypothetical market" for the asset required, provided that there is an actual demand for [the asset] on the part of undertakings which seek to carry on the business for which they are indispensable".[126]

This decision thus initiates a turnaround with regards to the applicability of the essential resources doctrine, which has been progressively extended from the exclusion of competition on an existing downstream market, to the impairment suffered by the undertaking requiring access and targeting a new market,[127] in which the dominant undertaking is not active yet, but could expand to.[128]

Under these premises, the approach to the essential facility doctrine appears to have changed, and broadened, in the Microsoft case.[129] Here, respectively the General Court and the European Court of Justice appear to have applied lower thresholds for the purposes of the essential facilities doctrine.

Indeed, in the Microsoft case, the General Court lowered the anticompetitive standard down to the existence of the *likelihood* that the refusal to access the facility would "eliminate all effective competition on the market",[130] this leading to a "limitation not only of production or markets, *but also of technical development*".[131]

The reference to technical development appears to signal a first application of the essential facilities doctrine to innovation markets, irrespective of the definition of a product or service that is meant to be developed by the company who requests the access. Indeed, despite the fact that the company seeking access to Microsoft's

---

[125] European Court of Justice, IMS Health GmbH & Co. OHG vs. Commission of the European Communities, C-418/01 (29 April 2004), para 49.

[126] European Court of Justice, IMS Health GmbH & Co. OHG vs. Commission of the European Communities, C-418/01 (29 April 2004), para 44–45.

[127] Rousseva (2010), p. 125.

[128] In a case where a company sought access to the facility in order to enter an existing market in which the dominant undertaking was not active, the European Court of Justice did not found the refusal of the latter to amount to an infringement of art. 102 TFEU given that the essential facility holder was not active in the downstream market, and the parties were thus not competitors. See European Court of Justice-Court of First Instance, Tiercè Ladbroke SA vs. Commission of the European Communities, C T-504/93 (12 June 1997), para 133. Moreover it can be argued that in case an undertaking seeks access to a facility for the entering of an already existing market, in which not the facility holder but other companies are active, the requirement of the essential nature of the facility would be missing. So Graef (13 May 2019), p. 20.

[129] As a consequence of the broadening of the interpretation of the essential facilities doctrine requirements, some strand of the literature has referred to it as the "convenient" facility doctrine. Ridyard (2004), pp. 669 ff.

[130] European Court of Justice- Court of First Instance, Microsoft Corp. vs. Commission of the European Communities, Case T-201/04 (17 September 2007), para 563. Emphasis added.

[131] European Court of Justice- Court of First Instance, Microsoft Corp. vs. Commission of the European Communities, Case T-201/04 (17 September 2007), para 647. Emphasis added.

interoperability information was not able to identify the new product or service it would have developed once it had gained access to the interoperability information, the requirement of prevention of new product development was considered as fulfilled by the General Court on grounds that the refusal of Microsoft had the effect of restricting technical development.[132]

Interestingly, the General Court highlighted that the restriction of technical development was not only to be suffered on the side of the company receiving the refusal but also on the side of the same incumbent, whose refusal would have consolidated its dominant company, ultimately leading to a decrease of the same incumbent's incentives to innovate.[133]

In this perspective, thus, also the risk of an impediment of competitors to autonomously run R&D processes for the placing on the market of new product or service has been held by the General Court as a sufficient ground for the identification of exclusionary anticompetitive effects of the refusal to give competitors access to research precious information, and thus for the activation of competition enforcement under the essential facilities doctrine.[134]

In the Microsoft decision, the essential facility-related remedy was even broadened beyond the objective of consumer welfare protection that had been highlighted in *Magill*, and widened to the achievement of more sectoral objectives, as the restructuring of the industry for the ultimate political purpose of the strengthening of the internal market and the achievement of wider European Union objectives.[135]

Interestingly, this broad conception of the new product requirement has been expressly acknowledged in the Commission Guidance on enforcement priorities under art. 82 EC, stressing that harm can be caused to consumers when "the competitors that the dominant undertaking forecloses are, as a result of the refusal, prevented from bringing innovative goods or services to market *and/or*

[132]European Court of Justice-Court of First Instance, Microsoft Corp. vs. Commission of the European Communities, Case T-201/04 (17 September 2007), para 665.

[133]European Court of Justice-Court of First Instance, Microsoft Corp. vs. Commission of the European Communities, Case T-201/04 (17 September 2007), para 697–698. This two-sided nature of the innovation impairment resulting from the refusal to give access to research valuable information has been particularly highlighted in the literature. See Lillà Montagnani (2007), p. 630.

[134]It needs to be recalled that the General Court's decision was not appealed by Microsoft, so the Court of Justice did not express its view on such a broad scope of the essential facilities doctrine as that affirmed by the General Court. Nonetheless, the further developments of the European Court of Justice's case law in the Intel decision, appear to place the General Court's decision in the Microsoft case in line with subsequent judgments of the European Court of Justice who likewise appears to have lowered the scope of the threshold for the essential facilities doctrine for the purposes of the protection of research in technological progress.

[135]This is directly acknowledged by EUI paper. Broulik and Diathesopoulos (22 May 2017), p. 22. See for example, the statements in European Court of Justice- Court of First Instance, Microsoft Corp. vs. Commission of the European Communities, Case T-201/04 (17 September 2007), para 647; 648; 649; 652; 653; 656.

where follow-on innovation is likely to be stifled".[136] In the Commission's view, this harm is especially likely to occur when the "business in need of supply does not intend to limit substantially the coping of products or services already offered by the dominant undertaking on the downstream market, but intends to produce new or improved products or services for which there is potential consumer demand *or is likely to contribute to technical progress*".[137]

It is not a coincidence that the Guidelines have been issued after the Microsoft case, as a definitive acknowledgment of the relevance of innovation as a direct object of harm that competition rules may directly, without the need for any intermediation by sector regulation, protect. These statements by the Commission ultimately appear to pose grounds for a new justification of the essential facility doctrine as a means to establish a level playing for research and innovation, when harmed by an abuse.

7.3.2.2 Sharing Remedies Over Digital Data: The Debate

The question of access to information is considered to be a central concern in contemporary competition law.[138] The core of the debate relates to the newly emerging link in digital markets, occurring between data "portability"—in the general sense of data sharing[139]—and competition.[140] The sharing of data has thus been increasingly regarded by the European competition authorities as a remedy capable of deconstructing big undertakings' self-generating market dominance in innovation, and thus of re-establishing a more homogeneous field of research and development.

The European Commission, on its side, has recently stated that general competition law is applicable in respect to data-driven business models, and its remedies can thus be invoked to claim wider access to data held by one market player.[141] The refusal to grant access to essential business data has been expressly recognised by the Commission as one of the principal unfair trading practices on online platforms.[142] In these regards, the sharing remedy under the essential facilities doctrine has been

[136]European Commission, Guidance on Enforcement Priorities in Applying Article 82 of the EC Treaty to Abusive Exclusionary Conduct by Dominant Undertakings, C 45/02 (24 February 2009), para 87. Emphasis added.

[137]European Commission, Guidance on Enforcement Priorities in Applying Article 82 of the EC Treaty to Abusive Exclusionary Conduct by Dominant Undertakings, C 45/02 (24 February 2009), para 87. Emphasis added.

[138]Waller (2012), p. 593.

[139]Data portability is here intended in the general, non-technical sense, that meaning not in the specific sense of the right established under art. 20 General Data Protection Regulation.

[140]Geradin and Kuschewsky (13 February 2013); European Data Protection Supervisor (March 2014).

[141]European Commission (10 January 2017e).

[142]European Commission (25 May 2016c), p. 12.

expressly put in connection by the Commission to the objective of the free flow of information in digital markets.[143]

Under this premise, the Commission appears to be in favour of the applicability of the essential facility doctrine framework also to data not covered by intellectual property rights.[144] This interpretation of the Commission's statements would imply a further stretch of the interpretative trend regarding the essential facilities doctrine initiated by the Court of Justice in respect to high tech markets. Indeed, such interpretation would also go beyond the statements made by the General Court in the Microsoft decision, which stated that the prevention of the development of a new product resulting from a refuse is "found only in the case law on the exercise of an intellectual property right",[145] but not in general refusal-to-deal cases.

7.3.2.2.1 The Arguments Against the Sharing Remedy Over Digital Data Under Art. 102 TFEU

The applicability of the essential facilities doctrine framework to digital data is object of a heated debate.[146] Also the literature that supports this interpretative solution, has highlighted some non-negligible challenges it brings about.[147]

These challenges attain to issues both newly arising from the specific properties of digital data; and traditionally associated with the features of the proactive sharing remedy the essential facilities doctrine triggers.

In respect to the difficulties of considering data as a facility under the essential facilities doctrine framework, a strand of the literature has stressed how digital data could not be eligible as an essential facility exactly because it could never really be deemed essential for the development of a new product or service.[148] Digital data can indeed be easily replicated, also through the recourse to data brokers.[149]

From a further standpoint, the same literature highlights that the link of digital data to a new product or service as the (earlier) essential facilities doctrine requires,

---

[143] European Commission (10 January 2017f), p. 21.

[144] This is observed by Maggiolino and Colangelo (2017), p. 267.

[145] European Court of Justice-Court of First Instance, Microsoft Corp. vs. Commission of the European Communities, Case T-201/04 (17 September 2007), para 334.

[146] Lao (2013), pp. 272 ff.; Abrahamson (2014), pp. 867 ff. and Meadows (2015), p. 795.

[147] See in particular Lindqvist (2016), pp. 16–18 and Drexl (2017), pp. 48–52.

[148] Maggiolino and Colangelo (2017), p. 256.

[149] See Free Trade Commission (2014). Executive Office of the President (2016), p. 5. See also statements of the European Commission in the Facebook/Whatsapp decision, stating that disregarding the creation of a data pool between the user data of Facebook and of Whatsapp, "there will continue to be a large amount of Internet user data that are valuable for advertisement purposes and that are not within Facebook's exclusive control". European Commission, Facebook/ Whatsapp, case COMP/M. 7217 (3 October 2014a), paras 188–189. The Commission refers here to advertisement purposes but these statement could be eventually applied also to data that are valuable for research purposes.

would be particularly hard to establish, especially beforehand.[150] However, it needs to be observed right from the beginning that this argument specifically relates to general big data, as search engine data or social network data, that is general runaway data[151] and not to more sophisticated types of digital data as health data.[152]

Shifting the perspective from the facility to the sharing remedy regarding digital data, instead, it has been observed that the proactive imposition by a competition authority of disclosure duties onto a dominant company is an operation of outright market design, affecting the structure of existing markets. More precisely, the imposition of a sharing remedy would ultimately accomplish distributive justice goals, through the surreptitious creation of a level playing field.[153] In this light, the expansive application in digital markets of the essential facilities doctrine under art. 102 TFEU would enlarge the scope of abusive conducts related to the refusal to share data in these same markets, this implying a use of competition rules, and in particular of art. 102 TFEU, for interventionist market regulation purposes.[154]

Moreover, the establishment of an information sharing remedy in the form of the imposition of a duty to deal on the dominant company, directly interferes with the same company's freedom to do business and to contract and to choose the trading partner,[155] as well as with its right to property, in case of the requested facility is protected under property schemes.[156]

The decision of a competition authority to impose a sharing duty onto a dominant undertaking requires indeed a delicate balancing between these constitutionally relevant interests and the one regarding the re-establishment/promotion of competition.[157]

---

[150] Maggiolino and Colangelo (2017), p. 269.

[151] On the notion of runaway data as defined by the European Medicines Agency see supra Chap. 2, Sect. 2.1.5.

[152] Stressing the fact that search engine data or social network data are just one type of digital data, Kathuria (2019), p. 90.

[153] European Court of Justice, Editions Odile Jacob v. Commission, C-551/10 (6 November 2012), paras 66–67.

[154] Graef (13 May 2019), p. 23.

[155] European Court of Justice- Court of First Instance, Bayer vs. Commission, C T-41/96 (26 October 2000), para 180 where the Court stressed the importance of safeguarding free enterprise when applying competition rules of the Treaty.

[156] Advocate General Jacobs (28 May 1998) Opinion in Oscar Bronner GmbH & Co. KG. vs. Mediaprint Zeitungs, C-7/97, para 56.

[157] European Court of Justice, Oscar Bronner GmbH & Co. KG vs. Mediaprint Zeitungs, C-7/97 (26 November 1998), para 57, where the Advocate General Jacobs in Bronner has well highlighted the relationship between increased intervention of competition rules into essential facilities and incentives to invest. More precisely, the Advocate has stressed the link between intellectual property rights and the creation/availability of creation resources for innovation through competition law. It indeed affirmed that "the justification in terms of competition policy for interfering with a dominant undertaking's freedom of contract often requires a careful balancing of conflicting considerations. In the long term it is generally por-competitive and in the interest of consumers to allow a company to retain for its own use facilities which it has developed for the purposes of its

With specific regards to the case of legally possessed intellectual property rights, deeming as abusive the refusal to share these with third parties, would amounts to an actual expropriation of the latter, forcing the holder to assist a competitor to the detriment of its interests.[158]

In these regards, a strand of the literature has also argued that a compression of the dominant undertaking's rights and the forcing of network owners to disclose the information resulting from their investments, would sensitively decrease the incentive to invest in technological innovation.[159] More precisely, an undue interference with the dominant undertaking's freedom to conduct business and right to property could have the effect of diminishing incentives for competitors and for the same dominant firms to innovate and develop substitutes for the existing infrastructure in the long term.[160]

In these regards, a strand of the scholarly literature has argued that a decision by a competition authority not to intervene in a certain market through sharing remedies would put greater pressure onto competitors to introduce new technologies in order to overtake the dominant position of the incumbent, thus advancing competition *for* the market.[161] The policy option not to impose a sharing remedy is said to safeguard at the same time the (intellectual) property rights of the dominant undertaking, and the incentives of new entrants to develop new technologies for the purposes of market overtake.[162]

According to this perspective, thus, the refusal to access intellectual property rights, should be considered as a natural (negative) expression of the incumbent's market power, as directly deriving from the competitive advantage acquired within

business. For example, if access to a production, purchasing or distribution facility were allowed too easily there would be no incentive for a competitor to develop competing facilities. Thus, while competition was increased in the short term it would be reduced in the long term. Moreover, the incentive for a dominant undertaking to invest in efficient facilities would be reduced if its competitors were, upon request, able to share the benefits. Thus the mere fact that by retaining a facility for its own use a dominant undertaking retains an advantage over a competitor cannot justify requiring access to it".

158 Graef (13 May 2019), p. 22. It is interesting to recall, in these regards, that Germany has normatively excluded the application of the essential facilities doctrine to intellectual property rights in the Section 19(4) GWB (Gesetz gegen Wettbewerbsbeschränkungen).

159 Spulber and Yoo (2014), p. 391, arguing in this sense that competition law would better "tolerate some degree of static inefficiency in order to promote dynamic efficiency". In this sense also Maggiolino and Colangelo (2017), p. 263.

160 European Court of Justice, Opinion of Advocate General Jacobs in Oscar Bronner GmbH & Co. KG. vs. Mediaprint Zeitungs, C-7/97 (28 May 1998), para 57.

161 This point is raised in Evans and Schmalensee (2002), p. 1; Geradin (2004a), p. 1539; and see in these regards already, Katz and Shapiro (1999), p. 57.

162 This is also claimed by Graef (13 May 2019), p. 10, citing the arguments raised by the US. Supreme Court in the Trinko judgment, where the Court argued that "the opportunity to charge monopoly prices- at least for a short period- is what attracts "business acumen" in the first place; it induces risk taking that produces innovation and economic growth". So US Supreme Court, Verizon Communications v. Law Offices of Curtis vs. Trinko LLP (Trinko), 540 U.S. 398 (2004), para 407.

the natural structure of the market and its operating conditions.[163] Such a refuse should thus not amount to an abuse under art. 102 TFEU, in the view of the self-correcting market safeguards, which are expected to temporarily restrain the incumbent's acquired dominance through an overtake by a new entrant.[164]

In line with these arguments, thus, the essential facilities doctrine should be restrictively applied, in order not to interfere with the rationale of protecting incentives to invest and to innovate that are incorporated within the possession of intellectual property rights, and that are effective also in the dynamics of digital markets.

7.3.2.2.2 The Arguments in Favour of the Sharing Remedy Over Digital Data Under Art. 102 TFEU

Within the frame of this debate, however, other scholars have observed how the protection of intellectual property rights can be justified until the protection itself, and thus the protection of its exclusive—and exclusionary—use by the owner, is beneficial to innovation.[165]

When the intellectual property holder has gained a dominant market position which entrenches the incumbent on the "technological frontier"[166] in a way that blocks the innovation pace that the same intellectual property rights aim to stir, thus ultimately distorting their essential function, then competition law-and in particular art. 102 TFEU—can have the integrative function of proactively imposing positive obligations perfecting market structure conditions.[167]

The sharing remedy under art. 102 TFEU can be a suitable a means for preventing dominant companies from extending and consolidating their dominance when this delays the start of a new round of competition for the market.[168] It is indeed functional to the re-establishment of the competitive pressure, in case the market dynamics fail to generate it on their own.[169] In these "exceptional circumstances" thus, the same competition law, and in particular art. 102 TFEU, disowns its traditional role to intervene as to correct active behaviours rather than to correct

[163] This is observed by European Court of Justice, European Court of Justice, Radio Telefis Eireann (RTE) and Independent Television Publications Ltd. (ITP) supported by Intellectual Property Owners Inc. (IPO) vs. Commission of the European Communities supported by Magill TV Guide Ltd., Joined Cases C-241/91 P and C-242/91 P (6 April 1995), para 49.

[164] Kathuria and Globocnik (2020).

[165] For an assessment of the complex link between intellectual property and "good" and "bad" innovation, see Lillà Montagnani (2007), pp. 630 ff.

[166] The "technological frontier" is the last advancement in technology in a certain sector, this is highlighted by Lillà Montagnani (2006), pp. 333 ff.

[167] In a similar sense European Court of Justice, Editions Odile Jacob v. Commission, C-551/10 (6 November 2012), paras 66–67.

[168] Pardolesi and Renda (2004), pp. 528–535.

[169] Graef (13 May 2019), p. 22.

negative behaviours, by invasively intervening in the market through the establishment of a positive obligation.[170]

Under these premises, the extensive application of the essential facilities doctrine to the case of digital data is exactly suggested by the specific market characteristics of digital markets in which data as a tradable commodity is (not) exchanged.

In digital markets, indeed the market position of incumbents is sustained and ultimately entrenched by network effects, high switching costs and lock-in effects.[171] Incumbents are thus facilitated to enter connected technological markets and to engage in "conglomerate strategies"[172] through which they partner or acquire new potential market entrants.[173] In this way, these potential new entrants are prevented to become competitors potentially displacing the same incumbents.[174]

These peculiar dynamics in which competition in digital markets proceeds weaken the self-correcting mechanisms of the market and risk to impair the development by other market players of innovative technologies, ultimately freezing competition for the market.[175]

These market failures encourage market tipping strategies in multisided markets. Tipping strategies exacerbate in turn the unavailability of the research valuable resources, thus impeding competitors to compete within a certain research market, with an ultimate negative impact on products' variety and prices.[176]

In this perspective, the existence of the peculiar market failures stemming from the presence of network effects or switching costs that lock-in the market, and consolidate dominant undertakings' dominance, can provide sufficient grounds for antitrust authorities to intervene, by imposing a duty to disclose that re-opens up and liquifies the competitive process.

It is thus exactly because of the very specific features of digital markets that the imposition of a sharing remedy potentially becomes extremely relevant for the protection of data-driven innovation, allowing competitors to acquire the research information that is necessary for the design of complementary products and the stirring of follow-on innovation.[177] Indeed, the availability of the resources needed to compete within an existing market can facilitate competitors' race in bringing to the market disruptive inventions and thus in gradually taking over the position of the dominant undertaking by making its dominance less significant.[178]

---

[170] Graef (13 May 2019), p. 22.

[171] This has been elsewhere observed supra Chap. 3, Sect. 3.1.1.2.

[172] So Graef (13 May 2019), p. 11.

[173] These market characteristics of digital markets are also stressed by Kathuria (2019), p. 90.

[174] It is the phenomenon of "market-tipping". See Lindqvist (6 November 2018) and in particular p. 24.

[175] So Graef (13 May 2019), p. 11.

[176] Van Roojen (2010), pp. 34–46.

[177] Graef (13 May 2019), p. 11.

[178] Surblyte (2011), p. 131.

Under this premise, when the protection of upstream rights or assets harms innovation, then the essential facilities doctrine under art. 102 TFEU can be an interesting remedy for safeguarding the availability of research and competitively valuable information within digital innovation markets, and thus stir competition for new digital products or services.

7.3.3 *Information Sharing Remedies in Health Data Pools*

Both the evolution of the European case law, which has defined a broad framework of the essential facilities doctrine in the context of high tech markets, and the scholarly debate regarding the extension of such doctrine to digital data, provide useful grounds for the assessment of whether digital health data can be considered an essential facility for the purposes of digital health research, and thus be object of a specific duty to share borne by companies that are dominant in the same market of health data-driven innovation.

In these regards, it needs to be first observed that differently from general big data's features,[179] research valuable health data is to be considered a specific research resource with well-defined features.

7.3.3.1 Health Data as Essential Research Facilities

Although in the digital environment the sources of sensitive health data have proliferated, it has been previously demonstrated that the research value of such differently captured sensitive health data, directly stems from the aggregation of different complementary health datasets, ranging from general runaway health data to more sophisticated scientific testing data.[180] This implies that the so formed health data pools are not ubiquitous, thus easily retrievable, as general big data are.[181]

Moreover, because they are the direct product of the research investments of the members of the health data pool, they are protected by more than one layer of intellectual property protection.[182]

In this perspective, hence, a refusal to share research valuable health data that are protected by intellectual property rights, would amount to a refusal to license intellectual property rights, as in the *IMS Health* and in the *Magill* case.[183]

---

[179] See Maggiolino and Colangelo (2017), pp. 249 ff.

[180] See supra Chap. 2, Sect. 2.1.1.

[181] See observations supra Sect. 7.3.2.2.1.

[182] See supra Chap. 2, Sect. 2.2.1.

[183] The fact that health data are mostly covered by some kind of intellectual property rights leaves aside the above-highlighted debate regarding the applicability of the essential facilities doctrine to data that is not protected under any intellectual property right.

With regards to the exclusive nature of some types of digital data, it has been rightly observed that exclusivity of a resource does not automatically amount to essentiality. The essentiality requirement indeed implies something more than simple exclusivity: it involves an outright monopoly power by the data holder in the collection and generation of these same data.[184]

However, the health data flown in the formed health data pools originate from and in turn themselves define the relevant health data-driven innovation market.[185] Indeed, both the complementary nature of the data and the technological assets pooled together and the indirect network effects existing between the markets of digital health services/products and the pure data-driven innovation market controlled by the members of the established health data pool, are very likely to place an established research consortium in a (quasi-) monopolistic position regarding a certain type of research valuable health data.

This implies, in turn, that the pooled health data is very likely to be essential for the satisfaction of a specific research demand connected to a relevant health data-driven innovation market as defined around a specific research sector, e.g. the research sector regarding diabetes as in the joint venture between Google and Sanofi; or regarding kidney injuries as in the partnership between Google DeepMind and the Royal Free Hospital.

The aggregated health data, together with the developed technological research infrastructure, can indeed be hardly replicated by competitors, and especially by smaller research consortia, which, as already shown, usually have just one type of research relevant health information.[186]

Following the above-recalled *Bronner* decision, it can be thus said that health data pools are if not impossible, "unreasonably difficult" to substitute from a technical, economic and legal perspective, even if the requesting firm would undertake investments similar to that of the dominant firm in order to reproduce the health datasets.

The corollary of this specific market features is that access to an established health data pool can become indispensable to enter a specific health-data driven innovation market and thus for the answering of a specific research question.[187]

Under these premises, it needs to be observed that health data can be considered essential facilities for health data-driven research purposes only in light of a broad interpretation of the essential facilities doctrine as detached from the strict requirement of the new product. This is because at the moment in which a competitor seeks access to the research facility, the new products or services that will follow from the analytical research processes of these facilities are mostly unforeseeable or at least not clearly defined. Indeed, research courses based on the analysis of data are

[184] Maggiolino and Colangelo (2017), p. 256.

[185] See supra Chap. 6, Sect. 6.4.1.

[186] See supra Chap. 2, Sect. 2.2.

[187] In these regards, health data sensitively differ from "general" big data, which, as has been stressed in the literature, are not gathered and organized in order to answer a specific research question, see Maggiolino and Colangelo (2017), p. 270.

open-ended processes that cannot be linked, especially in early stages of the research, to a precise product or service. This factual consideration thus suggests the opportunity that the requirement of the essential nature of the facilities for the purposes of the new entrants' market initiatives is not linked, as in the traditional conception of the essential facilities doctrine, to the development of a specific new product or service, but rather to the conduction of a research enquiry related to a specific sector.

As has been shown, the evolution of the above-recalled European case law appears exactly to admit to consider a facility *essential* also in respect to broader objectives of research and technological progress. Indeed, especially the *Microsoft* and *Intel* decisions, have employed the requirement of exclusion of competition in a more flexible way in respect to dynamic markets with a progressive detachment from the requirement of the exclusion of effective competition.

7.3.3.2 The Refusal to "License" Health Data as Abuse under Art. 102 TFEU

In the context of digital health markets, health data is the basis of research and development enquiries for the development of a wide range of new health technologies.

Following the above-mentioned European decisions regarding the essential facilities doctrine, a refusal to disclose health data by the members or by one member of a health data pool could be deemed abusive when it strengthens the market dominance of the facilities' holder(s) in the multisided digital health markets not only as a consequence of the restriction of competition in already established health products' or service' markets, but also as a result of the freezing of competition in innovation in a specific research market.[188]

Under these premises, the abuse stemming from the withdrawal of pooled health data, needs again to be deeper enquired and contextualised at the complex intersection between intellectual property, competition and innovation rationales.

In these regards, from an intellectual property standpoint, the blocking of *competition in the market*, which is mostly competition by imitation, through the retention of a specific protected resource, is to be considered as a legitimate entitlement directly stemming from the intellectual property protecting the resource at stake. Conversely, the blocking of *competition in innovation* as a result of such retention, would exactly go against the very goal of the promotion of technological progress the same intellectual property system is bound to.[189]

Under these premises, a careful consideration of the very features of digital health product/service markets provides some interesting suggestions as regards to when a

---

[188] Rousseva (2010), p. 125. See also Drexl (2017), pp. 282 ff.

[189] The different link between intellectual property rights and, respectively, competition by imitation and by substitution is made by Drexl (2004), p. 805.

refusal to license protected health data can be deemed abusive in the correspondent digital health research market.

Indeed, the already recalled market failures related to the direct network effects or users' high switching costs affecting an existing digital health product/service market in which the incumbent consolidates its market position, suggest that a disclosure of health data by the same incumbent to a new entrant, would presumably not be capable of undermining the dominant position the incumbent has acquired in these markets.

Indeed, the existence of these market failures would very probably impede that a disclosure of upstream data would trigger competition by imitation—or competition in the market—mechanisms that the same intellectual property apparatus structurally intends to retard.

This means, at a deeper level, that in the view of such market failures, the disclosure of the protected research data would hardly undermine intellectual property rights' physiological rewarding function of a dominant position in the digital health product/service markets.

This has been expressly proved in the *IMS Health* and *Microsoft* cases, where exactly the market failures prevented potential competitors from entering the considered market by introducing their own products since consumers were not interested in switching to a new type of brick structure or client PC operating system.[190]

However, such rewarding function of the intellectual property system turns out to be abused when the dominance assured by intellectual property rights is meant to be unduly extended onto other—related—markets, this ultimately going against the incentivising function of intellectual property rights.

Under these premises, thus, a refusal to access health data needed by new entrants to autonomously carry out research and development targeted at new markets, which may be related, but not coinciding, with the market in which the facility holder is dominant, would thus favour the incumbent's market tipping strategies, with that impeding new entrants' to engage in the competition for the market race. In this case, a similar refusal to access health data could amount to an infringement of art. 102 TFEU, triggering a sharing remedy necessary to restore competition in innovation, otherwise unduly frozen.

Ultimately, on a more general level, an interesting parallel can be drawn between the establishment of a duty to share research valuable health data under the essential facilities doctrine and the establishment of compulsory patent licenses granted for exceptional reasons of public interest.[191] The considerations of the public interest grounding the exception to the general individual freedom of the patent holder and thus the establishment of a compulsory license could provide further systemic arguments in favour of a licensing-based remedy regarding the sharing of health

[190] This is recalled by Graef (13 May 2019), p. 22.

[191] Richter and Slowinski (2019), p. 22.

data that are essential for the conduction of health research and thus for the achievement of the public interests that are related to it.[192]

7.3.3.3 The Sharing Remedy Over Health Data

The above made considerations support the application of the essential facilities doctrine in health data pools, for the ultimate protection of research patterns, which would be unduly blocked by the over-appropriation of research valuable facilities by an already dominant undertaking.[193] The related sharing remedy would indeed enable to lower the entry barriers that are rising in the digital health research environment because of digital markets' market failures related to lock-in and network effects, and to overcome the emerging abusive conducts of cutting off research facilities to downstream rivals.

The sharing remedy regarding health data under art. 102 TFEU would thus be directly functional to curb these distortions of digital health research outcomes, for the direct achievement of consumer welfare protection and internal market's consolidation objectives, which the same European Court of Justice has linked to the essential facility sharing remedy in the Magill and Microsoft decisions.

In respect to the case of health data, these objectives could be further concretised in respect to the identified emerging European policy objective of the free flow of scientifically valuable health information. The consideration of this last policy objective provides a ground of promotion of the information sharing remedy under the essential facilities doctrine, but also a starting point for considering the limits in which the same sharing remedy under art. 102 TFEU can be enacted. Indeed, the allocation of such economic regulatory function to the sharing remedy under art. 102 TFEU needs to be contained within well defined limits.[194]

Under these premises, the debate regarding the opportunity to apply the sharing remedy under the essential facilities doctrine in highly dynamic, technology-driven markets, needs to be contextualised in the very features of health data-driven research markets in which the access to health datasets is requested and the role that data availability has in the design of new digital services and products.

First of all, in order to avoid that the sharing remedy fulfils generic research promotion objectives, the sharing remedy needs to be confined to specific health datasets, which can be linked to a specific research sector—e.g. health data regarding diabetes or kidney injuries-, and thus to a well-defined innovation market. In respect

[192] These have been highlighted supra in Chap. 3, Sect. 3.3.1.

[193] The lowering of the threshold for the enactment of a sharing remedy based on the essential facilities doctrine has been proposed by a strand of the literature in respect to datasets that are generated as a by-product of the delivery of a service. See Schweitzer et al. (9 October 2018), pp. 5–6.

[194] For a broad discussion over the creeping of economic regulatory functions into the texture of competition law remedies, Maggiolino (2015), pp. 3 ff.

to the health sector, the relevant innovation market could be defined in respect to a specific field of diseases.[195]

In addition to this, a further limit to the extension of the research remedy should be given by the gravity of the above-mentioned market failures. In these regards, it has been rightly observed that the less severe the market failures are, the more the sharing remedy under the essential facility doctrine should be anchored to the prejudice not to general, although sector-specific, research objectives, but to the development of specific products or services which would result into a substantial utility for consumers.[196] For these purposes, it has been noted that the product to be introduced by the access seeker should have no or a relatively low degree of substitutability with the product or service already marketed by the facility holder.[197]

This stricter interpretation would be respectful of the reward function of the dominant undertaking's intellectual property rights, which would otherwise be threatened in case, thanks to the sharing remedy, new entrants could market products or services which imitate the protected ones developed by the dominant undertaking.

The above traced limits would maintain the sharing remedy confined to "exceptional circumstances", although within the more flexible context of research markets than the one of specific product or service markets.

Against this backdrop, the application of the essential facilities doctrine in the data-driven research context within the above-traced limits, ultimately suggests the opportunity of a more interventionist and market shaping role of competition enforcement under art. 102 TFEU, whenever digital health data-driven markets appear to lack self-correcting antibodies. In these specific cases, thus, an antitrust intervention, in the form of the establishment of a proactive obligation to share and specifically designed to encourage and incentivise a consumer welfare enhancing competition in health research, appears to be desirable.[198]

From a systemic perspective, moreover, the—although exceptional—configuration of a sharing remedy regarding health data under the essential facilities doctrine is consistent with other recent competition policies, developed by the European Commission for the protection of research efforts, as the ones lately developed in the context of mergers, under the new so-called "innovation theory of harm".

[195] In these regards, it needs to be observed that the definition of an innovation market is structurally affected by a certain vagueness, exactly because of the uncertain or- better- unexpected nature of research courses.

[196] Graef (13 May 2019), p. 22.

[197] Graef (13 May 2019), p. 22.

[198] For a critical assessment of the regulatory market function of competition remedies, especially in the form of information sharing obligations, see Page and Childers (2007), p. 77.

7.3.4 *Data Sharing Remedies in European Merger Policy*

7.3.4.1 The Innovation Theory of Harm in Merger Policy

Innovation considerations have been lately given particular attention by the European Commission in the context of mergers in the pharmaceutical market and also in the neighbouring chemical market.

In these contexts, the Commission has conducted an innovation-based assessment through express reference to innovation-markets.[199]

The Commission has assessed not the *pro*-competitive but rather the *anti*-competitive effect of the mergers on innovation aiming at creating new products, assessing, as has been stated, "the impact of the Transaction at the level of innovation efforts by the Parties and its competitors".[200]

Examples of this case-law can be found in the *Medtronic/Covidien* merger,[201] where the Commission found that the merger between the two medical devices producers would have restricted competition and thus diminished the level of innovation in the considered market, disincentivizing one of the parties to finish the testing procedures for a promising drug Stellarex.

Likewise, also in the acquisition by *Novartis* of the company *Glaxosmithklines' (GSK) oncology business,*[202] the Commission detected the risk that the merger would have stopped developing two important drugs for the cure of skin and ovarian cancer, thus negatively impacting on the market's innovation outcomes.

A third similar case is to be found in the merger involving *Pfizer* and *Hospira,*[203] which the Commission deemed to affect the development of an important biosimilar drug[204] treating autoimmune diseases. Pfizer, who was carrying out the testing of such drug, would have indeed retarded the testing phases after the merger or would have divested the research on the drug to the originator, thus hindering price competition.

---

[199] See European Commission, Ciba-Geigy/Sandoz, Case n. IV/M. 737 (17 July 1996), para 43, where the Commission assessed relevant R&D "in terms of its importance for future markets". European Commission, Glaxo Wellcome/SmithKline Beecham, Case n. COMP/M. 1846 (8 May 2000), para 174, where the Commission assessed "the impact of the transaction on existing markets and on R&D markets". See also European Commission, Upjohn/Pharmacia, Case n. IV/M. 631 (28 September 1995). For the chemical market, see European Commission, Dow/DuPont, Case M. 793227 (27 March 2017a), para 348.

[200] European Commission, Dow/DuPont, Case M. 793227 (27 March 2017a), para 348.

[201] European Commission, Medtronic/Covidien, Case N. Comp/M7326 (28 November 2014b).

[202] European Commission, Novartis/Glaxosmithkline Oncology Business, Case N. Comp/M. 7275 (28 January 2015a).

[203] European Commission, Pfizer/Hospira, Case N. Comp/M. 7559 (4 August 2015c).

[204] It needs to be recalled that biosimilar drugs have the same therapeutic principle than the patented original, without being a copy of it as generics. Thus they are expected to lower prices for the correspondent treatments and widen patients' access to biological drugs.

Ultimately, also in the merger between *Johnson & Johnson* and *Actelion,*[205] the Commission noted the risk that one of the two parallel projects for the development of a new insomnia drug would have been abandoned after the merger, thus, as in the previous cases, impairing innovation competition.[206]

The mentioned cases are particularly relevant because they signal an increasing employment of the innovation market paradigm within pharmaceutical sectors' enquiries,[207] and thus a growing attention by the Commission with regards to the (in)efficiency outcomes of a market transaction.[208] This orientation has been reaffirmed by the Commission also in other mergers in the neighboring chemical sector, as in the *Dow/DuPont*[209] and in the *Bayer/Monsanto*[210] cases, where just as in the mentioned pharmaceutical cases, the merging between research-based companies was investigated from the perspective of the impact on the development of new products.[211] More precisely, in the *Dow/DuPont* case, Commissioner Vestager has argued that: "we need to make sure that the proposed merger does not lead to higher prices or *less innovation* for these products".[212]

In all the considered cases, the findings were related to the forecast of an overall reduction in innovation efforts, substantiated in a decrease of the number and quality of new products, directly resulting from the "discontinuation, deferment or redirection of competing lines of research and early pipeline products".[213] In view of these statements, the literature has critically observed, in particular with regards to the *Dow/DuPont* merger, that the Commission is posing the grounds for a new theory of harm based on innovation unrelated to a specific product market.[214] By doing so, it

[205] European Commission, J&J/Actelion Case M. 8401 (9 June 2017c).

[206] See in these regards, the overview of European Commission (28 January 2019), p. 30.

[207] European Commission (28 January 2019) 4. See also Bundeskartellamt (November 2017), pp. 1 ff.

[208] For a reconstruction over the role of efficiency considerations in EU mergers, see Cardwell (2017), pp. 551 ff.

[209] European Commission, Dow/DuPont, Case M. 793227 (27 March 2017a). European Commission (6 February 2017b).

[210] European Commission, Bayer/Monsanto, Case M. 8084 (21 March 2018a).

[211] See the comment by See Ibanez Colomo (2018), pp. 561 ff.

[212] European Commission (11 August 2016d).

[213] European Commission, Dow/DuPont, Case M. 793227 (27 March 2017a) para 277. Similarly, European Commission, Bayer/Monsanto, Case M. 8084 (21 March 2018a), para. 82: "the investigation suggests that the Transaction would likely significantly diminish innovation competition in a number of innovation spaces within the crop protection and seeds and traits industries by encouraging the merged entity to curtail its innovative efforts and capabilities below the level that would prevail in the absence of the Transaction". For a comment, see Bushell (1 March 2017).

[214] Bundeskartellamt (November 2017), pp. 1 ff. Werner et al. (2018), pp. 133 ff.; Bushell (1 March 2017). See also Carlin et al. (October 2017). Overall, it can be said that the major strand of the scholarship is skeptical on the legitimacy of enquiries that significantly depart from traditional market analyses. According to these positions, the assessment of the innovation capabilities of agreements between companies is an excessively risky and uncertain task. For the economics

appears to uphold those economic theories showing that mergers tend to reduce overall innovation and, as a result, harm consumer welfare.[215]

7.3.4.2 Data Sharing Remedies Through Commitments: The Divestment of Research Poles

Despite the detection of the above-described anticompetitive effects, the cited mergers were approved by the European Commission upon the condition that specific remedies were enacted by the merging parties.

In these regards, for example, in the *Medtronic/Covidien* merger Medtronic committed to sell Covidien's *Stellarex* business including manufacturing equipment, related intellectual property rights as well as scientific and regulatory material needed to finish the drug's development.[216] In this way, the Commission assured that the development of the drug would have been completed by a third company, working under the competitive pressure to innovate and to quickly bring the product on the market.

Similarly, in the *Novartis/GSK Oncology Business*, Novartis committed to divest one R&D business related to one of the two considered drugs to a third company, and retransfer the R&D business of the other one to the same company that was the original licensor. In addition to this, the remedy envisaged a cooperation agreement between this company and another third party, securing the proper testing procedures for the two drugs enabled by such cooperation.[217]

Also, in the *Pfizer/Hospira* case,[218] the remedy was related to the divestment of the biosimilar drug's development to a third company. Ultimately, in the *Johnson & Johnson* merger with *Actelion,*[219] Johnson & Johnson committed not to influence any strategic decision regarding the development of Actelion's research pipeline regarding insomnia treatment, transferring the control of the development of its own product to a partner.

Overall, the cases at stake demonstrate- and partly confirm- the emerging practice by the Commission to impose commitments exactly in those areas, as innovation markets, where business models and partial integration render it very arduous to forecast with certainty the future effect of a transaction, given that the effect itself

---

literature criticizing the expression of "innovation theory of harm", which suggests a presumption that horizontal mergers only hamper innovation, See Denicolò and Polo (22 March 2018).

[215] See for example, Federico et al. (2017), pp. 136 ff.; Federico et al. (2018), pp. 1 ff. More recently, Haucap et al. (2019), pp. 283 ff. Less severe conclusions are reached by Motta and Tarantino (30 August 2017).

[216] European Commission, Medtronic/Covidien, Case N. Comp/M7326 (28 November 2014b). See European Commission (1 April 2016a), p. 4.

[217] European Commission, Novartis/Glaxosmithkline Oncology Business, Case N. Comp/M. 7275 (28 January 2015a).

[218] European Commission, Pfizer/Hospira, Case N. Comp/M. 7559 (4 August 2015c).

[219] European Commission, J&J/Actelion Case M. 8401 (9 June 2017c).

will be given by the market developments and by how the arrangements are implemented.[220]

In the cited merger decisions, indeed, competition enforcement intervention occurs through commitments that become an outright means to impose onto (otherwise dominant) merged entities pro-competitive information sharing obligations directed to other players in the same research market.

These commitments are specifically directed at safeguarding competitors' ability to compete in health data based markets, and with that protecting a consumer welfare-enhancing health innovation pace. Interestingly, in these regards, the commitments cover not only an actual overlapping process or product, but also the *ability to create* an overlapping process or product.[221]

Overall, thus, the mentioned commitments are specifically designed to assure the protection of innovation and thus to preserve the ability and incentives to innovate, with that restoring effective competition in innovation.[222] These commitments mostly assure that pipeline projects regarding important drugs are not abandoned and that these are taken up by a third operator,[223] acting as a new innovative competitor posing competitive constraints to preserve innovation.[224]

More precisely, the commitments regarding the divestment of research poles appear to imply exactly the sharing of research valuable information to competitors actually or potentially acting within the same research field, together with the needed technological research infrastructure.

As particularly well reflected in the *Novartis* merger, the commitments regarding the divestment of research poles, through the establishment of additional cooperation agreements, maximize the research expertise available in the market.

This appears to be very interesting for it shows how the Commission's intervention with regards to collaborations between pharmaceutical companies ultimately directs and gives expression to the innovative potential of a networked health research environment, where new (life-saving) drugs can be marketed faster when the competitive pressure on the market is greater.

Under these premise, the commitments reflect how the aggregation of different technological assets within concentrated research pipelines can be tailored to efficiency goals.[225] At a deeper level, the analyzed case law appears thus to suggest that

---

[220] This renders it particularly hard to assess if the transaction will lead to new products and when these new products will be placed on the market. See in these regards, Svetiev (2014a), p. 478.

[221] Emphasis added. For the literature Kokkoris (2020), p. 56 ff.

[222] European Commission (28 January 2019), p. 30. The Commission's decisions regarding mergers in other innovation markets such as the ones in the chemical sector, had similar outcomes. See European Commission (21 March 2018b).

[223] European Commission (28 January 2019), p. 4.

[224] De Coninck (2016), p. 43.

[225] This is supported also by economic findings, see in this respect Denicolò and Polo (22 March 2018), p. 26, concluding that that there are cases in which two merging firms share the basic innovation, thus increasing "the R&D investment both in the research stage and in the development stage. The investment in the research stage increases as the basic innovation can be applied to the

innovation market analysis in the pharmaceutical sector supports aggregation practices of technological research tools for their pro-competitive effects.[226]

7.3.5 *The Regulatory Dimensions of Competition Sharing Remedies of Research Data*

The above-traced analysis has shown the emergence within European competition policy of information sharing remedies specifically tailored to information flows objectives in the context of innovation markets.[227]

Indeed in both essential facilities cases in high tech markets and in merger decisions regarding pharmaceutical innovation markets, sharing remedies appear to have been expansively imposed by the European Commission, either in the form of a sharing obligation borne by an abusing dominant undertaking or in the form of a commitment by the newly merged entity to divest some research poles to competing parties. These sharing remedies appear to work as research and innovation catalysts in case of anticompetitive suspension of sectoral research and development interactions among different market players.

Under these premises, both the sharing remedy under art. 102 TFEU and the commitments regarding the divestments of research poles appear to work as "para-regulatory" competition remedies,[228] re-establishing threatened competition in innovation through greater availability of research information on the relevant innovation market.

More precisely, in light of the developments of both the essential facilities doctrine and the merger analysis regarding high-tech and innovation markets, the European Commission appears to have developed specific remedial tools for the restoration of (research) information asymmetries in the case these harm innovation. Given that information asymmetries are ever growing in the dynamics of digital markets and more precisely in the dynamics of digitised high-tech and innovation markets, it is very likely that these will result, amongst others, not only in informational imbalances between businesses and data subjects, but also in informational imbalances regarding different businesses' research capabilities.

---

research projects of both divisions of the merged firm and hence is more valuable. The investment in the development stage increases, on average, as it is more likely that R&D expenditure is more productive thanks to the basic innovation". Recognising, up to certain limits, the positive impacts on innovation of collaborations, Aghion et al. (2005), pp. 701 ff.

226 Carrier (2008), pp. 393 ff.

227 This is well highlighted also by Di Porto (2014), p. 312.

228 With regards to obligations to share information under art. 102 TFEU, see Di Porto (2014), p. 321 especially in the energy and network industry sector. With regards to the "para-regulatory" nature of commitments, see Wils (2006), pp. 345 ff.; Georgiev (2007), pp. 971 ff.

The emerging para-regulatory role of competition law[229] in the context of high tech and innovation markets,[230] are presumably destined to expand in the context of digital markets, and more precisely in the context of digital innovation markets, where imbalances exactly in respect to research-valuable resources are destined to become sharper.

Research imbalances may have pervasive effects in the structuring of the newly resulting product/service markets, by centralizing research assets under the control of closed research ecosystems, and thus becoming source of monopolization patterns in developing markets. In these terms, such a re-allocative intervention regarding research information appears to be justified from the perspective of both ordoliberalist rationales regarding the protection of competition processes' fairness and competing firms' economic freedom and of economic oriented stances of consumer welfare protection.[231]

However, as has been observed, this emerging regulatory drift of competition law enforcement disowns the traditional restrictive, *ex post* and facts-based attitude of competition law as conceived by the Chicago School, in order to embrace a new *ex ante* and forward-looking market shaping role.[232]

These developments are thus triggering deeper reflections in the scholarship with regards the actual relationship between these regulatory turnarounds of competition policies and economic regulation.[233] Such reflections have been mostly directed at finding parallelisms and eventual overlaps between para-regulatory competition remedies and sector-specific regulation.[234]

In respect to the sharing remedies regarding research information, this line of reasoning is particularly thought provoking in light of the existence of regulatory obligations to render research information available in publicly accessible databases controlled by regulatory agencies. It is the case, for example of clinical trials databases and safety information regarding medical devices, which respectively the Clinical Trials Regulation and the Medical Device Regulation demand to be accessible to competitors through the intermediary transparency role of regulatory agencies.[235]

---

229 Parcu (2013), pp. 321 ff.; More generally about the legal foundations of competition law remedies, see Lianos (2013), pp. 362 ff.

230 See Weber (2015), pp. 239 ff.

231 For the assessment of these two lines of development of competition policy, see supra Chap. 6, Sect. 6.2.

232 This point is stressed by Maggiolino (2015), pp. 15–16.

233 Svetiev (2014b), pp. 63 ff., in particular at 76–82, highlighting the new "problem-solving" and thus functional nature of the para-regulatory remedies developed by competition authorities.

234 In this regard, see observations by Monti (2008), pp. 123 ff. and Geradin (2004b); Weber (2015), pp. 239 ff.

235 See supra Chap. 2, Sect.2.1.5 at note 113 mentioning the case of clinical trials databases and safety information regarding medical devices.

The consideration of these sector-specific disclosure obligations regarding health research data, thus raises the question over the difference between specific sharing remedies under competition law and such regulatory disclosure obligations.

In these regards, it needs to be remembered that the latter assure the *ex ante* availability of research data employed in regulatory procedures for the obtainment of marketing authorisations. Conversely, having the objective of restoring harmed competition in innovation processes, the sharing remedies under competition law appear to refer to the deeper layers of research data pools, which are not disclosed in the course of regulatory procedures and which are thus not publicly accessible by competitors.

In this perspective, it could be thus argued that the difference between regulatory disclosure obligations regarding research information and sharing remedies under competition law is to be identified in the fact that the former regard research information which is strictly related to marketed health products or services, whereas the latter, in accordance with innovation market theory, is "pure" research information, which is not (at least, yet) directly linked to a specific product or service.

Another distinction between these two set of obligations regarding the disclosure of research information is to be found in the different impact on intellectual property rights: the regulatory disclosure obligations, implying a general and standardised public disclosure of research results, cannot impair businesses' intellectual property rights.[236] Conversely, sharing obligations imposed by competition authorities amount to exceptional market interventions implying the sharing of research information with one or more well identified competing undertakings. In these regards, the sharing remedy structurally implies the direct interference with the dominant undertaking's intellectual property rights. The disclosure obligations in these exceptional remedial cases take indeed the form of outright duty to license the (mostly intellectual property protected) research information.

From a further standpoint, the emergence of exceptional para-regulatory competition remedies regarding the re-distribution of information between competing research entities, could signal a legislative vacuum that would need to be filled with a specific normative intervention generalising the obligation to share health research results between health research undertakings.

Such a general sharing obligation regarding health data would be also in line with some recent legislative initiatives which have established outright sharing obligations among competitors in specific markets.

This is the case, for example, of the Payment Service Directive II, which has set an explicit obligation to share information onto payment service providers.[237] Similarly, also the EU Regulation on platform-to-business relations (P2B) provides

---

[236] See art. 89 Clinical Trials Regulation.

[237] Directive (EU) 2015/2366 of the European Parliament and of the Council of 25 November 2015 on payment services in the internal market, amending Directives 2002/65/EC, 2009/110/EC and 2013/36/EU and Regulation (EU) No 1093/2010, and repealing Directive 2007/64/EC (23 December 2012) art. 67.

a rule that a platform provider must be transparent with the data it collects for its business users and if it intends to give access to that data to its business users in a discriminating fashion, it needs to be transparent.[238]

Against the backdrop of these European normative developments, in a *de jure condendo* perspective, it would be desirable to have a similar obligation with regards to research entities to share their data with other actual or potential competitors acting within a specific health data-driven research market.

In these regards, it needs to be however specified that, in line with the connection of the information sharing remedy under art. 102 TFEU only to an *abuse* of *dominant* market power, such normative duty to give access to research data should be proportional also to the involved parties' individual market power. This means that a group of smaller research entities that pool together their data to gain a competitive advantage should not be compelled to share their pooled data with a larger self-standing established market player.[239] In the light of this risk, a normative mandatory sharing obligation posed onto research entities could be established independently of the occurrence of a market abuse, thus being broader in scope than the sharing remedy available under art. 102TFEU, but should be strictly anchored to the existence of a dominant market position of the addressees of such obligation. Otherwise, a normatively imposed sharing obligation of research data would risk to exactly facilitate the establishment of research information-based monopolies of the recipients of an information disclosure obligation.

7.3.6 *The Regulatory Design of Sharing Remedies Over Research Data*

The consideration of the para-regulatory nature of information disclosure obligations as remedies under competition law suggests some further reflections regarding the design that these sharing remedies regarding research information in innovation markets should have.

Indeed, in the moment competition law develops tools to intervene in innovation, through the definition of a relevant market and the development of adequate remedies to re-allocate innovation incentives in a more homogeneous way among existing market players in the innovation field, this regulatory task that competition authorities acquires should conform to the rules of other regulatory branches regarding research and innovation.

[238] Regulation EU 2019/1150 of the European Parliament and of the Council of 20 June 2019, on Promoting Fairness and Transparency for Business Users of online Intermediation Services (11 July 2019) art. 9. European Commission (30 September 2021).

[239] Lindqvist (6 November 2018), p. 23.

These regulatory branches of research and innovation are, traditionally, intellectual property law and, specifically regarding data-driven innovation, data protection law.[240]

The design of sharing obligations in competition remedies both regarding abusing dominant undertakings and merged entities, in the view of their function of restoring competition in innovation and thus promoting research and development enquiries, should thus conform to the principles and rules established in these other two branches of innovation regulation.

It is to these frameworks that competition authorities should thus look at for the design of the sharing obligations regarding research data.

However, if the conformation to some schemes drawn from intellectual property law is only desirable from a policy standpoint, for they would increase the research efficiencies stemming from health data pools, the conformation to data protection laws should be considered mandatory, given the existence of specific rules regarding the processing of sensitive personal data for research purposes.

Under these premises, since the imposition of sharing remedies regarding research data implies the transfer to a third party and thus a further processing of this same data, in designing the sharing remedies needed to open up established health data pools, competition authorities should conform the sharing remedies to the specific data protection rules set by the General Data Protection Regulation. This would require the necessary involvement of data protection authorities both in the definition and in the supervision of the enactment of sharing obligations regarding research valuable health data.

In this respect, it needs to be observed that the remedial imposition of sharing obligations towards a third party competitor by an established health data pool, equals to the creation of a new health data pool between these parties, circumscribed to the data either held essential for the specific research purposes—under the sharing obligation *ex* art. 102 TFEU—or forming the divested research pole—under a commitment decision. This means that from a data protection perspective, these sharing remedies should respect the above-defined data protection safeguards that the parties to a health data research pool have to obey to in order to be compliant to data protection law.

In these regards, however, since information sharing remedies enacted at competition enforcement level are exceptional and specific regulatory interventions, specifically designed by competition authorities in the exercise of their exceptional regulatory powers, it could be argued that by designing these remedies competition authorities could require a higher data protection threshold. This would need to be imposed together with data protection authorities and eventually also with relevant ethics committees.

Competition authorities, for example, could require that research data are shared anonymously.[241] As has been assessed above, the requirement of anonymity

[240] See supra Chap. 2, Sect. 2.2.2 and Chap. 5, Sect. 5.2.2.

[241] This has been suggested by Commissioner Vestager (29 September 2016).

regarding research data is not established as mandatory under the General Data Protection Regulation. The imposition of such a requirement by the competition authority could thus heighten the data protection threshold of health data pools mandatorily imposed through competition remedies in respect to that of "spontaneously" formed health data pools.

Moreover, competition authorities could refer to data protection law principles[242] in order to define the addressees of disclosure obligations regarding research information. In particular the principles of fairness and transparency of health data-driven research could suggest that the beneficiaries—that is the recipients of sharing remedies—are smaller private research entities or public research entities. The mentioned data protection law principles could thus ground, for example, a more flexible interpretation of the notion of essential facilities when the entity requesting access to research valuable information is a smaller private undertaking or a public undertaking who intends to enter a research field already controlled by a dominant (digital) research platform.[243] Likewise, in case of the divestment of research poles through a commitment decision, the same data protection law principles could suggest the direction of the research poles' divestment towards smaller undertakings or public research entities, which risk to be otherwise cut off research collaborations through the entrenching dominance of newly merged entities.

Against this backdrop, thus, data protection law, in its reaffirmed function of regulating data-driven innovation and data flows within the Digital Single Market,[244] could provide regulatory grounds for the design by competition authorities of sharing remedies regarding innovation valuable information.

In this respect, the incorporation of data protection law's rules and principles within "behavioural" information-based competition remedies, does not amount to an undue enforcement of these same rules and principles by competition authorities, and does not mean thus the encumbering of competition law with external values.[245]

To the contrary, such regulatory interaction appears to be exactly demanded by the object that competition enforcement would have in the context of health data pools, that is the restoration of the competition process in health data-driven innovation.

Since, as demonstrated above,[246] the General Data Protection Regulation requires that data-driven research, and thus the *ex ante* design of research based health data pools, should be fair, transparent and sustainable, these same principles should also

---

[242] See supra Sect. 7.2.1.

[243] In these regards, it is interesting to recall that the European Commission has opened an investigation regarding Dutch and Polish banks' behaviour of granting access to data only to established banks and not to smaller companies, as start-ups in the financial sector. European Commission (6 October 2017d).

[244] See supra Chap. 5, Sect. 5.2.2.

[245] This is the risk that a strand of the antitrust scholarship highlights with regard to the incorporation of data protection considerations within competition law assessments. See, amongst others, Colangelo and Maggiolino (2017), pp. 363 ff.

[246] See supra Sect. 7.2.1.

be followed by competition law authorities when intervening *ex post* in order to restore competition in health data-driven innovation through the mandatory creation of new health data pools between parties competing in the field of health data-driven research.

For the purposes of this form of para-regulatory competition enforcement, itself suggested by the European developments occurred in the context of information abuses under art. 102 TFEU and of recent commitment decisions in pharmaceutical markets, competition authorities cannot disregard the object of the imposed sharing remedy- that is (sensitive) personal data- and the rules that govern its sharing. This because the regulatory dimensions of health research as personal data processing and of health research as a market are just two sides of a same phenomenon. As a result, the rules requiring health data processing for research purposes to be fair, transparent and sustainable demand also the market of health data-driven research to be fair, transparent and sustainable.

Such interpretation, which intends to maximise the regulatory interactions between competition law and data protection law, in the moment the former intervenes in the market structuring of health data processing activities, is suggested by the principle of consistency and coherence of European law under art. 107 TFEU,[247] which points at the interdependency and mutual supportiveness between different branches of European law.[248] On a practical level, such consistency would be thus achieved through greater collaborative efforts between competition and data protection authorities.[249]

Different considerations need to be conversely made in respect to the regulatory support that intellectual property law can have in the shaping of competition remedies regarding the sharing of innovation sensitive information. Differently from the case of data protection law, which provides specific rules concerning the sharing of health data, which are thus directly applicable, intellectual property law's licensing schemes could be applied only in analogy. In these regards, for the purposes of health data pools' design, licensing schemes drawn from standard essential patents and from patent pools would be particularly interesting.

In these regards, it would be useful, as some strand of the literature has already suggested,[250] that the Commission would issue more specific Guidelines regarding data-driven cooperation, better defining the conditions under which intellectual property law schemes could be applied to data pools.

Upon the premise that more precise specifications would be needed through the Commission's soft law interventions, at a very general level, it can be said that the intellectual property-based schemes upon which competition authorities could rely on for the purposes of the design of pro-competitive health data pools, could

[247] Bertea (2005), pp. 154 ff.

[248] It needs to be however recalled that the principle of coherence within European law in highly debated, for an overview, see Prechal and Van Roermund (2008).

[249] Stressing this point Zingales (2018), p. 96.

[250] Lindqvist (6 November 2018), pp. 26–27.

be respectively found in the imposition (i) of FRAND terms, (ii) of grant back-clauses and (iii) of technical standards of openness regarding the sharing of research valuable health information.

(i) **FRAND Terms**: already in the *Asnef-Equifax* decision, the European Court of Justice stressed the importance of the non-discriminatory nature of the conditions of access to a data pool by competing parties.[251] For these purposes, the European Commission has argued in favour of taking inspiration from practices regarding certain standards setting concerning technologies under patent protection.[252] In these regards, with specific reference to the negotiation framework of standard essential patents, it has considered the possibility of establishing licenses of data on the basis of FRAND—*i.e.* fair, reasonable and non-discriminatory—terms.[253]

In the realm of intellectual property, these are licensing terms compelling standard essential patents holders to license their patents to any standard's implementer on FRAND terms.[254]

From the perspective of the considered competition sharing remedies regarding competitively relevant data, the imposition of FRAND terms would be a means to grant access to essential research data to minor undertakings.[255] Moreover, in the context of commitment decisions, the granting of access to research valuable data under FRAND terms could be a requirement conditioning the divestment of research poles to other big competing research actors, thus impeding the creation of research oligopolies. A similar commitment was offered by the parties in the *Siemens/Drägerwerk* merger, where the merging entities committed to ensure the continued interoperability between their medical equipment and patient monitors and their interoperability with hospital data management systems "on a non-discriminatory basis and free-of-charge".[256]

---

[251] European Court of Justice, Asnef Equifax v. Ausbanc, C-238/05 (23 November 2006), para 60.

[252] For the literature see Telle (2017), pp. 421 ff.

[253] European Commission (10 January 2017f), p. 12. See also with regards to the financial sector, European Commission (8 March 2018d), p. 7.

[254] On the pro-competitiveness nature of the FRAND terms, see Trabucco and Ghidini (2017).

[255] This is what the Commission and the Court of Justice stressed in the Microsoft decision: "Microsoft shall on reasonable and non-discriminatory terms, allow the use of interoperability information". European Court of Justice- Court of First Instance, Microsoft Corp. vs. Commission of the European Communities, Case T-201/04 (17 September 2007), para 193; 808; 1231 and 1261.

[256] So European Commission, Siemens/Drägerwerk, Case COMP/M.2861 (30 April 2003), para 156. It is interesting to recall that access to essential data under FRAND terms was object of commitments in other merger cases. See European Commission, Liberty Global/De Vijver Media, CASE M.7194 (24 February 2015b), para 624; 625; 655; 672, where the companies committed to grant access to critical television channels on FRAND terms to any interested TV distributor in Belgium. Similarly, see also European Commission, Worldline/Equens/Paysqaure M 7873 (20 April 2016b) where the companies committed to license key card and payment processing software, and also source code of the same software on FRAND terms to payment network service providers.

From an additional standpoint, the FRAND terms could also be a basis for the setting of remuneration rules for the data access provided to third parties.[257]

However, it needs to be observed that the implementability of FRAND terms in the context of data sharing remedies is largely obstructed by the lack of consensus regarding the actual definition of what these terms actually are as well as the procedures that need to be enacted in order to comply with a commitment based on the FRAND terms.[258]

The European Court of Justice has tried to fill some of these gaps in the Huawei decision, which has developed a negotiation framework for FRAND Royalties.[259] This framework has been explicitly referred to by the European Commission for the establishment of a framework of obligations to share data under competition law.[260] However, it has itself acknowledged that a proper framework regarding FRAND terms is far from being developed.[261] This has led some strand of the literature of questioning the opportunity of referring to FRAND terms as a relevant means for the promotion of pro-competitive data sharing.[262] Although this position may be commendable, it is here believed that the consideration of the FRAND terms, could nonetheless provide an interesting benchmark upon which more precise Guidelines regarding the remedial obligations of information sharing need to be developed for the purposes of competition enforcement. With specific regards to the sharing of health research relevant information, the definition of the principles regarding fair, reasonable and non-discriminatory access terms should be conducted with reference to the corresponding data protection principles, to which health data-driven research needs to conform under the General Data Protection Regulation.

(ii) **Grant Back Clause**: with regards to the establishment of grant back clauses, these could be conversely a means imposed by competition authorities to repair exclusionary conducts occurred within an established health data pool. It could thus assure that all the parties to a health data pool effectively get back the research information resulting from a research enquiry conducted, *inter alia*, with the data that they had initially shared within the pool.[263] The imposition of such clauses

[257] European Commission (10 January 2017f), p. 13; European Commission (25 April 2018c), p. 15.

[258] Colangelo and Borgogno (5 April 2019), p. 15.

[259] European Court of Justice, Huawei Technologies Co. Ltd. vs. ZTE Corp. and ZTE Deutschland GmbH, C-170/13 (16 July 2015), paras 44 ff.

[260] European Commission (10 January 2017f), p. 21.

[261] In focusing more on the procedural framework, the European Court of Justice has left unanswered some more substantial issues, as for example the definition of a dominant position in respect to standard essential patents or the possibility to apply the framework to non-competing parties. So Colangelo and Borgogno (5 April 2019), p. 15. In these regards the European Commission has defined key principles, contributing to the establishment of a more predictable framework regarding standard essential patents. European Commission (29 November 2017).

[262] Colangelo and Borgogno (5 April 2019), p. 15.

[263] See with regards to the establishment of grant back clauses in financial data pools Di Porto and Ghidini (25 June 2019).

would thus be a means to counterbalance the (growing) market power of a data pool's member,[264] which could be abused through the interruption of the provision to other members either of the provided research infrastructure or of a specific type of upstream data, as, for example, digital runaway data controlled by a digital company, as Google or IBM.[265] In respect to this scenario, a grant back clause would thus assure that all the members of the data pool, thus also the weakest members—as could be the case of pharmaceutical companies in respect to digital companies-, continue to have access to the pools' generated essential research facilities. Also in case of the divestment of research poles, and thus the imposition of a research collaboration with other competing parties as in the above-cited Novartis case, a grant back clause could block the attempt of (mis-)appropriation of competing parties of the research facilities built upon the research information provided by the merged entity through the divestment of the research pole.

The imposition of a grant back clause should however be only imposed as an *ex post* remedy in case of the occurrence of such abusive exclusionary conducts: indeed, as has been observed by a strand of the literature, the general obligation to insert such a clause in data exchange agreements could discourage a large external data holder from entering a pool, with that precluding the pool members to access needed technological infrastructures or specific types of research valuable data.[266]

(iii) **Technical Standards of Openness**: ultimately, just as patent pools, also data pools could be bound to the respect of certain technical standards of openness. In these regards, the European Commission has underlined that effective data sharing policies need to be "supported by appropriate technical standards in order to implement meaningful portability in a technologically neutral manner".[267]

In the context of the debate regarding *which* technical standards could effectively promote interoperability and data exchanges among platforms, application programming interfaces (APIs) have been looked at with increasing interest by both the European Commission[268] and the scholarship.[269]

[264] Stressing this effect of grant back clauses and cross-licensing covenants for future innovations Lindqvist (2014), pp. 229 ff.

[265] This scenario of exclusive conduct has been assessed above Sect. 7.3.1.2.

[266] Lindqvist (6 November 2018), p. 10.

[267] European Commission (10 January 2017f), p. 16.

[268] European Commission (10 January 2017f), p. 12. See also European Commission (25 April 2018c), pp. 5–6: "Providing access to dynamic data via application programming interfaces is particularly important, as it supports the open data ecosystem, saves time and costs through automation of the download process, and greatly facilitates the re-use of data for a wide range of new products and services. Sharing data via the correct and secure use of application programming interfaces can generate significant added value for different actors of the data value chain. It can also contribute to the creation of valuable ecosystems around data assets whose potential is often unused by data holders". Under these premises, the European Commission has also launched an assessment process aimed at investigating how to incentivize to adopt "open, standardized and well-documented APIs". European Commission (25 April 2018c), p. 8.

[269] Colangelo and Borgogno (5 April 2019).

Application Programming Interfaces are sets of protocols determining how software components communicate with each other, thus enabling a firm to access data controlled by another company. The relevance of these technical standards of openness for data sharing has been stressed by the Article 29 Working Party in respect to the implementation of data portability under the General Data Protection Regulation.[270] Here, the Working Party stressed the opportunity to define application programming interfaces for the purposes of data transfers in consistency with a sector-specific approach.[271]

Interestingly in these regards, some studies are enquiring the specific application of application programming interfaces for the purposes of the increasing the access and the sharing of health data among health providers.[272]

However, well before this sector-specific approach, the European Commission has stressed the importance to conform the structuring and the employment of application programming interfaces to the principles, amongst others, of "stability, maintainance over the lifecycle, uniformity of use and standards".[273] As the literature has stressed in these regards the definition of standardization features of these application programming interfaces is seen as an essential precondition for the establishment of the technical and thus legal certainty that is needed in order to promote efficient data sharing practices. The lack of the definition of uniform technical requirements results, to date, in a technical uncertainty that ultimately impairs the achievement of the set objective of efficient data sharing.[274]

For these purposes, the European Commission has programmed the establishment of a European support centre for data sharing, under the Connecting Europe Facility Programme, with the specific aim of assisting firms in developing sound application interfaces programmes with best-practices models, contracts and other technical and legal support.

Although it is still largely unclear who should define the standards for these application interfaces programs, it would be desirable that the participation to the standard setting procedure would be unrestricted and transparent, and that the resulting standard agreement should provide access to the standard on the condition of the respect of the above recalled fair, reasonable and non-discriminatory (FRAND) terms.[275] The lack of openness in the definition of such standards

---

[270] Article 29 Data Protection Working Party (13 December 2016, last Revised and adopted on 5 April 2017), p. 2.

[271] Article 29 Data Protection Working Party (13 December 2016, last Revised and adopted on 5 April 2017), p. 17.

[272] See Dullabh et al. (2019), pp. 201 ff.

[273] European Commission (25 April 2018c), p. 11, stressing that the structuring and the employment of application programming interfaces, should be grounded in the principles of "stability, maintainance over the lifecycle, uniformity of use and standards, user-friendliness and security". Colangelo and Borgogno (5 April 2019), p. 6.

[274] Colangelo and Borgogno (5 April 2019), p. 6.

[275] Lindqvist (6 November 2018), p. 26.

would risk to cut off from the adoption of such technology the market players that cannot autonomously keep pace with technological developments.[276]

7.3.6.1 Open Questions Over the Administrability of Sharing Remedies of Research Data

The support that both data protection rules and intellectual property schemes can give to the design of sharing remedies regarding research valuable information encounters some technical problems regarding the practical administrability of the licensing of digital health data.

First of all, in the context of the algorithmic processing of the data, it is very difficult to define which exact datasets are to be made object of the sharing obligation.[277]

In respect to essential facilities cases, the requesting firm, is indeed not able—exactly in light of the obscuring intellectual property rights over health data and of the generative nature of processing analytics—to know in advanced which datasets are essential for its research activities. Hence, From the perspective of the requesting firm, the exact content of health data pools is thus unspecified.[278]

Differently, in the context of commitments regarding the divestment of research poles and thus the sharing of health data pools, the question could arise whether the divested health data pools should concern a defined set of data or whether the licensed data should be updated in accordance to the pace of data analytics.[279]

The problem of the identification of the licensed data resource could be however partly overcome through a collaborative effort between competition and data protection authorities. Indeed, as has been shown above, data protection authorities have strong investigation powers established under the General Data Protection Regulation. In virtue of these auditing powers, mainly given by the analysis of data protection impact assessments, data protection authorities can access the most detailed information regarding the content and structure of health data pools, and can also access information protected under intellectual property rights.[280]

This means that the assessment by the competition authority over the essentiality of specific datasets can only be carried out through collaboration with the data protection authority, in order to define which information is to be captured by the sharing obligation. In this perspective, the joint assessment of research data pools by the involved authorities can also establish the limitation of the timeframe for which

[276] This is also stressed by Lynskey (2017), p. 807.

[277] Stressing this point Maggiolino and Colangelo (2017), p. 260; Kathuria and Globocnik (2020), p. 529.

[278] Maggiolino and Colangelo (2017), pp. 270–271.

[279] Maggiolino and Colangelo (2017), pp. 270–271.

[280] See supra Sect. 7.2.2.

also future, thus updated, data need to be shared,[281] respectively by the abusing dominant firm in case of a refusal to share under art. 102 TFEU and by the merging entity that has committed to share with other market players part of its research valuable assets. In these regards, the timeframe set for the licensing of future information should be carefully determined also in light of the risk that, by granting access to an excessively large dataset, the same competitors could be disincentivised from generating their own research data.[282]

A second concern regarding the administrability of the licensing of health data is given by the difficulty of assuring that the shared data are effectively employed by the competitors benefiting of the remedy for the purposes of health research and not for other ones.[283] In these regards it has been rightly acknowledged in the literature that an eventual limitation on the use of the licensed data only for the declared purposes would be impossible to monitor by a competition authority.[284]

However, it is here believed that it would be sufficient for the competition authority to monitor that the data licensed through the sharing remedy is effectively used for the health research purpose and is thus functional to the re-establishment of the harmed competition processes regarding health research. Conversely, uses of the licensed data for different purposes are not relevant for the competition dynamics of the considered innovation market. The monitoring of these should thus not be competence of competition authorities. The uses of data that fall outside the (imposed) licenses should be considered illegitimate under the relevant intellectual property or data protection laws.

Ultimately, also with the above-signalled restrictions, the administration of sharing remedies needs a constant monitoring and, if needed, also an outright re-calibration of the imposed obligations in accordance to the fast changing nature of the considered research environment.[285] It could indeed occur that the competing firm that is the addressee of the imposed information flows, as it is the firm requesting access to the research-essential facility or the firm to whom the research pole is divested as a result of a commitment, itself merges, creates a joint venture or establishes another type of research alliance with another market player, this rendering the sharing remedy not appropriate anymore for the purposes of the re-establishment on competition in innovation.[286] Such a scenario would thus require competition authorities to re-shape the occurred competition enforcement in light of the changed networked research ecosystem.

[281] Maggiolino and Colangelo (2017), p. 275.

[282] Kathuria and Globocnik (2020), p. 529.

[283] Health data could indeed be used for other purposes of commercial nature, which are not related to health research or the health sector. In these regards, see supra Chap. 3, Sect. 3.3.6.

[284] Stressing the difficulty for competition authorities of supervising the effective employment of the data for the purposes for which the data were deemed essential by the competition authority, Podszun (2017), pp. 406 ff. See in general Kennedy (March 2017).

[285] This was forecasted by Waller (2009), p. 26. Similarly, Svetiev (2014a), pp. 466 ff.

[286] Some strand of the literature has observed in these regards that the same fast changing nature of dynamic markets could render the remedies even useless. See Kokkoris (2020).

The above highlighted concerns regarding the administrability of big data relate to the ultimate question of the breadth of competition authorities' intervention powers in respect to behavioural remedies. For these purposes, both articles 7 and 9 of the Council Regulation 1/2003,[287] respectively regarding remedies under art. 102 TFEU and commitment decisions, confer to the Commission broad powers for ending an occurred infringement "through any behavioural or structural"[288] remedy, with the only requirement of the proportionality of such enforcement intervention under art. 7 of the same Regulation.

These "behavioural" enforcement interventions in the market need to be first of all rooted in specific antitrust harms. This means that competition authorities should thus abstain to assess what technical data is being collected and exchanged, as long as it does not interfere with antitrust harms to innovation in a well-defined research area.

In this perspective, competition enforcement need to be strictly rooted first of all in the ascertainment of a harm, even if the scope of such harms has been lately extended by both the European Court of Justice and the European Commission within innovation markets.

In these "exceptional circumstances", as the mentioned essential facilities' cases and the commitment decisions in the context of pharmaceutical mergers have shown, information sharing remedies need to be imposed by competition authorities on a careful case by case basis, through reliance of specialist expertise to make predictions with a certain degree of confidence.[289] In cases of sharing of personal data, as it is the case of health data, such expertise needs to necessarily be retrieved first of all from data protection authorities, and if needed also from scientific regulatory authorities, such as the European Medicines Agency at European level. The reliance on such expertise could thus help to fill some of the above highlighted administrability loopholes of competition remedies regarding the sharing of data, starting from the definition of which data need to me made object of the remedy in order to effectively restore the identified harm.

These last considerations suggest the opportunity to envisage a "collaborative governance" of competition remedies in highly networked data-driven innovation sectors, as the one of digital health.[290]

This decentralization of the design of competition remedies, through the involvement of other regulatory agencies, needs however to accompanied by a non-negligible note for caution, which relates to what is maybe the most serious

---

[287] Council Regulation (EC) N. 1/2003 of 16 December 2002 on the implementation of the rules on competition laid down in Articles 81 and 82 of the Treaty (4 January 2003) OJ L1/1 https://eur-lex.europa.eu/legal-content/EN/TXT/PDF/?uri=CELEX:32003R0001&from=EN.

[288] So art. 7 Council Regulation (EC) N. 1/2003.

[289] Svetiev (2015), p. 77, referring exactly to the cases of new market and industry settings and the ones where "technological innovation is rapidly changing market boundaries". More generally stressing the problem of the limits of knowledge of courts and regulators in deciding innovation-related competition cases, Drexl (2010), pp. 677 ff.

[290] This had been already foreshadowed by Svetiev (2010), pp. 79 ff.

criticality regarding the administrability of information-based remedies. The risk is indeed that competition authorities, as supported by the expertise of other regulators, enjoy a too broad discretion in shaping such information remedies and thus in deciding whether and which information should remain in the appropriability sphere of dominant or merged companies, or should be disclosed in order to advance competition in innovation.[291]

Such an excessive broad discretion would first of all go to the detriment of the legal certainty in competition enforcement endured by market players in respect to their decisions regarding how to manage their research valuable information assets, and thus regarding whether to share their data or to refuse to share their data. Moreover, such broad discretion in the design of information sharing remedies risks to bind these same remedies beyond their legitimate function of preserving sources of competitive pressure in research markets, and to encumber them with the regulatory function of structurally adjusting markets to promote innovation.[292]

The imposition of an obligation to share research valuable information entails per se a market shaping effect. This determines the above-mentioned para-regulatory nature of such remedies. However, in order to prevent an undue proactive market structuring effect through information sharing remedies, these should be strictly circumscribed to the elimination of the consequences of the anticompetitive behaviour. As the European Court of Justice has pointed out, behavioural remedies should be circumscribed to the provision of "advantages which have been wrongfully withheld".[293]

The definition of the extension of competition authorities' powers to re-establish such "wrongfully withheld" advantages remains an open question.

In these regards, a strand of the literature has argued that in some cases, in order to effectively restore the harmed competition process, competition authorities should restore competition not (only) at the level it was before the infringement but at the level it would have been at the moment of enforcement without the infringement.[294]

At the very opposite end of the spectrum, other authors have highlighted that demanding the sharing of data would be a form of "market engineering", which

[291] Stressing the problem related to authorities' discretion in shaping remedies for the purposes of preserving competition in innovation, Ibáñez Colomo (2016), p. 217.

[292] In this sense, Ibáñez Colomo (2016), p. 218. See in this regard, the observations made by the American District Court, pointing out that the Court's role is to end the illegal conduct and to make every effort to protect against conduct of the same type or class, not to engineer a particular market outcome". American District Court New York vs. Microsoft Corp. 224 F Supp. 2d 76, 95 (D.D.C. 2002).

[293] European Court of Justice, Istituto Chemioterapeutico Italiano and Commercial Solvents vs. Commission, Joined Cases C-6 and 7/73 (6 March 1974), para 45.

[294] Ritter (2016), pp. 587 ff., arguing for the opportunity of a "but for" the infringement enforcement policy.

would unduly try to protect competitors' instead of consumers welfare[295] and thus substitute competition enforcement to the market's self-correcting mechanisms.[296]

In respect to the competition in data-driven innovation, it is highly difficult to establish both the level of competition that existed before the infringement, or that would have developed if the infringement had not occurred, this rendering both of the mentioned positions of highly speculative nature.

However, in case an infringement is found under the essential facilities' reading of art. 102 TFEU or a merger is found to excessively centralise research resources with a resulting harm to competition in research endeavours, the sharing remedy becomes a means exactly to re-establish the well-functioning of the market through the provision of the input resource through which the market aliments itself.

Against the backdrop of the objective regarding the re-establishment of the well-functioning of the market, a "behavioural" competition intervention would be thus justified when the phagocyting dynamics of data-driven markets themselves appear to be uncapable of self-corrective reactions against occurred antitrust harms. Since, as the European policy declarations and legislative initiatives regarding the Digital Single Market suggest,[297] the existence of free-flows of information is regarded as a structural component of the well-functioning of data-driven markets, information sharing remedies would thus consistently meet this objective.

From this perspective, hence, the objective of the well-functioning of data-driven innovation markets, as achieved through free information flows, constitutes at the same time the justification and the limit of the enactment of competition remedies based on the sharing of research valuable information.

The assessment regarding how a specific sharing remedy is functional to the re-establishment of the well-functioning of the market as harmed as a result of businesses' anticompetitive conduct, needs to be necessarily conducted on a case by case basis.

This means that the question regarding how the information sharing should be designed and thus how the behavioural competition intervention is allowed to interfere with the free play of market forces cannot but be determined in light of the very specific circumstances of a case, as it occurs with any other competition remedy, also with prohibition decisions.

Nonetheless, the above-traced analysis has tried to trace some general boundaries for the discretionary enactment of sharing remedies and for their design: first of all, the existence of an antitrust harm; second, the respect of the regulatory dictates of other branches of the law- as data protection law and eventually intellectual property law-, which are directly applicable to the information that is made object of the sharing remedy; third, the involvement of other relevant regulatory authorities in the phases of both the design and monitoring of the remedies; ultimately, the tailoring of

---

[295] Kathuria and Globocnik (2020), pp. 523–524.

[296] Generally regarding behavioral remedies under article 7, Hjelmeng (2013), pp. 1024. Arguing in this direction also Ibáñez Colomo (2016), p. 218.

[297] See supra Chap. 4, Sect. 4.3.2.

information sharing remedies only *to the extent* they are necessary to the re-establishment of the (harmed) market functioning through the provision of necessary informational inputs.

References

Abrahamson Z (2014) Essential data. Yale Law J 124:867–881

Aghion P, Bloom N, Blundell R, Griffith R, Howitt P (2005) Competition and innovation: an inverted U relationship. Q J Econ 120:701–728

Almunia J (26 November 2012) Competition and Personal Data Protection, Speech given at the European Commission event, Privacy Platform Event: Competition and Privacy in Markets of Data. https://europa.eu/rapid/press-release_SPEECH-12-860_en.htm

American District Court New York vs. Microsoft Corp. 224 F Supp. 2d 76, 95 (D.D.C. 2002)

Art. 29 Data Protection Working Party (3 October 2017 last modified 6 February 2018) Guidelines on Automated Individual Decision-Making and Profiling for the Purposes of Regulation 2016/679. https://ec.europa.eu/newsroom/article29/item-detail.cfm?item_id=612053

Article 29 Data Protection Working Party (adopted on 13 December 2016, adopted 5 April 2017) Guidelines on the Right to Data Portability https://ec.europa.eu/newsroom/document.cfm?doc_id=44099

Article 29 Working Party (4 April 2017) Guidelines on Data Protection Impact Assessment (Dpia) and Determining Whether Processing is "Likely to Result in a High Risk" for the Purposes of Regulation 2016/769. https://ec.europa.eu/newsroom/article29/items/611236

Autorità Garante della Concorrenza e del Mercato (18 February 2010) Sapec Agro/Bayer-Helm, Case A415, Decision n. 22558. https://www.agcm.it/dotcmsDOC/allegati-news/old/A415_avvio.pdf

BBMRI-ERIC, Code of Conduct for Health Research: Taking Up Speed & Calling for your Input. http://www.bbmri-eric.eu/news-events/code-of-conduct-for-health-research/

Bertea S (2005) Looking for coherence within the European Community. Eur Law J 11:154–172

Braun J, Pugatch MP (2005) The changing face of the pharmaceutical industry and intellectual property rights. J World Intellect Prop 8:599–623

Broulik J, Diathesopoulos M (22 May 2017) The Conceptual Integration of Innovation into the Traditional Establishment of EU Competition Law: Connecting the Dots Between Static and Dynamic Competition

Bundeskartellamt (November 2017) Innovations-Challenges for Competition Law Practice. https://www.bundeskartellamt.de/SharedDocs/Publikation/EN/Schriftenreihe_Digitales_II.pdf?__blob=publicationFile&v=3

Bundeskartellamt (7 February 2019) Bundeskartellamt Prohibits Facebook From Combining User Data From Different Sources, Press Release. https://www.bundeskartellamt.de/SharedDocs/Publikation/EN/Pressemitteilungen/2019/07_02_2019_Facebook.pdf?__blob=publicationFile&v=2

Bundesministerium für Justiz und Verbraucherschutz (22 January 2020) Opinion of the Data Ethics Commission. https://www.bmjv.de/SharedDocs/Downloads/DE/Themen/Fokusthemen/Gutachten_DEK_EN_lang.html;jsessionid=A6A9519779DDF3581BA26837A1481B6D.1_cid334?nn=11678512

Bushell G (1 March 2017) EU merger control and the innovation theory of harm: fake news?. Kluwer Competition Law Blog. http://competitionlawblog.kluwercompetitionlaw.com/2017/03/03/eu-merger-control-and-the-innovation-theory-of-harm-fake-news/

Cardwell D (2017) The role of the efficiency defence in EU merger control proceedings following UPS/TNT, FedEx/TNT and UPS v. commission. J Eur Compet Law Pract 8:551–560

Carlin F, Batchelor B, Bushell G (October 2017) EU Merger Control: the Dow/DuPont Theory of Innovation Harm-Backer McKenzie Client Alert. Concurrences. http://awa2018.concurrences.com/articles-awards/business-articles-awards/article/eu-merger-control-the-dow-dupont-theory-of-innovation-harm

Carrier MA (2008) Two puzzles resolved: Schumpeter-arrow stalemate and pharmaceutical innovation markets. Iowa Law Rev 93:396–450

Casey B, Farhangi A, Vogl R (2019) Rethinking explainable machines: the Gdpr's "right to explanation" debate and the rise of algorithmic audits in enterprise. Berkeley Technol Law J 34:143–188

Clifford D, Ausloos J (7 August 2017) Data Protection and the Role of Fairness, CiTiP Working Paper 29/17. KU Leuven Centre for IT and IP. https://papers.ssrn.com/sol3/papers.cfm?abstract_id=3013139

Colangelo G, Borgogno O (2019) Data sharing and interoperability: fostering innovation and competition through APIs. Comput Law Secur Rev 35:105314

Colangelo G, Maggiolino M (2017) Data protection in attention markets: protecting privacy through competition? J Eur Compet Law Pract 8:363–369

Colomo PI (2016) Restrictions on innovation in EU competition law. Eur Law Rev 41:201–219

Comandè G (2019) Ricerca in sanità e data protection... un puzzle risolvibile. RIML 1:183–203

Commissioner Vestager (29 September 2016) Big Data and Competition. https://ec.europa.eu/commission/commissioners/2014-2019/vestager/announcements/big-data-and-competition_en

Council Directive 91/414/EEC of 15 July 1991 concerning the placing of plant protection products on the market (19 August 1991) OJ L 230/1, subsequently repealed by Regulation (EC) No 1107/2009 of the European Parliament and of the Council of 21 October 2009 concerning the placing of plant protection products on the market (24 November 2011) OJ L 309/

Council Regulation (EC) N. 1/2003 of 16 December 2002 on the implementation of the rules on competition laid down in Articles 81 and 82 of the Treaty (4 January 2003) OJ L1/1. https://eur-lex.europa.eu/legal-content/EN/TXT/PDF/?uri=CELEX:32003R0001&from=EN

De Coninck R (2016) Innovation in EU merger control: in need of a consistent framework. Compet Law Policy Debate 2:41–51

Denicolò V, Polo M (22 March 2018) The Innovation Theory of Harm- an Appraisal. SSRN. https://papers.ssrn.com/sol3/papers.cfm?abstract_id=3146731

Denozza F (2010) Il rifiuto di licenze come abuso: bilanciamento "ad hoc" o bilanciamento categorico? In: Giudici S (ed) Studi in memoria di Paola AE Frassi. Giuffrè, Milan, pp 149–179

Di Porto F (2014) Abuses of information and informational remedies: rethinking exchange of information under competition law? In: Di Porto F, Drexl J (eds) Competition law as regulation. Edward Elgar, Cheltenham, pp 296–340

Di Porto F, Ghidini G (25 June 2019) I Access Your Data, You Access Mine-Setting a Reciprocity Clause for the "Access to Account Rule" in the Payment Services Market. https://papers.ssrn.com/sol3/papers.cfm?abstract_id=3407294

Directive (EU) 2015/2366 of the European Parliament and of the Council of 25 November 2015 on payment services in the internal market, amending Directives 2002/65/EC, 2009/110/EC and 2013/36/EU and Regulation (EU) No 1093/2010, and repealing Directive 2007/64/EC (23 December 2012) OJ L 337/35. https://eur-lex.europa.eu/legal-content/EN/TXT/PDF/?uri=CELEX:32015L2366&from=EN

Dove ES (2018) The EU general data protection regulation: implications for international scientific research in the digital era. J Law Med Ethics 46:1013–1030

Drexl J (2004) IMS health and Trinko-antitrust placebo for consumers instead of sound economics in refusal-to-deal cases. IIC 35:788–808

Drexl J (2010) Real knowledge is to know the extent of one's own ignorance: on the consumer approach in innovation-related competition cases. Antitrsut Law J 76:677–708

Drexl J (2017) Designing competitive markets for industrial data: between propertization and access. JIPITEC 8:257–292

Dullabh P, Hovey L, Heaney-Huls K, Rajendran N, Wright A, Sittig DF (2019) Application programming interfaces (APIs) in health care: findings from a current-state assessment. Stud Health Technol Inform 265:201–206

European Commission (28 September 1995) Upjohn/Pharmacia, Case n. IV/M. 631 https://ec.europa.eu/competition/mergers/cases/decisions/m631_en.pdf

European Commission (17 July 1996) Ciba-Geigy/Sandoz, Case n. IV/M. 737. https://eur-lex.europa.eu/LexUriServ/LexUriServ.do?uri=CELEX:31997D0469:EN:HTML

European Commission (8 May 2000) Glaxo Wellcome/SmithKline Beecham, Case n. COMP/M. 1846. https://ec.europa.eu/competition/mergers/cases/decisions/m1846_en.pdf

European Commission (30 April 2003) Siemens/Drägerwerk, Case COMP/M.2861. https://eur-lex.europa.eu/legal-content/EN/TXT/PDF/?uri=CELEX:32003D0777&from=EN

European Commission (24 March 2004) Microsoft vs. Commission, Case C-3/37.792. https://fsfe.org/activities/ms-vs-eu/CEC-C-2004-900-final.pdf

European Commission (11 March 2008) Google/DoubleClick, Case N. Comp./M. 4731. http://ec.europa.eu/competition/mergers/cases/decisions/m4731_20080311_20682_en.pdf

European Commission (24 February 2009) Guidance on Enforcement Priorities in Applying Article 82 of the EC Treaty to Abusive Exclusionary Conduct by Dominant Undertakings, C 45/02. OJ C 45/7. https://eur-lex.europa.eu/legal-content/EN/TXT/PDF/?uri=CELEX:52009XC0224(01)&from=EN

European Commission (3 October 2014a) Facebook/Whatsapp, case COMP/M. 7217. https://ec.europa.eu/competition/mergers/cases/decisions/m7217_20141003_20310_3962132_EN.pdf

European Commission (28 November 2014b) Medtronic/Covidien, Case N. Comp/M7326. http://ec.europa.eu/competition/mergers/cases/decisions/m7326_20141128_20212_4138173_EN.pdf

European Commission (28 January 2015a) Novartis/Glaxosmithkline Oncology Business, Case N. Comp/M. 7275. http://ec.europa.eu/competition/mergers/cases/decisions/m7275_20150128_20212_4158734_EN.pdf

European Commission (24 February 2015b) Liberty Global/De Vijver Media, CASE M.7194. https://ec.europa.eu/competition/mergers/cases/decisions/m7194_20150224_20600_4264271_EN.pdf

European Commission (4 August 2015c) Pfizer/Hospira Case N. Comp/M. 7559. https://ec.europa.eu/competition/mergers/cases/decisions/m7559_20150804_20212_4504355_EN.pdf

European Commission (1 April 2016a) Competition Policy Brief- EU Merger Control and Innovation. http://ec.europa.eu/competition/publications/cpb/2016/2016_001_en.pdf

European Commission (20 April 2016b) Worldline/Equens/Paysquare, M 7873. https://ec.europa.eu/competition/mergers/cases/decisions/m7873_1821_3.pdf

European Commission (25 May 2016c) Communication from the Commission to the European Parliament, the Council, the European Economic and Social Committee and the Committee of the Regions, Online Platforms and the Digital Single Market – Opportunities and Challenges for Europe. https://eur-lex.europa.eu/legal-content/EN/TXT/PDF/?uri=CELEX:52016DC0288&from=EN

European Commission (11 August 2016d) Mergers: Commission Opens In-depth Investigation Into Proposed Merger Between Dow and DuPont- Press release. http://europa.eu/rapid/press-release_IP-16-2784_en.htm

European Commission (27 March 2017a) Dow/DuPont, Case M. 793227. http://ec.europa.eu/competition/mergers/cases/decisions/m7932_13668_3.pdf

European Commission (6 February 2017b) Dow/DuPont: Protecting Product and Innovation Competition, Competition Merger Brief 2/2017. http://ec.europa.eu/competition/publications/cmb/2017/kdal17002enn.pdf

European Commission (9 June 2017c) J &J/Actelion Case M. 8401. https://ec.europa.eu/competition/mergers/cases/decisions/m8401_740_3.pdf

European Commission (6 October 2017d) Antitrust: Commission Confirms Unannounced Inspections Concerning Access to Bank Account Information by Competing Services, Press Release. https://europa.eu/rapid/press-release_MEMO-17-3761_en.htm

European Commission (10 January 2017e) Communication from the Commission to the European Parliament, the Council, the European Economic and Social Committee and the Committee of the Regions-Building a European Data Economy. https://eur-lex.europa.eu/legal-content/EN/TXT/?uri=COM:2017:9:FIN

European Commission (10 January 2017f) Commission Staff Working Document on the Free Flow of Data and Emerging Issues of the European Data Economy. Accompanying the Communication Building a European Data Economy. https://eur-lex.europa.eu/legal-content/EN/TXT/?uri=CELEX:52017SC0002

European Commission (21 March 2018a) Bayer/Monsanto Case M. 8084 http://ec.europa.eu/competition/mergers/cases/decisions/m8084_13335_3.pdf

European Commission (21 March 2018b) Mergers: Commission Clears Bayer's Acquisition of Monsanto, Subject to Conditions. https://ec.europa.eu/commission/commissioners/2014-2019/vestager/announcements/mergers-commission-clears-bayers-acquisition-monsanto-subject-conditions_en

European Commission (25 April 2018c) Commission Staff Working Document, Guidance on Sharing Private Sector Data in the European Data Economy, Accompanying the Document Communication from the Commission to the European Parliament, the Council, the European economic and social Committee and the Committee of the Regions "Towards a Common European Data Space". https://eur-lex.europa.eu/legal-content/EN/TXT/PDF/?uri=CELEX:52018SC0125&from=EN

European Commission (8 March 2018d) Communication From the European Commission to the European Parliament, the Council, the European Central Bank, the European Economic and Social Committee and the Committee of the Regions, FinTech Action Plan: For a More Competitive and European Financial Sector. https://eur-lex.europa.eu/resource.html?uri=cellar:6793c578-22e6-11e8-ac73-01aa75ed71a1.0001.02/DOC_1&format=PDF

European Commission (28 January 2019) Report from the Commission to the Council and the European Parliament, Competition Enforcement in the Pharmaceutical Sector (2009–2017)-European Competition Authorities Working Together for Affordable and Innovative Medicines. http://ec.europa.eu/competition/sectors/pharmaceuticals/report2019/index.html

European Commission (30 September 2021) Online platform. https://digital-strategy.ec.europa.eu/en/policies/online-platfo

European Court of Justice (6 March 1974) Istituto Chemioterapeutico Italiano and Commercial Solvents vs. Commission, Joined Cases C-6 and 7/73. https://eur-lex.europa.eu/legal-content/EN/TXT/PDF/?uri=CELEX:61973CJ0006&from=EN

European Court of Justice (6 April 1995) Radio Telefis Eireann (RTE) and Independent Television Publications Ltd (ITP) supported by Intellectual Property Owners Inc. (IPO) vs. Commission of the European Communities supported by Magill TV Guide Ltd., Joined Cases C-241/91 P and C-242/91 P. http://curia.europa.eu/juris/showPdf.jsf?text=&docid=98207&pageIndex=0&doclang=EN&mode=lst&dir=&occ=first&part=1&cid=9564524

European Court of Justice (26 November 1998) Oscar Bronner GmbH & Co. KG vs. Mediaprint Zeitungs, C-7/97. https://eur-lex.europa.eu/legal-content/EN/TXT/?uri=CELEX%3A61997CJ0007

European Court of Justice (29 April 2004) IMS Health GmbH & Co. OHG vs. NDC Health GmbH & Co. KG, C-418/01. http://curia.europa.eu/juris/showPdf.jsf;jsessionid=E613B0D5914960FEE3A7299443789819?text=&docid=49104&pageIndex=0&doclang=EN&mode=lst&dir=&occ=first&part=1&cid=11184740

European Court of Justice (6 November 2012) Editions Odile Jacob v. Commission, C-551/10. http://curia.europa.eu/juris/document/document.jsf?text=&docid=129322&pageIndex=0&doclang=EN&mode=lst&dir=&occ=first&part=1&cid=9586400

European Court of Justice (17 July 2014) YS v Minister voor Immigratie, Integratie en Asiel, in Joined Cases C-141/12 and C-372/12. http://curia.europa.eu/juris/document/document.jsf?docid=155114&doclang=EN

European Court of Justice (16 July 2015) Huawei Technologies Co. Ltd vs. ZTE Corp. and ZTE Deutschland GmbH, C-170/13. http://curia.europa.eu/juris/document/document.jsf?text=&docid=165911&pageIndex=0&doclang=EN&mode=lst&dir=&occ=first&part=1&cid=9569566

European Court of Justice-Court of First Instance (12 June 1997) Tiercè Ladbroke SA vs. Commission of the European Communities, C T-504/93. http://curia.europa.eu/juris/showPdf.jsf?text=&docid=103416&pageIndex=0&doclang=EN&mode=lst&dir=&occ=first&part=1&cid=9574568

European Court of Justice-Court of First Instance (26 October 2000) Bayer vs. Commission, C T-41/96. http://curia.europa.eu/juris/showPdf.jsf?text=&docid=45755&pageIndex=0&doclang=en&mode=lst&dir=&occ=first&part=1&cid=9587269

European Court of Justice-Court of First Instance (17 September 2007) Microsoft Corp. vs. Commission of the European Communities, Case T-201/04. http://curia.europa.eu/juris/document/document.jsf?text=&docid=62940&pageIndex=0&doclang=EN&mode=lst&dir=&occ=first&part=1&cid=9565119

European Data Protection Supervisor (March 2014) Preliminary Opinion, Privacy and Competitiveness in the Age of Big Data: The Interplay between Data Protection, Competition Law and Consumer Protection in the Age of Big Data. https://edps.europa.eu/sites/edp/files/publication/14-03-26_competitition_law_big_data_en.pdf

European Data Protection Supervisor (23rd September 2016) Opinion on Coherent Enforcement of Fundamental Rights in the Age of Big Data. https://edps.europa.eu/sites/edp/files/publication/16-09-23_bigdata_opinion_en.pdf

European Data Protection Supervisor (February 2018) Accountability on the Ground: Provisional Guidance on Documenting Processing Operations for EU Institutions, Bodies and Agencies-Summary. https://edps.europa.eu/sites/edp/files/publication/18-02-06_accountability_on_the_ground_summary_en.pdf

European Data Protection Supervisor (6 January 2020) A Preliminary Opinion on Data Protection and Scientific Research. https://edps.europa.eu/sites/edp/files/publication/20-01-06_opinion_research_en.pdf

European Parliament (July 2019) How the General Data Protection Regulation Changes the Rules for Scientific Research-STOA Panel for the Future of Science and Technology. http://www.europarl.europa.eu/RegData/etudes/STUD/2019/634447/EPRS_STU(2019)634447_EN.pdf

Evans DS, Schmalensee R (2002) Some economic aspects of antitrust analysis in dynamically competitive industries. In: Jaffe AB, Lerner J, Stern S (eds) Innovation policy and the economy, vol 2. MIT Press, Boston, pp 1–49

Executive Office of the President (2016) Big Data: A Report on Algorithmic Systems, Opportunity and Civil Rights. https://obamawhitehouse.archives.gov/sites/default/files/microsites/ostp/2016_0504_data_discrimination.pdf

Federico G, Langus G, Valletti T (2017) A simple model of mergers and innovation. Econ Lett 157: 136–140

Federico G, Langus G, Valletti T (2018) Horizontal mergers and product innovation. Int J Ind Organ 59:1–23

Free trade Commission (8 June 1998) Complaint in the matter of Intel Corporation, N. 9288. https://www.ftc.gov/news-events/press-releases/1998/06/ftc-intel-abuses-its-monopoly-power-violation-federal-law

Free trade Commission (3 August 1999a) Docket n. 9288- Decision and Order. https://www.ftc.gov/sites/default/files/documents/cases/1999/08/intel.do__0.htm

Free Trade Commission (6 August 1999b) Statement of Chairman Robert Pitofsky and Commissioners Sheila F. Anthony and Mozelle W. Thompson in The Matter of Intel Corporation. https://www.ftc.gov/sites/default/files/documents/cases/1999/08/intelstatement_0.htm

Free Trade Commission (19 May 2014) Data Brokers: A Call for Transparency and Accountability. https://www.ftc.gov/system/files/documents/reports/data-brokers-call-transparency-accountability-report-federal-trade-commission-may-2014/140527databrokerreport.pdf

Garante per l protezione dei dati personali (19 dicembre 2018) Regole deontologiche per trattamenti a fini statistici o di ricerca scientifica, pubblicate ai sensi dell'art. 20, comma 4, del d.lgs. 10 agosto 2018, n. 101. https://www.garanteprivacy.it/web/guest/home/docweb/-/docweb-display/docweb/9069637

Georgiev GS (2007) Contagious Efficiency: The Growing Reliance on U.S.-Style Antitrust Settlemets in EU Law. Utah L Rev 971–1037

Geradin D (2004a) Limiting the scope of article 82 EC: what can the EU learn from the US Supreme Court's Judgment in Trinko in the wake of Microsoft, IMS, and deutsche Telekom? Common Mark Law Rev 41:1519–1553

Geradin D (2004b) Remedies in Network Industries: EC Competition Law vs. Sector-specific Regulation. Intersentia, Cambridge

Geradin D, Kuschewsky M (13 February 2013) Competition Law and Personal Data: Preliminary Thoughts on a Complex Issue. https://papers.ssrn.com/sol3/papers.cfm?abstract_id=2216088

Ghidini G, Arezzo E (2010) L'assalto fallito? Riflessioni sulla proposta di rivisitazione in chiave "più economica" dell'abuso di dominanza. Mercato Concorrenza Regole 12:115–137

Graef I (2016) EU competition law, data protection and online platforms – data as essential facility. Wolters Kluwer, Alphen aan den Rijn

Graef I (13 May 2019) Rethinking the Essential Facilities Doctrine in Digital Markets. https://papers.ssrn.com/sol3/papers.cfm?abstract_id=3371457

Graef I, Clifford D, Valke P (2018a) Fairness and enforcement: bridging competition, data protection and consumer protection. IDPL 8:200–223

Graef I, Husovec M, Purtova N (2018b) Data portability and data control: lessons from an emerging concept in EU law. German Law J 19:1359–1398

Hacker P (2018) Teaching fairness to artificial intelligence: existing and novel strategies against algorithmic discrimination under EU law. Common Mark Law Rev 55:1143–1185

Haucap J, Rasch A, Stiebale J (2019) How mergers affect innovation: theory and practice. Int J Ind Organ 63:283–325

Hjelmeng H (2013) Competition law remedies: striving for coherence or finding new ways? Common Mark Law Rev 50:1007–1037

Houdijk J (2005) The IMS health ruling: some thought on its significance for legal practice and its consequences for future cases such as Microsoft. EBOR 6:467–495. https://apps.eui.eu/EUI_API/EVENTSV2/Attachments/Index?id=13154

Ibanez Colomo I (2018) Competition law and innovation: where do we stand? J Eur Compet Law Pract 9:561–562

Kathuria V (2019) Greed for data and exclusionary conduct in data-driven markets. Comput Law Secur Rev 35:89–102

Kathuria V, Globocnik J (2020) Exclusionary conduct in data-driven markets: limitations of data sharing remedy. J Antitrust Enforce 8:511–534

Katz ML, Shapiro C (1999) Antitrust in software markets. In: Eisenach JA, Lenard TM (eds) Competition, innvoation and the microsoft monopoly: antitrust in the digital marketplace. Kluwer Academic Publishers, Dordrecht, pp 29–81

Kennedy J (March 2017) The myth of data monopoly: why antitrust concerns about data are overblown. ITIF. http://www2.itif.org/2017-data-competition.pdf.

Kokkoris I (2020) Innovation considerations in merger control and unilateral conduct enforcement. J Antitrust Enforc 8:56–85

Lao M (2013) Search, essential facilities, and the antitrust duty to deal. Northwest J Technol Intell Prop 11:272–319

Lianos I (2013) Competition law remedies in Europe. In: Lianos I, Geradin D (eds) Handbook on European competition law: enforcement and procedure. Edward Elgar, Cheltenham, pp 362–455

Lillà Montagnani M (2006) Predatory and exclusionary innovation: which legal standard for software integration in the context of the competition versus intellectual property clash? IIC 37:304–335

Lillà Montagnani M (2007) Remedies to exclusionary innovation in the high-tech sector: is there a lesson from the Microsoft Saga? World Compet 30:623–643

Lindqvist B (2016) Big data, open data, privacy regulations, intellectual property and competition law in an internet of things world-the issue of accessing data. Stockholm Faculty of Law Research Paper Series N.1, 2016. https://papers.ssrn.com/sol3/papers.cfm?abstract_id=2891484

Lindqvist B (6 November 2018) Data Collaboration, Pooling and Hoarding Under Competition Law Stockholm Faculty of Law Research Paper Series 61 https://papers.ssrn.com/sol3/papers.cfm?abstract_id=3278578

Linqvist B (2014) Standardization under EU competition rules & US antitrust laws: the rise and limits of self-regulation. Edward Elgar, Cheltenham

Lynskey O (2017) Aligning data protection rights with competition law remedies? The GDPR right to data portability. Eur Law Rev 42:793–814

Maggiolino M (2015) The regulatory breakthrough of competition law: definitions and worries. In: Drexl J, Di Porto F (eds) Competition law as regulation. Edward Elgar, Cheltenham, pp 3–26

Maggiolino M, Colangelo G (2017) Big data as a misleading facility. Eur Compet J 13:249–281

Maldoff G (12 February 2016) The 10 operational impacts of the GDPR: Part.8- Pseudonymization. https://iapp.org/news/a/top-10-operational-impacts-of-the-gdpr-part-8-pseudonymization/

Mantelero A (2018) AI and big data: a blueprint for a human rights, social and ethical impact assessment. Comput Law Secur Rev 34(4):754–772

Maxwell WJ (2015) Principle-based regulation of personal data: the case of 'fair processing'. IDPL 5:205–216

Meadows M (2015) The essential facilities doctrine in information economies: illustrating why the antitrust duty to Deal is still necessary in the new economy. Fordham Intell Prop Media Ent Law J 25:795–830

Meli V (2003) Rifiuto di contrattare e tutela della concorrenza nel diritto antitrust comunitario. Giappichelli, Turin

Mendoza I, Bygrave LA (2017) The right not to be subject to automated decisions based on profiling. In: Synodinou TE, Jougleux P, Markou C, Prastitou T (eds) EU internet law-regulation and enforcement. Springer, Cham, pp 77–98

Monti G (2008) Managing the intersection of utilities regulation and EC competition law. Compet Law Rev 4:123–145

Motta M, Tarantino E (30 August 2017) The Effect of Horizontal Mergers-When Firms Compete in Prices and Investments. https://pdfs.semanticscholar.org/2709/12148ff62a37fc2d572a8edf74b155299a96.pdf

Newman N (2014) Search, antitrust and the economics of the control of user data. Yale J Reg 31: 402–454

Osti C (2011) voce Abuso di posizione dominante. Enciclopedia del diritto- Annali 2011

Page WH, Childers SJ (2007) Software development as antitrust remedy: lessons from the enforcement of the Microsoft communications protocol licensing requirement. Mich Telecommun Technol Law Rev 14:77–136

Parcu PL (2013) On the convergence of antitrust and regulation. Concorrenza e Mercato:321–339

Pardolesi R, Renda A (2004) The European Commission's case against Microsoft: kill bill? World Compet 27:513–566

Podszun R (2017) Competition and Data. ZGE 406–410

Prechal S, Van Roermund B (eds) (2008) The coherence of EU law: the search for unity in divergent concepts. Oxford University Press, Oxford

Quinn P (2016) The anonymisation of research data- a pyric victory for privacy that should not be pushed too hard by the EU data protection framework? Eur J Health Law 24:1–21

Quinn P, Quinn L (2018) Big genetic data and its big data protection challenges. Comput Law Secur Rev 0:1–19

Regulation EU 2019/1150 of the European Parliament and of the Council of 20 June 2019, on Promoting Fairness and Transparency for Business Users of online Intermediation Services

(11 July 2019) OJ L 186/57. https://eur-lex.europa.eu/legal-content/EN/TXT/PDF/?uri=CELEX:32019R1150&from=EN
Richter H, Slowinski PR (2019) The data sharing economy: on the emergence of new intermediaries. IIC 50:4–29
Richter P (2016) Big Data, Statistik Und Die Datenschutz-Grundverordnung. Datenschutz und Datensicherheit 40:581–586
Ridyard D (2004) Compulsory access under EC competition law- a new doctrine of "convenient facilities" and the case for price regulation. Eur Compet Law Rev 25:669–673
Ritter C (2016) How far can the commission go when imposing remedies for antitrust infringements. J Eur Compet Law Pract:587–598
Rousseva E (2010) Rethinking exclusionary abuses in EU competition law. Hart Publishing, Oxford
Schneider G (2019) Algoritmi, "verificabilità" del trattamento automatizzato dei dati personali e tutela del segreto commerciale nel quadro europeo. Concorrenza Mercato e Regole 2:353–382
Schweitzer H, Haucap J, Kerber W, Welker R (9 October 2018) Modernising the law on abuse of market power- report to the German federal ministry for economic affairs and energy. https://papers.ssrn.com/sol3/papers.cfm?abstract_id=3250742
Spulber DF, Yoo CS (2014) Antitrust, the internet and the economics of networks. In: Blair RD, Sokol D (eds) Oxford handbook of international antitrust economics. Oxford University Press, Oxford, pp 380–403
Surblyte G (2011) The refusal to disclose trade secrets as an abuse of market dominance- Microsoft and beyond. Stämpfli Publishers Ltd., Bern
Svetiev Y (2007) Antitrust governance: the new wave of antitrust. Loyola Univ Chicago 38:593–694
Svetiev Y (2010) Networked competition governance in the EU: delegation, decentralization or experimentalist architecture? In: Sabel C, Zeitlin J (eds) Experimentalist governance in the EU: towards a new architecture. Oxford University Press, Oxford, pp 79–120
Svetiev Y (2014a) Settling or learning: commitment decisions as a competition enforcement paradigm. Yearb Eur Law 33:466–500
Svetiev Y (2014b) Settling or learning: competition commitments as an enforcement paradigm. Yearb Eur Law 33:466–500
Svetiev Y (2015) (re-)joining the regulatory fold? Problem-solving innovations in competitive enforcement. In: Drexl J, Di Porto F (eds) Compet law as regulation. Edward Elgar, Cheltenham, pp 63–86
Szyszczak E (2011) Controlling dominance in European markets. Fordham Int Law J 33:1738–1775
Telle S (2017) Daten und FRAND- Regulatorische Rahmenbedingungen von Datenzugangsverhältnissen. In: Taeger J (ed) Recht 4.0 – Innovationen aus den Rechtswissenschaftlichen Laboren. OlWIR Verlag für Wirtschaft, Informatik und Recht, Edewecht pp 421–436
Trabucco G, Ghidini G (2017) Il calcolo dei diritti di licenza in regime FRAND: tre criteri pro-concorrenziali di ragionevolezza. ODC 1:1–18
US Supreme Court (2004) Verizon Communications v. Law Offices of Curtis vs. Trinko LLP (Trinko). 540 U.S. 398
Van Roojen A (2010) The software Interface between copyright and competition law. A legal analysis of interoperability in computer programs. In: Hugenholtz PB (ed) Information law series. Alphen aan den Rijn, Kluwer Law International, pp 34–46
Vayena E, Blasimme A (2017) Biomedical big data: new models of control over access, use and governance. J Bioeth Inq 14:501–513
Wachter S (2018) The GDPR and the internet of things: a three-step transparency model. Law Innov Technol 10(2):266–294
Waller SW (2009) Past, present and future of monopolization remedies. Antitrust Law J 76:11–29

Waller SW (2012) Access and information remedies in high-tech antitrust. J Compet Law Econ 8: 575–593
Weber RH (2015) From competition law to sector-specific regulation in internet markets? A critical assessment of a possible structural change. In: Drexl J, Di Porto F (eds) Competition law as regulation. Edward Elgar, Cheltenham, pp 239–267
Werner P, Clerckx S, De La Barre H (2018) Commission expansionism and EU merger control-fact and fiction. J Eur Compet Law Pract 9:133 ff- 145
Wils WPJ (2006) Settlements of EU antitrust investigations: commitment decisions under article of regulation n. 1/2003. World Compet 29:345–366
Zarsky T (2017) Incompatible: the GDPR in the age of big data. Seton Hall Law Rev 47:995–1020
Zingales N (2018) Data protection considerations in EU competition law: funnel or straightjacket for innovation? In: Nihoul P, Van Cleynenbreugel P (eds) The roles of innovation in competition law analysis. Edward Elgar, Cheltenham, pp 79–130

Chapter 8
Research Results and Conclusions

The study has explored the emerging economic reality of health data pools from the perspective of European Union policy and law, with specific regards to European data protection and competition law. Against the backdrop of the contractual sharing of health data for research purposes and the growing emphasis placed at European policy level in respect to the free movement of research data within the Digital Single Market, the study has questioned whether and under which conditions health data pools are lawful under the two considered frameworks.

For these purposes the research has evolved around three main levels of analysis, employing different methodological tools and respectively referring to different fragments of the European regulatory framework regarding data-driven health innovation.

The first level of analysis has enquired the features of the newly emerging patterns of digital health research, demonstrating that for the purposes of innovation in digital health research, stakeholders are increasingly resorting to data pooling schemes as a means of concentrating complementary information-based technology resources. As has been illustrated, health data pools are a form of private ordering of digital health innovation, which can be considered as an evolution of patent pooling schemes in the datafied life sciences research sector. They are a direct expression of businesses' and research entities' freedom of contract and business in the digitised health research environment. From a further perspective, they are to be considered as a contractual response to research actors' growing reliance on technical and legal means of enclosure of information-based assets, increasingly entrenched in data silos.

Overall, health data pools reflect a newly emerging innovation-based paradigm centred upon the collaboration of a different range of stakeholders for the purposes of data sharing and aggregation. As has been shown, such paradigm is contractual-based and not intellectual property-based: from a more general regulatory perspec-

G. Schneider, *Health Data Pools Under European Data Protection and Competition Law*, Munich Studies on Innovation and Competition 17,
https://doi.org/10.1007/978-3-030-95427-7_8

tive this reflects the weakness and—as some authors[1] have suggested—the inadequacy of intellectual property laws for the promotion of data-driven innovation objectives; and conversely the growing relevance of "contractually reconstructed research commons" established through (health) data pools. The examined case studies of recently established health data pools have enabled the mapping of the various interests of both public and private nature underlying health data sharing practices.

The importance of contractual sharing of data for innovation purposes has been lately strongly stressed at European policy level within the Digital Single Market Strategy and the European Strategy for Data. In this respect, the European Union has interestingly chosen the policy option of shaping incentives for the sharing of data among various economic stakeholders instead of introducing compulsory access regimes through direct legislative interventions.[2] In this context, both digital health and the free flow of information are identified as strategic areas in respect to the set goal of maximising the innovation potential of the digital internal market.

Under these premises, the second level of analysis has questioned whether European data protection and competition law support data-driven innovation objectives and under which normative conditions. Ultimate goal of this part of the study has been that of measuring the contractual freedom of sharing research valuable data, as supported at European policy level, upon European data protection and competition laws' provisions regarding research.

From the perspective of data protection law, the analysis of the provisions related to health data treatment under arts. 9(2) lett. j; art. 5(1) lett. b); 6(4) and 89 GDPR has suggested the existence of an outright research exemption and a special data protection regime related to the processing of health data for research purposes. Under this special framework, thus, it appears that the GDPR allows health data pools in accordance with the objective of the promotion of the free flow of personal data within the European internal market, which is set in parallel to the other objective related the protection of the fundamental right to data protection. From this standpoint, it has been argued that the research exemption is a rule for the data economy, as the right to data portability, stimulating data mobility among businesses and thus directly serving innovation purposes.

From the different perspective of competition law, it has been shown that also European competition law entails a research exemption in the form of a block exemption for research and development agreements, equally pursuing objectives of economic and technical progress resulting from the sharing of research precious information. This part of the study thus has enquired the relevance of health data pools as research and development agreements under art. 101 TFEU, and the applicability of art. 101.3 TFEU and the related R&D Block Exemption.

This part of the research has demonstrated that both European data protection and competition law establish specific access regimes regarding research valuable health

[1] Hoffmann et al. (2020).

[2] This is well illustrated by Zoboli (2020).

data, ultimately enabling the contractual trading of such sensitive data. Both frameworks appear to encourage health data pooling practices carried out for scientific research purposes, subjecting these to specific conditions. This means that under both legal regimes, provided certain conditions are met, data pooling practices are considered lawful under an innovation-rationale. At a more general level, the analysis has suggested that under both data protection and competition law, European Union law establishes an innovation-defence framework for the sharing of health data for research purposes.

These findings have in turn triggered the question, addressed in the final part of the study, regarding the limits that the considered data protection and competition law frameworks set to the contractual freedom of health data sharing. For these purposes, after having acknowledged the alignment between the two legal frameworks in respect to the promotion of contractual exchanges of data and the related data-driven innovation objectives, this last level of analysis has explored the different roles that each of the considered frameworks have in the design of health data pools, identifying the requirements and remedies directly interfering and thus shaping economic actors' contractual freedom to share data.

In this respect it has been shown that data protection law sets ex ante design requirements in the form of data protection safeguards required under art. 89 GDPR and under other more general data protection obligations borne by controllers in data processing and thus data sharing operations. From the competition law side, conversely, the relevance of sharing remedies under both the essential facilities doctrine and commitment decisions in merger procedures has been evaluated for the purposes of the ex post design of health data pools, that is for the purposes of competition interventions over established data sharing agreements.

This part of the analysis has ultimately suggested newly emerging channels of interaction between European data protection and competition law in the regulation of the complex phenomenon of health data sharing. As said, both frameworks set invasive limits to the free trading and aggregation of health data.

However, if in respect to the identified research-enabling regimes—that are the GDPR's research exemption and the block exemptions under art. 101(3) TFEU—both frameworks appear to favour market-oriented innovation goals, in the different moment of the limits these same frameworks establish to contractual data aggregation, the objectives pursued by each of the considered regulatory scheme become different. Indeed, as has been illustrated, the data protection safeguards required by the General Data Protection Regulation for processing activities carried out for research purposes re-establish also in the context of the special data protection regime regarding research the external limit related to the protection of data subjects' fundamental rights and freedoms. In this way, the primacy of the General Data Protection Regulation's fundamental rights-based pillar over the market-oriented one is affirmed also, and especially, in respect to data processing activities carried out for research purposes.

Conversely, the analysis of the possible limits to the sharing of health data under competition law has shown how a sharing remedy regarding aggregated data could be justified exactly in light of the objective of protecting competing parties' ability to innovate and to stirring the technological progress. As has been demonstrated, innovation has become an increasingly important parameter in recent competition policy under both art. 102 TFEU and merger procedures. A competition-based sharing remedy over health data transfer agreements would assure that established data pools remain open also to weaker competitors, with that promoting the data-driven progress in the internal market.

Despite these very diverging objectives of data protection safeguards and competition remedies acting as regulatory constraints to the freedom of contract and business in data sharing, the analysis has also suggested a mutual supportiveness between data protection and competition law in the regulation of (health) data-driven innovation, which can be perceived in a bi-directional perspective.

First of all, it has been observed how competition-based sharing remedies could curtail controllers' over-reliance on data protection safeguards, which could abusively impair the flow of research valuable health data among economic actors. In this perspective, competition intervention could become a means to modulate the same data protection law's goal of promoting the free flow of personal data, by taking advantage of the same GDPR's regulatory flexibilities regarding research. Such competition-based sharing remedies regarding personal data would indeed be triggered there where the same data protection safeguards could be employed by controllers in a way that abusively consolidates their market power in a certain research sector, thus restraining the correspondent innovation path.

From an opposite perspective, it has been highlighted that the fundamental rights-oriented data protection safeguards required for research processing activities over sensitive data are not at all suspended in case of competition-based data sharing remedies. To the very contrary, exactly because the imposition of an obligation to share datasets implies a further processing of collected datasets, the compulsory sharing of such datasets would need to comply first of all with data protection requirements. As has been shown, thus, data protection safeguards constitute the external limit to the enactment of sharing remedies regarding personal data. In this perspective, thus, data protection law appears to have a fundamental guiding role over the design of behavioral competition remedies, as data sharing remedies.

Ultimately, data protection law, and more precisely the General Data Protection Regulation, sets the basic framework for health data sharing, occurring both in the form of free contractual sharing, encouraged in the Digital Single Market Strategy and the European Strategy for Data, and of externally imposed sharing obligations. This means that the research-based data protection regime illustrated in the present study constitutes a primary regulatory source of health data-driven innovation, shaping contractual parties' sharing arrangements as well as competition authorities' interventions onto data pooling operations.

For these last purposes, the study has ultimately suggested the opportunity of a stricter collaboration between data protection and competition authorities, to be grounded in the precious information regarding the structuring as well as the content of information technology pools, both authorities have access to.

This last consideration shows how, operationally speaking, the mutual supportiveness between data protection law and competition law in the regulation of data-driven research and innovation remains an open field of enquiry. This contribution has provided a first theoretical and normative analysis of the newly emerging challenges related to data-driven innovation in the healthcare sector. These are directly resulting from the collaborative organizational arrangements of data pools, to be considered as contractual-based ordering tools shaping research patterns, in respect to which data protection and competition laws have a growingly relevant regulatory impact.

The practical countenance of such an impact will need to be further explored: in particular the obstacles to a collaboration between data protection and competition authorities in the governance of data pools—as the one given by the limitation of competences of the two regulatory authorities—will have to be examined more in detail and addressed. Further research needs thus to be clearly conducted with regards to the operational balance and synergies between fundamental rights' protection objectives and market-oriented innovation goals in the creation of the common European health data space announced by the European Commission in the 2020 European Strategy for Data.

The urge to find such a complex balance has become even clearer in the wakes of contemporary events, where the pressure of unlocking the vital research value embedded in health datasets through collaborative sharing efforts should be carefully directed towards fundamental rights-shielding innovation schemes. This ethical, well before normative, precept will have to be taken seriously in the next European and global political and regulatory agenda so as to prevent that violations allowed for in emergency times end up to be stable models in future business models and science.[3]

References

Di Cataldo V (2020) Esiste uno stile giuridico neoliberale? Uno studio per Francesco Denozza. ODC 1:9–22

Hoffmann J, Hilty R, Scheurer S (2020) Intellectual property justification for artificial intelligence. In: Lee JA, Liu KC, Hilty RM (eds) Artificial intelligence & intellectual property. Oxford University Press, Oxford, pp 50–72

Zoboli L (2020) Fuelling the European data economy: a regulatory assessment of B2B data sharing. Eur Bus Law Rev 31:663–692

[3] Underlining the delicate task for legal scholars to find adequate legal frameworks regarding current changes in society and technology, Di Cataldo (2020).